CHAPTERS FROM
THE AGRARIAN HISTORY OF
ENGLAND AND WALES,
1500–1750

3

Agricultural Change: Policy and Practice,
1500–1750

CHAPTERS FROM THE AGRARIAN HISTORY OF ENGLAND AND WALES, 1500–1750

EDITED BY JOAN THIRSK

Sometime Reader in Economic History,
University of Oxford

VOLUME 3

Agricultural Change: Policy and Practice,
1500–1750

With new Introductory material by
JOAN THIRSK, ERIC EVANS AND MALCOLM THICK

EDITED BY

JOAN THIRSK

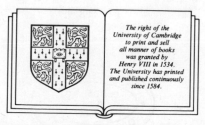

The right of the
University of Cambridge
to print and sell
all manner of books
was granted by
Henry VIII in 1534.
The University has printed
and published continuously
since 1584.

CAMBRIDGE UNIVERSITY PRESS

CAMBRIDGE

NEW YORK   PORT CHESTER   MELBOURNE   SYDNEY

Published by the Press Syndicate of the University of Cambridge
The Pitt Building, Trumpington Street, Cambridge CB2 IRP
40 East 20th Street, New York, NY 10011, USA
10 Stamford Road, Oakleigh, Melbourne 3166, Australia

First published 1990

Printed in Great Britain by the
University Press, Cambridge

British Library cataloguing in publication data
Chapters from the Agrarian History of
England and Wales, 1500–1750.
1. England. Agricultural industries,
ca. 1350–1870
1. Thirsk, Joan II. The Agrarian
History of England and Wales
338.1'0942

Library of Congress cataloguing in publication data
Chapters from the agrarian history of England and Wales. 1500–1750/
edited by Joan Thirsk.
p.   cm.
Rev. ed. of: Vols. 4 and 5 of the Agrarian history of England and
Wales. 1967–
Bibliography.
Includes index.
Contents: v. 1. Economic change/edited by Peter J. Bowden – v.
2. Rural society/edited by Christopher Clay – v. 3. Agricultural
change/edited by Joan Thirsk – v. 4 Agricultural markets and
trade. 1500–1750/edited by John Chartres – v. 5. The buildings of
the countryside. 1500–1750/edited by M. W. Barley.
ISBN 0 521 36884 7 (v. 1)
1. Agricultural – Economic aspects – England – History.
2. Agricultural – Economic aspects – Wales – History. 3. England – Rural
conditions. 4. Wales – Rural conditions. I. Thirsk, Joan.
II. Agrarian history of England and Wales.
HD1930.E5C47   1989
338.1'0942 – dc19   88-38786   CIP
ISBN 0 521 36882 0

CONTENTS

5 Tithes, 1640–1750

By ERIC J. EVANS, M.A., PH.D., F.R.HIST.S.,
Professor of Social History, University of Lancaster

6 Market gardening in England and Wales, 1640–1750

By MALCOLM THICK, B.SC.

7 Agricultural innovations and their diffusion, 1640–1750
By Joan Thirsk

PLATES

TABLES

EDITOR'S PREFACE

Since a survey of English agriculture is a large part of the economic history of England in the sixteenth to eighteenth centuries, it has seemed desirable to make the volumes of *The Agrarian History of England and Wales* available in a cheaper format to a wider readership. With this purpose in mind, each of the general chapters published in volume IV of *The Agrarian History*, and spanning the years 1500–1640, has been combined with its partner in volume V, 1640–1750, to give a survey covering two hundred and fifty years.[1] Here then is a view of a long chain of development. And while the individual authors fix a piercing gaze upon single themes in the sequence, the amalgamation of their studies reveals a larger pattern unfolding. Particularly striking are the differences in the economic circumstances ruling between the two periods, from 1500 to 1650 on the one hand, and from 1650 to 1750 on the other. Whereas rising food prices boosted the production of mainstream crops in the first period, stable or falling prices encouraged diversification, and the commercial production of a more varied range of plants and animals in the second. These differing circumstances also obliged landowners and all other classes living off the land to devise different strategies for survival. Changes in consequence did not follow one linear path. Human ingenuity turned in two different directions in the two periods, and, in fact, some of the subsidiary, not to say frivolous, activities in the first period (such as the production of luxury fruit and vegetables for the rich) proved to be among the most rewarding of the strategies for survival in the second.

The authors of all chapters in these two volumes have been given the chance to bring their surveys up-to-date by drawing attention to new work published since they first wrote. As volume IV was published in 1967, this means that they have more to say about their earlier writing than the later (published in 1985–6). These introductions should guide the reader to the most recent research. But it is also hoped that the juxtaposition of chapters from both volumes will offer a new perspective on the period as a whole, and so promote further discussion and

---

[1] The only chapters omitted from this paperback series, which appeared in the hardback version, are those describing regional farming systems, namely chapters I and II in volume IV, and all the chapters in part I of volume V.

understanding of the significance of the two phases within it. For while some of the solutions to problems in the second half of the period plainly sprang from developments in the first half, we must also bear in mind that within this whole web of human activity lay certain notable successes with new crops, new farming systems, and new ways of getting a living, which launched another phase of boisterous agricultural, and industrial, expansion in the later eighteenth century. To see agricultural development in a long view across two-and-a-half centuries is a particularly salutary experience for us who live in another changing agricultural world.

ABBREVIATIONS

Agric. Hist.	*Agricultural History*
AHEW	*Agrarian History of England and Wales,* Cambridge, 1967–
AHR	*Agricultural History Review*
Amer. Hist. Rev.	*American Historical Review*
AO	Archives Office
APC	*Acts of the Privy Council,* London, 1890–
Arch. Aeliana	*Archaeologia Aeliana*
Arch. Camb.	*Archaeologia Cambrensis*
Arch. Cant.	*Archaeologia Cantiana*
Arch. J.	*Archaeological Journal*
B. Acad.	British Academy
BE	N. Pevsner, *The Buildings of England,* London, 1951–74
BL	British Library
BM	British Museum
Borthwick IHR	Borthwick Institute of Historical Research
BPP	British Parliamentary Papers
Bull. BCS	*Bulletin of the Board of Celtic Studies*
Bull. IHR	*Bulletin of the Institute of Historical Research*
Bull. JRL	*Bulletin of the John Rylands Library*
CCC	M.A.E. Green, *Calendar of the Proceedings of the Committee for Compounding. etc., 1643–1660,* 5 vols. London, 1889–92
C,Ch.	Proceedings in the Court of Chancery
CJ	Commons Journals
CP 40	Court of Common Pleas, Plea Rolls, PRO
CPR	Calendar of Patent Rolls
CRO	Cumbria Record Office, Carlisle
CSPD	*Calendar of State Papers Domestic*
CW2	*Cumb. and Westmor. Antiq. and Arch. Soc.,* 2nd series
E	Exchequer Records, PRO
E 134	Exchequer, Depositions

E 159	Exchequer, King's Remembrancer, Memoranda Rolls
E 164	Exchequer, King's Remembrancer, Miscellaneous Books
E 178	Exchequer, Special Commissions
E 315	Exchequer, Augmentations Office, Miscellaneous Books
E 318	Exchequer, Augmentations Office, Particulars for Grants
E 321	Exchequer, Augmentations Office, Proceedings
EcHR	*Economic History Review*
EFC	M. W. Barley, *The English Farmhouse and Cottage,* London, 1961
EHR	*English Historical Review*
EPNS	English Place-Name Society
EVH	Eric Mercer, *English Vernacular Houses: A Study of Traditional Farmhouses and Cottages,* RCHM (England), London, 1975
GLCRO	Greater London Council Record Office
GMR	Guildford Muniment Room
Hist. Mon. C.	Historical Monuments Commission
HMC	Historical Manuscripts Commission
J.	Journal
JCH	*Journal of Comparative History*
JFHS	*Journal of the Friends' Historical Society*
JMH	*Journal of Modern History*
KRO	Cumbria Record Office, Kendal
LAO	Lincolnshire Archives Office
LJ	Lords Journals
LJRO	Lichfield Joint Record Office
LP	*Letters and Papers of Henry VIII*
LPL	Lambeth Palace Library
LR	Exchequer Office of the Auditors of Land Revenue, PRO
LUS	Land Utilization Survey
Mont. Coll.	Montgomeryshire Collections
NLW	National Library of Wales
NQ	*Notes and Queries*
PP	Parliamentary Papers
PP	*Past and Present*
PRO	Public Record Office, Chancery Lane and

	Kew, London
PS	*Population Studies*
RASE	Royal Agricultural Society of England
RCAM	Royal Commission on Ancient Monuments
RCHM	Royal Commission on Historical Monuments
Req., Req. 2	Proceedings in the Court of Requests
RHS	Royal Historical Society
RO	Record Office
Roy. Inst. Cornwall	*Royal Institution of Cornwall*
SC	Special Collections, PRO
SP	State Papers
T & C	*Seventeenth-Century Economic Documents,* ed. J. Thirsk and J. P. Cooper, Oxford, 1972
TED	*Tudor Economic Documents*, ed. R. H. Tawney and Eileen Power, 3 vols., London, 1924
UCNWL	University College of North Wales Library, Bangor
VCH (name of county in italics)	*Victoria County History*
Yorks. Bull.	*Yorkshire Bulletin of Economic and Social Research*

INTRODUCTION

The chapters of the *Agrarian History* assembled in this volume deal with farming techniques, changes in the use of land, including those associated with enclosure and the growth of horticulture, and the legislation which influenced the process, including that concerning tithe payments. They cover two and a half centuries of innovations during which the range of farm products entering commercial markets broadened substantially. Surveying the scene in 1500, historians concentrate their attention on grain, cattle, and sheep production, but by 1750 they must accommodate a much more varied selection of products, ranging from rapeseed, hops, fruit and vegetables, to walnuts, pigs, turkeys, pigeons, coach horses and racehorses. Each of these, and more, has its own history that rewards exploration, for apart from the fact that each activity contributed to farmers' incomes, and most have to be fitted somewhere into the history of the Englishman's diet, all new pursuits had to be accommodated within existing farming systems, thereby causing the main concerns for grain and meat to be correspondingly modified.

The discussion of changes in land use and farming techniques has broadened in certain directions since the first publication in 1967 of volume IV of the Agrarian History, but it continues to focus primarily on enclosure and the two new fodder crops, clover and turnips. It is to be hoped that the publication of volume V in 1985–6 will have shifted attention to other, significant innovations which deserve further investigation. Such a shift is being helped by one quite separate surge of interest in horticulture, which sprang originally from an enquiry into the decorative gardens of manor houses and then moved to consider their kitchen gardens and orchards. The consequences of this development of vegetable and fruit growing, making it a new branch of commercial agriculture was underlined in volume V, in the whole chapter devoted to it; it was reaffirmed, indirectly, in the section on tithes, which described the disputes centering upon some of the new crops. Horticulture is one of a variety of innovations that has to be accommodated in the fuller picture of long-term change.[1]

---

[1] See further below, pp. 8–12.

That enclosure history continues to absorb a large share of attention is evident in the recent literature: several different aspects have been reviewed in the last twenty years. The chronology of the movement is continuously being scrutinized. Ian Blanchard has pointed to the 1520s as the significant decade when land abundance and a shortage of people to cultivate it came to an end, causing the rising population from then onward to express most forcefully its resentment at the conversion of arable to pasture.[2]

An ingenious attempt by Ross Wordie at calculating the acreages involved in enclosure throughout England (including Monmouthshire) has concluded with the suggestion that far more land was enclosed in the seventeenth century than in either the sixteenth, eighteenth or nineteenth centuries.[3] Such calculations have been helped by the work of Michael Turner in revising and publishing W. E. Tate's study of Parliamentary enclosure in the eighteenth and nineteenth centuries, to which he added original work and analysis of his own.[4] This has given a firmer figure than before of the total of land enclosed after 1700 by Parliamentary acts. The calculations of Dr Wordie suggest that only 2 per cent of the land was enclosed in the sixteenth century, 24 per cent in the seventeenth, 13 per cent in the eighteenth, and 11.4 per cent in the nineteenth century up to 1914. This statistical venture, using the documents of governments which were only just beginning to think statistically, is extremely tentative, and the suggested progress of enclosure in the sixteenth century should be treated with deep scepticism. One has only to consider the incentives to enclose at that time, and the protests voiced against the hardships it caused. Some of the weaknesses in the calculations have already been pointed out.[5] Moreover, every local investigation continues to reveal a multitude of uncontested enclosures that left no documents at the time they occurred.[6]

It may not be far wrong to suggest that the acreage enclosed in the sixteenth and seventeenth centuries together roughly equalled that enclosed in the eighteenth and nineteenth centuries, and it is certainly

[2] Ian Blanchard, 'Population Change, Enclosure and the Early Tudor Economy,' EcHR, 2nd ser., XXIII, 3, 1970.

[3] J. R. Wordie, 'The Chronology of English Enclosure, 1500–1914', EcHR, 2nd ser., XXXVI, 4, 1983.

[4] For the latest summary, with a good bibliography, see Michael Turner, Enclosures in Britain, 1750–1830, London, 1984.

[5] John Chapman, 'The Chronology of English Enclosure', EcHR, 2nd ser., XXXVII, 4, 1984. See also J. R. Wordie, 'The Chronology of English enclosure: a reply', ibid.

[6] For a good example of this, see John Porter, 'Waste Land Reclamation in the Sixteenth and Seventeenth Centuries: the Case of South-Eastern Bowland, 1550–1630', Trans. Hist. Soc. Lancs. & Cheshire, CXXVII, 1978.

likely that somewhat more land was enclosed in the seventeenth than in the sixteenth centuries. If such impressions do not satisfy, then those who enjoy mathematical games can, and doubtless will, continue to juggle with the available figures, mostly taken from the official government enquiries. How trustworthy are they? That they did record enclosures that had actually occurred has been the recent verdict of John Martin, examining some of the reports collected by the 1607 commission. (Fundamental doubts had earlier been expressed about their credibility as historical evidence.)[7] But it is also worth emphasizing another passage in John Martin's article, citing contemporary views on the underlying intention of the enquiry, namely, to hold up for public disapproval the enclosures of prominent men, in order to teach a lesson to others.[8] We know already that statutes at this period were intended as cautionary exhortations, rather than as laws to be enforced universally. Despite the present-day liking for mathematical precision, we should heed these reminders of a different frame of reference for "enquiry commissions": they were not intended to embrace all cases and should not be ranked alongside twentieth-century censuses.

More helpful than quantification in deepening our understanding of the progress of enclosure is the qualitative analysis of its different regional forms, purposes and advances. A notable study along these lines was J. A. Yelling's book on *Common Field and Enclosure in England, 1450–1850* (1977), drawing on many local, and particularly Midland, examples for illustration.[9] Two more modest, but enlightening, studies of the enclosure history of Bowland in Lancashire and of north Buckinghamshire also deserve mention in this connection.[10] Still more refined have been the local studies which have given a step-by-step account of the negotiations, or wrangling, that led to individual enclosures, sometimes showing in the seventeenth century notable consideration for the poor.[11] These can be especially helpful in explaining why and how enclosure slowly became more acceptable, as

[7] John Martin, 'Enclosure and the Inquisitions of 1607: An Examination of Dr Kerridge's Article "The Returns of the Inquisitions of Depopulation"', AHR, xxx, 1, 1982. For the vigour with which prosecutions were conducted against enclosers who were reported to the 1517–18 enquiries, see J. J. Scarisbrick, 'Cardinal Wolsey and the Commonweal', in E. W. Ives *et al.* eds., *Wealth and Power in Tudor England: Essays presented to S. T. Bindoff*, London, 1978, pp. 55–67.

[8] Martin, *op. cit.*, p. 45.

[9] J. A Yelling, *Common Field and Enclosure in England, 1450–1850*, London, 1977.

[10] Porter, *op. cit.*; Michael Reed, 'Enclosure in North Buckinghamshire, 1500–1750', AHR, XXXII, 2, 1984, esp. p. 135.

[11] See, for example, A. Gooder, *Plague and Enclosure. A Warwickshire Village in the Seventeenth Century (Clifton-upon-Dunsmore)*, Coventry and North War. History Pamphlets of the Coventry Branch of the Historical Association, No. 2, 1965.

procedures were adjusted in order to promote agreement rather than dissension. When, furthermore, a local study of enclosure is set in the context of other enclosures that were in progress round about, it can be still more enlightening, for it can explain, on the one hand, the vehemence of the opposition from peasants, feeling they were trapped by a rapidly rising tide; on the other hand, it can explain the fervour of the support coming from some of the gentry, who believed that the tide was running strongly in the direction of enclosure, and that the only problem remaining to be solved was how to make a just allocation of land between the interested parties. The strength of this last viewpoint was strongly manifest in 1656, when the final Parliamentary attempt was made to regulate enclosure. But long before that, enclosures by agreement were, in practice, making much headway. This can now be much better investigated, thanks to the initiative of Professor Maurice Beresford; a considerable sample of Chancery Decrees has been indexed, and among these are many enclosure agreements.[12]

In tune with a wider interest in riots and revolts and how they start, some work has also been directed at the outbreaks of violence associated with enclosure. John Walter's article on the Oxfordshire rising of 1596, when a bad harvest drove up grain prices, is a good example, which examines the discontent at Bletchingdon alongside contemporary experience of enclosures in surrounding parishes. The identification of people, places, and the personal interconnections here goes a long way towards making the local controversy more intelligible, as well as helping to explain the background to the arguments used by individuals in Parliament in favour of the two fresh anti-enclosure acts, which were passed immediately afterwards, in 1597.[13] We also see in this example the possibility of learning more about the purposes of other agrarian legislation by enquiring into the circumstances and experiences of the MPs who spoke for it, in debates in the Commons or outside.

Agricultural techniques were comparatively briefly dealt with in vol. IV of the Agrarian History, although the one chapter devoted to them endeavoured to show the value of contemporary books of husbandry in describing practices not explained elsewhere. Since then the merits of the books and the personal experience of three authors have been further investigated, showing the close relationship between bookish

---

[12] M. W. Beresford, 'The Decree Rolls of Chancery as a Source for Economic History, 1547–c.1700', EcHR, 2nd ser., XXXII, 1, 1979.

[13] John Walter, 'A "Rising of the People"? The Oxfordshire Rising of 1596', *Past and Present*, 107, 1985. For a contribution on the social class of the ringleaders who broke down enclosures, see Roger B. Manning, 'Patterns of Violence in Early Tudor Enclosure Riots', *Albion*, VI, 2, 1974.

advice and practice found among both authors and readers.[14] There remain, however, many opportunities, not yet fully grasped, for using the textbooks to illuminate other records.

The major innovations in agricultural practice were handled in much more detail by Eric Kerridge in *The Agricultural Revolution*, published in 1967. He devoted seven separate chapters to ley farming, fen drainage, fertilizers, the floating of water meadows, new crops, new systems, and new stock.[15] Since he used the books of late eighteenth- and nineteenth-century writers to describe some of the earlier practices, however, care is needed when comparing these accounts with the evidence from earlier days, for it cannot be assumed that the procedures of 1800 were all as well developed two hundred years before.

Even in the seven chapters of Professor Kerridge's book, not all innovations received their due space. Least informative was the chapter of fifteen pages on new livestock, which discussed sheep and cattle but said nothing of pigs, and gave only a paragraph to horses. On the subject of livestock breeding, we now have a notable new study by Nicholas Russell on the breeding of horses, cattle, and sheep.[16] On rabbits a book-length study by John Sheail in 1971 has been supplemented by another article on their significance in agriculture between the sixteenth and eighteenth centuries.[17] No one has yet tackled the poultry business, though a hint of its commercial importance by the later seventeenth century around Horsham in Sussex occurs in Brian Short's account of poultry cramming in the late nineteenth century.[18]

Agricultural innovations leading to the improvement of grassland have been studied from several different angles. Carolina Lane has shown the new attention paid to the composition of grassland from the sixteenth century onwards, while John Broad has publicized a significant shift of interest from temporary leys to permanent pasture in parts of the East Midlands in the later seventeenth century.[19] Professor Kerridge's account of watermeadows, especially in Wiltshire, has been amplified by another careful study of their seventeenth-century spread

[14] Joan Thirsk, 'Plough and Pen: Agricultural Writers in the Seventeenth Century', in T. H. Aston *et al.*, eds., *Social Relations and Ideas. Essays in Honour of R. H. Hilton*, Cambridge, 1983.

[15] Eric Kerridge, *The Agricultural Revolution*, London, 1967.

[16] Nicholas Russell, *Like Engend'ring Like. Heredity and Animal Breeding in Early Modern England*, Cambridge, 1986.

[17] John Sheail, *Rabbits and their History*, Newton Abbot, 1971; *idem*, 'Rabbits and Agriculture in Post-Medieval England', *J. Hist. Geog.*, IV, 4, 1978.

[18] Brian Short, ' "The Art and Craft of Chicken Cramming": Poultry in the Weald of Sussex, 1850–1950', AHR, xxx, 1, 1982, p. 19.

[19] Carolina Lane, 'The Development of Pastures and Meadows during the Sixteenth and Seventeenth Centuries', AHR, xxviii, 1, 1980; John Broad, 'Alternative Husbandry and Permanent Pasture in the Midlands, 1650–1800', AHR, xxviii, 2, 1980.

in Dorset.[20] The use, or rather revived use, of lime in the sixteenth and seventeenth centuries has been traced in Devon, and its value described, not only on sour pastures, but in increasing the effectiveness of other manures used on arable land.[21]

Questions about new plant varieties, how and where they were introduced in the early modern period, have not yet been tackled, despite the hints given in contemporary writings, but the process by which new crops and systems were spread has excited considerable interest among both geographers and historians. The diffusion of turnips and clover in East Anglia is being studied in a new way, made possible by using the computer to record and map all references occurring in probate inventories.[22] In two other investigations with a somewhat different emphasis, the social history of diffusion has been extended by identifying the individuals, and hence the classes of people, who were responsible for the spread of clover in Wales, and of tobacco in England.[23]

Closer contact between botanists and historians has resulted in a lively debate on the possibility of dating hedgerows by counting the number of species of shrubs found in them. A large number of shrub species, it is suggested, denotes the much greater age of the hedge; the method has even been used to suggest the date of enclosure. Lively discussion on the reliability of this method of dating continues; in the end its validity can only be judged from a multitude of hedgerow samplings tested against sound documentary evidence. But it underlines the potential value of a closer alliance between botanists, ecologists, and historians.[24]

Agricultural tools have not yet found their historian, with the result that much remains to be learned of improvements in their design and their geographical distribution in the early modern period. The modest literature so far available on the subject can be gauged from a substantial bibliography, published in 1984, of wider chronological scope.[25] As

[20] J. H. Bettey, 'The Development of Water Meadows in Dorset during the Seventeenth Century', AHR, xxv, 1, 1977.

[21] Michael Havinden, 'Lime as a Means of Agricultural Improvement: the Devon Example', in C. W. Chalklin and M. A. Havinden, eds., Rural Change and Urban Growth, 1500–1800, London, 1974.

[22] Mark Overton, 'The Diffusion of Agricultural Innovations in Early Modern England: Turnips and Clover in Norfolk and Suffolk, 1580–1740', Trans. Institute of British Geographers, new ser., x, 1985.

[23] F. Emery, 'The Mechanics of Innovation: Clover Cultivation in Wales before 1750', J. Hist. Geog., II, 1, 1976; Joan Thirsk, 'New crops and their Diffusion: Tobacco-Growing in Seventeenth-Century England', in idem, The Rural Economy of England, London, 1985.

[24] See, for example, M. D. Hooper et al., Hedges and Local History, Standing Conference for Local History, National Council of Social Service, London, 1971; John Hall, 'Hedgerows in West Yorkshire: the Hooper Method Examined', Yorks. Archaeolog. J., LIV, 1982.

[25] Raine Morgan, Farm Tools, Implements, and Machines in Britain. Pre-history to 1945: a Bibliography, Univ. of Reading and British Agric. Hist. Soc., 1984.

regards transport on the farm, the use of more commodious farm wagons, in the seventeenth century, in place of two-wheeled carts, has been analysed regionally and chronologically in the county of Huntingdonshire.[26] It has yielded surprises, for it was expected to show their increasing use on grain farms, whereas, in fact, they first appeared in some numbers in the pastoral areas of the county. Also noticeable in this study, though less surprising, was their frequency on the larger, enclosed farms. The complexity of factors governing the spread of new ways in farming is clearly not yet well understood, and our inspired guesses can turn out to be very wide of the mark.

The productivity of agriculture in the early modern period has prompted much speculation by economic historians and some investigations of yields, costs, and prices. The larger framework of this question is presented in the chapters assembled in volume I of this paperback series. But the issue is also interwoven with the question of changing farming methods and the use of land, for every technical change can be assumed to have affected productivity in some way or other. Yet historians, speculating on this score, concentrate on certain innovations only, considering mainly those affecting grain. In general, it has been argued that agricultural improvements in the early modern period raised productivity per acre. Dr Outhwaite, however, has recently turned the other side of the coin, and reminded us that by extending the cultivated area on to less good land farmers may have lowered *average* arable productivity.[27] This is certainly thought to have occurred in not dissimilar circumstances, during the period of population growth before the Black Death. The clear evidence of a grain surplus by the mid-seventeenth century strongly supports the view that total grain production rose significantly between 1550 and 1650, but assertions about the rise of average productivity per acre may well be over-bold.

JOAN THIRSK

TITHES

While the introduction of new crops has not yet drawn more historians to study the tithe disputes which they provoked, two publications since

[26] Stephen Porter, 'Farm Transport in Huntingdonshire, 1610–1749', *J. Transport History*, 3rd ser., III, 1982.

[27] R. B. Outhwaite, 'Progress and Backwardness in English Agriculture, 1500–1650', EcHR, 2nd ser., XXXIX, 1, 1986. For a discussion of the separate issue of yields of wheat per acre, in the eighteenth century only, see M. Turner, 'Agricultural Productivity in England in the Eighteenth Century: Evidence from Crop Yields', EcHR, 2nd ser., XXXV, 1982, and two comments on this in EcHR, 2nd ser., XXXVII, 2, 1984.

1986 have added to our knowledge of the tithe controversy during the English Revolution. Dr Morrill has suggested that the main reason for the interruption of tithe payments was not principled Puritan objections to the compulsory maintenance of a clergy from the fruits of the land, but specific "tithe strikes" against the "intruded clergy", who replaced ejected ministers during the 1640s.[28] The instances cited are few in number but add to the increasingly persuasive case for only limited disruption to established religious practice in the provinces.

What gave ordinary parishioners little more trouble than normal in the 1640s and 1650s could, however, destroy any fragile unity which remained among the puritan sectaries and assorted religious zealots who lumbered and postured their way through the constitutional china shop. Professor Woolrych adds fresh evidence of the critical importance of the tithe question in effecting the collapse of the Barebones Parliament in 1653. The close vote to reject the Tithe Committee's proposal to maintain tithe payments for "approved" ministers was important both for itself and as final confirmation that the nominated Parliament could not perform the task which it had undertaken of effecting dutiful, principled government by the Godly. Cromwell's continuation of tithe payments until the system could be replaced by "a provision less subject to scruple and contention" was a barely concealed admission of the intractability of the tithe problem in republican England.[29]

The appearance of two major studies on the tithe files of the 1830s and 1840s has relevance for a student of tithes in the seventeenth and eighteenth centuries, since reference was frequently made in the files not only to disputes but also to earlier compromises and accommodations over tithe which were sanctioned or (less frequently) abandoned during the process of commutation.[30] These studies are a major advance in tithe scholarship and deserve wide consultation.

ERIC EVANS

MARKET GARDENING

Since no chapter in volume IV was devoted entirely to market gardening, and chapter 18 in volume V (ch. 6 below) concentrated mostly on market gardening in the period after 1640, more deserves to be said about the chronology of commercial gardening over the longer

[28] J. S. Morrill, 'The Church in England', in J. S. Morrill, ed., *Reactions to the English Civil War*, London 1982, pp. 89–114.

[29] A. Woolrych, *Commonwealth to Protectorate*, Oxford, 1982, pp. 235–50, 347, 373.

[30] R. Kain and H. Prince, *The Tithe Surveys of England and Wales*, Cambridge, 1985, and R. Kain, *An Atlas and Index of the Tithe Files of Mid-Nineteenth-Century England and Wales*, Cambridge, 1986.

period, and the social and economic status of gardeners pursuing this new occupation.

Long before the mid-sixteenth century, when the first professional market gardeners began trading in England, seeds, plants and vegetables were sold by the gardeners of large houses, royal palaces, colleges and monasteries both at the garden gate and in markets. A sizeable trade in seeds was carried on: onion, leek, and cabbage seed was purchased in bulk by colleges and monasteries from the thirteenth century onwards. Such institutions also sold surplus seeds, and common vegetable seeds could be purchased at fairs. Merchants sent packhorse loads of leek seed from England for sale in Scotland in the thirteenth century. Garden seeds were imported from the Low Countries in the sixteenth century, and it appears that foreign seeds shipped by London merchants supplied a large share of the domestic market until well into the seventeenth century.[31]

From at least the fourteenth century the poor grew vegetables for themselves, and they would, in times of plenty, have taken any surplus to market. Langland's peasants grew peascods, leeks, cabbages, onions, parsley and chervil, and Chaucer's poor widow in the Nun's Priest's Tale had a bed of 'wortes' (cabbages) in her yard. In the 1570s Tusser advised husbandmen's wives to keep a well stocked kitchen and herb garden and Harrison observed that vegetables grew in the gardens of the poor. Justices were told to encourage the poor to grow roots in the early seventeenth century and, when the Diggers tried to transform society in the 1640s by cultivating the commons, they were derided as "poor people making bold with a little waste ground in Surrey to sow a few turnips and carrots to sustain their families". By the 1660s John Worlidge found "scarce a cottage in most of the southern parts of England, but hath its proportionate garden, so great a delight do most men take in it".[32]

[31] H. T. Riley, *Memorials of London and London Life*, London, 1868, pp. 228–9; T. McLean, *Medieval English Gardens*, London, 1981, pp. 73–4; John H. Harvey, 'Vegetables in the Middle Ages,' *Garden History*, XII, 2, 1984, pp. 95–7; James E. Thorold Rogers, *A History of Agriculture and Prices in England*, Oxford, 1866–1902, I, p. 223; II, p. 594, III, pp. 206, 555, 559, 565; John H. Harvey, *Mediaeval Gardens*, London, 1981, p. 79; Dr. H. J. Smit, 'Brennen tot de Gerschiedenis von den hande met Engeland, Schotland, en Ierland,' *Rijks Geschiedkundige Publicatien*, 's-Gravenhage, 86, 1942, pp. 385, 523, 694; Brian Dietz. ed., *The Port and Trade of Early Elizabethan London: Documents*, London Rec. Soc., 1972, pp. 63, 78; Miles Hadfield, *A History of British Gardening*, London, 1969, p. 46; William Harrison, *The Description of England*, Georges Edden, ed., New York, 1968, p. 264; John Harvey, *Early Nurserymen*, London, 1974, pp. 30–1.

[32] William Langland, *Piers the Ploughman*, ed. J. F. Goodridge, London, 1959, p. 89; *The Works of Geoffrey Chaucer*, ed. F. N. Robinson, Oxford, 1966, p. 203; Thomas Tusser, *Five Hundred Points of Good Husbandry*, London, 1984, pp. 94–5; Harrison, *op. cit.*, p. 216; Norfolk RO, WLS XVII/2 410x5, f. 37 *recto* and *verso*; D. W. Petegorsky, *Left-Wing Democracy in the English Civil War*, London, 1940, pp. 164–5; John Worlidge, *Systema Horticulturae*, London, 1677, p. 175.

The development of full-time market gardening around London and other large towns was an inevitable result of the sustained growth of England's population in the century before 1640 and the consequent rise in population of the capital and most provincial towns. Given no dramatic changes in transport, the response of suburban agriculture to ever larger concentrations of landless town dwellers was, as von Thünen later postulated, more intensive food production as a whole, with most intensive production on land nearest the market. Producers turned increasingly to spade cultivation and row culture, to eliminating fallows, applying large quantities of fertilizers, and concentrating on high yielding vegetables: in short, gardening. Little horticultural expertise was needed to raise carrots, cabbages and turnips, and some of those who in sixteenth-century England grew these vegetables for their own families turned to full-time gardening.[33]

Certain accidents of history influenced the early years of market gardening. Dutch and Flemish gardeners who settled in East Anglia and Kent from the middle of the sixteenth century provided a vital boost to the infant industry. They were experienced in both the technical and commercial aspects of gardening, and their fellow immigrants provided an immediate source of demand. These foreigners took market gardening to many places in southern and eastern England; their success prompted Englishmen to emulate them.

The foreign gardeners and the experience of food shortages after the terrible grain harvests in the 1590s greatly stimulated gardening around London in the early seventeenth century. The Dutch gardeners in East Anglia shipped many tons of roots to London for sale to the poor in the famine years and were later credited with the introduction of gardening to Surrey in about 1600. Bulk production of carrots, turnips and parsnips by native producers to the west of London was much increased in the period 1600 to 1630, encouraged by the success of such vegetables as alternative food when grain was scarce.[34]

The shock of near famine encouraged Richard Gardiner of Shrewsbury to write, in 1599, by far the best practical work on vegetable gardening then published, forcefully advocating market gardening as the way to feed the poor. Other writers, such as John Norden, also urged root production to relieve hunger. An order from the Lord Chief

[33] *Von Thünen's Isolated State*, tr. C. M. Wartenberg, ed. P. Hall, Oxford, 1966; Hadfield, *op. cit.*, pp. 48–9; Tusser, *op. cit.*, p. 94.

[34] William Boys, *Collections for an History of Sandwich*, Canterbury, 1792, pp. 361, 747; *The Walloon Church of Norwich: Its Registers and History*, W. J. C. Moens, ed., Huguenot Soc. of London, I, 1887–8, p. 262; PRO,E190, 594/9; E190, 474/17; E190, 480/5; E190, 477/8; E190, 481/11; Samuel Hartlib, *His Legacie, or an Enlargement of the Discours of Husbandrie Used in Brabant and Flanders*, 2nd edn, London, 1652, pp. 8–9; Corp. of London RO, City Repertories, 49, ff. 261–3.

Justice to the Norfolk justices in the second decade of the seventeenth century to encourage root growing amongst the poor would imply some official endorsement of gardening. In the 1630s the need to ensure an unimpeded supply of roots for the London market was an important factor in defeating legal moves by the Gardeners' Company to enforce its restrictive regulations upon the market gardening husbandmen of Fulham. High grain prices were again a problem for a time in mid-century, and although around London "at present Gardening flouri-sheth much", it was also noted that in "divers other places ... a few Gardiners might have saved the lives of many poor people, who have starved these dear years".[35]

The continued spread of gardening in the century 1650–1750 was not, however, primarily a response to over-population and hunger but a consequence of much slower population growth, falling grain prices, falling farm incomes, and a widening consumer interest in, and taste for, more varied foodstuffs. Works on agricultural improvement reflected the changing situation by suggesting gardening, not as a way of feeding the poor, but as a way of increasing income. The gentry, who had long sent the surplus produce of their own kitchen gardens to market, benefited after the Restoration from the higher rents which garden land could command: "many Gentlemen have frequently repair'd or gain'd a sudden Fortune, with Plowing part of their Parks, and setting out their fat grounds to Gard'ners &c" wrote John Evelyn in 1669.[36]

Major new areas of production appeared. Sandy in Bedfordshire and the Vale of Evesham were noted for commercial gardening by the end of the seventeenth century. Gardening for the London market moved deeper into the surrounding counties. Around Colchester and Sand-wich old-established gardening areas found new markets by growing vegetables for seeds, setting up successful domestic competition against imported seeds. The new provincial areas of gardening adopted mainly farm-gardening; a small acreage only of an agricultural holding was devoted to vegetable production. Open fields were no barrier to the introduction of gardening; the husbandmen of Sandy quite happily devoted a large area of one of their fields to vegetables, as did their fellows in Fulham.[37]

[35] Richard Gardiner, *Profitable Instructions for the Manuring, Sowing and Planting of Kitchin Gardens*, London 1599; John Norden, *The Surveyors Dialogue*, London, 1607, p. 207; Norfolk RO, *loc. cit*; Corp. of London RO, *loc. cit*; Samuel Hartlib, *loc. cit.*

[36] John Evelyn, *Sylva, or a Discourse of Forest-Trees*, London, 1670, p. 212.

[37] F. Beavington, 'Early Market Gardening in Bedfordshire', *Trans. Inst. Brit. Geographers*, LXXVII, 1965; R. C. Gaut, *A History of Worcestershire Agriculture*, Worcester, 1939, p. 112; R. W. Sidwell, 'A Short History of Commercial Horticulture in the Vale of Evesham', *Vale of Evesham Hist. Soc. Research Papers*, II, 1969, pp. 43–51; Corp. of London RO, *loc. cit.*; F. Beavington, *op. cit.*, pp. 93–6. See also references in note 18 of the main chapter, p. 237.

The wealth and social status of gardeners were diverse. The most accomplished London nurserymen were often garden designers and past (or future) head gardeners in noble households. They had a close relationship with the nobility, considered themselves gentlemen, and most possessed the wealth to support such a position. London kitchen gardeners were also men of substance throughout the period; in 1747 capital of £100 to £500 was required to start a garden and the luxury goods found in gardeners' inventories confirm their wealth.[38]

The fortunes of provincial gardeners were more variable. Those who were farmer-gardeners usually died leaving moveable goods of more than £100; in other words they were substantial husbandmen. Kitchen gardeners outside London were less well off, and some left goods worth just a few pounds. Many of the poorer gardeners may have been labourers, old people or widows who sold what they could from their own small gardens to supplement their incomes.[39]

More research is needed into the profitability of market gardening and the amount of income it provided for those who were wholly or partially engaged in it. Other aspects worth further examination are: commercial gardening in England before 1500, and the role of immigrants from the Low Countries in encouraging gardening, including comparisons between their activities on the continent and in England. A study of the trade in garden seeds is under way.

Recently published works on market gardening include some local studies of the London area, and it is hoped that local historians in other parts of England will undertake similar research. Dr J. M. Martin, in an article on the origins of market gardening in the Vale of Evesham, has shown the importance of favourable social conditions and land tenure in stimulating gardening in areas away from the suburbs of large towns.[40]

MALCOLM THICK

As more and more is being uncovered concerning changes in techniques and systems of farming in the early modern period, one question will

[38] R. Campbell, *The London Tradesman*, London, 1747, pp. 335, 337, 338; Greater London RO,(M) AM/PI (I) 1718/10.

[39] Kent AO, PRC 10/57/6; PRC 11/57/55; PRC 11/76/85; PRC 11/79/74; Bodleian Library, MS Wills, Peculiar 48/1/20; 52/1/38; Norfolk RO INV/67, Box 190, no. 44; INV/78, Box 200A, no. 70; INV/79, Box 201b, no. 8; Norwich Archdeaconry INV. Case 33, Shelf E, pcl. 4, fol. 148.

[40] A. C. B. Urwin, *Commercial Nurseries and Market Gardens*, Twickenham Local History Society, 1982; Maisie Brown, *The Market Gardens of Barnes and Mortlake. The Rise and Fall of a Local Industry*, Barnes and Mortlake History Soc., 1985; J. G. L. Burnby and A. E. Robinson, *Now Turned into Fair Garden Plots (Stow)*, Edmonton Hundred Hist. Soc., Occasional Papers, n.s., XLV, 1983; Eleanor J. Willson, *West London Nursery Gardens*, Fulham and Hammersmith Hist. Soc., 1982; J. M. Martin, 'The Social and Economic Origins of the Vale of Evesham Market Gardening Industry', AHR, XXXIII, 1, 1985, pp. 41–50.

recur: did all this amount to an agricultural revolution, comparable with that which occurred in the later eighteenth and nineteenth centuries? A debate on this score was sparked off by Professor Kerridge, when he entitled his book on the earlier improvements *The Agricultural Revolution*. The validity of the term 'revolution' was subsequently discussed in a balanced survey by Donald Woodward in 1971, and considered again by Mark Overton in 1984.[41] The debate will doubtless continue, as will the discovery and evaluation of innovations, for, to quote Dr Outhwaite in his article on progress and backwardness in English agriculture, "there is much to be done ... [on] the changing efficiency with which our forebears cropped their fields".[42]

JOAN THIRSK

[41] D. Woodward, 'Agricultural Revolution in England, 1500–1900: a Survey', *The Local Historian*, IX, no. 7, 1971; M. Overton, 'Agricultural revolution? Development of the Agrarian Economy in Early Modern England', in A. R. H. Baker and D. Gregory, eds., *Explorations in Historical Geography. Interpretative Essays*, Cambridge, 1984. See also Joan Thirsk, *England's Agricultural Regions and Agrarian History, 1500–1700*, London, 1987, pp. 56–61.

[42] Outhwaite, *op. cit.*, p. 18.

FARMING TECHNIQUES, 1500–1640

A. INTRODUCTION

All periods of agricultural prosperity in England have given rise to a spate of literature on farming techniques. This was particularly true in the sixteenth and early seventeenth centuries, more especially after about 1560, when methods were more carefully examined and discussed than at any time since the thirteenth century, and the number of books published was greater than ever before. This reappraisal was prompted by the insistent demand for food, which made itself felt in every quarter of the kingdom. For as the population increased, not only were the towns obliged to seek larger supplies of food in the country-side, but every village too found itself supporting a larger number of families. Somehow the land in cultivation had to be made to grow more, the pastures had to be improved to support more stock, and the wasteland put to better use. It is not surprising that contemporary writings on husbandry are full of exhortations to improve the yield of the land and contemporary documents full of examples of how this was done. Men were imbued with the conviction that everything could and should be employed and improved. With economy and ingenuity every living thing, where possible, was pressed into the service of man—wild fruits, wild animals, weeds, wildflowers, insects— all found a use in agriculture or as medicines to promote the health of men and stock. Animals were cured of sicknesses with frogs, the earth of anthills, mugwort, rue, rosemary, savory, bloodwort, seeds of broom, herb robert, alder leaves, and a hundred and one other plants. In years of corn shortage the poor mixed beechmast and chestnuts in their breadflour, and when they were without ale they were urged to distil liquors from the birch tree and gorse flowers, aniseed, fennel seed, and caraway seed.[1]

This life of frugality and careful economy, far from being a painful necessity, was regarded as a positive virtue. Every hedgerow, men argued, could and should be planted with fruit trees. Hemp, they maintained, should be grown on every tiny weed-covered scrap of ground. On wet land, impossible to drain, willows would grow

---

[1] L. Mascall, *The Government of Cattle, passim;* Hugh Platt, *Sundrie New and Artificiall Remedies against Famine,* ff. A4ᵛ, C4ᵛ.

quickly; on the driest carrots would flourish. "I am of the opinion," wrote Norden, "that there is no kind of soil, be it never so wild, boggy, clay, or sandy, but will not yield one kind of beneficial fruit or another." Others evidently shared Norden's opinion. They offered remedies for all types of barren land overrun with heath and ling, sandy land covered with moss, waste moorland, marshes overflowed by the sea, land plagued with moles and anthills, and neglected fields rank with weeds. If men exploited their resources to the full, they argued, they would not need to settle new plantations overseas.[1]

That such comprehensive schemes of improvement were formulated in this period was proof of the favourable economic conditions surrounding the farming business. But every hopeful propagandist of improvement recognized the obstacles in the way of fulfilment. The majority of men, they admitted, were plain countrymen, who lacked resources or ambition or both. They carried on in the way of their forefathers, content with little, and loving leisure above the rewards of toil. "We have, indeed, a kind of plodding and common course of husbandry hereabouts," wrote Norden, "a kind of peevish imitation of the most, who (as wise men note) are the worst husbands." It was impossible to persuade such men to improve their land unless the scheme involved small expense. Hope lay in the ingenious husbandman who was willing to experiment. It was taken for granted that he would be master of his land, that is, that his arable and his pasture would be all, or at least mostly, enclosed.[2]

Even when this condition was satisfied, however, the diligent husbandman might be hindered by other obstacles. Some landlords deterred their tenants by refusing them long leases and by not allowing them compensation for improvements. The floating of land to improve fertility was prejudiced by millers who turned watercourses, and sometimes caused farmland to be flooded. Not all men were willing to co-operate in destroying molehills and anthills and keeping their fields clean, and their sins were visited on their neighbours. For even when land was enclosed and freed of the burden of common rights, few men owned ring-fence farms, completely separate from their neighbours. On the contrary their lands lay in scattered bits and pieces, and their neighbour's bad or indifferent farming touched them nearly.[3]

Many were the complaints about bad farming—about those who exhausted their land with a few seasons' crops and abandoned it again,

---

[1] J. Norden, *The Surveyor's Dialogue*, 1607, pp. 204–8; Adam Speed, *Adam out of Eden*, Preface.

[2] Norden, *op. cit.*, p. 226; Gervase Markham, *Farewell to Husbandry*, p. 57.

[3] Gabriel Plattes, *A Discovery of Hidden Treasure*, p. 29; Walter Blith, *The English Improver Improved*, pp. A3–B2, 11.

and those who skimped the ploughings and stirrings. We can see why common-field regulations, and indeed, all village by-laws were necessary to maintain minimum standards of husbandry. Indeed it is tempting to argue that some of the worst examples of bad farming must have come not from the common field but from the enclosed areas which were populated by small family farmers. But we cannot be sure.[1]

On land let by lease some rules of husbandry were enforced by the landlord, but they affected only a small part of the farmer's routine—the rotations he used in his fields, and the frequency with which he manured his crops. Many a landlord tolerated a low standard of farming without complaint. James Bankes of Winstanley, Lancashire, a considerate landlord if ever there was one, did not expect his tenants to marl their land, but was content to wait until their leases fell in and they claimed no renewal, to carry out this much-needed improvement himself.[2]

In the cultivation of land, contemporaries regarded the labours of the husbandman as a continuous war upon nature to preserve the land from reverting to scrub and woodland. They believed that most, if not all, land in the kingdom had once consisted of forest, and that by the efforts of man it had been transformed into pasture and cornland. This version of past history meant that the creation of corn land was the supreme end of the farmer's work. The arable farmer was always held superior to the pasture farmer.

B. ARABLE HUSBANDRY

The necessary tools and equipment of the arable husbandman were the plough, the harrow, the clodding beetle, the drag, roller, fork, weed-hook, reaphook, scythe, sickle, pitchfork, rake, flail, sled, and seedlip, the dung cart, and the corn cart or wain, sometimes with iron-bound wheels. Most of the tools were made by hand while the husbandman sat by the fire on winter evenings.

Many different ploughs were at his disposal, varying in shape and detail according to the depth and strength of the soil they were intended to plough, and in part according to local eccentricity and obstinacy which none could logically explain. "The differences," wrote John Mortimer, more sceptical than most, "proceed more from the custom of the country than any usefulness that belongs to them." Despite this diversity, however, it was usual to classify ploughs into four groups:

[1] Blith, op. cit., pp. 9–11.
[2] The Memoranda Book of James Bankes, 1586–1617, ed. Joyce Bankes, pp. 7–8.

the double-wheeled; the single-wheeled and foot ploughs; the ploughs without wheel or foot; and the Dutch or plain Dutch ploughs.[1]

The double-wheeled plough was used on flinty or gravelly soil—on the North Downs and in Hertfordshire, for example—where it stood the test of strength. It was drawn by horses or oxen double abreast, and the wheels could be adjusted deep or shallow. The turn-wrest or Kentish plough was also double-wheeled, having either two turnwrests, or one which moved from one side to the other when the plough reached the headland. Either way, the turnwrest enabled the ploughman to reverse at the furrow end without turning the plough. Theoretically the idea was good. In practice, it was less successful; the Kentish plough surpassed all others for weight and clumsiness.[2]

The one-wheeled plough was a short, neat implement which, on the lightest soils, such as the brecklands of Norfolk, where the going was easy, could be drawn by one horse. More usually, however, it required a man and two horses. With this complement, the Colchester one-wheeled plough could plough two acres a day, while on the sandy lands of Norfolk and Suffolk with the same man and horse-power, it was possible to plough two or even three acres a day. In the deeper claylands, such as those of Oxfordshire, the foot plough was preferred to the one-wheeled plough. It was drawn by horses in a string, walking in the furrow.[3]

The plain plough without wheel or foot was the common man's plough, the cheapest and simplest of all, usable in most conditions, and indispensable on uneven hilly ground, where the wheeled plough was useless.[4]

Finally, the Dutch plough was used in the fens and marshland where the soil was free from stones. It had a broad sharp share, one-and-a-half feet wide, which could deal with matted weeds and sedge.[5]

The plough was drawn by oxen or horses or both, and the respective merits of each were discussed on a practical basis. Tough land was best left to oxen, whereas on lighter soils horses were faster and nimbler, though more costly to keep. When too old for work, oxen could be sold to the butcher, whereas the horse was profitless, apart from its hide. On the other hand it was unwise to keep oxen if your neighbours kept horses or you would "want their companies in your journey." The same debate in the nineteenth century contained no more original arguments than these.

[1] John Worlidge, *Systema Agriculturae*, p. 228; Norden, *op. cit.*, p. 191; Blith, *op. cit.*, p. 198; John Mortimer, *The Whole Art of Husbandry*, p. 38.

[2] Blith, *op. cit.*, pp. 198–203; Worlidge, *op. cit.*, p. 224.

[3] Blith, *op. cit.*, p. 203; Mortimer, *op. cit.*, p. 39; R. Plot, *The Natural History of Oxfordshire*, p. 247.

[4] Blith, *op. cit.*, p. 215.   [5] *Ibid.*, p. 209; Mortimer, *op. cit.*, p. 39.

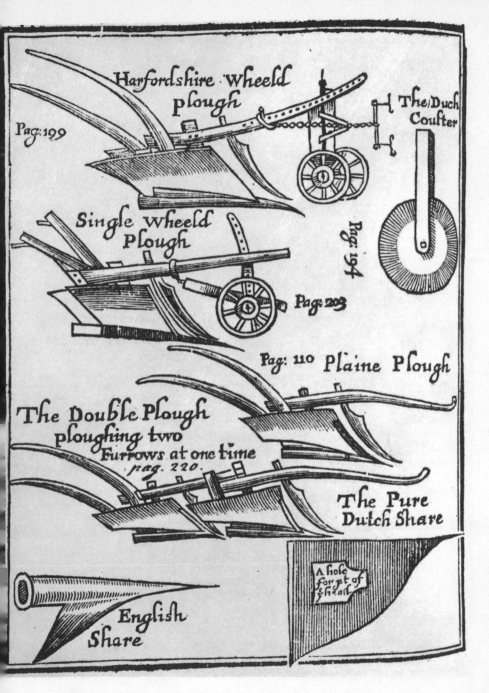

Types of plough illustrated in one of the best seventeenth-century books of husbandry: Walter [Bli]th, *The English Improver Improved or the Survey of Husbandry Surveyed, Discovering the Improveableness of all Lands*. 1652.

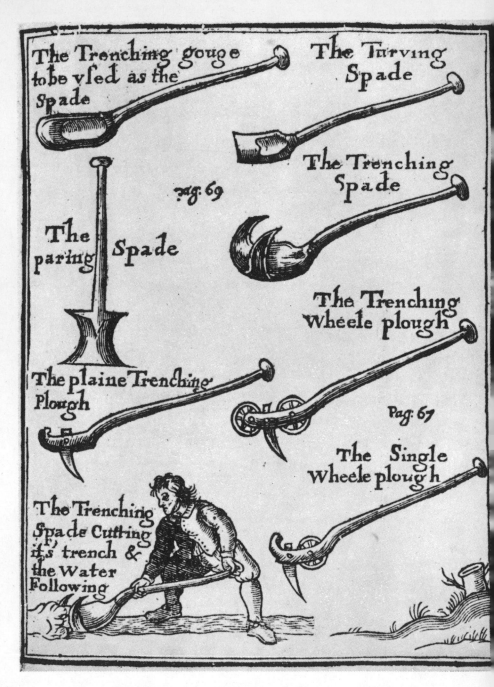

The Trenching gouge to be vsed as the Spade

The Turving Spade

pag: 69

The paring Spade

The Trenching Spade

The plaine Trenching Plough

The Trenching wheele plough

Pag: 67

The Single Wheele plough

The Trenching Spade Cutting it's trench & the Water Following

II. Farm tools from Walter Blith, *The English Improver Improved*, 1653.

1 *Auena Vesca.*
Common Otes.

2 *Auena Nuda.*
Naked Otes.

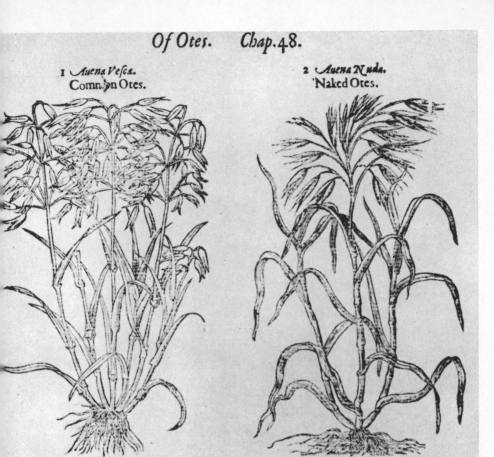

※ *The description.*

AVen: Vesca, common Otes, is called *Vesca à Vescendo*, bicause it is vsed in many countries to make sundry sorts of bread, as in Lancashire, where it is their chiefest bread corne for Iannocks, Hauer cakes, Tharffe cakes, and those which are called generally Oten cakes; and for the most part they call the graine Hauer, whereof they do likewise make drink for want of Barly.

2   *Auena Nuda* is like vnto the common Otes, differing in that, that these naked Otes immediately as they be threshed without helpe of a mill become Otemeale fit for our vse. In consideration whereof in Northfolke and Southfolke they are called vnhulled and naked Otes. Some of those good huswiues that delight not to haue store of any thing but from hand to mouth, according to our English prouerbe, may (whiles their pot doth seath) go to the barne, and rub foorth with their hands sufficient for that present time, not willing to prouide for to morrow, according as the Scripture speaketh, but let the next day bring with it.

* Tho

III.   Common and naked oats from John Gerarde, *The Herball or General Historie of Plantes*, 1597.

Tragopyron. Bucke wheate.

✳ The deſcription.

BVcke Wheate may very well be placed among the kindes of graine or corne, for that oftentimes in time of neceſſitie bread is made thereof, mixed among other graine. It hath round fat ſtalks ſomwhat creſted,ſmooth and reddiſh, which is deuided in many armes or branches, whereupon do grow ſmooth and ſoft leaues, in ſhape like thoſe of Iuie or Baſill; whereof *Taber montanus* called it *Ocymum Cereale:* the flowers be ſmall,white and cluſteſtered togither in one or moe tufts or vmbels, ſlightly daſht ouer heere and there with a floriſh of light carnation colour. The ſeedes or graines are of a dead or darke blackiſh colour, triangled or three ſquare like the ſeede of blacke Bindeweede, called of the ancient Herbariſts *Malacociſſos.* The roote is ſmall and threddie.

✳ The place.

It proſpereth verie well in any ground be it neuer ſo drie or barren, where it is commonly ſowen to ſerue as it werein ſteede of a dunging. It quickly commeth vp and is very ſoone ripe,

ripe, it is very common in and about the Namptwiche in Cheſhire, where they ſowe it aſwell for foode for their cattell, pullen and ſuch like, as to the vſe aforeſaid. It groweth likewiſe in Lancaſhire and ſome parts of our ſouth countrey, about London in Middleſex, as alſo in Kent and Eſſex.

✳ The time.
This baſe kinde of graine is ſowen in Aprill and the beginning of Maie, and is ripe in the beginning of Auguſt.

✳ The names.
Buckwheat is called of the high Almaines ꝓenkorn: of the baſe Almaines Bucken weiꝺ, that is to ſay, *Hirci Triticum,* or Goates wheate. Of ſome *Fagi Triticum,* Beech wheate. In Greeke τϝϛϙ πϓϛην: in Latine *Fago-Triticum:* taken from the faſhion of the ſeede or fruit of the Beech tree. It is called alſo *Fegopyrum* and *Tragopyron:* in Engliſh French wheate, Bullimong,and Bucke wheate: in French *Dragee aux cheueaux.*

✳ The nature.
Bucke wheate nouriſheth leſſe than wheate, rie, barlie, or otes; yet more than either Mill or Panicke.

✳ The vertues.
Bread made of the meale of Bucke wheat is of eaſie digeſtion, it ſpeedily paſſeth through the belly, but yeeldeth little nouriſhment.   A

IV.   Buckwheat from John Gerarde, *The Herball or General Historie of Plantes,* 1597.

The final decision in the sixteenth century rested not so much on the cost of draught animals as on the availability of fodder on the farm. In pastoral areas the grass was abundant, in arable areas oats could be grown. A horse could be tethered on balks in the common fields, oxen could not. Nor was it any good putting oxen to graze on a bare common pasture after a day's work, and expecting them to be fresh for work in the morning. They had to be put to lush grass that was only available in closes. So long as fodder was the decisive factor, then, the mixed farmer with sufficient pasture in severalty and the pasture farmer could keep oxen, although in mountainous districts the latter would have to keep horses as well for transport down the hillsides. The common-field farmer in the lowlands was more likely to use horses. The rich man used both.[1]

Methods of ploughing varied according to the different types of soil. On stiffish clay soils the land was thrown up into high ridges before sowing to lift the seed out of the damp, waterlogged furrows. This method was used in Bedfordshire, in the vale of the White Horse in Berkshire, in Buckinghamshire in the vale of Aylesbury, in the Weald of Kent, the vales of Gloucestershire, and in Durham. On the very heaviest clays, as in Essex, Middlesex, and Hertfordshire, the land was also ridged up but into narrow lands of no more than two or three furrows to prevent the soil from sticking together in a solid mass and to enable weeding to be carried out more easily. On the light soils of the chalk downlands and wolds, on the Isle of Portland, the warm soils of south Devon, and the East Anglian brecklands, the land was ploughed flat without water furrows in order to retain as much moisture as possible. It was in common fields in these areas that, for lack of water furrows, the grass balks were necessary, to define the boundaries of each man's strips.[2]

After the land had been ridged up on heavy soils in the common fields (and, for that matter, in enclosures also) adequate drainage was secured by directing the water from the ends of the furrows into gutters crossing the headlands, by cutting cross-gutters to drain the water to the sides of the fields, and by trenching. Trenching was often carried out at the expense of the whole community, and guttering too might be done on this basis, if it was not the responsibility of the individual.[3]

The work of guttering was carried out by a trenching plough,

---

[1] *The Book of Husbandry by Master Fitzherbert*, ed. W. W. Skeat, English Dialect Society, 1882, p. 15; Mascall, *op. cit.*, pp. 300–1; Markham, *op. cit.*, pp. 153–4.

[2] E. Kerridge, 'Ridge and Furrow and Agrarian History', EcHR, 2nd Ser., IV, i, 1951, pp. 14–20.

[3] E. Kerridge, 'A Reconsideration of Some Former Husbandry Practices', AHR, III, i, 1955, pp. 27–30.

wheeled or unwheeled (Plate II). The smaller type was owned by individuals, the larger, which belonged to the whole township and was maintained at its expense, was drawn by as many as eight or nine oxen, with two or four horses in front, ridden by boys to guide the whole equipage. The town plough, frequently with two coulters, cut drains about one foot deep. Trenching spades and shovels perfected the work of the plough, or if a plough was not to be had, the work could be done more laboriously with the spade alone. Manorial court orders afford ample evidence of the attention that was rightly given to this vital matter of drainage.[1]

Arable land was usually ploughed three times in the fallow year in preparation for wheat, four times by the industrious, twice only on some soils, and in other years only once or twice. In the fallow year a shallow ploughing, casting the ridges down, was given in April when once the crops were sown in the other fields. The second ploughing in about June went deeper than the first and included ridging up the land. The third was performed in July or August when the land was cast down again, if appropriate, or left ridged up if not. The land was then harrowed and sown and harrowed again, and any clods remaining were crumbled with the roller, or by hand with the mattock or clodding beetle, a tool which resembled a carpenter's mallet but with a longer handle. Spring crops were sown after one or two ploughings, and the available dung applied to the barley in April or the beginning of May.[2]

Ley ground, waiting to be ploughed again after several years of grass, was turned over soon after the beginning of the year, and oats were sown as the first crop. Wasteland, such as that on Dartmoor, which was being brought into cultivation for the first time, old pasture overgrown with moss or rushes, and fen and marshland being cultivated for the first time after drainage, was denshired. The turf was pared off with a paring plough in summer, piled into heaps and burned, and the ashes scattered over the land. If oats were not the first crop, then coleseed was recommended, particularly in the fens.[3]

Seed was carefully selected by the best farmers, and the sources of supply changed at regular intervals. In many cases it was bought from far afield, and if possible from a worse soil than that in which it was to be sown. North Staffordshire farmers bought their seed from south Staffordshire, and vice versa; wheat and barley seed for west Suffolk farmers came from Cambridgeshire; the best hempseed was imported

[1] E. Kerridge, loc. cit.; G. Atwell, The Faithfull Surveyour, p. 88.
[2] E. Maxey, A New Instruction of Planting and Setting of Corne, f. B3; Mortimer, op. cit., pp. 44–6; Fitzherbert, op. cit., pp. 24–8, 31–9; W. Ellis, Chiltern and Vale Farming, p. 308.
[3] Fitzherbert, op. cit., p. 17; E134, 4 Chas. I, Easter 9; Blith, op. cit., p. 61.

from Holland. Various steeps for seed were used before sowing, and many experiments were carried out to test their virtues, some prompting their inventors to apply for a royal patent granting them sole use of their invention. A much-used method was to steep the seed in brine and then mix it with unslaked lime. This prevented smut and deterred the birds. Another recipe used salt, red lead, and water, and yet another sheep dung steeped in water.[1]

Corn was either sown broadcast and harrowed in, ploughed under furrow, or set with a setting board. Peas, vetches, and beans were sown broadcast and ploughed or harrowed in; beans were sometimes set with a dibbler. At harvest wheat was reaped with a sickle or hook, barley and oats were usually mown with a scythe, peas and beans reaped or sometimes mown. Local practice differed according to custom or the fashion of the moment. Maxey tried to set the fashion of using a setting board for wheat, but the task must have been extremely tedious and he probably had few followers. In parts of Somerset around Martock wheat was shorn very low, the ears cut off, and the stalks used for thatching.[2]

For manure, anything and everything was put to use. At Newcastle-on-Tyne the burgesses cast their ashes and dung on a heap adjoining the castle walls in the middle of the town, which was carted away once a year by country farmers. Some of the muck from Newcastle was also carried away by water to country areas along the coast. Marl was dug from medieval marlpits in Lancashire, Cheshire, Shropshire, Somerset, Middlesex, Sussex, and Surrey. In Shropshire, Denbighshire, Flintshire, and later in Sussex, limestone was carried two to four miles from the hills to be burned in kilns in the fields and then cast on the land. Pebbles from the beaches of Kent, Sussex, and Suffolk were similarly burned and applied to the fields. Around Padstow in Cornwall people led their horses, laden with sacks of seasand, as much as six miles to their farms. In Hertfordshire farmers laid bracken in the lanes in autumn, and in March when it was well trodden down by the feet of horses and men and by the wheels of carts and carriages, it was carried on to the fields. In Sussex and Surrey the cleansing of the many fish-ponds provided more manure. Sludge from the river Colne was transported eight to ten miles to fertilize barren land in Hertfordshire, Buckinghamshire, and Middlesex, and from the river Avon into Hampshire. London's stable dung travelled down the Thames to

[1] Mortimer, op. cit., pp. 50–2; SP 14, 187, 22 A; Hugh Platt, The Garden of Eden, p. 91; E. Kerridge, 'The Notebook of a Wiltshire Farmer in the Early Seventeenth Century', Wilts. Arch. & Nat. Hist. Mag., CXCVII, 1952, p. 420.

[2] Fitzherbert, op. cit., p. 39; Ellis, op. cit., pp. 221, 230; J. Blagrave, The Epitomie of the Art of Husbandry, 1685, pp. 26–7; Plot, op. cit., pp. 255–6.

Chelsea, Fulham, Battersea, and Putney. Malt dust discarded by the maltsters, soap ashes cast out by the soap boilers, brine taken from the Nantwich salt pits, hair from the backs of animals, decaying fish, offal, beasts' entrails and blood, all were laid on the land.[1]

In addition to all this, the dung of cattle, sheep, pigs, horses, and pigeons was employed with the utmost diligence and economy. Pigeon dung was prized most highly, but it was not available everywhere; the counties with the most pigeons were Bedfordshire, Northamptonshire, and Cambridgeshire. For the majority of farmers, the best and strongest dung to be had was sheep's dung, and it was for this reason that sheep-folding on the common fields fertilized them so handsomely. Cattle dung was laid on warm soils, stable dung on cold land, and the better the horses were fed the better the dung. Corned horse dung was therefore richer than hay horse dung. Since barley benefited most from rich manure, the dung was usually laid on the barley at the end of April or beginning of May.[2]

The commonest arable crops were wheat, rye, barley or bigg, oats or haver, beans, and peas, with the addition of buckwheat, vetches, tares, and lentils in certain areas.

Both species of wheat were grown in England and Wales at this period, rivet or cone wheat (*triticum turgidum*) which produces a mealy flour suitable for biscuits, and bread wheat (*triticum vulgare*) which yields a strong flour, suitable for bread-making. The bread wheats, usually, though not always, beardless, seem to have been the most common, although some fifteenth- and sixteenth-century specimens of plant remains from Kent suggest that in this county, at least, rivet wheats may have predominated. Of bread wheats there were many varieties. The most notable were *flaxen wheat*, without awns, with a yellow ear, small straw, and small corn, which made the whitest bread and grew well on indifferent land; *pole-eared wheat*, also without awns and thickset in the ear; *white wheat* with a square ear; *red-stalked wheat*, more resistant to smut, which was said to have been first propagated at Dunstable in the 1620's, spread through Buckinghamshire, and became one of the commonest varieties grown in Oxfordshire fifty years later; and *white-eared red wheat*, introduced about the middle of the seventeenth century, which yielded twenty grains for one, far more than any other variety. When wheat and rye were sown

[1] E 134, 20 Jas. I, E 18; Norden, *op. cit.*, pp. 226–30, 219–22; H. Prince, 'Pits and Ponds in Norfolk', *Erdkunde*, XVI, i, 1962, *passim;* Hugh Platt, *The Jewell House of Art and Nature*, pp. 49, 50, 42, 59.

[2] Worlidge, *op. cit.*, pp. 66–8; John Smith, *England's Improvement Revived*, 1673, p. 174; Blith, *op. cit.*, pp. 147–8; Fitzherbert, *op. cit.*, p. 27; Norwich Public Library, MS 1505, Box 1, D 2.

together as maslin, the first three of these varieties were particularly recommended, since they ripened early and were ready with the rye. Rivet wheats, though less common, were growing on the rank clays of Oxfordshire when Plot wrote his *Natural History* of the county in 1676, and were specially resistant to mildew and lodging. A century and a half earlier, Fitzherbert's description of Peak wheat which had a red ear, was full of awns, and would not make bread, almost certainly refers to a variety of rivet wheat.[1]

Almost always wheat was sown in the autumn, and usually in September, but a March or summer wheat, sown in spring, was known in the northern counties, and was remarked by William Harrison when travelling in the neighbourhood of Kendal. The wheat of Heston, Middlesex, was among the most celebrated in England, but wheat was also the principal white grain in some other districts of the lowlands such as central Hertfordshire, the Lincolnshire marshlands and Holderness, the heaths and sands of Hampshire and Dorset, the vales of Taunton Deane and Wellington, and the Kentish downs. Mostly, however, it was second in importance to barley. This meant that barley, even in the lowlands, was the main breadcorn.[2]

Two varieties of rye were grown in the sixteenth century, a winter variety, sown in September, and often eaten down by sheep in the spring, and a spring variety, used in the northern counties, which was sown in March, produced a shorter straw and smaller ear, and made a very brown bread. Rye was a common crop for growing in small quantities, but larger acreages were to be found on gravelly, dry soils, such as the Archenfield district of Herefordshire, in the Wye valley around Clehonger, on the eastern sands of Suffolk, in the vale of York, on the Bunter Sandstones of the Cannock hills in Staffordshire, and in Shropshire. In this last county the spring variety was used and land was often measured according to the amount of rye required to sow it. Rye was also a common crop on the sour soils of the Yorkshire moors and dales, and on Dartmoor, before manuring made the soil fertile for barley. In all these districts rye was the principal, if not the only, grain used for bread, whereas elsewhere it was more commonly used in a mixture with wheat, for bread made from maslin was thought to keep moist longer than pure wheaten bread.[3]

[1] J. R. B. Arthur, *Plant Remains taken from Medieval Building Material*, n.d. (1963?), *passim*; Fitzherbert, *op. cit.*, p. 40; Plot, *op. cit.*, pp. 151–2; Worlidge, *op. cit.*, p. 36; J. M. Percival, *The Wheat Plant, a Monograph*, pp. 156–7, 241–3, 265–74, 289, 296; Henry Lyte, transl., *A Niewe Herbal*, p. 453.

[2] W. Harrison, *Elizabethan England*, ed. F. J. Furnivall, p. 98; W. Folkingham, *Feudigraphia*, p. 42.

[3] Lyte, *op. cit.*, p. 459; Beale, *Herefordshire Orchards*, p. 36; Salop RO, 167, 43; E 134, 3 & 4 Chas. I, Hil. 11.

Of all the white grains, barley was probably grown in largest quantity, for it served a triple purpose for bread, malt, and stock feed, and since it made fewer demands on the land than wheat, it would grow in the less fertile soils of the common fields. With good reason, then, it was dubbed "the countryman's tillage" (Plate III). The most usual variety of barley was two-rowed barley, of which there were two main kinds in the early sixteenth century, *long-ear*, being a form of *hordeum distichum*, and having a long, narrow ear and smallish corn, and *spratt*, a form of *hordeum zeocriton*, which possessed a larger corn and was considered the best barley. The latter was specially recommended for rank land since it had a stiff, erect straw, a characteristic which has commended it to barley-growers ever since. An early ripening or *rathe-ripe* variety of narrow-eared barley came to prominence in the seventeenth century, which could be sown in May rather than March and returned to the barn in two months or less. It was of the greatest value in wet, backward springs, and was known in Cornwall, and much grown in Oxfordshire. It originated, however, in Patney, Wiltshire, whence the seed was despatched far afield. Another less-celebrated rathe-ripe form of *hordeum distichum* was Scotch barley which was cultivated in Lincolnshire.[1]

Less popular than the two-rowed barleys was *naked* or *wheat* barley, also known as French barley, which resembled wheat in the ease with which the grain came from the ear. It made good bread and malt, and was popular in parts of Staffordshire, such as the Hamstall–Ridware district. The worst barley was six-rowed *bere* or *bigg*, which was spring or sometimes autumn sown and produced a harvest, though a poor one, on the dryest, poorest soils. William Harrison noticed it growing in the neighbourhood of Kendal, and it seems to have been the most common type of barley in Durham, Cumberland, Westmorland, and High Furness.[2]

Although the main uses of barley were for beer—that of Lincolnshire and the Hertfordshire Chilterns was mostly used for this purpose—and also for bread, it was widely used, usually in a boiled mash, for weaning and fattening pigs, and fattening capons, barren cows, oxen that were past work, and sheep that were short of grass in winter. A large amount of barley was used in this way in counties such as Hertfordshire and Leicestershire, particularly in the latter where barley was the main corn crop and lack of river transport prevented its being marketed far afield.[3]

[1] Worlidge, *op. cit.*, pp. 36–7; Fitzherbert, *op. cit.*, pp. 22–3; H. Hunter, *The Barley Crop*, 1952, pp. 5, 31–2; Plot, *op. cit.*, pp. 152–3; Lyte, *op. cit.*, pp. 460–1; Mortimer, *op. cit.*, p. 100.
[2] Mortimer, *op. cit.*, p. 100; Lyte, *op. cit.*, p. 460; *Elizabethan England*, p. 98.
[3] Worlidge, *op. cit.*, p. 51.

On the very poorest and wettest soils the only cereal that would succeed was oats. Hence it was the main crop of the Derbyshire Peak, the Staffordshire moorlands, the Yorkshire dales, south Lancashire, and parts of Wales, and came second only to bigg in all other parts of the northern counties. It was the largest crop on Dartmoor and in north Devon, and a common one elsewhere in Devon and Cornwall. It was also extensively grown in some pastoral areas in lowland England such as the Weald of Kent and Sussex.[1]

In mountainous counties where wheat-growing was rarely possible and barley was needed for beer, oats were used to make bread and sometimes for malting as well. But their main purpose was to make oatmeal concoctions, such as pottage, hasty pudding, gruel, washbrew, and gertbrew, which provided starch in the diet in more varied forms than oat bread and oat cake. Further south, oats were grown to feed cattle, pigs, horses, and poultry. The large acreages in Hertfordshire, for example, were intended for its many stables which provisioned horses on their way to and from London. In Somerset they were put to yet another use by clothiers who used them to thicken their mingled cloths.[2]

The varieties grown were white, black, and red oats. Red oats were best for oatmeal and were grown in Staffordshire and the north. Black (Tartarian) oats, found in Westmorland, for example, were sown early in spring, at the end of February or beginning of March, but made inferior oatmeal. White oats were sown in April and yielded the heaviest grain, good for both bread and pottage (Plate III).[3]

Of peas there were several sorts; white, green, grey, and black, and the local varieties of each were innumerable. *Hotspurs* were ripe soonest, *sugar peas* were the sweetest, the *White Hastings* were large and ready among the earliest, grey *Runcival* peas were the fullest, *Red Shanks* were best for freshly broken land, *Vale grey* for strong land, *Hampshire kids* for newly chalked land, and the *Cotswold* pea for gravelly land. Since beans required a strong soil if they were to do well, peas were the usual alternative for lighter land, though various mixtures were also sown. In Durham oats and peas were cropped together, and in other places beans and peas. Their principal use was for feeding horses, sheep, pigeons, and fattening pigs.[4]

[1] Mortimer, *op. cit.*, p. 105; E 134, 3 & 4 Chas. I, Hil. 11; W. J. Blake, 'Hooker's Synopsis Chorographical of Devonshire', *Devon Assoc.*, XLVII, p. 345.

[2] Markham, *Farewell to Husbandry*, p. 133; CSPD 1629–31, p. 406. For the difference between the oatbread of north-west England and the oatcake of north-east England, Scotland, and Wales, see F. Atkinson, 'Oatbread of Northern England', *Gwerin*, III, 1960–2, pp. 44 *sqq.*

[3] Mortimer, *op. cit.*, pp. 103–5; Worlidge, *op. cit.*, p. 37; Fitzherbert, *op. cit.*, p. 23.

[4] Lyte, *op. cit.*, pp. 474–5; Worlidge, *op. cit.*, p. 149; Plot, *op. cit.*, p. 153.

Among beans, the domestic variety was grown in gardens only, and the great field bean—usually white, but sometimes red or brown and flat in shape—made only a rare appearance. Much the most common were the small horse beans, which were sown in February, and when harvested in the north country and the Midlands, at least, were usually made into small ricks. But they were widely grown on all stiff clay soils, and of all pulses were probably grown in largest quantity. They were used to fatten pigs—a speciality of Leicestershire and Hertfordshire, for example—to feed pigeons, horses, sheep, and in lean years to make meal for bread.[1]

Lentils were highly praised by agricultural writers as the best of all pulses for feeding calves and pigeons, but if the evidence of farmers' inventories is to be trusted they were not a common crop, though they were found in south Lancashire and Oxfordshire.[2]

Winter and summer varieties of vetch were grown, but it was a crop of southern England and in the north seems to have been entirely neglected. In Oxfordshire the *Gore* and *Pebble* vetch were sown on sour land, the rathe-ripe or early-ripening variety on cold, moist ground. On the North Downs in Kent, a considerable acreage was grazed by cattle, and afterwards ploughed in. But when vetches were to be mown, they were often planted with a cereal, oats in particular, to act as a support.[3]

Lupines were recommended in at least one contemporary textbook of husbandry as a good crop in the arable rotation for sheep feed, but the exhortation to grow it seems to have been in vain. No reference to a growing crop of lupines has been found in documents, and it is probable, as some writers, indeed, imply, that it was a plant better known to gardeners and herbalists than to farmers.[4]

Buckwheat or French wheat was grown on barren, sandy land which would not grow much else, and was supremely good for fattening poultry and pigs, while in years of dearth it was used by the poor, mixed with barley, to make "a very hearty and well-relished bread." If it did not instigate, it certainly promoted the growth of the poultry business in Norfolk and Suffolk, for the largest acreages of buckwheat in the whole kingdom seem to have been grown on the sands and brecks, where hundreds of turkeys, geese, chickens, and ducks were fattened for the table. It was also grown on the Bagshot

[1] Lyte, *op. cit.*, pp. 472–3; Markham, *Farewell to Husbandry*, pp. 135–6; Mortimer, *op. cit.*, p. 107.

[2] Worlidge, *op. cit.*, p. 38; Mortimer, *op. cit.*, pp. 107–8; M. Havinden, 'Agricultural Progress in Open-Field Oxfordshire', AHR, IX, 1961, p. 82.

[3] Worlidge, *op. cit.*, p. 38; S. Hartlib, *His Legacie*, p. 49.

[4] Markham, *Farewell to Husbandry*, p. 43; Hartlib, *op. cit.*, p. 49; H. Lyte, *op. cit.*, pp. 480–1; Worlidge, *op. cit.*, p. 38.

heaths in Surrey, on the downlands of Hampshire, and in Essex (Plate IV).[1]

It is evident from this enumeration of the many varieties of common arable crops, both cereals and legumes, that considerable attention was paid to the quality of each variety, and that there were always men on the look-out for new strains that would yield better, prove more resistant to disease, or easier to harvest. In addition, some new, and some not so new, crops were being developed in special localities. Information about them was passed on to literate farmers by enthusiastic writers who thought it possible to extend to other places the cultivation of these less usual plants. One of these was coleseed or rape, a plant that was already indigenous on the seashores of this country. The full circumstances of its introduction as a field crop are not yet known, but Barnaby Googe, a Lincolnshire squire, publicized it in 1577 by translating *The Four Bookes of Husbandry* of Konrad Heresbach, landowner in the Duchy of Cleves, who commended it as green manure, sheep fodder, and for its oil. Since strenuous efforts were being made during the same decade to promote the manufacture of oil in England and so to reduce the imports of expensive foreign oils, it is unlikely that the usefulness of coleseed passed unnoticed, particularly since it was more productive of oil than either linseed or hempseed. Not until the 1590's, however, is there proof of coleseed being grown on a large scale, and by then it was being exported from eastern England, a fact which suggests that the volume of production was considerable.[2]

Most early references to coleseed relate to the fens and marshes of eastern England, where the soil was admirably suited to it. In 1593 it was being exported from Boston; in September 1599 a farmer of Terrington St Clements, Norfolk, was in possession of ten coombs of rapeseed; in 1611 and 1631 it was being exported from Maldon, and in 1631 from Colchester; in 1632 it was one of the crops sown on four thousand acres of Sutton Marsh, Lincolnshire, and was frequently mentioned as a crop in other Lincolnshire fens newly drained by the Dutch. The chronological order of these documentary references makes it impossible to continue to attribute the introduction of coleseed to the Dutch drainers who came to England with Vermuyden in the early seventeenth century. However, it is more than likely that the crop was introduced from the Netherlands, for it had been extensively grown there ever since the Middle Ages, and, since it seems to have been first deliberately cultivated in the field in Elizabeth's reign, and since all seed was always recommended to be brought from

[1] Worlidge, *op. cit.*, p. 37; CSPD 1629-31, p. 545; SP 16, 187, 12.
[2] G. E. Fussell, 'History of Cole (Brassica Sp.)', *Nature*, CLXXVI, no. 4471, p. 48; H. W. Brace, *History of Seedcrushing in Great Britain*, pp. 15-17. See also Thirsk, *Economic Policy and Projects*, Oxford; 1978; pp. 68-72.

Holland, it seems reasonable to guess that it was introduced by the refugees who settled in East Anglia and recognized the suitability of the crop in their new environment. Its value as oil seems to have been regarded as its first asset, but when the oil was pressed out, the residue was made into cakes for fodder and for fuel. Towards the end of the seventeenth century the value of the stubble as winter food for sheep was more widely publicized, and at the same time the acreage was greatly increased.[1]

Other crops urged upon the enterprising farmer were plants used for dyes. Weld, otherwise known as *dyer's weed*, which produced a yellow dye, was one of these. It needed a warm, dry soil, but since it did not produce a crop until the second year, it was recommended to be sown with barley or oats in the first year. Large claims were made for its profitability—that it would repay the farmer four times the charge of the land and its cultivation. However, the only known centre for the crop seems to have been the chalklands of Kent, particularly around Canterbury and Wye, where the seed was marketed.[2]

Greater success was had with woad owing to the additional propaganda of the government. Although woad grew wild in various parts of England, and had also been deliberately cultivated on some monastic estates in the Middle Ages, the necessity for growing it was not urged until the second half of the sixteenth century. The rising demands of the wool-textile industry induced farmers to plant more of it and thus enable the clothiers to dispense with imports from France. It had long been regarded as an exhausting crop. Now the opinion gained ground that it was, nevertheless, a very profitable one. A report of woad growing in Surrey in 1585 described the profit from two acres after all charges as five guineas, or, as another report put it, six times the profit of corn. The commercial attractions of the crop may also be inferred from a proclamation of 1587, a famine year, limiting the amount of woad that might be grown on individual farms and in parishes as a whole, and forbidding its cultivation near royal palaces, cities, market towns, and thoroughfares. Woad-growing had become so popular a business that it prompted the fear that land would be exhausted on a large scale, and the poor deprived of means to sustain them. The panic of 1587 was quickly allayed, however, and in 1589 a more liberal policy was announced allowing anyone to grow woad who wished.[3]

Because of the intensive cultivation necessary to grow woad, it is probable that the land benefited in the long run from this crop. As a

[1] H. W. Brace, *loc. cit.*; Fussell, *op. cit.*, pp. 48–9; Thirsk, *English Peasant Farming*, p. 133; SP 14, 180, 79; Blith, *op. cit.*, p. 249; Worlidge, *op. cit.*, p. 52; Mortimer, *op. cit.*, pp. 120–1.   [2] Blith, *op. cit.*, pp. 222–4.

[3] J. B. Hurry, *The Woad Plant and its Dye*, 1930, pp. 59–64; Thirsk, *Econ. Policy, op. cit.*, pp. 3–5, 27–30.

reporter from Surrey expressed it in 1585, "we have seen good wheat and barley after woad, which we take not to be because of the woad but the rather by so much marling, stirring, and soiling of the ground in far more better sort than they do for corn." Every one agreed, however, that after woad it was no good trying to grow grass for many years.[1]

One of the principal and earliest areas in which woad was grown in the Middle Ages was Somerset, but by the later sixteenth century there were woad farms in Hampshire, Bedfordshire, at Lathbury in Buckinghamshire, and at Alphamstone in Essex. By the mid-seventeenth century, it was also being grown in Worcestershire, south Warwickshire, Oxfordshire, Gloucestershire, Northamptonshire, Leicestershire, and parts of Rutland. It had to be cultivated in a deep, well-drained soil, and it was for this reason that many sites lay on alluvial land near rivers.[2]

Yet another dye plant was madder for red colouring. It was grown at Barn Elms, Barnes, in Charles I's reign, and at Deptford in the 1650's, but it was a crop that took three years to come to perfection, and was not likely to commend itself to many. It was more popular with gardeners who grew it for the apothecary.[3]

Saffron was used as a dye as well as a condiment, medicine, and perfume, and was a speciality in the neighbourhood of Saffron Walden, Essex, in Suffolk, around Walsingham in Norfolk, and in Cambridge-shire. It was planted at midsummer and was ready to yield a crop the following autumn. It was said to prepare the ground for splendid harvests of barley.[4]

Various plants for culinary use were grown as field crops in special localities. Caraway was grown in Oxfordshire at Clanfield. Mustard seed was grown in the Norfolk fens and around Tewkesbury, onions in the Lincolnshire fens, and liquorice at Worksop in Nottinghamshire, at Pontefract, Yorkshire, and at Godalming, Surrey. Carrots were grown in east Suffolk, at Orford, Ipswich, and along the coast; at Framlingham inland; at Bury St Edmunds in west Suffolk; at Norwich and other places in Norfolk; and at Colchester, Essex. At Fulham, near London, where market-gardening was becoming the principal occupation, carrots were grown together with parsnips, turnips, and other vegetables in common fields, parts of which were ploughed, parts dug with the spade, and all kept fertile by an occasional change from vegetable to wheat-growing. Although most of this crop was destined for the table, some carrots were used to feed poultry, and probably in Suffolk, at least, to feed cows and fatten bullocks thus leading men on

[1] Guildford Muniment Room, Loseley MS 1966, 3 and 1.
[2] Hurry, op. cit., pp. 65–70, 11.
[3] Blith, op. cit., p. 235.
[4] Folkingham, op. cit., pp. 31, 42; Blith, op. cit., p. 244.

to the idea of using turnips in the same way. The use of carrots for cattle is strongly suggested by an inventory of Robert Beversham of Sudbury, yeoman, who in January 1638 had eighteen cows, forty bullocks, 38 acres of rye, and five acres of carrots.[1]

More original than any of the plants mentioned already was tobacco, first cultivated in England about 1571. Experiments were made with both *nicotiana tabacum* and *nicotiana rustica* or yellow henbane, but by the early seventeenth century the latter had supplanted the former. Repeated attempts were made by the Crown in the reigns of James I and Charles I to suppress the cultivation of tobacco in England and Wales in order to ensure a market at home for the Virginian crop, but they had not the slightest effect. The acreage of land growing tobacco increased by leaps and bounds. In the early seventeenth century it was grown in yards and gardens in London and Westminster, in the Home Counties, the Channel Islands, in Lincolnshire and Yorkshire, Worcestershire, Warwickshire, and Wiltshire, and above all in Gloucestershire, where the districts around Winchcombe, Cheltenham, and Tewkesbury became the most important centres of tobacco-growing in the kingdom. The history of this crop illustrates better than any other, perhaps, how adventurous English farmers from all districts could be when once they had been persuaded of the success of a new farm enterprise.[2]

Another newly introduced plant of this period was hops, said to have been introduced into England at the time of the Reformation. They were first grown in Suffolk, Kent, Surrey, and Essex, and later moved westward into Hampshire and Herefordshire, where John Beale, a proud native of the latter county, claimed in 1657 that with the hops around Bromyard "we make haste to be the chief hopmasters in England." Despite high labour costs the financial rewards of hop-growing were attractive to large farmers who had suitable, well-drained soil: twenty acres of hop bines, growing at Earls Colne in Essex in 1631, were valued at £400.[3]

Among crops grown for the making and processing of various kinds of cloth and for the making of domestic goods such as baskets, some were common to most parts of England and Wales, some were confined to special areas. Among the latter were teasels, used in the

[1] Plot, *op. cit.*, p. 155; Folkingham, *op. cit.*, p. 42; Blith, *op. cit.*, pp. 246–8; Worlidge, *op. cit.*, p. 147; Norden, *op. cit.*, p. 207; P. McGrath, *The Marketing of Food, Fodder, and Livestock in the London Area in the Seventeenth Century*, London M.A. thesis, 1948, p. 197; Hugh Platt, *The Jewell House of Art and Nature*, p. 13.

[2] C. M. MacInnes, *The Early English Tobacco Trade*, pp. 76–93. Joan Thirsk, 'New Crops and their Diffusion', in *Rural Change and Urban Growth, 1500–1800*, ed. C. W. Chalklin and M. A. Havinden, 1974, pp. 76–103.

[3] Robert Reyce, *Suffolk in the Seventeenth Century*, p. 31; Norden, *op. cit.*, p. 206; John Beale, *Herefordshire Orchards*, p. 47.

finishing of cloth, which were grown in the Cheddar area of Somerset, and were considered excellent as a preparation for wheat, because their strong roots opened out the soil. Osiers were a speciality of the fens of eastern England and the Somerset Levels, and were used for making baskets. The more common crops were hemp and flax. They were grown in small tofts and crofts by the peasantry, who, after the harvest, found further employment in dressing them for the weaver. At the same time, some districts grew these crops on a larger scale, and here too the harvest, coming after other harvests, gave much-needed work to the poor. Hemp requires a rich, alluvial soil, and was particularly suited to fenland. It occupied a large acreage in the fens of south-east Lincolnshire, Norfolk, and the Isle of Axholme, and along the rivers in east Suffolk, Sussex, Dorset, and Somerset. Good flax land lay in Essex, along the rivers of Kent, particularly around Maidstone on the Medway (where the best thread in all England was spun), in Warwickshire, Worcestershire, the forests of Northamptonshire, and, finally, in Gloucestershire, where at Winchcombe in James I's reign an agriculturist who had formerly bought flax from the Eastland company to be dressed by the poor, planted 40 acres and claimed to employ eight hundred people in cultivating and dressing it. Both crops had many uses besides being woven into cloth. Linseed oil from flax was used in paint and soap, and the chaff and the stalks for fuel. Hemp made exceedingly strong ropes that were used as horse halters and for shipping purposes. The seed was good for feeding poultry.[1]

It is clear from the variety of crops grown in the kingdom, from the fact that some of the unusual ones such as teasels and saffron were fitted into the crop rotation of modest peasant farmers, while even market-gardening was carried on in common fields, that the cropping schedule of every locality, sometimes also of every field in one township, was subject to the greatest variety. On newly reclaimed land, and on all poor soils in the northern counties, the rotation often consisted of two, three, or four years of arable crops, followed by seven or eight years of leys. In Cumberland, for example, the rotation was oats, barley (usually bigg), oats, and then grass for seven to ten years. In the more fertile vale lands of the kingdom, including the lowlands of Durham, a more intensive rotation of two year's crops and one of fallow was the rule. Sometimes it consisted of winter corn, spring corn or pulses, and a fallow, as in the vale of Aylesbury, or wheat or barley one year, oats or pulses in the second, and a fallow in the third, as in the vale of York. In the marshlands of Lincolnshire and east Yorkshire a two-course rotation was customary, which meant that one field lay

[1] VCH Somerset, II, p. 542; Thirsk, English Peasant Farming, p. 30; Norden, op. cit., p. 207; Blith, op. cit., pp. 254–5; Worlidge, op. cit., pp. 40, 52; SP 14, 180, 79.

fallow while the other was divided into furlongs, some growing spring, some winter crops. On the brecklands of Norfolk a four-course rotation was followed, consisting of barley, rye, then barley or another spring crop, then fallow. In the fens of Lincolnshire some land alternated between arable and pasture, some supported crops year after year without a fallow. And in many parts of England farmers in common fields sometimes grew tares on parts of the common fields that would otherwise have lain fallow.[1]

It is impossible to discover all the various rotations that suited each locality and, indeed, each season. But one innovation affecting the rotations in mixed farming areas in the lowlands deserves special notice. It was the introduction of years of leys on arable land which had previously been subject to a regular course of grain, legumes, and one year's fallow. It is possible that the practice was suggested by rotations used in the north where leys of seven to ten years were not unusual. What is certain is that the use of leys in old arable fields revived a lot of ploughland which badly needed a rest under grass. The logic behind the system was described by Fitzherbert in his *Book of Husbandry* for the benefit of those who had enclosed lands. "And if any of his three closes that he hath for his corn be worn or wear bare, then he may break and plough up his close that he had for his leys, or the close that he had for his common pasture, or both, and sow them with corn and let the other lie for a time and so shall he have always rest ground, the which will bear much corn with little dung." The first reference so far found to leys in common fields relates to Wymeswold in Leicestershire in the early fifteenth century. In documents of the sixteenth and seventeenth centuries there are numerous examples of leys among the common fields and village agreements have been adduced to show how the system worked. It was necessary for the owners of the strips to agree to put them under grass, and when the ley was established it could be grazed by them all. How long the leys were left before they were ploughed up is a more difficult question to answer. It has been suggested on the evidence of leys in Cambridgeshire that some became permanent pasture, though termed 'leys'. But other references to leys newly ploughed or to "broken up leys" suggest that they were genuinely temporary, though they might last ten years or more.[2]

---

[1] See *supra*, p. 29; Ellis, *op. cit.*, p. 197; Thirsk, *op. cit.*, pp. 61, 23, 100; E 134, 4 Jas. I, E 26; Havinden, *op. cit.*, pp. 78–9; E. Kerridge, 'The Notebook of a Wiltshire Farmer in the early Seventeenth Century', *Wilts. Arch. & Nat. Hist. Mag.*, CXCVII, 1952, p. 419.

[2] TED, III, p. 23; W. G. Hoskins, *Essays in Leicestershire History*, pp. 139–43; Thirsk, *op. cit.*, pp. 100–1; M. Havinden, *op. cit.*, p. 75; Margaret Spufford, 'Rural Cambridgeshire, 1520–1680', Leicester M.A. thesis, 1962, p. 19, and correspondence with the writer.

Common-field farming might be an irksome system to the farmer in districts of mixed husbandry who wished to turn the bulk of his land to pasture, and to the individualist, like Henry Best, who hated to think that the fruits of his labour would be appropriated for the benefit of others, that his hay, for example, which he had to contribute along with other villagers to feed the village flock in the coldest days of winter, would be used to feed other men's animals. But by the standards of the plain countryman the system was efficient and flexible enough to suit his needs. The regular fallow every second or third year was essential to keep down weeds and restore the land if manure was not abundant, and was still used in the eighteenth century on lands that had long been enclosed. Changes of agricultural routine could be, and were, accepted after discussion in the manorial court. New crops and unusual rotations were introduced into common fields as well as closes. And for some farming systems such as the sheep-corn farming of the downlands, where sheep-folding by a communal flock was the foundation on which the success of the arable crops depended, the co-operation of the community was essential. Thus people were willing to tolerate the inconveniences of common fields—the risks of having other men's stock trampling their crops on intermingled strips, having their animals stolen overnight from the common pastures, or having the wool stolen from the sheeps' backs just before they were shorn. They tolerated these risks because there were others attending enclosure. Mildew in wheat, for example, was a serious disease in closes because the hedges prevented the sun and wind from drying the grain.[1]

The result of this attachment to a traditional system was not always third-rate farming. The two most famous corn-growing areas in the kingdom, where the greatest pains were taken in the preparation of the arable, were the vale of Taunton Deane—the *Paradise of England*, in Norden's words—which was mostly enclosed at this period; and the brecklands of Norfolk and Suffolk, which lay for the most part in common fields, and where farmers possessed the largest array of arable implements anywhere.[2]

C. GRASSLAND AND STOCK

Meadows, whether enclosed, or commonable after harvest as in common-field townships, were of two kinds. Dry upland meadows consisted of the best pasture shut up for hay. Low meadows lay along

[1] Henry Best, *Rural Economy in Yorkshire, 1641*, Surtees Soc., XXXIII, 1857, pp. 74, 94, 118; Ellis, *op. cit.*, p. 4; E. Kerridge, 'The Sheepfold in Wiltshire and the Floating of the Watermeadows', EcHR, 2nd Ser., VI, 3, 1954, pp. 283–4; Hartlib, *op. cit.*, p. 17; Markham, *The Inrichment of the Weald of Kent*, p. 6.

[2] Norden, *op. cit.*, p. 230.

river banks and in the fens and were overflowed in winter, thus making "the grass grow cheerful." Natural water meadows were far superior to dry meadows, and along the banks of the Dove, the Severn at Welshpool, in the vale of Taunton Deane, and at Crediton, were the best meadows in the kingdom. They lay under water during the winter, and in spring were drained off when the old sewers and water drains were cleaned out or renewed. Upland meadows had to be manured at least once every three years if they were to survive continual mowing. Chalk and lime, coaldust, ashes, chimney soot, and marl were applied, and in south-west England water, washed from the streets and ditches, was led into the meadows. Good grasses recommended for hay and grazing were clover, white melilot or sweet clover, milfoil or yarrow, septfoil or tormentil, cinquefoil, and ribgrass. Bare patches, advised Norden, should be resown with clover and grass honeysuckle or other seeds from the best hay. But if more drastic remedial treatment was needed, the meadow was ploughed in spring, left all summer, ploughed again in autumn, and sown the following spring with peas or vetches. This was followed by wheat, and in the third year by vetches or hayseed, after which the meadow was ready to be grazed once more. The fourth year it was ready to be mown again. That the value of clover in the meadow was already recognized is evident in the advice of Norden and Folkingham quoted above. Moreover, cloverseed was being imported into Norfolk in 1620. But whether the idea of the clover ley had yet been introduced is not certain. It was well-tried on the Continent, and since Norfolk was the centre of so many innovations in farming that seem to have been brought over by the Flemish immigrants, it is possible that the clover ley was also introduced by them. But it was not until the 1650's that its merits were advertised in print and that clover seed was being bought by farmers in quantity outside East Anglia.[1]

The great innovation in the management of meadows in the late sixteenth and early seventeenth centuries, which in western England solved the problem of finding fodder early in the year for increasing numbers of stock, was the deliberate flooding of upland meadows—a technique that was undoubtedly suggested by the natural action of the rivers in overflowing low meadows.

The first known experiment was made by Rowland Vaughan of New Court in the Golden valley in Herefordshire, who publicized his method and proclaimed his success in a book published in 1610,

---

[1] Norden, *op. cit.*, pp. 193–202; Folkingham, *op. cit.*, p. 25; G. E. Fussell, 'Adventures with Clover', *Agriculture*, LXII, 7, 1955, pp. 342–5; E. C. Lodge, *The Account Book of a Kentish Estate, 1616–1704*, p. 237. Honeysuckle was a common term for all the clovers.

entitled *The Most Approved and Long Experienced Waterworks*. In it, he implied that he had been engaged in this work for some years, possibly since the later 1590's.

To float a meadow, it was necessary first to construct a hatch to dam up the river. When this was opened, the water flowed through a specially dug main duct, and thence into a series of lesser ducts, spaced at intervals of 30–40 feet, all of which were floored and walled with timber. Between each duct a drain was dug to take the water off the meadow when necessary, and to lead it into a main drain and back to the river. The water was allowed through the hatch in November and covered the meadow to a depth of one inch. Not only was it charged with chalk and other deposits, so enhancing the fertility of the meadow, it also acted as a blanket, protecting the grass from frost. Thus the water was kept on the meadow until the danger of severe frosts had passed, and only if scum began to appear on the surface of the water was it necessary to drain it off temporarily and allow the grass to breathe. By about the middle of March the grass was five to six inches high, and the water was then drained off, and the meadow allowed to dry for a few days. It was then ready to be grazed by sheep. The farmer thus had rich grass at his disposal at least a month and sometimes nearly two months before most other farmers. In consequence, he could over-winter more stock, knowing that the lean month of April was catered for. He could also advance lambing time and so gain a considerable financial advantage when he came to sell early lamb to the butcher.[1]

At the end of April, when the grass had been eaten low, the meadows were floated again for a few days, and then put up for hay. The harvest in June was generally four times as heavy as from ordinary meadows. If necessary a second or even a third crop of hay could be had in one year by repeating the same procedure. Alternatively, and more usually, the farmer grazed the meadow with dairy cattle until about October, when the drains and ducts had to be cleaned out and the waters let in again for the winter.

The floating of meadows demanded skill and experience, and by the mid-seventeenth century it was customary to entrust the work to a professional 'floater'. The initial cost of construction was high, but it was not always necessary for one individual to bear a heavy burden of expense. Although Rowland Vaughan, working alone, spent £2,000 on his meadows, the work was carried out on some common meadows

---

[1] This and the following paragraphs are based on E. Kerridge, 'The Floating of the Wiltshire Watermeadows', *Wilts. Arch. & Nat. Hist. Mag.*, CXCIX, 1953, pp. 105 *sqq.*; id., 'The Sheepfold in Wiltshire and the Floating of the Watermeadows', *EcHR*, 2nd Ser., VI, 3, 1954, pp. 282 *sqq.*; *Rowland Vaughan, His Booke*, ed. E. B. Wood, 1897; Hugh Platt, *The Jewell House of Art and Nature*, p. 46.

in Wiltshire by agreement with, and at a cost that was shared between, the whole community.

Although Rowland Vaughan publicized his pioneer efforts through his book, the written word did not persuade many of his fellow farmers. His example was much more effective. His methods were adopted before the middle of the seventeenth century in several places on the chalk lands of Salisbury plain, notably on the estates of the earls of Pembroke, who had family connections with the Vaughans, and had presumably seen and applauded the result of his efforts in Hereford-shire. Indeed, Vaughan wrote a dedicatory letter to William, earl of Pembroke. As with some later farming innovations, the new technique seems to have spread first through personal recommendation and example. Experiments in Wiltshire were probably being made around 1616. On the authority of Aubrey, we know for certain that floated meadows were started at Wylye and Chalke about 1635 and in other Wiltshire villages in the 1640's. After the period with which we are concerned, the use of floated watermeadows spread into other down-land areas in Berkshire, Dorset, and Hampshire, even into the Midlands and eastern England. It led to a sharp increase in the number of cattle and sheep that could be maintained both in winter and summer.

Pasture for the grazing of stock was plentiful in some areas through-out the year except when snow fell. In others it was adequate in summer and meagre throughout the winter, though many farmers had a close or two near the house where they could graze some of their animals when the commons were bare. All except the minority, whose pasture as well as arable land was enclosed, depended on the commons for feeding their animals during the summer and autumn. The risks of infection among stock grazing together in large numbers were reduced by strict by-laws, which imposed penalties on anyone who allowed a sick animal on to the common.

The value of rights of common pasture varied greatly between mixed farming and pastoral regions. In the less fertile pastoral areas—in the Pennines, and on the fells of the northern counties—common pasture rights were unlimited, and it was not unusual for a holding to be without pasture closes, and to have all its cultivated land in use as arable and meadow. Near the Scottish border, in Tyndale and Redes-dale, so spacious and neglected were the more distant pastures that the inhabitants of the valleys still practised transhumance in the early seventeenth century. In less remote nucleated settlements in the north some improvement of these vast commons was carried out by enclosing a portion where stock could have shelter and graze without the attention of a cattleherd or shepherd. And wherever pasture was plentiful, it was customary for the commoners by agreement to take in some of the common when necessary, plough it for a while and then put it back to common again. There are abundant references to this practice in Staffordshire where the ploughing usually lasted about five years, and greatly benefited the subsequent pasture. In the northern counties this taking in of common was the usual way of replacing one worn-out common field by a fresh one.[1]

The quality of the grazing on most commons was as nature made it and the stock ate and fertilized it. The practice of folding deprived the commons of much needed manure, but on the other hand some bene- fited more than ever before from the increasing number of animals put out by the commoners. The larger the flocks and herds, the more effectively they kept down the bracken and coarse, sedgy grass. As one of the graziers of Dartmoor explained it, "Pasture is just as good when there are many sheep [as when there are few] because the lower the sedge and grass is eaten in spring, the sweeter the pasture all the year after and the sheep prove the better." The argument suggests that perhaps some of our hillsides which have been surrendered to bracken may have been more profitable to our forebears when there were more cattle, wild horses, and sheep in these lonely places to keep the bracken at bay.[2]

Common pastures were also unstinted in the forest areas of the lowlands, even in comparatively populous districts such as east Northamptonshire and the Weald of Kent, and in all fen areas in eastern England where some of the wet commons were being drained and made more profitable in the early decades of the seventeenth century. So abundant was the grazing in the fens of Lincolnshire, indeed, that the commoners were allotted each year a portion of the fen to be shut up for hay. And in years of special abundance when there was still grass to spare, the bailiff of the manor agisted strangers' cattle for the summer at a few pence per head. But on all commons, however spacious, restrictions on unlimited grazing were imposed indirectly, since no one was supposed to keep more stock in summer than he could support on his home farm in winter. The rule was intended to stop the greedy opportunist from taking more than his share of the common, and judging by the prosecutions for infringement, it was sometimes strictly enforced.[3]

Grazing was a comparatively scarce commodity in some pastoral areas of the west Midlands and in all mixed farming districts every-

[1] E 134, 8 Jas. I, Easter 15; 34 Chas. II, Mich. 10; *Star Chamber Proceedings, Henry VIII & Edward VI*, Wm. Salt Archaeolog. Soc., 1912, p. 169; *Chanc. Proc. temp. Eliz., ibid.*, 1926, pp. 91–2.

[2] G. Plattes, *A Discovery of Hidden Treasure*, p. 30; E 134, 17 Chas. I, Mich. 21.

[3] E 134, 17–18 Eliz., M 6.

where. The number of animals which each tenant was allowed to graze on the common was related to the size of his holding, and the seasons at which stock could be grazed were agreed in the manorial courts. These measures did not prevent over-grazing, however, for large increases in stock numbers were taking place everywhere in this period. In some cases, the commoners met the difficulty by introducing stints for the first time, or reducing old ones.

The majority of townships in England and Wales, as we have seen, had a fixed allotment of common land, which could be improved but not enlarged. Some coastal townships, however, were in the exceptionally fortunate position of being able to count on a gradual increase in their land resources through the action of the sea along the shore. Some stretches of the coastline, of course, were being eroded at the same time, for example, in Holderness, Yorkshire, along the Lincolnshire coast at Mumby Chapel, at Benington along the Wash, at Penychen in Caernarvon, Rhuddlan in Denbigh, and Overton in Lancashire. But the losses here were small in comparison with the gains elsewhere. Large-scale marshland reclamation was being carried out, as opportunity offered, during the reigns of Elizabeth, James I, and Charles I. On the Suffolk coast reclamation of saltmarsh was carried on at a number of places, including Hemley, Bawdsey, Lowestoft, and Walberswick. Along the southern edge of the Wash extensive reclamations became possible in the early seventeenth century, because, the inhabitants said, of a change in the course of the channel which occurred during a storm in or about 1592 and once thereafter. The coastline started to silt up rapidly and hundreds of acres of marsh were built up between the old seabank and the sea. As the men of Whaplode graphically described it, creeks of the sea on which the wives of fishermen had once stood to call their husbands home to dinner had now become dry land. In Romney Marsh, Kent, at Lydd and Broomhill, the existence of some hundreds of acres of saltmarsh outside the seawall attracted the notice of the queen, who was lord of the manor, and became the subject of litigation to establish the queen's rights to draw rent from them. Thereafter the Crown conducted regular enquiries into the extent of reclaimed marsh along the whole coast of England and Wales, and discovered further small acreages on the banks of the Severn, and along the Devon, Hampshire, and Welsh coasts.[1]

Saltmarsh was a valuable asset to the inhabitants of coastal areas since it added fresh acres of grazing to their existing resources and made good pasture for horses and sheep. Although the marsh was damp,

---

[1] E 178, 5922; 3382; 2195; 2917; 1078; 6016; 5629; 3409; E 134, 27 & 28 Eliz., M 15; 23 Eliz., E 11; PRO DL 44, 67; Ipswich & E. Suffolk RO, Blois Coll., 50, 22, 3-1; Thirsk, *op. cit.*, pp. 15-19, 62-6.

sheep were unaffected by foot rot because of the salt. As soon as the spring tides drained off the marsh, it was left for a few days until the rain had washed out some of the salt. It was then ready for grazing until the next spring tide. The use of these unprotected saltmarshes was not without risk. An unexpectedly strong tide might drown the marsh before the animals had been driven to higher pastures, but the danger was reduced in some places by the presence of shepherds who kept watch in huts on the marsh. As silting proceeded, the saltmarshes were raised above the level of the tides, and lost their saltiness. Samphire and cotton lavender began to grow and the marsh was soon covered with coarse sedgy grass. Gradually its quality improved and it became dry pasture and meadow. Later still it became possible to plough it: at Holbeach, for example, four hundred acres of wheat, oats, barley, and rye were growing on the marshes in 1640.[1]

Sheep and horses were not the only occupants of the saltmarshes. Saltcotes were dotted along the coast from the shores of Lincolnshire to Essex. The salt evaporated here could not have been more conveniently situated to serve the needs of the graziers who thronged the marshes. They could have their meat slaughtered nearby and immediately salted down for ships' victuallers. The industry, which had been carried on in some places since the Iron Age, did not survive throughout this period, however. It came to an end in Lincolnshire at the beginning of the seventeenth century, possibly, as one contemporary alleged, because of the large imports of salt from Scotland at the accession of James I, possibly, as a recent writer has suggested, because of the dearth of turves as fuel for boiling the salt, caused by the gradual flooding of the turbaries during the later Middle Ages. Thereafter salt came to Lincolnshire by sea or by road, along the Salt Way which led from the saltmines at Droitwich in Worcestershire and entered the county near Saltby.[2]

Since common rights were granted to all men possessing a house and some arable land, and in some places, where pasture was plentiful, to all inhabitants whether they had land or not, there were few men who did not have an animal of some kind, usually a cow, sometimes a couple of sheep, and sometimes a horse, since the owner of a horse could always get a living as a carter. A cow was the most usual possession of the small man, whatever else he lacked, so that he could have milk, cheese, and butter even if he was too poor to buy meat. Among large farmers, for whom cattle breeding or fattening was a business, it was not unusual to find between forty and eighty animals in the yards and the fields.

[1] Thirsk, op. cit., pp. 17, 133.
[2] H. E. Hallam, 'Saltmaking in the Lincolnshire Fenland during the Middle Ages', Lincs. Archit. & Arch. Soc., NS VIII, 1960.

In the cattle-breeding areas of the north and west, whence stores were sold into the lowlands, and where it was important to give the calves a good start, they were left to run with the cows all the year. In the dairying areas they were weaned at between two and eight weeks and the milk sent to the dairyhouse throughout the summer and autumn for making into butter and cheese. In Hertfordshire, Essex, and other counties round London, calves were fattened for the butcher as there was a good market for veal in London. Otherwise, it was years before beef was ready for the butcher, and by that time many a bullock had come a long way from its birthplace. From the cattle-breeding areas of the north, west, and south-west stores were sent to the fattening areas of the Midlands, the Home Counties, and East Anglia. In the mixed farming areas cattle that were not bred on the farm were bought in between August and October and fattened for sale in winter or spring. In pastoral areas in the lowlands and on some enclosed farms elsewhere some cattle were overwintered, and more were bought in in spring to be ready for the butcher between July and September. Barren cows and oxen were used for draught until they were about ten years old and then fattened on hay, vetches, peas, boiled barley, or beans, and sold to the butcher.[1]

Contemporary writers on husbandry distinguished three principal breeds of cattle which they considered gave England its high reputation. First were the long-horned cattle, which were the main breed in York-shire, Derbyshire, Lancashire, and Staffordshire—black-haired, with large white horns tipped with black, square stately bodies, and short legs. They were especially good for tallow, hide, and horn, but also made good milkers and were strong in labour. Second came the Lincolnshire cattle of the fens and marshes, pied, but more white than anything else, with small crooked horns, tall, large bodies, and large but lean thighs. They were the strongest of all cattle for work and made good meat. The third type were the red Somerset and Gloucestershire cattle, with tall, large bodies, and small horns. They made excellent milkers.[2]

In addition to these, there were many other local breeds which did not enjoy the same celebrity. Woodland Suffolk, for example, had its polled dun-coloured cow, which produced the milk for Suffolk cheeses. Anglesey and Wales had a breed of black cattle that were considered excellent for fattening on barren or poor land, and were distinct from the red and brown cattle of the more fertile lands in south and central Wales. North Devon fostered a breed of red cattle, excel-lent for draught, and Sussex and Kent a dark red animal, also esteemed for draught and for beef. Cheshire cattle were large, big-boned long-

---

[1] Mortimer, *op. cit.*, pp. 168, 171; Mascall, *op. cit.*, pp. 52–8, 61.
[2] Markham, *Cheap and Good Husbandry*, pp. 85–6; Folkingham, *op. cit.*, p. 9.

horns, which yielded milk for cheese or good beef for those who wanted it.[1]

Despite the existence of these local breeds the fields in every shire were liable to hold a motley collection of cattle, for the trade in live-stock reached into every corner of the kingdom. There were red cattle in Durham, Cumberland, and Furness, as well as the black and brown longhorns. There are signs that imported Frisian cattle were already in Cumberland and Furness in the 1590's, if that is the correct interpreta-tion of references to *Frisent* and *Fristneck* cattle. The wild white cattle were to be found in Cumberland, at Gilsland and probably elsewhere. Irish cattle were imported in great numbers into Somerset and other counties in the west country. Indeed, it was alleged, in the House of Commons in 1621, that 100,000 Irish cattle came into the kingdom each year. In the lowland areas where fattening was the business, it was still more difficult to distinguish the most favoured breed, since cattle were brought in from Wales and the north. There were Welsh and northern steers in the Weald of Kent and in Essex, black and brown cattle in Hertfordshire.[2]

If cattle, and particularly cows, were considered the most desirable farm animals, sheep undoubtedly came next. "Sheep in mine opinion," wrote Fitzherbert, "is the most profitablest cattle that a man can have," and this belief was reflected in the care lavished on them. In southern England, at least, they were regarded as tender animals, prone to disease, and unable to endure the cold. Hence houses were recommended for them in winter, and were certainly used in Gloucestershire and Herefordshire. In arable areas having common fields and meadows, lambing took place between the beginning of January and the end of March so that the lambs would be strong enough before May to be moved out of the meadows, then being closed for hay, and to follow the ewes over the rough stubble and water furrows of the common fields. Pasture sheep dropped their lambs in April when the grass was ready for them, and were weaned at 16–18 weeks, or at 12 weeks if the ewes were to be milked for cheese, as in the Derbyshire Peak. Meat from suckled lambs was considered vastly preferable, however, to that of grass lambs.[3]

Sheep were normally shorn about mid-June and culled at Michael-mas, when a great movement of sheep took place from breeding to feeding grounds and from feeding grounds to the butcher. The regular slaughter of stock at Michaelmas is a myth: it occurred in

[1] R. Trow-Smith, *A History of British Livestock Husbandry to 1700*, pp. 197, 210; Mortimer, *op. cit.*, p. 166.

[2] Notestein, Relf, and Simpson, *Commons Debates, 1621*, III, p. 214; V, p. 492.

[3] Fitzherbert, *op. cit.*, p. 42; Mascall, *op. cit.*, pp. 202, 229; Beale, *op. cit.*, p. 54; Markham, *Cheap and Good Husbandry*, pp. 105, 108, 113.

occasional years when the hay crop had been exceptionally poor, but otherwise the only slaughter that took place was of fat animals. In the winter sheep were fed on grass, hay, or straw, chaff, peas in the straw, or mashes of barley, beans, and acorns. In the worst of the winter ash and elm leaves and holly were used for fodder. In the spring the sheep were driven into the fields to graze the tares, where grown, or the green shoots of rye and wheat. Ewes before lambing were put on the best pasture available, or fed on threshed oats or peas and oats in the straw. Before taking the ram they were brought into good condition with oat or barley stubble. Wethers were finished for the butcher at four or five years either on grass during the summer or on peas during the winter, to be ready for sale between December and May. Lamb was in the shops at any time from Christmas onwards, for the sheep of Dorset, Hampshire, and Wiltshire lambed about November, and many ewes in lamb were bought up by Middlesex graziers for early sale at Christmas. Otherwise lambs fattened for the butcher were not ready until July.[1]

The soundest precept offered to the purchaser of sheep was that he should buy from land of poorer quality than his own, so that his flock would thrive when moved to better grazing. The best cure for sick sheep and the best way to increase the milk from ewes was a change of pasture. The principal diseases were liver fluke and rot, the latter avoided by moving the sheep regularly to fresh pastures, the former cured quickly (without much loss to the farmer) by despatching the animal to the butcher.[2]

In all areas of mixed farming, the folding of sheep on the arable was a pillar of the farming system, and the breeds of sheep used for this purpose were specially conditioned to it. In common-field areas the sheep were put into a common village flock, since a small flock was useless, hurdled at night, and the pens moved from one part of the field to another daily. On enclosed farms the farmer needed a large flock or the system did not work. A thousand sheep would fold an acre of common-field land in a night, and folding was arranged so that each field should be dunged in time for sowing. Folding was only possible on land that was fairly dry, otherwise the sheep were liable to rot. In Wiltshire on the warm chalk soils of the downs folding continued all the year round. But in other places it was carried on during the summer months only, between about May and September.[3]

Contemporaries believed that environment and feed were the main

[1] A.S., *The Husbandman's Instructor*, p. 53; Trow-Smith, *op. cit.*, pp. 242–4; Mascall, *op. cit.*, pp. 303–4, 306; Mortimer, *op. cit.*, p. 180.   [2] Beale, *op. cit.*, p. 54.
[3] E. Kerridge, 'The Sheepfold in Wiltshire', *loc. cit.*, pp. 284–5; Mortimer, *op. cit.*, p. 180; Mascall, *op. cit.*, p. 230; Henry Best, *op. cit.*, p. 14.

factors which shaped the breeds, and that all sheep were liable to change their characteristics when moved from one place to another. Strangely, they attached no importance to the effects of selective breeding, though their textbooks insisted on this matter, and the results of selection, haphazard though it may often have been, cannot have been negligible. Thus while modern geneticists give much more weight to the effects of selection than to environment, contemporaries considered the influence of the latter paramount and so did not attempt to enumerate all the many local breeds and define their relationships. All we can do, therefore, is to note the principal types, knowing that minor deviations occurred in every locality.[1]

All the mountain breeds were small, horned animals, some white, some black-faced, usually wild and restless, and producing a sometimes hairy but often fine wool, and excellent mutton. Many reared on the mountains were sold at two or three years or thereabouts into the lowlands, sometimes far distant, where they were fattened for the butcher. Wales had a breed of mountain sheep, horned, small-bodied, usually dark in colour, either black, grey, or brown; Cornwall had a sheep similar to the Welsh, called the South-West Horned. In the hilly areas of the north Midlands and beyond, the principal breed was the black-faced heath sheep, otherwise known as the Lintons, big-boned with large spirally twisted horns, and carrying rough, shaggy, hairy wool. From this breed are descended the modern Scottish Blackface, the Rough Fell, the Swaledale, and the Dalesbred breeds. In the Lake District the Herdwick—a white-faced horned breed—was more favoured. They were the very smallest of the hill sheep, and extremely agile at climbing rough mountain sides. Their wool was grey in colour and coarse in texture, and was already used for making carpets. The sweet taste of their mutton was said to be enhanced by the holly and ash leaves fed to them in winter. Numerous local breeds, descended from these two types of black-faced and white-faced horned mountain sheep, were to be found in the forests and on the moors of the Midlands and the south-west. Dartmoor had one type, Exmoor another, the Mendip forest another, Cannock another, Delamere another, Charnwood another. Their faces and legs were sometimes white, but generally black, grey, or dun-coloured, and usually they had horns. But all yielded fine wool and fine-flavoured mutton.[2]

[1] Markham, *Cheap and Good Husbandry*, p. 103; A.S., *op. cit.*, p. 48. The following account has benefited greatly from discussions with Dr Michael Ryder and his article, 'The History of Sheep Breeds in Britain', AHR, XII, 1964.
[2] David Low, *On the Domesticated Animals of the British Islands*, 1845, pp. 64–8, 80–4; Mortimer, *op. cit.*, p. 177; Markham, *op. cit.*, p. 104; Sydney Moorhouse, 'Herdwick Sheep of the Lake Country', *Wool Knowledge*, III, 12, 1956, pp. 14–19.

The finest wool of all, however, came from the short-woolled sheep of the lowlands, all reared on sweet, but short, not to say scanty, herbage. The best producers of fine wool were the Ryelands, which came from Herefordshire, particularly around Leominster, Shropshire, and Worcestershire, though they were also to be found in various forest districts in the neighbourhood, such as the Forest of Dean, and even in Wales. They were small white-faced animals, with a short delicate fleece, weighing between one and two pounds. These were the animals which were housed at night in the belief that this preserved the fineness of their fleeces.[1]

Dorset had another breed of white-faced short-wool sheep which was unique in that the ewes received the ram early in the season and produced lambs in October which were ready for the butcher by Christmas. Hence some ewes in lamb were sold to Middlesex graziers for the supply of the gourmet's table in London. This long breeding season is still exploited in the modern Dorset Horn breed. The Dorset sheep had white legs and faces, small horns in both sexes, long limbs, low shoulders, and a fleece of medium-fine wool. They were hardy and suited to folding. But the best breeds for this last purpose were the Old Wiltshires of Wiltshire and Hampshire, the Southdown—the "hillish breed" kept by Toke of Godinton, Kent, in the early seventeenth century—and the Norfolk sheep. The Wiltshires were the largest of the white-faced short wools, with clumsy heads, arched faces, horns in male and female, long, straight back, and long, large-boned legs. Their mutton was tolerable but they were slow to fatten, and usually it was not for the butcher that they were kept. Their great virtue was their ability to be driven long distances up hill and down dale from the downland pastures to the fold on the arable fields, and to make good on scanty herbage. Their fleeces were fine and weighed about two pounds. Equally suited to the fold were the black-faced short wool Southdowns and Norfolks. The Southdown was a small animal, with light fore-quarters, narrow chest, long neck, and the long limbs characteristic of most fold sheep. Its home was the Sussex downs. The Norfolk had a long body and legs, was a sturdy walker, and a producer of sweet mutton as well as wool. It was a popular breed on the brecklands of Norfolk and Suffolk and in Cambridgeshire.[2]

Long-woolled sheep were the sheep of the rank marshes and fens and of the fertile vales inland. The Lincolnshire marsh and fen sheep was a Lustre Longwool, like the Midland sheep, and the largest of all, with

---

[1] Mortimer, *op. cit.*, p. 177; Markham, *op. cit.*, p. 103; Beale, *op. cit.*, p. 54; Low, *op. cit.*, pp. 155–7.

[2] Low, *op. cit.*, pp. 120–4, 162–3, 187, 114–16; E. Kerridge, 'The Sheepfold in Wiltshire', EcHR, 2nd Ser., VI, 1954, p. 283; Folkingham, *op. cit.*, p. 9.

long legs, a long naked belly, admirably adapted to survive on lush but damp grazing. It fattened slowly but butchers liked it nevertheless for its large proportion of fat. It had a heavy fleece of long, coarse wool. The Romney Marsh sheep—a Demi-lustre Longwool—was bred in a similar environment. It is a more primitive breed than the Midland Longwool, with which it too has affinities, but on the fat grazings and under the harsh climate of the marsh it had developed in flesh, wool, and hardiness. As a meat animal it was as slow to mature as the Lincolnshire, but again it yielded a large quantity of fat and offal. Its principal asset, however, was its fleece, which although shorter than the Lustre Longwool commonly weighed three to five pounds.

The sheep of the inland vales were again Lustre Longwools—the large Teeswater on Teesside and the Midland Longwool sheep, found in Warwickshire, east Worcestershire, Leicestershire, Buckinghamshire, Northamptonshire, and most of Nottinghamshire except Sherwood Forest. The Midland was a large-boned lank-bodied animal with a coarse head, and produced a medium-fine fleece weighing two to three pounds. When kept in enclosed pastures, as opposed to common fields, all these qualities of size and weight were further exaggerated.[1]

The two main types of horse used in agriculture were the packhorse for cross-country transport and the cart-horse for labour in the fields. In addition, farmers had to satisfy a considerable demand for saddle and coach-horses. These were usually of cart-horse stock mixed with other, mainly foreign breeds, for horses were imported from abroad more often than any other farm animals. Thus Gervase Markham recommended that for the saddle an English mare be bred with a Turk or Irish Hobbie, for coach and cart with a Flanders or Friesland horse, and for heavy transport with a German horse. And in suggesting this mixing of breeds, he claimed to have had practical experience of the results.[2]

Horses were reared in considerable numbers in all the forests of England. Some were wild, like the ponies of the New Forest, some were farm-bred. The wild horses were usually of pony size, though better grazing sometimes produced a larger animal. Others were of mixed blood and included horses for the hunt, and towards the end of the period, for the racecourse. Their importance among horse fanciers may be judged by the fact that many horse fairs were held in towns within or adjoining the forests: for example, at Woodstock, Rothwell, Northampton, and Brewood. The common packhorse, which carried cloth from the Yorkshire dales to the towns and ports, coal from the

[1] Markham, *op. cit.*, pp. 103–4; Low, *op. cit.*, pp. 171, 176; A.S., *op. cit.*, p. 49; E. Topsell, *The History of Fourfooted Beasts*, p. 484; Mortimer, *op. cit.*, p. 177.
[2] Gervase Markham, *Cavalarice or the English Horseman*, 1625, p. 18.

coalpits, and peat and fuel from the moors of Cornwall and Devon, was probably descended from the same stock of forest ponies. He was a small, sure-footed animal, also used for riding.

The vales of England bred larger horses which were used for draught. They were not speedy but had great strength. Some were mixed with foreign blood to produce saddle horses and lighter carriage horses, but their quality of endurance was best revealed in work on the farm. There were many local breeds known to contemporaries, of which we have no record. But there are incidental references to coach-horses which came from Rothwell fair, near Kettering; plough and cart-horses from Durham; horses from Cleveland, Yorkshire, the Cleveland bays, in other words, excellent for ploughing lighter soils; and the chestnut-coloured Suffolk Punch from wood-pasture Suffolk, which, with its thickset body and short legs, was an ideal horse for work on heavy soils, and would pull a heavily laden wagon till it dropped. The Lincolnshire fens bred horses for the coalpits of Nottinghamshire, the leadmines of Derbyshire, and for Yorkshire breeders who mated fenland mares with their local types.[1]

As we have seen, horse-breeding was mainly the speciality in pastoral areas, where it was usual to have a team of mares and work them gently till near foaling. Hence the preoccupation with horse-breeding in the Lincolnshire and Norfolk fens, the Somerset Levels, the Essex marshes, the Yorkshire dales, Cannock Chase, the forests of Pickering, Maccles-field, Northamptonshire, and Arden, and the New Forest. In mixed farming areas, with more arable land at their disposal, horses and geldings were a better proposition. These were the choice in south Hertfordshire and Cambridgeshire, counties which were traversed by main roads into London, and had to meet a large demand for coach-horses. Hertfordshire horses were bought in as colts from Leicestershire, at two or three years, and sold at six years.[2]

Pig-keeping was regarded as one of the peasant's standbys. It was a common saying that "he that hath sheep, swine, and bees, sleep he, wake he, may thrive." Many a peasant, therefore, kept a pig or two as "the husbandman's best scavenger, the housewife's most wholesome sink." And in due course he had meat that hung in the roof and kept better than all other flesh. It would be an exaggeration, however, to think that all peasants kept pigs. Many a family did not have enough kitchen waste to keep even one pig: in Northumberland, Durham, Cumberland, and Westmorland, therefore, the majority of peasants had none at all. Thus, although pig-keeping enabled the small peasant

[1] David Low, *op. cit.*, pp. 521, 524, 602, 619; vol. IV of this series, pp. 88–9; Robert Reyce, *Suffolk in the Seventeenth Century*, pp. 42–3; Thirsk, *op. cit.*, pp. 176, 32.

[2] Worlidge, *op. cit.*, p. 160; Mortimer, *op. cit.*, p. 149.

to enjoy meat at the lowest cost, to produce pigs for the market was mainly a business for the larger farmer, or for the specialized husbandman who happened to have suitable feed that cost him little. Thus, dairymen kept pigs in large numbers to consume the whey from the dairy. In the forests they were fattened in droves on acorns, beechmast, crab apples, medlars, and hazelnuts, and in Herefordshire, when nuts were short, on elm leaves. In mixed farming areas, however, particularly in the Midlands, they were fattened, not on kitchen waste or on the common harvest of the woods, but on grain and pulses, specially grown for their benefit. In Germany at this period this would have been regarded as a most uneconomic and extravagant method of farming.[1]

The best pig was considered to be one that had a long, deep-sided, deep-bellied body, with thick thighs, short legs, and a thick neck. They might be pink, sandy, or white, but very few were black. They were fattened in various ways according to the facilities available. In forest areas they were turned into the woods for fattening in six to eight weeks, and were then brought home, and finished off in sties, feeding for ten to fourteen days on old dried peas, split beans, or tares. In Elizabeth's reign a dispute developed between two men who arranged to send 240 pigs from Buckinghamshire and Oxfordshire to be fed in the woods of Sussex and Hampshire, and to receive them back "well and sufficiently fed for bacon." It was this kind of forest pig-keeping that made Hampshire hogs "allowed by all for the best bacon." This business maintained many a peasant in the Chilterns and the Shropshire and Herefordshire forests. In Suffolk's wood-pasture region the pigs were reared with the dairy, and then fed on the mast and acorns of the woods. Acorns were claimed to make the hardest, firmest flesh which salted down the best.[2]

In the neighbourhood of towns such as London and York pork and bacon were much in demand, and for that reason pigs were kept in great numbers in Hertfordshire and in the vale of York. One of the feeding methods was to put them in sties and feed them on the dregs and offal of tallow, mixed with a warm wash, till the pigs fattened up, when their flesh was hardened off with peas. This procedure produced bacon speedily, though, as may be imagined, it lacked much flavour. For lard or brawn swine were fed with barley mash, followed by raw malt and dried peas, washed down with sweet whey or the dregs of ale barrels.[3]

[1] Blagrave, *op. cit.*, p. 73; Mascall, *op. cit.*, p. 257; Speed, *Adam out of Eden*, p. 86; Markham, *Cheap and Good Husbandry*, p. 121.
[2] G. Markham, *op. cit.*, pp. 122, 128; PRO Req. 2, 270, 39; VCH *Hants.*, v, p. 496; Reyce, *op. cit.*, p. 37; A.S., *The Husbandman's Instructor*, p. 74.
[3] Markham, *op. cit.*, pp. 129–30.

The largest pigs, and the very best meat of all, came from Midland counties, such as Leicestershire and Northamptonshire, where peas and beans were grown in quantity, mainly for the purpose of feeding pigs. At nine months or a year old, they were shut up in sties and fattened in four to five weeks, or turned out, as in Leicestershire, to feed from the peas ricks in the fields.[1]

Another source of food for the modest husbandman was poultry. All but the poorest had a few hens, chickens, and sometimes ducks, while those who enjoyed generous common rights kept geese as well. Hence the fenlanders of eastern England and the foresters of Dartmoor kept geese in large numbers and earned something from the sale of feathers and grease as well as meat. At the same time a poultry-keeping industry was already in existence in Norfolk and to a less extent in Suffolk. Not only were chickens fattened for the market but ducks, geese, and turkeys, too. Turkeys were not introduced into Europe from Mexico until the second decade of the sixteenth century but by the end of Elizabeth's reign there were already considerable numbers in Norfolk.

Buckwheat was one of the foods most used in East Anglia for fattening poultry. But in the 1590's, carrots and turnips also were used for this purpose which may have suggested their use for cattle too. Various other grains served their turn when available. Turkeys were fed on sodden barley and oats, and sometimes on bruised acorns; chickens were crammed with wheat meal and milk for fourteen days; capons were crammed with corn and peas at the barn door, or penned and fed with barley malt. Geese were fed on grass or other pastures; the young were fattened with ground malt and milk, old and stubble geese with new malt. Outside East Anglia poultry-keeping as a speciality was the eccentric choice of individuals, but it is worth mentioning William Dockray of Matterdale, Cumberland, whose labours suggest that the market for poultry was not restricted to London. In 1639 Dockray possessed 160 head of poultry, worth £42.[2]

Finally, among the activities of the peasant, from which the poor were not debarred by the cost of equipment, was bee-keeping. Since honey was the main sweetening agent in the kitchen, there were beehives everywhere. In the forests they were made of hazel wood, in champion country of long rye straw, and in the west country of wheat straw. If they were more in evidence in some districts than others, it was on the moorlands where heather honey was produced.[3]

[1] Mortimer, *op. cit.*, p. 184; Markham, *op. cit.*, pp. 128–9; A.S., *op. cit.*, pp. 73–4.
[2] H. Platt, *The Jewell House of Art and Nature*, p. 13; Markham, *op. cit.*, p. 139; Worlidge, *op. cit.*, p. 165.
[3] Markham, *op. cit.*, p. 169.

Goats were kept only in mountainous areas, in High Furness, for example, Northumberland, and Wales, where "cattle of better profit can hardly be maintained." Besides giving milk to their owners, their skin was useful for clothing, their hair excellent for ropes, since it did not rot in water, and their flesh when young as tasty as venison.[1]

Deer which had been kept in parks in the Middle Ages were gradually thrust out in the second half of the sixteenth century by deliberate action on the part of lay landowners, and by neglect on the part of the Crown in administering royal chases. Almost everywhere, even in Cumberland, where it might be thought that land was not always put to the most profitable use, deer gave way to more profitable cattle.[2]

Rabbits were not regarded as pests but as a valuable source of additional income for those who were willing to go to the expense of making a warren. For besides providing meat at six weeks, the rabbit had a skin that made a useful fur. For those whose crops were liable to be eaten by rabbits they were a nuisance but not an incurable one. Rabbits could be contained in the warren if good banks were erected and maintained around the perimeter. Most warrens were situated on heathy, sandy, or other waste land that was of little use for other purposes. There were warrens on the Yorkshire and Lincolnshire wolds, on the moors of Barnsley, in Sherwood Forest, on the Northamptonshire heaths, on the Norfolk brecklands, on the eastern sands of Suffolk, and on the heath at Wrotham, Kent, where one warren owner paid his rent with the profit of his rabbits.[3]

D. FRUIT AND MARKET-GARDENING

Finally, two branches of farming which assumed a new importance in this period and which have since become the principal, and sometimes the only activity, of some farmers, were fruit-growing and market-gardening. Great emphasis was placed on fruit-growing as a profitable enterprise with an assured market in the sixteenth century. In most of the fruit-growing counties—Kent, Hertfordshire, Worcestershire, Gloucestershire, Herefordshire, Somerset, and Devon, fruit trees grew in every hedgerow, and farmers elsewhere were urged to plant them likewise. But in these counties orchards too were rapidly increasing in number.[4]

[1] Markham, *op. cit.*, p. 116; A.S., *op. cit.*, p. 91; Worlidge, *op. cit.*, p. 162.
[2] Norden, *op. cit.*, pp. 114–15.
[3] Speed, *Adam out of Eden*, p. 3.
[4] This and the following three paragraphs are based on Alicia Amherst, *A History of Gardening in England*, 1895, pp. 93–8, 143–55; Norden, *op. cit.*, pp. 208–9; S. Hartlib, *op. cit.*, p. 20; John Beale, *op. cit.*, pp. 3, 10, 32. I wish to thank Miss W. Dullforce for help with the bibliography of this subject.

Fruit-growing seems to have benefited greatly from royal encouragement, for it was to royal gardens that attention was always directed by contemporaries whenever they discussed the history of fruit-growing in their own lifetime. Henry VIII's gardener, Richard Harris, is said to have been among the first to import French grafts of cherry, pear, and apple, and among apples "especially pippins, before which time there were no pippins in England." The anonymous writer of this account (1609) added that Harris's orchard at Teynham, Kent, was "the chief mother of all other orchards for those kinds of fruit in Kent and divers other places." The apricot, too, was a novelty of the first half of the sixteenth century, probably introduced by Henry VIII's gardener, Wolf, about 1524, while among the first gooseberries to be planted in gardens were those growing in Henry VIII's garden in 1516.

By Charles I's reign the varieties of apples were too numerous for the compilers of botanical descriptions to list them all. Of pears there were at least sixty-five varieties, of cherries thirty-five, of plums sixty-one, and of apricots six, including one brought back from "the Argier voyage" against pirates in 1620 by John Tradescant, a great fruit-grower who "laboured to obtain all the rarest fruits he can hear of." The fruits of warmer summers than those enjoyed in England were still patiently coaxed and coddled. Lord Burghley planted vines at Hatfield about 1607, and having an orange tree already, ordered a lemon tree from abroad. The peach was grown but not with much success, its fruit being soft and fleshy and "hoary without." James I tried hard to encourage the planting of mulberry trees and issued a circular letter to Lords Lieutenant of the counties in 1609 announcing that he would be sending one thousand mulberry trees to each county town the following March, and requiring the inhabitants to plant them.

The fruits that reached the market in largest quantity were cherries, apples, and pears, and the connoisseur knew the best varieties from each part of the country. Hertfordshire and Kentish apples and Hertfordshire pears were sold in London as fruit. Perry was best made from west country and Kentish pears. Pippins, that is to say dessert apples, and cherries were a speciality in Kent around Faversham and Sittingbourne. Cherries grew plentifully at Ketteringham, Norfolk. Worcestershire grew pears and cherries better than Herefordshire. Herefordshire grew excellent cooking apples but for lack of river transport had difficulty in selling its cider.

Market-gardening developed rapidly in the late sixteenth century—mainly in the 1590's—with the encouragement and active participation of alien immigrants from the Low Countries. The areas around London which specialized in this activity can be gauged from the addresses of members of the Gardeners' Company, which received its first charter in 1605, and quickly grew in importance. Some of the centres of market gardening were Westminster, Lambeth, Battersea, Fulham, Putney, and Brentford, and, in the opposite direction along the Thames, Whitechapel, Stepney, Hackney, and Greenwich. These were all districts with easy access to the river, which enabled market produce and the dung that was essential in large quantities for this kind of intensive cultivation, to be transported by water. More distant from London were market-garden centres in Surrey, Essex, and Kent, particularly at Colchester and Sandwich. The Sandwich carrot, indeed, was as famous as the Fulham parsnip and the Hackney turnip.[1]

E. CONCLUSION

We have enumerated the various branches of farming in which both plain countrymen and ingenious husbandmen were engaged in the sixteenth and early seventeenth centuries. The individual's choice of a suitable combination of these activities was to a large extent determined for him by the condition of his land—its soil and topography, and the climate of the district—and by the routine that was necessary to maintain each branch of farming. Some activities could be undertaken together by a peasant family with little land and large pasture commons, which were out of the question for the man with a virgate of land and small pasture rights. The main specialities, however, can be summarized thus: pastoral areas were engaged either in cattle or sheep breeding, fattening, dairying, pig-keeping, or horse-breeding, or, more usually, doing something of each. The main stock-breeding areas lay in the moorland and mountainous parts of the highland zone, most stock fattening was done in the vales, dairying was carried on in both, pig-keeping and horse-breeding were the specialities of the forests, but pig-keeping was also an adjunct to the dairy. Always the arable land in these regions was no more than adequate to satisfy domestic and farm needs for grain, and the large-scale market production of arable crops was impossible. The mixed farming areas usually contained far more ploughland than pasture, except perhaps in parts of the Midland counties such as Leicestershire and Northamptonshire, where enclosure in some areas had wrought drastic changes in the proportions of each. Mixed farming regions specialized in growing grain and fodder crops. Cereals were marketed, if water transport by river or sea was available, and if not, were used to feed and fatten stock for the butcher. Some mixed farming areas, in consequence, had the same objectives as the

[1] P. McGrath, 'The Marketing of Food, Fodder, and Livestock in the London Area in the Seventeenth Century', London M.A. thesis, 1948, pp. 193–206; Norden, *op. cit.*, pp. 229–30; Folkingham, *op. cit.*, p. 42.

pastoral vales, though their methods were different. Less usual crops such as saffron, teasels, and vegetables for the table, which were grown in specialized areas, were not necessarily products of enclosed farms, but were incorporated in arable rotations in common fields. Hemp and flax, of course, were grown everywhere in crofts and closes beside the house, though some pastoral districts, such as the fens, specialized in them.

Although much specialization was an ancient tradition, it was not a fixed and unchanging one. Slight modifications, and some more drastic ones, can be observed in the course of this century and a half. Some breeding areas, such as Arden in Warwickshire, for example, turned to dairying; fruit growing spread from the Canterbury area of Kent to other districts on the edge of the Weald; dairying in the Weald disappeared for good and cattle fattening became the principal activity. Moreover, as one region prospered by means of its speciality, it influenced its neighbours. Cheese production in the wood-pasture region of Norfolk, for example, spread into the sheep-corn region, and the dairying of the Arden in Warwickshire infected the Felden.

The land's capacity, the custom of the country, capital resources, and the influence of market prices were paramount influences governing the choice of speciality by individual farmers. But no mean consideration was the cost of labour. We catch fragments of the discussion on this matter in the advice given by James Bankes of Winstanley to his son. He was lord of the manor and an employer of labour on his demesne. Writing in 1600 he recommended corn growing "for in breeding of cattle is great loss." "Make tillage of your best land that is good and therein your gain will be greatest for corn is ready money and cometh once a year." By 1610 experience had caused him to revise his ideas. His labourers had caused him much anxiety and trouble, and he had decided that a system of pasture farming which required the least labour paid best.

"Make no more tillage to get corn than to serve your house, for I have been hindered by keeping of servants in getting of corn that I have rather desired to die than to live for they care not whether end goeth forward so that they have meat, drink, and wages. Small fear of God is in servants, and thou shalt find my counsel just and most true."

This problem of the labourer's inefficiency and its influence upon the farming programme of the larger farmer is also referred to in a letter by a Yorkshire steward to his master in the 1620's. "Nothing is more unprofitable than a farm in tillage in the hands of servants where the master's eye is not daily upon them."[1]

[1] Joyce Bankes, op. cit., pp. 23, 28; Sheffield RO, Strafford Letters, WWM, 20(a), 17

In the course of the sixteenth century, most noticeably after about 1560 when our records become abundant, farm production made rapid strides. It is impossible to say how far yields per acre were raised during this period since there were wide differences in the rate of seeding and in the yields from different kinds of soil, and documentary evidence between different periods never affords comparisons of like with like. But we can confidently speak of other reasons for the increase in agricultural production: namely, the use of more intensive rotations, accompanied by heavier manuring; the use of improved varieties of grain; and, probably most important of all, the impressive increase in the total acreage of land under the plough as a result of the reclamation of waste and the conversion of pasture. This increased acreage, it should be noted, was regarded by contemporaries as the main explanation for the improved supply of corn. It led an unknown writer to the Commissioners for Pardons to write in 1621 that "there is no want of cornland at this time, but want of pastures and cattle, for much woodlands and barren grounds are become fruitful corn lands instead of pasture." Heavier manuring of the arable, of course, was made possible by keeping larger numbers of animals, which resulted in a great increase in the supply of meat and wool and other animal products. Heavier rates of stocking were made possible by the improvement of pastures and meadows by fertilizers, by the improved supply of spring grazing, through the watering of meadows in the west country, the growing of tares elsewhere, and by the increased supply of summer grazing through the use of leys and the reclamation of coastal marshland and fen. Thus improvements in arable and pastoral husbandry went hand in hand, each helping the other, and both serving to promote the specialization and interdependence of regions.

2

ENCLOSING AND ENGROSSING, 1500–1640

A. INTRODUCTION

Enclosing and engrossing were two of the most controversial topics in sixteenth-century England. They provoked animated discussion in the alehouses, inspired outspoken sermons from the pulpit, and stirred passions and community loyalties in the fields as men ploughed their strips side by side in the common fields and muttered imprecations against the selfish and the rich. They incited many minor local riots and one larger disturbance which spread across three Midland counties. Popular indignation prodded the government into action, and commissions of enquiry, proclamations, and statutes form a continuous series from the beginning of Henry VII's reign to the end of Elizabeth's and beyond.

A movement which was so widespread, in which so many people of all classes participated, and yet which aroused such loud popular outcry, poses problems for the historian. He cannot make sense of the seeming contradictions without recognizing first that the word 'enclosure' was a very loose general term for a number of different dealings concerning land and changes in land use, and, secondly, that the economic advantages and social consequences of enclosing and engrossing differed profoundly from one region to another. To those who observed or experienced some of the more ruthless enclosures of land in the Midland counties, all enclosers were agents of Satan and all enclosures inflicted grievous harm on the community. Such hardened opponents of change would hardly have recognized as part of the same movement the amicable enclosures taking place at the same time in some of the northern and west Midland counties.

To arrive at a fair definition of enclosing and engrossing, it is first necessary to strip the subject of all reference to the controversies which surrounded it in the Tudor period. To enclose land was to extinguish common rights over it, thus putting an end to all common grazing. To effect this, it was usual for the encloser to hedge or fence the land. Thus in contemporary controversy anger was directed mainly at the hedges and fences—the outward and visible signs of enclosure. To make it economically worth while, enclosure was often preceded by the amalgamation of several strips by exchange or purchase. If the enclosed land lay in the common arable fields or in the meadows, the encloser now had complete freedom to do what he pleased with his land throughout the year, instead of having to surrender the stubble or aftermath after harvest to the use of the whole township. On the pasture commons, enclosure by an individual signified the appropriation to one person of land which had previously been at the disposal of the whole community throughout the year. All enclosures, then, whether they concerned land in the common fields, in the meadows, or in the common pastures, deprived the community of common rights. The seriousness of the loss depended entirely on whether the needs of the villagers' stock were adequately met by the common grazing which remained. Engrossing signified the amalgamation of two or more farms into one. The superfluous farmhouse was either left to fall into decay, or, with a small piece of land attached to it, was down-graded to accommodate a cottager. Engrossing and enclosing were frequently referred to in the same breath as twin evils in the countryside. But they did not inevitably accompany one another. Many an encloser was innocent of the charge of engrossing. Many an engrosser of land was free of all temptation to enclose. The two sins ranked together because, by different means, they both caused depopulation.

To analyse the significance of enclosing and engrossing first of all in the electric atmosphere of sixteenth-century popular agitation is to see two commonplace changes in the use and distribution of land at one special moment in history when tempers were high and perspective was distorted. Enclosing and engrossing were as ancient as farming itself. They could and did occur without riot or revolution, and, in less inflammable situations, were regarded as part of a sensible and reasonable plan of agrarian improvement.

Much enclosure had already taken place without trial or tribulation in the early Middle Ages. Enclosure from the waste had been as commonplace a part of the farming round as ploughing. And as long as the commons remained plentiful, such enterprise went unchallenged. Individuals who wished to enlarge their holdings cleared an acre or two on the vacant land adjoining their farms, if possible, or at a convenient distance. Others made a small clearing in the forest, and started a pioneer operation which was not completed for several generations. Their labours might end in the creation of a family farm, or even in a small hamlet. Settlements like this of medieval origin are scattered all over England, and lie usually on the fringes of parishes. Sometimes a group of farmers, or even whole villages, enclosed some common land by agreement and by co-operative labour. In this way, much land in the fen was diked, drained, enclosed, and then partitioned among the tenants of the fen villages. The community thus added to its land resources as population grew.

The growth of population, indeed, had been the sharpest goad behind the enclosure of pasture and waste in the Middle Ages and continued so until the nineteenth century when the movement virtually reached completion. At the beginning of settlement all townships had had extensive wastes for which they had no immediate use. As population increased, this land formed a reserve upon which the community could draw to support its growing numbers. So long as the reserves remained plentiful, no one counted the loss of a few acres enclosed here and there to provide a better living for one member of the community, while manorial lords welcomed all improvements which increased their income from rent. Indeed, as late as the sixteenth century in thinly populated districts—for example in many parts of Lancashire, Yorkshire, and the more northern counties, neighbouring villages intercommoned on the waste lying between their townships without observing any frontiers.

Serious disagreements between villages did not arise for centuries, often not until the Tudor age, when the diminishing waste and the growth of population taught people to look at first anxiously, and then angrily, at the slightest new encroachment on their commons. They learned at last, by bitter practical experience, that the commons were not unlimited, and that their diminution beyond a certain point could pose grave economic problems. The changing situation in the sixteenth century is best described by a tenant of Holme on Spalding Moor, Yorkshire, giving evidence in 1620 in a dispute about common rights. A cottage built on the common some sixty years before had enjoyed common rights "by sufferance or negligence of the freeholders," for at that time "the freeholders made little reckoning of common for so small goods [i.e. so few stock] as was then put upon the said common by the said tenants." The situation changed radically in the next two generations. The population as a whole increased, and this cottage, originally a small hut 15 feet by 12 feet, containing two small rooms, was altered to accommodate another and more affluent farmer who added a parlour, a chamber over the parlour, a milkhouse, a stable, and at the end of the building a new hall house, kitchen, barn, and beast-house. He had a great many stock and claimed the right to graze them all on the commons.[1] Since this kind of incident recurred many times in townships all over England, it is not difficult to see how in the end the enclosure of the waste became a highly controversial issue. The same episode serves to illustrate a further point, namely, that the crisis of land shortage was liable to occur at different times in different districts, for not all townships grew in population at the same pace, nor did they start with the same amount of land. Hence in Shropshire or

[1] E 134, 18 Jas. I, Hil. 15.

Lancashire in the sixteenth and early seventeenth centuries enclosure was usually an amicable and peaceable proceeding, which reflected the fact that land was still an abundant commodity. The indignation which enclosure aroused at the same period in the east Midlands, on the other hand, leaves no doubt that in this region the shortage of common grazings had reached a critical point.

The enclosure of strips in the common fields and meadows raised much the same issues as the enclosure of commons, for it further reduced the area of common grazing land. But again the significance of the problem differed from district to district and period to period. In some parts of England and Wales common arable fields were neither extensive nor of great economic importance. In the Pennine Hills, for example, arable fields were usually small and were separated from each other by large areas of pasture; moreover, the farmer's livelihood depended more on the exploitation of his pastures than on his corn harvest. In certain counties much common-field land was enclosed before 1500. Sixteenth-century writers regarded the counties of Suffolk, Essex, Hertfordshire, Kent, Devon, Somerset, Cornwall, Shropshire, Worcestershire, and Herefordshire as completely, or largely, enclosed. And although no one nowadays would agree that any of these counties was completely without common fields, and many still had large areas of common pasture, the historian accepts the substantial truth of these generalizations. Somehow in the Middle Ages these counties had put an end to most of their common fields and common rights without commotion.[1]

In districts of England which possessed large areas of old enclosed land, or a local system of husbandry which was not yet endangered by shortage of land, the enclosure controversy had little meaning and stirred few passions. But in others the zeal to enclose caused the maximum social disturbances and distress. What elements in the local situation signalled danger for the intending encloser in the Tudor period, and where were they most commonly found? The most inflammable situations seem to have arisen in lowland villages possessing attenuated common pastures, large areas of common field, and an increasing population which leaned heavily on its common grazing land for the feeding of its animals. In such villages no one could enclose without risk of hurting others. Even when the individual

---

[1] W. Cunningham, *The Growth of English Industry and Commerce in Modern Times*, 1921 ed., II, pp. 898–9; E. F. Gay, 'Inclosures in England in the Sixteenth Century', *Qtrly J. Econ.*, XVII, 1903, p. 593; *A Discourse of the Common Weal of this Realm of England*, ed. E. Lamond, 1954, p. 49; John Nichols, *History and Antiquities of the County of Leicester*, IV, i, 1807, p. 99; A. H. Johnson, *The Disappearance of the Small Landowner*, 1909, p. 39.

encloser surrendered a proportion of his share in the common grazings to compensate for the close he had made in the arable fields, the remaining commoners might derive less benefit from their commons than before, because the enclosure divided the land into scattered bits and pieces, and forced men to keep moving their stock from one small piece of grazing to another, thus damaging the grass, and often rendering it almost worthless. Moreover, every argument against enclosure carried extra weight because the enclosure of the common fields *and* the waste was often under way at the same time. When the process took place on both fronts in a single township, the farming routine of the community was liable to be severely disrupted by the sudden reduction in its total resources of common pasture.[1]

Why was the demand for grassland so insistent in the sixteenth century? The answer lies in the economic trends of the period, in the rise of population, and the prosperity of farming. After the Black Death, labour had been short and land plentiful. This situation did not endure. After a little more than a century of stagnation, population began to grow again. The increase cannot be measured by any exact counting of heads, but it was apparent from 1470 onwards in the rising price of land.[2] By the beginning of the seventeenth century it was sufficiently obvious to contemporaries to call for public comment. No doubt, the rate of increase differed from region to region, and no full understanding of economic and social changes in the countryside at this period will be attained until this subject is examined in greater detail. But here it is sufficient to note that it was a national phenomenon. The population of Leicestershire, for example, increased by 58 per cent between 1563 and 1603, that of 74 parishes in Hertfordshire by the same amount.[3] In other parts of England, the increase has not yet been studied in the same detail but it manifested itself to contemporaries in other ways. They noticed first of all the number of new houses built in their townships, and then the increasing numbers of stock which were put out to graze on the commons. In the Isle of Axholme, the inhabitants of Epworth manor observed one hundred extra cottages built between about 1590 and 1630. At Misterton, in the same district, thirty new cottages were erected in forty years. Equally good examples could be drawn from other English counties. The consequence everywhere was a substantial increase in the numbers of cattle, sheep, horses, pigs,

---

[1] PRO C 78, 1581, 5.

[2] M. M. Postan, 'Some Economic Evidence of Declining Population in the later Middle Ages', EcHR, 2nd Ser., II, 1950; E. Kerridge, 'The Movement of Rent, 1540–1640', EcHR, 2nd Ser., VI, 1953.

[3] VCH *Leics.*, III, p. 140; L. Munby, *Hertfordshire Population Statistics, 1563–1801*, 1964, p. 21.

and geese seeking herbage on the commons. Many of the predominantly pastoral counties could absorb this increase without practical
inconvenience. Others could not. They became involved in innumerable lawsuits concerning common rights, or they solved the problem
with less expense by reducing the number of stock which each tenant
was entitled to put on the commons. In some townships stints were
already in operation, and these were reduced to give every commoner a
fair share and at the same time preserve the common from ruin by
over-grazing. In other places, stints were introduced for the first time
in the Tudor period. In others, for example in the fenland of Lincolnshire, stints were discussed but never operated.[1]

Apart from the difficulty of finding pasture for a rising population,
most villages were subject to additional stress and strain because large
farmers wished to increase the scale of their undertakings. Rising prices
for agricultural produce throughout the sixteenth century stimulated
enterprise among all farmers who produced a surplus for the market.
Its effects can be observed in indirect ways—in the growing number and
size of markets, and in increasing specialization by the farmers themselves. It can be illustrated more directly in complaints from villages
all over the country against John Brown and Henry Smith who over-
charged the commons with their herds and flocks, brought in strangers'
cattle to graze on the summer pastures, or kept more stock on the
commons in summer than they could support in winter on their home
grounds. The complaints were all of one kind, recording the resentment
of the many at the selfish ambitions of the few. And they echoed from
Solway Firth to the East Anglian fens, from the Essex marshes to
Land's End.

The demand for pasture reflected agricultural prosperity and the
pressure of a rising population. It demonstrated too the basic impor-
ance of livestock in all farming systems. The land could not be made to
yield more until more manure was put into it. All over England farmers
were making the most of their local resources with this end in view.
Marl, chalk, seasand, alluvial silt, seawrack, night soil from the towns—
all were spread upon the land where available. But the distance and
costs of transport were considerable, and none was as efficient in
increasing yields and maintaining humus as dung. To get more manure
it was necessary to keep more animals. Hence in all farming regions,
both those which concentrated on crops and those specializing in
animal production, more intensive farming could only be achieved by
carrying more livestock. Hence the universal pressure on grazing.

Public hostility to engrossing was prompted by the same economic

[1] Joan Thirsk, 'The Isle of Axholme before Vermuyden', AHR, I, 1953, p. 24;
Tudor Enclosures, Hist. Ass. pamphlet, General Series, 41, 1959, p. 6.

stresses and strains as enclosure. Modern agricultural economists recommend engrossing, or, as we would term it today, the amalgamation of farms, as a means to more efficient business. The adverse social consequences weigh lightly in the scale of modern values. But in the sixteenth century, when most country people expected to get their living by farming, and when the idea of an ordered society in which no man took advantage of his neighbours was regarded as the only philosophy by which communal farming could work, the social drawbacks of engrossing carried greater weight than the economic advantages. Hence the outcry against it was vociferous, and claimed as much attention from the government as enclosure. Though Tudor landlords might prefer to let their land to one man rather than to many, they were constantly thwarted by the more powerful social argument that engrossing constituted the loss of a holding which could have supported a deserving family. As the vicar of Quinton in Gloucestershire observed bitterly to the President of Magdalen College, Oxford, in the early part of Henry VII's reign, "To let your lordship to one man, to prefer him, and he to keep under your tenants, and have all the vayle and they the burden, will there none tenants come to the town."[1]

Hunger for land and particularly for pasture impelled both those who enclosed and those who resisted. The two opposing attitudes towards enclosure mirrored two different ways of farming—the individualist and the communal systems. We have seen the simpler and more immediate reason for the opposition to enclosure—that it deprived the community of common rights. Others, more involved, however, weighed strongly in the formation of public opinion. They concerned first and foremost the adverse social consequences which followed when land was put to a new use, especially when old arable was put under pasture.

The regulations governing the common fields had never been so rigidly enforced as to preserve a permanent equilibrium between the arable and pasture of a township. But so long as a community pursued its traditional course of husbandry, some such balance tended to be preserved naturally. This did not mean that the same land remained under the plough or in grass century after century, without any change of use. The drawbacks to any such permanent routine were obvious when yields were reckoned up after harvest. It was usual for individuals and whole communities to alter the use of land as occasion required. By village agreement arable strips were converted into common pasture and a piece of common taken in to make a new

[1] W. Denton, *England in the Fifteenth Century*, 1888, p. 318. See also Warws. RO L2, 86.

arable field. In Northumberland villages, the redistribution of land was frequent and radical, and is probably to be attributed to the fact that good pasture did not last long in this wet climate and, unless ploughed out at frequent intervals, became overgrown with moss. In many pastoral districts where the commons were still plentiful, it was customary for whole communities to agree upon a change of land use from time to time. Alternatively, a man was permitted by custom to enclose and cultivate a piece of land from the common at any time, so long as the community was compensated by an equivalent piece of formerly enclosed land. In these ways a rough balance was always maintained between plough and pasture. And so long as the traditional system of husbandry was observed, the balance was not too rudely shaken even though the commons continued to undergo piecemeal enclosure.

The rapid spread of enclosure in the fifteenth and sixteenth centuries, however, was accompanied by some radical changes in the traditional husbandry of the different regions. Enclosure liberated men from restrictions and communal regulations. They used this liberty to alter their system of husbandry. In some places the old equilibrium of plough and pasture abruptly disappeared. In the fifteenth century the conversion of arable to pasture was so usual after enclosure in parts of England that in the sixteenth it was popularly regarded as the inevitable consequence. And since it was generally admitted that land in grass employed fewer hands than land under corn, the drastic fall in the arable acreage threatened to create serious unemployment among wage workers. Of the justice of popular complaints on this score there is no doubt. Unemployment and depopulation were writ large across the face of the landscape. Already by the accession of Henry Tudor hundreds of deserted or decaying villages gave a miserable daily reminder to all neighbours and travellers that this was the meaning of enclosure.

To contemporaries, in brief, enclosure signified first the loss to the community of common rights, and, when arable land was converted to pasture, depopulation. Engrossing likewise caused depopulation. Herein lay the logic behind all contemporary allegations that enclosure impoverished and depopulated the countryside. What, then, were its advantages to the encloser? By extinguishing common rights it freed men from subjection to the rules of communal husbandry. From the landlord's point of view this meant that the land was worth more and the rent could be increased. An acre enclosed, declared John Norden, was worth one and a half in common. Writing in 1641 Henry Best thought enclosed land was worth thrice the value of common land. Its benefits to the farmer depended entirely on the way the land was employed after enclosure. This in turn depended on the farming system of the locality and the policy of the individual farmer. The advantages of enclosure were as varied as the farming types.[1]

The least contentious enclosures were those which effected no change in land use or else resulted in the conversion of pasture to arable. These were common enough in the mainly pastoral districts where grass was a more successful crop than corn and where grazing was still relatively plentiful. Pasture from the commons was sometimes enclosed and kept in grass, because its feeding capacity could be improved by controlled grazing and more systematic manuring, and because the hedges of a close provided better shelter for stock than that afforded on a wind-swept open common. Sometimes pasture was enclosed and put under the plough because the inadequacy of the arable land caused a shortage of fodder or domestic corn and made the farmer undesirably dependent upon purchased foodstuffs. The fenland peasant, for example, whose arable land on average amounted to no more than eight acres, and who enjoyed unstinted grazing rights on the common, was more likely to turn pasture into cornland than the reverse. Hence the meagre crop of enclosure cases found in the Lincolnshire fenland by the commissioners of 1607.[2]

Sometimes the conversion of pasture to arable after enclosure was accompanied by the conversion of an equivalent amount of arable to pasture. Many such rearrangements were described in detail in the lawcourts after the enclosure commissioners had reported on one half of the operation, the conversion of arable to pasture, and neglected to mention the other. Here the enclosure and change of land use preserved the same balance of corn and grassland as before, but improved the yield of both by introducing a convertible husbandry. The wisdom of this practice had long been recognized. It had prompted many redistributions of land in the Middle Ages when common was put under the plough and cornland reverted to common. But now men were beginning to see the benefits of a change in land use accompanied by enclosure, and undertook both operations together. They justified it by describing the progressive exhaustion of their arable. Their observations led Miss Harriet Bradley, some forty years ago, to argue the universal exhaustion of the soil in England by the end of the Middle Ages. It was a greatly exaggerated hypothesis, quickly discredited when others were able to demonstrate from monastic estate records of the same period an impressive series of rising corn yields. The two opposing arguments can only be reconciled by admitting the truth of

---

[1] J. Norden, *The Surveyor's Dialogue*, p. 97; Henry Best, *Rural Economy in Yorkshire, 1641*, Surtees Soc., XXXIII, 1857, pp. 129–31.

[2] E 134, 2 Jas. I, Mich. 33; Thirsk, *Tudor Enclosures*, pp. 14–15.

both. There *were* estates on which crop yields increased. Equally, there were farmers, more particularly perhaps those farming on a small scale, who noticed diminishing yields and recognized its cause, namely that the fields had been too long cropped without respite and needed a rest under grass.[1]

The solution to the difficulty did not inevitably lie with enclosure. The radical redistribution of land by common agreement but without enclosure was one alternative and had long been customary in Northumberland. Another was to let some arable strips in the common fields lie in ley. The ley strips were fenced off in order to permit stock to graze them when the adjoining arable land was in corn. Alternatively, the stock grazing on the leys were tethered. This compromise, which stopped short of enclosure, worked well enough. It could be carried out by a number of tenants agreeing together to leave a whole furlong in ley, or it could be undertaken by individuals converting a few of their own strips. The only disadvantage lay in the necessity for fencing or tethering cattle. The tenants of Fulbeck in Lincolnshire found themselves tethering 300 draught cattle and milch kine in the township on leys, headlands, and small pieces of ground in the cornfields and suffering constant damage to their corn when the animals broke loose. The inhabitants were driven in the end to accept the final remedy—to agree upon the consolidation of strips and enclosure.[2]

The most contentious enclosures of all, however, which vexed the government, and caused the greatest hardship, and the loudest popular outcry, were those which led to the permanent conversion of arable to pasture. To understand the economic motives for this movement it is necessary to refer briefly to agrarian changes in the century before 1500. The disastrous mortality in the plagues of the mid-fourteenth century had radically altered the relationship of land and labour. Land became plentiful and labour short. Men acquired holdings easily and large demesne farmers found it difficult to hire sufficient labourers to work their land efficiently. Some ceased to farm and leased their land to tenants, but others solved the problem of dear and scarce labour and untenanted holdings by turning their land over to sheepwalk and cattle pasture. Their labour costs fell, and the land was kept in use.

The demand for wool to supply the expanding wool trade and cloth industry justified the keeping of increasing numbers of sheep. Less is known about the parallel increase in the keeping of cattle at this time, but it is probable that with the spread of pasture farming it was as

---

[1] E 178, 3749; E 134, 23 Eliz. H6; TED I, pp. 61–2; Harriet Bradley, *The Enclosures in England—an Economic Reconstruction*, 1918; R. Lennard, 'The Alleged Exhaustion of the Soil in Medieval England', *Econ. J.*, cxxxv, 1922.

[2] C 2, Jas. I, F 135.

marked in some regions as was sheep-keeping in others. Dairying developed in the wood-pasture region of Suffolk, for example, in the fifteenth century. When the vaccaries of Rossendale ceased to be managed by the great lords and were leased to smaller tenants from the fourteenth century onwards, there is nothing to suggest that they did not continue in use as cattle rather than sheep farms. The full story of regional specialization in the Middle Ages has yet to be told, but when complete, it is unlikely that the sheep will be allowed to dominate the historical scene as they have done in the past. Flocks were certainly conspicuous in the landscape, particularly on the hills throughout southern England, where a sheep-corn husbandry prevailed, but in other grassland regions, where better water supplies were available, it is likely that some of the beef and dairy cattle, which were well in evidence by the sixteenth century, were already in occupation of the pastures.[1]

For the present the place of sheep and cattle in the agrarian changes of the late Middle Ages cannot be assessed, but there is no doubt of the increasing popularity of pasture farming in areas where formerly a mixed corn and cattle husbandry had prevailed. Economically it had every advantage for the large farmer. But by the end of the fifteenth century, when population had begun to rise again, more attention was given to the awkward social problems it created. As common field arable was turned over to grass, the fall in the demand for labour caused unemployment; the profits of pasture farming tempted the larger farmers to overstock the common pastures with their animals and then to engage in illegal and ruthless measures for getting control of more land, and driving out the commoners. In one way and another the small farmer and the hired man were being edged off the land. In the worst cases small hamlets were completely abandoned and larger villages seriously depopulated. At the accession of Henry VII the increase in pasture farming had already cost the country a heavy price in human suffering.[2]

And yet the movement continued for a time into the Tudor period. Population rose, and the prices of farm produce and rents followed suit. Now the cloth industry was expanding, and the demand for wool rose to new and hitherto undreamed of proportions. Indeed, in areas marginal to corn, it is probable that the profit from wool in the early part of the sixteenth century was higher than for any other produce of

[1] A. H. Denney, *The Sibton Abbey Estates. Select Documents*, Suffolk Rec. Soc., II, 1960, pp. 26–7; G. H. Tupling, *The Economic History of Rossendale*, Chetham Soc., NS LXXXVI, 1927, p. 39; R. H. Hilton, 'A Study in the Pre-History of English Enclosure in the Fifteenth Century', *Studi in Onore di Armando Sapori*, pp. 680–2.
[2] *The Anglica Historia of Polydore Vergil*, ed. D. Hay, Camden Soc., LXXXIV, 1950, p. 277; Maurice Beresford, *The Lost Villages of England, passim.*

the farm. Not that this is anywhere explicitly stated in contemporary records, but in 1539 Fitzherbert held the view that "of all stock the rearing of sheep is most profitable," while the superior profits of sheep *and* cattle production over other farm enterprises are to be inferred from Sir Thomas Smith's suggested remedy for enclosure in 1549—to permit corn export and prohibit wool in order "to make the profit of the plough to be as good, rate for rate, as the profit of the graziers and sheepmasters." In the end, of course, this aim was achieved in the second half of the century through the impersonal intervention of economic forces.[1]

The decline of the cloth trade after 1551 dealt the wool producer a serious blow and farmers' interests shifted somewhat from wool to meat and cheese production. While some grassland regions concentrated on meat, others in west and north-west England showed signs (from about 1590 onwards) of shifting their interests from meat to cheese and butter production. Furness farmers engaged in cheese-making and invested less capital in cattle fattening; the small farmers of the Warwickshire Arden began to keep fewer bullocks and feeding oxen, and to fill their yards with cows and heifers—a trend which became more and more noticeable under the early Stuarts.[2]

Meanwhile the demand for farm produce of all kinds was growing in the towns. London began to sprawl further along Thames side; the cloth-producing areas of the west country and west Yorkshire became more populous; the metal-working centres around Birmingham and the coalmining towns of Durham called for more and more workers. All these industrial centres depended increasingly on all kinds of produce—not merely meat and cheese but grain as well—brought to the market by local farmers. And local farmers responded. Two excellent examples of regions catering particularly for the needs of the town lie ready to hand in eastern Durham, sending meat, cheese, and grain to the coalminers around Newcastle, and central Hertfordshire supplying pork, bacon, beef, and wheat to London. Neither, it should be noticed, displayed an overweening desire to convert all its ploughland to pasture.

The 1590's mark a turning point in the agricultural history of this period. They include a run of bad harvests which caused grain shortages, plague, and near famine. Thereafter, profit margins no longer favoured grass at the expense of grain. The enclosure movement did not cease, but the conversion of arable to pasture did not hold out the attractive possibilities of two generations earlier.

[1] R. H. Tawney, *The Agrarian Problem in the Sixteenth Century*, pp. 195 sqq.; *A Discourse of the Commonweal of this Realm of England*, p. 53.

[2] See *AHEW*, IV, p. 94.

The generalizations offered here concerning the economic incentives in farming during the period 1500–1640 must not be allowed to dominate this account of the enclosure movement. Indeed, they are dangerously misleading unless handled in their proper context. Farming is not a highly flexible business which can twist and change direction at every trick and turn of the price curve. The land and its buildings impose severe limitations on most farmers. Moreover, within the framework of what is practicable, the successful farm business is a union of several interlocking enterprises. Complex problems arise for the man who makes a change in any one of them. Even if he can reorganize and rearrange them satisfactorily, he may find the short-term benefits cancelled out by the long-term disadvantages. Understandably, then, the ordinary farmer is rarely a revolutionary, and often his knowledge of his land and his experience of the vagaries of the market will make him a hardened conservative in agricultural matters. When we speak of changes in the relative profits of wool, meat, dairy produce, and grain, therefore, we describe economic forces which left thousands of farmers unmoved. They could not or would not respond. The downland farmers who at one time found themselves able to take advantage of rising wool prices and to keep more sheep were not able at another time to change over to preparing beef for the butcher. Those who reared cattle in Lancashire and the west Midlands could turn to dairying if they chose, but the farmers on the light lands of Norfolk and Suffolk were chained to a sheep-corn husbandry with no room to manœuvre. The farmers on the lower slopes of the Pennines could alter within limits the proportion of sheep to cattle as prices lured them, but the farmer on the damp waterlogged clays of the Weald of Kent could never do any good with sheep and was bound to rest his fortune on other stock. As circumstances changed through this century and a half, the trend towards increasing specialization affected every corner of the kingdom, but it led the farmers of the different regions in various directions. Every region possessing common fields or common pastures had some experience of enclosure. But it was not equally advantageous to the individual everywhere nor equally injurious to the community. And when enclosures were accompanied by the conversion of cornland to grass, not every farmer was prompted by the desire to accommodate a larger sheep-flock.

B. PUBLIC OPINION, POPULAR COMMOTION,
AND LEGISLATION

Throughout the sixteenth century Tudor governmental enquiries and legislation reflected concern at the progress of enclosing, the conversion of arable to pasture, and engrossing. But policy vacillated between mild and rigorous measures, from acts which were vaguely phrased and could not be enforced to strenuous county-by-county enquiries, followed by prosecutions in the courts and heavy money fines. In addition to these direct attacks on the problem, a number of statutes were passed which struck a glancing blow at enclosure and engrossing by attacking sheepmasters and those who leased cottages without sufficient land to support their occupants. Under James I and Charles I, however, the government lost much of its zeal for the cause. Indeed, after 1607, when the last large-scale enclosure enquiry took place, it abandoned all opposition to the principle of enclosure, but continued to keep up the appearance of opposing it in practice. Commissions were issued from time to time for the discovery of offenders, but their crimes were pardoned on payment of a money fine. The punishment of enclosers had degenerated into a revenue-raising device and little else.[1]

Some of the reasons for this change of attitude can be inferred from the preceding pages: as economic circumstances altered, so did the pace, purpose, and social consequences of enclosing and engrossing. It is now necessary to consider the legislation against the movement, in order to see more clearly the gradual growth of understanding in Parliament of its multifarious causes, and to set alongside all this the evidence of public opinion in so far as it can be gauged in political and other literature, and was revealed in popular disturbances.

The first acts to deal with the problems of depopulation at the beginning of Henry VII's reign did not appear like bolts from the blue. Some public complaint against the effects of enclosure had already reached the ears of Parliament, though just how vociferous the outcry had been it is impossible to say. But since, in the words of John Hales writing in 1549, "the chief destruction of towns and decay of houses was before the beginning of the reign of King Henry VII," it is certain that before the Tudor age began tempers in the countryside already ran high, and that the country gentry who sat as members of Parliament at Westminster were well aware of local grievances. But as yet people had no easy means of gaining wide publicity for their distress through the printed word, and the surviving evidence of popular

[1] M. Beresford and J. K. St Joseph, *Medieval England. An Aerial Survey*, p. 120.

complaint is extremely meagre. Two petitions to Parliament in 1414 from the Crown tenants of Darlton and Ragnall in Nottinghamshire against enclosure, and from the inhabitants of Chesterton, tenants of the prior and canons of Barnwell in Cambridgeshire, against engrossing, together with a petition by John Rous to the Parliament at Coventry in 1459, are the only protests known to have been presented formally to Parliament. But at the opening of Parliament in 1484 a reference by the lord chancellor to enclosures and depopulation implied that the government considered these matters urgent enough to call for action.[1]

The first act, passed in 1488, concerned the Isle of Wight. It was an attack on engrossers who took many farms into their hands and turned them all into grazing grounds for cattle and sheep. The government expressed dismay at the depopulation which followed, and the consequent threat to the defence of the kingdom, and enacted penalties for anyone who engrossed holdings whose total value exceeded ten marks a year. This was followed by a general statute in 1489 "agaynst pullyng doun of tounes" prompted by the same considerations as the act of 1488. Its provisions, however, were framed differently, and were preceded by a more verbose preamble. Deploring the decay of villages and the conversion of arable to pasture, the act enumerated all the evil consequences thereof: the growth of unemployment, the decay of tillage, the destruction of churches, and the weakening of England's defences against her enemies. Finally, it provided that all houses with twenty acres of land should be preserved with all necessary buildings and land for the maintenance of tillage. Until the decayed buildings were rebuilt, offenders had to surrender half the profits of the holding to the lord of the fee. It was a vaguely worded act and a little muddled. Despite the preamble which deplored the conversion of arable to pasture (without, be it noted, mentioning enclosing), the act was in fact directed against engrossing. It is true that both these things *and* enclosure were inextricably mixed in contemporary discussion and blended together into one massive agrarian problem. But this does not excuse a muddled act. The legislature seems to have been no more clear-headed on the subject than the public.[2]

No further acts against engrossing and the conversion of arable to pasture were deemed necessary for almost another generation. In 1515 the issue flared up again, at the same time as London officials were

[1] *A Discourse of the Commonweal of this Realm of England*, p. lxiii; E. F. Gay, *Zur Geschichte der Einhegungen in England*, Inaugural Dissertation zur Erlangung der Doktorwürde, Friedrich-Wilhelms-Universität zu Berlin, 1912, pp. 23–5. I wish to thank Professor Herbert Heaton for the loan of this thesis.
[2] Beresford, *The Lost Villages of England*, pp. 103–4; TED I, pp. 4–6.

anxiously investigating the export of corn. The immediate cause, therefore, may well have been fear of corn shortage in the capital. An undated bill against engrossing, and a proclamation against the conversion of arable to pasture, were drafted at about the same time. The bill inveighed against the engrossers of farms, and named in particular the merchant adventurers, clothmakers, goldsmiths, butchers, tanners, and other artificers who held sometimes ten to sixteen farms apiece, and were totally unable to maintain tillage in all of them. It deplored the consequent scarcity of victuals, and the depopulation of townships, which had once possessed twenty or thirty dwellings, and now were populated only by a neatherd, a shepherd, or a warrener. In short, it attacked merchants who engrossed farms, engaged in pasture farming, and kept cattle, sheep, and rabbits, at the expense of tillage. Having delivered this thrust at townsmen-turned-farmers, it suggested that no one should be allowed to occupy more than one farm. It was a sweeping, and also an illogical proposal. It would not by itself have arrested the spread of pasture farming, while to prohibit engrossing throughout the whole of England was an unworkable scheme and economically undesirable. Not surprisingly, then, this draft bill was discarded. The act of 1515 followed much more closely the lines of the draft proclamation, also drawn up in 1514, which dealt with the conversion of arable to pasture. The proclamation alluded to complaints from justices of the peace and commissioners of shires concerning the continued scarcity of grain owing to the conversion of arable to pasture, and the engrossing of farms. It laid special stress on the "infinite number of the king's subjects, [who] for lack of occupation, have fallen and daily do fall into idleness and consequently into theft and robberies." It then proposed that all land in tillage in 1485 should revert to tillage. Like the bill on engrossing, this proclamation was phrased in sweeping general terms with little regard for the practical difficulties of enforcing its provisions throughout the kingdom.[1] The act which finally emerged in 1515, and was made perpetual in 1516, showed more understanding of regional diversity, and seems to have been modified under pressure from members of Parliament who knew something of the variety of local conditions. For "advoidyng pullyng downe of townes" the act declared that all villages and habitations which on the first day of the present Parliament were for "the more part" occupied in tillage were to continue so; all buildings which were decayed were to be rebuilt within a year; and all land turned to pasture since 1 February 1515 was to be restored to arable "after the maner and usage of the countrey where the seid lond lyeth." The penalty for disobedience was again

[1] N. S. B. Gras, The Evolution of the English Corn Market, p. 223; LP I, ii, pp. 1493, 1494.

the forfeiture of half the profits from the holding to the lord of the fee so long as the offence continued. The act, in brief, attempted to arrest the decay of farm buildings (through engrossing), and the conversion of arable to pasture. It legislated for the districts where a substantial proportion of land was under the plough, and omitted the predominantly pastoral areas from the reckoning.[1]

Two years later Wolsey appointed a commission of enquiry into depopulation—a more effective instrument for measuring the scale of the problem than any used hitherto. It reflected the importance attached to the subject by the government, and, presumably, the complete failure of the earlier legislation. The commissioners were ordered to conduct investigations in all but the four northern counties of England, to report on villages and houses pulled down since 1488, the amount of land then in tillage and now in pasture, and the amount of parkland enclosed for the preservation of wild animals. In 1518, when the commission was still conducting enquiries, the first offenders began to appear in Chancery, and in a decree of the court issued that year it was ordered that all who pleaded for pardon should, within forty days, pull down all enclosures made since 1485, unless they could prove that their enclosures were beneficial to the commonwealth. Failure to obey the court's decrees laid the offender open to a penalty of £100. Prosecutions, consequent upon the information gathered in 1517 and 1518, continued for the next twenty years, but always they were initiated by the Crown. Although the immediate overlords of enclosing tenants had equal rights with the Crown to start proceedings, they utterly failed to do so. Herein lay the chief obstacle in the way of enforcing the early anti-enclosure legislation. The interests of landlords were identical with those of enclosing tenants. Their land was far more valuable enclosed than open. The Crown could not hope to find many allies among landlords.[2]

Prosecutions by the Crown in the court of Chancery and in the court of King's Bench continued for the next two decades. At the same time the acts of 1489 and 1515 remained on the statute book, and public attention was drawn to them from time to time by proclamation. In May 1528, for example, the lord chancellor asked for information to be passed to him secretly of all persons who kept more than one farm and made enclosures. In February 1529, again by proclamation, all enclosed grounds were ordered to be laid open and the hedges or palings removed before the following Easter. For nearly two decades

[1] *Statutes of the Realm*, III (1509–47), p. 176.
[2] I. S. Leadam, *The Domesday of Inclosures, 1517–18*, I, pp. 1–11; E. F. Gay, 'Inquisitions of Depopulation in 1517 and the Domesday of Inclosures', RHS NS XIV, 1900, p. 235; Beresford, *The Lost Villages of England*, pp. 106–10.

the hunt for engrossers, enclosers, and converters was carried on with the imperfect weapons forged in 1489 and 1515–1517. Then in 1533 the government turned to attack the problem from another angle.[1]

In a new act (25 Hen. VIII, c. 13) with a freshly-worded preamble it fastened responsibility for the spread of enclosure on the "great profit that cometh of sheep" and declared (a little wildly, perhaps) that some individuals had five, six, ten, twenty, even twenty-four thousand sheep apiece. Henceforth no person was to keep more than two thousand sheep, reckoned by the long hundred, i.e. 2,400 animals, on pain of forfeiting 3s. 4d. for every sheep above that number. The act then enumerated various important exceptions to the new ruling. "Spiritual persons" and lay lords occupying their own demesnes could keep as many sheep as they liked. So could those who needed them for household consumption. Lambs under one year did not count as sheep according to this definition, so that the breeder of sheep was less hampered in his business than those who specialized in wool and meat production. Finally, the act legislated against engrossing. No one after Christmas was to take up more than two farms or tenements, and those who had two holdings must dwell in the parishes in which they lay or forfeit 3s. 4d. for every week in which their offence continued. The act was a puppet, wearing a bold face but stuffed with straw. Indeed, it has every appearance of having been put forward by the government in strong terms, and modified subsequently under pressure from the large landlords sitting in Parliament. The explanatory clauses of the final act enabled them to escape from its restrictions almost scotfree, leaving the smaller farmers to submit. In one respect, however, the act proclaimed stern intentions. Responsibility for the discovery of offenders was placed for the first time on private informers as well as on the Crown, and the former were encouraged to produce information about enclosing and engrossing by the promise of an equal share with the Crown in the money penalties imposed on offenders. Informers had now taken the place of landlords in implementing the law, and were to share with the Crown the fines imposed on offenders. Common informers were used by Tudor and early Stuart governments on many other occasions for enforcing the law. Indeed, they have been called the "chief instrument for the enforcement of economic legislation" between 1550 and 1624, and though their performance was uneven, and their motives and methods always questionable, their poking and prying doubtless had a deterrent effect.[2]

[1] J. L. Lindsay, *Bibliotheca Lindesiana. Bibliography of Tudor and Stuart Proclamations*, nos. 111, 115.

[2] *Statutes of the Realm*, III, p. 451; M. Beresford, 'The Common Informer, the Penal Statutes, and Economic Regulation', EcHR, NS x, 1957, pp. 221 *sqq.*

If the sheep population was increasing as fast as the government feared, this was due to the remarkable expansion of the cloth industry in Henry VIII's reign. Export figures suggest a steady upward movement from the beginning of the reign, and it is reasonable to suppose that the demand for wool had prompted more and more farmers to concentrate on this branch of farming. At the same time, pamphlets were beginning to appear emphasizing the rôle of sheep in the depopulation of villages, and these helped further to tilt the argument against sheep rather than against the evils of pasture farming in general.[1]

Meanwhile the earlier acts of 1489 and 1515 continued in operation though the machinery for enforcing them had proved ineffective. To remedy this weakness another act was passed in 1536 (27 Hen. VIII, c. 22). It did not introduce any new crimes, but its preamble observed that while the king had taken steps to enforce the earlier acts on Crown land, manorial lords had entirely neglected their duty of enforcing the law on their own estates. The new statute provided that if a landlord did not prosecute a tenant who let a house of husbandry fall into decay or converted arable to pasture, then the king was entitled to take the profits due to the immediate overlord so long as the offence continued. In other words, the new act allowed the Crown to take the initiative in prosecuting all enclosers, whether Crown tenants or not. Two further clauses took account of varied regional conditions. They conceded the existence of local husbandry practices in a vague phrase which stated that when pasture was converted to arable again, it should be done "according to the nature of the soil and course of husbandry used in the country where any such lands do lie." Secondly, the act applied only in the counties of Hertfordshire, Cambridgeshire, Lincolnshire, Nottinghamshire, Leicestershire, Warwickshire, Rutland, Northamptonshire, Bedfordshire, Buckinghamshire, Oxfordshire, Berkshire, Worcestershire, and the Isle of Wight. This choice of counties may not seem entirely logical, but it was doubtless arrived at, as was the list of counties in the later tillage statute of 1597, after much debate in Parliament and after many interventions by local members. Its merits were that it grouped together, in one large region, thirteen contiguous counties, all of which possessed a considerable amount of arable land or common field or both; and it concentrated on the portion of central England from which most complaints emanated, as well as including others on the fringe of this area.[2]

It is worth speculating, however, whether the act of 1536 would not have contained different provisions if it had been deferred for a few

[1] F. J. Fisher, 'Commercial Trends and Policy in Sixteenth-Century England', EcHR, x, 1940, pp. 96–7.
[2] *Statutes of the Realm*, III, p. 553.

months. For in the late summer of 1536 disturbances broke out in the North Riding of Yorkshire, Cumberland, and Westmorland which were not unconnected with enclosure. They could easily have been used to justify the inclusion of these counties in the act of 1536.

The main strength of the rebellion in 1536, as its name—the Pilgrimage of Grace—implies, was drawn from discontent at religious innovations, in particular the dissolution of the monasteries, and it recruited its most enthusiastic supporters in the north and in Lincolnshire. But social and economic issues were inextricably intertwined with religious dispute in the north-west, for the monasteries and their farms often constituted the social centre of community life as well as its economic framework. When Furness Abbey was dissolved, the people of the district described how hitherto they had supplied various provisions to the monastery and received in return "almost as much as they supplied," namely sixty barrels of single beer or ale, thirty dozen loaves of coarse wheat bread, iron for their ploughs, and other farm tools, and timber to repair their houses. Moreover, everyone having a plough was allowed to send two people to dinner in the refectory one day a week from Martinmas to Pentecost, all tenants were allowed to send their children to school in the monastery, and to dinner or supper in the refectory each day; and if any child was "apt for learning," he was elected a monk, or given a post in the monastery in preference to all others. Finally, the monks paid all the charges for repairing the banks of the Isle of Walney. At the dissolution, the abrupt end of this mutual aid in Furness and elsewhere dealt a severe blow to those relatively poor communities in the highland parts of England who derived little benefit from the life-bringing arteries of national commerce. If their new landlord proved to be a non-resident country squire, or an absentee merchant, who expected his land to bear him financial profit before all else, he was a miserable substitute for the monastic brotherhood.[1]

The principal agrarian grievances voiced in 1536, therefore, arose from changes in lordship and landownership following the dissolution of the monasteries. Enclosure was only one, and seemingly a lesser cause of complaint, than quarrels about the rights and duties of customary tenants. Customary tenure was the most common tenure in the four northern counties, and because it laid onerous obligations on tenants—they were obliged to render border service, when necessary, to protect their land from the incursions of the Scots, and this was

---

[1] LP XII, i, p. 405; Thomas West, *The Antiquities of Furness*, 1805, p. 195. This and the following paragraphs are based on M. H. and Ruth Dodds, *The Pilgrimage of Grace, 1536–7, and the Exeter Conspiracy, 1538*, 1915, and R. H. Tawney, *The Agrarian Problem in the Sixteenth Century*, pp. 318 *sqq.*, and the authorities therein cited.

more than a nominal duty—their rights were more generous than those customary in the south. The rebels who assembled at Doncaster in 1536 had evidently come fresh from wrangles with their landlords on the meaning of "tenant right," and their chief claim, therefore, was that lands in Westmorland, Cumberland, Kendal, Dent, Sedbergh, Furness, and abbey lands in Mashamshire, Kirkbyshire, and Nidderdale should be held by "tenant right," and that the customary payments for entry fines should be two years' rent. Enclosure was mentioned only once in a plea that the statutes against it should be enforced— a difficult task in this region where local government officials were too few to make much impression—and that intakes of land made since 4 Henry VII (except those made in mountains, forests, and parks) should be laid open. This seems to be a reference to the enclosure of commons, which became much more frequent in this part of the country later in the century without arousing any loud outcry. It seems probable, therefore, that it loomed large at this time because the traditional life of the community was under attack from many different directions, and this grievance was magnified in the light of all the rest. New interpretations of tenant right, rent increases, enclosure, and the knowledge that justice was expensively bought, made the inhabitants of these remote highland valleys feel themselves beleaguered and defenceless against their new landlords.

The northern rebels who joined the Pilgrimage of Grace gathered under the leadership of certain men of Richmondshire, a district in the north Yorkshire dales inhabited by many small pasture farmers, whose poverty was later alleviated by the growth of a secondary occupation— the knitting of stockings—to supplement their meagre farm earnings. Their leaders were called the four captains of Penrith: Faith, Poverty, Pity, and Charity, and judging by the confessions later elicited from two of the rebels, their support was drawn almost entirely from north-western England, the highland districts of north-west Yorkshire, Westmorland, and Cumberland, where people were poorer and, owing to the meagre quantity of their arable land, lived in more congested conditions than in the north-east. Not surprisingly, these northern insurgents who set agrarian grievances alongside the religious in their campaign did not co-operate easily with the leaders of the religious insurrection. Indeed, how could it have been otherwise, since the background of their experience was entirely different from that of the rebels in the lowlands of East Yorkshire and Lincolnshire?[1]

The whole outbreak was ruthlessly put down in the early months of 1537 and the executions that followed terrorized the rebellious into subjection. A more powerful and authoritative King's Council in the

[1] LP xii, i, pp. 300–4.

North was set up to administer the five northern counties, and to hear and deal with agrarian grievances. The rebellion of 1536 did not necessitate any new agrarian legislation, but more conscientious efforts were made in the north at least to enforce existing acts.

The problem simmered for more than a decade until a new government under a Protector who lent a fresh and sympathetic ear to complaints from the peasantry unwittingly·fomented unrest until it issued forth in another political crisis. But by that time economic conditions had undergone a profound change since 1536. The country was now living through a period of sharp inflation. Three debasements of the coinage in 1542, 1547, and 1549, accompanied by harvest failures in 1545, 1549, 1550, and 1551, contributed to a sharp rise in prices, notably of food. The price index of articles consumed in the ordinary labourer's household, which stood at 100 in 1508, had risen to 231 by 1547, and rose again to 285 in 1551.[1]

The price revolution, which had made a slow start in the first three decades of the century, had now gathered such speed in the forties that it was racking the foundations of the economy. The sins of the government were at once laid at the door of the pasture farmer, and particularly the sheepmaster. He was charged with the responsibility for everything, for the poverty of the poor, the high price of food, and even the high price of wool. He was the canker that poisoned the economy at its roots, forcing it into complete servitude to the foreign cloth market. The remedy for this imbalance seemed to Somerset's advisers to lie in curbing the activities of the sheepmaster, and this, as Sir Thomas Smith, an influential figure in government circles, defined it, lay in making "the profit of the plough to be as good, rate for rate, as the profit of the graziers and sheepmasters." In March 1549, persuaded by these arguments and the propaganda of the Commonwealth men, Parliament sanctioned a novel tax on sheep and cloth. Although its overt objective was to raise money, its promoters were evidently well aware of its wider repercussions on agriculture.[2]

The idea of a tax on the cattle grazier or sheepmaster had been in the air since the beginning of Edward VI's reign. An estimate had been made about October 1547 (the document is undated, so this date is conjectural) by an unknown writer of the probable sum of money which would accrue from a tax on sheep and fat cattle. It involved elaborate calculations concerning the amount of wool, woolfells, and

[1] See vol. 1 of this series, p. 50; Y. S. Brenner, 'The Inflation of Prices in Early Sixteenth-Century England', EcHR, NS XIV, 1961, pp. 231–2; E. H. Phelps-Brown and Sheila V. Hopkins, 'Seven Centuries of the Prices of Consumables compared with Builders' Wage Rates', Economica, NS XXIII, p. 312.

[2] Discourse of the Commonweal, p. 53.

cloth exported in the reign of Edward III and in 1546, and the number of sheep which must have accounted for this output. It arrived at an estimate of nearly seven million sheep in the mid-fourteenth century and nearly 8½ million in the mid-sixteenth—a calculation, incidentally, which suggests a rather modest increase in sheep numbers, hardly supporting the wild allegations of contemporaries that sheep-keeping had displaced all other kinds of husbandry. The memorandum then went on to make a number of alternative proposals, one for a tax on sheep, wool, cloth, fat cattle, and leather, and another on sheep alone. When John Hales presented his *Causes of Dearth*, probably in a speech to Parliament in the summer of the following year, he engaged in similar estimates of sheep numbers, which betrayed the influence on his thought of the earlier draft proposal. On this occasion, however, the tax on sheep and cloth was proffered as a substitute for revenue that would be lost by the suggested abolition of purveyance. Parliament accepted it: purveyance was abolished for three years, and in an act of March 1549 a "relief" on sheep and cloth was imposed in its place. It entailed a nation-wide, parish-by-parish census of sheep, which was scheduled to take place in June of that year. But the incidence of the tax was modified according to the amount which taxpayers paid at the same time on personal goods. This clause seems to have been an amendment insisted on by Parliament, since it did not appear in Hales's original proposal, and it had the effect of easing the burden on the rich while leaving it on the poor. The act, therefore, defeated its author's intentions before it even reached the statute book.[1]

Parliament rose in the middle of March, and the commissioners began their enquiries that summer. But general discontent in the countryside, coupled with political manœuvring at Westminster, wrought the downfall of Protector Somerset that autumn, and he was succeeded by the more cautious Northumberland. When Parliament met again in November 1549, it repealed the tax on sheep. The preamble of the act (3 & 4 Edward VI, c. 23) explained that the tax had fallen harshly on the poor commoners—a result that might have been foreseen—and that the money had been cumbrous to collect—a readily credible statement. So the tax by which Hales had hoped to redress the balance between tillage and pasture was abandoned before it had time to show effect.[2]

The vigorous opposition to the sheep tax of 1549 and its speedy repeal early the following year cannot be fully understood, however, without due reference to more serious agrarian disturbances that

---

[1] TED I, pp. 178 *sqq.*; *Discourse of the Commonweal*, pp. xlii *sqq.*; M. Beresford, 'The Poll Tax and Census of Sheep, 1549', AHR, I, 1953, pp. 9–15; II, 1954, pp. 15–29.
[2] *Statutes of the Realm*, IV, p. 122.

occurred in the same year. Before the tax on sheep was introduced, Somerset's government had dealt another blow at enclosure by initiating in 1548 an enclosure enquiry on the same lines as that of 1517. A principal instigator, and one of the commissioners appointed to undertake local enquiries, was again John Hales. Before this, a proclamation had been issued on 1 June 1548, inveighing against engrossing, enclosing, and the conversion of arable to pasture, declaring that rots and murrains were the punishment, sent by God, for "this uncharitable conduct," and ordering the laws of Henry VII and VIII to be put into execution. The enclosure commissioners in the same month were given precise instructions to enquire into the towns, villages, and hamlets decayed and laid down to pasture by enclosure since 1488, to discover the number of ploughs put down, the houses fallen into decay, the number of parks created or enlarged, the names of the persons responsible, the names of those who kept over 2,400 sheep, those who had robbed their tenants of their commons, and those who occupied more than two farms. The commissioners were despatched first of all to the Midland counties and later to other areas as well.[1]

Sponsored by a government which promised to show special sympathy for the poor, the commission raised hopes for the redress of grievances which could not but be frustrated by promises of legal prosecutions that might take years to produce results. Riotous attacks on enclosures broke out all over the country, and the commissioners who had been bidden to work for "a charitable and quiet reformation by the order only of the law" encountered a peasantry with staves and bludgeons in their hands ready to effect quicker remedies. Three anxious proclamations in 1549, in May, mid-June, and mid-July, betrayed an ugly situation. By exhortation and the threat of dire penalties, they tried to repress seditious and disobedient persons, and to put an end to riotous assemblies. All three proclamations dealt particularly with enclosure disturbances and associated the outbreaks of violence with the enclosure commissioners' enquiries.[2]

The uproar was widespread in southern England. It had started in Hertfordshire before the enclosure commission set to work, and spread to Buckinghamshire, Wiltshire, Sussex, Hampshire, Kent, Gloucestershire, Suffolk, Warwickshire, Essex, Leicestershire, Worcestershire, and Rutland. For the most part the outbreaks were disorganized and uncoordinated, but eventually the uproar crystallized in two more formidable risings centred upon widely separated districts—the south-west, and Norfolk. And although neither of these outbreaks was expressly concerned with enclosure, nor the two districts much plagued by the

[1] Lindsay, *op. cit.*, no. 333; TED I, pp. 39–44; S. T. Bindoff, *Tudor England*, p. 134.
[2] Lindsay, *op. cit.*, nos. 353, 356, 362.

movement, their leaders recruited many aggrieved men with personal experience of agrarian abuses, including enclosure and engrossing, whose enthusiasm for their cause sprang from a seedbed of many discontents. Sir William Paget, for example, expressing some personal knowledge of the circumstances behind the rising in the west country, dwelt not only upon religious indignation, provoked by Cranmer's new prayer book, but also upon high prices and enclosures. This view of the causes of discontent is confirmed by the character of the disturbances in many scattered places throughout southern England.[1]

In Norfolk, where the disturbances of 1549 took the form of an open rebellion, led by Robert Ket, agrarian discontent was outspoken. The rebels came mostly from the populous district of north and east Norfolk, where pressure on the land within a community of small farmers had bred tension enough to kindle a riot at the smallest provocation. But enclosure was not the outstanding grievance; it was not even mentioned directly in Ket's programme, and the only reference to enclosure was ambiguous, and seemed to concern closes reserved for saffron-growing. But underlying the particular list of abuses concerning selfish lords who overgrazed the commons with their animals, kept dovecotes, allowed their pigeons to damage their tenants' crops, and kept rabbits in unprotected cony warrens, was general exasperation at the shortage of land and the greedy exploitation of the commons by the few. Local discontents mirrored the economy and the social structure of the region as they had done in 1536 in north-western England. But all were rooted in the shifting sands of a changing economy, a growing population, and expanding agricultural enterprise.[2]

Ket's rebellion failed miserably, the Western rebellion was crushed, and Somerset was overthrown. The government learnt its lesson and was not disposed to embark again on legislation which would act as a clarion call to a restive peasantry. The sheep tax had gone. The enclosure enquiry of 1548 was prematurely brought to an end, and the only surviving information collected by it relates to Warwickshire and Cambridgeshire. But despite the general verdict that Northumberland was the friend of the large landowner, his period of government saw the passing of two agrarian statutes in 1550 and 1552 to help the homeless cottager find accommodation in the countryside, and to maintain tillage. Though hardly forceful enough, they at least made a show of defending the poor against the powerful. The first act of 1550 "concerning the ymprovement of comons and waste groundes," was in fact concerned with protecting small cottagers who sought to build a

---

[1] E. F. Gay, 'The Midland Revolt and the Inquisitions of Depopulation of 1607', RHS, XVIII, 1904, p. 200; Strype, *Ecclesiastical Memorials*, 1822, II, ii, p. 432.

[2] S. T. Bindoff, *Ket's Rebellion, 1549*, pp. 7–10, 17–18.

house and take a small plot of land on the wastes. It reaffirmed the principles set out in the Statutes of Merton and Westminster in 1235 and 1285 that lords might improve their commons so long as they left enough for their free tenants, but reminded them that houses built on the waste with not more than three acres of land "dothe noe hurt and yet is muche commoditie to the owner thereof and to others." Only when more than three acres of land were annexed to the cottages was an offence committed, and the land ordered to be laid open to common again. In short, the act recognized that housing had to be found for increasing numbers of people, that squatting on the commons was the only solution to the housing shortage in many places, and that some distinction had to be made between such encroachments and enclosures by farmers who sought to carve out more substantial farms.[1]

The second statute, in 1552 (5 & 6 Edward VI, c. 5), reverted to the familiar problem of maintaining and increasing tillage. It harked back to the beginning of Henry VIII's reign and ordered that all land which had been in tillage for four years at any time since 1509 should be put back to tillage. The act thus instituted an enquiry into the use of land over the previous forty-two years. Another clause excluded land that had lain in pasture for forty years, and all land on marshes, heaths, common downs, fens, and moor, which had not been ploughed for forty years, as well as pasture kept only for the maintenance of houses and hospitality. It also exempted from penalty all those who, having converted arable to pasture, converted an equivalent amount of land in the same township from pasture to arable. Commissioners were to be appointed to discover the lands which offended against the new regulations, cases were to be heard in the court of Exchequer, and a penalty of 5s. was imposed on every acre discovered which was not put back into tillage. The act was to endure for ten years at least and after that to the end of the next Parliament.[2]

Under Mary Parliament reiterated and elucidated the meaning of the old statutes of husbandry. It provided for the appointment of commissioners to see that the statutes were observed, while allowing some latitude in the enforcement of the acts in areas where it was considered unnecessary to insist on the strict letter of the law. It also attacked another problem, which had been voiced much earlier in the century, though it is not easy to measure its importance beyond the clauses of the statute. In 1556 it was ordained that all men who kept more than 120 sheep should keep one cow per sixty sheep and rear one calf for every 120 sheep. The preamble justifying the act tells us that "of late yeres" people had turned their land over to the feeding of sheep, oxen, steers, heifers, etc., and in concentrating on meat produc-

[1] *Statutes of the Realm*, IV, pp. 102–3.   [2] *Ibid.*, pp. 134–5.

tion had neglected rearing, and so caused a shortage of store cattle. This complaint had already been made by Thomas More in his *Utopia* (1516). The decline of cattle breeding, he had argued, was due to the fact that rich men preferred to engage in the more profitable pursuits of keeping sheep or fattening bullocks. The argument was repeated by John Hales in his *Causes of Dearth* (1548): the universal dearth of victuals, he said, resulted from the failure to breed and rear cattle and poultry. By 1555 Hales had ceased to have any influence on government policies, but this proposition, following so closely the reasoning in *Utopia*, probably expressed a widespread popular notion about the causes of high food prices.[1]

Judging by the records we possess of the animals kept by the larger farmers in the sixteenth century, there were few men keeping large numbers of sheep who did not also keep a sizeable herd of cows and rear calves. Nor did the act, having attacked the producers of mutton as well as beef, suggest how to compel those who fattened sheep to give attention to rearing them. It was certainly true that some regions tended to concentrate more and more on fattening—this was the trend in the Weald of Kent, for example—but then these districts were served by farmers from north and west where rearing was the principal business. Towards the end of the sixteenth century the tendency grew for the rearing regions to engage in a certain amount of fattening as well. The farmers in the four northern counties, for example, seem to have taken more interest in fattening, probably in response to a larger demand for meat from the local cloth- and coal-producing towns. This may well have reduced the number of store cattle available for sale to the farmers of the Home Counties, who concentrated on fattening because of their favourable geographical position in relation to London. By the beginning of the seventeenth century, moreover, there were other signs that the home production of store cattle was inadequate. The gap was being met by imports from Ireland, a solution which prompted bitter complaint from some of the breeders in Somerset.[2]

It would not, therefore, have been surprising to see the act of 1556 in the 1590's or at the beginning of James I's reign. But it is difficult to show that fifty years earlier it dealt with an urgent problem. Rather it would seem likely that increasing specialization on meat production in certain districts around London had forced itself upon the notice of contemporary writers and politicians, and persuaded them that this was the trend all over England. Had this been true, it would certainly have been arguable that legislation was needed to encourage cattle

---

[1] *Statutes of the Realm*, IV, pp. 274–5; *The Utopia of Sir Thomas More*, ed. H. B. Cotterill, 1937, p. 30; *Discourse of the Commonweal*, p. xlii.

[2] See also p. 41; CSPD 1619–23, p. 291.

breeding again. In fact, it was not, and there is nothing to suggest that at this date the breeding regions failed to supply all the needs of the fattening areas.

It is noteworthy that the attack on sheepmasters, which had prompted punitive legislation in 1533, had now died away. The one and only statute which had singled out the wool producers rather than the pasture farmers as a whole was a period piece, belonging to a decade when cloth exports were reaching their peak. By 1550 the Crown had turned its attention elsewhere—to the graziers who produced meat by buying in their store animals from elsewhere. And in the nineties, when bad harvests and high food prices yielded signs of considerable rural distress and occasioned a fresh burst of legislation, it was again meat producers who were cast in the rôle of villains of the piece, while the sheepmasters were allowed to retreat into the shadow. The change of emphasis between 1533 and 1555 seems to reflect a change of opinion concerning the mainspring of the enclosure movement. The profit from sheep had been regarded as the main motive until the middle of the century. Now it was the profit from fat cattle.

Enclosure cases presented in the court of Exchequer from 1517 onwards dwindled to a mere trickle after 1556. This slackening off in the zeal of informers explains the provisions of a new act for maintaining tillage, passed early in Elizabeth's reign (1563). It repealed all agrarian statutes passed under Edward and Mary on the grounds that they were imperfect, in some cases too mild, and did not produce results, and it ordained that the acts of Henry VII and VIII should continue in force, that from 1564 all land tilled for four successive years at any time since 20 Henry VIII (1528–9) should continue in tillage, that all arable converted to pasture between 7 and 20 Henry VIII should be restored to tillage, and that no further conversions from arable to pasture should be carried out anywhere. The act heralded a new enclosure enquiry, which began in 1565. For some reason, not yet clearly understood, however, this commission came to a premature end, and the only surviving returns consist of fragments relating to Leicestershire and Buckinghamshire.[1]

Before the dearth of the nineties again focused anxious attention on enclosure, one other agrarian statute was passed in 1589, dealing with the problem of landless cottagers. It forbade the building of cottages with less than four acres of land. This may have been inspired by the

---

[1] Beresford, *The Lost Villages of England*, p. 115; E. F. Gay, 'Inclosures in England in the Sixteenth Century', p. 577. Gay suggests elsewhere that the enquiry of 1566 ended abruptly because Parliament did not renew the act of 1563. The Crown had to rest content with a proclamation in 1568.—E. F. Gay, *Zur Geschichte der Einhegungen in England*, p. 45.

Crown's own experience of the problem as landowner. As population increased in certain areas, holdings and tenements were being divided in order to provide accommodation for everyone, sheds and barns were being turned into dwellings, and cottages were being built by freeholders on small sites as a speculation. Often they lacked any land, and became a desperate refuge for paupers who had little hope of supporting themselves and who made heavy demands on the charity of the rest of the community. The new legislation, therefore, was designed to preserve the principle that all countrymen should have some land for their essential support.[1]

The act of 1563 for maintaining tillage had contained nothing novel, and the enquiry of 1565 had proved abortive. We must conclude from this and the fact that the rebellion of 1569 did not let loose an avalanche of agrarian complaints that enclosing and engrossing had lost some of their sting. Not that the movement came to a halt in the second half of the sixteenth century—it did not. But it may well have slowed down. This seems to have occurred between 1530 and 1580 in Leicestershire, for example, one of the counties most plagued by enclosures in the Tudor period. Moreover, the idea that enclosure had some merit was gaining ground, as reasonable methods of carrying it through became more common and the peasantry shared in its benefits. Finally in the Parliament of 1593 the Commons decided "because of the great plenty and cheapness of grain," and partly because of "the imperfection and obscurity of the law" that the statutes against the conversion of arable to pasture should be discontinued. It proved to be an ill-chosen moment at which to loosen the reins. The autumn of 1594 brought a disastrous harvest failure, and this was but the first of a series of four. The subsistence farmer was quickly reduced to abject helpless misery; he could not feed his family, let alone pay his rent. The middling farmers could support themselves but had nothing to sell at the market; they too fell in arrears with their rent. Only the large farmer who still had a considerable surplus to sell did well out of the famine.[2]

In 1597 Parliament took fright and decided to revive the statutes against enclosing and engrossing. In doing so, it expressed the conviction that enclosing had greatly increased since 1593, and this statement has been confirmed by detailed investigation in one Midland county— Leicestershire—showing a great burst of activity between 1591 and

---

[1] *Statutes of the Realm*, IV, pp. 804–5; PRO DL 44, 398.
[2] L. A. Parker, *Enclosure in Leicestershire, 1485–1607*, London Ph.D. thesis, 1948, p. 189; TED I, pp. 84–5; C 2 Eliz., P 7, 34; P 1, 5; D 8, 31; H 11, 46; Thirsk, 'Industries in the Countryside', pp. 82–3; CSPD 1595–7, p. 348. The influence of the harvests on this legislation is analysed in W. G. Hoskins, 'Harvest Fluctuations and English Economic History, 1480–1619', AHR, XII, 1964, pp. 28–46.

1597. The loosening of the reins had evidently accelerated the movement in the Midlands towards the conversion of arable to pasture and convertible leys.[1]

E. F. Gay once remarked of the anti-enclosure legislation of the sixteenth century that most of it coincided with periods of dearth. Legislation became necessary because the government feared the social tension bred by these changes within a community of hard-pressed anxious peasants. Nothing illustrates this better than the legislation of 1597. From all parts of the country the Privy Council received news of meagre corn supplies and plague. Enclosing and engrossing, the old bones of contention, seemed doubly offensive to the peasantry, and were doubly dangerous to the government, as a threat to social peace. Fear and reality were brought face to face in disturbances in Oxfordshire "to overthrow enclosures, and to help the poor commonalty that were to famish for want of corn."[2]

The two statutes of 1597 emerged as a result of the initiative taken by the Commons. The first act against the decaying of towns (39 Eliz. c. 1) tackled engrossing by ordaining that all houses of husbandry (i.e. all houses having twenty acres or more of land) which had been allowed to fall into decay within the last seven years should be rebuilt and forty acres of land (or if so much land was not available, twenty acres) laid to them. Half the houses decayed for *more than* seven years were to be rebuilt with the same allotment of land. The second act "for the maintenance of husbandrie and tillage" (39 Eliz. c. 2), having stated in the preamble that the repeal of the old statutes in 1593 had caused more depopulations by turning tillage into pasture than at "anie time for the like number of yeares heretofore," ordered that lands converted since 1588 into sheep pastures or used for the fattening or grazing of cattle, and having been tilled for twelve years before conversion, should be restored to arable before May 1599. Certain exceptions followed, however, which show that by now members of the Commons were well drilled in the routine of pointing out the unpractical and unrealistic aspects of the tillage statutes. The act did not apply to lands converted to pasture in order to regain heart by being grazed—official recognition, at last, for the virtues of ley farming. The act did not apply to common graziers or butchers who needed only grazing grounds for the temporary keep of fat beasts and sheep. Nor did it apply to commons and wastes which were unsuited to corn. Finally, the statute was ordered to

---

[1] Parker, *op. cit.*, pp. 93, 189.
[2] E. F. Gay, 'The Midland Revolt and the Inquisitions of Depopulation of 1607', RHS, XVIII, 1904, p. 213 note; Henry Barnes, 'Visitations of the Plague in Cumberland and Westmorland', *Cumb. & Westm. Antiq. & Archaeolog. Soc.*, XI, 1892, pp. 178–9; SP 14, 28, 64.

be kept in certain counties only. The original bill, having been designed to apply throughout the kingdom, was amended in committee to omit Devon, Cornwall, Shropshire, Staffordshire, Cheshire, Lancashire, Cumberland, Westmorland, and all counties in eastern England lying east of a line drawn through Hampshire, Berkshire, Buckinghamshire, Bedfordshire, and Cambridgeshire. The reasoning behind the geography of this act is not readily obvious. But it seems to have been decided upon after vigorous discussion in committee, as a result of intervention by members of Parliament with local knowledge of farming in their own counties. One member, for example, remarked in debate that Shropshire was wholly given over to woodland, oxen, and dairies—in other words, it was a pastoral county. To include it in the act would breed a greater scarcity than the scarcity of corn. This then explains the omission of Shropshire from the act, while Herefordshire, one of the counties described as "the barns for the corn" in this part of the country, was included. Sir John Neale has expressed the view that some counties suffered inclusion in the act simply for want of an M.P. to speak for them. But all in all the counties selected for investigation seem to have been wisely chosen. They were counties with common fields and considerable arable land, while many, though not all, the omitted counties lacked common fields or were mainly engaged in grassland farming. The final singular exception in this statute related to land "lying within two miles of Watling Street leading from Dunstable to Westchester so that the same ground be not above five miles from the parish church of Dunstable nore within two miles thereof." This clause smacks especially of strong intervention by a member of the Commons with local interests, and may have been designed to ensure that the drovers of cattle had sufficient pasturage at this halting place on their road to London. But it will require a local historian to settle this problem with certainty.[1]

Surviving records of the Commons debate on these two statutes in 1597 suggest that the anti-enclosure bill met much opposition while that against engrossing did not. It was, indeed, difficult to defend engrossing against those who argued the paramount importance of defending the realm and the necessity for keeping the country well populated with husbandmen and yeomen. Economic rationalism— the strongest argument in favour of engrossing—could not compete against the patriotic appeal for military security at home. But enclosure had become a highly controversial subject, because greater knowledge had shown it to be a many-sided issue. Nothing illustrates better the

[1] J. E. Neale, *Elizabeth I and her Parliaments, 1584–1601*, pp. 337–45; *Statutes of the Realm*, IV, pp. 891–6; A. F. Pollard and Marjorie Blatcher, 'Hayward Townshend's Journals', *Bull. IHR*, XII, 1935, p. 16.

increasing awareness of its complex nature than the tone of the speeches in debate, and the content of some of the rejected clauses of the Act against the Decaying of Towns. At one stage a clause was proposed to allow any tenant to enclose land belonging to his farm if he had the consent of his lord. Another amendment suggested allowing anyone to enclose as much land as he desired, so long as it was for the maintenance of his household. In the midst of these debates, a bill "for the most commodious usage of land dispersed in the common fields" was presented. This also must have been intended to assist consolidation of holdings, if not enclosure. The discussions leading up to the legislation of 1597 were throughout hampered by uncertainties about the wisdom of anti-enclosure legislation. For the immediate cause of the proposed acts was the shortage of grain, and who could be certain that this was really due to the decay of tillage? In the opinion of one speaker in debate, the true cause was the weather. If pasture were converted to arable, it would raise the rents of pasture, cause cattle and sheep to be scarce, wool to fall short of demand, grain to be overabundant, and its price to fall unduly low. Here, indeed, was displayed a much fuller understanding of the complementary nature of arable and pastoral husbandry than in any of the statutes passed earlier in the Tudor period.[1]

The two statutes of 1597 served their turn while high prices lasted. But in 1601 they fell under criticism again, for the previous harvest had been good, and grain prices had fallen. The Commons began to consider the possibility of repealing them. Policy was now vacillating and uncertain. The conviction that enclosure was wrong and the tillage laws were right, which had governed opinion at Westminster for so long, had gone. The statutes seemed necessary when grain prices were high, but when they fell, some politicians, at least, saw the folly of compelling men to convert pasture to arable to grow more grain and so force the price of corn even lower. "In the time of dearth, when we made this statute [for the maintenance of tillage]," said Mr Johnson in the Commons in 1601, "it was not considered that the hand of God was upon us; and now corn is cheap. If too cheap, the husbandman is undone, whom we must provide for, for he is the staple man of the kingdom. And so, after many arguments, he concluded the statute to be repealed." Sir Walter Raleigh also argued in favour of repeal, desiring to leave every man free, "which is the desire of a true Englishman." Cecil, on the other hand, was against repeal because he believed that in years of abundance the surplus corn could be

[1] Neale, *op. cit.*, pp. 342–3; M. Beresford, 'Habitation versus Improvement. The Debate on Enclosure by Agreement', *Essays in the Economic and Social History of Tudor and Stuart England*, ed. F. J. Fisher, pp. 52–3.

readily exported, and national defence demanded a good supply of ploughmen.[1]

Cecil's speech shows that the government opposed repeal of the tillage statutes, and on this occasion its view prevailed. But the tenor of the debates of 1597 and 1601 suggests that the weight of opinion in the House was gradually shifting towards a *laissez-faire* attitude, leaving "every man free" as Raleigh phrased it. Probably the tillage laws would have been discarded altogether in the next ten years had the harvests been plentiful. But events took another turn. Suddenly in 1607, with little warning, an angry peasantry in three counties rose in revolt against enclosure, and in a matter of days the Midlands were ablaze with tumult and rumours of worse to come.

A full explanation of the outbreak of 1607 must wait upon a local historian who can examine in detail the enclosure history of all those villages in Northamptonshire, Leicestershire, and Warwickshire which were the ringleaders of the revolt. All five villages lay within a small tract of country—none more than twenty miles from any other—between Rugby, Kettering, and Market Harborough, a district now given over almost entirely to grazing and dairying, where the enclosure movement had made rapid strides in the Tudor period. No national legislation touching enclosure can be blamed for encouraging the insurgents, nor had Westminster recently intervened with economic aid or promises of aid to raise hopes of a remedy for agrarian distress. The long-term irritant was almost certainly the prolonged agricultural distress, which had begun with a bad harvest in 1594, and had continued with a whole series of misfortunes, mounting grain shortage, high prices, and sickness among men and stock. A contemporary reporter described the purpose of the revolt in 1607 as the desire "for reformation of those late inclosures which made them of the porest sorte reddy to pyne for want." In the light of other information about this decade, it seems that enclosures were the scapegoat for other more immediate ills. We have noticed already how in depression falling profits drove the larger farmer to economize in the employment of labour. This immediately aggravated the plight of the poor by increasing unemployment just at the time when food was in short supply and expensive. Even those who had some land of their own reaped such a meagre harvest in bad years that they had nothing to sell, and were driven, if they had money enough, to buy domestic supplies at the market. Everything conspired against the labourer and small farmer in bad times, and it was almost certainly in a situation like this, of mounting

[1] Bland, Brown, and Tawney, *English Economic History. Select Documents*, pp. 274–5. It seems to have been a conventional assumption that "shepherds be but ill archers."— TED III, p. 55.

economic difficulty offering little hope of a speedy remedy, that the Midland revolt broke out.[1]

The disturbance started with a riot in Northamptonshire on the last day of May. Already in 1604 complaints had been heard in this county against "the depopulation and daily excessive conversion of tillage into pasture." Parts of Northamptonshire, like Leicestershire, had fallen readily into the grasp of the enclosing farmer, for its soils were nowhere specially fertile for corn whereas it grew good grass, and was eminently suited to cattle and sheep grazing. Thus although bad harvests between 1594 and 1597 had raised the price of grain and so encouraged the large corn-grower, the difficulties of distributing corn in these east Midland counties, and the hazards of growing it, were too great to divert the farmer from his course. The extent of the enclosure movement can be roughly measured by the reports submitted to the enclosure commission later in 1607. The acreage of Northamptonshire reported enclosed since 1578 was far higher than in any other Midland county investigated by the commission. Over 27,000 acres were reported, affecting 118 townships.[2]

As for the immediate cause of the revolt, it is evident that grain shortage had raised prices in the Midlands by the spring of 1607, though they were not as high as they were to be on the eve of the harvest of 1608; Arthur Standish who referred in *The Commons Complaint* (1611) to mutinies "only for the dearth of corn in Warwickshire, Northamptonshire, and other places" can only have been referring to the troubles of 1607. Since this was a district which could export little grain for lack of good water transport, and so presumably did not normally produce much more than it consumed, it was easy enough for a bad year to precipitate a serious crisis. Certainly, on the eve of the harvest of 1608 the shortage of grain was unmistakable in the Midland counties. William Combe wrote to Lord Salisbury from Warwickshire foreseeing trouble because of the dearth of corn, and because of the activities of maltsters in the bigger towns engrossing barley under the very eyes of the justices of the peace.[3]

Hunger and threatening starvation drove the peasants to vent their wrath on the most obvious offenders, the enclosing farmers. The first rising in Northamptonshire was followed by others at Hillmorton in Warwickshire, Cotesbach in Leicestershire, and Rushton, Pytchley, and Haselbeech in Northamptonshire. Parts of Bedfordshire were affected, and in Derbyshire people were restive. The local circumstances of the

---

[1] Gay, 'The Midland Revolt', p. 215.
[2] *Ibid.*, pp. 212, 240.
[3] *Ibid.*, p. 213, note 3; J. D. Gould, 'Mr Beresford and the Lost Villages: a Comment', AHR, III, 1955, p. 112; PRO SP 14, 113, 90; SP 14, 34, 4.

outbreaks have not yet been examined in detail except in the case of Cotesbach, but this one example is enough to illustrate the bitterness of local quarrels about enclosure which had frayed tempers to breaking-point.[1]

Cotesbach lies in the southern tip of Leicestershire on the borders of Northamptonshire and Warwickshire. The bulk of the land in the parish belonged to the Devereuxs of Chartley (Staffs.) until 1591 when the estate was sold to pay off heavy debts. By 1626 it had passed through the hands of six different owners. Except for the enclosure of the demesne—some 200 acres, or one-fifth of the lordship—which took place at the beginning of the sixteenth century, the organization of farming at Cotesbach had undergone no fundamental alteration for a hundred years. Then suddenly, between 1603 and 1612, everything was changed. The lordship was enclosed and the income of the lord was doubled. The revolution was brought about by John Quarles, a London merchant, who bought the estate in 1596 and promptly had it wrested from him by the Crown to pay off the debts of the previous owner. He did not recover possession until about 1601–2, when he resolved to recoup his losses. His tenants' leases had expired, and he offered them new agreements at a rent of £5 per yardland, which they refused. He therefore resolved to enclose the lordship. He bought out one of the four freeholders, came to agreements with the second freeholder, and with the rector, owner of the glebe, and ignored the fourth, who, in any case, had only two acres of freehold land. The leaseholders were given another opportunity to renew their leases, but again refused. In 1603 Quarles procured a royal licence to enclose, and the courts turned down a petition of the tenants against it. After enclosure, the tenants had no option but to accept new leases or leave the village. Some remained but took up less land than before, since the new rents were appreciably higher; some rented cottages only and refused all land, contenting themselves with grazing rights at 6d. per cow on the lord's closes; others declined the new terms altogether and left the village. The tenants had suffered a complete defeat and their numbers had been reduced by about a half. No wonder that seething discontent boiled over in revolt in 1607. Cotesbach became the rallying point in Leicestershire where "there assembled of men, women, and children to the number of full five thousand" to cast down the hedges. But the revolt did not spread. Indeed, both here and in Northamptonshire and Warwickshire the term *revolt* exaggerated the scale of the disturbances. A gallows was erected in Leicester as a warning to miscreants on 6 June, and the borough, expecting worse violence, began to train the militia. The gallows were torn down by an angry

[1] Gay, 'The Midland Revolt', pp. 215 *sqq.*

crowd on the 8th, but no worse commotion occurred, and by 14 June the trouble was over.[1]

Brief though the disturbances were—they lasted little more than a month—they caused enough alarm in government circles to prompt the appointment of a new enclosure commission in August 1607. Its work was limited to seven Midland counties: Northamptonshire, Warwickshire, Leicestershire, and Bedfordshire, which had set the stage for the summer disturbances, together with Huntingdonshire, Buckinghamshire, and Lincolnshire. Oxfordshire, which had shown itself to be a much-enclosed county in 1517, was unaccountably ignored, and so was Derbyshire, where the alarm had been sounded in 1607, though all fears in that quarter had proved groundless.

This first and last enquiry of James I's reign harked back thirty years and called for a return of the townships depopulated since 1578, the land enclosed and converted to cattle and sheep pasture, the land severed and engrossed, the farmhouses vacant or turned into cottages, the farm buildings decayed, the tenants evicted, the highways blocked up or diverted, and the churches decayed. The results of the enquiry filled in some of the background to the Midland revolt by showing that the acreage of the county reported to be affected by enclosure was far higher in Northamptonshire than in any other county, while Lincolnshire, Leicestershire, and Bedfordshire each reported over 10,000 acres of enclosure and over sixty villages affected. The enquiry of 1607 was followed up by numerous prosecutions and fines in Star Chamber, but much resentment lingered in the Midlands owing to the universal belief that nothing was being done to bring offenders to book. From Northamptonshire, for example, came a report to Salisbury in August 1608 of fresh enclosures and a burning sense of grievance among the people "that no reformation doth follow." Nothing further occurred, however, to fan these embers into flame.[2]

Viewed in the light of changing public opinion towards enclosure, the Midland revolt was something of an anachronism. At Westminster, where the problem was discussed in its national setting, passions were no longer deeply engaged. Politicians forgot that in certain districts, particularly in Leicestershire and Northamptonshire, people had had to swallow a highly concentrated pill, and were still brooding over their long and bitter memories. The appointment of the enclosure com-

---

[1] L. A. Parker, 'The Agrarian Revolution at Cotesbach, 1501–1612', *Studies in Leicestershire Agrarian History, Leics. Arch. Soc.*, XXIV, 1948, pp. 41 *sqq.*

[2] E. F. Gay, 'Inclosures in England in the Sixteenth Century', *Qtrly J. Econ.* XVII, 1903, p. 581; John Gould, 'The Inquisition of Depopulation of 1607 in Lincolnshire', EHR, LXVII, 1952, pp. 392–5; L. A. Parker, 'The Depopulation Returns for Leicestershire in 1607', *Leics. Arch. Soc.*, XXIII, 1947, p. 4; SP 14, 48, 4; SP 14, 35, 52.

mission of 1607 showed that the government was not disposed to overlook the causes of the Midlander's discontent. But neither was it to be driven into panic legislation. Nothing could be better reasoned or more reasonable than the memorandum of July 1607—*A Consideration of the cause in question before the lords touching depopulation*—apparently prepared for the benefit of the Privy Council immediately after the revolt, and arguing the *pros* and *cons* of enclosure. It claimed, quite rightly, that enclosure did not inevitably cause depopulation, and cited Somerset as an example of an enclosed, wealthy, *and* populous county. It pointed out that open fens and forest commons were often the nurseries of beggars, while enclosed land in counties like Essex, Devon, and Somerset afforded fuel for the poor, and work in hedging and ditching. It reached the heart of the matter by concluding that depopulation was the evil to be rooted out, and not enclosure, and that depopulation was as readily caused by engrossing as converting. "By redressing the fault of depopulation and leaving enclosing and converting arbitrable as in other shires, the poor man shall be satisfied in his end, habitation, and the gentleman not hindered in his desire, improvement."[1]

The *pros* of enclosure were beginning to outweigh the *cons*, and, not surprisingly, the 1607 commission turned out to be the last large-scale enquiry. In 1618 the government decided that "tillage is become much more frequent and usual, corn is at reasonable rates," and appointed a commission of judges and others to grant exemptions from the tillage statutes in order that "the rigor of the statutes may be mitigated according to these present times and occasions." It was admitted that legislation had forced men to put land in tillage which was unsuitable for crops, and that the work of informers in exposing the crimes of those who converted arable to pasture had been more of a nuisance to the king's subjects than a benefit to the commonwealth—"some great offenders were spared by connivance of the informer, and others that were innocent were vexed without end." Finally, in 1624, when Parliament agreed that the nation's corn supply was no longer in danger, the tillage statute of 1563 was repealed, while those of 1597 died for want of enforcement. In the words of Chief Justice Coke, they had been "so like labyrinths, with such intricate windings or turnings as little or no fruit proceeded from them." It was at about this time that John Shotbolt, in his *Verie necessary considerations for the Weale publique*, put forward a plan for a general permission to enclose land by exchange, believing that the public might now be willing to accept "so good a business . . . for so general enriching to

[1] W. Cunningham, *The Growth of English Industry and Commerce in Modern Times*, II, pp. 898–9.

all sorts." The idea of enclosure had, indeed, "hardened and become more durable."[1]

The last attempt by the Crown to flog a dead horse into life was made in the 1630's, when bad harvests caused alarm and the Privy Council instituted another investigation into enclosure. This last enquiry began in 1630 and has been termed a display of "paternalism and pick-pocketry," for it brought benefits to the Crown in the shape of fines, and appeared to appease the victims of enclosure. But it did nothing to sweeten relations between Charles I and his subjects, for, in fact, the commission condoned as much enclosure as it condemned. In any case, public opinion had undergone a considerable change: in 1644, when Archbishop Laud was tried for high treason, the charges against him included the allegation that "he did a little too much countenance the commission for depopulations." A century before, such a charge, far from causing the bishop to be arraigned before Parliament, would have endeared him to it.[2]

By 1640, then, a strenuous attack on enclosers was no longer the sure way to court popularity. Depopulation was still universally condemned, but people no longer assumed that enclosure was always and alone responsible. They saw more clearly the tangled complexity of the problem, and, moreover, they now knew by experience the shortcomings of penal legislation against enclosure which was enforced regardless of individual circumstances. Private informers, who had been made responsible for the first time in 1538 for bringing offenders against the tillage statutes to book, had done as much as anything to antagonize the public. Indeed, the commission of 1618 to compound with enclosers justified itself on these grounds. More than this, people had groped their own way towards a solution of their difficulties. Increasingly efficient methods were being employed for carrying out enclosure, without depopulation, by agreement. Private agreements between individuals for the exchange of land as a preliminary to enclosure show the principle at work in its simplest form in the Tudor period. Private agreements on a larger scale, between lords and their tenants, were not uncommon in the later sixteenth century. Finally, to save the parties to these agreements from the fear of later litigation, the habit developed of getting them enrolled in one of the

[1] Beresford, 'Habitation versus Improvement', pp. 49–50, 55 note, 54; *Commons Debates, 1621*, ed. Notestein, Relf, and Simpson, VII, p. 512; E. Gay, 'Inquisitions of Depopulation in 1517 and the Domesday of Inclosures', RHS, NS XIV, 1900, pp. 236, 240; *The Anglica Historia of Polydore Vergil*, ed. Denys Hay, Camden Soc., LXXIV, 1950, p. 277.

[2] See, for example, SP 16: 531, 82; 187, 7; 184, 7; 181, 6; 185, 86; 176, 11; E. M. Leonard, 'The Inclosure of Common Fields in the Seventeenth Century', RHS, NS XIX, 1905, pp. 127 *sqq.*; CSPD 1631–3, p. 490; Beresford, 'Habitation versus Improvement', p. 50.

courts at Westminster. Tenants of the Crown had enjoyed this privilege in the sixteenth century when seeking permission to improve land. When their landlord investigated the situation and agreed, he gave his endorsement by having the agreement enrolled in the court of Exchequer. At some time in the early seventeenth century private lords began to follow this example, and secured the enrolment of their agreements in the court of Chancery. The parties claimed, truthfully or otherwise, that the agreement was being challenged by a few wanton troublemakers. They brought a lawsuit into the court, the result of which was a decree approving the enclosure, which was duly registered on the Chancery rolls. The date of the first of such Chancery decrees cannot yet be ascertained owing to the deficient indexes to this large class of records. But in the 1630's enrolled agreements were not unusual, and after 1633 the court of the Palatinate of Durham also began to sanction and record enclosure agreements.[1]

C. PAMPHLET LITERATURE

The pamphlet literature of this century and a half of enclosure controversy reflects the changing moods of the public in much the same way as do the statutes and parliamentary debates. The subject remained controversial, but the indignation which charged the pens of writers at the beginning of the period was much diluted with tolerance and sweet reasonableness at the end. The matter could still provoke fierce debate in the 1650's within the Midland shires. It prompted a petition from Leicestershire to the Council of State in November 1655, and a bill in Parliament to regulate enclosure in 1656. But three years earlier, when John Moore, minister of Knaptoft, Leicestershire, rose up like a ghost from the past to launch a bitter attack on enclosures in *The Crying Sin of England of not caring for the Poor*, he found an equally redoubtable adversary in Joseph Lee, rector of Catthorpe, who from his own personal experience could compile an impressive list of Leicestershire villages which had been enclosed in the previous fifty years without depopulation and without the decay of tillage.[2]

Viewed as a whole, the pamphlet literature mirrors as many different aspects of depopulation as anyone seeking local differentiation could wish for. Even Thomas More, whose impassioned and dramatic passage in *Utopia* is the best remembered of all the diatribes against depopulation, in fact castigates a regional phenomenon only, the increase of sheep in those areas which were already dedicated to sheep-keeping and which grew the finest wool. It is true that his remarks

---

[1] Beresford, *op. cit.*, pp. 49, 53 *sqq.*; L. A. Parker, 'Enclosure in Leicestershire', pp. 190–1; TED I, p. 61; Leonard, *op. cit.*, p. 109.   [2] VCH *Leics.*, II, pp. 218–19.

begin with a general comment on the sheep which cause depopulation, and this has resulted in their being generally remembered as an indiscriminate and vigorous onslaught upon enclosure for sheep every-where. "Your sheep, that were wont to be so meek and tame and so small eaters, now, as I hear say, be become so great devourers and so wild, that they eat up and swallow down the very men themselves. They consume, destroy, and devour whole fields, houses, and cities." But in fact More particularizes in the very next sentence. The passage continues, "For look, in what parts of the realm doth grow the finest and therefore dearest wool, there noblemen and gentlemen, yea and certain abbots, holy men, no doubt, not contenting themselves with the yearly revenues and profits that were wont to grow to their forefathers and predecessors of their lands, nor being content that they live in rest and pleasure, nothing profiting, yea much noying the weal public, leave no ground for tillage." More, in short, was as precise a reporter on the evils of his day as were the members of the House of Commons defend-ing the local interests of their constituencies against the tillage statutes.[1]

The dominant theme of the pamphlet literature of 1500–1640 was depopulation and its varied causes. But different writers singled out different abuses for special attention. Altogether, they were five in number: first, enclosure of the common pastures and fields, and the subsequent conversion of arable to pasture, which deprived the poorer people of common grazing and reduced employment in arable farm-ing; secondly, sheep-keeping on a large scale—the crime of the rich and ambitious farmers—because it too reduced employment as well as causing beef, dairy produce, and corn to be scarce and dear; thirdly, cattle-keeping, which, when more exactly defined, meant fattening, again because it employed few hands and caused a scarcity of young cattle and dairy products; fourthly, engrossing of farms, because it drove small men off the land—another crime usually attributed to the rich and powerful farmers and landlords, and sometimes coupled with the crime of rackrenting; fifthly, the making of parks and chases for deer, which again reduced the amount of land in tillage. This last recreation of the landed gentleman was a fashion in vogue in the first half of the sixteenth century, but it received less attention in the literature than other agrarian changes because it passed out of favour in the second half of the century when many of the parks were turned to more profitable use for cattle grazing.[2]

---

[1] *The Utopia of Sir Thomas More*, ed. H. B. Cotterill, 1937, p. 28.
[2] See the list of contemporary pamphlets and sermons on enclosure in Conyers Read, *Bibliography of British History. Tudor Period*, 1933, p. 169, and Godfrey Davies, *Bibliography of British History. Stuart Period*, 1928, pp. 203–4; E. Kerridge, 'The Revolts in Wiltshire against Charles I', *Wilts. Arch. & Nat. Hist. Mag.*, LVII, 1958–9, p. 64.

D. THE LOCAL HISTORY OF ENCLOSING
AND ENGROSSING

Through the eyes of pamphleteers and politicians, we have observed a large-scale enclosure movement in the period 1500–1640, concentrated mostly in the Midland counties, and provoking great controversy there because it served as the prelude to the conversion of much arable to pasture, and the increase of stock farming at the expense of corn. Regional differences can now be elaborated, using the more detailed evidence of the contemporary enquiry commissions, and other miscellaneous documentary material now available to the historian.

The evidence of the enclosure commissions is, of course, woefully imperfect. The 1517–19 enquiry was directed at only twenty-three counties, and the surviving documents even from these twenty-three are incomplete. All that remains of the report of 1548 concerns two counties only, Warwickshire and Cambridgeshire, and from the commission of 1566 there survive only fragments for Leicestershire and Buckinghamshire. In 1607 seven Midland counties were surveyed, and reports are at hand for all of them. But though they are packed with information, they reveal only too clearly the difficulties of the commissioners' task, and the imperfections of the final result. The returns were collected hundred by hundred from empanelled juries who can never have hoped to collect information of all enclosures in the area. Moreover, the reports submitted were usually inaccurate in minor ways, and sometimes complete distortions of the truth.[1]

Taking the information submitted to the enclosure commissioners, the lawsuits that followed, together with other evidence from local records, however, certain general observations seem to be justified. Enclosing and engrossing were taking place all over England, but unemployment and depopulation which accompanied these changes were mainly Midland problems. Clement Armstrong's *Treatise concerning the Staple* (c. 1519–35) spoke of enclosure "in the middle parts of the body of this realm." And we have traced already in the statutes and enquiries the government's growing recognition that the worst distress was indeed concentrated there. Whether engrossing was a Midland rather than a national matter is less certain. It was liable to occur wherever land was in short supply and farming seemed a profitable business. Many enclosed counties, therefore, must have been as much plagued by engrossers as the common-field areas. However, the government clung to the view that the two things were inseparable,

---

[1] Gay, 'Inquisitions of Depopulation in 1517', p. 238; E. Kerridge, 'The Returns of the Inquisitions of Depopulation', EHR, LXX, 1955.

and never considered asking for reports of engrossing from counties that were already enclosed.[1]

In counties with common fields there was plentiful evidence of both enclosing and engrossing. But the two problems were not evenly distributed everywhere. Enclosure and conversion to pasture, for example, were unusual in the Lincolnshire marshlands. As various inhabitants pointed out when accused of this crime in 1607–8, they had little arable land, the district comprising "almost all pasture and feeding ground, employed for the feeding and grazing of sheep and cattle." On the other hand, because of the excellent feeding qualities of the land, engrossing was a common grievance. Indeed, the occupation of marshland by farmers from other districts was a continual annoyance to the inhabitants until the eighteenth century, when the upland farmer finally found a way of fattening his sheep on his own land.[2]

The surviving returns of the enclosure commissions of 1517–19 are so incomplete that no conclusions about the extent of enclosing and engrossing can be built upon them. The more impressive figures—showing over 4,000 acres of land enclosed and over fifty farmhouses decayed or reduced to cottages—relate to ten counties:

Table 1. *Findings of the 1517–19 Enclosure Commission in ten counties*

County	Acreage affected by enclosure	No. of villages from which returns are available	Houses of husbandry		No. of[a] persons displaced
			Decayed	Made cottages	
Nottinghamshire	4,470	80	71	—	188
Warwickshire	9,694	70	189	18	1,018
Leicestershire	5,780½	49	136	12	542
Northamptonshire	14,081½	112	345	9	1,405
Oxfordshire	11,831	107	176	10	720
Buckinghamshire	9,921	70	160	12	887
Bedfordshire	4,137	36	89	—	309
Berkshire	6,392	86	116	—	588
Lincolnshire	4,866½	63	70	—	158
Norfolk	9,334	122	70	—	—

[a] I. S. Leadam, *The Domesday of Inclosures*, 1897, I, pp. 38, 40.

For 1548 and 1565 the returns are so fragmentary as to be valueless; they have survived by chance and merely record what would in any case have been assumed, that enclosing and engrossing were still in

[1] TED III, p. 100.
[2] PRO St Ch. 8, 17, 23; Thirsk, *English Peasant Farming*, pp. 154–6, 177.

progress. In 1607, when the returns were confined to seven Midland counties, the following acres were reported.

Table 2. *Findings of the 1607 Enclosure Commission*

County	Acreage enclosed and converted to pasture	No. of villages from which returns are available	Houses of husbandry Decayed	Made cottages	No. of[a] persons displaced
Warwickshire	5,373	28	62	26	33
Leicestershire	12,290½	70	151	21	120
Northamptonshire	27,335½	118	201	157	1,444
Buckinghamshire	7,077½	56	29	51	86
Bedfordshire	10,004	69	47	75	259
Huntingdonshire	7,677½	52	59	87	290
Lincolnshire	13,420	?	⌐—1,290—⌐		?

[a] Gay, 'Inclosure in England in the Sixteenth Century', p. 581; Gould, 'The Inquisition of Depopulation of 1607 in Lincolnshire', p. 395.

None of these figures bears close examination. In the first place, no county investigation was thorough and complete. In the second place, each county was made up of two or more regions, each with a different farming routine and a different social structure, and they were not all equally susceptible to enclosing and engrossing. No fair statistical comparison between the counties, therefore, is possible. In the third place, the allegations which were made against enclosers to the commissioners were often found later to be based on flimsy evidence, to distort the true facts, or even to be downright falsehoods. The courts investigating these cases afterwards rejected many as unfounded, and listened sympathetically to the extenuating circumstances surrounding others. All that the enclosure enquiries do is to point an accusing finger at certain counties in the Midlands which had suffered more, or at least complained more, than the rest. Those which attracted notice consistently throughout the period were Leicestershire, Lincolnshire, Warwickshire, Northamptonshire, Bedfordshire, and Buckinghamshire. In the agrarian history of these counties, then, we may expect to find the explanation for the controversial nature of enclosing and engrossing in the period 1500–1640. Other counties await the closer attention of the local historian. Oxfordshire, Berkshire, Norfolk, and Nottinghamshire kept Wolsey's clerks busy in 1517–19, and were included in the tillage statutes of 1597, but were passed over in 1607. Huntingdonshire did not attract attention in 1517–19 or in 1597, but justified the visit of the enclosure commissioners in 1607 by producing evidence of considerable engrossing and over 7,500 acres enclosed. Its sudden appearance on the stage in the final act of the drama is not easily explained, but it was probably due to the intervention of a local member of Parliament who could argue from experience the necessity for governmental interest in this usually neglected county. Some hint of what was afoot may be found in statements made in Charles I's reign that many citizens of London owned land in the county and leased it to tenants, while the county as a whole was complaining of its poverty and inability to contribute to a levy. Since the county was proving an attractive field of investment to the London business man, its experiences of enclosing, and, more noticeably, of engrossing may well derive from this fact.[1]

Before considering the special circumstances of the Midland counties, some brief observations on enclosure in other parts of England and Wales must be made. Wales was not singled out for special mention in legislation until 1597, when the tillage statute of that year included Pembrokeshire at the suggestion of the House of Lords. Before this the government at Westminster had not considered that Wales had any serious enclosure problem, although the Council of Wales, being obliged to enforce the laws of England, had been instructed from time to time to investigate the decay of tillage and the enclosure of commons, and had heard appeals from injured parties against enclosure. However, the loss of most of the records of the Council of Wales makes it impossible to say how large the problem loomed in its deliberations. That enclosure was under way throughout Wales there is no doubt. The country had plentiful open commons and wastes, and much arable land which was divided into scattered strips, some of it subject to common rights, and which required consolidation. And since Welsh farmers were subject to the same economic stimuli as English farmers, they too responded by specializing more than hitherto, cultivating their land more intensively, keeping more stock and threatening to overcharge the commons, using temporary leys, clearing fresh land from the waste, and enclosing their common pastures and arable fields. But Wales was for the most part a pastoral country depending on its sheep and cattle for a living, and like the pastoral districts of England, it possessed the secret of enclosing land amicably. Since common rights over the arable were not greatly valued, and sometimes did not exist at all, many fields were enclosed without opposition of any kind. Enclosure of the commons was more liable to provoke disturbance, and did so in Monmouthshire and Carmarthenshire, where protests were accompanied by some colourful incidents: at Ffinnant, Breconshire, in 1560

[1] Kerridge, 'The Returns of the Inquisitions of Depopulation', *passim;* SP 16, 8, 44 and 86.

the hedges were overthrown and their planters tied to the tails of horses; at Dreuthen, Monmouthshire, in 1619 the tenants gathered to watch the enclosures, saying "Work if you will, for it shall not stand very long." Nevertheless, even the enclosure of commons did not inevitably enrage or injure the community. Many commons were so large that the allotments after partition satisfied everyone, while in the most thinly settled mountain districts enclosure often resulted from customary usage rather than deliberate agreement; people used different portions of the mountain as their sheepwalk until at length they claimed them as their own. Viewed as a whole, enclosure made more progress in this period in the eastern half of Wales than in the west, particularly in north Monmouthshire and the more accessible parts of Radnorshire and Breconshire, which were more influenced by English developments and the English market than west Wales. But nowhere did the movement cause wild commotion. The pastoral husbandry of the country, like that of highland England, could accommodate enclosure without disrupting social peace and destroying the poor.[1]

The government's lack of concern for the four northern counties of England at the time of the 1517–19 enclosure commission can be explained as a tradition of much economic legislation and one which persisted to some extent throughout the century. It was not intended to imply that enclosure was unknown in this area. But it would have been as futile to attempt an enclosure survey in 1517 as it was to collect a subsidy. The gentry, on whom the Crown relied to do the donkey work, were too few and too remote from central control, and the government, therefore, had to admit its inability to administer this distant territory efficiently. Later on, these four counties were included in some of the tillage statutes, since after 1536 the Crown had a reconstituted council sitting in the North which could deal with enclosure information and put the statutes in execution. But even then little concern was shown for the northern counties in this matter, and this attitude was in part justified by the knowledge that they were not corn-growing counties, and were not likely to be much distressed by the "decay of tillage." They were not, however, immune from the effects of depopulation, and in 1597, when some exemptions to the tillage statutes were being considered, the dean of Durham pleaded for the inclusion of Northumberland, Cumberland, and Westmorland. "The decays are not, as supposed, by the enemy, but private men have

[1] Beresford, 'Habitation versus Improvement', p. 48; T. I. J. Jones, *The Enclosure Movement in South Wales in the Tudor and early Stuart Periods*, Univ. of Wales M.A. thesis, 1936, *passim;* David Williams, *A History of Modern Wales*, pp. 83–4; John Rhys and D. Brynmor-Jones, *The Welsh People*, p. 432. I owe this paragraph to Mr Frank Emery.

dispeopled whole villages." In the end, Northumberland alone was included in the provisions of the act but was omitted in 1601 when the statute was re-enacted.[1]

Much work could profitably be done on the enclosure history of these northern counties, for the chronology, and the means by which enclosure was carried through, are still not yet fully understood. Westmorland and Cumberland seem at first glance to have suffered more depopulation from Scottish raids than from enclosing and engrossing, for except on the coastal plains, their common fields were small, and their unstinted commons extensive. And wherever enclosure occurred, it tended to take place silently and painlessly. Northumberland and Durham did not escape some depopulation, however, particularly during the last years of Elizabeth. But engrossing seems to have been a more common cause of the demise of villages than enclosing, and the problem was localized—in the eastern plain and in the wider valleys inland, which possessed large common fields, grew corn in some quantity, and were accessible to good markets and ports. By the end of Elizabeth's reign enclosure agreements were fairly common. Farmers in the more mountainous western parts of these counties, however, were more interested in pasture-farming than in corn-growing, and since, in the words of a reporter writing on rural conditions on the border, "the people that inhabit there are very poor and rude, having much more ground than they can manage, not having stock to store a third part thereof," there was no purpose in engaging in depopulating enclosure. Even the acquisitive instincts of their landlords were held firmly in check by the physical difficulties of getting their goods to market. We should not, therefore, expect to find many of Philip Stubbs's "caterpillars and locusts that massacre the poor and eat up the whole realm" in this part of the kingdom.[2]

Other counties of the north, west, and south-west, for example, Lancashire and Yorkshire, Cornwall and Devon, Cheshire, Shropshire, and Derbyshire, were omitted from the later enclosure commissions because they too were largely grass-growing counties, and the government was concerned with those which lay "for the more part" in tillage. Some of these counties had fertile districts of mixed farming, but they were small enclaves in predominantly pastoral regions and could safely be ignored in the spacious generalizations of the politicians.

[1] CSPD 1595–7, p. 542; Beresford, 'Habitation versus Improvement', p. 48.
[2] Beresford, *The Lost Villages of England*, pp. 172–7, 372–3; H. L. Gray, *English Field Systems*, pp. 207, 105–7; G. Elliott, 'The System of Cultivation and Evidence of Enclosure in the Cumberland Open Fields in the Sixteenth Century', *Cumb. & Westm. Antiq. & Arch. Soc.*, NS LIX, 1959, pp. 85, 89; *Phillip Stubbes's Anatomy of Abuses in England in Shakespere's Youth*, ed. F. J. Furnivall, 1877–9, part i, p. 117; SP Jas. I, IX, 97.

Some of these counties, also, were, or were reputed to be, largely enclosed. And although the modern historian can produce evidence of enclosure in the sixteenth century from all of them, it was either small in scale, or if extensive, was of an amicable kind. In pastoral districts the path for both the enclosing landlord and the enclosing peasant seems to have been smoothed by the common assumption that enclosure was a reasonable and not an anti-social improvement of land, and that so long as others were not injured thereby, an enclosure would normally be approved by the community, often in the manorial court. Rossendale in Lancashire yields perhaps the best evidence of the enclosure of small pieces of waste, a process which was deemed thoroughly commonplace, and passed unchallenged since land was plentiful. Shropshire yields good evidence of the enclosure of strips in the common fields. Agreements, by deed, to exchange strips and consolidate them, are plentiful in the local records of this county and were the avowed prelude to enclosure. In Wiltshire too, most enclosures were carried out by agreement, not by force. Why agreements were so much more numerous in the pastoral counties than in the mixed farming areas is a subject which deserves closer investigation than it can receive here. But we may see some part of the explanation in the fact that grazing rights over the arable were not so jealously guarded in a pastoral county, nor was land so scarce. The documents relating to an enclosure at Ilminster in Somerset convey to us something of the surprise of the inhabitants that any one should object to the enclosure of strips in the common fields. In reply to the charge that arable land had been converted to pasture, Joan Bonvile replied that there was no custom in the manor of Ilminster preventing the enclosure of arable land and its conversion to pasture. She had known the copyhold tenants for half a century to convert arable to meadow or pasture "at their will and pleasure without denial of anyone." Some such basic attitude, which was entirely foreign to the eastern Midlands, seems to have been usual in the pastoral counties, and to account for the generally peaceable progress of enclosure.[1]

The counties of southern and eastern England were exempt from the plague of enclosure for other reasons. Kent, Sussex, and Essex were by this time commonly deemed enclosed counties. East Anglia was regarded as enclosed, though in fact only the wood-pasture region was

[1] J. Lister, 'Some Local Star Chamber Cases', *Halifax Antiq. Soc.*, XXIV, 1927, p. 199; G. H. Tupling, *The Economic History of Rossendale*, Chetham Soc., NS LXXXVI, 1927, pp. 47 *sqq.*; Nat. Lib. Wales, Pitchford Hall Coll., nos. 2434, 2029, etc.; C 2 Eliz., A 7, 28; VCH *Wilts.*, IV, p. 47; Woburn Abbey Muniments, Court Roll of the earl of Bedford's manor of Werrington, 21 September 1557. I owe this reference to the kindness of Professor H. P. R. Finberg.

enclosed and much of the light lands and brecks lay open. Only about 9,000 acres of newly enclosed land were reported from Norfolk in 1517–19, and in 1549 Ket's complaints suggest that engrossing and encroachments by large farmers were a greater irritant than enclosure. To this extent official unconcern for the problem of enclosure in these districts was justified.[1]

The government, therefore, appraised the situation as accurately as it could when it sought in the Midlands for the heart of the matter. But even then, in designating whole counties for investigation, it was making only a rough and ready generalization. Even within the Midland shires certain regions of fen and forest were almost untouched by the controversies about depopulation. Most of the deserted villages in Warwickshire listed by Rous at the end of the fifteenth century, as well as those where enclosure was reported to the Tudor commissioners, were situated in the common-field districts of south Warwickshire, and not in the forest area of Arden in the north. The fenland and forest districts of Northamptonshire, the Chiltern forest areas of Oxfordshire, and the fens of Lincolnshire were likewise oases of peaceful farming, standing apart from the turmoil of the common-field areas in the same counties. Even Midland England then was not all of a piece.[2]

But since the government administered affairs by counties, and not by farming regions, it was not far wrong in directing its whole attention to the Midland shires. What, then, can we add by way of explanation?

In the first place, the Midland counties were among the most densely populated of the common-field counties. The poll tax returns towards the end of the fourteenth century suggest that Leicestershire, Rutland, Northamptonshire, Bedfordshire, East Anglia, and the fens of Lincolnshire were the most populous districts of England, and this may be taken as a guide to the situation at the beginning of the sixteenth century. In many townships the farming community had used up all the waste land on which it had formerly relied for accommodating an increasing population. Few Leicestershire townships except those lying in Charnwood forest had any waste by the sixteenth century, and many others had only small amounts of regulated common pasture. Grazing thereon had to be carefully controlled, in consequence, and the overcharging of the commons was jealously watched. Young men wishing

---

[1] M. R. Postgate, 'The Field Systems of Breckland', AHR, x, 1962, pp. 85–6; K. J. Allison, 'The Sheep-Corn Husbandry of Norfolk in the Sixteenth and Seventeenth Centuries', AHR, v, 1957, pp. 13, 22–3; 'The Lost Villages of Norfolk', *Norfolk Archaeology*, XXXI, 1955, pp. 134 *sqq.*
[2] M. Beresford, 'The Deserted Villages of Warwickshire', *Birmingham Arch. Soc.*, LXVI, 1950, p. 80; *The Lost Villages of England*, pp. 234–7, 379.

to make a living in their native places were hard put to it to find land to farm, and as village populations grew—the population of Leicester-shire increased by almost a half between 1563 and 1603—stints of stock on the common pastures had to be reduced, to ensure that all had their fair share. The whole community tended to feel oppressed by the irksome restraints imposed by its straitened land resources. Enclosing or engrossing in such circumstances only made matters worse. And yet, from the point of view of the individual, such measures were one of the few means left of increasing efficiency and so making the best use of a restricted supply of land. Deprived of the chance to change things by enclosure, they were trapped. For price changes whipped up ambition and offered to farmers a golden chance to make more money if their husbandry could be made more flexible, at the same time goading the landlord with the certain knowledge that by enclosure he could raise the rents on his estate.[1]

Large populations and land shortage explain why it was difficult to enclose and engross land in the Midlands without injuring the com-munity and arousing hostility. Further trouble arose after enclosure because so much land was put down to pasture. The advantages of pasture farming have already been described in general terms. Good prices were paid for meat, wool, sheep skins, leather, and tallow, and the labour costs of pasture farming were lower than for crop-growing. But over and above this, local circumstances pulled in the same direc-tion. The Midland counties had difficulty in exporting grain for lack of a convenient river system. Two contemporary comments underline the seriousness of this handicap. In defence of enclosure, a writer of a memorandum to the Privy Council in 1607 argued that the Midland shires should be allowed to develop naturally into pasture counties, because of their poor transport facilities, "the charge far exceeding the full worth of the corn they sell." In 1620 the same point was underlined yet again when the Leicestershire justices argued the absence of any need for a local storehouse for corn, "the county being remote from any means of exporting grain."[2]

Yet another more technical reason for the conversion of arable to pasture must be emphasized. Large areas of the Midlands are covered with a heavy clay soil. Even today it is difficult to grow crops on this land. The conversion of arable to permanent pasture was a change of

[1] H. C. Darby, *An Historical Geography of England before A.D. 1800*, 1936, p. 232; W. G. Hoskins, 'The Leicestershire Farmer in the Seventeenth Century', *Agric. History*, xxv, 1951, p. 10; SP 16, 402, 12 and 13; PRO C 78, 526, 8; C 78, 67, 21; Leicester City RO, Clayton MSS, 35'29, 292; 383; 447; 57; John Rylands Library, Ry. Ch. 2659.

[2] W. Cunningham, *The Growth of English Industry and Commerce*, ii, pp. 898–9; CSPD 1619–23, p. 124, quoted in J. Gould, 'Mr Beresford and the Lost Villages', p. 112.

use which subsequent generations of farmers have applauded and endorsed. East and south Leicestershire, for example, which underwent much enclosure in the Tudor period, have remained for the most part in permanent grass to this day. In short, while the prices of pastoral products rose in the Tudor period, and the Midland movement was much influenced by this fact, we must not ignore the sound technical reasons also which justified it.

Another system of cultivation favoured on the lighter clay soils of the same region was that known as convertible husbandry, whereby the arable land was put under grass for a number of years in order to "regain heart" and old pastures were ploughed up. The conversion of arable to pasture frequently proved to be one stage of a programme for introducing ley farming. It gave rise to the usual complaints on the grounds that the plough had been permanently put down, but often what looked like another permanent pasture was in fact a temporary ley. Here again the modern farmer can help us to see the issue in better perspective, for he understands the issues involved. In the last thirty years the principles of ley farming have been scientifically analysed and diligently publicized. The system is now widely understood and practised by English farmers.

The spread of permanent pastures and of convertible leys in the Midlands, therefore, had a technical justification as well as an economic one. And since the ordinary peasant undoubtedly understood the practical problems of agriculture better than the economics, it would be unwise to assume that he attached more weight to the financial than to the technical arguments in favour of growing grass. It is worth noting, for example, how often technical arguments were used in the law-courts to defend enclosure. Moreover, this was an age of practical farming manuals, and although the majority of peasants could not read, they could certainly talk. Indeed, the social life of the village community in common-field England probably gave more time and opportunity for talk and the exchange of ideas than that enjoyed by the modern farmer. The advantages of temporary leys and permanent pasture may well have been as much argued in the alehouses as Elizabeth's religious settlement.[1]

While the increase of pasture was the commonest consequence of enclosure in the Midlands, the farming system carried on in the new closes differed from region to region. In general it may be said to have accentuated the existing specialization of the district. On the Lincolnshire wolds and the limestone edge, and in the eastern uplands of Leicestershire, enclosures were used to extend the area of sheepwalk and to increase the quantity of sheep feed in winter. But while sheep

[1] E.g. SP 16, 183, 25.

were profitable in themselves, they were also essential for manuring the thin soils of the uplands and increasing the yield of corn. For the upland farmer, therefore, the sheep flock was only one pillar of his system; his arable, and particularly his barley or wheat crop, were an equally important part of his farming business, even though the profits were not as spectacular, as those from his sheep. The same system ruled farming in parts of Oxfordshire and Buckinghamshire, and explains why the writer of *The Decaye of England only by the great multitude of shepe* (1550–3) drew particular attention to these two counties as well as Northamptonshire. The generalization would have been more precise had it been made of farming regions, and not counties. On the Cotswold hills of Oxfordshire a sheep-corn husbandry similar to that of the chalk and limestone hills of Lincolnshire was the general rule. Even without enclosure, therefore, the incentive to keep more sheep was so strong, that we may accept without undue scepticism the charge that enclosure here had led to an increase of sheep numbers.[1]

Northamptonshire had other reasons for its addiction to sheep. In the Middle Ages more than half the county lay within the royal forests of Rockingham, Salcey, and Whittlewood, and this had undoubtedly acted as a brake upon the improvement of the land for cultivation by the plough. Much of this forest land, therefore, lay under grass in the sixteenth century as it had done in the Middle Ages. The special attractions of pasture farming in the period did not procure as complete a revolution as has sometimes been suggested. Moreover, as a modern account of Northamptonshire farming tells us, "no part of the county is remarkable for the exceptional productivity or fertility of its arable land." Even in 1939 "the most outstanding feature of Northamptonshire farming" was the amount of land laid to grass; the county carried more sheep per hundred acres of grass crops and rough grazings than any other lowland county of England. Since the present-day farmer with all the resources of science at his command cannot find a better use for his land than in sheep-keeping, we cannot altogether condemn the gentry and husbandmen who were perspicacious enough to see this four hundred years ago. The Ishams of Lamport, who purposefully reorganized their estates between 1560 and 1584 in order to expand their wool dealing business to include wool production, the Spencers of Althorp, and the Treshams of Rushton, who concentrated on fattening mutton for the butcher, were all making good use, and perhaps the best use, of their land. Despite the predominance of sheep, however, the county had other goods to sell. Many farmers were producing beef for the market, and many bred horses for sale at the

---

[1] Thirsk, *English Peasant Farming*, pp. 84–6, 88–9; TED III, p. 52; M. A. Havinden, 'Agricultural Progress in Open-Field Oxfordshire', AHR IX, 1961, p. 81.

horse fairs at Rothwell and Fotheringhay. Nevertheless, all these activities only served to emphasize the county's predilection for pasture-farming.

In explaining the outcry against enclosure in Northamptonshire, however, what was just as significant as the increase of grazing was the fact that Northamptonshire was generally acknowledged to be a densely populated county, and was becoming more so as its forest areas with their ample commons continued to attract immigrants throughout the period. Enclosure and conversion to pasture stood condemned, therefore, mainly for its harmful social consequences. It satisfied the ambitions of the larger farmers, but only at the expense of the small men and the many poor.[1]

In Warwickshire enclosure and the conversion of arable to pasture in the fifteenth century had had disastrous effects in depopulating common-field villages in the southern half of the county. Many large farmers and landlords had turned from mixed farming to sheep-keeping on a large scale, and the worst depopulations had certainly occurred before the reign of Henry VII. But the movement to evict men for the benefit of sheep lost much of its force in the next four reigns, even though some eighteen more villages were depopulated between 1485 and 1558. By the end of the sixteenth century the Warwickshire Felden was still a country of mixed farming, growing large corn crops as well as keeping stock. True, it boasted some large sheep-flocks, but the production of store cattle was also a considerable business, and by the early seventeenth century, dairying also. The northern half of the county, the Arden or forest region, on the other hand, suffered little from the pangs of enclosing, converting, and depopulation, for its economic and social organization was quite different from that of the Felden country. It had many similarities with the wood-pasture region of Suffolk and the dairying districts of Wiltshire, and it too specialized in the same kind of farming. Indeed, the fact that the Arden had organized the markets and the means of transport for the sale of dairy produce probably explains the trend towards dairying in the Felden in the early Stuart period.[2]

In south, and parts of east, Leicestershire, where the heavy clay soils favoured the spread of permanent pastures, new closes were most frequently used for cattle fattening. Here was land which later enjoyed a high reputation for its feeding quality. Already by the late sixteenth

[1] *Land Utilization Survey: Northamptonshire and the Soke of Peterborough, parts 58, 59,* pp. 349, 355, 361; Mary Finch, *Five Northamptonshire Families,* Northants. Rec. Soc., xx, 1956, *passim;* P. A. J. Pettitt, *The Economy of the Northamptonshire Royal Forests, 1558–1714,* Oxford Univ. Ph.D. thesis, 1959, pp. 35–6, 269, 303, 306–7.

[2] Beresford, 'The Deserted Villages of Warwickshire', pp. 80, 85.

century south Leicestershire as well as parts of Northamptonshire had become acknowledged suppliers of beef to the butchers of the Midland towns and London. In west Leicestershire on the poor soils in and around Charnwood forest the traditional pasture-farming of the region tended to develop a special emphasis on breeding and dairying, and this trend was accelerated in some places by enclosure. But enclosure was not nearly so common in west Leicestershire as in the eastern half of the county, and the breeding of cattle with butter and cheese-making were common on open as well as on enclosed lands. The technical arguments in favour of this specialization were stated in an enclosure report in 1631. Pleading the case in extenuation of an enclosure at Market Bosworth, the justices of the peace explained that some part of the land "is of indifferent quality for corn, the rest unfit for corn or sheep pasture, but most fit for milch kine and breeding of cattle, being of a sour, cold, and wild nature." At Nailstone they described the land as "all, or the greatest part, of a light wild nature, full of springs of a spongey nature, wet and cold, not fit for continual tillage. And yet in the best use of husbandry must in eight or ten years be ploughed to destroy the broom, gorse, and heath it is subject to bear." At Donington on the Heath (Charnwood area) the land was deemed of the same quality as at Nailstone, "but worse, greatest part thereof rocky, stony, cold and moorish, only fit for breeding cattle [if] without the help of lime." So, they concluded, "in our opinion, there is no likelihood of depopulation or decay of tillage."[1]

These more detailed explanations in defence of enclosure indicate the complexity of local circumstances surrounding the spread of the movement. Over and over again, farmers argued that their newly converted land was better suited to pasture than to arable. And if they did not plead this excuse, then they extolled the virtues of ley farming. John Bluett of Harlaxton, in Lincolnshire, for example, defended his conversion of 200–300 acres of arable as a means of building up fertility. For the time being, he explained, he was using the land as meadow, eating part of it every fourth year and mowing it in the other three years, grazing part for two years and mowing for two years, and mowing and grazing the rest every other year. Arable which he had converted already had been the means "to make good corn ground of that which before was very barren and bare and lay waste by reason there was not sufficient grass ground to maintain stock to manure it before this was converted. For," he continued, "we find that one land well manured is better than two that want heart."[2]

Apart from the technical reasons for enclosing and converting arable to pasture, practical convenience moved many a landlord and farmer

[1] SP 16, 183, 17.   [2] PRO St Ch. 8, 17, 23.

to enclose or to engross after a change of occupier had taken place. These cases illustrate another set of circumstances justifying changes in land arrangement. William Walcote, esquire, defended the conversion of sixty acres of arable to pasture at Walcot in Kesteven on the ground that he needed the additional pasture to maintain his household because his mother had an estate for life in half his land. Thomas Manisby had a farm of 100 acres in Cadeby and another farm in Binbrook, Lincolnshire, and was using the two in conjunction, altering the use of the land in each in order to achieve a proper balance of husbandry over the whole. Sir Edmund Bussey, having land in Heydour, Oseby, Aisby, and Culverthorpe, Lincolnshire, claimed that when he entered into possession the manor house was in ruin and the land inadequate to keep his household. A considerable reorganization of houses and land was necessary until everything was arranged to his liking. From the details which he gave, it would have required a Solomon sitting in judgement to determine whether the new pattern of occupation was less socially desirable than the old. Sir Thomas Cony claimed that his manor and demesne in North Stoke, again in the same county, had been let to a tenant who had divided the house and land among several undertenants, and that all he did on taking possession again was to restore the *status quo*, moving the three tenants elsewhere " to their better contentment."[1]

The justices who sat in Star Chamber and listened in 1608 to these and many more circumstantial explanations in defence of enclosing and engrossing must have ended that year of hearings chastened and wiser men. For in all the lawsuits arising from the enclosure enquiry in these seven Midland counties they heard many reasonable arguments in favour of enclosure, which bore eloquent witness to the desire of optimistic and hopeful farmers to make changes in order to improve their land and their yields.

The lawsuits of 1608 emphasized the rational advantages of the enclosure movement. But it was, of course, in the interests of every defendant to present a sweetly reasonable case. We must not be too gullible. The stories of evicted peasants departing their villages in tears and lamentation showed the other side of the medal. And the two differing accounts of one and the same episode were not necessarily deliberate or gross distortions by one or other party, but merely the forceful expression of two strongly held and different points of view. A course of action which seems reasonable to a man who has bought an estate and sets about organizing it to his liking will appear ruthless and inexcusable to his tenants whose forefathers have long occupied farms on the estate. The dispute at Cotesbach, which ended in a riot,

[1] PRO St Ch. 8, 17, 23; 8, 10, 4.

admirably illustrates the irreconcilable attitudes of two opposing sides, while each party justified itself to its own satisfaction.[1]

At the same time, it must be acknowledged that the reasonable tone of the arguments heard in the court of Star Chamber by 1608 agrees with many of the expressions of public opinion on the subject at the same period. The changing attitude towards enclosure was already evident by the end of Elizabeth's reign. Its explanation lay partly in the strength of the technical arguments in favour of enclosure, and secondly in the gradual change of procedure by which it was carried out. For the peasantry had learned the advantages of enclosure from the gentry. The evidence of enclosure in Leicestershire, for example, suggests that in the early years of the sixteenth century it was mainly the work of the nobility, gentry, and religious houses. Something like 70 per cent of the reported enclosures in the period 1485–1550 were carried out by the nobility and squirearchy alone. But in the second half of the sixteenth century the peasantry of this Midland county began to take the initiative, and between 1551 and 1607 were responsible for 19 per cent of the land reported enclosed. Moreover, the method of enclosing land changed. Since the very word 'enclosure' had become an incitement to violence, landlords were forced to proceed more cautiously. And statutes, government proclamations, and public opinion generally were not without their deterrent effect. Amicable agreements became more common. William Brocas of Theddingworth, Leicestershire, for example, came to an agreement with his freeholders in 1582, giving " gratuities and leases of good value" in addition to land in compensation. At least six and possibly a dozen enclosure agreements in Leicestershire date from the second half of the Tudor period. And what was happening in Leicestershire was happening also in other Midland counties.[2]

In the course of the next fifty years, the machinery for carrying out enclosure agreements was improved, and gave such satisfaction that the parliamentary enclosure commissioners a hundred years later were disposed to copy it in some detail. An agreement to enclose was accompanied by the appointment of (usually) five referees and two surveyors, chosen by all parties, who were responsible for allotting the new holdings. They were obliged to pay due regard to the "quantity, quality, and convenience of every man's land;" cottagers with common rights were granted land in compensation; the poor were provided for, frequently by a piece of open common. The final agreement was made binding on all parties by being enrolled in the court of Chancery after a fictitious suit had been brought to test it.

---

[1] See *supra*, pp. 88 *sqq*.
[2] L. A. Parker, 'Enclosure in Leicestershire', pp. 83, 149, 114.

Friendly agreements which dealt fairly with tenants' claims took the sting out of the enclosure movement. And in 1656, when the last bill to regulate enclosure was introduced into the House of Commons by Major-General Edward Whalley, the governor of five of the Midland counties, it was rejected. Thus ended all attempts by the government to arrest the progress of enclosure, and for a time, until the movement entered upon another energetic phase in the mid-eighteenth century, it ceased to be an urgent subject of public debate.

By 1640 few strong arguments could be advanced in favour of common fields and pastures. And not surprisingly, the strongest of them all was one which no contemporary ever mentioned, for it was one which only the observer from a later age could appreciate. Common fields and pastures kept alive a vigorous co-operative spirit in the community; enclosures starved it. In champion country people had to work together amicably, to agree upon crop rotations, stints of common pasture, the upkeep and improvement of their grazings and meadows, the clearing of ditches, the fencing of fields. They toiled side by side in the fields, and they walked together from field to village, from farm to heath, morning, afternoon, and evening. They all depended on common resources for their fuel, for bedding, and fodder for their stock, and by pooling so many of the necessities of livelihood they were disciplined from early youth to submit to the rules and the customs of their community. After enclosure, when every man could fence his own piece of territory and warn his neighbours off, the discipline of sharing things fairly with one's neighbours was relaxed, and every household became an island unto itself. This was the great revolution in men's lives, greater than all the economic changes following enclosure. Yet few people living in this world bequeathed to us by the enclosing and improving farmer are capable of gauging the full significance of a way of life that is now lost.

3

SELECT BIBLIOGRAPHY, 1500–1640

Alcock, L., and Foster, I. Ll. (eds.). *Culture and Environment*. London, 1963.

Allan, D. G. C. *Agrarian Discontent under the early Stuarts and during the last Decade of Elizabeth*. University of London M.Sc. (Econ.) thesis, 1950.

—— 'The Rising in the West, 1628–31', EcHR, 2nd Ser., v, 1952.

Allen, J. Romilly. 'Old Farmhouses with Round Chimneys near St David's', *Arch. Camb.*, II, 1902.

Allison, K. J. 'Flock Management in the Sixteenth and Seventeenth Centuries', EcHR, 2nd Ser., XI, 1958.

—— 'The Sheep-Corn Husbandry of Norfolk in the Sixteenth and Seventeenth Centuries', AHR, v, 1957.

—— *The Wool Supply and the Worsted Cloth Industry in Norfolk in the Sixteenth and Seventeenth Centuries*, University of Leeds Ph.D. thesis, 1955.

Ambler, L. *Old Halls and Manor Houses of Yorkshire*. London, 1913.

Ascoli, Georges. *La Grande-Bretagne devant L'Opinion Française au XVIIe Siècle*. Travaux et Mémoires de l'Université de Lille, NS, Fascicule 13, I, Paris, 1930.

Ashley, Sir William J. *The Bread of our Forefathers*. Oxford, 1928.

Ashton, T. S. *An Economic History of England: the Eighteenth Century*. London, 1955.

—— *Economic Fluctuations in England, 1700–1800*. Oxford, 1959.

Aylmer, G. E. *The King's Servants*. London, 1961.

—— 'The Last Years of Purveyance, 1610–1660', EcHR, 2nd Ser., x, i, 1957.

Bacon, Nathaniel. *Annalls of Ipswiche*. Ipswich, 1884.

Bailey, J., and Culley, G. *General View of the Agriculture of the County of Northumberland*. London, 1813.

Bankes, Joyce (ed.). *The Memoranda Book of James Bankes, 1586–1617*. Inverness, 1935.

Barley, M. W. *The English Farmhouse and Cottage*. London, 1961.

Barnes, D. G. *A History of the English Corn Laws from 1660 to 1846*. London, 1930.

Barnes, T. G. *Somerset Assize Orders, 1629–1640*. Som. Rec. Soc., LXV, 1959.

Bates, E. H. *The Particular Description of the County of Somerset, 1633*. Somerset Rec. Soc., XV, 1900.

Batho, G. R. 'The Finances of an Elizabethan Nobleman: Henry Percy, Ninth Earl of Northumberland', EcHR, 2nd Ser., IX, 1957.

—— *The Household Papers of Henry Percy, ninth Earl of Northumberland*. Camden Soc., XCIII, 1962.

Beale, John. *Herefordshire Orchards, a Pattern for all England*. London, 1657.

Bean, J. M. W. *The Estates of the Percy Family, 1416–1537*. London, 1958.

Bell, H. E. *An Introduction to the History and Records of the Court of Wards and Liveries*. Cambridge, 1953.

Bennett, M. K. 'British Wheat Yield Per Acre for Seven Centuries', *Economic History*, III, 1935.

Beresford, M. W. 'Glebe Terriers and Open-Field Buckinghamshire', *Records of Bucks.*, XVI, 1953–4.

—— 'Habitation versus Improvement. The Debate on Enclosure by Agreement', *Essays in the Economic and Social History of Tudor and Stuart England*, ed. F. J. Fisher. Cambridge, 1961.

—— 'A Journey to Elizabethan Market Places', chapter VI in *History on the Ground*. London, 1957.

Beresford, M. W. *The Lost Villages of England*. London, 1954.
—— 'The Lost Villages of Medieval England', *Geog. J.*, CXVII, 1951.
—— 'The Lost Villages of Yorkshire', *Yorks. Arch. J.*, XXXVIII, 1952.
Best, Henry. *Rural Economy in Yorkshire in 1641, being the Farming and Account Books of Henry Best of Elmeswell in the East Riding*, ed. C. B. Robinson. Surtees Soc., XXXIII, 1857.
Beveridge, Lord. 'British Exports and the Barometer', *Economic J.*, XXX, 1920.
—— 'The Yield and Price of Corn in the Middle Ages', *Economic History*, II, 1927.
—— 'Wages in the Winchester Manors', EcHR, VII, 1936–7.
—— 'Weather and Harvest Cycles', *Economic J.*, XXXI, 1921.
Beveridge, Lord, and others. *Prices and Wages in England from the Twelfth to the Nineteenth Century*. London, 1939.
Bickley, W. B. *Abstract of the Bailiffs' Accounts of Monastic and other Estates in the County of Warwick*. Dugdale Soc., II, 1923.
Bindoff, S. T. *Ket's Rebellion, 1549*. Hist. Assoc. Pamphlet, General Series 12, 1949.
—— *Tudor England*. London, 1950.
Birch, Walter de Gray. *A Descriptive Catalogue of Penrice and Margam Manuscripts*, Series I–IV. London, 1893–5.
Blagrave, J. *The Epitomie of the Art of Husbandry*. London, 1669.
Blake, W. T. 'Hooker's Synopsis Chorographical of Devonshire', *Devon Assoc.*, XLVII, 1915.
Bland, A. E., Brown, P. A., and Tawney, R. H. *English Economic History. Select Documents*. London, 1914.
Blith, Walter. *The English Improver Improved*. London, 1652.
Blome, Richard. *Britannia*. London, 1673.
Bouch, C. M. L., and Jones, G. P. *The Lake Counties, 1500–1830*. Manchester, 1961.
Bourne, George. *The Bettesworth Book. Talks with a Surrey Peasant*. London, 1920.
—— *Memoirs of a Surrey Labourer: a record of the last years of Frederick Bettesworth*. London, 1911.
Bowden, P. J. 'The Home Market in Wool, 1500–1700', *Yorks. Bull. of Econ. and Soc. Research*, VIII, ii, 1956.
—— *The internal Wool Trade in England during the Sixteenth and Seventeenth Centuries*. University of Leeds Ph.D. thesis, 1952.
—— 'Movements in Wool Prices, 1490–1610', *Yorks. Bull. of Econ. and Soc. Research*, IV, 1952.
—— *The Wool Trade in Tudor and Stuart England*. London, 1962.
Brace, H. W. *History of Seed Crushing in Great Britain*. London, 1960.
Bradley, Harriet. *The Enclosures in England—an Economic Reconstruction*. New York, 1918.
Brenner, Y. S. 'The Inflation of Prices in Early Sixteenth Century England', EcHR, 2nd Ser., XIV, 1961.
—— 'The Inflation of Prices in England, 1551–1650', EcHR, 2nd Ser., XV, 1962.
Brett-James, N. G. *The Growth of Stuart London*. London, 1935.
Brown, E. H. Phelps, and Hopkins, Sheila V. 'Seven Centuries of Building Wages', *Economica*, NS, XXII, 1955.
—— 'Wage-rates and Prices: Evidence for Population Pressure in the Sixteenth Century', *Economica*, NS, XXIV, 1957.
—— 'Builders' Wage-rates, Prices and Population: Some Further Evidence', *Economica*, NS, XXVI, 1959.
Browning, Andrew (ed.). *English Historical Documents, 1660–1714*. London, 1953.
Brunskill, R. W. 'An Appreciation of Monmouthshire Houses', *Mont. Coll.*, LIII, ii, 1954.

Brydson, A. P. *Some Records of two Lakeland Townships—Blawith and Nibthwaite—chiefly from original documents.* Ulverston, 1908.

Burton, William. *The Description of Leicestershire.* London, 1622.

Caley, J., and Hunter, J. (eds.). *Valor Ecclesiasticus temp. Hen. VIII....* (6 vols.). London, 1810–34.

Camden, W. *Britannia,* trans. R. Gough. 3 vols., London, 1789.

Campbell, Mildred. *The English Yeoman Under Elizabeth and the Early Stuarts.* New Haven, 1942.

Carew, Richard. *The Survey of Cornwall.* London, 1602.

Carpenter, H. J. 'Furse of Morhead', *Devon Assoc.,* XXVI, 1894.

Cave, T., and Wilson, R. A. (eds.). *The Parliamentary Survey of the Lands and Possessions of the Dean and Chapter of Worcester.* Worcs. Hist. Soc., 1924.

Chalklin, C. W. 'The Compton Census of 1676: the dioceses of Canterbury and Rochester', *A Seventeenth Century Miscellany.* Kent Arch. Soc., Records Publication Committee, XVII, 1960.

—— 'The Rural Economy of a Kentish Wealden Parish, 1650–1750', AHR, X, 1962.

—— *Seventeenth Century Kent.* London, 1965.

Charles, B. G. 'The Second Book of George Owen's Description of Pembrokeshire', *Nat. Lib. Wales J.,* V, 1947–8.

Charman, D. 'Wealth and Trade in Leicester in the early Sixteenth Century', *Leics. Arch. Soc.,* XXV, 1949.

Cheke, Val. *The Story of Cheese-making in Britain.* London, 1959.

Chippindall, C. L. W. H. (ed.). *A Sixteenth-century Survey and Year's Account of the Estates of Hornby Castle, Lancashire.* Chetham Soc., NS, CII, 1939.

Cipolla, C. M. 'La prétendue "révolution des prix." Réflexions sur l'expérience italienne', *Annales E.S.C.,* 10e année, 4, 1955.

Clapham, Sir J. *A Concise Economic History of Britain from the Earliest Times to 1750.* Cambridge, 1949.

Clark, G. N. *The Wealth of England from 1496 to 1760.* Oxford, 1947.

Clarkson, L. A. 'The Organization of the English Leather Industry in the Late Sixteenth and Seventeenth Centuries', EcHR, 2nd Ser., XIII, 1960.

Clay, J. M. *Yorkshire Monasteries: Suppression Papers.* Yorks. Arch. Soc. Rec. Ser., XLVIII, 1912.

Clay, T. *Briefe, Easie and Necessary Tables of Interest and Rents Forborne.* London, 1624.

Cliffe, J. T. *The Yorkshire Gentry on the Eve of the Civil War.* University of London Ph.D. thesis, 1960.

Coleman, D. C. 'Industrial Growth and Industrial Revolutions', *Economica,* NS, XXIII, 1956.

—— 'Labour in the English Economy of the Seventeenth Century', EcHR, 2nd Ser., VIII, 1955–6.

Collier, C. V. 'Burton Agnes Courts, Miscellanea II', Yorks. Arch. Soc., Rec. Ser., LXXIV, 1929.

Collis, I. P. 'Leases for Term of Years, determinable with Lives', *J. Soc. Archivists,* I, 1957.

Considerations Touching Trade, with the Advance of the King's Revenue..., 1641.

Cooper, J. P. 'The Counting of Manors', EcHR, 2nd Ser., VIII, 1956.

—— 'The fortune of Thomas Wentworth, Earl of Strafford', EcHR, 2nd Ser., XI, 1958.

Cordingley, R. A. 'British Historical Roof Types and their Members', *Ancient Monuments Soc.,* NS, IX, 1961.

—— 'Stokesay Castle, Shropshire: The Chronology of its Buildings', *The Art Bulletin* (U.S.), XLV (2), 1963.

Cornwall, J. C. K. *The Agrarian History of Sussex, 1560–1640.* University of London M.A. thesis, 1953.

Cornwall, J. C. K. 'English Country Towns in the Fifteen Twenties', EcHR, 2nd Ser., xv, i, 1962.
—— 'Farming in Sussex, 1560–1640', Sussex Arch. Coll., xcii, 1954.
Cox, J. C. (ed.). The Records of the Borough of Northampton, II. Northampton, 1898.
Craig, Sir J. The Mint. A History of the London Mint from A.D. 287 to 1948. Cambridge, 1953.
Cramer, J. A. (ed.). The Second Book of the Travels of Nicander Nucius of Corcyra. Camden Soc., xvii, 1841.
Creighton, C. A History of Epidemics in Britain from A.D. 664 to the Extinction of Plague. Cambridge, 1891.
Crook, Barbara. 'Newnham Priory: Rental of Manor at Biddenham, 1505–6', Beds. Hist. Rec. Soc., xxv, 1947.
Cross, M. Claire, 'An Exchange of Lands with the Crown, 1587–8', Bull. IHR, xxxiv, 1961.
Cunningham, W. The Growth of English Industry and Commerce in Modern Times, II. Cambridge, 1919.
Daniel-Tyssen, J. R. 'The Parliamentary Surveys of the County of Sussex', Sussex Arch. Coll., xxiii, 1871.
Darby, H. C. The Draining of the Fens. Cambridge, 1940.
—— (ed.). Historical Geography of England before A.D. 1800. Cambridge, 1936.
Darby, H. C., and Saltmarsh, J. 'The Infield-Outfield System on a Norfolk Manor', Economic History, iii, 1935.
Davies, D. J. The Economic History of South Wales prior to 1800. Cardiff, 1933.
Davies, Elwyn. (ed.). Celtic Studies in Wales. Cardiff, 1963.
Deane, Phyllis, and Cole,W. A. British Economic Growth. 1688–1959. Cambridge, 1962.
Defoe, Daniel. A Tour through England and Wales. Everyman edn., London, 1959.
Dendy, F. W. 'The Ancient Farms of Northumberland', Archaeologia Aeliana, 2nd Ser., xvi, 1894.
Denney, A. H. The Sibton Abbey Estates: Select Documents, 1325–1509. Suffolk Rec. Soc., ii, 1960.
Dexter, R., and Barber, D. Farming for Profits. London, 1961.
Dickens, A. G. 'Estate and Household Management in Bedfordshire, c. 1540', Beds. Hist. Rec. Soc., xxxvi, 1956.
—— The Register or Chronicle of Butley Priory, Suffolk, 1510–35. Winchester, 1951.
Dietz, F. C. English Government Finance, 1485–1558. University of Illinois, Studies in the Social Sciences, ix, 3. Urbana, 1920.
—— English Public Finance, 1558–1641. New York, 1932.
Dodd, A. H. Studies in Stuart Wales. Cardiff, 1952.
Edwards, Ifan Ab Owen (ed.). A Catalogue of Star Chamber Proceedings relating to Wales. Cardiff, 1929.
Eland, G. (ed.). Thomas Wotton's Letter-Book, 1574–1586. London, 1960.
Ellis, Sir Henry (ed.). Speculi Britanniae Pars: an Historical and Chorographical Description of the County of Essex by John Norden, 1594. Camden Soc., ix, 1840.
Elsas, M. J. 'Price Data from München, 1500–1700', Economic History, iii, 1935.
—— Umriss einer Geschichte der Preise und Löhne in Deutschland vom ausgehenden Mittelalter bis zum Beginn des Neunzehnten Jahrhunderts, i, ii. Leiden, 1936–49.
Elton, G. R. The Tudor Constitution. Cambridge, 1960.
—— The Tudor Revolution in Government. Cambridge, 1953.
Emerson, W. R. The Economic Development of the Estates of the Petre Family in Essex in the Sixteenth and Seventeenth Centuries. University of Oxford D.Phil. thesis, 1951.
Emery, F. V. 'West Glamorgan farming circa 1580–1620', Nat. Lib. Wales J., ix, x, 1955–6, 1957–8.

Emmison, F. G. *Tudor Secretary: Sir William Petre at Court and Home.* London, 1961.

Ernle, Lord. *English Farming Past and Present.* New (sixth) edn., London, 1961.

Evans, A. 'Battle Abbey at the Dissolution', *Huntington Lib. Qtrly.*, IV, 1941–2.

Evans, Elwyn. 'Two Machynlleth Toll-Books', *Nat. Lib. Wales J.*, VI, 1949–50.

Evans, G. Ewart. *The Horse in the Furrow.* London, 1960.

Everitt, Alan. *The Community of Kent and the Great Rebellion, 1640–60,* Leicester, 1966.

—— *The County Committee of Kent in the Civil War.* Leicester, Dept. of English Local History, Occasional Papers, 9, 1957.

—— *Kent and its Gentry, 1640–1660: a political Study.* University of London Ph.D. thesis, 1957.

—— *Suffolk and the Great Rebellion.* Suffolk Rec. Soc., III, 1961.

Farrer, W. *Chartulary of Cockersand Abbey*, III, iii. Chetham Soc., NS, LXIV, 1909.

Feaveryear, A. E. *The Pound Sterling. A History of English Money.* Oxford, 1933.

Felix, D. 'Profit Inflation and Industrial Growth', *Qtrly. J. of Economics*, LXX, 1956.

Fiennes, Celia. *The Journeys of Celia Fiennes.* ed. C. Morris. London, 1947.

Finberg, H. P. R. 'An Early Reference to the Welsh Cattle Trade', *AHR*, II, 1954.

—— *Gloucestershire Studies.* Leicester, 1957.

—— 'The Gostwicks of Willington', *Beds. Hist. Rec. Soc.*, XXXVI, 1956.

—— *Tavistock Abbey.* Cambridge, 1951.

Finch, Mary. *The Wealth of Five Northamptonshire Families, 1540–1640.* Northants. Rec. Soc., XIX, 1956.

Fisher, F. J. 'Commercial Trends and Policy in Sixteenth Century England', *EcHR*, X, 1939–40.

—— 'The Development of the London Food Market, 1540–1640', *EcHR*, V, 1935.

—— 'London's Export Trade in the Early Seventeenth Century', *EcHR*, 2nd Ser., III, 1950.

Fisher, H. A. L. *The History of England, 1485–1547.* London, 1906.

Fishwick, H. (ed.). *The Survey of the Manor of Rochdale.* Chetham Soc., NS, LXXI, 1913.

Folkingham, W. *Feudigraphia.* London, 1610.

Fowler, J. T. *The Coucher Book of Selby Abbey, II.* Yorks. Arch. Soc., Rec. Ser., XIII, 1893.

Fowler, R. C. 'Inventories of Essex Monasteries in 1536', *Essex Arch. Soc.*, NS, X, 1909.

Fox, Sir Cyril. *A Country House of the Elizabethan Period in Wales: Six Wells, Llantwit Major, Glamorganshire.* Cardiff, 1941.

—— 'The Round-chimneyed Farm-houses of Northern Pembrokeshire', *Aspects of Archaeology in Britain and Beyond, Essays presented to O. G. S. Crawford,* ed. W. F. Grimes. London, 1951.

—— 'Three Rounded Gable Houses in Carmarthenshire', *Arch. Camb.*, 1951.

Fox, Sir C., and Raglan, Lord. *Monmouthshire Houses: A Study of Building Techniques and Smaller House-Plans in the Fifteenth to Seventeenth Centuries.* 3 vols. Cardiff, 1951–4.

Fussell, G. E. 'Adventures with Clover', *Agriculture*, LXII, 7, 1955.

—— 'Cornish Farming, A.D. 1500–1910', *Amateur Historian*, IV, 8. 1960.

—— *The English Rural Labourer.* London, 1949.

—— 'Four Centuries of Cheshire Farming Systems, 1500–1900', *Hist. Soc. Lancs. & Cheshire*, CVI, 1954.

—— 'Four Centuries of Farming Systems in Derbyshire, 1500–1900', *Derbyshire Arch. & Nat. Hist. Soc.*, LXXI, 1951.

—— 'Four Centuries of Farming Systems in Dorset, 1500–1900', *Dorset Nat. Hist. & Arch. Soc.*, LXXIII, 1952.

—— 'Four Centuries of Farming Systems in Hampshire, 1500–1900', *Hants. Field Club & Arch. Soc.*, XVII, iii, 1949.

Fussell, G. E. 'Four Centuries of Farming Systems in Shropshire, 1500–1900', *Salop Arch. Soc.*, LIV, i, 1951–2.

—— 'Four Centuries of Nottinghamshire Farming', *Notts. Countryside*, XVII, 2, 1956.

—— 'History of Cole (*Brassica* Sp.)', *Nature*, 4471 (9 July), CLXXVI, 1955.

—— *Robert Loder's Farm Accounts, 1610–1620*. Camden Soc., 3rd Ser., LIII, 1936.

Fussell, G. E., and Goodman, Constance. 'The Eighteenth-century Traffic in Milk Products', *Economic History*, III, 1937.

Gardiner, Dorothy (ed.). *The Oxinden Letters, 1607–1642*. London, 1933.

Gardiner, S. R. (ed.). *The Constitutional Documents of the Puritan Revolution, 1625–1660*. 1906 edn., Oxford.

Gay, E. F. 'Inclosures in England in the Sixteenth Century', *Qtrly. J. of Economics*, XVII, 1903.

—— 'Inquisitions of Depopulation in 1517 and the Domesday of Inclosures', RHS, NS, XIV, 1900.

—— 'The Midland Revolt and the Inquisitions of Depopulation of 1607', RHS, XVIII, 1904.

—— 'The Rise of an English Country Family: Peter and John Temple, to 1603', *Huntington Lib. Qtrly.*, I, 1938.

—— 'The Temples of Stowe and Their Debts: Sir Thomas Temple and Sir Peter Temple, 1603–1653', *Huntington Lib. Qtrly.*, II, 1938–9.

Gerard, J. *The Herball or Generall Historie of Plantes*. London, 1597.

Glass, D. V. 'Gregory King's Estimates of the Population of England and Wales, 1695', *Population Studies*, III, 1950.

Gough, R. (ed.). *Description des Royaulmes d'Angleterre et d'Escosse composé par Etienne Perlin, Paris 1558*. London, 1775.

Gould, J. D. 'Mr Beresford and the Lost Villages: a Comment', AHR, III, 1955.

—— 'The Inquisition of Depopulation of 1607 in Lincolnshire', EHR, LXVII, 1952.

Grafton, Richard. *A little Treatise conteyning many proper Tables and Rules, very necessary for the use of all men*. 1602 edn., London.

Gras, N. S. B. *The Evolution of the English Corn Market...*, Cambridge, Mass., 1926.

Gray, H. L. *English Field Systems*. Harvard Historical Studies, XXII, 1915.

Green, Mrs J. R. *Town Life in the Fifteenth Century*. London, 1894.

Habakkuk, H. J. 'The Long-term Rate of Interest and the Price of Land in the Seventeenth Century', EcHR, 2nd Ser., V, 1952.

—— 'The Market for Monastic Property, 1539–1603', EcHR, 2nd Ser., X, 3, 1958.

Haldane, A. R. B. *The Drove Roads of Scotland*. London, 1952.

Hallam, H. E. 'Some Thirteenth-century Censuses', EcHR, 2nd Ser., X, 3, 1958.

Hallett, G. *The Economics of Agricultural Land Tenure*. London, 1960.

Hamilton, E. J. 'American Treasure and Andalusian Prices, 1503–1660', *J. Econ. & Bus. Hist.*, I, 1928–9.

—— *American Treasure and the Price Revolution in Spain, 1501–1650*. Harvard, 1934.

—— *Money, Prices, and Wages in Valencia, Aragon, and Navarre, 1351–1500*. Harvard, 1936.

—— 'The Decline of Spain', EcHR, VIII, 1938.

Hammarström, D. I. 'The Price Revolution of the Sixteenth Century: Some Swedish Evidence', *Scand. Econ. Hist. Rev.*, V, 1957.

Hammersley, G. 'The Crown Woods and their Exploitation in the Sixteenth and Seventeenth Centuries', *Bull. IHR*, XXX, 1957.

Harland, John (ed.). *The House and Farm Accounts of the Shuttleworths of Gawthorpe Hall...*, Parts I and II. Chetham Soc., XXXV, XLI, 1856.

Harris, A. 'The Agriculture of the East Riding of Yorkshire before the Parliamentary Enclosures', *Yorks. Arch. J.*, CLVII, 1959.

Harrison, William. *Harrison's Description of England in Shakspere's Youth*, ed. F. J. Furnivall, New Shakspere Soc., 6th Ser. I and VIII. London 1877 and 1881.

Hartlib, Samuel. *Samuel Hartlib his Legacie*. London, 1652.

Harvey, N. 'Farm and Estate under Elizabeth the First', *Agriculture*, LX, 1953.

Hasbach, W. *A History of the English Agricultural Labourer*. London, 1908.

Hasted, Edward. *History of Kent*. Canterbury, 1797–1801.

Havinden, M. 'Agricultural Progress in Open-field Oxfordshire', AHR, IX, 1961.

Hembry, P. M. *The Bishops of Bath and Wells, 1535–1647: a social and economic study*. London University Ph.D. thesis, 1956.

Hemp, W. J., and Gresham, Colin. 'Park, Llanfrothen and the Unit System', *Arch. Camb.*, XCVII, 1942.

Henman, W. N. 'Newnham Priory: a Bedford Rental, 1506–7', *Beds. Hist. Rec. Soc.*, XXV, 1947.

Hervey, Lord Francis (ed.). *Suffolk in the Seventeenth Century. The Breviary of Suffolk by Robert Reyce, 1618*. London, 1902.

Hexter, J. H. *Reappraisals in History*. London, 1961.

Heylyn, Peter. *A Help to English History*. 1709 edn., London.

Hill, C. *Economic Problems of the Church, from Archbishop Whitgift to the Long Parliament*. Oxford, 1956.

Hill, J. W. F. *Tudor and Stuart Lincoln*. Cambridge, 1956.

Hilton, R. H. *The Social Structure of Rural Warwickshire*. Dugdale Soc. Occasional Paper, 9, 1950.

—— 'Winchcombe Abbey and the Manor of Sherborne', *Gloucestershire Studies*, ed. H. P. R. Finberg. Leicester, 1957.

Hirst, L. F. *The Conquest of Plague*. Oxford, 1953.

Hobsbawm, E. 'The General Crisis of the European Economy in the Seventeenth Century', *Past and Present*, V, VI, 1954.

Holdsworth, W. S. *An Historical Introduction to the Land Law*. Oxford, 1927.

Hopkins, E. *The Bridgewater Estates in North Shropshire in the First Half of the Seventeenth Century*. University of London M.A. thesis, 1956.

Hoskins, W. G. *Devon*. London, 1954.

—— 'English Provincial Towns in the early Sixteenth Century', RHS, 5th Ser., VI, 1956.

—— *Essays in Leicestershire History*. Liverpool, 1950.

—— 'Harvest Fluctuations and English Economic History, 1480–1619', AHR, XII, 1964.

—— *Industry, Trade, and People in Exeter, 1688–1800*. Manchester, 1935.

—— *The Midland Peasant*. London, 1957.

—— 'The Reclamation of the Waste in Devon', EcHR, XIII, 1943.

—— *Two Thousand Years in Exeter*. Exeter, 1960.

Hoskins, W. G., and Finberg, H. P. R. *Devonshire Studies*. London, 1952.

Howells, B. E. 'Pembrokeshire Farming *circa* 1580–1620', *Nat. Lib. Wales J.*, IX, 1955–6.

Hudson, W. H. *A Shepherd's Life*. Everyman edn., London, 1949.

Hughes, H. 'Notes on the Architecture of some old houses in the neighbourhood of Llansilin, Denbighshire', *Arch. Camb.*, XV (5th Ser.), 1898.

Hughes, H., and North, H. L. *The Old Cottages of Snowdonia*. Bangor, 1908.

Hulbert, N. F. 'A Survey of the Somerset Fairs', *Som. Arch. and Nat. Hist. Soc.*, LXXXII, 1937.

Hull, F. *Agriculture and Rural Society in Essex, 1560–1640*. University of London Ph.D. thesis, 1950.

Hurstfield, J. 'Corruption and Reform under Edward VI and Mary: the Example of Wardship', EHR, LXVIII, 1953.
—— 'The Greenwich Tenures of the Reign of Edward VI', Law Qtrly. Rev. LXV, 1949.
—— 'Lord Burghley as Master of the Court of Wards', RHS, 4th Ser., XXXI, 1949.
—— 'The Profits of Fiscal Feudalism', EcHR, 2nd Ser., VIII, 1955.
—— The Queen's Wards: Wardship and marriage under Elizabeth I. London, 1958.
Jackson, J. N. 'Some Observations upon the Herefordshire Environment of the Seventeenth and Eighteenth Centuries', Woolhope Nat. Field Club, XXXVI, i, 1958.
James, M. E. Estate Accounts of the Earls of Northumberland, 1562–1637. Surtees Soc., CLXIII, 1955.
Jefferies, Richard. Field and Hedgerow. Being the Last Essays of Richard Jefferies. London, 1904.
—— The Toilers of the Field. London and New York, 1892.
Jevons, W. S. Investigations in Currency and Finance. 2nd edn., London, 1909.
Jevons, H. S. The Causes of Unemployment, the Sun's Heat, and Trade Activity. London, 1910.
—— 'Trade Fluctuations and Solar Activity', Contemporary Rev., August, 1909.
Johnson, A. H. The Disappearance of the Small Landowner. New edn., London, 1963.
Jones, Emyr G. (ed.). Exchequer Proceedings (Equity) concerning Wales, Henry VIII–Elizabeth. Cardiff, 1939.
Jones, E. L. 'Eighteenth-century Changes in Hampshire Chalkland Farming', AHR, VIII, 1960.
Jones, Francis. 'An Approach to Welsh Genealogy', Trans. Cymmrodorion Soc., 1948.
Jones, S. R., and Smith, J. T. 'The Houses of Breconshire, Part I', Brycheiniog, 1963.
Jones, T. I. Jeffreys (ed.). Exchequer Proceedings concerning Wales in Tempore James I. Cardiff, 1955.
Kennedy, J. The Dissolution of the Monasteries in Hampshire and the Isle of Wight. London University M.A. thesis, 1953.
Kenyon, G. II. 'Petworth Town and Trades, 1610–1760: Part I', Sussex Arch. Coll., XCVI, 1958.
Kerridge, E. 'Agriculture, c. 1500–c. 1793', VCH Wilts., IV, 1959.
—— The Agrarian Development of Wiltshire, 1540–1640. University of London Ph.D. thesis, 1951.
—— 'The Floating of the Wiltshire Watermeadows', Wilts. Arch. & Nat. Hist. Mag., LV, 1953.
—— 'The Movement of Rent 1540–1640', EcHR, 2nd Ser., VI, 1953.
—— 'The Notebook of a Wiltshire Farmer in the early seventeenth century', Wilts. Arch. & Nat. Hist. Mag., LIV, 1952.
—— 'A Reconsideration of some Former Husbandry Practices', AHR, III, 1955.
—— 'The Returns of the Inquisitions of Depopulation', EHR, LXX, 1955.
—— 'The Revolts in Wiltshire against Charles I', Wilts. Arch. & Nat. Hist. Mag., LVII, 1958–9.
—— 'Ridge and Furrow and Agrarian History', EcHR, 2nd Ser., IV, 1951.
—— 'The Sheepfold in Wiltshire and the Floating of the Watermeadows', EcHR, 2nd Ser., VI, 1954.
—— 'Social and Economic History of Leicester', VCH Leics., IV, 1958.
—— Surveys of the Manors of Philip, First Earl of Pembroke, 1631–2. Wilts. Arch. and Nat. Hist. Soc., Records Branch, IX, 1953.
King, G. Natural and Political Observations and Conclusions upon the State and Condition of England. 1696.
Klotz, E. L., and Davies, G. 'The Wealth of Royalist Peers and Baronets during the Puritan Revolution', EHR, LVIII, 1943.

Knocker, H. W. 'Sevenoaks: the Manor, Church and Market', *Arch. Cant.*, XXXVII, 1926.

Knowles, D. *The Religious Orders in England*, III. Cambridge, 1959.

Knox, Ronald. *Enthusiasm: a Chapter in the History of Religion.* Oxford, 1950.

Koenigsberger, H. G. 'Property and the Price Revolution (Hainault, 1474–1573)', EcHR, 2nd Ser., IX, 1956.

Lambarde, William. *A Perambulation of Kent.* 1826 edn., Chatham.

Lamond, E. (ed.). *A Discourse of the Common Weal of this Realm of England.* Cambridge, 1954.

Laslett, T. P. R. 'The Gentry of Kent in 1640', *Camb. Hist. J.*, IX, 1948.

Leadam, I. S. *The Domesday of Inclosures, 1517–18.* 2 vols. RHS, 1897.

Le Hardy, W. *County of Buckingham: Calendar to the Sessions Records, I, 1678–1694.* Aylesbury, 1933.

Leland, J. *Itinerary in England*, ed. L. Toulmin Smith. 5 vols. London, 1906–8.

Lennard, R. 'The Alleged Exhaustion of the Soil in Medieval England', *Econ. J.*, CXXXV, 1922.

—— 'English Agriculture under Charles II: The Evidence of the Royal Society's "Enquiries"', EcHR, IV, 1932.

—— *Rural Northamptonshire under the Commonwealth.* Oxford Studies in Social and Legal History, V, 1916.

Leonard, E. M. 'The Inclosure of Common Fields in the Seventeenth Century', RHS, NS, XIX, 1905.

—— 'The Relief of the Poor by the State Regulation of Wages', EHR, XIII, 1898.

Lewis, E. A. (ed.). *An Inventory of the Early Chancery Proceedings concerning Wales.* Cardiff, 1937.

—— 'The Toll-Books of some North Pembrokeshire Fairs (1599–1603)', *Bull. BCS*, VII, 1934.

Lewis, E. A., and Davies, J. Conway (eds.). *Records of the Court of Augmentations relating to Wales and Monmouthshire.* Cardiff, 1954.

Lipson, E. *The Economic History of England*, III. London, 1947.

Lisle, E. *Observations in Husbandry*, II. London, 1757.

Lister, J. 'Some Local Star Chamber Cases', *Halifax Antiq. Soc.*, 1927.

—— *Yorkshire Star Chamber Proceedings*, IV. Yorks. Arch. Soc., Rec. Ser., LXX, 1927.

Lloyd, Nathaniel. *A History of the English House from primitive times to the Victorian Period.* London, 1931.

Lodge, E. C. *The Account Book of a Kentish Estate, 1616–1704.* Records of the Social and Economic History of England and Wales, VI. London, 1927.

Low, David. *On the Domesticated Animals of the British Islands.* London, 1845.

Lyte, Henry. *A Niewe Herbal or Historie of Plantes...translated out of French by H.L.* London, 1578.

McGrath, P. V. *The Marketing of Food, Fodder, and Livestock in the London Area in the Seventeenth Century.* University of London M.A. thesis, 1948.

Malfatti, C. V. *Two Italian Accounts of Tudor England.* Barcelona, 1953.

Markham, Gervase. *Cheape and Good Husbandry.* 1623.

—— *Markham's Farewell to Husbandry.* London, 1625.

Marshall, William. *The Rural Economy of Norfolk.* London, 1787.

—— *The Rural Economy of the Southern Counties.* 2 vols., London, 1798.

Mascall, L. *The Government of Cattell....* London, 1620.

Matthews, C. M. 'Annals of the Poor: taken from the Records of a Hertfordshire Village', *History Today*, V, 1955.

Maxey, E. *A New Instruction of Plowing and Setting of Corne, Handled in Manner of a Dialogue betweene a Ploughman and a Scholler.* London, 1601.

Meekings, C. A. F. *Dorset Hearth Tax Assessments, 1662–1664*. Dorset Nat. Hist. and Arch. Soc., Occasional Publications, Dorchester, 1951.

Mercer, E. 'The Houses of the Gentry', *Past and Present*, v, 1954.

Miller, H. 'The Early Tudor Peerage' (thesis summary), *Bull*. IHR, xxiv, 1951.

—— 'Subsidy Assessments of the Peerage in the Sixteenth Century', *Bull*. IHR, xxviii, 1955.

Minchinton, W. 'Bristol—Metropolis of the West in the Eighteenth Century', RHS, 5th Ser., iv, 1954.

Moore, H. L. *Economic Cycles: their Law and Cause*. New York, 1914.

—— *Generating Economic Cycles*. New York, 1923.

More, Sir Thomas. *The Utopia of Sir Thomas More*, ed. J. H. Lupton. Oxford, 1895.

Mortimer, J. *The Whole Art of Husbandry*. London, 1707.

Morton, J. *The Natural History of Northamptonshire*. London, 1712.

Mousley, J. E. 'The Fortunes of Some Gentry Families of Elizabethan Sussex', EcHR, 2nd Ser., xi, 1959.

Munby, L. *Hertfordshire Population Statistics, 1563–1801*. Hitchin, 1964.

Nalson, John. *An impartial Collection of the great Affairs of State*. i. London, 1682.

Nef, J. U. 'A Comparison of Industrial Growth in France and England, 1540–1640', EcHR, vii, 1937.

—— 'Mining and Metallurgy in Medieval Civilisation', *The Cambridge Economic History of Europe*, ed. M. Postan and E. E. Rich, ii. Cambridge, 1952.

—— 'Silver Production in Central Europe', *J. Polit. Econ.*, xlix, 1941.

—— *The Rise of the British Coal Industry*. London, 1932.

—— 'The Progress of Technology and the Growth of Large-scale Industry in Great Britain, 1540–1640', EcHR, v, 1934.

Norden, John. *Speculum Britanniae. An Historical and Chorographical Description of Middlesex and Hartfordshire*. London, 1723.

—— *The Surveyors Dialogue*. London, 1607.

Notestein, W., Relf, F. H., and Simpson, H. (eds.). *Commons Debates, 1621*. 8 vols. New Haven, 1935.

Oschinsky, D. 'Medieval Treatises on Estate Accounting', EcHR, xvii, 1947.

Owen, George. *Description of Pembrokeshire*, 2 vols. ed. H. Owen. London, 1892.

—— *The Taylors Cussion*, ed. E. M. Pritchard. London, 1906.

Owen, G. Dyfnallt. *Elizabethan Wales. The Social Scene*. Cardiff, 1962.

Owen, L. 'The Population of Wales in the Sixteenth and Seventeenth Centuries', *Hon. Soc. Cymmrodorion*, 1959.

Page, F. M. *Wellingborough Manorial Accounts*, A.D. *1258–1323*. Northants. Rec. Soc., viii, 1936.

Palmer, A. N. *History of Ancient Tenures of Land in the Marches of North Wales*. Wrexham, 1883. Second edition in collaboration with Edward Owen, 1910.

Parenti, G. *Prime ricerche sulla rivoluzione dei prezzi in Firenze*. Florence, 1939.

Parker, L. A. 'The Agrarian Revolution at Cotesbach, 1501–1612', *Studies in Leicestershire Agrarian History*, Leics. Arch. Soc., xxiv, 1948.

—— 'The Depopulation Returns for Leicestershire in 1607', *Leics. Arch. Soc.*, xxiii, 1947.

—— *Enclosure in Leicestershire, 1485–1607*. University of London Ph.D. thesis, 1948.

Parliament. House of Commons. *Journals*, i, ii, 1547–1642.

Pearce, Brian. 'The Elizabethan Food Policy and the Armed Forces', EcHR, xii, 1942.

Peate, I. C. *The Welsh House, A Study in Folk Culture*. Liverpool, 1944.

Pelc, J. *Ceny w Krakowie w latach 1369–1600, Badania z dziejow spolecznych i gospodarczych*. Lwow, 1935.

Pierce, T. Jones (ed.). 'An Anglesey Crown Rental of the Sixteenth Century', *Bull*. BCS, x, 1940.

Pierce, T. Jones (ed.). *A Calendar of Clenennau Letters and Papers.* Aberystwyth, 1947.
—— 'The Law of Wales—the last Phase', *Trans. Cymmrodorion Soc.*, 1963.
—— 'Notes on the History of Rural Caernarvonshire in the Reign of Elizabeth', *Trans. Caernarvons. Hist. Soc.*, 1940.
—— 'Pastoral and Agricultural Settlements in Early Wales', *Geografiska Annaler*, XLIII, 1961.
Platt, Sir Hugh. *The Jewell House of Art and Nature....* London, 1594.
Plattes, G. *A Discovery of Infinite Treasure Hidden Since the World's Beginning.* London, 1639.
Plot, R. *The Natural History of Oxfordshire....* Oxford, 1677.
Plymley, Joseph. *General View of the Agriculture of Shropshire.* London, 1803.
Pollard, A. F., and Blatcher, M. 'Hayward Townshend's Journals', *Bull. IHR*, XII, 1934–5.
Postan, M. M. 'Some Economic Evidence of Declining Population in the later Middle Ages', *EcHR*, 2nd Ser., II, 1950.
—— 'The Chronology of Labour Services', *RHS*, 4th Ser., XX, 1937.
—— 'The Fifteenth Century', *EcHR*, IX, 1939.
Pribram, A. F. *Materialien zur Geschichte der Preise und Löhne in Österreich.* Vienna, 1938.
Pringle, A. *General View of the Agriculture of the County of Westmorland.* London, 1813.
Public Record Office, London. *Acts of the Privy Council, New Series, 1542–1630.*
Pugh, R. B. *Antrobus Deeds before 1625.* Wilts. Arch. & Nat. Hist. Soc., Records Branch, III, 1947.
—— *The Crown Estate, An Historical Essay.* London, 1960.
Pugh, T. B. (ed.). *The Marcher Lordships of South Wales, 1415–1536.* Cardiff, 1963.
Purvis, J. S. 'A Note on Sixteenth-century Farming in Yorkshire', *Yorks. Arch. J.*, XXXVI, 1944.
—— *A Selection of Monastic Records and Dissolution Papers.* Yorks. Arch. Soc. Rec. Ser., LXXX, 1931.
Ramsay, G. D. (ed.). *John Isham, Mercer and Merchant Adventurer: Two Account Books of a London Merchant in the Reign of Elizabeth I.* Northants. Rec. Soc., XXI, 1962.
Rathbone, A. *The Surveyor in Foure Bookes.* London, 1616.
Rea, W. F. 'The Rental and Accounts of Sir Richard Shireburn, 1571–77', *Hist. Soc., Lancs. & Cheshire*, CX, 1959.
Rees, W. *A Survey of the Duchy of Lancaster Lordships in Wales, 1609–13.* Cardiff, 1953.
Reid, Rachel R. *The King's Council in the North.* London, 1921.
Rew, R. H. *An Agricultural Faggot. A Collection of Papers on Agricultural Subjects.* Westminster, 1913.
Richards, Thomas. *A History of the Puritan Movement in Wales, 1639–53.* London, 1920.
Richardson, H. *Medieval Fairs and Markets of York.* St Anthony's Hall Publications, 20. York, 1961.
Richardson, W. C. *History of the Court of Augmentations, 1536–1554.* Baton Rouge, 1961.
—— *Tudor Chamber Administration, 1485–1547.* Baton Rouge, 1952.
Robinson, Thomas. *The Common Law of Kent; or, the Customs of Gavelkind. With an Appendix concerning Borough English.* London, 1822.
Rodgers, H. B. 'Land Use in Tudor Lancashire: the Evidence of the Final Concords, 1450–1558', *Trans. Inst. British Geographers*, XXI, 1955.
—— 'The Market Area of Preston in the Sixteenth and Seventeenth Centuries', *Geographical Studies*, III, i, 1956.
Rogers, J. E. T. *A History of Agriculture and Prices in England.* Oxford, 1866–1900.
—— *Six Centuries of Work and Wages.* London, 1894.

Rogers, P. G. *Battle in Bossenden Wood*. London, 1961.

Rowse, A. L. *The England of Elizabeth*. London, 1950.

—— *Tudor Cornwall, Portrait of a Society*. London, 1941.

Royal Commission on Ancient Monuments in Wales and Monmouthshire. *Anglesey Inventory*. London, 1937.

—— *Caernarvonshire Inventory*, 3 vols. London, 1956–64.

Royal Commission on Historical Monuments. *Monuments threatened or destroyed: a Select List*. London, 1963.

Royal Commission on Land in Wales and Monmouthshire. *Report*. London, 1896.

Royce, D. (ed.). *Landboc sive Registrum Monasterii...de Winchelcumba...*, II. Exoniae, 1903.

Russell, J. C. *British Medieval Population*. Albuquerque, 1948.

Rye, W. B. *England as seen by Foreigners*. London, 1865.

Sabin, A. *Some Manorial Accounts of Saint Augustine's Abbey, Bristol*. Bristol Rec. Soc., XXII, 1960.

Salter, E. Gurney. *Tudor England through Venetian Eyes*. London, 1930.

Salter, H. E. *Cartulary of Oseney Abbey*, VI. Oxford Hist. Soc., CI, 1936.

Saltmarsh, J. 'A College Home-farm in the Fifteenth Century', *Economic History*, III, 1936.

—— 'Plague and Economic Decline in England', *Camb. Hist. J.*, VII, 1941.

Savine, A. 'Bondmen under the Tudors', RHS, NS, XVII, 1903.

—— *English Monasteries on the eve of the Dissolution*. Oxford Studies in Social and Legal History, ed. P. Vinogradoff, I, 1909.

Sayce, R. U. 'The Old Summer Pastures, Pt II', *Mont. Coll.*, LV, i, 1958.

Schenk, W. *The Concern for Social Justice in the Puritan Revolution*. London, 1948.

Scott, W. D. Robson. *German Travellers in England, 1400–1800*. Oxford, 1953.

Simiand, F. *Recherches anciennes et nouvelles sur le mouvement général des prix du XVI* au XIX* siècle*. Paris, 1932.

Simpson, A. *The Wealth of the Gentry, 1540–1660: East Anglian Studies*. Cambridge, 1961.

Skeat, Rev. W. W. (ed.). *The Book of Husbandry by Master Fitzherbert*. English Dialect Soc., 1882.

Skeel, Caroline. 'The Cattle Trade between Wales and England...', RHS, 4th Ser., IX, 1926.

Slack, W. J. *The Lordship of Oswestry, 1393–1607*. Shrewsbury, 1951.

Smith, J. T. 'The Long-house in Monmouthshire: a Reappraisal', *Culture and Environment*, ed. Alcock & Foster, 1963.

—— 'Medieval Roofs: A Classification', *Arch. J.*, CXV, 1958.

Smith, P. 'The Long-house and the Laithe-house', *Culture and Environment*, ed. Alcock & Foster, 1963.

—— 'Plas Teg', *J. Flints. Hist. Soc.*, XVIII, 1960.

Smith, P., and Gardner, E. M. 'Two Farmhouses in Llanbedr', *J. Merioneth Hist. and Rec. Soc.*, III, iii, 1959.

Smith, P., and Owen, C. E. V. 'Traditional and Renaissance Elements in some late Stuart and early Georgian Half-timbered Houses in Arwystli', *Mont. Coll.*, LV, 1958.

Smith, R. A. L. *Canterbury Cathedral Priory, A Study in Monastic Administration*. Cambridge, 1943.

Smith, W. J. (ed.). *Calendar of Salusbury Correspondence, 1553–1700*. Cardiff, 1954.

Somerville, R. *History of the Duchy of Lancaster*, I, 1265–1603. London, 1953.

Speed, Adolphus. *Adam out of Eden...*, London, 1659.

Speed, Adolphus. *The Husbandman, Farmer, and Grazier's...Instructor...or Country-man's Guide.* London, [1705 or later].

Spratt, J. *Agrarian Conditions in Norfolk and Suffolk, 1600–1650.* Univ. of London M.A. thesis, 1935.

Steer, F. W. (ed.). *Farm and Cottage Inventories of Mid-Essex, 1635–1749.* Chelmsford, 1950.

Stone, L. 'The Anatomy of the Elizabethan Aristocracy', EcHR, XVIII, 1948.

—— 'The Elizabethan Aristocracy—a Restatement', EcHR, 2nd Ser., IV, 1952.

—— 'Elizabethan Overseas Trade', EcHR, 2nd Ser., II, 1949.

—— 'The Fruits of Office: The Case of Robert Cecil, first Earl of Salisbury, 1596–1612', *Essays in the Economic and Social History of Tudor and Stuart England,* ed. F. J. Fisher, Cambridge, 1961.

—— 'The Nobility in Business, 1540–1640', *The Entrepreneur,* Harvard University, 1957.

—— 'State Control in Sixteenth-century England', EcHR, XVII, 1947.

Straker, E. 'Ashdown Forest and its Inclosures', *Sussex Arch. Coll.,* LXXXI, 1940.

Straton, C. R. *Survey of the lands of William, first earl of Pembroke.* Roxburghe Club, 2 vols., 1909.

Summerson, Sir J. N. *Architecture in Britain 1530 to 1830.* London, 1953.

Supple, B. E. *Commercial Crisis and Change in England, 1600–1642.* Cambridge, 1959.

Sylvester, D. 'The Open Fields of Cheshire', *Hist. Soc. Lancs. & Cheshire,* CVIII, 1956.

Sylvester, D., and Nulty, G. *The Historical Atlas of Cheshire.* Chester, 1958.

T., R. Gent. *The Tenants' Law, or the Laws Concerning Landlords, Tenants and Farmers.* London, 1666.

Tables of Leases and Interest..., London, 1628.

Tawney, R. H. *The Agrarian Problem in the Sixteenth Century.* London, 1912.

—— *Business and Politics under James I: Lionel Cranfield as Merchant and Minister.* Cambridge, 1958.

—— 'The Rise of the Gentry, 1558–1640', EcHR, XI, 1941.

—— 'The Rise of the Gentry: A Postscript', EcHR, 2nd Ser., VII, 1954.

Tawney, A. J. and R. H. 'An Occupational Census of the Seventeenth Century', EcHR, V, 1934–5.

Tawney, R. H., and Power, Eileen (eds.). *Tudor Economic Documents,* 3 vols. London, 1924.

Taylor, H. *Old Halls of Lancashire and Cheshire.* Manchester, 1884.

Thirsk, Joan. *English Peasant Farming.* London, 1957.

—— 'Industries in the Countryside', *Essays in the Economic and Social History of Tudor and Stuart England,* ed. F. J. Fisher. Cambridge, 1961.

—— 'The Isle of Axholme before Vermuyden', AHR, I, 1953.

—— *Tudor Enclosures.* Hist. Assoc. Pamphlet, General Ser., 41, 1959.

Thomas, D. R. *The History of the Diocese of Saint Asaph.* 3 vols. Oswestry, 1908.

Thomas, Lawrence. *The Reformation in the Old Diocese of Llandaff.* Cardiff, 1930.

Thompson, Flora. *Lark Rise to Candleford.* 1957 edn., London.

Thorpe, S. M. *The Monastic Lands in Leicestershire on and after the Dissolution.* University of Oxford B.Litt. thesis, 1961.

Topographer and Genealogist, I. London, 1846.

Torr, Cecil. *Small Talk at Wreyland.* 1926 edn., Cambridge.

Trevor-Roper, H. R. 'The Elizabethan Aristocracy: an anatomy anatomized', EcHR, 2nd Ser., III, 1951.

—— *The Gentry, 1540–1640.* EcHR Supplement, I, 1953.

Trow-Smith, R. *A History of British Livestock Husbandry to 1700.* London, 1957.

Tupling, G. H. 'An Alphabetical List of the Markets and Fairs of Lancashire recorded before the Year 1701', *Lancs. and Ches. Antiq. Soc.*, LI, 1936.

—— *The Economic History of Rossendale*. Chetham Soc., NS, LXXXVI, 1927.

—— 'Lancashire Markets in the Sixteenth and Seventeenth Centuries', *Lancs. and Ches. Antiq. Soc.*, LVIII, 1947.

—— 'The Origin of Markets and Fairs in Medieval Lancashire', *Lancs. and Ches. Antiq. Soc.*, XLIX, 1933.

Tyack, N. C. P. *Migration from East Anglia to New England before 1660*. University of London Ph.D. thesis, 1951.

Upton, A. F. *Sir Arthur Ingram, c. 1565–1642*. London, 1961.

Utterström, G. 'Climatic Fluctuations and Population Problems in Early Modern History', *Scand. Econ. Hist. Rev.*, III, 1955.

Verlinden, C. and Others. 'Mouvements des prix et des salaires en Belgique au XVIe siècle', *Annales E.S.C.*, 1955.

Wales. A Bibliography of the History of Wales. Cardiff, 1962. *See also* Supplement I, *Bull.* BCS, 1963.

Walford, Cornelius. *Fairs, Past and Present: a chapter in the History of Commerce*. London, 1883.

Walker, F. *Historical Geography of South-West Lancashire before the Industrial Revolution*. Chetham Soc., NS, CIII, 1939.

Wallen, W. C. 'Tilty Abbey', *Essex Arch. Soc.*, NS, IX, 1904–5.

Watkin, Dom Aelred. 'Glastonbury 1538–9 as shown by its account rolls', *Downside Review*, LXVII, 1949.

Wedgwood, C. V. *The Great Rebellion: II, The King's War, 1641–1647*. London, 1958.

West, T. *The Antiquities of Furness*. Ulverston, 1805.

Westcote, Thomas. *A View of Devonshire in MDCXXX*. Exeter, 1845.

Westerfield, R. B. *Middlemen in English Business, particularly between 1660 and 1760*. Transactions Connecticut Academy of Arts and Sciences, XIX, Connecticut, 1915.

White, Gilbert. *The Natural History of Selborne*. Everyman edn., London, 1945.

Wiebe, G. *Zur Geschichte der Preisrevolution des XVI und XVII Jahrhunderts*. Leipzig, 1895.

Willan, T. S. *The English Coasting Trade, 1600–1750*. Manchester Economic History Series, XII. Manchester, 1938.

—— *River Navigation in England, 1600–1750*. London, 1936.

Willan, T. S., and Crossley, E. W. (eds.). *Three Seventeenth-Century Yorkshire Surveys*. Yorks. Arch. Soc. Rec. Ser., CIV, 1941.

Williams, Clare. *Thomas Platter's Travels in England, 1599*. London, 1937.

Williams, Glanmor. *The Welsh Church from Conquest to Reformation*. Cardiff, 1962.

Williams, N. J. *The Maritime Trade of East Anglian Ports, 1550–1590*. University of Oxford D.Phil. thesis, 1952.

—— 'Sessions of the Clerk of the Market of the Household in Middlesex', *London and Middlesex Arch. Soc.*, XIX, ii, 1957.

—— *Tradesmen in Early-Stuart Wiltshire*. Wilts. Arch. and Nat. Hist. Soc., Records Branch, XV, 1960.

Williams, W. Ogwen. *Calendar of the Caernarvonshire Quarter Sessions Records*. Cardiff, 1956.

Wilson, Rev. J. M. (ed.). *Accounts of the Priory of Worcester for the year 13–14 Hen. VIII, A.D. 1521–2*. Worcs. Hist. Soc., 1907.

Winchester, Barbara. *Tudor Family Portrait*. London, 1955.

Wolffe, B. P. 'The Management of English Royal Estates under the Yorkist Kings', EHR, LXXI, 1956.

Wood, E. B. (ed.). *Rowland Vaughan, His Booke*. London, 1897.

Wood-Jones, R. B. *Traditional Domestic Architecture in the Banbury Region*. Manchester, 1963.

Woodward, G. W. O. *The Benedictines and Cistercians in Yorkshire in the sixteenth century*. Trin. Coll., Dublin, Ph.D. thesis, 1955.

Woodworth, Allegra. 'Purveyance for the Royal Household in the Reign of Queen Elizabeth', *American Philosophical Soc.*, NS, xxxv, 1946.

Worlidge, John. *Systema Agriculturae; the Mystery of Husbandry discovered:...* 2nd edn. *with additions by the author*. London, 1675.

Wright, T. *Three Chapters of Letters relating to the Suppression of the Monasteries*. Camden Soc., 1843.

Wynn, Sir John. *History of the Gwydir Family*. Cardiff, 1927.

Wynn of Gwydir. *Calendar of Wynn of Gwydir Papers, 1515–1690*. Aberystwyth, 1926.

Youings, J. A. *Devon Monastic Lands: Calendar of Particulars for Grants, 1536–58*. Devon and Cornwall Rec. Soc., NS, I, 1955.

—— 'The Terms of the Disposal of the Devon Monastic Lands, 1536–58', EHR, LXIX, 1954.

Young, F. Brett. *Portrait of a Village*. London, 1937.

4

AGRICULTURAL POLICY: PUBLIC DEBATE AND LEGISLATION, 1640–1750

A. GENERAL INTRODUCTION

Official agricultural policy before 1600 may be fairly summarized as a series of *ad hoc* measures to guard against any threat of turbulence and riot because of food scarcity. In order that men should have bread, corn supplies had to be protected, and the government intervened in agricultural matters only when these threatened to run short. All sixteenth-century legislation against the enclosure and conversion of arable to pasture was concerned first and foremost with maintaining the plough, and ensuring a livelihood to ploughmen who would produce corn. That ploughmen would additionally serve their turn in war, since arable husbandry strengthened their muscles and made them strong soldiers, was a fortunate coincidence which fortified the other consideration.

In the last two decades of the sixteenth century, however, and more especially in the years 1600–40, discussions on matters of agricultural policy took new directions, and entered upon more complex matters. More precise knowledge of regional differences in farming systems, and of divergent farming interests, widened the horizon of debate, and it was no longer axiomatic that corn growers should receive all consideration, and other agricultural producers none. Public opinion was shifting its ground for several different economic reasons: some growers were turning against grain because of labour problems, and were attentive to other ways of using their land. The attention of other agricultural improvers shifted from the corn-growing areas of the south and east to the pastoral areas, especially of the fens in East Anglia and the forests in the west Midlands. When the agricultural limitations and social constraints in areas of dense population are allowed for, it may fairly be said that much corn-growing country left little room for improvement, whereas large tracts of semi-derelict grassland invited attention elsewhere. Many influential men at the heart of politics were gradually persuaded of better agricultural possibilities in long-neglected pastoral areas of the kingdom.

When men acted upon this knowledge, however, they came face to face with a resentful pastoral population, determined to resist their well-meant improvements. Existing pastoral routines had merits, which could always be defended against those who wished to transform them into something entirely different. Waving cornfields made a brave sight, but meat, cheese, and butter had to come from somewhere. A growing acquaintance with the pastoral countryside, therefore, taught many lessons, and forced policy makers to consider the value of foodstuffs other than grain. This they were the more prepared to do since other developments were leading them to appreciate a more varied diet, in which vegetables and fruit had a larger place. They learned to welcome new flavours: cider was accepted alongside beer; strong waters (distilled liquors) became familiar as a refreshment, not merely as a medicine; malt vinegar displaced wine vinegar; and men discovered and savoured the distinctive differences among the cheeses, the butter, and the salt of different localities, all made available to them through an improved marketing system.

In considering agricultural policy, then, we shall observe the government's interest extending to broader agricultural issues than those that dominated debate before 1600. In this survey, it will not be enough to name only the acts that were finally passed in parliament. All the many proposals for legislation that were unsuccessful deserve attention too, for they show what issues were arousing concern. The fact that many bills came to nothing did not mean that the problems they were trying to solve were a mirage. Usually they were real problems, sometimes of some urgency; they failed because members of parliament could not agree on satisfactory ways of solving them, or alternatively because other more urgent business intruded and squeezed them out. Sometimes one controversial clause in a bill killed the whole. This was alleged in relation to the bill to ban wool exports in 1673; it miscarried in the House of Lords because Ireland was included.[1]

No casualty of parliamentary debate represented altogether wasted words and energy, however. Each sheds light on the way members of the Commons and the Lords gradually acquired a better understanding of England's interlocking and complementary regional economies, and of changes in economic conditions that were affecting farmers' choice of specialities. Debates that ended in deadlock imparted a great deal of information to MPs on the current profits being made from products such as hops, cheese, hemp, and flax. And since landowning gentlemen and peers were in the majority in parliament, they carried away news of some practical value to their estates and constituencies. In November 1656, for example, thousands of hop planters and dealers from twenty counties petitioned the Committee on Trade, and their complaint was duly read in the Commons. We know nothing of their grievances, but the petition undoubtedly apprised MPs of the state of hop cultivation in twenty counties.[2] When the Commons debated

---

[1] CSPD, 1673, p. 382.

[2] CJ, VII, 1651–9, p. 454. It is possible that the complaints from the hopmasters of 20 counties had something to do with a new outburst of enthusiasm for hop growing, alluded to by John Beale in Herefordshire in 1657 as a development of the past three years. Prudent men were planting an abundance of hops: "We make haste to be the chief hopmasters in England." Were they possibly glutting the market? – J. Beale, Herefordshire Orchards, London, 1657, p. 47.

a statute in 1676–7 intended to compel farmers to grow half an acre of hemp or flax for every hundred acres of land, every member of the House who was present learned from Mr Swinfen, member for Tamworth in Staffordshire (a considerable hemp- and flax-growing county in the second half of the seventeenth century), that flax and hemp were then going out of favour because there was no profit in them. Colonel Birch told the House that he had grown none for seven years.[3] Thus, even when such debates did not eventuate in firm acts of policy, they distributed useful information that might be an adequate substitute. In this case the information was more likely to discourage the growing of hemp and flax than otherwise, but other debates, like that to encourage the growing of the new dye plant, safflower, could have promoted its growth.[4] Certainly it publicized it, which was the first necessity.

Effective policy making, moreover, was not achieved only by statutes that passed through parliament. The Council of State and Privy Council also took decisions that had consequences for agriculture. One such decision was made by the Council of State in 1653 when drainage of the Great Level of the fens was resumed. A letter went to the Adventurers there encouraging them to grow hemp, and, at the same time, a warrant was sent to the Navy Committee directing them to purchase the same hemp at 3s. per stone.[5] This could be highly effective policy making: it was agriculturally realistic, for the fens had always been good hemp country, and commercially realistic, since hemp growers were now guaranteed a market. Hemp *was* grown in large quantity after the drainage, and we must concede the possibility that this action of the government stimulated it.

All discussions of agricultural policy, in parliament and outside, no matter what their immediate effectiveness, must be heeded, for many were of significance for the future. It was a fact of life in the seventeenth century that new measures gestated very slowly; indeed, some of the proposals which aroused greatest interest in the 1650s, and were implemented in the 1660s and 70s, had first been voiced not forty but one hundred years earlier; many proposals that were new between 1640 and 1660 did not harden into policy enactments until after the Restoration. It behoves us, therefore, to consider carefully all expressions of opinion, in order to trace the beginnings of the many new themes in agricultural policy.

The Commonwealth period was undoubtedly the most fertile in original ideas, but the years after 1660 heightened the urgency of problems calling for action. The solutions chosen were at first deeply coloured by views that had crystallized in an earlier and different age. But gradually the enthusiasm and originality that had infused parliamentary debates on agricultural matters under the Commonwealth faded, and after 1700 parliament was increasingly

[3] *Cobbett's Parliamentary History of England, IV: 1660–88*, col. 835.
[4] See below, pp. 168–9.   [5] *CSPD*, 1652–3, pp. 144, 146.

inclined to let agriculturalists sort out their own problems. Parliament intervened less and less and took longer and longer to make up its mind, though in dire emergencies, such as that occasioned by the cattle plague, the King's Council was a brisk and effective agent in taking initiatives. Nevertheless, at the end of the period parliament and government held a realistic view of agriculture as a many-sided business, in which cider, rhubarb, liquorice, and coleseed had a place alongside grain for bread and drink. In this respect it reflected accurately the economic experience of the world outside where grain for a century was so plentiful and offered such moderate rewards to its growers that men had had to diversify or fail. Agricultural policy ranged over a much broader territory in 1750 than in 1600.

B. 1640–1660

1. Introduction

Between 1640 and 1650 politics and the Civil War engrossed attention, and for a whole decade little thought was spared for economic policy. Yet the problems of agriculture obtruded ever more conspicuously. The war imposed the heaviest burden of all on the farming community, by destroying crops and animals, and yet demanding food supplies to be available at a moment's notice in random places dictated by the constantly changing location of the main battlefields. Moreover, the farming community was required to pay its full share of taxation; its farming had to produce a sufficient surplus to earn the cash to meet these increasing demands. In the event, the problems of agriculture forced themselves upon the attention of politicians while the war was still in progress, though little could be done about them. Bad weather ruined the harvests of corn and hay for five years from the autumn of 1646 onwards, and every succeeding year until the harvest of 1651 exacerbated the problems left by the previous one.[6] The price index for a collection of foodstuffs which stood at 574 in 1645 reached 821 in 1649, and was to rise to 839 in 1650.[7] Petitions from London on behalf of "all the poor of this nation" were handed in to the Commons, and committees were set up to consider how to keep down corn prices.[8] Epidemics deepened the sense of foreboding as one bad season of weather led to another. But a still more serious preoccupation of government in 1649 was the general economic depression which pervaded industry and overseas trade, induced by bad harvest, the war, and political uncertainty. Under this heading parliament also gave attention to the problems of ensuring reasonable wages to labourers and creating more employment.[9]

[6] T & C, pp. 48–51.
[7] E. H. Phelps Brown and S. V. Hopkins, 'Seven Centuries of the Prices of Consumables, compared with Builders' Wage Rates', Economica, XXIII, 1956, p. 313.
[8] CSPD, 1649–50, pp. 60–1, 113.   [9] CSPD, 1651–2, p. 551.

Somehow the demand for food for the soldiery and for horses for battle had to be met. Yet the dearth of food supplies had become acute by the early months of 1649, and this reflected itself most plainly in military correspondence. Army commanders were alarmed at the mounting hostility of civilians towards soldiers requiring quarter, and gave orders that the latter should be satisfied with plain food, pay punctiliously for it, and not make extravagant demands of their hosts "in this great and unusual dearth".[10] Even when the war in England ended, the army still needed large quantities of food for its campaigns in Ireland and Scotland. Bulk orders for Cheshire cheese to be supplied at a moment's notice – 200 tons for the army in Ireland in February 1652, for example – say much for the resilience of the Cheshire dairy industry.[11]

The times were certainly not favourable to the expansion of agricultural production, and yet military demands undoubtedly exerted some stimulus, and this quickly showed its effects when peace and good seasons returned. Food supplies in the mid 1650s were thought so secure that the Protectorate government finally passed an act in November 1656 permitting, and, indeed, encouraging, their export. It thereby reversed the policy that had prevailed for a century; enactments that had been anxiously designed to ensure adequate food supplies at home by restricting exports overseas were brought to an end.[12]

The effects of the war on food production may thus be discerned, albeit in a shadowy form. Exact information about how the increase was achieved is lacking. We have to rely on general indications. Provision merchants supplying food in bulk for the army guaranteed to deliver many tons of biscuit, oatmeal, cheese, and malt, and lesser quantities of beef and butter. They placed their orders in specialist farming regions: cheese was sought mainly in Cheshire and to a lesser extent in Suffolk; butter was bought principally from Suffolk.[13] Supplies of more perishable foods like eggs, vegetables, and fruit were procured locally, and so their purchase does not feature in documents of state. Nor does the purchase of horses which were also sought locally rather than ordered in large numbers from dealers.[14]

Thus, by both methods of provisioning, the army enhanced the specialization of regions. The appearance of merchants negotiating bulk contracts always sent up local prices sharply, a fact which producers noted for future reference. And when relying on food bought locally, the military had to adapt their demands to what the neighbourhood could supply. Again this could have the effect of intensifying specialization. The full consequences of army victualling can only be guessed at, but a suggestive illustration comes from

[10] CJ, VI, 1648–51, pp. 136, 441, 486.
[11] Ibid., pp. 160, 201, 375, 416.   [12] See below, p. 134.
[13] See e.g. CSPD, 1645–7, p. 210; 1651–2, pp. 551, 561; 1650, p. 501.
[14] P. R. Edwards, 'The Horse Trade of the Midlands in the Seventeenth Century', AHR, XXVII, 2, 1979, p. 100.

the cider-producing regions of the west country. Because the territory was much fought over by royalists and parliamentarians, soldiers were introduced to the staple drink of the locality — cider — and acquired a taste for it. John Evelyn in *Pomona* explained that Charles I and his courtiers enjoyed cider during several summers spent around Hereford, where it sold cheaply for 6d. a quart.[15] The rank and file of the army must have appreciated its cheapness even more. It thus became a familiar, not to say fashionable, drink, and this advertisement for it in wartime promoted its sales nationwide after the Restoration. Efforts at increasing cider production and improving its quality in the later seventeenth century can only fully be understood when seen against this wartime experience. Nor is there reason to confine the stimulating consequences of war to cider production. It is likely that other specialities of regions attained a wider renown in the same way. That supplies increased in response must be inferred from the larger quantities of foodstuffs made available by the 1650s of which parliament finally took cognizance by its legislation in 1656.

Fruitful discussions about an agricultural policy began after the execution of Charles I in 1649. They were part of a wider debate about economic and social policy in general that accompanied the setting up of the new Commonwealth, on which high hopes were placed. Among members of parliament, officers and soldiers in the army, government servants at Westminster, and committee members in the counties, idealist dreams of a new world inspired far-ranging plans and programmes. Our documents reveal no more than a hundredth, or perhaps only a thousandth, part of the ideas then in circulation. They are best mirrored in the correspondence of Samuel Hartlib and in published books and pamphlets. They are seen only in the most shadowy form in the journals of the houses of parliament, and in the diaries of parliamentary debates. Nevertheless, the parliamentary journals remind us how many men were informed and involved in agricultural policy making, while Hartlib allows us to eavesdrop on their informal conversations. Pamphlets, memoranda, and correspondence emanating from the Hartlib circle and other interested parliamentarians disclose four main themes of policy affecting agriculture which were under public discussion between 1640 and 1660, every one of which was inherited from the previous generation. These can be ranked in order of priority, according to the time they occupied in Commons debates, the quantity of state documents generated by them, and the resultant acts and ordinances:

(a) The encouragement of agricultural production (particularly by freeing exports and discouraging imports) and its diversification;

---

[15] John Evelyn, *Sylva...to which is annexed Pomona*, London, 1664, *Pomona*, p. 4. According to John Beale, few cottagers and even few of the wealthiest yeomen in Herefordshire tasted any drink in the family other than cider and perry, except at a special festival two or three times a year. It was not a hardship but a choice. So the soldiers billeted locally must have had to fall in with the same habits — Beale, *op. cit.*, p. 7.

(b) The improvement of neglected land, notably wastes, fens, forests, and chases;

(c) The regulation of enclosure;

(d) The provision of more work for the poor.

2. Encouraging agricultural production and diversification

Discussions outside parliament that were deliberately directed at members of parliament were lively and stimulating, especially in the years 1649–56. Walter Blith addressed both houses of parliament in the introduction to his new book of husbandry in 1649, and in pointing out the main obstacles to agricultural improvement he brought the argument down to an unusual level of detail. In his view, they were: the absence of compensation to tenants for improvement (whereas in Flanders this problem had been solved); contentions about water supplies between farmers and millers, which hindered the floating of meadows; the intermixture of land in common fields, which discouraged individual improvers; the grazing of common pastures without stint, which ruined the grass and which, once in every four or five years, caused outbreaks of sheep rot; men's failure to search for mineral fertilizers, like lime and chalk; their failure to eradicate moles, to plough up mossy, neglected land, to straighten water courses, and to preserve timber; and finally men's slothfulness in general.[16]

The principal message of Blith's book was to urge all men to make the most of all their lands, whether arable, meadow, pasture, or woodland, and especially to promote tillage, for he held to the traditional view that this was the most profitable use of land both to landlords and tenants. To achieve this, he favoured leaving men complete freedom to use their best land as they wished. But to remove other obstacles to improvement, he favoured legislation. He wanted a law to make men destroy moles, a law to make men plant trees whenever they felled any (as was the custom in other countries), compulsion to plough up mossy pasture, and some government initiative in searching for minerals. Faced with the problem of resolving deadlock between improvers and traditionalists, where the obstinacy of one man could deprive a dozen others of benefit by innovation, the only remedy he could see was to offer compensation for damage, to be assessed by competent judges. Blith skirted the question how to compel a stubborn man to accept compensation, but others faced it soon after. Joseph Lee, a neighbour of Blith in the village of Cotesbach, Leicestershire, and a stout defender of enclosure so long as it was fair to all parties, insisted that the will of the majority should prevail, as it did in all public affairs in church and state.[17]

16 W. Blith, The English Improver, London, 1649, pp. A1v–A6v.

17 Ibid., passim; [J. Lee], Considerations concerning Common Fields, London, 1654, p. 28.

Blith's book of 1649 inaugurated prolonged discussions on ways of improving agricultural output. Debate was especially vigorous among members of the Hartlib circle – notably, country gentry and parsons – and it was the more effective because it coincided with a great flurry of activity in government and parliament to devise new economic policies in general. The first Council of Trade had been set up in August 1650 and by November 1651 it had made seven reports to the Council of State and seven to parliament.[18] Hence, some of the effect of these public discussions outside parliament was reflected in parliamentary acts and in the Council of State's ordinances, though for the most part their influence lurks in the background in the form of basic assumptions, or developing ideas that needed more time to mature, and did not bear fruit until after 1660. Nevertheless, parliament had to respond to immediate problems, and its measures allowed some new propositions, especially those in favour of a more diversified agriculture, to creep in by the back door if not through the front.

(a) Encouraging exports

Until 1650, the old statutes concerning the export of corn and other foodstuffs continued in operation. Export was permitted only when prices at home did not exceed a certain level, and domestic conditions did not favour much export during the 1640s, certainly not after 1646. Indeed, considerable sums of money were spent on importing grain in the later 1640s, and fresh prohibitions on export were issued from time to time.[19] One such order was called for in 1643 to prevent the export of corn, butter, cheese, wool, and fullers' earth; a similar order from the Council of State in March 1649 to the Commissioners of Customs forbad the export of corn without the express licence of parliament or the Council of State.[20] This edict was prompted by the news of corn going to the rebels in Ireland, and is one of several examples reminding us that important decisions affecting the farming community at this period passed at short notice to responsible officials, without leaving much trace in central government records.[21]

Until good seasons returned in 1652 parliament was preoccupied with curbing excessive food prices, preventing the waste of grain, prosecuting

[18] C. M. Andrews, *British Committees, Commissions, and Councils of Trade and Plantations, 1622–75*, Johns Hopkins Univ. Stud., ser. XXVI, nos. 1–3, Baltimore, 1908, pp. 24–5.

[19] *CSPD*, 1650, p. 179, printed in T & C, p. 59. For quantities of grain imported into London in autumn 1647, see C. Fitz-Geffrey, *God's Blessing upon the Providers of Corne*...London, 1648, p. 1.

[20] CJ, III, 1642–4, p. 359; *CSPD*, 1649–50, *passim*, but esp. p. 35.

[21] C. H. Firth and R. S. Rait, eds., *Acts and Ordinances of the Interregnum, 1642–60*, 3 vols., London, 1911, *II*, p. 442; CJ, VI, 1648–51, p. 441. For the pamphlet discussion and petitions preceding this act, see M. James, *Social Problems and Policy during the Puritan Revolution, 1640–1660*, London, 1930, pp. 264–6, and N. S. B. Gras, *The Evolution of the English Corn Market*, Cambridge, Mass., 1926, pp. 462–3.

hoarders, and curbing secret dealings; it gave little thought to positive measures for increasing food production. Six months after the first good harvest for many years, in autumn 1651, men began to take the full measure of national food production. On the last day of April in 1652 parliament ordered an act to be brought in repealing the statute that restrained the export of butter.[22] The bill continued under discussion into June but then disappeared from sight. The problem of a surplus of foodstuffs became more serious still in the course of 1653, as two letters from eastern England bear witness. One in May from John Maynard in Holbeach marsh, Lincolnshire, mentioned that "corn is cheap and money scarce", while tenants from St Faith's in Norfolk in December 1653 pleaded for the forbearance of their landlord in paying their rents since "neither corn nor cattle nor butter nor cheese will give any price". From Oxford in May 1653 it was reported that a bushel of wheat, which some years before cost 10s., was being sold for 2s. 6d. and 3s. In September 1653 parliament resolved to refer to the Committee for Trade "the transportation of corn". Agricultural production appeared to be more than sufficient for the nation's needs, and the policy towards export was in need of review. Moreover, in addition to the earlier discussions about butter, pressure had been put on parliament in February 1653 to allow the export of horses.[23] But political affairs always took precedence, and nothing was done. By October 1654 discontent was being expressed at "the low prices of corn in the nation" and, indeed, at "the cheapness of commodities" in general. The year 1654 had brought "plenty of corn, butter, and cheese".[24]

What precise information reached parliament's committee about the abundance of foodstuffs, and farmers' difficulties in disposing of it, we can only guess, but private correspondence suggests that it was accurate enough. A letter from William Turnbull of Easthampstead, Surrey, early in 1654 spoke of the cheapness of everything "not only in the northern parts but also throughout this nation", while from Norfolk in 1655 came more news of "the hardness of the times by which grain is so cheap as has not been known in late days".[25] A free-trade lobby was strong in the Commons, as we may judge from the instructions issued to the Council of Trade in 1650 and the vigorous, and sometimes angry, debates in favour of a free trade in industrial manufactures that followed in the Commons.[26] Members were quick to offer the same remedy for the depressed sales of foodstuffs. To encourage corn

---

[22] CJ, VII, 1651–9, pp. 129, 136, 138.

[23] Norfolk RO, Hobart MS NRS 15,994; Essex RO, Belhus MS D/DL/C2/5; Sheffield Univ. Library, Hartlib, "Ephemerides", 1653, JJ–JJ2; CJ, VII, 1651–9, pp. 319, 259.

[24] Diary of Thos. Burton, ed. J. T. Rutt, 4 vols., London, 1828, I, pp. xlix, lxxxv.

[25] Berks. RO, D/ED/C24; Norfolk RO, Hobart MS NRS 15,994. See also vol. II of this series, p. 357.

[26] T & C, p. 502. For a lively, hard-hitting debate on free trade in 1656–7, see Diary of Thos. Burton, I, pp. 308–10.

sales, they were even ready to consider allowing engrossing "without the danger of the law", as well as encouraging corn exports.[27] They also deemed it necessary to consider "what may be fit to be done for the transportation [i.e. export overseas] of butter and cheese".[28] The Committee of the Commons got as far as recommending the prices at which wheat, rye, barley, malt, peas, beans, and butter might be exported, and agreed to consider allowing the export of beer. Debates on the floor of the house led to the ceiling price of peas and beans being set at 24s. a quarter (instead of the 18s. recommended by the Committee). The house also voted on the price ceiling for butter, though this divided the members sharply, 92 favouring a ceiling price of 6d. a pound, which was agreed upon, though 62 voted against it.[29] A record of this debate would doubtless shed much light on the current development of the dairy industry. All that is clear is parliament's inclination to free food for export; its purposes were frustrated only by other business. The bill in question was on the brink of being accepted in November 1654 when the question of making Cromwell Lord Protector engaged attention. On the very day when the bill for transporting corn was to be reported, members spent all day debating the title that he should assume. The bill disappeared without trace for two years, even though its purposes were closely connected with the need to improve the nation's ability to bear taxation. The government was anxious in 1654 to increase its revenues, in order to pay its debts to soldiers and other creditors, and the country was growing restive at the mounting financial burden. Men feared that taxation "will make the poor tenant and farmer to run too; and ere long the very landlord himself".[30] Allowing freer exports of food would have been a timely measure to help the farming community find outlets for its produce and secure a better income. Yet it had to wait till the end of 1656 before such a measure was agreed. The decision was finally taken in November 1656 in an act which firmly stated its purpose. It would help towards establishing a favourable balance of trade. Since England's foodstuffs were in demand from other nations as well as from English plantations in America, and since supplies were abundant at home, corn, beer, cattle, horses (geldings only), butter, cheese, beef, pork, bacon, calfskins and sheepskins, and candles were allowed to be exported when supplies did not exceed a certain price.[31] The price ceilings were those suggested in 1654 for all items except wheat, where a more generous policy was favoured in 1656 than in 1654: export was allowed when wheat was 40s. a quarter, not 36s.

The 1656 act gave substantial encouragement to agriculturalists by widening their markets, and undoubtedly played a part in furthering

[27] Diary of Thos. Burton, I, p. xlix.
[28] CJ, VII, 1651–9, p. 374.   [29] Ibid., pp. 379–80.
[30] Diary of Thos. Burton, I, p. lxxxvi.
[31] Firth and Rait, op. cit., II, p. 1,043; CSPD, 1656–7, p. 174; Diary of Thos. Burton, I, p. lx.

Prices at which export was permitted

	In the 1654 bill	In the 1656 act
Wheat	36s. qtr	40s. qtr
Rye	24s. qtr	24s. qtr
Barley & malt	20s. qtr	20s. qtr
Oats	—	17s. qtr
Peas	24s. qtr	24s. qtr
Beans	24s. qtr	24s. qtr
Beef	—	£5 per barrel of 36 gal
Pork	—	£6 10s. per barrel of 36 gal
Bacon	—	6d. per lb
Butter	—	£4 10s. per barrel of 4 firkins (each firkin of 56 lb)
Cheese	—	£1 10s. per cwt
Candles	—	5s. per dozen lb
Other exports	—	No price specified

agricultural improvement. In addition to promoting food production, it assisted the horse breeders. War had immensely encouraged the latter in the 1640s, but when hostilities ceased, buyers disappeared. Demand from overseas then made itself felt, but the new outlets were artificially restricted by a continuing prohibition on the export of horses. In consequence, the Council of State received a swollen stream of petitions for special licences to export them. Dignitaries from all over Europe, princes, ambassadors, noblemen, and gentry, asked to ship five, ten, twenty, fifty English horses apiece back to their native countries, and a flourishing trade in the illicit export of horses developed. Gradually the Council of State became aware of an unprecedented demand for English horses in Europe, and the new legislation in 1656 liberated the trade in horses, as well as the trade in foodstuffs, from irksome restrictions. The status of the buyers and the prices they paid enable us to judge how much the condition of horses had improved since the sixteenth century, when Englishmen were more assiduous buyers of horses on the Continent than sellers.[32]

(b) Discouraging imports

Food imports did not generally arouse concern, since the quantities involved were comparatively small. Grain imports were needed only in periods of dearth, and then they were counted a blessing which none wished to criticize. This occurred in 1647 when a pamphleteer, inveighing against the hoarders of corn in 1648, recorded grain imports into London in the period August

[32] J. Thirsk, *Horses in Early Modern England: For Service, for Pleasure, for Power*, Stenton Lecture, 1977, Reading, 1978, p. 27; Edwards, *op. cit.*

to November 1647, showing how "the extremity of the times" had rapidly increased London's reliance on overseas supplies.[33] It was, in fact, only the beginning of several years of dependence, which raised the bill for imports at a time when the export trade was depressed, thus worsening the unfavourable balance of trade – a matter for weighty concern by 1650.[34] Nevertheless, it was an expense that could not be avoided. In addition to grain, Dutch cheese was imported to feed the army on a regular basis,[35] and modest quantities of vegetables and fruit were always imported from France and Holland to feed the gourmets. Dyestuffs, hemp, and flax were regularly imported to supplement home-grown supplies, but again without objections being raised, for it was generally recognized that whatever the size of the English crop, it could never meet the total demand whether for quantity or quality. The imports which were resented were Irish foodstuffs, especially cattle. Opposition was simmering for a very long time before any positive action was taken, but experience under the Commonwealth undoubtedly fuelled it. It had burst forth in the depression of 1621 in a protest by Sir Edwin Sandys against Irish cattle, beef, and butter imports, said to be worth £10,000 per annum,[36] and it was voiced again in 1637 at a meeting of the Committee of Trade. In February 1656, when the act to encourage exports was near realization, Sir John Reynolds and William Wheeler presented a report from the Committee on Trade to the Council of State "concerning transportation of corn and cattle out of Ireland". That this phrase signified serious public concern over the scale of Irish imports seems likely, although, since Sir John Reynolds was the grantee of a substantial estate in Ireland, it may be that he favoured the continuation of the trade.[37] In the event, no ban on Irish imports followed, but a body of hostile opinion was building up support for one. Action at this time may have been frustrated by the arguments of farmers from the south-west – from Cornwall, Devon, Somerset, and Dorset – who profited much from the sales of foodstuffs to Ireland.[38] The controversy ran underground until the Restoration.

(c) *Timber trees and fruit trees*
The first ideas for diversification to be urged upon parliament concerned tree growing. Serious timber shortages were feared, and a general policy, if heeded by private landowners, could bring benefits to the Commonwealth in the future. Hartlib chronicled public concern at the very beginning of his diary. In 1634 he recorded in a detached way "the business of the forests" as of

---

[33] Fitz-Geffrey, *op. cit.*, p. 1.   [34] *CSPD*, 1650, pp. 178–9.
[35] *CSPD*, 1649–50, p. 454.
[36] T & C, pp. 1, 3.
[37] *CSPD*, 1637, p. 47; 1655–6, p. 192; *DNB*, *sub* Sir John Reynolds. Information on William Wheeler, for which I thank the History of Parliament Trust, does not explain his interest in this matter. He lived at Westbury, Wilts.   [38] *CSPD*, 1656–7, p. 219.

great importance "not questioned these three hundred years". In 1651 a Mr Hartwel visited him and expressed the need for attention to be paid to forests and the planting of timber. Lord Scudamore was commended for having been a great preserver of woods against the day of England's need. By 1652 Sylvanus Taylor thought "all men's eyes were upon the forests", as, indeed, they were, now that the sale of crown forests was in prospect. But how could the timber of the whole kingdom be secured for the future?[39]

The policy that was many times discussed was that of compelling the planting of two or three trees for every one cut down. An anonymous writer in 1653 of *Proposals for the Improvement of Waste Ground*, who directed his remarks to the Committee for Trade, suggested that such a clause be inserted in leases.[40] The idea, as others explained, came from Germany.

The planting of fruit trees was similarly commended to private landowners not merely for their fruit but also for fuel, joinery wood, and drink; walnut, pear, and apple wood made better tables, chairs, and stools than other kinds, it was alleged (and certainly walnut became a fashionable wood for fine furniture by the 1690s). Apples and pears would yield cider and perry, thereby reducing beer consumption and saving the many thousand loads of wood used in malting. This in turn would save many acres of barley land. That cider was being treated seriously as an alternative to beer was one result of the Civil War armies' long sojourn in Herefordshire, Worcestershire, and Gloucestershire. The earl of Southampton was reported in 1653 to be planting 15,000 fruit trees near Portsmouth and to have a special design for making cider. In 1656 came news that cider in Germany had been brought to such perfection that the Elector of Cologne feared its damaging effect on wine sales.[41]

With encouragement from Hartlib, Ralph Austen wrote from Oxford urging a government policy to promote the planting of fruit and timber trees. First he drew up a humble petition to the Council of State, then wrote an eloquent book, *A Treatise of Fruit Trees* (1653), of which half the original printing of 500 copies was to be sent to MPs.[42] As soon as Austen heard rumours of government action in 1653 to prohibit any further growing of tobacco in Gloucester – tobacco had been prohibited in 1619 but the

[39] Hartlib, "Ephemerides", 1634, E–F15; 1651, A–B3; Beale, *Herefordshire Orchards*, p. 38; Sylvanus Taylor, *Common Good; or, the Improvement of Commons, Forrests, & Chases by Inclosure* (BL, Thomason Tract, E 663(6)), London, 1652, f. 29.

[40] BL. Thomason Tract, E 715(18).

[41] Sheffield Univ. Library, Hartlib MS 66/22; R. Austen, *The Spiritual Use of an Orchard; or, Garden of Fruit Trees*, Oxford, 1653, 'Epistle Dedicatory'; Hartlib, "Ephemerides", 1653, JJ–JJ4; 1656, 44–44–5. See also below, pp. 279–80.

[42] Hartlib MS 66/22; C. Webster, *The Great Instauration*, London, 1975, p. 478. Austen had already urged the policy in an earlier work, *A Designe for Plentie*, London, 1652. His ideas were anticipated by John Thomas, gardener, in a humble representation to the Council of State, *c.* 1650; he wanted fruit trees planted in hedges and waste places to the number of 10 trees per acre – Hartlib MS 62/12/1–3.

government had so far turned a blind eye to its continuance – he asked Hartlib for news of the Committee for Trade's intentions, wishing to suggest a law for planting fruit trees.[43] A month later he had more specific proposals to make to the committee: every £5 of "plantable land" should be planted with ten apple or pear trees. Justices of the peace should appoint surveyors, as they did for the highways; books on trees and skilled men should be made available; tenants should be allowed to hold orchards after the end of their leases until they had reaped a fair reward for planting them, and "honest men" should judge when that reward had been obtained.[44]

Thus in the early 1650s we can see serious moves being made to frame a policy for tree planting. The concern of private landowners and professional woodmen was brought to the attention of the House of Commons, through petitions and the deliberate circulation of a book. By 1656 men in the Hartlib circle were canvassing the idea of a more general act to encourage husbandry. It did not earn mention in the Commons journals, and it may never have reached the floor of the house, because the act to allow the export of foodstuffs devoured all available parliamentary time, but one of the provisions suggested for it was an obligation to plant timber and fruit trees.[45] Interest in a policy was slowly accumulating which gained greater precision after 1660.

3. Land improvement

(a) Confiscated lands

The crown as landholder had set the example of improving wastes, fens, forests, and chases in the late sixteenth and early seventeenth centuries. Much greater opportunities came the way of the Commonwealth, when it confiscated the lands of the church, the crown, and private royalists. For a while it simply acted as a collector of rents, and local sequestration committees were set up to administer these proceedings. They occasionally had the task of nominating tenants to vacant holdings, but we know nothing of the way such matters were negotiated, though it is difficult to believe that a man like Walter Blith, sequestrator in Warwickshire, did not favour putting in an improving tenant whenever such a choice came his way.[46]

When parliament decided subsequently to sell confiscated lands, it removed the responsibility for improvement from the government to the private individuals buying the lands, but again some of its aspirations could be – indeed, were – fulfilled by purchasers who were parliament's warm

---

[43] Hartlib MS 41/1/46. For the history of tobacco growing in the 1650s, see Joan Thirsk, 'New Crops and their Diffusion: Tobacco-Growing in Seventeenth-Century England', in C. W. Chalklin and M. A. Havinden, eds., *Rural Change and Urban Growth, 1500–1800*, London, 1974, pp. 94–7.

[44] Hartlib MS 41/1/52. [45] *Ibid.*, 53/20.

[46] CCC, *III*, p. 2,029.

supporters. Ralph Austen, author of some influential books on fruit trees, declared an interest in buying ten or twelve acres of Shotover Forest (Oxon.) when it was sold, remarking that his example might influence others. Presumably he intended to plant an orchard.[47]

Parliamentary sales undoubtedly furthered improvement, though this has to be set against the fact that some land, especially woodland, was despoiled for short-term gains. Bitter complaints were made in 1660 of the spoil of timber. Nevertheless, some of the agricultural changes wrought by purchasers were in accord with progressive thinking. Forms of 'improvement' were, of course, many, but in general it meant increasing the productivity of the existing land, and providing more work for the poor (see below, pp. 321ff). For Ralph Austen, improvement meant planting fruit trees in former woodland or scrub. For others it meant putting park and forest land under the plough, as did Sir John Done, keeper of Delamere forest c. 1650, who marled some land and then planted French wheat (i.e. buckwheat) and rye.[48] For others, parkland improvement entailed dividing the land into small holdings, thereby creating many new farms for husbandmen. Part of Windsor Great Park, for example, was so transformed. Marylebone Park in London was turned into dairy farms, representing again a more intensive use of the grassland.[49] But in common parlance in the first half of the seventeenth century, improvement meant putting land under the plough: arable was still conventionally deemed a more advantageous use of land.

(b) Fenlands

The drainage works carried out in the fen in Charles I's reign had been all but destroyed in the turmoil of the Civil War in the 1640s. Parliament turned early to the question of repairing the damage: in 1647 a parliamentary committee decided that draining the Great Level would be profitable to the Commonwealth:[50] in 1649 an act for draining the Great Level of the fens was passed. One definition of land improvement was clearly expressed in the preamble: the drainage would enable the land to bear coleseed for oil for the soap and cloth industries, it would improve the pasture for breeding and feeding cattle, it would afford more land for corn and also for hemp and flax, which would make cloth and cordage, and it would give work to the poor. William Dugdale's account of his journey through the Great Level in 1657 showed how these hopes were realized. All these arable and industrial crops were seen growing, and more besides, and it became a common opinion, voiced as early as 1653, and more confidently still after 1660 when the abundance of foodstuffs and their low price caused concern, that the

---

[47] Hartlib MS 41/1/58.
[48] Ian Gentles, 'The Management of the Crown Lands, 1649–60', AHR, XIX, 1, 1971, p. 33; Cheshire RO, DAR H/16.   [49] Gentles, op. cit., pp. 27, 38–9. See also below, p. 150.
[50] H. C. Darby, The Draining of the Fens, 2nd edn, Cambridge, 1956, pp. 66–7.

productivity of the fens was one factor in this great transformation. Certainly in turning livestock grazing into corn land, the drainage increased the grain harvest, thereby aggravating the problems after 1660 of grain in superabundance.[51]

None of this helped parliament to establish good relations with the fen commoners, despite alleged concern for their interests. The drainers overturned the old pastoral economy, and the fenlanders responded angrily with riots and lawsuits, in which they were helped by individual parliamentarians like John Wildman and John Lilburne who sympathized with their viewpoint. The fenlanders had a perfectly arguable case. Fish and fowl were disturbed in their traditional habitats by the drainage, wet land that had afforded lush pasture in summer was drained dry and robbed of the nutrients it had formerly received annually from winter flooding, and, in addition to all this, the commons were reduced to one-half or one-third of their former size. However much it tried, parliament could not possibly improve the fens without disturbing the commoners. In making a choice between two irreconcilable purposes, it chose to impose upon the commoners an improvement which it believed to be for their own good despite their opposition to it. In this policy, it was implementing the conclusions of Walter Blith, who similarly claimed sympathy with the commoners but gave to land improvement a still higher priority.[52]

The pattern of farm holdings that was created after fen drainage would repay more detailed investigation than it has yet received. In theory parliament favoured leasing new holdings to the local inhabitants. In practice the inhabitants were so bitterly opposed to the drainage works that they would have nothing to do with the new farms, of which the drainage engineers and investing Adventurers were usually the owners.[53] In consequence, Dutch and French were encouraged to take the land. A Cromwellian ordinance in 1654, a month after the Dutch war ended, invited foreign Protestants to become farmers and promised them the rights of free denizens. Moreover, since Dutch and Scotch prisoners had been employed as labourers, it is likely that some of them took up land also. The size and layout of their holdings, compared with those of the native fenlanders living in established villages nearby, is a matter of some interest. The evidence points to a mixture of large and small holdings: in the Great Level, for example, some fifteen-acre lots were offered in the early 1650s; but at the same time many large allotments went to Adventurers to repay them for their investments. Yet these

[51] Ibid., p. 68; BL, Lansdowne MS 722, ff. 29–30, 38v; Hartlib, "Ephemerides", 1653, OO–OO4,

[52] Darby, op. cit., pp. 76, 69; Joan Thirsk, 'The Isle of Axholme before Vermuyden', AHR, I, 1953, pp. 26–8; W. Blith, The English Improver Improved, 1652 edn, 'Appendix' (unpaged).

[53] This was the reaction of the commoners at the disafforestation of Galtres Forest, Yorks. – G. H. Overend, 'The First Thirty Years of the Foreign Settlement in Axholme', Proc. Huguenot Soc. of London, II, 1887–8, p. 301.

did not necessarily determine the pattern of working farms, which was shaped rather by the creation of many sub-tenancies. It may well be that smallish or medium-sized farms dominated the scene – at least in the short term. But none of this was the result of any deliberate government action to encourage a certain size of holding.[54]

(c) Forests

Large areas of royal forest came into the hands of the Commonwealth when the royal estates were confiscated. The decision to sell them, however, was not a foregone conclusion. The Act for the Sale of Crown Lands in 1649 excluded all forests and chases, as well as all trees growing within fifteen miles of a navigable river.[55] The government was primarily anxious to guard its supplies of timber for shipping, and was well aware of the scandalous waste of wood that had occurred since the outbreak of the Civil War in the Forest of Dean, one of the principal sources of naval timber. But whether the forests should be sold or leased was not an easy decision: even when it was decided in November 1653 to sell certain forests, others were excluded from the sale and the issue remained contentious to the end of the Interregnum. As late as October 1659 a new bill for the sale of the remaining forests and chases was down for discussion in the Commons.[56] A review of the issues will explain why forest management was a lively concern of agriculturalists and remained so for the rest of the period.

England's overseas adventures in the 1650s in the West Indies and against Holland made urgent demands for new naval vessels, and underlined the importance of conserving England's timber resources. The scandal of royalist depredations in the Forest of Dean first came to the notice of the Commons in April 1649, and thereafter many hours of Commons debates were taken up with it. Nor could the most loyal parliamentarian entirely ignore the spoil of woodlands carried out by members of his own party when they bought up confiscated land. Thenceforward, the nation's timber loomed large in public discussion.[57] Woodland management appeared alongside other measures for improving arable, meadow, and pasture in the books of husbandry. Walter Blith's contribution was included in the second edition

---

[54] Darby, op. cit., p. 76; H. Peet, transcr., *Register of Baptisms of the French Church at Thorney, Cambs., 1654–1727*, Huguenot Soc., XVII, 1903, pp. xii–xiii. For an illustration of large holdings in 1640 in Hatfield Chase, see PRO, SP 46/88, f. 173, showing how the land of Mr Rombout Jacobson (a Dutchman?) was disposed.

[55] S. J. Madge, *The Domesday of Crown Lands*, London, 1968 edn, pp. 79, 90; Ian Gentles, 'The Sales of Crown Lands during the English Revolution', EcHR, 2nd ser., XXVI, 4, 1973, p. 616.

[56] *Diary of Thos. Burton, II*, pp. 238–43; Madge, op. cit., p. 120.

[57] On the waste of timber at many different hands between 1640 and 1660, see Gentles, 'Management of the Crown Lands', pp. 25–41 *passim*. For a survey of the literature at this time, see Lindsay Sharp, 'Timber, Science and Economic Reform in the Seventeenth Century', *Forestry*, XLVIII, 1, 1975, pp. 56–9.

of his book on husbandry, *The English Improver Improved* (1652 and 1653), in an appendix entitled "Remonstrance to the Honourable Committee of Parliament for taking of grievances for regulating forests, wastes or commons within the Commonwealth". Despite his sympathy with the commoners, Blith argued warmly for improvement, on the grounds that the inhabitants got inadequate rewards for their labour under the existing regime.[58] But his central concern was to establish principles, not to enunciate the strategy and tactics of procuring improvement. The thorny business of overcoming the commoners' opposition, and of devising the practical details of a workable policy, he left to the politicians.

Here lay the kernel of the matter. Alternative courses of action were debated at length. The forests could either be leased or sold: in the first case, commoners would be left in possession of their rights but obliged to exercise them under the strict supervision of the keepers of the forest; in the second case, their rights as commoners would be extinguished in return for compensatory allotments. If the long-term interests of the nation were paramount, then clearly the forests ought not to be sold. Several writers of this mind argued vehemently for a policy of leases. Sylvanus Taylor, an influential committee man in Herefordshire, wanted the state to retain possession, or, if it did not, then he wanted purchasers to undertake to supply specified quantities of timber each year – as a kind of rent charge.[59] Another anonymous pamphleteer in 1653, aiming his remarks directly at the Committee for Trade, was equally strongly opposed to any outright sale. He rejoiced at the idea that "the name of state's land" should be stamped upon the forests "that the state may stand as the public landlord". But he also wanted to see the commoners justly dealt with, and suggested that they be given first offer of leases at something less than market rate. By orders and rules it was essential that the rich did not trample on the poor. The right of first (did he mean second?) refusal was also to be offered to parliament's supporters who had lent and spent their estates in the cause, to demobilized soldiers, and to those impoverished by warfare, plunder, or free quarter.[60] But if leases were to be the answer, then strict supervision of the commoners was necessary, as was recommended for Windsor Forest in 1654, and certain areas would have to be enclosed for the preservation of young timber. Yet control savoured of the old forest laws, of "former oppressions and extravagancies" which aroused strong emotions inside the Commons as well as outside. While the legislature vacillated, the spoil of the forests continued unabated.[61]

A more hard-headed realism was shown by two writers, Dr John Parker

58 Blith, *The English Improver Improved*, 1652 edn, 'Appendix' (unpaged).
59 Taylor, *Common Good*, pp. 42, 48–9.
60 T & C, pp. 135–40, esp. pp. 138–9.
61 CSPD, 1654, pp. 9–12; *Diary of Thos. Burton, I*, pp. 228–9.

and Edward Cresset, who jointly prepared a report arguing for the outright sale of the forests. Only by acquiring a freehold interest would men be willing to undertake the large capital investment that was necessary to improve them. This had been proved in the fen drainage project; no alternative solution would work.[62] Their view carried the day (though long-term forest improvement was a less crucial factor in the final decision than the desperate need to pay the state's creditors quickly), and Parker and Cresset were among the trustees appointed in the Act for the Disafforestation, Sale, and Improvement of the Forests, passed in November 1653.[63]

Even then the practicalities proved to be far from simple. The commoners' rights had to be determined and satisfactory compensation for them settled; in addition, purchasers had to be found who would buy forest land, from some of which the valuable timber had already been removed, while other parts lay on poor soil and had no great immediate value. Discussions in the House of Commons soon revealed the wild optimism of the paper proposals. The Commonwealth above all had to show regard for the forest commoners, for they had made a substantial contribution to parliament's victory against the crown. One diarist's record of the debate in the Commons shows us the tenor of the argument. The commoners had fought on parliament's side for liberty, not expecting to lose it by the imposition of a new forest law, or worse, by the outright sale of the forest. If some purchasers were found to buy odd bits of forest land, their cash payments were not likely to amount to anything very significant in alleviating the state's debts.[64] Behind a report from Alderman John Fowke and George Glapthorne in April 1654 lie further indications of the daunting difficulties in devising a satisfactory policy. The authors underlined the great damage being done to the forests while matters remained uncertain and while the forest laws were suspended. They suggested leasing the state's allotment for not more than twenty-one years at rack rents, while selling other parts, always reserving the timber for the state. To carry out the plan they envisaged a careful investigation of claims and many surveys. Their hope was to make the forests more productive in timber and other produce; accommodate more farmers, rich and poor; and, through the rents from leases, increase the state's revenues. What they could not guarantee was enthusiastic lessees and buyers to take up this challenge.[65]

By August 1654 the Act for Sale was deemed impracticable, and commissioners were appointed to survey the forests and put forward a fresh plan for their improvement. In 1655 they reported their failure either to sell or to lease, uncertainty about the claims of commoners being a principal

[62] PRO, SP 18/69.

[63] Firth and Rait, *Acts and Ordinances of the Interregnum, II,* pp. 783ff. For the steps leading to the act of 1653, see Madge, *op. cit.,* pp. 107–15.

[64] *Diary of Thos. Burton, I,* pp. 228–9. The same claim for freedom against those who felled woods and trees on common ground was put by Gerrard Winstanley – BL, Thomason Tract, E 557/9.   [65] *CSPD,* 1654, pp. 97–8.

obstacle.[66] In the end the only forests that appear to have been sold were Inglewood in Cumberland, Duffield Frith in Derbyshire, Bestwood in Nottinghamshire, and Kingswood in Gloucestershire.[67] The campaign waged by the forest inhabitants of Needwood in Staffordshire against the government decision to sell their forest in order to pay the army's arrears gives us a clue to the fierce local resistance to forest sales. In 1654, shortly after the inhabitants learned of the government's decision, a petition with twelve pages of signatures was collected in Marchington and Hanbury. On it were inscribed 834 names; whole families assembled, and each of its members, five, six, and eight of the same surname in many cases, signed one after the other. The grand jury at Quarter Sessions supported the petitioners, pointing to the heavy burden of poor relief that would result if the forest were sold. The justices of the peace echoed these sentiments and added their own. The Commonwealth surveyors, arriving to partition and stake out the allotments, needed a party of horsemen quartered nearby to save them from constant interruptions and threats to their lives.[68] Theoretical arguments about improvements that would follow the sale of the forests were alluring, but finding the purchasers was fraught with problems which the Commonwealth never solved. In the end the Protectorate did not sell the forests, nor did it pursue an active policy of leasing parts for improvement. It kept the situation uncertain to the very end: surveys were still in progress between September 1656 and March 1658 in Ashdown Forest; a new bill for the sale of the forest was under discussion in 1659.[69] Meanwhile the commoners exercised their customary rights and, doubtless, rather more than their rights, seeing no security for the future. The policy was the very worst that could have been devised, for it positively encouraged the waste of resources that would take decades to make good.[70]

4. The regulation of enclosure

After the mid 1630s, the enclosure of land lost its place among the topics urgently calling for close government scrutiny, largely because its advantages

[66] P. A. J. Pettit, The Royal Forests of Northamptonshire: A Study in their Economy, 1558–1714, Northants. Rec. Soc., XXIII, 1968, pp. 70–1.   [67] Madge, op. cit., pp. 388, 240.

[68] Joan Thirsk, 'Horn and Thorn in Staffordshire; The Economy of a Pastoral County', N. Staffs. J. Field Stud., IX, 1969, pp. 4–5.

[69] J. R. Daniel-Tyssen, 'The Parliamentary Surveys of the County of Sussex, 1649–53', Sussex Arch. Coll., XXIII, 1871, pp. 217ff; XXIV, pp. 190ff. On the shortcomings of the legislation to sell bishops' lands, see Ian Gentles, 'The Sales of Bishops' Lands in the English Revolution, 1646–1660', EHR, XCV, 1980.

[70] Violence was liable to break out at any time, as it did in the Forest of Dean as late as 1659 – CJ, VII, 1651–9, pp. 648–9 (11 May 1659) – but a complete view of forest administration in the 1650s is not yet possible. Hart's study of the Forest of Dean does not give a clear picture of the consequences of the Commonwealth's administration there – C. E. Hart, The Commoners of Dean Forest, Gloucester, 1951, p. 54.

loomed larger than its drawbacks, and men had arrived at a reasonably fair way of procuring enclosure by agreement.[71] Landholders in village or parish brought a fictitious action in the Court of Chancery, whereby they procured an enrolled Chancery decree, recording the agreement of all parties to enclosure. This procedure was not entirely satisfactory, inasmuch as the descendants of landholders subscribing to these agreements could, and did, go back on them. But for the time being the enclosure agreement was infinitely preferable to the old ways, and afforded a satisfactory means of enclosure so long as all landholders in a community could be persuaded to consent.[72]

In the turmoil of the 1640s a certain amount of illicit enclosure was carried out by tenants at the expense of landlords. A sour comment on this score was made by the vicar of Hainton, Lincolnshire, when he asserted his belief that the first enclosure of the fields in his parish "was clandestinely supported by the confusion and iniquity of the times. A great many enclosures in this county are of no better extraction than this, and a base one it is."[73]

But the most serious grievances that burst forth against enclosure in the 1640s occurred in forests and fens, where large-scale crown projects for enclosure and improvement in the earlier years of the seventeenth century had disturbed large numbers of commoners and left a legacy of deep resentment. Elsewhere, especially after 1649, many enclosures in individual parishes went peaceably ahead, as the study of individual counties bears witness, although the clergy expressed themselves deeply aggrieved at the Restoration at their failure to secure tithe or compensation for tithe.[74] The literature of agricultural improvement, moreover, was generally favourable to enclosure, assuming that it could be accomplished without hardship to the poor and without causing depopulation. It was no longer deemed inevitable that enclosure meant the conversion of arable to permanent pasture; the object of enclosure was to permit the flexible use of all land and improve its fertility.

A pamphlet written in 1652 by Sylvanus Taylor, a Herefordshire parliamentarian, entitled *Common Good; or, the Improvement of Commons, Forrests and Chases by Inclosure* reveals clearly how attention had shifted from the enclosure of good arable land to second- and third-rate grassland, where

---

[71] Although it should be said that R. Powell in *Depopulation Arraigned...*London, 1636, p. 1, considered that the offence of depopulation had grown "giant-like". But his attitude may have been inflamed by the appointment of the enclosure commissions of 1632, 1635, and 1636.

[72] Above, p. 92. For a full account of this development, see M. W. Beresford, 'Habitation versus Improvement', in F. J. Fisher, ed., *Essays in the Economic and Social History of Tudor and Stuart England*, Cambridge, 1961, pp. 49, 53ff.

[73] LAO, D & C DIV/59.

[74] See e.g. *VCH Leics.*, II, pp. 254–64; for the grievances of the clergy of Leicestershire, voiced by the bishop of Lincoln, see Bodleian Library, Clarendon MS 77, f. 157. However, levelling enclosures were reported in Gloucestershire in 1650 – *CSPD*, 1650, p. 218.

the economic benefits were more conspicuous than the social injuries. Even here, in appraising the advantages of enclosure, men were realistic. The benefits were not in all cases clear cut. Taylor did not, for example, believe that the downland commons of Wiltshire and Hampshire necessarily required enclosure, but he emphatically favoured the enclosure of furze-ridden, heathy woodland, and forests and chases, where one-fifth more people might be supported, than at present. The method of enclosure which he advocated was to divide the commons into four parts: one part should be set aside for cottagers' holdings, allowing between twenty and forty acres per cottage, and charging only a small rent; one part should be allotted to the lord; the remainder should be allotted to freeholders and copyholders, who in their turn would provide work for labourers. Enclosure, designed to create many new farms for yeomen, husbandmen, and cottagers, where corn, hemp, flax, vegetables, and fruit trees would replace scrubby woodland and deer, promised undeniable advantages.[75] But it took one fact for granted that could not be so readily assumed: woodland soils were not all amenable to this new use.

Nevertheless, the optimistic assumptions of Sylvanus Taylor represented a strong current of opinion. Enclosure should, and could, be beneficial to all parties. Only in the Midlands did a serious controversy break the surface of the new complacency, causing old arguments against enclosure to be reiterated, though vainly, against the overwhelming tide of opinion favouring enclosure. The outcry against unjust, depopulating enclosure was launched by John Moore, minister of Knaptoft, Leicestershire, when he preached a sermon at Lutterworth in May 1653 entitled *The Crying Sin of England of Not Caring for the Poor*. In veiled language, he attacked those who made men beggars by enclosure and depopulation. Joseph Lee, rector of Cotesbach, replied anonymously in 1654, castigating Moore for his biased argument and failure to consider the general issue fairly. In 1651 Lee and Walter Blith were neighbours in Cotesbach, and plainly shared the same views on agricultural improvement.[76] Lee's writings in reply to Moore portray a fair-minded man who did not confuse the particular with the general. He denounced enclosures that caused depopulation as a canker of the Commonwealth, but he deemed acceptable enclosure on the lines advocated by Taylor, that made due

[75] Taylor, *Common Good, passim,* but esp. pp. 19, 29–33, 35–9. Taylor was deeply involved in implementing parliamentary policy during the Interregnum as a parliamentary committee man in Herefordshire, administrator for the sale of crown lands, assessment and militia commissioner for Westminster, Herefordshire, and Radnorshire, and assessment commissioner for Middlesex – Ian Gentles, 'The Debentures Market and Military Purchases of Crown Land', unpub. London Univ. Ph.D. thesis, 1969, p. 60.

[76] J. Moore, *The Crying Sin of England of Not Caring for the Poor,* London, 1653; [Lee], *Considerations concerning Common Fields.* Another pamphlet of 1650 denouncing enclosure in the same vein as Moore's was *Inclosure Thrown Open: or Depopulation Depopulated...*(BL, Thomason Tract, E 619(2)).

provision for the poor. And in line with current trends, he favoured settlements enrolled in Chancery. He was even prepared to go one step further and advocate that the decision of a majority of landholders to enclose should prevail over a reluctant minority. This, he reminded his readers, was the procedure followed in the government of state and church.[77]

John Moore was probably better informed on particular instances of unjust enclosure in south Leicestershire than Lee, and had little difficulty in gathering support for his anti-enclosure lobby. The mayor and aldermen of Leicester supported him. One surviving petition to the Commons, in 1653, though damaged, bears 175 signatures; in addition, support for Moore's petition came from counties outside Leicestershire.[78] When Edmund Whalley became major-general in charge of the Midland counties in 1655 an authoritative peacemaker entered upon the scene. His correspondence makes plain his endeavour to reconcile opposing views of enclosure rather than to support one against the other. When Major-General Whalley presented to the Commons in December 1656 a bill for improving waste grounds, regulating commons, and preventing depopulation, it is likely, though the bill is nowhere fully set out, that it tried to steer a middle course in order to improve waste land and yet protect the commoners. In a letter to Thurloe in April 1656 Whalley had reported a successful formula that he had devised with the aid of the grand juries of Leicestershire and Warwickshire. Two-thirds of all arable land should be kept in tillage, the value of benefices should not be lessened (by changing land use), and the poor should be amply provided for. An earlier idea had been mooted in a Leicester petition for the management of enclosure by a body "in the nature of a corporation", which would direct the work and protect the interests of the poor. When enclosure was decided, it was to be implemented even without the commoners' unanimous consent. In these details we may recognize ideas that were to mature in Whalley's bill. A few details, indeed, were vouchsafed in debate: the division of commons was evidently entrusted to three commissioners acting with a jury. Yet the bill found no favour. The main criticism was that it invaded rights of property, and gave inordinate power to justices of the peace whose motives might not always bear examination. "Time was when I durst hardly have trusted the justices of peace with determining of a cow grass", declared William Lenthall, Speaker of the Commons. "You have good justices now; who can tell what may be hereafter?" Even the presence of a jury alongside the JPs could not convince that all would receive a fair deal. Final condemnation came from Mr Fowell, who thought the bill

[77] [Lee], op. cit., pp. 38, 28–9.

[78] Ibid., p. 37; John Goodacre, 'Lutterworth in the Sixteenth and Seventeenth Centuries: A Market Town and its Area', unpub. Leicester Univ. Ph.D. thesis, 1977, pp. 45–7. I wish to thank Dr Goodacre for permission to use his thesis, which for the first time makes intelligible, in their local setting, many of the arguments deployed by Moore and Lee. Parliamentary discussions on enclosure and depopulation are mentioned in 1653 in Diary of Thos. Burton, I, p. xiv.

"the most mischievous that ever was offered to this house. It will wholly depopulate many and destroy property." The bill did not get beyond a first reading.[79]

It was clear that no general act promoting enclosure and protecting the poor could satisfactorily be drafted. It seemed a defeatist verdict, yet we should not forget that parliament was still wrestling with the problem of the forests and fens. It had not yet found a satisfactory and peaceable way to enclose and improve those areas. It might well shrink at more contentious legislation, affecting perhaps half the land of the kingdom.

5. Work for the poor

The end of the Civil War, and the trade depression into which the kingdom was plunged in 1649, created a serious problem for the new Commonwealth of finding work for the unemployed and for demobilized soldiers.[80] Poor men came to the very doors of the Commons begging for jobs, and debates on this score punctuated proceedings in the Commons in 1650, 1652–3, 1656, and 1659. In the intervals between these dates the topic lapsed, probably because the urgency of the problem temporarily diminished.

Plainly agriculture in this period offered great opportunities for employing the poor. Any improvement of land was likely to involve much work in clearing woodland, planting hedges, ditching, draining, and manuring. All special crops being recommended to improvers – vegetables, hops, dye plants, hemp, and flax – called for much hand labour, and in lively discussions outside parliament most improvements were justified in part at least because they would afford much work to the poor. Ralph Austen, for example, who canvassed the extension of orchards, underlined in one of his books the work they would give to the poor, making particular reference "to the late consultations of the parliament".[81]

Hence, it was not without approval in principle, though not in practice, that the Diggers, inspired by Gerrard Winstanley, dug up commons to create holdings for the poor at St George's Hill, near Cobham, Surrey, growing for their first crops corn, parsnips, carrots, and beans. But by intruding upon the commons of others they turned their theoretical friends into enemies. Walter Blith put the objections thus: "Though the poor are or ought to have advantage upon the commons, yet I question whether they, as a society gathered together from all parts of the nation, could claim a right to any particular common." And characteristically for a practical man, with a

[79] G. Jagger, 'The Fortunes of the Whalley Family of Screveton, Notts....', unpub. Southampton Univ. M.Phil. thesis, 1973, pp. 187–91. I wish to thank Mr Jagger for permission to quote from his thesis. Diary of Thomas Burton, I, pp. 175–6.

[80] For a general discussion of the government's action for relief of the poor, see James, Social Problems and Policy, pp. 283–7.

[81] Austen, The Spiritual Use of an Orchard, 'Epistle Dedicatory'.

greater interest in the agricultural potential of land than in property rights, he added the opinion that St George's Hill in Surrey was not the best choice of a common for the purpose. "If there be not thousands of places more capable of improvement than theirs, and that by many easier ways and to far greater advantages, I will lay down the bucklers."[82]

Parliamentary spokesmen and their advisers failed to produce any precise and practical proposals to implement their theoretical ideas for employing the poor. What their debates achieved was to advertise the benefits to the poor of improvement schemes, thereby encouraging adventurers and improvers to go ahead with private ventures. One theorist, a Dr Tong, canvassed the idea of erecting workhouses, but forty years were to pass before his design was revived. Parliamentary policy reverted instead to the old Elizabethan solution of finding parish work stocks. A committee set up in March 1649/50 to peruse all former laws on poor relief, to summarize them, and to suggest how to set the poor on work, recommended that local charities be scrutinized and given new life, and that redundant churches be pulled down and sold to raise money for a work stock.[83] When the same topic came up for discussion in 1652, and the Committee for the Poor was set up, some of the amendments, cryptically recorded in the Commons journals, suggest that a measure to enforce the growing of hemp was contemplated, along with a suggestion that tithes on hemp and flax should not exceed 3s. per acre.[84] Even this measure failed to pass, for reasons that may be guessed: all the indications after 1660 suggest that tithe was considered the great stumbling block to any compulsory scheme for growing special crops. Industrial tasks for the poor, on the other hand, did not raise these vexed questions. Hence, spinning and weaving constituted the only parish work in view in 1652, and no fresh ideas were put forward in 1656 or 1659. Parish work stocks remained the readiest solution to the problem of unemployment throughout the Interregnum.[85]

Nevertheless, other government measures to sell forfeited lands, improve the forests, and drain the fens undoubtedly came to the rescue in some areas. Fen drainage created so much work that not enough voluntary labour could be found. When the act of 1651 for draining the Great Level revived that project, wage rates locally rose from 6d. to 12d. per day. Even so, labourers were insufficient, and Scottish prisoners were drafted into the area to help:

---

[82] L. Hamilton, ed., *Gerrard Winstanley: Selections from his Works*, London, 1944, p. 2; Blith, *The English Improver Improved*, 1652 edn, 'Epistle to the Reader'.

[83] A. L. Beier, 'Poor Relief in Warwickshire, 1630–60', *PP*, no. 35, 1966, p. 93; Hartlib, "Ephemerides", 1657, 50–50–6; CJ, VI, 1648–51, pp. 375, 481, 535.

[84] CJ, VII, 1651–9, pp. 127, 190, 255, 259–60. The Commons journals record amendments of the words "hemp", "50 acres", and "25 acres", which suggest that a plot of hemp was to be planted for every so many arable acres.

[85] CJ, VII, 1651–9, pp. 439, 766. See also *Diary of Thos. Burton*, I, p. clxxxiii; W. Goffe, *How to Advance the Trade of the Nation and Employ the Poor*, Harleian Misc., IV, pp. 385–9.

in October 1651 1,000 were ordered to be sent, of whom some duly arrived later at King's Lynn.[86] It is tempting to speculate on whether Walter Blith's experience with recalcitrant workmen in the fens, briefly described in his book, brought him into contact with these Scotsmen.[87] At all events, sufficient labourers were somehow found to complete the task, and William Dugdale's statement, when he visited the fens around Ely in 1657, that no fewer than 11,000 men had been employed at one time in recent years, gives some idea of the magnitude of the work.[88]

More lasting work for the unemployed resulted from the creation of new farms in the fenland. Not all were laid out for substantial yeomen. Some fell within the means of small husbandmen: land in the neighbourhood of Thorney, Cambridgeshire, for example, was offered in lots of fifteen acres. Some of these small freeholds were taken up by French and Flemish refugees who removed themselves from Hatfield Chase after the great riots of 1650–1 had destroyed their settlement at Santoft. But as the Bedford Level extended over 95,000 acres, not all new farms went to foreigners; some Englishmen, including parliamentary officers, took up holdings, as well as some Scots labourers.[89] And among the crops grown in the fens, some were of the labour-intensive kind, like hemp, flax, and onions, which provided much work for labourers. William Dugdale described Colonel Castle's farm in Ewell Fen, growing onions, peas, and hemp; Sir Edward Partridge's in Mildenhall Drove growing fruit and garden vegetables, woad, flax, hemp, and coleseed; and Colonel Underwood's at Whittlesea growing fruit trees, vegetables, and willows.[90] Every one of these farms had an experimental air about it. Every one would entail more work for labourers.

The sale of crown estates elsewhere similarly led to the creation of many new farms, calling for much labour. Land belonging to Theobalds Palace in Hertfordshire was divided into about thirty holdings, while thirty acres around the house were divided into sites for the farmhouses. It became what Fuller called "a little commonwealth, so many tenements like splinters having flown out of the materials thereof". Windsor Great Park was similarly divided into one hundred parcels, and new houses, barns, and stables built on them, and the land grubbed, ploughed, and manured with chalk and lime. Already by 1654 in Windsor Little Park the land had been fenced and grubbed, molehills destroyed, and the ground put into cultivation.[91] The conversion of all this land from mainly decorative to economic uses

[86] *CSPD*, 1651, pp. 458, 471–5. See also Darby, *Draining of the Fens*, pp. 76–7.

[87] See ch. 7 below.

[88] Overend, 'The First Thirty Years of the Foreign Settlement in Axholme', p. 323; BL, Lansdowne MS 722, f. 29v.

[89] Peet, *Register of Baptisms...at Thorney*, pp. xii–xiv; Samuel Wells, *The History of the Drainage of the Great Level...*2 vols., London, 1830, I, p. 244.

[90] BL, Lansdowne MS 722, ff. 29–30, 35.

[91] Gentles, 'Management of the Crown Lands', pp. 36, 38–9.

undoubtedly created much work, and since these estates were scattered all over the kingdom, they contributed much in particular localities to the relief of the poor.[92]

6. Conclusion

The ideas for an agricultural policy on which parliament deliberated in the 1650s were clearly as wide-ranging as the contemporary literature on husbandry, and they reached down to the smallest details. Legislators became better informed on the means of agricultural development than ever before, and with this knowledge went an interest in new measures of agricultural policy and new hope for agricultural change. The legislation that emerged was, nevertheless, extremely limited in scope, as parliament hesitated to take any fresh action that lacked a legitimate pedigree in accepted tradition or encroached upon individual rights of property. But underlying the abortive discussions, certain newish trends of thought were gaining ground. Parliament was reluctant to coerce agriculturalists, and became even more reluctant as better experience taught the complexity of local circumstances. It preferred to leave men free to work out their own solutions. But having shown a preference for economic freedom – which was displayed in its policy towards other sectors of the economy at the same time – parliament also advertised certain preferred goals for individual enterprise. Self-sufficiency in agricultural production was one, since the war against the Dutch and the brushes with Spain had obstructed trade and made clear the wisdom of subsisting "without the help of others".[93] A more sympathetic attitude towards pasture farming was also emerging – encouraged by the fall of grain prices, and bolstered by the evidence that pasture employed more labour, and that conversion of arable to pasture did not necessarily cause depopulation. The facts were adduced by Robert Child in an analysis called *The Defects and Remedies of English Husbandry* in 1652. Commodities from livestock, e.g. cloth, stuffs, stockings, butter, cheese, hides, shoes, and tallow, were far more stable in price than corn. Impressive numbers of people could work on the wool of 200–300 sheep; similarly, dairying engaged many more than the single cowherd. Child ventured to the extreme point of this argument by saying that it would be no loss to England if men did not plough at all, so long as they could get corn at reasonable rates.[94] At that date Child's opinion was at variance with the conventional view, and did not even accord with the advice of Walter Blith, but after 1660 it was given a fairer hearing. Finally, self-sufficiency and the desire to create as many farm holdings as possible enhanced men's appreciation of the role of intensive cultivation. Child was

[92] Beier, *op. cit.*, pp. 88, 96–8.
[93] Austen, *The Spiritual Use of an Orchard*, 'Epistle Dedicatory'.
[94] S. Hartlib, *His Legacie, or An Enlargement of the Discours of Husbandrie*, 2nd edn, London, 1652, pp. 43–4.

the most discerning observer of its merits and well in advance of his contemporaries. By using more land in gardens and closes, improved yields would certainly result.[95] Crops that called for intensive cultivation, moreover, had two further points in their favour. They gave work and they brought unusually large profits at the market. Diversified agricultural production was coming to be recognized as more advantageous than the monotonous insistence on corn.

c. 1660–1750

1. Introduction

Practical difficulties in devising legislation that coped with all situations satisfactorily obtruded more prominently still after 1660, with the result that parliament intervened in agriculture more decisively by indirect methods, by controlling marketing rather than production. When it attempted directly to dictate the activities of the farming community, as it had done so confidently before 1640, its proposals were likely to run into the sand; one example is the way measures to promote the growing of more hemp, flax, and madder were frustrated by disputes about tithes.

The discussion of policy measures in parliament, nevertheless, continued to serve as a valuable means of disseminating facts and opinions. Bills went to committees composed of ten, twenty, even thirty members of the Commons, who received petitions for and against from interested parties, and studied reports.[96] Men like John Evelyn and William Coventry, who sat on these committees after 1660, and voiced firm opinions on agricultural policy outside parliament, doubtless formed their views from information partly collected inside the house. The net effect was to confirm the belief in the less intervention the better. Nevertheless, the government did help the farming community at its very weakest points, supporting grain farmers with bounties on export which continued well into the eighteenth century, and livestock farmers with money compensation during the cattle plagues of 1714 and 1745–59. As for parliament's increasing concern with marketing rather than production, experience between 1660 and 1700 did not win over all

---

[95] Hartlib, "Ephemerides", 1650, G–H4.

[96] This statement is based on cursory impressions only of committee work in the House of Commons at this time. For evidently hard-working and interested committees of the House of Commons after 1660, including one at which over 100 MPs were present, see C. A. Edie, *The Irish Cattle Bills: A Study in Restoration Politics*, Amer. Philos. Soc., NS LX, 2, 1970, *passim*, but esp. p. 19. But a full study of Commons procedures in the seventeenth century is urgently needed for the argument advanced here is at variance with the conclusion of S. Lambert in *Bills and Acts: Legislative Procedure in Eighteenth-Century England*, Cambridge, 1971, pp. 99–100, who believes that in the eighteenth century committees were extremely perfunctory, sometimes assembled a bare quorum, and presumably sometimes did not achieve that. It should not be assumed that this was the case in the later seventeenth century.

parties even to this degree of indirect intervention. Sir Josiah Child protested vehemently in 1694 against the vanity of laws which forbad the engrossing of corn, "there being no persons more beneficial to a trade in a nation than engrossers". He also inveighed against laws charging customs duties on exports of beef, pork, bread, beer, "for which I think in prudence the door should be opened wide to let them out". Such arguments against export controls, even extending to wool, won stronger support still in the half-century up to 1750.[97]

The most notable features of the period 1660–1700 that profoundly influenced agricultural decisions were declining grain and wool prices. A general economic depression had cast a shadow in 1658, when men complained of the deadness of trade,[98] but for corn farmers the outlook was at first less dismal; poor seasons in 1657, 1658, and 1659 caused grain prices to rise, and this trend continued at the Restoration, when the harvests of 1660 and 1661 were also deficient.[99] From 1664, however, abundant crops lowered prices sharply, and they continued low to the end of 1672. The government's concern to encourage corn production by paying bounties on exports must be set against this background.[100]

Deeper-seated rumblings of discontent emanated from livestock producers complaining about the competition from Irish cattle, some of which were brought in fat, but most of which were imported lean to be fattened in England. Alarm had already been voiced in the 1620s, in 1637, and in the 1650s, but complaints grew to a loud chorus in the later 1660s when the falling rents of pasture, especially in the Home Counties, were blamed on low profits from livestock fattening, which were attributed in their turn to large Irish imports. That these complaints now received serious attention was due to the conjuncture of falling rents with a trade depression that inspired many pamphlets from 1667 onwards. Livestock imports were investigated as part of the wider problem of "the fall of rents and decay of trade".

The use of a slogan like "the fall of rents and decay of trade" (trade here meaning overseas trade) in itself reflects the limited outlook and interests of two groups in rural society – landowners, and farmers with large surpluses, of whom the majority were engaged in traditional corn and livestock

---

[97] Sir Josiah Child, *New Discourse of Trade*, London, 1694, p. 72. It is characteristic of parliaments' *laissez-faire* attitude that the enclosure of commonable grounds engaged the interest of the Commons in 1715 only as a device to endow poor rectories and vicarages – CJ, XVIII, p. 123. But the two interests – financial and agricultural – were skilfully combined in Mr Torriano's speech in the House of Lords in 1713 when he stressed the importance of the revenue from malt, cider, perry, and molasses, along with the importance of distilleries in taking up the products of barley growers and sugar refiners – *House of Lords Papers*, NS X, 1712–14, p. 133.

[98] *CSPD*, 1658–9, p. 114.

[99] See M. Beloff, *Public Order and Popular Disturbances, 1660–1714*, Oxford, 1938, pp. 58–75, for riots occasioned by the export of grain from south-coast ports in 1662 and the first half of 1663.

[100] See vol. I of the paperback series, Table XVII. For a comment from Yorkshire on low grain prices in 1668, see Sheffield City Library, Wentworth Woodhouse MS WWM BR 75/40.

farming. For them conditions were, indeed, discouraging. Two writers, one anonymous in 1673 and Sir Josiah Child in 1694, defined the problems in much the same terms. The value of land was falling because corn prices were low and interest rates (at 6 per cent) too high to encourage the investment of capital in land. Other forms of investment, primarily loans to the government, brought better returns for less effort. Other European countries were alleged to enjoy lower labour costs (high wages in England received particular attention from the middle 1670s), and this was given as one of the reasons why foreigners could sell agricultural (and industrial) products cheaper than the English. Therefore, even though policy makers were attempting to help the agricultural interest by encouraging exports, foreign competitors in European food markets still undercut the English farmer. A further complaint from landowners concerned their share of national taxation: the brunt fell on land and so they paid far more than any other class in society.[101]

These preoccupations are reflected in much farming correspondence throughout the period 1670 to 1691. Neither corn nor stock fattening yielded fair returns to the farmer, and on all sides landlords were being met with requests for rent reductions or threats by tenants to throw up their farms. Circumstances altered briefly with the bad harvest of 1692, which inaugurated a series of poor grain years that lasted until 1699. But while they temporarily yielded high profits to small numbers of grain farmers who had a surplus crop, in general the high prices of scarcity could not bring prosperity to the majority of those who had complained earlier of low prices.[102]

Nevertheless, the misfortunes of farmers growing none but traditional crops should not disguise the fact that some groups in the farming community, including many small farmers, were varying the conventional routine of corn and cattle to include special crops for which domestic demand remained buoyant throughout the period to 1750. The advice of the pamphleteers was given clearly enough in 1677: "our lands fall for want of being improved *some other way* [my italics], besides planting corn, breeding for wool, etc., which are become so low a price as scarce to turn to account".[103] Many more farmers took the hint after 1660, and fought off disaster by mixing traditional farm products with others that were more

---

[101] *Plain English in a Familiar Conference betwixt Three Friends, Rusticus, Civis, and Veridicus concerning the Deadness of our Markets*, London, 1673 (see p. 6 for reference to excessive wages), and Child, *op. cit.*, pp. 45–8, 223–9. In addition, and in vein similar to *Plain English*, see J. B[riscoe], *A Discourse on the Late Funds of the Million Act, Lottery Act, and Bank of England*, London, 1694, pp. 19–20, 28. For examples of falling rents on an estate in E. Bradenham, Norfolk, in 1674, see Norfolk RO, Clayton 17 MS 3,226.

[102] *CSPD*, 1676, pp. 113, 414; CJ, VIII, 1660–7, pp. 733–4; A. H. John, 'The Course of Agricultural Change, 1660–1760', in L. S. Pressnell, ed., *Studies in the Industrial Revolution*, London, 1960, p. 134.

[103] *Proposals for Building in Every County a Working Alms-House*, Harleian Misc., IV, 1745, p. 465.

remunerative. Parliamentary debates show well enough that members were familiar with these more profitable enterprises. Understandably, however, policy remained primarily concerned with the standard products of agriculture, corn, cattle, and wool, and throughout the 1670s and 80s the most persistent theme in debates was how to maintain the prices of these commodities. The problem subsided in so far as grain was concerned during years of scarcity but re-emerged intermittently to the end of the period.

2. Encouraging agricultural production and diversification

Plentiful food supplies encouraged increasing sophistication in the market, which was reflected in unwonted parliamentary concern for standardizing weights and measures for grain and, more significantly, for dairy produce. Marketing arrangements in the dairying business were evidently still primitive, even barbarous, judging by the emphasis placed in parliamentary discussions on improving sales procedures and removing abuses in packing and weighing. The time spent on these matters was so great that it must surely reflect the enhanced importance of dairy production in the national market; dairying had entered upon a new era of growth that was qualitatively different from any previous period. Possibly it reflected the success of the artificial grasses in improving the fat content of milk. Certainly, development was reflected in a geographical extension of the dairying regions, and in a more intense specialization in the traditional ones.[104]

(a) Cereals

As we have seen, the government was anxious from the mid 1650s to encourage corn growers to persist with tillage by allowing exports, but the consequences for trade defy measurement for lack of port books during that decade. One leading economic writer of the 1640s and 50s, Henry Robinson, had suggested reducing tithes on land that was growing corn, in order to encourage the plough; but neither he nor anyone else in that period seems to have reached the point of suggesting bounties to encourage exports.[105]

In the first year after the king's Restoration different measures were briefly needed. Corn shortages in 1661 provoked distress that was reflected in a

---

[104] An act for the better packing of butter and the redress of abuses in selling by unwarranted weights was passed in March 1649/50 – Firth and Rait, *Acts and Ordinances of the Interregnum*, II, p. 362. There had been only one statute relating to butter and cheese in the previous 100 years, that of 3 & 4 Ed. VI, c. 21 – a short act of 14 lines, – forbidding people to buy butter and cheese to sell again unless they sold retail. For Andrew Yarranton's statement on the improvement of cheese and butter after clover, see his *England's Improvement by Sea and Land*, London, 1677, p. 28. On dairying, see regional chapters in pt 1 of AHEW, V.

[105] Henry Robinson, *Certain Proposals in Order to the People's Freedom*...London, 1652, p. 7.

tumult of 500 angry women at Weymouth in December 1662, protesting at a shipment of corn overseas in a time of dearth. Consequent government action, asking JPs to survey corn stocks to see that they were not engrossed or hoarded, smacked of Charles I's personal rule. But a fair harvest in 1662 dispelled fears of scarcity, and by April 1663 a Commons committee was recommending a return to the policy of the Commonwealth of promoting corn exports.[106] The reasoning behind it was spelt out in the preamble of the subsequent act of 1663 "for the encouragement of trade": only if agriculture were profitable would waste land be brought into cultivation, more corn and cattle produced, more people employed, and "other lands also rendered more valuable". In consequence, this act, among other measures, allowed the exporting, and engrossing, of cereals and pulses when internal prices were at a specified low level, while charging a high duty on corn imports at the same time. In the words of N. S. B. Gras, "this was the first time in English history that English agriculture was protected by high import corn duties".[107] Thereafter, the corn bounties that were introduced from 1673 onwards, in his view, carried the same policy to its logical conclusion.

Before this happened, however, the government pressed its existing policy further by a proclamation in 1667 lowering yet again the prices at which grain exports were allowed, suspending all imports by proclamation in 1669, and then by statute in 1670 abolishing altogether the floor prices governing exports and laying down ceiling prices for imports. This intervention occurred in the course of the debates on the fall of rents and decay of trade. Such a policy, still following familiar lines, was judged by Sir William Coventry good, but "no way sufficient for the entire cure".[108] The Lords committee on the depression heard repeatedly in 1669 of the plenty of corn – "the usual plenty", as Josiah Child expressed it.

Since domestic supplies seemed secure, only two alternative policies presented themselves: a larger overseas market had somehow to be found for the surplus, or domestic corn production had to be reduced. Such a reduction in corn growing was indeed discussed: Sir William Coventry, c. 1670, favoured as alternative uses for land the planting of woad and the growing of hemp and flax, while Sir Richard Haines in 1674 recommended only hemp and flax.[109] As we shall see below, these policies for encouraging

[106] CJ, VIII, 1660–7, pp. 350, 467; CSPD, 1661–2, p. 602; R. B. Outhwaite, 'Dearth and Government Intervention in English Grain Markets, 1590–1700', EcHR, 2nd ser., XXXIII, 3, 1981, pp. 389–406.

[107] Statutes of the Realm, V, pp. 449–52 (15 Chas II, c. 7); Gras, Evolution of the English Corn Market, pp. 148–9.

[108] R. R. Steele, Bibliotheca Lindesiana, V, A Bibliography of Royal Proclamations of the Tudor and Stuart Sovereigns...2 vols., Oxford, 1910, I, nos. 3,503, 3,525; T & C, pp. 160–2, 80; Outhwaite, op. cit., p. 392.   [109] T & C, pp. 72, 70, 80–1, 90–1.

industrial crops were advocated for other reasons too. But the immediate solution chosen to alleviate the discomfiture of corn growers was to promote the export of grain by awarding bounties to farmers. It was a radical new departure in English policy, and yet, surprisingly, it was not a subject of pamphlet debate. D. G. Barnes searched hard in 1930 to find any discussion in print alongside the many pamphlets on trade and industry, but found none.[110] Grand explanations for this innovation have since been offered by historians, but it seems fairly certain that bounties were awarded in direct imitation of French policy. Benjamin Worsley pointed out in evidence to the Lords committee in 1669 that "the French have set up a Council of Trade and the king hath given a very large bounty and largesses to encourage trade". This was a reference to Colbert's policy which was now actively assisting French industrial enterprises to gain a footing in overseas markets by granting bounties on exports. The best-known case was Colbert's support of the languishing Languedoc cloth industry, which had been edged out of the Levant trade by the English: in 1667 and 1668 he arranged to pay a bounty of 10 *livres* on every cloth exported to the Levant, and in 1669 this was increased to 16 *livres*; the system of bounties continued well into the eighteenth century. Plainly, the device made its impression on English planners, and the granting of bounties to encourage corn exports neatly adapted French industrial experience to solve English farming problems.[111]

The act of 1672 giving bounties was designed to continue in force for five years, but the evidence for actual bounty payments shows them to have been paid up to 1680–1, though they temporarily lapsed thereafter.[112] They were not simply a gift to corn producers, but were intended to assist landowners to pay heavier taxation. The king needed £1¼ million in 1672 for his "extraordinary occasions", and, in imposing this burden on the gentry as the class bearing the main brunt of the levy, parliament agreed to award corn bounties in order to give husbandmen a better price for their corn, "now...already at a very low rate", whereby they could pay their rents; the "decay of rent" would thus be arrested, and landlords would then be better able to pay the taxes due on land.[113] There seems no reason to doubt this simple explanation for the new policy; it then served as a precedent when the problem of low corn prices again came up for discussion in parliament in 1688. In 1687 farmers had received a wheat price that was 33 per cent

[110] D. G. Barnes, *A History of the English Corn Laws from 1660–1846*, London, 1930, repr. New York, 1965, p. 16.
[111] T & C, p. 71; C. W. Cole, *Colbert and a Century of French Mercantilism*, 2 vols., New York, 1939, *II*, pp. 134, 156–8, 512–15.
[112] A. H. John, 'English Agricultural Improvement and Grain Exports, 1660–1765', in D. C. Coleman and A. H. John, eds., *Trade, Government and Economy in Pre-Industrial England*, London, 1976, p. 47; Barnes, *op. cit.*, p. 10.
[113] *Statutes of the Realm*, *V*, pp. 780–2, repr. in T & C, pp. 162–4.

below the price received in 1684.[114] The act of 1689 revived the payment of bounties (1 Wm & M., c. 12), stating that corn exports had proved a great advantage to landowners and trade and should be renewed. When a new land tax was imposed on landowners in 1693, the renewal of bounties was regarded as the *quid pro quo* – a compensation for land tax.[115]

When bounty payments started in 1674, contemporaries immediately noticed a boom in corn exports at outports such as Truro and Falmouth in the south-west and Bridlington in East Yorkshire, and even feared shortages and high prices at home.[116] But the more considered verdict of their long-term effect was that bounties stabilized the price level, and so gave much-needed encouragement to corn producers, while ensuring a steadier supply of corn to consumers. Between 1660 and 1672, before the bounty system started, probably no single English port exported more than 2,000 quarters of grain, at least officially, in any year. After 1674, the first year in which bounties were paid, King's Lynn, a well-placed port for disposing of East Anglian grain, exported 23,000 quarters, and Yarmouth, similarly well situated, over 24,000 quarters.[117] Between 1675 and 1677, when Holland and France were at war, and demand overseas was exceptional, bounties were paid on 217,976 quarters of grain from the outports and on 85,949 quarters from London. The largest number of such shipments from London (149 out of 355, or 42 per cent), went in 1677–8 to Spain and the Canaries, the remainder to America, the Straits, Scandinavia, and the Mediterranean. Markets served by the outports were Ireland reached from Bristol, and Norway from King's Lynn. Sums paid in bounties in 1675–6 show the largest exporting outports to have been (in order of importance) Hull, King's Lynn, Yarmouth, Dover, Exeter, Southampton, Boston, and Ipswich.

In short, the corn-exporting areas benefiting most from bounties in these two exceptional years were plainly the most highly specialized corn regions of the east and south, having accessible coastal ports. These were the East Riding of Yorkshire, Lincolnshire, East Anglia, the Kentish North Downs, the Hampshire downlands, and south Devon. The mixed farming regions of central England, some of which were increasing their corn production, but had inferior transport facilities, almost certainly did not benefit much from bounties in the 1670s, but may well have shared more of this cash after 1700 when exports underwent more sustained and, indeed, remarkable

---

[114] W. G. Hoskins, 'Harvest Fluctuations and English Economic History, 1620–1759', AHR, XVI, 1, 1968, p. 30.

[115] Bounties as a recompense for land tax are mentioned in a pamphlet published 75 years later, in 1768. See John, 'English Agricultural Improvement', pp. 47, 65 n. 9. This verdict on bounties does not accord with that of some historians, who have seen them as a measure to encourage more corn. Cf. C. H. Wilson, *England's Apprenticeship, 1603–1763*, London, 1965, p. 149.

[116] CSPD, 1675–7, pp. 377, 403, 433, 379.

[117] E. Lipson, *The Economic History of England*, 3rd edn, 3 vols., London, 1943, *II*, p. 458; Wilson, *op. cit.*, p. 148; Gras, *op. cit.*, p. 113.

expansion. They reached 2.8 million quarters in the ten years 1700–9, and moved upward especially rapidly in the 1730s, to reach over 6 million quarters per decade between the 1740s and the 1760s.[118]

In years of poor harvest, the government readily used its powers to curb or prohibit exports of grain, as well as malt and liquors using grain, but the period of restraint was made as brief as possible. After 1680 such emergencies arose on only four occasions, in 1699, 1709, 1728, and 1740. After one year's ban on export from January 1699, which meant the suspension of bounties also, opinion was exactly divided in the Commons for and against a renewal of the ban, and the Speaker's vote was needed to allow the bill even to be read. When once it was read, the bill was firmly rejected by fifty-eight votes, as was a proposal to continue suspending the payment of bounties.[119] When the next ban on exports was needed, in November 1709 (see AHEW V, ii, p. 830), it provoked vehement objections from the grain producers in East Anglia, who claimed in the last twenty years (i.e. since 1689) to have become heavily dependent on the export of malt to foreign countries. This was evidently more profitable than exporting grain for bread, and it made use of some poor quality barley, which had to be malted and disposed of quickly if it was not to go entirely to waste. One petition from Norfolk went so far as to maintain that barley was the only cereal which brought any profit to the county's grain growers.[120] The ban on grain export nevertheless passed into law (8 Anne, c. 2). and again it included malt and liquors, but lasted only a year.[121]

Nearly twenty years passed after this emergency before the government needed to intervene again to safeguard domestic grain supplies. High prices in 1727–8 prompted another general ban on exports, although the shortages of grain were not uniform throughout the country (see Appendix III, Table I). And by 1729 prices had fallen again.[122] Ten years later, in a worse crisis,

---

[118] Gras, op. cit., pp. 114–16, 418–19; John, 'English Agricultural Improvement', pp. 48–9; D. Ormrod, 'The English Grain Export Trade: The Appropriation and Distribution of Food Supplies within a System of Capitalist Agriculture, 1700–1760', pp. 5, 8–9. I wish to thank Dr Ormrod for allowing me to make use of this unpublished account. For an example of the large increase in grain, as well as malt, exports from one outport, Chichester in Sussex, between 1710 and 1750, see J. H. Andrews, 'The Port of Chichester and the Grain Trade, 1650–1750', Sussex Arch. Coll., XCII, 1954, pp. 102–3.

[119] CJ, XII, 1697–9, pp. 355, 450, 466–7; XIII, 1699–1702, pp. 138, 167, 172, 179, 181–3; Statutes of the Realm, VII, p. 454 (10 Anne, c. 3), p. 456 (10 Anne, c. 4), p. 544 (11 Anne, c. 1). For a special appeal in Nov. 1699 from Portugal to be allowed to import grain from England and more especially from Ireland, see CSPD, 1699–1700, p. 285. For a slightly different explanation of the arguments from E. Anglia, see Bodleian Library, f. Θ 665, no. 9, f. 656. The petition was alleged to emanate from Kent and Essex, as well as from Suffolk and Norfolk, whose barley was too damp to be fit for brewing or distilling, but could be dried and exported, and would serve as bread for the poor overseas, especially in Portugal. The petitioners appealed to be allowed to export beans, oats, and barley, not wheat.

[120] CJ, XVI, pp. 214–15, 222, 227.   [121] Statutes of the Realm, IX, p. 177.

[122] UCNWL, Penrhos i, 807; CJ, XXI, p. 309; LJ, XXIII, pp. 418, 421. For the consequences

unusually prompt action was taken in anticipation of a bad harvest in 1740. The clamour against expected high prices began in July, and Orders in Council were speedily issued against the engrossing of corn. Some gentry showed considerable concern, and took their own private measures: in Herefordshire they joined together to subscribe money to buy corn and supply it to local labourers at reduced rates; the price charged to the poor was set at 6–7s. when the current market price for wheat was 8–9s. per bushel. Such high prices prompted legislation to halt exports for the year, but by 1741 prices had fallen below average (they were to fall even more sharply the following year), and the ban was lifted.[123]

Thus, special measures to protect the grain consumer were not often agreed. As for the survival of grain growers, exports helped to keep them in business in years of fair harvests, and were especially effective when other exporting countries were struck down by a bad season. English farmers exploited such an advantage in 1734. One writer from Wiltshire was confident that recent large exports of corn had been responsible for raising local grain prices from the abysmally low price of 2s. a bushel to 4s.; farmers on Salisbury Plain had large stocks of old grain awaiting a more favourable turn, and had quickly seized the chance to dispose of between 2,000 and 7,000 bushels. Surveying land values on the Isle of Wight in 1737, Sir John Oglander of Nunwell firmly believed that if foreign demand for English grain failed for two years "the present rent of land must be sunk".[124]

The increase of exports was achieved despite severe competition in overseas markets. A careful analysis of "the corn affair" prepared in 1734 by a Pembrokeshire man, William Allen, dwelt on England's difficulties in the export trade. Ireland and the Baltic countries had an advantage over English farmers in their cheaper labour costs. The American Plantations too were a threat to Englishmen, for they traded their grain to the Straits, Lisbon, and Ireland. It was true that now and then crop failures in supplying countries helped English farmers for a season, but these random windfalls were no substitute for protection of a more permanent kind. Protection seemed the only answer, and was in line with the recipes offered to other sectors of the economy. So corn bounties continued (though they were not increased as William Allen wished), and other preferential terms were offered to exporters of malt, and of liquors using grain.[125] Whether parliament foresaw the full consequences of its financial concessions to exporters is doubtful. They led to all kinds of manoeuvres and innovations in the drink trades. But the net

of this ban on export in west Yorkshire, see the letter from Thos March at Bilbrough in March 1729, alleging that the act against distilling Geneva had barred the use of 100,000 qtr of wheat and barley that would have been exported, reduced barley prices from 30s. the year before to 11–15s. that year, and made it impossible for farmers to pay their rents – Leeds Archives Dept, He 37(a).

[123] UCNWL, Penrhos i, 587; i, 883; Barnes, op. cit., p. 16.
[124] Clwyd RO, D/GW534; Isle of Wight RO, OG/72/25.
[125] W. Allen, Ways and Means to Raise the Value of Land, London, 1736, pp. 12–16, 32, 42–5.

result was to expand a market for grain growers that was not confined to those growing the best-quality crops.

(b) Beer and spirits

Beer exports had been permitted by the act of November 1656, in order to encourage a flourishing trade in foodstuffs, but the consequences of this liberating measure are not easily investigated.[126] Beer brewing had undergone a major revolution in the period 1500–1640, as hopped beer superseded ale, and brewing, which had been done in villages in the Middle Ages, especially by alewives, became an urban occupation. Breweries, in consequence, tended to become larger business enterprises, making barley purchases on contract and with increasing discrimination. Their scale of operation would indicate an ability to trade overseas, if opportunity offered. That home consumption rose steadily must be inferred from the increase of population and the fact that more people became engaged in dusty, dirty, thirst-producing industrial occupations that only alcohol could assuage. But when the act to encourage overseas trade was passed in 1663, it did not sanction the export of beer along with grain. That proposal came to mind only when parliament discussed measures to counteract the decay of rents and trade in the later 1660s. Then the proposal to allow beer exports won ready support; additional members of parliament were added to the committee framing the legislation, and finally beer, ale, and mum were all included in the statute of March 1670.[127]

When the act of 1670 was about to expire in 1676, its continuation won approval, and it was re-enacted yet again in 1685.[128] By 1692 Ireland was on the way to becoming a not inconsiderable recipient of English beer, and a request came from Whitehall (from the earl of Nottingham) for exact information on the quantity of ale and beer sent there.[129] The Secretary for War may have been entertaining the idea of raising the export duty, but in the end it was the excise which was greatly increased in 1693 to pay the costs of the naval and armed forces needed for service in 1694. Thereafter exports to Ireland improved gently until the 1790s, then surged ahead, and reached over 100,000 barrels per annum in the 1790s, only to fall away to nothing by 1820, when the Irish brewers managed to brew their own.[130]

[126] Firth and Rait, *Acts and Ordinances of the Interregnum*, II, p. 362. But for beer exported to Ireland from Southampton, see the port book of 1648–9 – PRO, E 190/825/6. The evidence of export to Ireland from Chichester, Sussex, is mystifying. The malt trade to Ireland was buoyant in the Civil War period but not at any other time, judging by the port books. Yet two nineteenth-century authors claimed that great exports of malt and beer to Ireland founded the wealth of four principal Sussex families. Relying on the accuracy of the port books, J. H. Andrews discounts this story. See J. H. Andrews, *op. cit.*, pp. 99–100.

[127] CJ, IX, 1667–87, pp. 138, 150, 152, 153, 172, 178, 184, 186, 193, 215, 217; *Statutes of the Realm*, V, pp. 685–6.

[128] CJ, IX, 1667–87, pp. 404, 660, 682, 720, 744; *Statutes of the Realm*, VI, pp. 21–2.

[129] CSPD, 1691–2, p. 472. It is noteworthy that the Irish Cattle Act of 1667 was said to have diminished sales of English hops and beer to Ireland – Lipson, *op. cit.*, III, p. 200.

[130] CJ, XI, 1695–7, p. 81. Beer exports from London from Michaelmas 1662 to Michaelmas

Another way of consuming more corn in these years of abundance was to make stronger beers of many new kinds, which used larger quantities of barley; this was a noticeable trend in the later seventeenth and early eighteenth centuries. Yet another was to make brandy, *aqua vitae*, and spirits. At the beginning of the seventeenth century, these had been valued as medicines; now they were coming to be regarded as daily refreshment. Hence the stimulus given in England (and in other European countries too) to the distilling and export of spirits. It caused one pamphleteer in 1736 to regard this use of grain as a veritable lifesaver: "Whatever would become of our corn injured by bad harvests were it not for distilling?" he asked.[131]

The activity of distillers, then, rose noticeably in this period, and the value of using up grain in this way was officially recognized in William III's reign: the government chose to attack French trade in 1688 by, among other things, prohibiting the import of French brandies and spirits (1 Wm & Mary, c. 34), and in the following year explicitly encouraging the use of malted English corn in spirits (2 Wm & Mary, c. 9) "for the greater consumption of corn and the advancement of tillage". The encouragement lay in charging a particularly low duty of 1d. per gallon on low wines (the first liquid coming off the distilling process) from malted corn, compared with higher duties of 3–12d. on low wines from other materials. Furthermore, it encouraged exports by allowing a drawback of 3d. per gallon on all spirits made from malted corn sent overseas.[132]

Thus, the gin drinking of this age was not an altogether accidental social development; it was positively promoted by those who wished to help English grain farmers, and by its legislation the government assisted them generously. Furthermore, from 1697 onwards, the excise paid by all maltsters on malt destined for domestic consumption was repaid on whatever quantities were sold overseas. This 'drawback' reduced the price of English malt in Holland to a level lower than that at which the Dutch could make it from barley bought in the Baltic. In consequence, English malt exports surged ahead. The Dutch, in effect, were receiving subsidized malt for their breweries and distilleries, at the expense of the English taxpayer. But farmers in eastern England were more than content, for they had a reliable outlet for their barley, and one which did not insist on the highest quality grain. More profitably still, some English maltsters resorted to the device of swelling the malt artificially, by which means they received more in drawback than

1663 were said to be 568 tons, worth £2,272. This was very much less than the value of *aqua vitae* exported (£10,615 8s.) – BL. Add. MS 36,785. For later developments, see P. Mathias, *The Brewing Industry in England, 1700–1830*, Cambridge, 1959, pp. 151–5.

[131] Allen, *op. cit.* For Poland's output of spirits, see W. Kula, *An Economic Theory of the Feudal System*, London, 1976, p. 137, citing an eighteenth-century gentleman: "In our country the vodka distilleries could be called mints, because it is only thanks to them that we can hope to sell off our grain in years when there is no famine."

[132] I thank Dr Peter Clark, who is my informant on stronger beers. On spirits, see CJ, XXIII, pp. 583–4; *Statutes of the Realm*, VI, pp. 98, 236. See also *CSPD*, 1700–2, pp. 557–8.

the sum originally paid in excise. By 1717 this ruse was especially prevalent in East Anglia, whence so much barley and malt was being shipped to Holland, but it was checked (though not ended) in 1726 when the duty on malt was abolished.[133]

The help to barley growers by this development of the overseas trade in malt before 1726 is indicated in malt exports in the year Christmas 1702 to Christmas 1703. Malt exports amounted to 123,291 quarters, whereas wheat exports amounted to 103,835 quarters and barley to 71,523 quarters.[134] In 1707–8 exports from the outports for one year were similarly far larger for malt (83,923 quarters) than for any other grain, the next nearest quantity being 30,488 quarters for wheat.[135] After the abolition of the malt duty in 1726, malt exports fell back, while those of barley increased; but after 1745 both moved up sharply to the end of the period.[136]

Though distilling started as an offshoot and prop of the farming business, it developed into a major industrial enterprise in this period, generating fierce controversies among the many different participants within it. It was still a highly experimental business, and better and cheaper ways of distilling spirit had large consequences for the different interested parties, including not only grain farmers, but pig farmers as well. The ramifications were surprising and unforeseen. Legislation in 1732–3 that was intended to encourage English distilling from corn, and which set out a fresh tariff of drawbacks and bounties to encourage the export of spirits gave a financial advantage to distillers who used unmalted, rather than malted corn. This then had the effect of reducing the demand for grain, for 75 quarters of barley could now do the work of about 95 quarters of barley turned into malt. The chief complainants against this new development were farmers and maltsters from the south-eastern counties of Middlesex, Essex, Surrey, and Kent, presumably some of the chief suppliers to the distilleries. But their protests revealed issues more complex than those touching grain farmers' interests alone. Spirits made from unmalted barley were stronger, and so could be very cheaply diluted with the addition of water, though this, it was argued, made an inferior spirit, less likely to find a market abroad. Nevertheless, it was cheaper. Moreover, unmalted barley produced a larger quantity of waste grains for fattening pigs, which further lessened the quantity of grain needed to fatten pigs in the normal way, and injured country pig producers. One distiller acknowledged fattening 600 to 700 hogs at a time, at a much cheaper rate than could country farmers. Yet such carcasses were not thought so suitable for salting as those fed on beans and peas in the farmyard. Country-fed pork was worth 2s. 6d.

[133] *Statutes of the Realm, VII*, pp. 247–57 (8 & 9 Wm III, c. 22); Ormrod, *op. cit.*, pp. 13–22.

[134] *House of Lords Papers, NS VI*, 1704–6, p. 107.

[135] *House of Lords Papers, NS VIII*, 1708–10, p. 306.

[136] B. R. Mitchell with Phyllis Deane, *Abstract of British Historical Statistics*, Cambridge, 1962, p. 96.

a stone, whereas that fed on distillers' wash was worth no more than
1s. 6d.[137]

The issue was argued out again in 1744, when more opinions were voiced
for and against, and more facts adduced. By this time it was said that
three-quarters of all Kent corn passing to London was destined for the
distillers. Kentish objections to the use of unmalted grain were backed up
by the Norfolk farmers, and in 1745 all were rehearsed by the farmers of
Kent, Surrey, Middlesex, Buckinghamshire, and Northamptonshire.[138]
Clearly, more unmalted corn was being used than ever. Whereas two-thirds
of all corn used for spirits had been malted in the years between 1726 and
1731, by 1744 only one-fifth was malted. The unmalted grain enabled the
distillers to fatten many more pigs; one witness had seen 2,000 hogs in a
distiller's yard at Deptford, "kept always drunk", and fattened in something
like twelve to thirteen weeks (in 1740 they were said to require sixteen weeks'
fattening by the distillers). In spite of their softer, inferior fat, and their poorer
keeping qualities, especially in summer, distillers' hogs ruled prices in the
market: bacon had fallen in price from 28d. per stone in 1722 to 20d. by
the 1740s, causing some conventional farmers to give up feeding and breeding
pigs altogether. The Navy Victualling Office, which always accepted the
lowest tender for pork, had long since ceased to deal with farmers, and
country-fed pork had become a quality meat, reserved for private families
in London. It was also alleged that marshland farmers (in Essex?) had suffered
severely through their failure to compete in price with the distillers, and
believed that rents had fallen as a result – in one instance from £120 to £80.
The only dissenting voices to these arguments were raised by some yeomen
and farmers from east Kent who claimed that some barley in late and wet
harvests could nevertheless be used unmalted for hogs and horses when
maltsters could not or would not accept it. Moreover, they feared that the
price of spirits would rise if legislation obliged distillers to use only malted
corn; this would reduce home consumption and increase the smuggling of
French brandy. A processing industry, originally encouraged for the benefit
of grain farmers, now gave rise to multiple disputes among distillers,
maltsters, grain farmers producing different quality barleys, graziers, and pig
fatteners, not to mention consumers of high quality versus cheap quality meat.
By 1750 it had also given rise to great social and moral concern at the " great

[137] CJ, XXIII, pp. 583–4, 628–30. The last reference shows that the distillers in fact used a mixture
of unmalted and malted grains, in a proportion of something like 4:1. Nevertheless, it seems to
have been true that 20–30 per cent more grain was used in spirits when malted rather than unmalted
(p. 629). See also P. Mathias, 'Agriculture and the Brewing and Distilling Industries in the
Eighteenth Century', in id., The Transformation of England, London, 1979, pp. 252–5.

[138] CJ, XXIV, pp. 739, 837, 764; XXV, pp. 43–4, 68, 73–7. The report of the parliamentary
committee of 1744 (CJ, XXIV, pp. 833–7) was ordered to be printed, and the resulting pamphlet
is in London Univ., Goldsmith's Library (no. 8,140 in Canney and Knott, Catalogue of the
Goldsmith's Library, I).

and pernicious use of spirituous liquors". Gin drinking might help the farmers but it destroyed many working people.[139]

As the issues involved in bounties and drawbacks became more complex, it is not surprising that lively arguments developed by the middle eighteenth century concerning the effect of these subsidies in enhancing domestic prices and laying heavy burdens on the English taxpayer. The fact remains that traditional corn farms were sustained in business and in hope for a long period by these measures, when their alternative fate could have had very much more damaging consequences for the nation's food supply. The bounties and other concessions may have increased prices, but the poor were not short of bread and beer, and the farmers *were* short of encouragement. Rent arrears and untenanted farms could have been far more serious without these supports. As it was, larger farmers stayed in business (many smaller farmers did not) and they showed a moderate interest in persisting with improvements.[140]

(c) Special crops
The abundance and low price of corn, as we have seen, turned the attention of politicians and political economists to the desirability of using agricultural land for other purposes. One use was for gardening, the high productivity of which had elicited regular comment in the agricultural literature for half a century. John Houghton's pages of his weekly newspaper, *A Collection for Improvement of Husbandry and Trade*, was full of information and recommendations in this period to produce things other than corn and wool, while his advice on books to read, with regular lists of gardeners' names and addresses, kept special crops in the public eye. This was influential among Londoners and also among visitors to London.[141] Horticulture inspired a bill, presented in parliament in February 1696 by Lord Coningsby, MP for Leominster and landowner in Herefordshire, "to encourage the trade of gardening". Nothing is known of the bill's contents, however, and it did not receive a second reading.[142]

Other uses for land lay in growing industrial crops, hitherto imported in large quantities from abroad. Hemp and flax featured most prominently, but there were others: rapeseed for oil and for cattle cake was proving to be a versatile – indeed, indispensable – crop; home-grown madder came and went in favour according to the ups and downs of Dutch prices; and safflower (*Carthamus tinctorius*, or bastard saffron) attracted interest as a scarlet, pink, or rose-coloured dye used in silk manufacture, of which increasing quantities were needed, most of it being imported from around Strasbourg in Germany.

---

[139] CJ, XXIV, pp. 833, 835–6, 764; XXIII, p. 630; *Free and Candid Disquisitions on the Nature and Execution of the Laws of England…with a Postscript relating to Spirituous Liquors*, London, 1751, app.

[140] For a recent survey of this debate, see Ormrod, *op. cit.*, pp. 40–50, 68–70.

[141] See e.g. V, 102 (13 July 1694), p. 3; no. 114 (5 Oct. 1694), p. 3; VIII, 172 (15 Nov. 1695), p. 3.   [142] CJ, XI, 1695–7, p. 461.

Parliamentary discussions on special crops only palely reflected interest and experiment in the farming world, but they illuminate the problem of foreign competition. In fostering special crops England followed in the wake of European countries and, for the most part, did not match their successes because of her high labour costs.

(i) *Hemp and flax.* A bill to encourage hemp and flax growing by stipulating the proportions of land on a farm that must carry these crops was fast on the way to becoming an act in April 1662 when the vexed question of tithe payments was raised (a rate of 1s. per acre was suggested), together with the length of time that the act should last. A proposal of twenty-one years divided the House of Commons and did not secure a majority, and even when seven years was agreed, the bill remained lodged in controversy and lapsed.[143] The same happened in February–March 1663, in December 1664, and in October 1665. In October 1666, when the bill of 1665 was resuscitated, a tithe payment of either 2s. 6d. or 5s. per acre was debated, and 2s. 6d. was finally agreed on. An amendment was also introduced for restraining tenants from growing hemp and flax without their landlord's leave. Yet the session ended and still no bill had passed.[144] Yet another bill was presented in October 1670 and its title agreed in March 1671, but it too disappeared from view. The same happened again in February–March 1677, but on this occasion we have some record of the tone of the debate. In the background loomed the problems of labour shortage and low corn prices (they were now 22 per cent below average as a result of the good harvest of 1676; as one pamphleteer put it, when wheat was less than 4s. a bushel "it is known the farmer cannot live".[145] As some MPs saw the situation, lack of work in the countryside was driving labourers to London, thereby creating such labour shortages on the farms that farmers were having to thresh their own corn. Corn was so cheap, moreover, that no servants would stay their full term in service. By ordering more hemp and flax to be grown, it was thought that much extra work would be created in country areas, thereby keeping labourers at home. Members pointed out that 20s. worth of flax created far more work than £10 of wool; and imported linen was costing the kingdom £150,000, or, as Sir George Downing wildly estimated, £500,000 for French linen alone.

The arguments against the bill concerned the agricultural practicalities. In its provisions it insisted on half an acre of hemp or flax being grown for every hundred acres of land. But some land would not grow hemp; as one member put it, one might as well legislate to grow olives, oranges, or pomegranates. It was necessary to define the regions where such crops were suitable. By

---

[143] CJ, VII, 1660–7, pp. 412, 413, 415, 416.

[144] *Ibid., passim*; HMC, Eighth Report, *House of Lords*, 1665–71, p. 101; CJ, IX, 1667–87, pp. 158, 195, 211, 225. On tithe policy in general, see below, pp. 216ff.

[145] Hoskins, 'Harvest Fluctuations', p. 29; *Harleian Misc.*, IV, p. 468.

far the most incisive criticism came from Mr Swinfen, an MP for Stafford, a major hemp-producing county, saying that neither flax nor hemp was then profitable. "The sowing of it goes out because people make no profit of it. If it were for their advantage, men would turn all their lands to it...Is it imaginable this [bill] can take any effect?" Moreover, since the bill imposed penalties on those who did not sow their due proportion of hemp and flax, MPs guessed that the act would produce far more surveyors, officers who turned a blind eye, and universal penalties than it would yield help for the poor. The wisest judgment came from Sir William Coventry, concluding the debate. He wanted to see more hemp and flax growing, but saw that compulsion was inappropriate. The bill went back to the committee, requesting it to think of inducements and encouragements rather than compulsion.[146] Still it failed to materialize, and the same fate befell another such bill in June 1678. Repeated failures, following, we may guess, repetitious debates, eventually taught a lesson. When a bill to encourage the sowing of hemp and flax came up yet again in November 1691, it was speedily transformed into a bill for better ascertaining the tithes of hemp and flax; it was deemed more effectual to encourage than to compel, and after nearly thirty years of argument, an agreed tithe charge was settled of 5s. an acre.[147] Even then the act of 1691 left some minor problems unresolved which MPs tried unsuccessfully to clear up in 1693. However, the 1691 statute proved adequate, was re-enacted for another seven years in 1699, and re-enacted when necessary to the end of the period.[148]

The measure to encourage hemp and flax growing by fixing tithe payments supplemented a tariff policy, beginning in 1690, which discriminated against foreign linen, and was first and foremost designed to pay the costs of war. In the same year that the tithe charge was re-enacted, 1699, parliament received an eloquent petition from Somerset, from the inhabitants of Yeovil, Wincanton, and district, where flax growing and linen manufacture were thriving, in favour of yet more protective duties against foreign linen. Because of lower wages on the Continent "with which an Englishman cannot subsist", they claimed that English linen was being undercut by the foreign. A strong argument in favour of protection for the English product was that it employed great numbers of poor, and sympathy for this viewpoint was one of the themes running through subsequent discussions of tariff revisions. As a result, duties on foreign linen, which amounted to $7\frac{1}{2}$ per cent before 1690, were gradually increased, reaching 15 per cent by 1704 and on some linens reaching over 50 per cent after 1714. These high tariffs fostered the development of the Irish and Scottish industries as well as the English, and

[146] CJ, ix, 1667–87, pp. 387, 390; Cobbett's Parliamentary History, IV, 1660–88, p. 835.
[147] CJ, ix, 1667–87, p. 502; x, 1688–93, pp. 558, 568, 573, 574, 584; Statutes of the Realm, VI, p. 257 (3 Wm & Mary, c. 3).
[148] CJ, x, 1688–93, pp. 781, 784, 848; Statutes of the Realm, VII, p. 606 (11 Wm III, c. 16).

although much Irish and foreign hemp and flax were imported, and English-grown hemp and flax made only a modest contribution to the total supply of raw materials used in domestic manufacture, they were not insignificant supplementary crops in certain regions and counties, notably Dorset, Somerset, the Lincolnshire fenlands, Staffordshire, Yorkshire, and probably Lancashire.[149]

(ii) *Madder*. Madder growing had inspired considerable enthusiasm in the 1620s because of the high price of the Dutch article. Its growth had started seriously in 1621, encouraged by politicians like George Calvert, James I's Secretary of State, urging experiments on dyers and others interested in the clothing trade (see Chapter 7, pp. 268–9), but it seems to have lost ground, or did not gain more ground, after the later 1630s. Interest revived at the Restoration, however, as is clear from a private bill to encourage madder growing in England, put forward in the House of Commons by James Smith the younger in 1664. The bill was set aside, but the same man, as later litigation bears witness, went ahead undeterred, growing madder on a considerable scale in the Wisbech area. No further official attempt to promote madder was made until Dutch madder prices became exorbitant in the 1750s, when the same method of encouragement was found as for hemp and flax in 1757 – the tithe charge was fixed.[150]

(iii) *Safflower*. Safflower seems first to have attracted official attention in 1663 when Eustace Burnby, a projector who had already asked for a patent in 1662 to prepare barley in the French manner, now asked for monopoly rights in growing safflower, a skill he had learned in Alsace.[151] He secured his patent in 1670 and in 1673 was said to have planted 200–300 acres, though whereabouts was not stated. His fields may have lain in Oxfordshire, for Robert Plot knew the crop to be grown at North Aston (south of Banbury) by Colonel Edward Vernon.[152] Like other innovations, it was thought to be very profitable: Carew Reynel in 1674 reckoned the net gains at £20–30

---

[149] CJ, xii, 1697–9, p. 406; N. B. Harte, 'The Rise of Protection and the English Linen Trade, 1690–1700', in N. B. Harte and K. G. Ponting, eds., *Textile History and Economic History*, Manchester, 1973, pp. 76–8, 82, 86, 105–6, 109. Some later figures (1782–5) on English flax production, based on the payment of bounties, are given on p. 106 of this article.

[150] CJ, viii, 1660–7, pp. 539, 544.

[151] *CSPD*, 1661–2, p. 480; 1663–4, pp. 217, 378.

[152] HMC, Ninth Report, *House of Lords*, p. 28a (March 1672–3); Bennet Woodcroft, *Alphabetical Index of Patentees of Inventions*, London, 1969, p. 84; Robert Plot, *The Natural History of Oxfordshire*, Oxford, 1705, pp. 157–8. Colonel Vernon was the son of a Derbyshire family, and in 1680 was JP for Staffordshire. He did not hold the manor at North Aston. He was evidently interested in agricultural innovation, for he was said to have been responsible for spreading in England the Nonpareil apple, brought from Normandy to North Aston. I wish to thank the editors of *VCH Oxon.* for this information, and Mr Frank Emery for the notes from Robert Plot's MS showing that he saw Colonel Vernon's field of safflower in June 1674.

per acre. However, the English crop in 1669 was said not to amount to more than 2,000 lb a year, whereas 54,530 lb were being imported. Hence when Burnby promoted a self-interested campaign as grower to check imports by imposing duties on foreign safflower, dyers were quick to denounce the idea. They relied heavily on imports to produce the delicate-coloured carnation pink, rose, and scarlet dyes for silk ribbons, etc., and, having the edge over their competitors at Lyons, they wished to keep it. Nor could they believe that English safflower would ever be produced as cheaply as in Germany, where labourers were paid 1d. and 2d. a day, compared with 8d. and more in England.[153]

Parliamentary debates on safflower were not reported in the journals of Commons or Lords, but the manuscripts of the House of Lords show that some first-hand information on the crop was presented in committee by Burnby. In the event, the crop was left to make its own way without official support. It was mentioned by John Mortimer in *The Whole Art of Husbandry* (1707) as still growing at North Aston and Norton (presumably Chipping Norton) in Oxfordshire, and in 1694–5 some attempt was being made to grow it in Ireland, but it did not gain favour and it disappeared from view in the eighteenth century.[154] Some plausible reasons for its failure were offered in 1683: that the crop was inconvenient because it ripened at the same time as wheat; and that English seed was not as good as German, and continual imports of German seed were expensive. Safflower was also thought to impoverish the land, though this, as we have seen, was never a deterrent to woad and tobacco, so long as the profit was satisfactory. Sources of manure could always be found – at a price.[155]

(iv) *Tobacco*. Tobacco established itself as a field crop in England in 1618, but was banned by the government in 1619 to assist the Virginia colony, whose staple crop was tobacco. This did not prevent its continuing to be grown by poor men on small plots in an increasing number of English and Welsh counties. At various times between 1620 and 1680 it was grown in twenty-six counties of England and Wales and in the Channel Islands. But because it involved only poor men, the government, until the time of the Commonwealth, turned a blind eye. It was only when the Council of State reviewed its commercial policy in the early 1650s that it decided to enforce the law more rigorously (doubtless because of complaints from Virginia), and forbad tobacco growing by act in April 1652. The growers in Gloucestershire immediately protested so loudly that a compromise was

---

[153] Carew Reynel, *The True English Interest*, London, 1674, p. 87; PRO, SP 29/443, no. 43; HMC, Eighth Report, *House of Lords*, p. 134.

[154] J. Mortimer, *The Whole Art of Husbandry*, London, 1707, p. 131; *CSPD*, 1694–5, p. 32.

[155] J. Houghton, *A Collection for Improvement of Husbandry and Trade*, ed. R. Bradley, 4 vols., London, 1727–8, *III*, p. 354. The writer of this account had persuaded "an adventurer" to grow 25 acres at Evesham, Glos.

agreed to in September 1653: they could grow tobacco on payment of an excise. But this was intolerable to the more influential Virginia merchants; the Council of State acquiesced, therefore, in a fresh ordinance in April 1654 ordering the act of 1652 to be fully enforced. After March 1655 no exceptions were allowed, and yet the crop persisted.

At the Restoration the Virginia merchants promptly rehearsed their objections to home-grown tobacco and procured a new act in 1660, and another in 1670–1, prohibiting the crop. The Privy Council kept up its continuous pressure against it for the next twenty-eight years, sending out letters of reminder to the counties where most tobacco was grown – especially Gloucestershire, Worcestershire, Herefordshire, Warwickshire, and Monmouthshire. In the 1660s and 70s troops of horse were regularly used in summer to break down the growing crops. The last Privy Council orders were issued in 1690, when the battle against the tobacco growers had evidently been won. The price of Virginia tobacco had fallen so low that its cultivation in the unreliable English climate was no longer worth while.[156]

(v) *Hops*. Hops had been the subject of three statutes between 1571 and 1604 (in 1571, 1580, and 1604), but received no further attention until after 1700, when some expansion of the acreage must be inferred from parliamentary interest.[157] Ascertaining the tithe of hops had become a vexatious issue, and a bill to settle the charge was suggested in 1702. The tithe of hops was still taken in kind, and the bill probably represented an attempt to establish a fixed money charge. It did not pass, but interested parties, in Kent at least, evidently settled matters for themselves: a money composition had become the normal method of payment by 1751, and growers reacted sharply to a new agitation (possibly emanating from tithe owners at a time when hop prices were buoyant) to revive payment in kind. When we encounter statements, as in 1744, that hopgrounds around Farnham in Surrey let at £7 or £8 an acre, we have clues to the profits from the crop. It explains the statement of a Sussex man, John Fuller, somewhat earlier, in 1736, that "everybody is now in the humour of planting hops". Fuller was treating with a prospective farm tenant who insisted on turning a barn into an oast house and on securing permission to plant one or two acres of hops. Here is another effective illustration of the way farmers clutched at special crops to supplement other enterprises as soon as they felt certain of their financial advantage.[158]

The expansion of beer brewing required the expansion of the hop acreage,

---

[156] J. Thirsk, 'New Crops and their Diffusion', pp. 76–103. For the statutes of 1660 and 1670–1, see *Statutes of the Realm*, V, pp. 297 (12 Chas II, c. 34) and 747 (22 & 23 Chas II, c. 26). The act was renewed in 1685; see *ibid.*, VI, p. 20 (1 Jas II, c. 17). See also AHEW, vol. v, pt 1, ch. 6, pp. 169–70.

[157] A debate on hops in 1656 produced no action – *CSPD*, 1651–9, p. 454. See above, p. 126 and n. 2.

[158] CJ, XIV, p. 11; XXVI, p. 98; GMR, 51/5/67; E. Sussex RO, Sussex Arch. Soc. MSS, RF 15/25, under date 30 July 1736. See also vol. 1 in this series, pp. 285ff.

and demand was so strong that something of a hop-growing mania resulted in the 1730s and more especially in the 1740s. It was a risky crop, but in a good season it was extremely profitable, and in some southern counties it found many enthusiastic growers. In 1711 home-grown hops were made subject to a duty of 1d. per pound weight; this was surely a sign of the flourishing condition of hop growing. It is not surprising that in line with other action the legislature seized on this crop in order to raise its revenues.[159]

(vi) *Conclusion.* Parliamentary debates shed light on one of the major obstacles to the spread of special crops in England. Labour costs were high in comparison with those in Europe. Hence, any plants which could be imported without damage from overseas had the edge over the English product. Hemp and flax production increased modestly, but not spectacularly, for that reason, while madder growing boomed when Dutch prices were high but slumped again when they fell. The only effective way of promoting dye crops and other industrial plants, therefore, was by protective duties against imports. Hemp and flax growing benefited from such measures against foreign canvas and linen, but they sprang more from a consideration of industrial than of agricultural benefits. The special crops that did thrive were hops (which were indispensable in beer) and vegetables and fruits which could not be readily transported by sea and arrive in the same fresh condition as home-grown supplies. The local producer within walking or riding distance of his consumers was king in this market. These explanations do not account for the success of rapeseed, however. Its secret lay in its industrial value: an increasing number of uses were found for it, and it could easily be fitted into ordinary arable rotations, substituting for a less remunerative grain crop. It required more labour than grain, but it employed that labour in otherwise slack weeks of the farming year. It fitted superbly into a system of alternate husbandry, for after several years of pasture the ground was rich enough to grow rape without manure, and it suited the regime of ordinary corn–livestock farmers in more ways than one, for it fed their sheep usefully in autumn or spring.[160]

(d) Fruit trees and fruit drinks

The enthusiasm shown under the Commonwealth for fruit-tree growing persisted at the Restoration and was promoted by John Evelyn's appendix to *Sylva*, entitled *Pomona*. In it he expressed the hope that parliament would order the planting of two or three fruit trees for every acre of land. His hope was not fulfilled, but some manorial customs in the later seventeenth century, like those of Ombersley (Worcs.), show obligations to plant four fruit trees

[159] CJ, XVI, pp. 484, 485, 565, 618, 638, 668.

[160] Gertrud Schröder-Lembke, *Studien zur Agrargeschichte*, Stuttgart, 1978, pp. 188–91; M. Falkus, 'Lighting in the Dark Ages of English Economic History: Town Streets before the Industrial Revolution', in *Trade, Government and Economy in Pre-Industrial England*, ed. D. C. Coleman and A. H. John, London, 1976, pp. 248–73.

for every one cut down.[161] Where parliament effectively promoted the spread of orchards was by encouraging cider exports.

In 1660 cider was not considered an article for export, and in 1670–1 an act allowing the export of beer, ale, and mum omitted any reference to cider. But when the same act came up for renewal in 1676 the inclusion of cider was requested, in the very year that a writer in the *Philosophical Transactions* of the Royal Society claimed that the society's efforts at agricultural improvement, especially at promoting cider orchards, had taken "so good effects in the southern parts of England that they are much enriched thereby".[162]

Cider was not included in the act of 1680 or 1685, but when the measure was re-enacted in 1688 it did include cider.[163] Hopes of marketing more cider were high, and they must be associated with the many experiments in improving its quality which were in full spate in the 1670s.[164] Some Herefordshire cider already went by coastal barque to London in the 1660s, but, as John Beale had bewailed in 1657, "transport from Herefordshire was defective". It could have been transformed if the Wye had been made navigable, and since one of the earliest proposals for river improvement after the Restoration was to make the Wye and Lugg navigable, it is fairly certain that the cider producers supported it.[165] Trading figures have not been assembled as yet to mirror progress thereafter, but, as the excise accounts bear witness, by the eighteenth century cider production for domestic consumption was substantial.[166]

In the later 1690s experiments were being made in distilling brandy from cider.[167] These were stimulated by the sudden cessation of government

---

[161] P. Large, 'Economic and Social Change in North Worcestershire during the Seventeenth Century', unpub. Oxford Univ. D.Phil. thesis, 1980, pp. 40–1.

[162] *Statutes of the Realm*, V, pp. 199, 723 (22 & 23 Chas II, c. 13); CJ, IX, 1667–87, p. 404; *Philos. Trans. Roy. Soc.*, X–XII, p. 796. The writer of this optimistic account of southern England regretted the slow progress of cider orchards in central and northern England.

[163] *Statutes of the Realm*, VI, p. 87 (1 Wm & Mary, c. 22).

[164] See above, p. 130 and below, ch. 7, pp. 292ff; *Statutes of the Realm*, VI, p. 87; J. Beale and A. Lawrence, *Nurseries, Orchards, Profitable Gardens and Vineyards Encouraged*...London, 1677, p. 14.

[165] Evelyn, *Sylva...Pomona*, p. 33; Beale, *Herefordshire Orchards*, p. 32. The first act for improving the rivers Wye and Lugg was passed in 1662 – *Statutes of the Realm*, V, p. 434. Another act was passed in 1696 (7 & 8 Wm III, c. 14). But for objections to this last, see *House of Lords Papers, NS II*, 1695–7, pp. 201–2.

[166] Cider does not appear in goods exported overseas from London from Michaelmas 1662 to Michaelmas 1663 (BL, Add. MS 36,785), but it does appear in other sampled port books. See e.g. shipments from Truro to Plymouth and London, 1690–1, and to Truro from Bristol, 1703–4. (PRO, E 190/1,053/8 and E 190/1,063/11). See also W. Minchinton, 'Cider and Folklore', *Folklife*, XIII, 1975, p. 66, referring to Excise Accounts, 1662–1827, acct no. 11,894, showing quantities of cider sold retail, 1684–1828. The original document is at HM Customs and Excise Library, King's Beam House, London. See also vol. IV of the paperback series, p. 245.

[167] *CSPD*, 1696, p. 390. Captain Wintour claimed to have set up a distillery in 1691 which had paid £17,000 in excise by 1696.

policies promoting the use of corn for this purpose. A ban on the import of *aqua vitae* and other spirits from France had been imposed in 1689, and although an act in 1690 encouraged the distilling of brandy and spirits from home-grown corn in order to make good the deficiency, corn shortages resulting from the bad harvests of the later 1690s bred resentment at its use in distilleries. When an act to prohibit the excessive distilling of spirits and low wines from corn was passed in 1698, men embarked on the distilling of cider.[168]

What impact the campaign to grow more fruit trees made upon the fruit market it is impossible to say. Since the government favoured increasing the duty on imported apples and pears, as, for example, in 1721–2 and 1736, these measures may also have stimulated the laying out of more orchards at home. The impression that orchards were being extended is certainly conveyed by early-eighteenth-century estate archives and farm accounts. This, together with the fact that parliament's debates took cognizance of English fruit and cider in relation to overseas supplies and markets, mirrors the progress that had been made with this branch of farming enterprise since the middle seventeenth century.[169]

(e) Cattle

The fall of rents after 1660 sparked off a major new controversy about policy as it affected livestock production.[170] This aspect of farming had hitherto received little attention from parliament; a statute obliging all men who kept above 120 sheep to keep, as well, 2 kine and 1 calf had been enacted in 1556, but nothing more than this had been done to encourage cattle breeding for a century. Cattle producers were not influential in politics, in contrast to corn growers, who always had the ear of government. Hence the policy introduced in 1663 and 1667 banning cattle imports from Ireland, and so obliging English breeders to rear all replacements for themselves, was a novelty, calling for explanation. Indeed, it might be called a major landmark inasmuch as it denoted a changed official view of England's agricultural economy: grain supply was no longer the only concern; other products of farming were coming to be regarded as essential elements of the whole.

Yet while men's views of agriculture were broadening, the immediate discussion of cattle producers' interests against Irish competition was a tangled

[168] 1 Wm & Mary, c. 34, and 2 Wm & Mary, c. 9. The complex consequences that were feared to follow from this measure are indicated in the protests of the Distillers' Company and the sugar refiners – *House of Lords Papers*, NS II, 1695–7, p. 248. For the 1698 act, see 10 & 11 Wm III, c. 4. For petitions prompted by this bill from distillers using malted corn, see *House of Lords Papers*, NS II, 1695–7, pp. 285–8.

[169] J. E. O. Wilshere, *The Rev. William Hanbury, 1725–1778, of Church Langton, Leics: A Bicentenary Assessment*, Leicester, 1978, p. 4; CJ, XIX, pp. 701, 734; XXII, pp. 816, 881. See AHEW, vol. V, pt I, esp. chs. 6, 9; see also ch. 7 below.

[170] I wish to thank Mr Donald Woodward for his help with this section.

web of muddled ideas and highly debatable imputed interconnections among prices, rents, and agricultural prosperity in general, which cannot easily be sorted into a harmonious relationship. It should, of course, be remembered that the Irish trade did not concern cattle only. Exports to Ireland consisted of many textiles and miscellaneous goods, and, as these were paid for by imports from Ireland, some views on the cattle trade were coloured by vested interests in other branches of commerce. Other opinions owed more to personal enmities towards powerful politicians who had estates in Ireland than to serious thought on the future of agriculture and trade. The debate on cattle was, indeed, muddled; and a further explanation may be that the subject was so novel in parliamentary debate that the issues were not yet fully understood – in the same way that it took many decades in the sixteenth century before the arguments for and against enclosure were clarified.

The passage of the two cattle acts of 1663 and 1667 through parliament, and their impact on the Irish economy, have been described by Carolyn Edie, and their effects on English trade assessed by Donald Woodward. Yet the personalities who pushed them through remain somewhat shadowy, since almost no record of the parliamentary debates of the time remains, and the motives and full consequences of the acts for English livestock producers have yet to be uncovered in all but general terms.[171] The meagre contemporary discussions that do survive deserve careful scrutiny, therefore, for the light they shed on conflicting agricultural interests in the matter.

A deep prejudice against the import of large numbers of Irish store cattle had been voiced in Commons debates in 1621, though contemporaries plainly exaggerated their number. We have seen how economic ideas gestated for decades in the seventeenth century before any action was taken; this time too nothing was done. It should be noted, however, that the main concern at this date was the *loss of money* in payment for Irish cattle, beef, and butter.[172] Those who favoured Irish imports and pointed to the high prices of meat in London had no difficulty in persuading their opponents that these would not be lowered by excluding Irish cattle. Falling land values were also mentioned in this debate, but no indication was given as to which areas of the kingdom were affected. It may have been the south-west, for, in a report of 1621, the subsidy commissioners of Somerset, a county that accepted large numbers of Irish cattle for rearing and feeding, complained specifically of the decay of trade and scarcity of money "occasioned chiefly by the import of Irish cattle".[173] Such protests subsided for the time being, revived momentarily in 1637, but are not known to have appeared on the agenda again until 1656, when they featured at a meeting of the Council of Trade,

---

[171] Edie, *The Irish Cattle Bills*; D. Woodward, 'The Anglo-Irish Livestock Trade in the Seventeenth Century', *Irish Hist. Stud.*, XVIII, 72, 1973.

[172] See above, p. 136; T & C, p. 1; Edie, *op. cit.*, pp. 6–10. Woodward believes the Irish cattle trade increased between 1600 and 1640 – *loc. cit.*, p. 496.   [173] Edie, *op. cit.*, pp. 9–10.

at the same time that an act was being passed to promote the export of all kinds of agricultural produce, including cattle. Still no action was taken against them, and it is more than likely that further enquiries revealed the complementary nature of Irish and English interests in this trade: Irish stores coming into England could, after all, be fattened and re-exported as English beef.[174]

After the Restoration, Irish cattle became entangled again with the earlier preoccupation, namely, falling land values. These had not been mentioned in 1656, doubtless because rents in general had risen sharply in 1651 and 1652 alongside a reduction in interest rates.[175] But now the old linkage was revived, particular attention being directed to the difficulty of letting grasslands for grazing. Some of the loudest complaints now came from a much more politically influential group of landowners in the Home Counties, whose lands had been enclosed and turned over to permanent pasture in the sixteenth century, but who now found that the demand for old grassland was slackening. The truth was that arable farmers elsewhere were finding their own improved summer grass adequate, and were making good hay from their own clover leys.[176]

Nevertheless, discontented landlords of permanent grasslands in southern and eastern England were unwilling to accept this as the explanation of their troubles, for old prejudices against Irish cattle imports were latent, waiting to be invoked. When a review of tonnage and poundage charged in the Book of Rates was undertaken in July 1660, the Commons decided to lay 2s. 6d. per head on all beasts imported from Ireland. In other words, discrimination against Irish cattle had begun: the former rate of 2s. had stood since 1627; now it was being raised to 2s. 6d.[177] It was evidently the subject of some reflection and hesitation, however, for a fresh vote was taken on the following day to decide whether the earlier decision should be reconsidered. The voting was close, 83 being in favour and 86 against. The previous decision was upheld. Four days later, when the Lords returned the bill with their agreement, members again voted on whether they adhered to their former decision. This time the majority in favour of maintaining the earlier decision

---

[174] See above, p. 136.

[175] T & C, pp. 72–3.

[176] For a study of rents on estates in Bucks., Northants., and War., see Margaret Gay Davies, 'Country Gentry and Falling Rents in the 1660s and 1670s', *Midland Hist.*, IV, 2, 1977, pp. 86–96. But see vol. 1 of the paperback series, p. 415 for references to low rent in Wales also in 1670, attributed to the cheapness of corn and scarcity of money. For the support of the Verneys, Buckinghamshire landowners, for the Irish Cattle Act, see D. T. Witcombe, *Charles II and the Cavalier House of Commons, 1663–74*, Manchester, 1966, p. 60.

[177] CJ, VIII, 1660–7, p. 96. The debate on revised customs duties took place in the morning of 20 July 1660, and was interrupted by a message from the Lords. The first decision in the afternoon concerned the rate to be imposed on Irish cattle, and therefore seems to relate to the same debate. For the earlier rates charged on Irish cattle, see Woodward, *op. cit.*, p. 492.

was much greater: 219 were for, and 80 against. Thereafter tonnage and poundage on Scottish cattle were also considered, and a rate of 8d. per head proposed. This time 131 were in favour, but 140 votes were cast against such a levy; Scottish cattle thus escaped any charge.[178]

The different treatment given to Irish and Scotch cattle, of course, opened up many possibilities of evasion. George and Jos. Williamson, in correspondence in December 1660 about the king's future customs receipts, prophesied that if customs on Scottish beasts entering England were abolished, then all Irish cattle would pass into England via Scotland. They estimated the consequent loss of customs at £1,000 p.a., evidently reckoning on a trade, at 2s. 6d. per head, totalling 8,000 cattle. The same figure of £1,000, or even £1,100, p.a. was given in (April) (?) 1661 by the customs commissioners as the likely revenue accruing to anyone who farmed the customs on the Irish cattle trade.[179]

By 1663, much stronger animus against Irish and Scottish cattle had been whipped up, for a clause was inserted in the Act for the Encouragement of Trade (the Staple Act, whose purpose was to encourage tillage and raise land values by encouraging exports and favouring the use of English shipping) laying the prohibitive levy of 40s.[180] per head on all Irish cattle imported between 1 July and 20 December each year, and on Scottish cattle between 24 August and 20 December, while 10s. was charged on sheep from both countries between 1 August and 20 December.[181] Woodward argues convincingly that this clause was intended to stop fat Irish and Scottish livestock coming into England in late summer, but not to stop lean cattle coming in in spring.[182] As such, it was a device endearing itself most to graziers of the south and east, and represented a sound and rational expression of their interests. This interpretation of its intentions is supported by another piece of evidence: when the same restraint was proposed on Scottish cattle, it drew from one MP from Norfolk, Sir John Holland of Quiddenham, a clear-sighted denunciation of the adverse consequences that this ban would have for Norfolk graziers. They did not buy in beasts in spring, but rather relied on buying Scottish cattle at fairs held during September, which they then overwintered on pastures that would feed "none but of the Scotch breed".[183] The speech drew into alliance all graziers who, even though they worked on different feeding systems, wanted to buy lean store cattle and did

---

[178] CJ, VIII, 1660–7, pp. 97, 102, 103; Statutes of the Realm, V, p. 186.

[179] CSPD, 1660–1, pp 408, 577.

[180] Edie, op. cit., p. 11, mistakenly states 20s.

[181] The policy towards sheep is dealt with more fully below; see pp. 190–3.

[182] Woodward, op. cit., p. 499. This purpose was explicitly stated by Heneage Finch in a speech in the Commons in 1666. Recalling the purpose of the clause in the 1663 act, he described it as "the total prohibition of all fat cattle". It met the demands of "those English counties which wanted lean cattle to feed" while still leaving some trade in cattle for the Irish to enjoy – PRO, SP 63/323/193.

[183] Edie, op. cit., p. 12.

not want competition for their fattened beasts. For them the dates in the act were the most controversial item, and there were bound to be differences of viewpoint if some bought Irish and Scottish beasts in the spring to fatten in summer while others bought in autumn for overwintering. A ban for a short summer period would suit them all best.

In the end the clause passed into law as it was originally proposed, and the only recorded opposition, apart from that of the Norfolk MP already mentioned, was that of the Lord Privy Seal, John, Lord Robartes, and the earl of Anglesey in the House of Lords – men with mixed and possibly conflicting interests in Ireland and Wales as well as England. But strangely, the Secretary of State, Henry Bennet, justified the bill to the duke of Ormonde, Lord Lieutenant of Ireland and the richest landowner in that kingdom, as correcting "the infinite prejudice" which cattle imports inflicted on the north and west of England.[184] In other words, Bennet seemed to see this clause in the 1663 act as a measure to help livestock breeders (mostly found in the north and west) rather than graziers (mostly found in the south and east). Yet the timing of the ban during the summer months would clearly have helped the graziers most. Despite the confusion introduced by this comment, other circumstantial evidence points to the conclusion that the clause in the act of 1663 had as its main object help for the cattle graziers in southern and eastern England. Not until 1666 did other interests find voice.

When once the Staple Act passed into law, Irish cattle breeders took prompt evasive action. The policy urged upon them by Lord Anglesey was to stall-feed their cattle in winter and send them over to England between March and June; Lord Ormonde looked to the opening up of other new channels of foreign trade, having in mind, no doubt, stronger ties between Ireland and the Continent.[185] Both pieces of advice were taken, but the first noticeable effect on England was in line with Lord Anglesey's counsel. The act failed to eliminate all Irish imports; it simply altered the shipping season. Cattle shipped to Minehead, for example, were shipped from January onwards instead of waiting till April. Total numbers between 1663 and 1665 were reduced by only 4,000 p.a., from 61,000 to 57,000.[186]

Since the Staple Act of 1663 had hardly staunched the flow of Irish cattle to England, Sir Richard Temple, a Buckinghamshire landowner from grazing country that was much affected by falling rents, brought in another bill in October 1665 totally prohibiting Irish cattle imports. Now he had support from Yorkshire too, from breeders as well as fatteners, neither of whom could compete with low Irish prices: thirty-five men representing the grand jury of Yorkshire complained that Scottish and Irish cattle were being brought in "as a novelty practised only within a few years", which, "being fed, maintained and fatted with far less charge than can possibly be done in

[184] *Ibid.*, pp. 13, 14.   [185] *Ibid.*, pp. 15–16.
[186] Woodward, *op. cit.*, pp. 499–500; Edie, *op. cit.*, p. 21.

England, they fill and glut the markets in the beginning of spring and after in autumn, and undersell those of English breeding and feeding so much that the farmer who formerly furnished other parts must and do give over breeding and are forced to buy for themselves of that sort [i.e. Irish stores?] to their utter undoing, and the grazier cannot sell his fat cattle for the price they cost". The Yorkshiremen asked that Irish cattle be banned even earlier in the summer, and later into the winter, i.e. between June and February, leaving only three open months, from March to May.[187] Plainly the problem had changed complexion; all Irish beasts, lean and fat, were now thought to undermine the living of both breeders and fatteners. The only opponents of the bill were those who valued Irish trade in general and wanted to ensure a continuing exchange of goods, including industrial commodities, between the two countries. Such spokesmen were evidently few when ranged against a united agricultural interest.

At an early stage in the debate the king's ministers, who were lobbied by Irish opponents of the bill, believed that parliamentary opinion was so strongly in favour of Temple's bill that it would undoubtedly pass. Even though Sir Heneage Finch, Solicitor-General, argued that Irish cattle could take no blame for the fall of rents since they had been coming in ever since 1603, his strong words of sympathy for the Irish economy fell on stony ground. Two days later, Finch put his argument about rents still more vehemently: rents had fallen just as much in Norfolk and Suffolk, where high profits had been earned from the import of lean Irish cattle, as in the north and west, which claimed to suffer from Irish competition. The agricultural decline was a national phenomenon, and the fall of rents only one symptom; plague and the Dutch war were more likely causes than Irish cattle. Yet in one short week of debates the bill won the support in the Commons of 80 votes against 68 dissentients, and looked like receiving support in the Lords. Its passage was checked only because Charles II, who was known to oppose the bill, prorogued parliament.[188]

MPs swiftly returned to the subject in September 1666, at the beginning of the new session, when a fresh bill was proffered. The graziers from East Anglia who relied on buying lean Irish stores for fattening forcefully prophesied damage to their interests: Sir Heneage Finch deemed it a selfish measure that would benefit the north and west at the expense of Norfolk, Suffolk, Kent, and Ireland. But the clarity of his argument was clouded by new developments. The king's known opposition to the bill, and parliamentary suspicions towards the influential duke of Ormonde, now imparted a political, faction-ridden complexion to the controversy. The king's need for money to pay for his wars and other extravagancies became contingent upon

[187] Edie, op. cit., pp. 17–18. For the full text of the original document, as cited here, see PRO, SP 29/133, f. 90.
[188] Edie, op. cit., pp. 18–21; Woodward, op. cit., p. 489.

the passing of the Irish cattle bill. Heneage Finch probably got nearest to expressing the truth of the matter when he said that "This whole bill, for matter and forms, is carried on by such secret reasons as neither are, nor can be, openly avowed". Plainly, the best interests of English livestock producers as a whole were no longer at the centre of the argument. English graziers, who had first raised the outcry against Irish cattle, were now, so it was said, "exceedingly perplexed that it [the bill] should pass"; a different desire had taken hold – to curb Irish competition now that Irish soils had shown their ability to yield much the same produce as English soils. More than this, a blow had somehow to be struck at rich noblemen, flaunting their Irish wealth above that of the English nobility.[189]

The cattle bill passed the Commons by 165 votes in favour and 104 against. It also found favour in the Lords, although Lord Anglesey fought hard against it, and the debate was heated, acrimonious, disorderly, and unparliamentary. Those in favour were said to be fewer but more vocal than those who opposed it. In the Lords, as in the Commons, the act had become a pawn in a game inspired by other passions. The duke of Buckingham and Lord Ashley (later Lord Shaftesbury) were in favour of the act, partly to spite the king and his court favourites, partly to protest against the overweening influence of the duke of Ormonde, and partly to ventilate their prejudices against Ireland. Complaints against Scottish cattle resulted in attempts to comprehend them in the bill, but these failed. Many other contentious details took up parliamentary time which would have killed a bill of less universal interest. As it was, the Commons bullied the Lords into agreement, and the king was obliged to withdraw his opposition for fear of losing a vote of supply from the Commons. The Speaker of the House of Commons in presenting the bill for the royal assent worded its justification in such a way as to slur over the differences of interest between cattle breeders and cattle fatteners, also leaving unclear regional differences in men's experience of falling rents. The act was needed, he said, because "the infinite number of foreign cattle that were daily imported did glut our markets and bring down the prices of both our home-bred cattle and our lands". The act was passed to last for seven years, and then until the end of the first session of the next parliament.[190]

The two acts against Irish cattle imports benefited different interests. The difference between them may possibly reflect a change in the volume and structure of the Irish cattle trade between 1663 and 1666, or else a change in the alignment of the interested parties who lobbied parliament between those two dates. The 1663 act was a measure to help graziers, for it charged prohibitive duties at times of the year when the Irish were most likely to be sending fat, or nearly fat, cattle to England. It was not overtly designed to help breeders. Disclosures of interest in the parliamentary debate suggest

[189] Edie, *op. cit.*, pp. 23–6, 55–7.   [190] *Ibid.*, pp. 26–7, 29, 30–5.

that all cattle fatteners wanted the measure, so long as the closed months coincided with their routine of cattle buying. The views of north- and west-country breeders at this time are not made clear; MPs from those areas who opposed the act defended, not the cattle breeders, but the port towns which would lose shipping business. The 1667 act, in contrast, was a very different measure with a different impact, for it banned all Irish cattle, fat and lean. It could still help English graziers by eliminating the competition of fat Irish cattle, but it could harm them even more by substantially reducing the total numbers of lean cattle for purchase at fairs, thereby increasing their price. This was recognized in Heneage Finch's speech in the Commons, and in another speech briefly reported in Cobbett's Parliamentary History. To cattle breeders in England, Wales, and Scotland, on the other hand, it offered entirely new benefits: by excluding all lean Irish cattle, it made them the sole suppliers of stores to the graziers. It is not surprising that in the first years of the act's operation the price of stores rose so high that graziers got no profit out of fattening.[191]

The subsequent history of the Irish Cattle Act has been told mainly from the viewpoint of the Irish, who turned this seemingly heavy blow at their economy to advantage by expanding their cattle and beef trade with the continent of Europe, specializing in the victualling of vessels passing from Europe to America, and expanding sheep and wool production. Seen from the English point of view, its effects were not those anticipated. At first, smuggling continued on such a scale that it is doubtful if the ban was much more than a nuisance. Even when Irish cattle were seized at the ports, and a forfeit paid, they still sold in England at a price that brought profit to the importer. Not until May 1668 was an additional act passed which closed loopholes and much reduced smuggling. Yet Sir Josiah Child, in October 1669, deemed the act ineffectual, and in 1672 a petitioner for a licence to transport 10,000 cattle from Ireland to England claimed that "this is no more than is done every day by stealth, and in smaller numbers". The forfeitures that were paid could in some places amount to large sums: Ottery St Mary in Devon received far more cash in this way than it needed to relieve its poor, and in 1675 £500 was invested in land which was still distributing Cow Charity in the parish in 1916.[192]

The ban on Irish cattle was evaded, but its effect in the long term was considerable. Contemporaries claimed that meat prices rose in anticipation of the passing of the act, but this trend did not last. Indeed, for the next two decades beef prices tended to fall. Those who benefited most were the

[191] PRO, SP 63/323/193; Cobbett's Parliamentary History, IV, p. 338. This record also corroborates the remarks made by the grand jury of Yorkshire that the breeders' complaints (as opposed to the graziers') were recent. "The complaint was of so new a nature that it had never been heard of in England till some few months before this meeting in Parliament; only it had been mentioned in the Parliament at Oxford as a grievance to the northern counties."

[192] Edie, op. cit., pp. 37–42; Woodward, op. cit., pp. 500–1.

English, Welsh, and Scottish breeders at the expense of the graziers of the south Midlands, East Anglia, and the south-east, who were denied a source of cheap leanstock. Sir Edward Dering even attributed the decay of rents in Kent c. 1670 partly to the Irish Cattle Act, without remarking on the irony that the act had originally been designed to correct this very problem: "we are forced to buy at dear rates, and sometimes cannot get wherewith to stock our land unless we will buy lean cattle as dear as we can sell them when fat". Losses were experienced at English ports that had hitherto sold barrelled beef to seagoing vessels, and, indirectly, English farmers felt the draught of competition from larger supplies of Irish wool.[193]

Hopes of lifting the ban on Irish cattle were raised after cattle sickness in some parts of England in the winter of 1673–4 threatened a livestock shortage. A bill to lift the embargo on Irish cattle was compiled at this time, but there is no evidence that it was actually discussed in parliament. It *was* debated at the next opportunity, in spring 1677, when men's opinions were said to vary greatly "according to the different interests of their counties". Sir Edward Dering took the chair at a Grand Committee and may be assumed to have had strong views against the act. The voting showed a lively division of opinion, although those in favour of continuing the act carried the day in committee by 145 to 128, and in the house the following day by 129 to 91. In favour of its renewal were those who wanted to keep up the prices of English-bred lean cattle, while its opponents asked why they should pay inflated prices "solely to enrich the stockbreeders of the northern and western counties". Thomas Papillon, a London merchant and MP for Dover, described the act as an experiment that had not had the expected results, and since eight in ten Englishmen had neither breeding nor feeding land, the majority interest lay in getting cheap food. When the retort came that landowners and farmers bore the main burden of taxation, Papillon replied that of the one-fifth part of the nation that were landowners, owners of feeding lands bore two-thirds of the extraordinary taxes: in other words, if landowners had the right to dictate policy, the heavily taxed graziers deserved more consideration than the lightly taxed breeders.[194]

These arguments were, of course, only a fraction of the full debate, which turned also on England's attitude towards the Irish economy, and the effect the ban was having on the sale of English manufactures to Ireland. A multitude of conflicting interests had to be weighed in the balance. But the issue was not decided in 1679. Delaying tactics were successfully used by opponents of the act and so it lapsed with the end of the parliamentary session in May 1679, leaving the trade free from June 1679 until February 1681. In the interval, cattle imports resumed at a brisk rate. In 1679, 8,062 head of

---

[193] Edie, *op. cit.*, pp. 42–3; T & C, p. 85. Sir Edward Dering's view was echoed by Roger Coke in *Discourse of Trade*, London, 1670, p. 33.

[194] Edie, *op. cit.*, pp. 45–50. A draft bill, dated 1677, is in Derbs. RO, D239/309.

cattle and 37,647 sheep arrived in England and Wales from Ireland; in 1680, 24,116 cattle and 83,452 sheep. Plainly, English demand exceeded the supply, and the Scots had not filled the gap. But in February 1681 the ban fell again when a new act was passed, and fifteen years later English farmers had so accommodated themselves to the situation that John Houghton declared in 1696: "'tis plain our people find so great an advantage that even the talk of repealing that act is no ways heard". The Irish Cattle Act continued in force until 1759 – nearly eighty years. Scottish cattle continued to be imported, however, for a bill before parliament in 1681 to ban them failed to pass.[195]

In the long term, the Irish Cattle Act does not seem to have raised meat prices unduly; or, at least, the influence of the act cannot be separated from other factors. While the act seemed likely to make meat more expensive – Cheshire graziers confidently expected this in 1680, for example – in the event, contemporaries thought that subsequent increases in cattle production in England particularly, through the drainage of the fens and improvements in the quality of grasslands elsewhere, cheapened it again.[196] But the act certainly redistributed the profits from livestock production, giving more to the breeders of the north and west, and leaving less for the graziers of south and east. This, in company with other economic developments in northern and western England, and the relatively low level of taxation imposed there, accelerated agricultural improvements, especially of grassland. In a laboured calculation of the existing, and likely, revenues of the kingdom by Charles Davenant in 1695, he concluded that the Irish Cattle Act was wholly beneficial to the northern and western counties; it had improved the value of their land, but was "hurtful to the rest of England". He was also convinced that the low proportions of national taxation paid in the north and west were due to the political strength and eloquence of their MPs in preserving the old system. Whether this also accounted for their success in maintaining the Irish Cattle Act in operation until 1758/9 remains unclear.[197] Their success in getting the act passed in 1667 seems rather to have been a happy accident for them, partly attributable to factious intrigues in parliament, partly to prejudices against Ireland that had little to do with the interests of pasture

---

[195] Woodward, op. cit., pp. 502–3, 519; Edie, op. cit., p. 50. The slack demand for Welsh cattle at Shrewsbury in June 1679 was attributed to "the transporting of the Irish cattle" – Herts. RO, D/ELW, E60. For the level of Scottish cattle imports, see D. Woodward, 'A Comparative Study of the Irish and Scottish Livestock Trades in the Seventeenth Century', in L. M. Cullen and T. C. Smout, eds., Comparative Aspects of Scottish and Irish Economic and Social History, 1600–1900, Edinburgh, 1977, pp. 150–4. Woodward does not believe that the Scots appreciably expanded their sales of cattle to England after 1667. For John Houghton's remark, see Collection, ed. Bradley, II, p. 3.

[196] Cheshire RO, DCH/K/3/4; CSPD, 1675–6, pp. 369–70.

[197] T & C, pp. 807, 800–1. Edie thinks these counties were over-powerful in parliament – op. cit., pp. 53–4.

farmers in the highland zone, and partly to muddled ideas about the livestock business, which was a complex and unfamiliar subject at Westminster.

The ban on Irish cattle fostered English livestock production by means of a protective policy at the expense of Ireland. Other legislation was passed in 1670 (at the time of the debate on the decay of rents and trade) on the same principles that guided corn policy, encouraging the export of livestock and livestock products by abolishing duties (22 Chas II, c. 13).[198] It followed the same lines as the act of 1656; and the same purpose, of encouraging the breeding and feeding of cattle, was reiterated, and the same measures adopted in 1691 (3 Wm and Mary, c. 8). Whether these statutes had any appreciable effect on quantities exported, it is impossible to say. One would not expect the London port records to provide any fair guide to national exports, and the records of individual outports await examination. Livestock products like butter, cheese, and bacon were undoubtedly an item in export trade, but it seems likely that other meat and live cattle featured only exceptionally.

In 1696, when the war against France had to be financed, some consideration was given to the idea of an excise on livestock (cattle, horses, sheep, and pigs) and livestock products, to be paid when the beasts and other commodities changed hands at public markets or fairs.[199] This was a time when every item in general trade was liable to be viewed as a source of revenue. But the proposal came to nothing. The livestock side of the English farming business, therefore, received no further government attention until the epidemic of cattle distemper reached England from the continent of Europe.[200]

Englishmen had plenty of warning of the impending cattle plague (rinderpest), for it was endemic in certain areas of Europe: in 1683 the Royal Society received a report on it, and when a more serious outbreak occurred in 1711, Englishmen were quickly made aware. When it reached England in July 1714, therefore, the English already knew something of the countermeasures used on the Continent.[201] A detailed contemporary account of action taken to combat the spread of the disease affords a remarkable illustration of how effectively agricultural policy could be decided at this time, not by MPs debating at length in parliament, but by government officials, centrally and locally, using their influence without compunction in a spirit of benevolence and determination. In emergency, they did not hesitate

[198] *Statutes of the Realm*, V, pp. 685–6; VI, p. 311.

[199] For an elaborate calculation of the expected revenues, see Somerset RO, DD/SF 2,805, 2,870.

[200] Except for an act in 1714 (a low price year for cattle, which makes the act difficult to explain) to prevent the killing and stealing of cattle – *House of Lords Papers, NS X*, 1712–14, pp. 354–5. Similar complaints were discussed in the Commons in January 1741, when the graziers of Middlesex, Essex, Surrey, and Kent were most affected – CJ, XXIII, pp. 572, 585–6.

[201] C. F. Mullett, 'The Cattle Distemper in Mid-Eighteenth Century England', *Agric. Hist.*, XX, 3, 1946, pp. 145–6. I have benefited from Dr John Broad's recent thorough reappraisal of this episode in AHR, XXXI, 2, 1983.

to harangue and bully farmers, without always knowing for certain that their assurances and promises would be implemented.

The man appointed to investigate the infection, which first attacked livestock in Islington, was Thomas Bates, a surgeon in the king's household, who practised in London, moved in court circles, and was asked to undertake this task by the Lords Justices, the seven "kinglings" who had originally been appointed by William III to administer the realm in his absence after Mary's death. Bates received his authority from Lord Harcourt, the Lord Chancellor. Four justices of the peace for Middlesex, accompanied by Bates, interviewed the three farmers affected, and received at first hand descriptions of the symptoms of the disease. Having talked also with veterinary experts, they issued stern instructions on how to proceed in the future. Some of the sick cows were to be housed with other livestock in order to see whether the contagion would affect other animals. Bates promptly reported to the Lords Justices the opinions he had gathered on the outbreak, and was ordered to deliver next day written proposals for action. His suggestions were as follows: (a) all cows in the herds of the three affected farmers were to be bought, killed, and burned; (b) cattle houses were to be washed clean, fumigated, and left unused for three months; (c) fields were to be left for two months before being grazed again; (d) persons looking after sick cattle were not to have any dealings with those that were healthy; (e) all future infections were to be reported and dealt with in the same way; (f) cowkeepers were to keep their animals in small herds of ten to twelve animals in a field, and to be allowed such monetary compensation for complying with these proposals as the Lords Justices should think fit. The day after receipt of Bates's proposals, the Lords Justices gave the four Middlesex JPs authority to adopt them, and to pay 40s. compensation for every sick cow that was burnt. When the infection nevertheless spread elsewhere, they summoned all cowkeepers in the county, gave the same orders, and promised the same compensation. To ensure speedy action, the 40s. was promised only to those who destroyed their cows within twenty-four hours of their sickening. Some cowkeepers were discontented with the regulations, and tried to sell their animals at distant markets. But the JPs forestalled this manoeuvre by ordering butchers to watch the grounds of such men, count the numbers of their animals every morning, and follow those which were sent to market. At the market they prevented them from being sold by disclosing whence the animals came. The justices also encouraged cowkeepers to report outbreaks of infection promptly by holding out hopes of a charitable collection. But they insisted that only those who complied strictly with their directions would have any benefit from it. Accordingly, they kept a daily account of the conduct of each cowkeeper, and so allowed or disallowed their claims to compensation.[202]

Not surprisingly, it proved difficult to persuade cowkeepers that this

[202] Thomas Bates, 'A Brief Account of the Contagious Disease Which Raged among the Milch Cowes near London in the Year 1714', Philos. Trans. Roy. Soc., xxx, 1718, pp. 872–85.

procedure was in their best interests, but, in Bates's view, the gentry spared no effort to accomplish this end. They summoned cowkeepers once or twice a week, urged all to comply, and omitted no warrantable means to frustrate those who would not. Bates himself attended most of the JPs' meetings, while also conducting his own scientific enquiry into the origins of the disease, discussing it with cow leeches, consulting books, and dissecting sixteen infected cows. Bates was given orders to try a cure from Holland, but found it did no good. His own verdict was that the dry spring and the lack of lush grass at that time had inhibited the usual purging of cattle, and so caused internal obstructions leading to putrefaction and contagion. He was asked by the Lords Justices to examine the truth of an allegation that the feeding of cows on distilled grain was a new practice, and was the cause of the disease. He investigated this, but found that distillers' grains had been used for the last twenty years without trouble. Others thought the disease was due to the lack of water; Bates, however, could report that the Islington farmers always had water from the New river running through their very grounds.[203]

When at the end of September 1714 the disease spread further, and it proved impracticable to burn all cattle, Bates recommended that carcases should be buried fifteen to twenty feet deep, having previously been covered with quicklime. Finding also that cowkeepers normally sent calves at one week old to Romford market, where they might be the cause of spreading the infection more widely, Bates ordered their keepers to bury the calves as well. For this they were paid 5–10s. per calf. Again Bates received all possible support from the Privy Council. By the beginning of October the disease was spreading to Norfolk, Suffolk, and Hertfordshire, and Bates feared it would become more widespread still. He reported to a committee of the Privy Council his principal anxiety, that infected cattle were not being buried deep enough, whereby infection could spread. Writers on medicine also feared the spread of infection to men; an earlier mortality among cattle, and carelessness in burying their carcases, was thought by some to have given rise to the Great Plague of 1665.[204]

Bates's personal efforts and investigations were remarkably thorough, and showed close contact with, and intelligent use of, foreign experience. Moreover, his advice was promptly heeded by the authorities. To prod the government to further action, he reminded them that other states like Prussia and Holland had adopted very severe decrees and orders, commanding men to bury their infected cattle even upon pain of death. His alarm did not carry the King's Council quite so readily; it decided not to take such drastic action unless the distemper spread. In the event, the measures that were taken succeeded in containing the disease; the infection died away in the autumn of 1714. It had lasted three months in England, whereas in several European countries it lasted two or three years. Bates confidently, and probably rightly,

[203] *Ibid.*   [204] *Ibid.*

attributed the success of the English to the compliance of the cowkeepers, overawed, perhaps, by the four JPs of Middlesex "who gave daily attendance both early and late". In that epidemic England escaped lightly – losses in Middlesex, Essex, and Surrey were 5,418 cattle and 439 calves destroyed – whereas Holland lost more than 300,000 animals. Compensation at 40s. per cow and 10s. per calf amounted to £6,674 1s. 1d., which was paid by the king as a royal bounty from his own Civil List. It did not nearly compensate farmers, whose cows averaged £6 in value, and who were thought to have lost a further £4 apiece on servants' wages, rent, and contracts already entered into to purchase feeding grains from the brewers. A charity collection yielded disappointing returns, because false reports devalued the farmers' losses. Instead of the £24,500 hoped for, only £6,278 2s. 6d. was collected. Thus, from this source cowkeepers received for every cow £1 10s. 9d. to add to the original £2, to set against a loss of £6–10.[205]

This is a revealing episode in the history of agricultural policy, for, without Bates's detailed narrative, one would be inclined to look to parliamentary debates for the source and inspiration of the measures taken. In fact, quicker decisions were made, and remarkably speedily implemented, by high-ranking men in government, who had no hesitation in acting on their own initiative without parliament. In this case, they made promises they hoped they would eventually be able to fulfil, and they prevailed on the king to foot the bill. It is noteworthy that they were guided by knowledge of a policy already adopted in some European countries, though they modified the severe orders laid down by some states like Prussia.

In eighteenth-century politics the power of patronage and influence, wielded by the nobility and gentry, looms large, and the less socially exalted but more experienced practical men – the parsons and professional surveyors, for example, who had busied themselves in discussion and correspondence on agricultural matters under the Commonwealth and in the first decades after the Restoration – seem to have made little mark in the political arena. But the evidence of this emergency in 1714 shows the two groups in close alliance. Aristocrats in government evidently placed respectful trust in the views of medical men, and in collaboration with country gentlemen could take enlightened, realistic, and determined action in a dictatorial yet paternal spirit. Such dictatorial action, moreover, won sufficient approval for the same to be countenanced by parliament when a much more serious outbreak of cattle plague occurred in 1745.

The second outbreak of rinderpest in England spread from Holland, probably in imported calf hides, and was much less successfully contained, though the same countermeasures were taken. It reached Essex and Berkshire first, and was reported around London and in Leicestershire before the end of 1745. By January 1746 it was reported at Wisbech, Stamford, and

[205] *Ibid.*

Grantham, and it surrounded the duke of Bedford's estate at Thorney, Cambridgeshire; his estate correspondence contains orders for the control of cattle movements through his land. By 1747 the disease was widespread in the Midland counties – the area where some of the heaviest cross-traffic in cattle always occurred, and by December it had reached York.[206]

Following medical advice, the government issued regulations similar to those of 1715, and appointed salaried inspectors to enforce its commands. The same monetary compensation was offered: 40s. per head of cattle, and 10s. for calves that were promptly slaughtered. The stern watchfulness of parish officers – constables, churchwardens, and overseers – was enjoined, and many orders passed along the chain of command from Westminster to the county JPs and thence to the parishes. Desperate efforts were made locally to keep the epidemic from crossing major boundaries like rivers: when the epidemic reached York in December 1747, the East Riding authorities kept watch at the ferries crossing the rivers Humber, Ouse, Aire, and Trent. Such efforts proved of no avail, for during 1748 and 1749 the epidemic spread into Yorkshire and Lancashire, Cheshire, parts of Wales, and Somerset.[207]

From 1745 until February 1759, when a thanksgiving prayer in all churches signalled the end of the infection, the government regularly revised, amended, and improved its regulations in the light of experience.[208] The financial, as well as other measures, invoked considerable public support. Indeed, some landlords' actions indicated the belief that, financially, they did not go far enough. When farmers whose herds were badly affected could not pay their rents, some landlords made rent allowances, although money alone was not sufficient to put farmers on their feet again. The problem of restocking at a time when cattle were scarce, and all were suspect, was formidable; many farmers turned over to sheep or to tillage, against the wishes of their landlords. In many pastoral counties, therefore, land values fell sharply: an estate in Cheshire valued in 1746 at £5,000 was expected to sell in the early 1750s at only £3,600.[209]

General consent for the government's policy at the beginning of the outbreak was somewhat less unanimous by the end, some twelve to fourteen years later (though scattered cases of infection continued into the late 1760s).

[206] Mullett, op. cit., p. 146; Hants. RO, 27M54/3; Derbs. RO, D231M/E4,477; Beds. RO, R4/4,055/8; R4/4,021/16; Coventry City RO, A131; Leeds Archives Dept, He 35.

[207] E. Riding RO, QSF Christmas 1747/D4–10; Derbs. RO, D231M/E4,525; Cheshire RO, DTD/9/5 and 7; Somerset RO, Q/S Papers, Brewton 1748.

[208] GMR, PSH/OCK/1/1; Mullett, op. cit., pp. 150, 153, 155. It did not change the monetary compensation, although a proposal was discussed in the Commons in 1754 (but rejected in committee by the Lords) to compensate owners to the full value of their first, second, and third beasts, killed and buried according to the government's orders – G. Fleming, *Animal Plagues, their History, Nature, and Prevention,* 2 vols., London, 1871–2, I, pp. 287–9.

[209] Cheshire RO, DTD/9/9 and 27; GMR, LM778/35/20; Oxon. RO, DIL xvii/C/72; Leeds Archives Dept, NH 2,332; Mullett, op. cit., p. 156; Cheshire RO, DBN/C/17B/2.

Many different explanations were offered for its virulence, and many different remedies, but none of them did more than alleviate the sickness. Some criticisms of the countermeasures were simply administrative: not all farmers received all the compensation to which they felt themselves entitled; the authorities were indolent and unhelpful, or refused to accept valuations; and frauds were rife. More fundamental was another argument, that a farmer could be better off by refusing to slaughter his beasts, and taking a chance on the survival of at least one-third of their number. The survivors would be stronger, whereas buying new stock laid him open to another bout of infection. If he did not positively gain financially by this procedure, his loss, compared with the bounty, was small. The pamphleteer who presented this argument was prompted by concern for the expense of compensation falling on taxpaying freeholders, and by disappointment at the ineffectiveness of the measures taken.[210] The fact remains that at a time when the study of comparative pathology had not yet begun in England, the government's measures to deal with this epidemic were relatively enlightened, being modelled on the best medical opinion of the day, and, in the opinion of Broad, who has recently reviewed the whole episode, well ahead of the measures taken in other European countries. Livestock farmers probably lost at least half a million animals, but they were not left totally without financial compensation; it was better than nothing at all.

By the 1740s the government was not generally in a mood to intervene in agriculture; as we have seen, belief in *laissez-faire* was gathering strength. But enough vestiges of a former disposition to maintain the farming community in adversity survived; the name given in some documents to the compensation paid for slaughtered cattle was called a 'bounty', reviving a memory of the aid that had been given to corn farmers.[211]

(f) Dairy produce

Legislation governing dairy production was noticeably concerned to remedy abuses in the weighing and packing of butter and cheese. Some of the trouble was due to the diversity of local measures, but some was due to deliberate deceits about weights. After discussion of the matter in 1661–2, an act was passed in 1662–3 which declared in its preamble that butter was one of the principal commodities produced in the kingdom, and was transported in very great quantities overseas. In consequence, the use of false measures and other deceits, such as concealing bad butter under a thin layer of good butter, and packing stones, wet salt, and other trash in the middle of barrels, were

[210] Wilts. RO, Calley MSS unsorted, acc. 1,178; Kent AO, Q/SB1748; GLCRO, E/BER/S/E/8/1/2; *Observations on the Regulations...for Preventing...the Distemper among the Cattle, 1750*, in Goldsmith's Library. London Univ.

[211] Mullett, *op. cit.*, p. 144. For the term 'bounty', see Coventry City RO, A131. £220,000 was paid in compensation during 14 years of the cattle plague, compared with £1.5 million in corn bounties between 1740 and 1750 – Broad, *loc. cit.*

deplored, for they gave English butter a bad reputation.[212] Measures taken to check the abuses applied only to butter, but other abuses were evidently rife in the cheese trade, for in 1678 bullying by the London cheesemongers prompted a strongly worded petition from gentleman landowners and farmers of Suffolk in favour of legislation to control the quality of cheese. The cheesemongers were alleged to be wielding excessive power, holding the dairy producers to ransom by inspecting the butter and cheese at the ports long after the producers had sold it satisfactorily to factors calling at their doors. The port inspectors then found fault with it and made arbitrary price reductions.[213] A bill was drafted to meet these complaints, but no legislation was enacted then, nor did any action follow a counter-petition from the cheesemongers in 1692 calling for a remedy against the deceits perpetrated by the dairymen. The legislation finally passed in 1692 (4 Wm & Mary, c. 7) dealt with the grievances of 1678, namely, the inspection of butter and cheese by London cheesemongers at seaports, and last-minute deductions of price. Thenceforward, butter casks were to be sealed by buyers immediately upon purchase, and no recriminations against sellers could follow thereafter.[214]

The meagre details emerging from these discussions of butter and cheese marketing suggest that a few London cheesemongers had a stranglehold over the trade, and were at loggerheads with a mounting number of producers in many scattered regions of the kingdom. The cheesemongers with a tight control over the Suffolk dairy trade were said to number 22 who lodged in Thames Street. Out of a total of 250 cheesemongers in London, they were the butt of the fiercest criticism. Their power was so great that they would sometimes keep the butter for a month before they deigned to inspect it.[215] Moreover, they evidently had the hoymen, who shipped the butter and cheese to London, in thrall, denying them the right to carry the goods of anyone they pleased.

No doubt the cheesemongers also had cause for complaint, that quality was very variable; we have already noted some of their grievances. It seems fair to deduce from all this that quantities reaching the market were rising, quantity was endangering quality, and so long as a few London cheesemongers

---

[212] LJ, XI, pp. 420a–430a, 472a; Statutes of the Realm, V, p. 421 (14 Chas II, c. 26). The scale of butter and cheese exports deserves further investigation. Butter exports from Yarm, for example, rose rapidly in 1638–75 – D. Pearce, 'Yarm and the Butter Trade', Cleveland & Teesside Loc. Hist. Soc., no. 9, June 1970, pp. 10–12.

[213] CJ, X, 1688–93, p. 475. See also vol. IV of the paperback series, pp. 237–8.

[214] HMC, Fourteenth Report, App. VI, House of Lords, 1692–3, pp. 76, 75; CSPD, June 1687–Feb. 1689, p. 117; CSPD, 1700–2, p. 575; Statutes of the Realm, VI, pp. 388 et seq. (4 Wm & Mary, c. 7). Quarter Sessions records for the N. Riding of Yorkshire in 1685–6 show many presentments against producers who sold butter that was rancid, underweight, unbranded, etc. Yarm was a notable butter market – N. Riding RO, Quarter Sessions Books.

[215] The best glimpse of the wrangle between producers and traders is seen in 1692 in HMC, Fourteenth Report, App. VI, House of Lords, 1692–3, pp. 106–9, 353–6.

monopolized sales there was bound to be friction. One clause in the act of 1692, insisting that trade in butter and cheese should be free to all cheesemongers who were free of the City of London, and should not be engrossed by a few individuals, sounds like a sensible measure to promote a wider trade, perhaps to assist the sales of a wider range of qualities. But too little is known as yet of the personalities in the trade, and of their main buying and retailing connections, to pass any sound judgment. Suffice it to say that the cheese and butter trades were a matter for animated debate in parliament after the Restoration until the end of the century: that in itself indicates a quickening farming business, lacking as yet a smoothly working marketing system. After 1700 cheese producers played an active role in promoting river improvements – with the same goal in view, to improve marketing.[216] Those involved are indicated in a bill "to encourage the cheese trade" which was considered in 1737. The number of cheese-producing counties, from which MPs were selected for a Commons committee, were fifteen in England and Wales: Cheshire, Lancashire, Shropshire, Staffordshire, Derbyshire, Flintshire, Denbighshire, Gloucestershire, Wiltshire, Somerset, Dorset, Warwickshire, Suffolk, Oxfordshire, and Middlesex.[217]

The export of dairy produce was encouraged by the same statutes that promoted the breeding and feeding of cattle. Duties on butter and cheese exports were removed in 1670, and again in 1691 (having been briefly reintroduced in 1690). Exports were a regular but small item in overseas trade from London: in 1662–3 London sent cheese to the Plantations, Italy, Holland, and elsewhere, and butter to many more countries, especially Flanders. No doubt, the outports sent more. Certainly Newcastle was exporting butter to Holland, for in 1668 Sir William Temple described how the Dutch bought cheap butter in northern England and exported their own best butter.[218]

(g) Wool and sheep

Wool was a reasonably satisfactory farm product at the beginning of the seventeenth century, though a comparison of relative prices (ignoring costs and yields) suggests that it was not keeping pace with most other agricultural commodities. But from about 1614 the wool and cloth trade began to suffer troubles born of a number of changing circumstances in Continental cloth markets. The competitive textile industries of Europe reduced the demand

[216] LJ, XXI, pp. 252a. 303b, 273b, 277a, 281a, 288a; A. Henstock, 'Cheese Manufacture and Marketing in Derbyshire and North Staffordshire, 1670–1870', Derbs. Arch. J., LXXXIX, 1969, p. 41. See also vol. IV of the paperback series, p. 239.

[217] CJ, XXIII, p. 69. See also P. R. Edwards, 'The Development of Dairy Farming on the North Shropshire Plain in the Seventeenth Century', Midland Hist., IV, 3–4, 1978, pp. 175ff, and Henstock, op. cit., pp. 32–46, esp. pp. 33, 35.

[218] Statutes of the Realm, V, pp. 685–6 (22 Chas II, c. 13); VI, p. 311; BL, Add. MS 36,785; W. Temple, Observations upon the United Provinces...London, 1673, p. 208.

for English cloth, and since Englishmen thought that the foreigners' success derived in part from their use of English wool, they pressed eagerly for a ban on wool exports, securing this in 1614. The ban remained for 150 years.[219]

Such a policy plainly suited clothmakers but did not benefit wool growers. Already in the early 1620s they were complaining bitterly of low prices, yet much worse was to follow. Prices fell sharply in the 1650s, and more dramatically still in the 1680s, though a substantial recovery occurred in the 1690s.[220] Yet throughout the seventeenth century the cloth manufacturers' interests prevailed over those of the wool producers, although powerful voices proclaimed that their interests were identical. The first step in such an argument was easy. It was common ground between growers and manufacturers that the price of English wool had to be raised. It was admitted that its low price injured farmers and landowners, and accounted in part for arrears of rent, falling rents, and falling values of land.[221] If the same solution had been chosen for wool as for grain, exports would have been encouraged. But instead, because wool sustained a powerful native industry, the argument was given another twist: wool was cheap, not because it was over-plentiful in the domestic market, but because native cloth could not find sufficient trading outlets. If English textiles were protected against foreign competition, they would sell abroad and wool growers would then benefit from higher wool prices. By preventing foreigners from obtaining English wool, therefore, it was thought that their products would not be able to compete in quality with English cloth. Since much attention was also given to schemes for promoting employment for the poor, the interests of the textile industry swayed the policymakers more readily than did isolated sheep farmers.[222]

The ban on the export of English wool, therefore, was re-enacted in 1648, and again at the Restoration in 1660 and 1662. Fresh bills were debated in 1668, 1670–8, and 1685, and the law reiterated and strengthened in 1688, 1695–6, and 1698.[223] A scheme to check smuggling from Kent and Sussex, set up under the act of 1698, required an immense amount of paperwork: all wool owners within ten miles of the sea in these two counties had to account for all their fleeces when newly shorn, and give the names and addresses of the prospective buyers. No wonder that a scheme to operate nationally in the same way was rejected in 1732 by the Commissioners for Trade and Plantations because of the "multiplicity of accounts" involved. Even so, the City of London revived the idea of a public register of wool

[219] E. Lipson, *A Short History of Wool and its Manufacture*, London, 1953, p. 25.

[220] T & C, p. 24; P. J. Bowden, *The Wool Trade in Tudor and Stuart England*, new impr., London, 1971, p. 220.   [221] Bowden, *op. cit.*, pp. 214, 211.

[222] *Ibid.*, p. 215. A succinct example of this argument is in *CSPD*, 1675–6, pp. 373–4.

[223] For the 1648 ordinance, see Firth and Rait, *Acts and Ordinances of the Interregnum*, I, pp. 1,059–61. For the acts of 1660 and 1662, see *Statutes of the Realm*, V, pp. 293ff, 410ff; VI, pp. 96ff; VII, pp. 118, 421ff.

in 1741, though again the courage to undertake such a heroic enterprise failed.[224]

As problems associated with this single-minded policy deepened, more voices were raised to question its wisdom. When the government with fresh rigour insisted that Irish (and much less effectively) Scottish wool should not reach the Continent, larger wool supplies came on the English market in consequence, and English wool prices continued their fall. At the same time, low prices made English wool increasingly attractive abroad, and smuggling became an ever more serious and worthwhile business, especially from the south coast and Scotland. One contemporary believed that some of the smuggled English wool yielded a 50–60 per cent profit. It is thus hardly surprising that smugglers became better organized, moving about in armed companies, and shipping their wares from creeks in order to avoid the ports. Commentators agreed that the prohibitions were "but a cobweb".[225]

The ineffectiveness of the ban on wool exports must have conferred some benefit on wool growers, especially those who disposed of their clip in the vicinity of coastal ports.[226] But as a group the sheep farmers were disorganized, and their point of view was not strongly argued until the early eighteenth century, when the tide of opinion was running more strongly in favour of free trade in general, and, in Lipson's words, "the graziers raised a violent agitation against their confinement to the home market" which they carried on in an unceasing stream of pamphlets. A monumental investigation was conducted by the Reverend John Smith of Lincoln (centre of a prime wool-growing county) into past policy and debates on wool, which he published in 1747. At last farmers and landowners had an eloquent spokesman: "why must the interest of the grazier, the grower of wool, be the only sufferer?" he asked, when, in reality, the wool manufacturers and traders depended on the prosperity of growers, for they fostered employment and domestic demand. A wiser policy to benefit traders and the landed interest was to pay bounties on exported woollen goods and allow wool export under duty.[227]

[224] Lipson, *Short History of Wool*, pp. 24–5. For the constitutional novelty of the measures of 1698, see R. M. Lees, 'The Constitutional Importance of the "Commissioners for Wool" of 1689: An Administrative Experiment of the Reign of William III', *Economica*, XIII, 1933, pp. 147–68, 264–74.

[225] Bowden, *op. cit.*, pp. 203–9, 194–8; Lipson, *Short History of Wool*, pp. 23, 25; HMC, Eighth Report, *House of Lords*, pp. 127–8. For informed statements on the relative prices of Irish and English wool in 1698, see *House of Lords Papers, NS III*, 1697–9, pp. 108–9.

[226] For the argument in 1669 that wool from Sussex went to Saint-Valéry and Calais, and constituted two-thirds of the trade thither, see HMC, Eighth Report, App., *House of Lords*, p. 127.

[227] Lipson, *Short History of Wool*, p. 26; J. Smith, *Chronicon Rusticum-Commerciale; or Memoirs of Wool*, 2 vols., London, 1747, I, pp. 522–3; also pp. 80–90, 506, 511, 520–2; J. de L. Mann, *The Cloth Industry in the West of England from 1640 to 1880*, Oxford, 1971, p. 268. Mann does not positively identify Smith's proposals to the Commons in 1744 with the scheme in his *Memoirs of Wool*, but suggests the likelihood.

But to no avail. The export of wool was not officially allowed until 1824.[228] In consequence, farmers who persisted with sheep keeping set their hopes of profit on meat rather than on wool, and this may well have meant that sheep went to the butcher at a younger age than formerly. Whether numbers of sheep declined in proportion to cattle is doubtful; and certainly, following the two cattle plagues in 1714 and 1745, the very reverse occurred. The suggestion has been made by Charles Wilson that corn bounties were partly intended to compensate farmers for the handicaps they suffered from the national wool policy. But this seems to present what were accidentally favourable consequences for the farmers who specialized in sheep and corn in the guise of deliberate intentions to favour this one group. The truth is we lack as yet an informed assessment of the full impact of wool policy on the many different kinds of sheep farmer.[229]

(h) Game

A remarkable upsurge of interest, first of all in deer keeping, and then in preserving other game, revealed itself after 1660, which was noticeably at variance with trends in the previous sixty years. A full explanation is called for, for its consequences were far-reaching. The preservation of game became a serious occupation of the gentry, absorbing grain and other agricultural resources which in an age of less abundant foodstuffs could not have been so deployed. So determined were the gentry to persist with game keeping that, in some places, they thoroughly poisoned their relations with their tenants and other classes in rural society.[230] Their efforts developed and culminated with the Black Act in 1723, which, in the view of one criminal lawyer, probably instituted more capital provisions in one single statute than the whole criminal code of any other country. Looking a century ahead, E. P. Thompson has summed up the Black Act as the signal for "the onset of the flood tide of eighteenth-century retributive justice".[231]

Until the Civil War deer parks had to be licensed by the crown, and such a licence evidently gave valued legal protection against poachers. Thus a statute of 5 Eliz., c. 21 (1562–3) protected licensed parks from the unlawful hunting of deer. But it did not protect unlicensed parks, nor did it protect parks licensed after 1563. This latter legal oversight proved sufficiently inconvenient to prompt a further statute of 3 Jas I (1605–6) embracing parks enclosed and licensed after that date. But beyond these two acts, with more than forty years between them, no undue concern for protecting deer was shown for a century, between 1560 and 1660. Nor is this surprising. In

---

[228] Lipson, Short History of Wool, p. 104.
[229] Wilson, England's Apprenticeship, p. 149.
[230] Thoughts on the Present Laws for Preserving the Game and Some Methods Proposed for Making a Game Law Both Useful and Effectual, London, 1750, p. 13.
[231] E. P. Thompson, Whigs and Hunters: The Origin of the Black Act, London, 1975, p. 23.

practice, many gentry had abandoned their deer parks in the later sixteenth century, and turned the land over to more profitable cattle grazing, while in royal forests the crown allowed the commoners so much freedom that its herds of deer were greatly depleted by James I's reign, and in some areas the crown abandoned attempts at keeping deer altogether.[232] Under the Commonwealth, writers on husbandry showed no great interest in deer or game. The only intervention by the government occurred in 1651 with an act to prevent the killing of deer in forests, which took cognizance of the fact that the commoners in many forests whose future was uncertain had seized their chance to drive out the deer and replace them with sheep and pigs.[233]

In general, though of course there were exceptions, the gentry seem to have lost much of their interest in deer parks and deer keeping in the course of the later sixteenth and early seventeenth centuries. Their enthusiasm revived after 1660. The State Papers are full of plans for restocking deer parks destroyed during the Interregnum,[234] the system of licensing parks was gradually abandoned, and unusual attention was paid to legislation supporting the nobility and the gentry in their attempts to stop poaching. At the earliest moment after the Restoration in 1661 (13 Charles II, c. 10) a statute was passed to prevent the unlawful coursing, hunting, or killing of deer. Four years later, in 1665, a bill to restrain artificers and labourers from destroying hares, pheasants, partridges, and other game failed to pass through parliament.[235] But in 1670–1 nobility and gentry had their way by means of another statute, establishing their claim to reserve all game to themselves, and excluding the lower orders. The act not only preserved deer but secured warrens and fisheries against all poachers with guns, nets, and snares, and, moreover, allowed the employment of gamekeepers, and gave them authority to search suspected poachers.[236]

This legislation reflected heightened concern for game by the gentry alongside a heightened interest by others in sharing its delights. Poachers continued to poach, alone and in companies. A new Deer Killing Prevention Bill was drawn up in 1678, imposing financial penalties on poachers, or, if

[232] Statutes of the Realm, IV, 1, pp. 449–50; IV, 11, pp. 1,088–9; J. Thirsk in AHEW, IV, p. 18, and above, pp. 49, 93, citing esp. J. Norden, The Surveyor's Dialogue, London, 1607, p. 115. See also William Vaughan, The Golden Fleece, London, 1626, p. 60. The statement in vol. 5 of this series, p. 101, n. 31, that walled parks doubled in Hertfordshire between 1596 and the early eighteenth century prompts the question whether more were created after 1660 than before.

[233] Steele, Proclamations of the Tudor and Stuart Sovereigns, I, no. 2,938. Sheep and pigs were driven into the forest at Hatfield Broad Oak, where the deer had been kept, allegedly without interference from the commoners, until the Civil War – Essex RO, D/DB/LI/2/16.

[234] See e.g. CSPD, 1661–2 and 1663–4, passim.

[235] E. P. Shirley, Some Account of English Deer Parks, London, 1867, p. 51; Statutes of the Realm, V, p. 314; CJ, VIII, 1660–7, p. 616.

[236] Statutes of the Realm, V, pp. 745–6 (22 & 23 Chas II, c. 25).

they could not pay, committing them to one year's hard labour in a house of correction (six months had been the punishment laid down in the 1661 act) or to the common gaol; the death penalty was to be imposed if they killed a gamekeeper.[237] This bill did not then pass the Commons, but a similar statute with severe penalties received the royal assent in 1691, designed to check whole fraternities of poachers who, because of the small financial penalties earlier levied, were buying off their fellows when they were caught.[238] As poaching was becoming a better-organized business, so the legislation was changing character to correspond.

It is important not to exaggerate the size of the problem lying behind the legislation of 1660–1750. Some public acts concerned with other offences can be shown to have dealt with relatively local problems. This is made clear in the case of an act of 1670–1 to prevent the malicious burning of houses and stacks of corn and hay, and the killing and maiming of cattle. The preamble claimed that this was a nocturnal activity in several parts of the kingdom. The only evidence, other than the act, shows it to have been rife in the neighbourhood of Kempsey in Worcestershire; it may have occurred in a few other places, but there is nothing to suggest that it was a widespread nuisance.[239] In the same way highly purposeful, professional poaching may have been a localized problem, which a coterie of influential landowners with power in parliament managed to turn into a national issue.[240] The fact remains, however, that the Deer and Game Acts of 1661 and 1670 inaugurated a long series of unprecedentedly harsh game laws, which steadily and purposefully extended the gentry's control over foodstuffs that had once been much more fairly shared by all. An act of 1706 for the better preservation of game, re-enacted with minor alterations in 1711, gave particular attention to the preservation of hares, pheasants, partridges, and grouse, and, in the second act, to the taking of wildfowl in decoys.[241] Decoys were another of the alternative enterprises that engaged landowners in this period as a source of food and profit; the mounting number of such traps for wildfowl, and consumer demand for their meat, inevitably attracted the poachers.[242]

Alarm at the poaching of deer in parks (linked, it should be said, with

[237] LJ, XIII, pp. 258, 268. For the text of this bill, see HMC, Ninth Report, App., House of Lords, pp. 119–20.

[238] Statutes of the Realm, VI, pp. 312–13 (3 Wm & Mary, c. 10). For deer hunting, the penalty was £20, but for deer wounded or killed the penalty was now £30. A raid on the deer park of Sir John Banks at Aylesford, near Maidstone, Kent, was carried out in 1697 by more than 40 armed horsemen – Steele, op. cit., p. 505, no. 4,231.

[239] Statutes of the Realm, V, p. 709 (22 & 23 Chas II, c. 7); CSPD, 1671, pp. 18–19. The rioters around Kempsey were called Levellers, but in a 3½-page report about the disturbances no clue was given to the rioters' motives – PRO, SP 29/287/62.

[240] Cf. Thompson, op. cit., passim.

[241] Statutes of the Realm, VIII, p. 585 (6 Anne, c. 16); IX, p. 492 (9 Anne, c. 27). During the discussion of the first bill, a suggestion was made that the bounds of forests and chases be redefined, but it was rejected – CJ, xv, p. 297.   [242] See ch. 7 below, p. 307.

alarm at the damage done to new tree plantations) was at its height in the second and third decades of the eighteenth century. It culminated in the passing of the Black Act in 1723, punishing people going armed and disguised (i.e. blacking their faces and going under the name of Blacks). The act has been described by Sir Leon Radzinowicz as an "extremely severe criminal code", since it created five hundred new capital offences at a stroke. For ten years poaching by Blacks continued, until it finally died out in 1734, and, in the royal forests of the south at least, some of the forest laws were again relaxed.

Sir Leon Radzinowicz suggested that the Black Act owed its rapid passage through parliament to an extreme emergency. And certainly contemporaries saw a connection between the operations of Blacks and the general confusion following the collapse of the South Sea Company. But in his detailed investigation of the circumstances E. P. Thompson has traced long-smouldering grievances rather than a sudden crisis. He shows how in a royal forest like Windsor the court's enthusiasm for the hunt had not been matched for many years by care for the upkeep of the park and forest. Hence, when George I arrived in England from Hanover and took an unwonted interest in tightening administration of the forest – it is almost certain that he demanded standards of efficiency that prevailed at the time in German forests – he precipitated a conflict that might otherwise have smouldered but not burst into flame.[243] But underlying the increasingly embittered relations between game owners and poachers lay still deeper changes in attitudes and in the disposition of resources affecting all classes in rural society.

In the first place, a qualitative change seems to have occurred in attitudes to leisure. Among the nobility and gentry the pursuit of pleasure became as serious an activity in life as the performance of their day-to-day duties in running their households and estates, and discharging their obligations in local government. The process by which the pursuit of pleasure became a more deliberate and organized affair was a slow development. Its beginnings may be illustrated around 1600 in the remarkable growth of interest in horse racing. This began to be a fashionable and highly demanding occupation, calling for heavy expenditure on fine horses, the setting up of racecourses, and the organization of publicity, rules, prizes, and ordered public meetings.[244] By the early eighteenth century the use of leisure had become a commercialized business with many more facets. In the intervening hundred years, moreover, some subtle changes had taken place in the philosophical outlook of the landed classes to life and recreation. The value of outdoor pursuits "to the increasing of health and vigour" became an intellectual conviction. Exercise of the body

---

[243] Thompson, *op. cit., passim*, but esp. pp. 21–4, 41–4, 114, 142–5, 235, 238–9; *Remarks on the Laws relating to the Game and the Association Set on Foot for the Preservation of it...* London, 1753.
[244] J. H. Plumb, *The Commercialisation of Leisure in Eighteenth-Century England*, Reading Univ., 1973, pp. 16–17. See also Thirsk, *Horses in Early Modern England, passim*.

was as necessary as exercise of the mind.[245] But the profoundest change occurred because many of the gentry returned to their estates in 1660 after years of deprivation, and were determined to enjoy life and make good the wasted years. They had learned a lot about the pleasures of horsemanship, the hunt, and the chase on the continent of Europe.[246] They also learned how strictly game and game rights were preserved, especially in France. They returned to life in a country which had lost its fears of famine, and was looking instead for ways to dispose of an embarrassing surplus of grain. There was thus plenty of scope for feeding game and horses for pleasure as well as the human population of the kingdom. Gamekeeping and horse breeding became more highly skilled activities, in which more and more gentlemen took delight. Hunting was no longer the monopoly of kings, but consumed the zest, energy, and ability of nobility and lesser landowners, and called on them to show their skill and prowess with horses, dogs, and guns in the field, in place of their old enthusiasms for the joust and, more recently, the indoor manège.

Exactly how and when the lawyers and legislators managed to claim for the landed classes the exclusive right to take game is beyond the scope of this study. The basic principles had been enunciated in medieval legislation,[247] but the stricter interpretation, or manipulation, of the rules in the later seventeenth century almost certainly reflected increasing pressure on the uncultivated lands of the kingdom, formerly available for hunting, whether officially or unofficially, by all classes. Enclosure had made such rapid progress in the course of the sixteenth and seventeenth centuries, at least in Midland and southern England, that the waste and woodland over which deer and other wild life could roam had been drastically curtailed. Parks were urgently needed to protect deer from extinction. The game acts may thus be seen as a mirror of the successful seventeenth-century campaign to improve wastes, forests, and chases.

Yet another explanation for the gentry's interest in game lies in the economics of corn–livestock farming in this period. The gentry with other farmers were turning to special activities other than the everyday produce which yielded so little profit. Variety of diet was a consolation for other disappointments on the farming scene. Venison, game birds, and fish were more highly valued than ordinary meats, and even when the gentry did not engage in commercial sales, they valued their ability to make gifts of these luxury foodstuffs. Such presentations to patrons and friends could bring rewards more valuable than money.[248]

---

[245] This viewpoint is clearly stated in R. Blome, *The Gentlemen's Recreation*, London, 1686, pt II, pp. 1, 5, and 'Preface to the Reader'.

[246] *The Game Law: or a Collection of the Laws and Statutes Made for the Preservation of the Game of this Kingdom*, London, 1705, p. iii.

[247] *Thoughts on the Present Laws*, pp. 1ff.   [248] See ch. 7 below, p. 300.

At the moment when the gentry began to put fresh money and effort into keeping game on more restricted areas of land, however, the middle classes in society were finding equally good reasons for challenging their claim to this exclusive enjoyment of its pleasures. Hitherto the theory about gentlemen's exclusive rights to game, and the practice whereby all classes hunted it, had remained happily divergent; now they were converging uncomfortably, at the expense of the middle classes, who, in many other branches of life, were enjoying privileges that had formerly been reserved for the rich but were being now made more freely available to others.[249] The problem was put by a near-contemporary in 1750 thus: hunting had once been the privilege of kings; then it came to be enjoyed by the gentry; now men with more or less land, especially the middle classes, whose substance was increasing, claimed to share its pleasures too. Alternatively, if they did not wish to hunt for themselves, they appreciated delicacies like game at the table, and were prepared to pay for it. So long as this situation continued, others would be ready to supply their desires.

The competition for game among the classes was heightened by one further development, only dimly perceived before 1700, but blatantly clear by 1750. Gentlemen were employing "all manner of engines" in their sport. Nets, and then more efficient guns, enabled them to return from their day's adventures "as laden as they can". By 1750 men readily understood why "there was never a greater scarcity of game than at present".[250] Gentry and peasantry were engaged in a bitter battle for deer and other game by increasingly destructive methods. Pleasure for one, food for both – its pursuit brought forth legislation which greatly widened the social gulf between them.

3. Land improvement

The Commonwealth had given fresh momentum to the policy already inaugurated by the first two Stuarts of improving run-down land. It took pains to underline the fact that its methods were different – in particular, it endeavoured to see that justice was done to the commoners – but its goals were the same, to increase the productivity of underused, if not wholly derelict, pasture, woodland, and fen, and create more work on the land, thereby to support a larger population capable of contributing more to the state's revenues. The momentum of this policy was maintained after 1660, because such projects offered additional land for some of the most profitable

[249] J. Thirsk, *Economic Policy and Projects: The Development of a Consumer Society in Early Modern England*, Oxford, 1978, esp. ch. v. That the most persistent opposition to the game laws came from middle-class farmers and craftsmen is also brought out by E. P. Thompson in his investigations in Windsor Forest, *op. cit.*, pp. 84–94. For their resentment at the all-embracing nature of the laws' provisions, see also pp. 99–100, which express an attitude generalized in *Thoughts on the Present Laws*, pp. 17–19.   [250] *Thoughts on the Present Laws*, pp. 8–17; *CSPD*, 1673–5, 411.

crops then in cultivation. Rapeseed, flax, hemp, and vegetables from the newly drained fenland, timber from improved woodlands, and fruit trees from new orchards – often established on poor pasture – did not suffer from the falling prices that afflicted grain crops. Landowners, farmers, and adventurers saw in this policy possibilities of personal gain, as well as the promotion of the common good. Thus, at one of the first meetings of the Georgical Committee of the Royal Society in 1664, members took up Mr Howard's offer to find out ways of improving wastelands, heathy grounds, and bogs.[251] Prospects for increasing agricultural production and supporting a larger population stretched ahead in a long, almost unending vista. Hence, when Sylvanus Taylor's pamphlet *The Improvement of Commons, Forests and Chases by Inclosure*, originally published in 1652, was reissued in 1692, it had lost none of its force; indeed, its aspirations to promote "the advantage of the poor, the common plenty of all, and the increase and preservation of timber" read as fresh as the day when first written.[252] The campaign to improve land won enough public support to need only occasional assistance from parliament.

(a) Fenlands

So far as fen drainage was concerned, official support consisted of legislation to spell out the authority of drainers and their right to continue drainage works. Most of it was designed to overcome difficulties left unsettled by the Commonwealth. The General Drainage Act of 1663, for example, set up a Company of Conservators of the Great Level of the Fens, tacitly approving the measures taken in 1649 to enable the earl of Bedford and his co-adventurers to continue their drainage works and levy taxes to maintain them.[253] The northern fenlands of Lincolnshire reverted to the care of the Court of Sewers, but in Deeping Fen the task of drainage was given afresh in 1665 to the earl of Manchester to complete the work within seven years – a period which was extended in 1670 for a further three years.[254]

The problems of drainage in this period were less political than legal, administrative, and financial, and above all technical, such that no policy makers could solve. Public opinion in the meantime had shifted so far in favour of draining the largest area of fens around the Wash and turning its pastoral economies over to arable that, despite the perpetual difficulties of maintaining the dykes, and the new problems created by peat shrinkage and falling land levels, no one contemplated allowing the fens to return to their former state. Nevertheless, all plans were cautiously laid. An account of work under way in Wildmore Fen in April 1663 combined a concern to maintain

---

[251] T & C, pp. 150–1.   [252] BL, Thomason Tracts, E 663 (6).

[253] Darby, *Draining of the Fens*, p. 78; *Statutes of the Realm*, V, pp. 499–512 (15 Chas II, c. 17). See also the latter, pp. 643–6 (19 & 20 Chas II, c. 13).

[254] Darby, *op. cit.*, pp. 80–1; *Statutes of the Realm*, V, pp. 559–68 (16 & 17 Chas II, c. 11); V, pp. 687–9 (22 Chas II, c. 14).

local good will with a realistic assessment of the policies needed to achieve this end. "The ordinary sort of people and middle sort are very well pleased with what we have done, and as yet we have heard of no man that in the least is displeased, all sorts being desirous to be tenants both in Boston and all the country over...For one, two or three years we must let great penniworths that the meaner sort of people may give us good words and their helps to enclose."[255] But the Lindsey Level in Lincolnshire, which was less damaged by flooding, waited until the early eighteenth century for a new drainage scheme, and, when it came, the House of Lords' discussions in 1701 and 1711 showed that memories of past confrontations with the commoners were still green. The fen, it was said, was "everyone's property". The parliamentary committee could agree on nothing except the title of a bill and a preamble. All else was in dispute, and so the plan to drain the Lindsey Level was abandoned.[256]

After 1700 interest in fen drainage languished noticeably, for its chief advantage was to increase the arable area, and yet corn at this time was too cheap to yield much return to the farmer. Hence landowners in the fens summoned little enthusiasm, while onlookers who had land on the higher chalk and limestone hills were actively hostile to any such projects, seeing, if the fen were drained, a threat to their livings from the competition of farmers producing more corn, more wool, and more meat from more fertile soils.[257]

Nevertheless, while interest in large capital undertakings evaporated, the natural condition of the fens did not remain unchanged. Rather they deteriorated for lack of expenditure in keeping existing channels clear. This problem was only one facet of a general unwillingness at this period to spend money on scouring field ditches.[258] In the Ancholme Level, Lincolnshire, bitter complaint was made in 1698 that the drainer, Sir John Monson in Charles I's reign, had not been required, after the first drainage scheme was complete, to keep the Level drained. In 1704 the sluices and drains were said to have been out of repair for more than twenty years, and every year the Level lay under water.[259] Conditions further south were not much different. In the Kesteven fens, one writer in 1721 described such neglect of the Forty Foot Drain that Holland Fen was under water, and the Kesteven fens were threatened. If they flooded, five hundred landowners would be ruined.[260] Lands in Deeping Fen, which had been drained by virtue of an act of 1666,

[255] PRO, SP 29/71, no. 95.

[256] J. Thirsk, English Peasant Farming: The Agrarian History of Lincolnshire from Tudor to Recent Times, London, 1957, pp. 126-7.

[257] LAO, Mon. 7/12/80, letter from William Jackson to Sir John Newton, 1693.

[258] See e.g. Norfolk RO, HOW 731/1, and Leeds Archives Dept, He 37(a). For the same unwillingness to push ahead with the draining of the Somerset Levels, see Michael Williams, The Draining of the Somerset Levels, Cambridge, 1970, pp. 110–18.

[259] CJ, XII, 1697–9, p. 120.

[260] LAO, Asw. 1/25, Notes by Thos. Reeve [2 Mar. 1721].

were under water by 1738 "through the defects of their outfalls to the sea and other causes".[261]

The drowned condition of many fens after 1700 was not due entirely to neglect of the dykes and outfalls, however. Part of the trouble was caused by the shrinkage of the land, for which there was only one solution: windmills were needed to lift the water from one level to another. Parliament heard arguments in favour of mills in 1726, when a bill for draining Haddenham Level in the Isle of Ely was discussed. This passed as a private act, and was a landmark, inaugurating a new phase when groups of local landowners attempted to overcome the inadequacies of the larger drainage plans by devising their own district schemes. Private acts resulted in the extensive Bedford Level being divided into sub-districts, each organizing its internal drainage and the discharge of its waters into the central drain. Thus, separate interests set their hopes on achieving small gains, because a comprehensive programme was unattainable.[262] Yet they could not avoid the inevitable outcome, a fierce clash of interests among them all making a larger plan imperative. Such grander schemes were discussed in the 1720s without effect, lapsed in the 1730s, but revived in the 1740s, as the pamphlet literature bears witness.[263] They did not, however, lead to action until the later 1750s, and more especially in the 60s, when corn growing became decisively profitable once more and activated a fresh round of bolder improving enterprises.

(b) Forests

If, after 1660, the fens could safely be left to private adventurers, now sobered by their harsh earlier experiences, this was not thought wise for the forests. The Commonwealth had pursued no decisive policy, wavering but never committing itself firmly to anything.[264] Meanwhile the timber resources of the nation had been extravagantly and, indeed, wastefully used. Much woodland that had belonged to the crown, and to royalist landowners whose estates were confiscated, had been bought by men who were not sure of holding it for long, and had to take their profit quickly. The stocktaking in 1660 was a sadly sobering exercise. Yet the writers on a forest policy under the Commonwealth, and indeed before, had pronounced clearly on what was needed – "positive governmental action, founded on accurate information, equitable legislation, and rational planning". A programme was thus available in 1660 as well as convincing evidence of its urgency. Forest preservation became a matter of high priority among policy makers.[265]

---

[261] Thirsk, *English Peasant Farming*, pp. 127, 206. See also Darby, *op. cit.*, pp. 94ff.

[262] Darby, *op. cit.*, pp. 119–22.   [263] *Ibid.*, pp. 291–2.   [264] See above, pp. 141–4.

[265] Sharp, 'Timber, Science and Economic Reform', p. 59 *et passim*. For current concern for timber supplies, see many references in *CSPD*, e.g. 1664–5, *passim*. But see G. Hammersley, 'The Crown Woods and their Exploitation in the Sixteenth and Seventeenth Centuries', *Bull. IHR*, xxx, 1957, pp. 136–61, who argues that the alarms were exaggerated and cites Sir William Petty in support.

The Royal Society gave urgent attention to woodlands, entrusting the main investigation to John Evelyn. His *Sylva*, the most influential book on the subject to be published in this period, was delivered to the Royal Society in October 1662, at an appropriate moment when the Navy Commissioners were putting questions to the Royal Society about securing their future supplies for shipbuilding. *Sylva* was intended to be of immediate practical value in several different ways, by describing planting procedures for foresters, and by suggesting laws to be enacted for the preservation and improvement of woods. Much of this last advice was culled from European, especially French, German, and Spanish experience. In Biscay, as Evelyn explained, officers carefully supervised the marking of trees for felling for navy purposes and proprietors planted three trees for every one felled.[266] Dr Merrett had already reported on the French and German systems of dividing woods into eighty sections, felling one every year. The contrasting English policy of keeping crown forests "folded up in a napkin", uncultivated and neglected, was deemed thoroughly reprehensible. An active policy of constant care and supervision was needed that would preserve and exploit the royal forests to the full, and also give opportunities to buy naval timber from private woodlands. As for general laws against damage to woodland, Evelyn deplored their weakness in punishing wood stealers, and the laxness with which good laws, like those prohibiting assarts, were in force. He was plainly the enemy of commoners in forests everywhere; their cattle especially were the ruin of young nursling plantations.[267]

Legislation after the Restoration demonstrating current concern for English woodlands started with an act of 1663 (15 Chas II, c. 2) punishing the unlawful cutting of timber. Many more proposals to improve timber supplies followed between 1667 and 1676, and again in 1696, together with a measure to bring down the price of timber in 1667–8. In 1674 a bolder Wood and Timber Preservation Bill was discussed in parliament; it would have enabled forest owners to agree with their commoners to enclose portions of their forests and hold them free of common rights, or, if the commoners failed to agree, to have recourse to six or more local JPs to designate a plantation. The object was to remedy the serious scarcity of timber for houses and ships; but such proposals laid a minefield through the territory of private property rights, and not surprisingly never emerged from committee.[268]

The disafforestation of a number of crown forests – Ashdown, Needwood, and Delamere – was contemplated in this period, and yet again in none of these cases did the plans proceed.[269] Parliament could only agree when it was necessary to rescue particular royal forests from serious deterioration.

[266] Evelyn, *Sylva*, title page and p. 110.   [267] *Ibid.*, pp. 108–12.
[268] *Statues of the Realm*, V, pp. 441–2; HMC, Ninth Report, *House of Lords*, pp. 41–2; Index of CJ, VIII–XI, under 'Timber'.
[269] E. Sussex RO, Glynde MS 3,162; *CSPD*, 1663–4, pp. 29, 308; HMC, Eighth Report, App., *House of Lords*, p. 105. For the discussion surrounding the disafforestation of Delamere Forest in 1660–1 and the decision in 1673 not to disafforest it, see Cheshire RO, DAR A/14, A29 H/10.

The Forest of Dean occupied much parliamentary time in the 1660s in an attempt to extricate it from a tangle of concessions made before the Civil War. Sir John Winter was at the centre of a long-drawn-out dispute with the commoners and with the crown. It seemed to be settled in 1665 when Winter was entrusted with improving the forest as a nursery of timber (having previously been accused of making much spoil there). But his lease was withdrawn in 1668, and some enclosure was carried out in order to create nursery plantations for the future supply of timber. Even then, no satisfactory long-term settlement was achieved with the commoners in Dean. Riots broke out in 1680 and 1688, even though far more parliamentary time was spent on discussing the Forest of Dean than on any other royal forest.[270]

Enclosures to establish nurseries for young trees were a principal objective of general forest policy, and this was the purpose of an act in 1695–6 (9 Wm III, c. 33), but still applying to the New Forest only, allowing an immediate 2,000 acres of waste, and another 200 acres yearly for twenty years, to be enclosed to establish nursling plantations. The preamble of this statute spoke of the great waste of timber of late years, imperilling supplies to the navy. The problems of day-to-day supervision of the forests were nowhere solved and anxieties on this score persisted into the late 1690s.[271] Nevertheless, Evelyn's pleas in *Sylva* for more skilled woodland management flowed with the economic tide, and so won support from many landowners, who were ready to put their own houses in order, so profitable was it. "Who would not preserve timber", Evelyn had exclaimed, "when within so few years the price is almost quadrupled". Hence his suggestion for growing half an acre of timber for every twenty acres of pasture – advice which Evelyn thought especially appropriate for counties bereft of timber like Northamptonshire, Lincolnshire, and Cornwall – was in line with other similar legislative proposals discussed in parliament, though they were unable ever to win general assent. But as a principle of good timber management the precept appealed to many gentleman readers of Evelyn's book, and entered into their estate plans. Finally, Evelyn suggested the appointment of deputies to the Navy Commissioners in every county to see that so many trees were planted per hundred acres. Custodians of the forest were needed, he declared, like those set up in Aristotle's *Politics*. Yet again no legislation followed, but the Navy Commissioners seem to have established a system of active collaboration with some owners of woodland near rivers, buying their shipping timber and encouraging them to grow more. This is one example of administrative procedures that are found working in the later seventeenth century, which were in line with prevailing policy recommendations and informed opinion, but which were not spelt out in legislation.[272]

[270] Hart, *Commoners of Dean Forest*, pp. 54–60, 68–71, 74–5.

[271] *Statutes of the Realm*, VII, pp. 405–8; LJ, XVI, pp. 248b, 277a. See also below, p. 293.

[272] Evelyn, *Sylva*, pp. 114, 116, 119. Sir Edward Dering sold his timber to the Chatham

After 1700, when private plantations flourished and timber supplies in general were thought satisfactory because of satisfactory prices, attention shifted to the need to punish malicious damage by the opponents of afforestation. An act of 1715 (1 Geo. I, c. 48) to promote the growing of timber, fruit, and ornamental trees was passed in answer to this need, and was a punitive act against malefactors.[273] In the next decade more room for plantations was sought on common lands. When a mild interest in enclosure and drainage revived in 1724, a tentative proposal for a bill to improve commons and wastes was linked with a scheme to plant timber in such places. This bill never materialized, but its intentions mirror private aspirations which were, if anything, more resolute than ever before. The career of William Hanbury, the parson of Church Langton, Leicestershire, best exemplifies the passion that lay behind some of them. Hanbury was inspired with a missionary zeal for tree planting as an undergraduate at Oxford in the 1740s, and launched into action in the 1750s, when he was established in a secure church living in Leicestershire. He planned to use the wastes and commons of his parish for grand tree plantations that would earn funds for a charitable trust. He was not allowed a smooth passage. Two ladies of the manor of West Langton, equally charitable inasmuch as they left £12,000 to hospitals, became his arch enemies, deliberately procuring the destruction of his tree nurseries. But Hanbury was plainly putting into practice a scheme that lurked in the back of many minds. The same ideas impelled lords of nine Surrey manors to petition the Commons in 1757 for leave to plant many thousand acres of wasteland with trees for the benefit of the poor. The land was deemed unfit for tillage or pasture but capable of producing "great numbers of different kinds of trees".[274]

In an unusually informative account in the Commons journals of the committee's investigations into this bill, we learn the names and authority of those who gave evidence in support of the Surrey gentry's plea. Philip Miller, gardener to the Apothecaries' Company, and a highly popular author of gardening textbooks, joined forces with the Hon. Charles Hamilton and another unnamed MP in advising that Scotch firs and beech would grow successfully on the hilltops; birch, hazel, oak, and chestnut on the hillsides; and oak in the bottoms. Other members of the committee emphasized from personal knowledge that the plantations of the dukes of Bedford and of Argyll had shown how profitable and how economical such plantations

dockyards – CSPD, 1664–5, p. 298. For sales by Sir Roger Twysden of E. Peckham, Kent, to the Navy Commissioners, see CSPD, 1668–9, pp. 126, 325–6, et passim.

[273] For an investigation into timber supplies for the navy in 1708, see House of Lords Papers, NS VII, 1706–8, pp. 352–7. For the act of 1715, see Statutes at Large, V, 1768, pp. 85–6. Lord Coningsby was one of the MPs nominated to prepare this bill. He had proposed a bill to promote the trade of gardening in 1696 – CJ, XI, 1693–7, p. 461.

[274] CJ, XX, p. 386; Wilshere, The Rev. William Hanbury, pp. 1–5; CJ, XXVII, pp. 379, 465, 574–5; XXVIII, p. 198.

could be. These opinions heralded the day some forty years hence when the forestry skills of Scotland would be as celebrated as the arable farming of England.[275]

Other supporting evidence disclosed the financial stimulus behind this use of waste land: timber prices were rising and shortages were causing alarm. Two tanners in 1756 emphasized the scarcity of bark, since many woods had recently been grubbed up and none replanted. A shipbuilder spoke of higher prices in the past fifty years and large imports. Shortages, mounting prices, and imports were underlined by a surveyor of the royal forests, a surveyor of the navy, a purveyor of timber for Woolwich Yard, a timber merchant, and a customs officer. The parliamentary committee gave its verdict in favour of the enclosure of commons for the planting of timber, and the House of Commons subsequently passed (1755–6) a general act, rather than a particular bill for the benefit of Surrey landowners.[276]

Government legislation to assist timber production did not in the end amount to much, but the subject was discussed sufficiently often to keep it before the public eye. Reading between the lines, one can readily see how the incentive of profit from woodlands was solving the problem, while parliament encouraged gentry from the sidelines, even to the point of allowing some enclosures of low-grade commons for the extension of woodland. Such endeavours relaxed towards the middle of the eighteenth century, however, when landowners turned back again to their old farming interests in corn and livestock.

4. The regulation of enclosure

No statutes regulating common fields or facilitating enclosure were passed between 1660 and 1700, but it was not for want of trying. In the 1660s in particular considerable concern was shown for the better management of common fields through orders and by-laws. Perhaps this was a legacy from Commonwealth days – it followed so closely the views of Gabriel Plattes. Bills in parliament were considered in 1661, 1662, 1663, and 1664, and although they were not successful, their purpose is almost certainly summarized in a petition c. 1661, now housed in the Guildford Muniment Room. It pertained not to Surrey alone but to the whole kingdom and deplored the overstocking of common fields with sheep and cattle, failure to trench the ground for drainage, constant tillage which wore out the arable, too frequent mowing of the meadows, the lack of wood in common fields, and lack of interest in planting any. It appealed for an act obliging the majority of landholders and commoners to order a stint of cattle and levy a fine for

---

[275] CJ, xxvii, p. 575. In *Caspar Voght und sein Mustergut Flottbek*, Hamburg, 1969, pp. 69–70, Gerhard Ahrens shows how respected were Scottish foresters by German landowners in the 1790s.
[276] CJ, xxvii, p. 575; *Statutes at Large*, VII, pp. 719ff (29 Geo. II, c. 36).

breaches thereof. It implied a serious breakdown of manorial court regulations in some areas; yet it failed to win support.[277]

In 1666 another bill was presented to confirm enclosures that had been registered in courts of equity in the past sixty years and had not been contested for twenty years. This last bill was intended to end the vexations caused by people who raised objections to enclosures decades after they had been signed, sealed, ratified by decree, and acted upon. It too met opposition and was dropped.[278]

Meanwhile piecemeal enclosure by agreement went ahead. Its geographical concentration varied and cannot be exactly mapped, but while some counties like Leicestershire underwent more enclosure in the first half of the seventeenth century than in the second, others like Northumberland and Durham experienced the reverse.[279] All over the country enclosure was now generally accepted as part of the normal process of change in agriculture, and the existing machinery, while capable of improvement, worked reasonably satisfactorily. Some landlords were prepared to offer inducements to their tenants to hasten matters, as did Thomas Erle of Charborough, a hamlet in east Dorset, in an agreement with his copyhold tenants in September 1695: in order to achieve an enclosure "both freely and voluntarily", he promised not to raise fines or rents above the former rates during his lifetime, and undertook to give his less secure and affluent tenants (having estates for one life only or land under £10 in value) the coppice wood needed for fencing.[280] Other landlords, whose desire to enclose was frustrated by their tenants, waited for an opportune moment to buy up freeholds and gradually cajole or coerce their copyholders.[281]

As more agreements were concluded, so impatience mounted in places where a majority of tenants were in favour of enclosure but could not procure unanimity. John Houghton in 1681 and again in 1700 advocated a general permissive act to allow enclosure, but to no effect.[282] Meanwhile pressure was beginning to be exerted from an unexpected quarter. A measure to

---

[277] CJ, VIII, 1660–7, pp. 278, 318, 384, 438–9, 466, 555; GMR, LM 1,734.

[278] LJ, XII, pp. 20b, 28a, 37a, 40a, 66b. For a specimen of a Chancery decree, see A. E. Bland, P. A. Brown, and R. H. Tawney, eds., English Economic History: Select Documents, London, 1914, pp. 525–6.

[279] J. A. Yelling, Common Field and Enclosure in England, 1450–1850, London, 1977, pp. 18–19, 26–9. For the newly prepared list of enclosures by decree in the Chancery rolls, see M. W. Beresford, 'The Decree Rolls of Chancery as a Source for Economic History, 1547–c. 1700'. EcHR, 2nd ser., XXXII, 1, 1979, pp. 1–10.

[280] Dorset RO, D131 uncatalogued. For another example of an enclosure agreement (of 1667–9), see that between Charles, earl of Derby, and the copyholders of W. Derby and Wavertree – Lancs. RO, DDM/52/38.

[281] Bland, Brown, and Tawney, op. cit., pp. 526–7.

[282] See e.g. CJ, VIII, 1660–7, pp. 573, 575; IX, 1667–87, p. 72; LJ, VIII, Mar. 1667/8; and HMC, Eighth Report, App., House of Lords, p. 119. On parliamentary interest and Houghton's opinion, see E. C. K. Gonner, Common Land and Inclosure, London, 1912, p. 58.

explain the ancient Statute of Merton and its intentions regarding the improvement of the commons was debated in 1697. It seemed at first sight to have general implications, but in fact it was initiated by the inhabitants of Kingston upon Thames, Surrey, who were prepared to set up schools to teach paupers and children how to weave linen and canvas cloth, if only they could be permitted to use some of their commons to grow flax and hemp. This proposal, of course, coincided with other energetic attempts that were a special feature of the 1690s to devise work for the poor; but it was unusual in proposing a combination of parish work on the land with work in manufacture, and also in designating the commons for more productive cultivation. It did not get past a second reading in the Commons, and no strong movement to use townships' commons for community purposes followed But, as we have seen above, the idea of using some for woodland plantations that would yield cash to support the poor inspired more than one private venture after 1700.[283]

How and why the private bill was finally resorted to, thus starting a new phase of enclosure history, appears a relatively simple question, and yet it is difficult to answer. The already established procedure of enclosing by agreement continued in use, such agreements being subsequently made secure by Chancery decrees. But that security proved far from complete. Successors in title to land could, years later, raise objections to enclosure, and a way round this difficulty had to be sought. The procedure was then developed further when acts were used, first to overcome the opposition of a minority to an agreement, and then to initiate enclosure after an agreement in principle had been reached. When this happened, the enclosure was finally completed not by the act, but by an award which followed some time later, and which was legally binding.[284]

Lord Ernle interpreted this development as evidence of the way the monarch's authority was weakened and parliamentary authority strengthened. This verdict is possible if one stands back after 150 years of enclosure by parliamentary act and surveys the full consequences. When first used, however, it seemed to be more of an empirical device, forced upon enclosers by the ineffectiveness of Chancery decrees in contentious cases. As we have seen, increasing numbers of private acts were being passed to enable private landowners to improve or protect their property. Private enclosure acts were one group in this larger whole, though they eventually swamped the others in importance.[285]

Thus, although the parliamentary enclosure act paved a very broad highway to enclosure, it is likely that the trail was blazed by other users of

[283] CJ, XI, 1695–7, pp. 718, 725.

[284] W. E. Tate, *The English Village Community and the Enclosure Movements*, London, 1967, pp. 49–50: Gonner, *op. cit.*, pp. 55–6, 60–2. For an act to overcome the obstruction of two proprietors who would not say yea or nay, see LJ, XXIII, p. 691a.

[285] Gonner, *op. cit.*, p. 50. See also p. 214 below.

private acts. They in turn were exploiting a system of investigation and decision that was more promptly efficacious than lawsuits. The parliamentary procedure for public bills had long allowed objectors to be heard; and in many cases, parliamentary committees listened patiently to a remarkable number of objectors from far and wide. It would seem in theory, therefore, that objectors to an enclosure would be sure to have a fair hearing. If so, the use of bills could have been encouraged by that assurance. In practice, of course, objectors to a parish enclosure could not usually organize their opposition as effectively as, say, the yeomen and gentry of a whole county, who managed to raise loud voices against some public bills with an agricultural content. Objectors to one parish enclosure were a much smaller group who usually lacked the financial resources, as well as experience in the ways of political manoeuvring at Westminster. Moreover, a parliamentary committee was composed of persons interested in a bill, and MPs interested in enclosure were likely to have only one viewpoint, favouring their class rather than paying much heed to small men's interests; the strongest opponents of enclosure, on the other hand, were likely to be small men, unable to assert their viewpoint to equal effect.[286] An early hint of possible abuses in the procedure is conveyed by a report from a Lords committee in 1732 on an enclosure act that was alleged to have been obtained by surprise. But generally the weaknesses of the procedure by parliamentary act became much clearer in the second half of the eighteenth century as more experience accumulated. Before 1750 most interest focused on the benefits of the new procedure – its speed and the security it offered for the future – in contrast to the disadvantages of enclosure by decree. Flagrant abuses emerged only gradually as the procedure hardened, and they were not deemed flagrant enough to be corrected until 1744, when parliament drew up standing orders for dealing with enclosure bills.[287]

The momentum of enclosure by act built up only slowly between 1700 and 1750. Eight enclosure acts were passed between 1724 and 1729, thirty-nine in the 1730s, and thirty-nine in the 1740s. The liveliest interest in the first two decades was shown in Gloucestershire and Warwickshire, which, between 1726 and 1739, secured six and nine acts respectively. But the strongest impetus was not felt until cereal prices improved after 1750. In Leicestershire, for example, only two enclosure acts were passed between 1730 and 1740 and only one between 1741 and 1750, whereas twenty-three were

[286] The discussions of a Lords committee early in 1721 – before enclosure acts became generally accepted – "to consider the method of passing bills for enclosing of commons" may imply some unease about the proceeding. It was prompted by a bill for improving Stokesby common, Norfolk – LJ, XXI., pp. 408a, 416a. For the way private promoters of bills secured their friends' support at the committee stage, see the instructive evidence from Warwickshire in J. M. Martin, 'Members of Parliament and Enclosure: A Reconsideration', AHR, XXVII, 2, 1979, pp. 101–9.

[287] LJ, XXIV, pp. 190b, 226b. For the adverse criticisms of enclosure after 1750, see Tate, op. cit., pp. 84ff.

passed between 1751 and 1760. A survey of the chronological spread of parliamentary enclosure acts is set out in Gilbert Slater's study *The English Peasantry and the Enclosure of Common Fields*, showing acts beginning to be used more frequently in the 1730s, but not popular until the 1750s. It took time before the merits of the act were deemed to outweigh those of a Chancery decree. On the practical side, the methods of surveying and allotting the new enclosures were much the same in both cases. The difference lay in their expense and legal effectiveness: an act was far more expensive than a decree, but its legally binding effect proved to be the decisive consideration. And the cost was less of a deterrent when once cereal prices began to rise. Thus a fairly close correspondence has been found between agricultural prices and enclosure throughout the period of parliamentary acts, "upswings in prices being followed after a short interval by upswings in enclosure".[288]

5. Work for the poor

Success in finding work for the poor proved so much greater in the countryside than in towns that rural poverty drew little comment compared with the situation under the Commonwealth. It is true that the burden of poor relief falling on landowners and farmers was deeply resented. But this grievance only strengthened the argument in favour of labour-intensive farming pursuits, which would provide work instead of relieving the poor while keeping them in idleness. When writers and politicians wished to publicize horticulture or other new branches of farming enterprise, and underlined their capacity to employ more labour, they uttered what were now acknowledged commonplaces. More probing questions revealed a serious interest in the exact costing of such activities. Thus a letter in the *Philosophical Transactions* on agricultural improvement in Cornwall in 1675 recommended sand as a fertilizer, and promptly drew a reply urging that the costs should be reckoned first. Even so, the writer conceded that if the husbandman profited only a little, he should bear in mind the benefit that was conferred by employing the poor.[289]

Other enterprises were known to benefit the public weal still more, as, for example, when hop gardens were dug with a spade, or hemp and flax were grown to provide for linen and canvas weaving.[290] Another school of thought turned an old argument against pasture farming upside down,

---

[288] G. Slater, *The English Peasantry and the Enclosure of Common Fields*, London, 1907, pp. 268–313; *VCH Leics.*, II, p. 229; Tate, *op. cit.*, pp. 107–8; J. D. Chambers and G. E. Mingay, *The Agricultural Revolution, 1750–1880*, London, 1966, pp. 78–84. For recent surveys, see Yelling, *op. cit.*, and M. Turner, *English Parliamentary Enclosure*, London, 1980, esp. p. 68.

[289] *Plain English in a Familiar Conference betwixt Three Friends*, pp. 13–14; *Philos. Trans. Roy. Soc.*, x, 113–14, 1675, esp. p. 306.

[290] Ralph Arnold, *A Yeoman of Kent*, London, 1949, p. 35. See also p. 207 above.

by proclaiming its advantages over arable farming in employing many more people. Since many of the raw materials for industry like wool, leather, tallow, etc. were pastoral products, pasture farming could fairly be said to create more work than tillage.[291] All these arguments pushed traditional corn farming into the background, but there was logic in this since grain prices were so depressed. Few could look realistically for salvation to larger grain acreages. On the contrary, as Carew Reynel argued, "variety of husbandries" was the best recipe for the times, along with "variety of manufactures".[292]

As the evidence shows (in Chapter 7 below), much work was created by diversifying farming and rural industrial occupations – so much so that when the problems of poor relief thrust themselves to the forefront of discussion in the 1680s, and more urgently still in the hard years in the later 1690s, attention was focused on the burden in towns, and most hope was set on the introduction of industrial occupations that had already proved so valuable in the countryside: linen and canvas weaving, woodcrafts, pinmaking, stocking knitting, lacemaking, netmaking and sailmaking. A whole chapter of a treatise by Sir Josiah Child, written in 1693, on the relief and employment of the poor made clear on the second page that it was the poor in "the outparts of cities and great towns" which concerned him, not the rural areas.[293]

Sir Matthew Hale in 1683 had urged groups of parishes to raise a workstock to set up workhouses and instruct children in work. This revived a proposal from the Commonwealth period. Now the idea won support on all sides, and great enthusiasm was shown for procuring private acts to erect hospitals and workhouses, but it was towns like Exeter, Tiverton, Crediton, and Colchester that led the way. Even John Bellers in his proposals for establishing a College of Industry, where people would cultivate land as well as set up manufactures, thought first of Colchester, Taunton, and Stroud – all clothmaking towns – for his first colleges.[294]

The government's lack of concern to provide work in rural parishes is also to be explained by reference to the changing relation of labour supply to demand. Men continued without thinking to remind each other of the need to create work for the poor, but here and there shortages of labour were already appearing. Areas in which one would first expect to encounter the problem were those undergoing dramatic agricultural improvement – the

[291] Samuel Fortrey, *England's Interest and Improvement*, Cambridge, 1663, p. 19; Charles Davenant, *An Essay upon the Probable Methods of Making a People Gainers in the Ballance of Trade*, London, 1699, p. 89.

[292] Reynel, *The True English Interest*, 'Preface' and p. 19.

[293] Child, *New Discourse of Trade*, p. 56.

[294] Sir Matthew Hale, *A Discourse Touching Provision for the Poor*, London, 1683, p. 13; Child, op. cit., pp. 75, 77–9. On the many parliamentary discussions from 1698 onwards, see CJ, XII–XV, passim; *Statutes of the Realm*, VII, 1695–6, index; John Bellers, *Proposals for Raising a College of Industry*, London, 1696, p. 14.

East Anglian fens in the 1650s, for example, where drainage transformed a one-time pastoral economy making modest labour demands into an arable-cum-horticultural system requiring much labour. Not surprisingly, John Maynard, employing labour there in 1655, was found bemoaning "the great charge of managing tillage, being enforced to give greater wages than ever in my time".[295] The signs of rural labour shortages were more widespread after the Restoration. A bill to prohibit building in London *c.* 1673 complained of London attracting so many people from the country that "there are not enough left to manage land".[296] At the same date another pamphleteer inveighed against high wages and the incorrigible idleness of the poor even while the markets were dead.[297] In a period of slow population growth, cheap and adequate food supplies, and proliferating employment in specialized agriculture, in horticulture, and in industries and servicing trades, these complaints reflected the rational movement of labour away from traditional corn–livestock farming.

As the cost of poor relief rose alarmingly in the early eighteenth century, more schemes for workhouses in towns went ahead. For a long time they were set up by private acts. A public bill for providing work for the poor through a joint stock company was before parliament in 1698, and other public bills presented different schemes with the same object in view between 1702 and 1706, but none were passed.[298] Hence, the workhouse idea made little general impact until the Workhouse Test Act of 1723 empowered all parishes to set up workhouses and to form unions of parishes if desired; thereafter it was the towns which showed most energy and interest in establishing them. In rural areas, judging by the examples of Cambridgeshire and Nottinghamshire, parishes sometimes chose to build workhouses, but more often showed a readiness to maintain a parish stock, usually of wool or hemp, to provide work.[299]

It has been suggested that public attitudes to the poor were hardening by 1723, and so the workhouse, which was originally designed in a philanthropic spirit to give work to the poor, degenerated into a "stable of slavery".

---

[295] Norfolk RO, NRS 15,994.

[296] HMC, Ninth Report, App., *House of Lords*, p. 26.

[297] *Plain English*, p. 6.

[298] One of the bills discussed at this time, which nearly passed, was Sir Humphrey Mackworth's bill. It would have used the poor rate to buy materials and provide working capital to employ the poor of all ages and both sexes, for wages. If they had refused, they would have surrendered all claim to relief – S. Webb and B. Webb, *English Poor Law History*, pt 1, London, 1963 edn, pp. 113–14.

[299] D. Marshall, 'The Old Poor Law, 1662–1795', EcHR, VIII, 1937–8, pp. 43–4; J. D. Chambers, *Nottinghamshire in the Eighteenth Century*, 2nd edn, London, 1966, pp. 233–4; E. M. Hampson, *The Treatment of Poverty in Cambridgeshire*, Cambridge, 1934, pp. 93–8. Barley refers in vol. 5 of this series, pp. 140–1, to some good buildings erected in parishes for the aged poor and the education of the young, but was not able to identify any portions that were plainly set aside as workshops.

Though it reduced expense – in one rural parish of Olney, Buckinghamshire, where the management of the workhouse was privately contracted, the poor rate was reduced as a result from 3s. 9d. to 1s. 9d. in the pound – it discouraged the poor from entering it.[300] At the same time, it is well known that a great diversity of practice in administering poor relief was possible between parishes, and we do not yet know the full range of work provided. Were the occupations always handicraft ones, like hemp and wool spinning, weaving, and lacemaking? Hampson's examples from rural Cambridgeshire show the poor employed in field keeping, cutting willows, and gathering and carting stones. It is not impossible that some parishes provided work on parish land which they turned over to vegetable gardens or hemp and flax plots.[301]

People certainly mulled over the lessons of practical agriculture when seeking better ways of relieving the poor. The poor harvests and food shortages that punctuated this half-century had the effect of stimulating interest in food crops other than grain, and vegetable growing meant food *and* work for the poor. Thus the severe winter of 1729 caused Professor Bradley of Cambridge to write eloquently in favour of potatoes for the poor, especially in pastoral country. He also urged the growing of vegetables in gardens, following the example of Europeans, who, he claimed, relied for a quarter of their food on vegetables such as cabbages, turnips, parsnips, and carrots. He expected to encounter some prejudices against vegetable eating from the poor, who, in his view, were accustomed to much flesh in their diet. But he proposed to win them over by telling them that most gentlemen of quality in England took pleasure in food from the garden.[302] Bradley was thinking along lines similar to, but less institutional than, Lawrence Braddon, who in 1723 proposed to relieve the poor by employing them profitably in gardening, ploughing, planting trees, etc. Correctly, he argued that one acre of garden ground, judiciously managed by a skilful gardener, would produce a far greater weight of turnips, carrots, and cabbage than the grass and hay from fifty acres of meadow. Warming to his ideas, he proposed that, if gardening once began to employ the poor successfully, colleges might be set up to teach the young husbandry, gardening, and forestry. The circulation of a beguiling pamphlet such as his helps to explain the stout-hearted conviction with which William Hanbury pursued his idiosyncratic tree-growing project in Leicestershire.[303]

In general, it seems that hopes of keeping the poor employed and

300 W. A. Speck, *Stability and Strife: England, 1714–60*, London, 1977, pp. 77–8.
301 Hampson, *op. cit.*, p. 187.
302 R. Bradley, *A Philosophical Enquiry into the Late Severe Winter*...London, 1729, pp. 16, 36–7.
303 [Lawrence Braddon], *To Pay Old Debts without New Taxes*...London, 1723, pp. xiii–xvi. I wish to thank Dr Stephen Macfarlane for drawing my attention to this pamphlet. On William Hanbury, see above, p. 204.

self-supporting faded in the course of the eighteenth century because projects failed to become efficient businesses. Workhouses degenerated into deterrent institutions, and the poor survived with the aid of makeshift payments of outdoor relief and pensions.[304] But the range of measures taken in rural parishes to provide work for the poor before 1750 has not yet been adequately explored. Public discussion hints at more private endeavour and local ingenuity than have yet come to light.

6. Conclusion

In so far as the century 1640–1750 can be seen as a coherent whole, it must be viewed as a period when new directions for agriculture were being sought, while only in extremity were old undertakings propped up with government support to ensure their continuance. The economics of traditional corn and livestock farming pushed rural communities in this period more strenuously in search of other activities to top up their incomes. The government was sufficiently alert to the threat that farmers might abandon these essential activities to relax its regulations on the export of foodstuffs, and to show especial generosity to grain growers by paying bounties on export and encouraging the use of more grain for malt, in beer, and in spirits. This was its most positive and far-sighted act of intervention, for it thereby kept the efficient corn-growing farmers in business with more enthusiasm and less dispirited resignation. But industrial interests were too powerful to allow the same decision regarding wool export to help sheep farmers. Meat production was their alternative.

Livestock farmers were less effectively assisted, except during the cattle plagues. The ban on the import of Irish cattle and sheep did not help them all, since many different interests were involved when animals passed through several hands before they reached the butcher. Initiated by the graziers, the Irish Cattle Act helped the livestock rearers more, and thus gave a new thrust to agricultural improvement in the highland zone. It helped to draw the north and west more positively into the commercial marketing network. Pig keepers were pushed this way and that by policies that were directed for the benefit of malt producers and distillers. Their share in the meat market was growing, but they were a divided group; country pig producers faced harsh competition from town distilleries, and from other, urban pig keepers using brewers' and distillers' grains and feedstuffs to produce much cheaper bacon and pork. Nevertheless, the 71 per cent rise of pig prices in the course of the period suggests that they had no reason to be dissatisfied with their lot. Dairy producers for different reasons were similarly weak in political

[304] A. W. Coats, 'The Relief of Poverty, Attitudes to Labour, and Economic Change in England, 1660–1782', *Int. Rev. Soc. Hist.*, XXI, 1, 1976, pp. 106–8; Marshall, *op. cit.*, pp. 43–7; Webb and Webb, *op. cit.*, pp. 168–72, 399–400.

influence, and failed to extricate themselves from the stranglehold of the London cheesemongers. Some tougher, more commercially minded dairymen did enter the political arena in this period, however, to expose their conflict with the cheesemongers, but without resolving it.[305]

At the same time, alternative agricultural pursuits introduced a much greater variety of produce into the markets, and the government gradually recognized this by encouraging with legislation some enterprises like flax, hemp, and madder growing, by protecting some English products like apples against foreign imports, and by choosing some products, like hops and cider, to bear new or larger excise duties in order to raise state revenues.

Farmers, of course, manoeuvred under general economic constraints which affected not only England but other west European countries as well. But they probably succeeded better than some others in expanding their food exports, which had been negligible before 1640, even though these remained a small proportion of national output. The government intervened here and there to assist, or to exploit, the changing pattern of landed produce entering into trade. But in general freedom was conceded to farmers to do what they liked with their land before it was conceded to merchants. The state was obviously incapable of controlling a large and dispersed community of landholders, pursuing very varied systems of farming. Its best strategy was to think of "inducements and encouragements" – in the words of Sir William Coventry – rather than passing sweeping acts that called a vast bureaucracy into being.

As the government retreated from compulsion, it silently gave encouragement to the use of private acts. Landowners took the hint, and cast their aspirations in local terms, thus significantly decentralizing policy making. A great increase in private bills with public objectives resulted. They first rose conspicuously in number in the reign of William III, and this may have been due to procedural difficulties in congested parliamentary sessions. Afterwards they fluctuated in number from year to year but still maintained a high level. In William's reign (1689–1702) 466 private acts were passed; in George II's reign (1727–60), 1,244. Only a minority of these concerned agricultural projects, of course, but others affected farming prosperity by initiating road improvements and bridge repairs.

Private bill procedure undoubtedly offered greater chances of getting economic measures successfully passed. Large issues of general principle were not called in question: the bill was debated in terms of local conditions, and an MP's loyal friends could be relied upon to give support with local anecdote and detail. A private bill, moreover, received all the advertisement it needed to encourage others. If it inaugurated a successful project, more private acts

---

[305] See vol. 1 of the paperback series, p. 190. Edwards, in 'The Development of Dairy Farming', p. 177, emphasizes, alongside the small dairy farmers, the emergence of more commercially minded farmers with large herds in north Shropshire in the seventeenth century.

would follow, as occurred with enclosure schemes and plans for workhouses to employ the poor in towns.[306]

Samuel Hartlib's purposes in 1653, when publicizing schemes of improvement, were thus fulfilled in ways that he could not have foreseen. He hoped his agricultural projects might find acceptance "if not so far as to be set by authority, yet to be understood by private persons".[307] By 1750 it could be said that authority had given much publicity to new designs, without imposing anything much by force; and that publicity had conveyed much encouragement to private persons, who were also given much freedom to pursue the paths that suited them best. Small vegetable gardeners availed themselves of these opportunities as readily as large landowners. But more varied agricultural enterprises meant more competition for land; such competition led to a sharp conflict in some forests in southern England, which anticipated the larger and longer contest between owners of land and commoners when enclosure gathered momentum in the century after 1750. But between this period and the next the general economic circumstances radically changed. Before 1750 land was desired for hop gardens, market gardens, orchards, woods, and warrens. After 1750 the improvers were again seeking land for corn.

[306] P. D. G. Thomas, *The House of Commons in the Eighteenth century*, Oxford, 1971, pp 45–61; index of private acts in *Statutes at Large, II* and *III*. I have benefited from discussion of this problem with Dr Stephen Macfarlane. See also above, pp. 207, 210.

[307] See Hartlib's introduction to Cressy Dymock, *A Discovery for Division or Setting Out of Land*, London, 1653, p. Aa.

5

TITHES, 1640–1750

As it had evolved by the middle of the seventeenth century the tithe system was awesome in its complexity. The simple Old Testament injunctions to Moses and Jacob to give one-tenth of all the produce of the land for the work of God, the foundation of the right to take tithes, had become overlaid by a bewildering array of customs, variations, and caveats.[1] The payment of tithes in England seems to have become a legal obligation by the end of the eighth century. Tithe claims by our period could be pursued either in the ecclesiastical courts or at common law and equity. In the early seventeenth century common lawyers were busy establishing precedents by which cognizance of tithe cases could be transferred from ecclesiastical to temporal courts by means of 'prohibitions' against the former. Before the Civil War, tithe law was one of the battlegrounds on which Archbishop Laud waged his war against the growing power of temporal authority.

It is central to an understanding of tithes to appreciate that they were not purely an ecclesiastical property. The right to collect them had been enjoyed by some influential laymen as early as the twelfth century, but it was the Reformation which brought into being that important class of tithe owners known as lay impropriators. Tithe rights, which had been extensively enjoyed by the monasteries, were forfeit to the crown at the Dissolution along with other forms of monastic property. In the generation which followed, most of these tithes were granted out or sold by the crown to courtiers, noblemen, and important officials. They thus became private property which could be further sold, leased, or purchased at will. In the middle of the seventeenth century about one-third of all tithes were owned by laymen; many more were leased out by cathedral chapters and by ordinary beneficed clergymen to men skilled in the tricky and frequently abrasive art of collection.

Important consequences flowed from lay involvement. The very fact of lay ownership fatally corrupted the pristine purity of tithing as a sacrament appropriate to the maintenance of the church and its ministers. Lay ownership

---

[1] Leviticus 27: 30–3; Genesis 28: 21–2. John Selden, *The Historie of Tithes*, London, 1618, provides a full account of the early precedents and customs. For modern interpretations, see G. Constable, *Monastic Tithes from their Origins to the Twelfth Century*, Cambridge, 1964, for the medieval period, and Christopher Hill, *Economic Problems of the Church*, Oxford, 1956, pp. 77–167, for the early modern. See also Eric J. Evans, 'A History of the Tithe System in England, 1690–1850, with Special Reference to Staffordshire', unpub. Warwick Univ. Ph.D. thesis, 1970, pp. 1–19.

did not necessarily imply financial support for the minister of the parish to which the tithes had once been attached; some lay impropriators lived at the other end of the country from their tithe property. Lay ownership also strengthened the radical case against tithes. They had always produced massive inequity in the distribution of church wealth; now some of the richest fruit was not even picked by the church. On the other side of what was to become during the Civil Wars and Interregnum a central issue of religious and social dispute, tithes augmented the property of the landed class. An attack on tithes, whatever its motivation, was also an attack on property rights. Parliamentary discussions and decisions on tithe between 1640 and 1660 need to be appraised in this context.

Tithes were divided into 'great' and 'small' to identify kinds of ownership. Great tithes were usually of corn, hay, and wood and belonged either to a rector, who had the right to all tithes in his parish, or to a lay impropriator. These tithes were almost always the most valuable. Small tithes were traditionally payable to vicars, those *vicarii* who had been placed in a living by a monastery during the Middle Ages to discharge its duties as designated deputy. In our period, tithes in impropriated parishes were usually shared between lay impropriator and vicar. Small tithes were those of livestock, wool, and, usually, non-cereal crops. Curacies traditionally were not supported by tithes but by remuneration provided by a lay impropriator.

Custom provided many exceptions to these general rules. In the 1690s, for example, it was by no means uncommon for a vicar to be in receipt of hay tithes. Of thirty four vicarages in Staffordshire for which adequate documentation survives, twenty-three took hay tithes, despite the guidance of law books to the contrary. Similarly, the vicar of Bramley (Hants.) was receiving tithe hay in addition to that from fruit trees, hemp, flax, and honey in 1674, as was the vicar of Rushmere (Suffolk) in 1745.[2] Nor was it uncommon for small portions of the corn tithes to be allowed to the impropriator as a much-needed supplement to income. Thus, in Bramley grain tithes arising from gardens, orchards, and 'backsides' were payable to the vicar "as grain elsewhere payeth to the impropriator". At Hanbury (Staffs.) in 1718 the vicar took corn tithe from Newborough and Agarsely Park, while the remaining corn tithes were the property of the bishop of Lichfield and Coventry as clerical appropriator.[3]

Some perpetual curacies also held limited tithe rights, usually by specific grant of an impropriator. Fourteen of Staffordshire's perpetual curacies in the 1690s took some tithes, including the curate of Maer, who had been given "by Mrs. Elizabeth Ashe late deceased all the tithe corne of the said parish except the tythes of Sidway Hall demean" and three other smaller plots. Where tithes were not valuable but difficult to collect, it clearly made sense

[2] LJRO, Glebe Terriers series, B/V/6; Bodleian Library, Oxford, MS Top, Hants.e.8; E. Suffolk RO, HD 6/2/6.   [3] LJRO, B/V/6: Hanbury.

for an absentee impropriator to pass on the burden of collection to a curate in preference to monetary provision.

Tithe was also classified according to produce. Two categories, 'predial' tithes for those arising directly from the ground (corn, hay, wood, fruits, etc.) and 'mixed' tithes for livestock nourished on the ground, were relatively straightforward. The third, 'personal' tithes, had been particularly contentious during the sixteenth century. According to one expert, personal tithes were meant to cover "such profits as do arise by the honest labour and industry of man".[4] They thus covered both wages and profits from industry and commerce. Such payments were extremely difficult to assess, and evasion was common. In some towns, private acts of parliament had settled rates.[5] Generally, however, small fixed payments were being substituted for tithes of wages; these naturally advantaged the payer as prices rose. Payments of 2–6d. for each servant were common.[6] Meanwhile a statute of 1548 formally exempted day labourers from payment of tithe.

Attempts to tithe profits were generally unsuccessful. Tithe owners rarely had either the knowledge to make an accurate assessment of a merchant's or a mine owner's profits or the resources successfully to prosecute an alleged defaulter. They normally took what they could get by means of customary payment or 'modus'. Occasional references are made in glebe terriers to payments in lieu of the profits from iron forges. At Wombourne (Staffs.) in the 1730s the vicar took payments of 3s. 4d. and 2s. 4d. for Heath Forge and Swindon Forge, while 'hammermen' paid 6d. a year as a tithe on their skill. At North Wraxall and North Newton (Wilts.) in the early 1700s compositions of 11s. 4d. and 6s. 8d. were payable in lieu of mill tithes.[7] The law, however, had long since compounded the difficulties of tithe owners. In 1549 the profits of new iron mills, fulling mills, and copper and tin mines were declared non-tithable unless continuous payment over the previous forty years could be established; similar evidence was necessary to sustain claims for tithes of particular skills or of fish.[8] Though occasional controversy stirred when incumbents tried to revive ancient rights, most tithe owners had admitted defeat on personal tithes by 1640. They generally survived only as devalued customary payments. In consequence, tithe ceased to be a live issue in the towns. It is difficult to dissent from Archbishop Whitgift's lugubrious assessment, given as early as 1585, that personal tithes "are in a manner wholly gone, because there is no way to recover them, but by the large conscience of the parishioners".[9]

[4] R. J. Phillimore, *The Ecclesiastical Law of the Church of England*, 2nd edn, 2 vols., London, 1895, I, p. 1,484.

[5] C. Cross, 'The Incomes of the Provincial Urban Clergy', in R. O'Day and F. Heal, eds., *Princes and Paupers in the English Church, 1500–1800*, Leicester, 1980, pp. 68–9.

[6] See e.g. the terriers of Chebsey, Trysull, Wednesbury, and Wombourne – LJRO, B/V/6.

[7] Salisbury Diocesan RO, Bishop's Admin., Terriers, Wilts.   [8] 2 & 3 Edw. VI, c. 13.

[9] Hill, *op. cit.*, p. 91. See also A. G. Little, 'Personal Tithes', EHR, ccxxxvi, 1945, pp. 67–88.

During the dislocations of 1640–60, tithe became a central political issue. Not only did the suspension of church courts after 1641 make the maintenance of clerical tithe rights much more difficult. The very institution of tithe as the primary means of spiritual maintenance was anathema to most radical groups. These advocated separate churches, funded by voluntary contributions of the faithful. Tithes, objectionable in themselves to Levellers, Fifth Monarchists, and the like, became also the softest target in a much more ambitious campaign against a state church and, in large measure, against the very institution of property.[10] Examples from a uniquely extensive polemical literature might be taken almost at random. The Leveller leader, Richard Overton, urged in 1647 that "the grievous oppressions by tythes and forced-maintenance for the ministry be removed, and that the more easie and evangelicall practice of contribution be granted, and confirmed for the benefit of the subject". The Quaker Edward Burrough caught the growing mood of popular anticlericalism in the late 1640s when he declared that "these men called ministers in this nation, the way of their setting up and sending forth, and the way of their maintenance…they are the greatest and most woeful oppression in the nation".[11]

Despite the direct representation of tithe owners by the gentry who sat in the Long Parliament and the Rump, tithes only narrowly escaped extinction. Parliament passed an ordinance in November 1644 insisting on the payment of tithes: "divers persons within the realm…taking advantage of the present distractions and ayming at their own profit, have refused and still do refuse to set out, yield, and pay tythes".[12] Complaints for redress were to be heard before two justices of the peace. In 1647 a further ordinance confirmed that ministers placed by parliament in livings held under sequestration should receive tithes. This was an important clarification, since almost 30 per cent of parochial clergy were ejected from their livings during the Civil War and Interregnum.[13] By 1647, however, anti-tithe petitions and propaganda were bombarding parliament. The *Husbandman's Plea against Tithes* (1647) encompassed a petition from the counties of Hertfordshire, Bedfordshire, and Buckinghamshire urging abolition, since "tithe mongers" took away "other men's goods which they are not able to spare".[14] The

[10] An excellent guide to the vast polemic literature on radical religion and politics is C. Hill, *The World Turned Upside Down*, London, 1972.

[11] D. M. Wolfe, ed., *Leveller Manifestoes of the Puritan Revolution*, New York, 1945, pp. 193–4; Hill, *World Upside Down*, p. 83.

[12] C. H. Firth and R. S. Rait, eds., *Acts and Ordinances of the Interregnum, 1642–60*, 3 vols., London, 1911, I, pp. 567–9.

[13] *Ibid.*, pp. 996–7; I. M. Green, 'The Persecution of Parish Clergy during the English Civil War', EHR, xciv, 1979, pp. 507–31. Petitions complaining of non-payment of tithes to ministers in sequestered parishes are found in LJ, ix, pp. 344–5.

[14] M. James, 'The Political Importance of the Tithes Controversy in the English Revolution, 1640–60', *History*, xxvi, 1941, pp. 1–18.

explicit references to reducing the inequalities between rich and poor, however, alarmed MPs, paralleling as they did Leveller agitation within the army. The Leveller Petition of March 1647 and the Second and Third Agreements of the People both proposed the abolition of tithes as part of a grandiose plan of social reconstruction with implications as fundamental for landlords as for churchmen. The Long Parliament's affirmation of support for tithes was, therefore, an affirmation of property rights.

The execution of the king and the purging of the Long Parliament to produce the Rump greatly encouraged the radicals in their hopes of real church reform. The sale of episcopal lands to provide for poorer livings seemed to presage a redistribution of income in the church, however chaotically it actually worked.[15] The Act for the Maintenance of Preaching Ministers (1649) prescribed that the now appropriated tithes of the church hierarchy, together with the impropriations of delinquents, be administered by a body of trustees, who would augment poorer livings. That same act, however, held fast to the principle of tithing, the Rump having defeated by a single vote a proposal to refer to a committee the issue of tithes as an appropriate means of support for a preaching ministry.[16] Prodding by the Council of State in the direction of abolition was unavailing. It was probable that a majority could be fashioned in the Rump against the principle of tithing, but only a minority were prepared to abolish tithes first and search for alternative maintenance afterwards. Nor was that minority's position helped by the wilder utterances of the radical sects, whose confidence grew after the royalist defeat at Worcester in 1651, and who were now prepared to attack moderate independents and Presbyterians with that self-righteous fervour which was not the least unattractive of their many rebarbative qualities.

During 1652 anti-tithe petitions circulated freely again. Pamphlets such as Lupton's *The Tithe Takers Cart Overthrown* and Gerrard Winstanley's *Law of Freedom in a Platform* inflamed anticlerical passions. Independents in the Rump, concerned for orderly church government, became thoroughly alarmed, especially when a Declaration of the Army in 1652 called both for the abolition of tithes and for law reform. A counterattack produced a resolution by the Rump to persevere with tithes until a better means of maintenance could be found, and petitions from the shires indicated that radical ideas did not meet with universal favour outside parliament.

Inevitably, Cromwell's 'Parliament of the Saints' appraised the tithe question afresh in 1653. Reform of both legal and ecclesiastical systems was

---

[15] On the complex administration of this thorny area, see R. O'Day and A. Hughes, 'Augmentation and Amalgamation: Was There a Systematic Approach to the Repeal of Parochial Finance, 1640–1660?' in O'Day and Heal, *op. cit.*, pp. 167–93, and I. Gentles, 'The Sale of Bishops' Lands in the English Revolution, 1646–60', EHR, XCV, 1980, pp. 573–96.

[16] D. Underdown, *Pride's Purge*, Oxford, 1971, p. 272.

debated against the usual barrage of pamphlets. A temporary victory by the radicals in November and early December precipitated what many have seen as the crisis of the Revolution. Once Barebones had agreed to abolish ecclesiastical patronage and, by two votes, to reject committee proposals safeguarding legal rights to take tithes, the more conservative members of the assembly hastened to surrender their now dangerous authority to Cromwell.[17]

During Oliver Cromwell's Protectorate tithes remained secure. Though the Protector retained a preference for their eventual supersession by a rational means of maintenance, the alarms of 1652–3 with their implications for property rights exercised a fierce brake on reforming initiatives. The Instrument of Government (1653) anticipated eventual reform but insisted that tithes be paid in the meantime. The proposed Parliamentary Constitution of 1655 repeated both the pious aspiration, and the present aversion, to hasty change. Cromwell's increasing irritation with the self-righteousness and intolerance of the sects served to strengthen the security of tithe holders. The Fifth Monarchist John Rogers was told in 1655: "You fix the name Antichristian upon anything...and so all is Antichristian and tithes are so too, with you, but I will prove they are not." Cromwell told parliament in September 1656 that he would consider it "very treacherous if I should take away tithes, till I see the legislative power to settle maintenance to them another way".[18] He knew, of course, that this 'legislative power' would not be forthcoming from members who shared his own distaste for the 'overturning' schemes of the sectaries. Clause 11 of the Humble Petition and Advice (1657) anticipated the religious intolerance of the Restoration. It proposed maintenance for ministers prepared to make a "publique profession" of their belief in "the true Protestant Christian religion". "But for such persons who agree not in matters of faith with the publique profession aforesaid, they shall not be capable of receiving the publick maintenance appointed for the ministry."[19]

The struggle between reform and the security of property tithe owners, whether lay or clerical, benefited property owners. It is not necessary to accept Christopher Hill's assertion that "the whole history of the 1650s can be told in terms of tithes" to appreciate their importance in the ideological struggles of the Interregnum.[20] After Oliver's death in 1658, tithes were pushed once again to the forefront during the death throes of the English Revolution.

The army's reinstatement of the Rump in May 1659 initiated a period of short but intense ferment. The arguments were similar to those heard in

[17] Ibid., pp. 330–1; C. Hill, God's Englishman: Oliver Cromwell and the English Revolution, London, 1970, pp. 133–5; James, op. cit., p. 11.

[18] W. C. Abbott, The Writings and Speeches of Oliver Cromwell, 4 vols., New York, 1937–47, III, p. 614; IV, p. 272.

[19] Firth and Rait, op. cit., II, pp. 1,053–4.   [20] Hill, World Upside Down, p. 187.

1652–3, but their context had changed. In 1659, unlike 1653, the English gentry were eminently persuadable that a restored monarchy was preferable to incessant sectarian strife. The sects, indeed, were going about this persuasion with a will. During the spring and summer, the old anti-tithe arguments were prominently paraded in works such as *Englands Safety in the Laws Supremacy*, *The Moderate Man's Proposall to the Parliament about Tithes*, and *An Indictment against Tythes*. The means of alternative maintenance, whether by taxes, sale of tithes, or voluntary contributions of the faithful, divided the authors. One of the strongest voluntarists was John Milton, who weighed in with *The Likeliest Means to Remove Hirelings out of the Church* in August 1659.[21] Milton believed it "a rule of common equitie which proportions the hire as well to the abilitie of him who gives as to the labor of him who receives, and recommends him only as worthy, not invests him with a legal right...The church of Christ was founded in poverty rather than in revenues, stood purest and prospered best without them."

As before, petitions accompanied the pamphlets. One from Somerset, Wiltshire, Devon, Dorset, and Hampshire was received in June 1659 calling for an alternative to tithes. On the Speaker's casting vote, consideration of alternative provisions was referred to a grand committee of the house. When the Quakers followed up this success with a further petition from "many thousands of free-born people", it encountered sterner parliamentary resolution: tithes must continue until a better means be found. Judges were to remind citizens of this necessity as they travelled on circuit.[22]

The heavy involvement of low-born Anabaptists and Quakers in the anti-tithe campaign rallied landed opinion. John Prynne remarked in *Ten Considerable Quaeres concerning Tithes* that most of their opponents were too poor to pay them anyway, and that this attack was a cover for more dangerous designs. Their true aim, as he suggested elsewhere, was "to extirpate the church and ministry of England, advowsons, glebes, tithes, and demolish all parish churches as antichristian; to extirpate the law root and branch under pretext of reforming and new-moulding it".[23] Prynne probably did not know that Anthony Pearson, whose *The Great Case of Tythes* (1657) had become one of the most influential Quaker tracts, had purchased several forfeited estates at low prices while acting as secretary to the still more voraciously acquisitive republican Arthur Heselrige. The evident desire of the army's lower ranks to have done with tithes once Lambert had forcibly dispersed parliament evoked unpleasant gentry memories of Putney in 1647. This strengthened Monck's hand in mounting

---

[21] *Complete Prose Works of John Milton*, rev. edn, London, 1980, pp. 77–95, 277–321. See also D. M. Wolfe, *Milton in the Puritan Revolution*, London, 1941, pp. 102–10.

[22] CJ, VII, p. 694. See also G. Davies, *The Restoration of Charles II*, Oxford, 1955, pp. 25, 119–21, and James, *op. cit.*, p. 17.

[23] Underdown, *op. cit.*, p. 349.

a successful counter-thrust. Monck himself specifically mentioned the anti-tithe campaign as a critical factor justifying his actions. As the Restoration approached, the conservatives in the restored Rump asserted themselves. Vicars obtained clear powers to recover predial tithes, and the Rump's last enactment before dissolution in March 1660 was 'An Act for Ministers and Payment of Tithes'. By it, all ministers settled in livings were fully entitled to recover tithes; cases of dispute were referable to two JPs.[24]

While tithes survived the Interregnum, the manifold uncertainties and dislocations made collection doubly difficult, especially in those southern and eastern counties where the sectaries were strongest. Legal redress against defaulters virtually ceased in many areas after the abolition of the church courts. Evidence thus becomes frustratingly slender, but this was clearly not a period in which to assert new tithe rights or seek to overturn inflation-damaged customary payments. Incumbents were doubtless also anxious to avoid drawing attention to themselves by zealous pursuit of claims when sequestrators and county committees were considering their work and witness. Every incentive existed for incumbents to keep their heads down and pray for more settled times. The diary of Ralph Josselin, vicar of Earls Colne, Essex, an area of some Puritan influence, indicates the difficulties encountered. In 1641 he complained that "when tithes come I must doe it myself: I compounded: with all my toyle I think that yeare I could make them [tithes] amount not above £33 and since then they are come to lesse, and all the losse to this day hath fallen upon my shoulders". By 1648 he was complaining that he was "forsaken and neglected by the inhabitants of Earls Colne, and destitute of a competent maintenance to live upon". He had just "received in from the towne, at several times with much calling upon: £25 6s. 9d.", and "let any understanding man judge whether £80 be not as little as a man can live on in these times". He was promised augmentations from the Committee for Plundered Ministers and the Trustees for the Maintenance of Ministers, but, probably characteristically, received only £113 3s. 8d. of the £600 he had been expecting during the late 1640s and 1650s.[25]

It was naturally anticipated that the return of Charles II would bring a change of fortunes. With the exception of the hated High Commission, the judicial activities of the Church of England were restored in 1660–1 along with the episcopacy. The church courts began to hear again the defamation, matrimonial, testamentary, and tithe cases which had been their stock-in-trade before 1641. Public penance and excommunication also reappeared as

---

[24] CJ, VII, p. 880; Firth and Rait, op. cit., II, pp. 1,467–8.
[25] A. Macfarlane, ed., Diary of Ralph Josselin, British Acad. Rec. Soc. & Ec. Hist., NS III, 1976, pp. 11, 135–6, 221, 446; A. Macfarlane, The Family Life of Ralph Josselin, Cambridge, 1970, p. 35; O'Day and Hughes, op. cit., pp. 173, 180–90.

traditional sanctions.[26] The conservatism of the Restoration Church Settlement was most evident, and it by no means worked to the long-term
advantage of the church. Projects for parochial and financial reform were
out of favour, being branded by their sectarian associations during the
previous two decades; this despite the bishops' recognition of the need at
least to raise the incomes of the poorer clergy to respectable levels. Since the
prime reason for the poverty of livings was the absence or inadequacy of
tithe income, and since most of those absent revenues were pocketed by lay
landowners whose support had helped to restore the king, the delicacy of
the position needed no emphasis. English landowners welcomed the Church
of England and its bishops back in 1660 – but on their own terms.

Post-Restoration England, nevertheless, did witness some score-settling
over tithes. Church courts were busy as never before, determining disputes
and re-establishing rights endangered or extinguished during the Interregnum.
The Court of Arches, the court of appeal from the diocesan courts in the
province of Canterbury, heard a total of 587 tithe appeals between 1660 and
1876. No fewer than 227 of these (39 per cent) were heard between 1660
and 1674.[27] Not only were incumbents reasserting themselves. Many new
clergy had to be found after 1660, and a change of incumbent often provoked
litigation as fresh minds found old payments inadequate or incomplete.[28]
As the vicar of Swaffham Prior was to note in 1713, he had obtained tithes
from some 600 acres in his parish, "which tithes my predecessors had not
courage to sue for".[29] The vicar of West Hoathly (Sussex) took Thomas
Comber to court in 1671 for non-payment of tithe on milk, cheese, fruit,
and hops. At Benacre in Suffolk two defendants were cited in 1665 for
non-payment of wool, livestock, barley, and oats. William Taylor of
Worfield (Salop.) was accused in 1675 of paying no tithe on clover, peas,
and turnips, while Bartholomew Garrett was alleged to have evaded payment
of any tithe from the fruit and vegetables grown on land he had rented in
Abingdon in 1674 and 1675.[30] Francis Chamberlayne gave as a subsidiary
reason for his intention to quit a tenancy at Cold Overton (Leics.) from 1672

---

[26] I. M. Green, *The Re-Establishment of the Church of England, 1660–1663*, Oxford, 1978;
E. A. O. Whiteman, 'The Re-Establishment of the Church of England', RHS, 5th ser., v, 1955,
pp. 111–31. On the work of the ecclesiastical courts, see R. A. Marchant, *The Church under the
Law: Administration and Discipline in the Diocese of York, 1560–1640*, Cambridge, 1969, C. Hill,
Economic Problems, and C. I. A. Ritchie, *The Ecclesiastical Courts of York*, Arbroath, 1956.

[27] Calculations from data in J. Houston, ed., *Cases in the Court of Arches*, British Rec. Soc.,
LXXXV, Chichester, 1972.

[28] Eric J. Evans, *The Contentious Tithe*, London, 1976, pp. 48–9.

[29] Cambs. RO, P150/8/2.

[30] E. Sussex RO, Add. MSS 3,302, 3,307; E. Suffolk RO, FAA/3/9; LJRO, B/C/5, 1675,
Worfield; Bodleian Library, MS Oxf. Archdeacon's Papers, Berks., c.149, ff. 40–1. See also Francis
Clarke's attempt to get satisfaction from one Richard Webb of Falmer (Sussex) in 1660, since
Webb's "is a dangerous example to the rest of the inhabitants who may withold their tithes too"
– E. Sussex RO, Add. MS 1,902.

the rector's determination to sue him "for payment of corn, hay & herbage in kind. If he can get it it will advance his tithes very much."[31]

It is in some respects unfortunate that so much of our knowledge about the tithe system derives from litigation documents.[32] The impression that all tithe owners were involved in incessant battles must be resisted. Yet the uncertainties of tithe law and custom did engender an enormous number of cases. This was particularly true when, as in our period, farming patterns underwent radical change and tithe owners stood to gain large amounts by establishing rights to a full tenth of a new crop or to improved yields via new methods of husbandry. Between 1660 and 1750, as in the period which followed up to the passage of the Tithe Commutation Act in 1836, tithe owners were playing for high stakes.

Most tithe cases were begun because owners wished to assert rights which had either fallen into disuse or had been openly flouted by parishioners. It was well known that the collection, especially of small tithes in large parishes, was an arduous and a vexatious business. Many incumbents opted for a quiet life and did not press their claims to the fullest extent. One such, evidently, was William Royston, rector of the Staffordshire parish of Haughton in the 1710s and early 1720s. When Randall Darwell succeeded him he sourly reported that "as to the small tythes and customary dues of the parish, there has been such confusion and irregularity in the gathering of 'em that 'tis next to an impossibility to ascertain the just right". Darwell's subsequent attempts at ascertainment saddled his parishioners with almost fifty years of intermittent litigation, from which he was to gain little but the lasting odium of his flock.[33] The dilemma for conscientious clergymen was acute. Either they tried to realize their full tithe income (and many calculated that they collected little more than half their dues) and risked fracturing pastoral relationships, or they effectively connived at lowering the value of an estate in which they were only life tenants by forgoing legitimate claims.

Against the less important parishioners clergymen might expect speedy success when they pursued ordinary claims, such as those made by Lancelot Charleton, vicar of Padworth (Berks.) against George Burges in 1720 for non-payment of tithe from five acres of wheat and 84 sheep 'depasturing on grass', or that against Jeffrey Pinnel of Olveston (Glos.) in 1701 for withholding tithe hay.[34] Some tenants calculated that tithe owners would not go to law. When disabused, as the deputy diocesan registrar of Lichfield would explain to a prospective litigant in 1830, a mere citation to appear

[31] E. Sussex RO, FRE 8,977, letter from Francis Chamberlayne to Mrs Turner, 14 Sept. 1671.

[32] For amplification of this point, see Evans, thesis, pp. 109–46, and id., Contentious Tithe, pp. 42–58.

[33] LJRO, B/V/6, Haughton terriers.

[34] Bodleian Library, MS Oxf. Archd. Papers, Berks., c.150; Bristol RO, Consistory Court Papers EP/J/2/1, bdle 5.

in the ecclesiastical court would produce the desired result. "In these cases the question seldom arises at a plea – the citation generally brings them to their senses, and they quietly pay the sum claimed with the costs."[35]

Tithe owners, particularly vicars, however, could find themselves out-matched. If wealthy defendants were prepared to contest a claim, then the complexities of the law were so arcane and the rules of admissible evidence in the various courts so confusing that it was an unresourceful lawyer indeed who could not string out proceedings at least until the litigant's cash ran out. Cases begun in church courts could be 'prohibited' from determination there if a litigant raised any question of title. Such cases, and there were many, were then transferred to equity courts, either Exchequer or Chancery, where timetables were leisurely and lawyers' fees lavish. Juries might be sworn locally to hear evidence before commissions sent out from London to establish particular facts. A case which was heard to the end frequently took ten years to complete, and many dragged on even longer. A suit begun by the rector of Checkley (Staffs.) in 1712 was protracted by various means for twenty-two years until two defendants were finally ordered to pay the tithes demanded.[36]

In such situations, issues were often determined on resources rather than right. In advance of litigation, prospective plaintiffs might agree to share costs. At Barthomley (Cheshire) in 1724 the patron, John Crewe, agreed with the rector to combine to sue for tithe corn "by a proper process of law or equity…It is further agreed that if the case goes against the rector Crewe shall bear all costs and charges. But if the corn tithes are recovered the rector is to allow Crewe all the sd. tithes until the costs of the recovery are reimbursed."[37] Reciprocatory confederations of landowners and tenants were not unusual.[38] Against powerful adversaries, tithe owners could not expect much protection.

Most lengthy tithe disputes turned on the validity or otherwise of a modus, or fixed customary payment in lieu of tithe. In general, equity courts would uphold a modus if payment could be proved to have been fixed and unalterable over many years and if its amount was judged a feasible bargain between tithe owner and proprietor at a time beyond the limit of legal memory (i.e. before 1189). Many specific exceptions to this general rule,

---

[35] LJRO, B/A/19, Letter Book 'C', Haworth to Graysbrook, 6 Feb. 1830.

[36] PRO, E 112/892 nos. 97–8; E 126/21 p. 313; E 134/4/Geo. I/178. The gist of the case is reported in Hutton Wood, *A Collection of Decrees by the Court of the Exchequer in Tithe Causes*, 4 vols., London, 1798–9, *II*, p. 122.

[37] Cheshire RO, DCR/27/7. In order to ease the burden of costs the dean and chapter of Canterbury agreed to pay one-half of the cost of a tithe dispute in 1753 in the hope of maximizing the value of the tithe estate – D. A. Heaton, 'A Study of the Corporate Estate Management of the Dean and Chapter of Canterbury, 1640–1760', unpub. Kent Univ. M.A. thesis, 1971, p. 161.

[38] See e.g. the defence subscriptions at High Offley and Wolstanton (Staffs.), William Salt Library, Stafford, M68, and Keele Univ., Sneyd MSS S95 and S97.

however, filled the lawbooks on the subject.[39] Since inflation had rendered many modus payments nearer one-hundredth than a tenth of the true value, the breaking of moduses was an issue of prime importance. Considerable successes were chalked up by determined tithe owners because ordinary occupiers were unable to provide evidence of fixed payments over sufficiently long periods to satisfy the courts. When lands were turned over from corn to hay, threatening the value of the tithes, many suits were begun to destroy moduses of 1d., 1½d., or 2d. an acre, made originally when the hay tithes were too troublesome and insufficiently valuable to collect in kind.

Rather less success was usually achieved in attacking larger customary payments which discharged tithes from particular parts of a parish. Such moduses usually derived from old demesne land and were often still occupied by the more substantial proprietors. The rector of Cheadle (Staffs.) in 1732 failed in his attempt to break a 4d. modus in lieu of all tithes from Thornbury Hall farm. John Green vigorously defended a modus of 14s. exonerating hay and small tithes from 120 acres which he occupied at Bushbury. Green knew that his chances of success depended not on justice but upon his ability to outspend the vicar and keep the case going.[40]

The introduction of new crops often provoked disputes, and this became a particular problem when fodder crops and artificial grasses came into widespread use in the second half of the seventeenth century. Glebe terriers often list new crops. At Godalming in 1697, for example, "all tithes of corn, grain, clover stfoin & of all upland grass" were noted as payable in kind, with "all tithes of set peas and beans (& of peas and beans drilled & hoed in...Tithes of gardens & orchards & fruit trees & shrubs in fields and elsewhere. Also tithes of hops, flax, hemp, rape, woad, saffron, coleseed, plants & all small tithes."[41] George Fakes of Bury St Edmunds found himself cited in the Sudbury Archdeaconry Court in 1693 for non-payment of tithe on turnips which were assessed at 2s. an acre. A dispute arose in 1709 at Nash (Kent) over ground newly sown with sainfoin. The rector of Purley (Berks.) in 1711 had to sue a tenant, Mrs Mary Blagrove, for non-payment of clover tithe: "The chief reason for her refusal to pay tithe in kind and afterwards ye value was to save money. But what she gave out was that she was unwilling to begin a custom for paying tithe for that particular sort of grass."[42]

[39] See e.g. W. Blackstone, *Commentaries on the Laws of England*, 4 vols., London, 1765–69, R. Burn, *Ecclesiastical Law*, 4 vols., London, 1763–5, F. K. Eagle and E. Younge, *A Collection of the Reports of the Cases, the Statutes and Ecclesiastical Laws Relating to Tithes*, 4 vols., London, 1826, and H. Gwillim, *A Collection of Acts and Records...Respecting Tithes*, 4 vols., London, 1801.

[40] LJRO, B/C/5, 1733–4; B/C/2/98, p. 273; PRO, E 112/740, no. 64.

[41] GLCRO, DW/S53. On glebe terriers as a source of information for new crops, see Eric J. Evans, 'Tithing Customs and Disputes: The Evidence of Glebe Terriers, 1698–1850', AHR, XVIII, 1970, pp. 17–35.

[42] W. Suffolk RO, E14/7/2; Cornwall RO, DD Bu764, letter from Lewis to Buller, 7 Nov. 1709; Berks. RO, D/P/93/1/1. References to new crops in tithe records are frequent. Only some

Despite the difficulties occasioned by alterations in husbandry, establishment of tithe rights to new crops was relatively straightforward if the tithe owner had the resources to pursue his claim in the courts. More difficulties arose when crops had a dual purpose. The impropriator of Shireoaks and other townships in north Nottinghamshire and south Yorkshire took legal advice in 1747 when farmers, having previously paid 2s. or 1s. an acre for turnip tithes, refused to continue the payment, arguing that since cattle fed on the turnips the tithe owner already gained tithe value from the animals thus nourished. Also "turnips are sown for the improvement of the land by being eaten thereon and thereby manuring the same the succeeding crops are greatly increased and they being sown when the land would otherwise be fallowed and afford no profit...they insist no tithe is due". Legal opinion distinguished between turnips taken from the ground, on which tithe was due in kind, and turnips eaten by cattle, for which a money payment based on the value of the land might be appropriate. If cattle were kept for milk rather than fattening, no tithe was due.[43]

Since the middle of the sixteenth century proprietors had been given statutory protection from tithes when they improved land previously barren. Erstwhile common and waste lands were exempted for the first seven years after improvement to compensate the landowner for heavy initial investments. The terrier of North Meols (Lancs.) in 1696 thus noted that "no lands are tythe free save the newly improved moss for the first seven years only".[44] As with so much else in tithe law, however, uncertainties were legion and opportunities for evasion plentiful. Many proprietors avoided payment once the seven-year period was up and until litigation was threatened. The definitions of common and waste ground were imprecise. Some indications suggested that fenland did not qualify – a matter of much moment in Cambridgeshire and Lincolnshire. When the earls of Portland and Bedford agreed to drain Whittlesey Fen in 1639 one of the conditions was that the lands to be set out should be "discharged from all payment of tithes of hay and fodder, the tenants paying to the owners of the several rectories or parsonages $\frac{1}{2}$d. per acre per an."[45] The rector of Swaffham Prior, on the other hand, recorded proudly in 1713 that he had won tithes from some 600 acres "taken out of the intercommon fen of Swaffham Prior and Swaffham Bulbeck which tithes my predecessors had not courage to sue for". He was able to afford £300 in litigation to establish his rights against the vicarage of Swaffham Bulbeck to tithe from fenland. The Exchequer suit "lasted

representative examples are here cited. On turnips, see E. Suffolk RO, FF569/S112; Essex RO, D/DP/L20/1; Sheffield City Library, ACM W164; LAO, 3 Anc 7/14/31. On clover, see Shrewsbury Public Library, Deed 9,632; Kent AO, U120/E4; Shropshire RO, Worfield Parish Records, 1,374/17. On sainfoin, see Cambs. RO, P150/8/2; Kent AO, DRG/At 3; U791/E81. On coleseed, see Norfolk RO, B. Lawrence viii d (2); Hare 544; W. Suffolk RO, E14/7/1.

[43] Sheffield City Library, Arundel Castle MSS W164; see also the opinion of J. White of Lincoln's Inn, LAO, 3 Anc 7/14/31.

[44] 2 & 3 Edw. VI, c. 13; Lancs. RO, DRL/3/8.   [45] Cambs. RO, R59/12/14.

several years and had divers trials". Litigiousness rewarded, the rectory was enriched to the tune of £15 a year.[46] It may readily be appreciated why many incumbents neither could nor would follow this example.

Potatoes rapidly became a profitable tithe once they were introduced as a cash crop on the Lancashire mosses from the late 1660s. By 1716 the Aughton glebe terrier noted a composition payment of 8s. an acre in lieu of potato tithe, a rate much higher than most compositions, even for wheat.[47] Potato tithing caused acrimony for two main reasons. Some doubts existed as to its status as a great or small tithe. In some parishes, especially in the plain lands of the north-west, potatoes were the most extensive and valuable crop by the 1730s. Lord Chief Justice Hardwicke's judgment in 1742 that they should be considered a small tithe even when widely grown in the open fields caused consternation among impropriators.[48] The other source of discontent concerned potatoes grown in small quantities in cottage gardens and allotments for the domestic consumption of labourers and the poor. Technically, these were tithable, and while most vicars were prepared to forgo their legal dues in the interests of charity and parochial harmony, this was not an invariable reaction.[49]

The importance accorded by many MPs to the growing of flax and hemp in the Restoration period has been explained elsewhere. Repeated attempts were made to limit tithe demands before success was finally achieved in 1691 with the act 'for the better Ascertaining the Tythes of Hemp and Flax'.[50] Its preamble declared that "the sowing of hemp and flax is and would be exceedingly beneficial to England by means of the multitude of people that are and would be employed in the manufacturing of these two materials". Since tithing these new crops was "exceeding difficult, creating grievous chargeable and vexatious suits and animosities", a maximum tithe of 4s. per acre was set. The decision was hotly contested by the owners in parts of East Anglia where hemp was being extensively grown, and in 1693 the bishop of Lincoln, acting for many incumbents in his diocese, tried to get an amendment such that land "anciently sown" with hemp or flax should be exempted from the new provisions. Whig anticlericalism diverted this challenge with comfort and the only amendment came in 1699 when the maximum tithe was raised to 5s. an acre. The act was made perpetual at the beginning of George I's reign.[51] The precedents thus set were not followed

---

[46] *Ibid.*, P150/8/2.   [47] Lancs. RO, DRL/3/1.

[48] In *Smith* v. *Wyatt*, in Gwillim, *Collection of Acts and Records*, II, p. 777. See also the opinion of J. Morgan in Feb. 1745 when a Norfolk landowner was reminded of this judgment: "potatoes were a small tithe although the greatest part of the land in the parish was set with potatoes" – Norfolk RO, Hare 5,444.

[49] Evans, *Contentious Tithe*, pp. 46–7.

[50] See ch. 4 above, p. 167; 3 Wm & Mary, c. 3.

[51] H. Horwitz, ed., *Parliamentary Diary of Narcissus Luttrell, 1691–3*, Oxford, 1972, p. 476; 11 & 12 Wm III, c. 16 and 1 Geo. I, c. 2.

up. The only other crop to receive similar protection was madder, which was likewise restricted to a tithe of 5s. per acre in 1757 as "an ingredient essentially necessary in dyeing and calicoe printing, and of great consequence to the trade and manufactures of this kingdom".[52]

Litigants in tithe causes received only the most modest protection even during the 1690s when many Whigs were anxious to cut Tory bishops and ordinary clergy down to size. After 1696 summary jurisdiction of small-tithe claims up to £2 could be obtained before two JPs, who also had power to distrain goods to recover payment. In the case of Quakers, a central tenet of whose faith was non-payment of tithes, the upper limit was set at £10.[53] Recourse to summary jurisdiction remained optional, and many clerics preferred the protection of the church courts for small claims. Tithe litigation also enabled the plaintiff to make an example of defendants and thereby, he hoped, dissuade others from similar non-payment. For this purpose speedy settlement before local JPs was not necessarily the best course.

Tithe collected in kind offered greater prospects of parochial discord. Not only was it awkward for farmers to set out the tenth shock of corn or to reserve the tenth pig or goose, but also local customs varied so much that new incumbents or new tenants might inadvertently infringe them and provoke dispute. The opportunities for deliberate vexation were also considerable. Typical was the behaviour of two inhabitants of Elstead (Surrey) who in 1668 and 1670 would not allow the incumbent to make his own cock of grass on their land without payment.[54] The tithe owner could make things awkward too. Legal decisions gave him the right to collect his tithe later than the rest of the harvest, thereby delaying any post-harvest pasturage or resowing. The expense of collecting less valuable tithes from large, scattered, upland parishes was also great.

So the advantages of moving towards money compositions were considerable if a suitable rate could be agreed. The drift away from in-kind payments becomes more pronounced in this period, though as late as 1750 tithing in kind of the more valuable and easily collected crops was by no means unusual, except in parts of the Midlands.[55] At Long Newton (Durham) the rector in the 1660s generally agreed a total composition sum for small tithes, while he collected corn in kind. At Stanhope between 1700 and 1714 compositions were regularly taken for sheep, lambs, and calves; at Whickham hay and corn tithes were compounded. At Barrow on Soar (Leics.) most tithes were

[52] 31 Geo. II, c. 12.

[53] 7 & 8 Wm III, c. 6; 7 & 8 Wm III, c. 34. On Quaker resistance to tithe payments, see Evans, thesis, pp. 178–239, A. Braithwaite, 'Early Tithe Prosecutions – Friends as Outlaws', *J. Friends' Hist. Soc.*, XLIX, 1960, pp. 148–56, and Eric J. Evans, '"Our Faithful Testimony" – The Society of Friends and Tithe Payments, 1690–1730', *ibid.*, LII, 1969, pp. 106–21.

[54] GMR, PSH/EL/12/1 (5). For similar examples, see, from Tamworth, LJRO, B/C/5, 1711–12; Kingswinford, PRO, E 112/740, no. 78; and Alton, Staffs. RO, D554/42.

[55] This revisionist assertion is more fully examined in Evans, *Contentious Tithe*, pp. 21–6.

taken by composition in the early eighteenth century, though some in-kind payment, including fleeces of wool, were received.[56] The transfer to cash payment described at Empingham (Rutland) in 1729 is probably typical: "tyth hay, corn, lambs, wool was paid in kind until about 10 or 12 years ago when Sir Thos. Mackworth for convenience & ease of his tenants let them be laid to the farms and since then they have been paid in composition money".[57]

After compositions had been agreed, tithing in kind could still be reimposed. This was done frequently in advance of litigation to establish the custom of the parish against an actual or prospective defendant. At Twineham (Sussex) in 1757 the rector gave notice to occupiers to set out their tithes in kind just before he began a tithe suit. A defendant ruefully noted: "There is no particular custom or manner of taking tithes in the parish as they have never been known to be taken in kind til very lately." John Dearle, vicar of Baswich (Staffs.) from 1710 to 1749, usually took compositions, but when he sought to establish his right to potato tithes in 1741 he demanded payment in kind. Defaulters were proceeded against in the Lichfield Diocesan Court.[58]

Even when compositions per crop or per acre were securely established, tithe remained an unpopular property. Tithe leases were difficult to arrange because of their uncertainty and the steady prospect of disagreement leading to litigation. Lessees well knew how sly and practised tenants had become in evading or minimizing their tithe dues. It was reported of the Holker estates in the Furness district of Lancashire in 1746: "I can't meet with any person willing to farm the tithe corn of Flookburch and Holker." At Birdsall (Yorks. E.R.) the tithes could not be let in 1702, and during a thin harvest at Bilborough in 1728 (Yorks. W.R.) enormous collection difficulties were experienced.[59] In Staffordshire in 1726 one observer suggested that tithes were "what no person desires to buy but to free their own estates from lay demands of".[60] In the mid eighteenth century tithe-free estates commanded higher rents. Landowners had persuasive reasons for seeking to rid their estates of tithe altogether when the parliamentary enclosure movement got under way in the 1760s.

Tithe was not a general disincentive to agricultural improvement in this period. Evasion was relatively easy and the pronounced trend towards composition payments, particularly for 'new' crops, eased the burden when

[56] Durham RO, Lo/F/192/4; EP/St1; EP/WL 31; Leics. RO, DE 108/15; DE 108/29. Examples of tithe in kind, selected to show regional coverage, may be found from Barningham and Staveley (Yorks.) in the 1730s, Leeds Archives Dept, RD/RG/2/2; Rokeby in the 1660s, N. Riding RO, ZNQ iv/7; Godalming (Surrey) in the 1690s, GLC RO, DW/S 53; Badwell Ash (Suffolk) in the 1720s, Suffolk RO (Bury St Edmunds), E3/10/10/2/26; Babworth (Notts.) in the 1670s, Reading Univ. Library, NOT/5/1/1; Newchurch (IOW) in the 1630s, Isle of Wight RO, SW/990.   [57] LAO, 3 Anc 7/16/6.

[58] E. Sussex RO, Hickstead Place MSS 1,101; William Salt Library, Stafford, S.Ms. 429/iii.

[59] Lancs. RO, DDCa/22/17/7; Leeds Archives Dept, TN/BL/C69; He37(a). See also Derby Public Library, Gale Bequest, bdle 3, Queries at Brassington, 1667.

[60] Staffs. RO, D1,790(W)/D/3/2.

investment decisions were made. Isolated references to disincentives can be found, of course. A Shropshire farmer asserted in 1747 that he would improve a piece of boggy ground by planting potatoes on it but only "provided the vicar were not to have the tithe". The earl of Suffolk was supposed to have converted ground in Saffron Walden to hop cultivation at about the same time only because it was tithe-free.[61] Landlords would naturally await the outcome of litigation when it was in progress before deciding on major improvement schemes. Overall, however, the main improvements were not directly threatened by tithes. Movements to convert from arable to grass usually had advantages for the tithe payer, since pasture land produced less valuable tithes and, very often, low monetary compositions in lieu of tithe. At Brassington (Derbs.) in the 1660s it was reported that "The tithes are much decayed as the town....is enclosed, yet formerly maintained tillage which was chargeable in ploughing, sowing, keeping servants etc....Now by mowing the ground they get real profit with less labour and charge...and tithe hay is not worth $\frac{1}{4}$ money that corn is."[62]

Offers to commute tithe during enclosure discussions were much less generous in the late seventeenth and early eighteenth centuries than would be the case during the parliamentary enclosure movement.[63] The inference is that proprietors were under less pressure to rid themselves of tithes than their early-nineteenth-century successors would be. An enclosure at Walton upon Trent (Derbs.) in 1652 gave the rector £66 10s. in lieu of all tithes in perpetuity, a bargain which no tithe owner would have countenanced in, say, 1790. The discussion of enclosure at Birdsall in 1669 included an offer to give the impropriator a straight tenth of the land to be enclosed, an almost equally unattractive offer by later standards.[64] Nevertheless, the practice of allotting land to exonerate tithe rights was gaining momentum in the early eighteenth century and protests such as that by the bishop of Lincoln in 1735 that proprietors should be content "with improving their own estates without attempting to sink other mens estates into them" cut little ice.[65] The interests of the church were by no means so extensively harmed as during the widespread conversions from arable to pasture in the late sixteenth and early seventeenth centuries, but its ability to strike hard bargains with landlords was not yet pronounced. In enclosure arrangements, as in leasing policy, it seems, the church remained on a "country gentleman's ramp" until the second half of the eighteenth century.[66] Tithe itself, whatever its individual vexations and even harassments, cannot plausibly be characterized as a crippling burden weighing down the landed interest.

[61] Shropshire RO, 112/box 20; Essex RO, D/DBY E9.
[62] Derby Public Library, Gale Bequest, bdle 3.   [63] Evans, *Contentious Tithe*, pp. 94–114.
[64] Derbs. RO, D1,129A/PZI; Sheffield City Library, WWM 76/29
[65] LAO, Mon 7/10/42.
[66] Hill, *Economic Problems*, pp. 100–6; C. Clay, '"The Greed of Whig Bishops"? Church Landlords and their Lessees, 1660–1760', *PP*, no. 87, 1980, pp. 128–57.

MARKET GARDENING IN ENGLAND AND WALES, 1640–1750

A. BEFORE 1640

Regular markets for horticultural produce pre-date the appearance of the first market gardeners in England and Wales. Garden wares were sold at St Paul's in London in the fourteenth century, and Colchester had a well-established vegetable market by 1529.[1] At such early markets, gardeners in the employ of the crown, of monastic institutions, and of the richer citizens sold surplus produce from their masters' gardens. Vegetables imported from Europe were sold in London from the early sixteenth century.[2]

It is not possible to say exactly where and when the first market gardeners in England and Wales began their trade. In the middle of the sixteenth century, however, there were men in London who made a living by tending their own or rented gardens and selling the produce.[3] By the first decade of the seventeenth century commercial gardening had spread to a number of places in England, mostly in the south and almost always near large towns. London had the largest number of market gardeners, some of whom held land within the city in the sixteenth century. By 1600, however, the relentless spread of buildings had pushed market gardens into the suburbs and surrounding countryside north and south of the Thames. Gardening was well established at Norwich by 1575. In Kent, Sandwich and Canterbury possessed market gardeners before 1600, as did Colchester in Essex. At Sandy in Bedfordshire, market gardening was started early in the seventeenth century. Gardeners at Worksop in Nottinghamshire and Pontefract in Yorkshire were growing liquorice in the second half of the sixteenth century.[4]

---

[1] H. T. Riley, *Memorials of London and London Life*, London, 1868, pp. 228–9; Philip Morant, *The History and Antiquities of the Most Ancient Town and Borough of Colchester*, London, 1748, bk I, p. 76.

[2] George W. Johnson, *A History of English Gardening*, London, 1829, p. 56; William Harrison, *The Description of England*, ed. Georges Edden, New York, 1968, pp. 263–4; T. McLean, *Medieval English Gardens*, London, 1981, pp. 73–4; Brian Dietz, ed., *The Port and Trade of Early Elizabethan London: Documents*, London Rec. Soc., 1972, pp. 152–5.

[3] John Stow, *A Survey of London*, ed. C. L. Kingsford, 2 vols., Oxford, 1908, *I*, pp. 126, 129; Ralph Agas, *Civitas Londinium c. 1560* (map), London, 1874.

[4] John Gerarde, *The Herbal, or General Historie of Plantes*, London, 1636, p. 232; W. Folkingham, *Feudigraphia*, London, 1610, p. 42; Thomas Fuller, *The History of the Worthies of England*, London, 1662, pp. 76–7; Samuel Hartlib, *His Legacie, or an Enlargement of the Discours of Husbandrie Used in Brabant and Flanders*, 2nd edn, London, 1652, pp. 8–9; Kent AO, PRC 10 box 2, f. 12; William

Although commercial gardening was a relatively new craft in the early seventeenth century, methods of production and crops grown could vary considerably from area to area and gardener to gardener. The majority of market gardeners grew edible vegetables, some also grew fruit and flowers, and a few raised and sold nursery wares. Some occupied relatively small pieces of land, often under ten acres, used only hand tools for cultivation, and, by dint of much labour and manuring, produced very high outputs per acre. Such gardeners were called kitchen gardeners because their gardens resembled those beside private houses which provided fresh vegetables for the table. In contrast, 'farmer-gardener' is the term which will be used to describe those market gardeners who cultivated farms on which both field and garden crops were grown. Such farms were usually larger than kitchen gardens, and in most cases only a small part of the total arable land on each farm-garden was cropped with spade-cultivated garden crops in any one year.

The trades of nurseryman and seedsman had hardly emerged as distinct occupations by 1640. Gardeners in private employment who tended the pleasure gardens of the rich obtained the plants they needed mostly by raising them themselves, buying them from other private gardeners or from kitchen gardeners, or in some cases sending abroad for them. The large number of private gardens in and near London and Westminster, however, led to the development of a regular trade there in nursery wares and to the establishment of a few full-time nurserymen in the area.[5] The small amount of evidence so far discovered suggests that most garden seeds sold in England and Wales before 1640 were imported from Europe via London by English and foreign merchants and retailed by market gardeners and shopkeepers.[6]

Most of the increase in the demand for market-garden produce in the sixteenth and early seventeenth centuries was for edible vegetables. Both rich and poor in the early sixteenth century probably regarded much garden produce as inferior food. In the seventeenth century some of the nobility and gentry continued to despise vegetables as fit only for the poor or foreigners. Others, however, copied the French upper classes in admitting vegetables to their tables, albeit usually exotic or delicate vegetables too expensive for the poor. Even so, garden produce played a minor part in meals, which were

Boys, *Collections for an History of Sandwich*, Canterbury, 1792, pp. 361, 747; F. Beavington, 'Early Market Gardening in Bedfordshire', *Inst. Brit. Geographers*, XXXVII, Dec. 1965; Richard Holmes, ed., *Collections towards the History of Pontefract, I*, Pontefract, 1882, p. 240; W. Camden, *Britannia*, 1695, facs., Newton Abbot, 1971, pp. 485, 712, 715; *The Walloon Church of Norwich: Its Registers and History*, ed. W. J. C. Moens, Huguenot Soc. of London, I, 1887–8, p. 262; *Returns of Aliens*, ed. R. E. G. Kirk and E. F. Kirk, Huguenot Soc., X, iii, Aberdeen, 1907, pp. 139, 140, 147, 166, 168, 170, 171, 173, 231, 340, 400, 423; *Register of Baptisms in the Dutch Church at Colchester*, ed. W. J. C. Moens, Huguenot Soc., XII, Lymington, 1905, pp. 95–101, 105–6.

[5] John H. Harvey, *Early Nurserymen*, London, 1974, pp. 30, 32, 39, 40, 41; Harrison, *op. cit.*, p. 264.

[6] Harvey, *op. cit.*, pp. 30–1; Harrison, *op. cit.*, p. 264; Dietz, *op. cit.*, pp. 63, 78.

still dominated by meat. Many of the vegetables eaten by the rich came not from the market but from their own gardens.[7]

The poor took to vegetables not out of choice but of necessity, supplementing their meagre diet with them because of the rising prices of grain and animal products. Peas, beans, cabbages, carrots, parsnips, turnips, radishes, Jerusalem artichokes, onions, and summer salad stuff were eaten in quantity by the poor of London and other large towns and by some country folk by 1600. Root vegetables in particular formed a substantial part of the diet of some. Dutch immigrants introduced the commercial production of root crops (carrots, turnips, and parsnips), and by the 1570s the poor of Norwich were sustained by roots grown by Dutch settlers.[8] In the famine years of the 1590s large shipments of roots were sent from Norwich via the port of Yarmouth and from Colchester to London. From Yarmouth to London, between the months of October and March in each case, the following tonnages of roots were shipped: 1593–4, 280; 1597–8, 812; 1589–90, 639; 1600–1, 112.[9] In the early seventeenth century the inhabitants of Bristol and Manchester supplemented their diet with turnips, and a few years earlier the Welsh were said to eat them raw. By the end of the sixteenth century parsnips and carrots were "common meate among the common people, all the time of autumne, and chiefly uppon fish daies".[10]

The continuing demand for roots in London encouraged farmer-gardeners and kitchen gardeners to grow them in the country around the capital. At the end of the sixteenth century Hackney supplied turnips to London markets. Subsequently Fulham, Kensington, and Chelsea, furnished much of the capital's needs, sending 20,000 loads of roots per year to the markets of London and Westminster by 1635.[11]

Immigrants played an important part in the early history of market gardening in England and Wales. Among the many Dutch and French Protestant refugees who fled to England in the sixteenth century were some, mainly Dutch, who were market gardeners or gardeners' labourers. These men quickly began to practise their trade in England, setting up market

[7] Ben Johnson, Epigramme CXXXIV, The English Poets, ed. S. Johnson, V, London, 1810, p. 515; Tudor Economic Documents, ed. R. H. Tawney and E. Power, III, London, 1924, p. 41; Harrison, op. cit., pp. 264–5; John Parkinson, Paradisi in Sole, London, 1629, p. 466; HMC, Rutland MSS, IV, 1905, pp. 462, 468, 469, 471, 476, 479, 498, 543; Sir Thomas Overbury, The Overburian Charactery, ed. W. J. Taylor, Oxford, 1936, pp. 74, 59–60; J. C. Drummond and A. Wilbraham, The Englishman's Food, rev. D. Hollingsworth, London, 1957, pp. 49, 53, 54–5.

[8] The Walloon Church of Norwich, p. 262; Parkinson, op. cit., pp. 461, 469, 518, 521, 522; Gerarde, op. cit., p. 232; Harrison, op. cit., p. 216; Thomas Cogan, The Haven of Health, London, 1596, pp. 61, 63, 74.

[9] PRO, E 190, 594/9; E 190, 474/17; E 190, 480/5; E 190, 477/8; E 190, 481/11.

[10] Cogan, op. cit., p. 63; John Aubrey, The Natural History of Wiltshire, ed. John Britton, Wilts. Top. Soc., London, 1847, p. 36; Gerarde, op. cit., p. 232; E. Kerridge, The Agricultural Revolution, London, 1967, p. 340.

[11] Folkingham, op. cit., p. 42; Corp. of London RO, City Repertories, 49, ff. 261–3.

gardens at Sandwich, Colchester, Norwich, Canterbury, Maidstone, and London. Except in London, they were the first market gardeners at these places.[12]

Coming from that part of Europe where market gardening and intensive arable husbandry were most highly developed, they brought with them a great deal of practical and commercial expertise. The agriculture which they and their descendants practised at Sandwich was akin to that in operation in parts of the Low Countries. It was the Dutch who first grew turnips and other roots for sale in England; they were probably the first commercial florists in this country; they introduced canary seed as a farm-garden crop to east Kent; and they may well have been the first to raise seeds for the market at Sandwich and Colchester. In spreading market gardening to many parts of southern England, and in showing the profitability of horticulture, they did much to stimulate this new branch of agriculture.[13]

B. 1640–1750

By 1640 market gardeners occupied land at many places in southern England and in a few locations in the north. Root crops were raised for human consumption in Wales by either market gardeners or farmers. In the places where the immigrant gardeners of the sixteenth century had started gardening, their descendants and others carried on the trade.[14]

London in 1640 had market gardens on all sides; to the west at Westminster, Kensington, Chelsea, Fulham, Isleworth, and Twickenham; to the north and east at Spitalfields, Hackney, Shoreditch, Stepney, and Smithfield; to the south across the Thames at Barnes, Putney, Battersea, Lambeth, Southwark, and Bermondsey. London's demand for food also encouraged gardening at Gravesend in Kent at this time.[15] In the provinces there were market gardeners around Oxford, Banbury, Henley, York, Nottingham, Bristol, and Ipswich, and in the parish of Sandy in Bedfordshire.[16] The occurrence of one or two gardeners in villages not

[12] *Lists of Foreign Protestants and Aliens*, Camden Soc., London, 1862, p. 11; *The Walloon Church of Norwich*, p. 262; *Returns of Aliens, loc. cit.*; *Register of Baptisms in the Dutch Church at Colchester*, pp. 105–6; Boys, *op. cit.*, pp. 742, 743, 747; Hartlib, *op cit.*, pp. 8–9; Fuller, *op. cit.*, pp. 76–7.

[13] B. H. Slicher van Bath, *The Agrarian History of Western Europe*, tr. O. Ordish, London, 1963, p. 241; *The Walloon Church of Norwich*, p. 262; G. W. Johnson, *op. cit.*, p. 132; I. Elstob, *The Garden Book of Sir Thomas Hanmer Bart.*, London, 1933, p. xxviii; J. C. Loudon, *An Encyclopaedia of Gardening*, London, 1822, p. 81.

[14] Gerarde, *op. cit.*, p. 232; Aubrey, *op. cit.*, p. 36.

[15] John Norden, *The Surveyor's Dialogue*, 2nd edn, London, 1610, p. 168; Folkingham, *op. cit.*, p. 42; Hartlib, *op. cit.*, p. 9; HMC, *Egmont, I*, 1905, p. 531; (map) Moses Glover, *Istelworth Hundred Being the Manor of Sion etc.* (1635), Edward Stanford, London, 1880; Guildford MR, MS 3,389/2, Abstracts of Wills, in PCC 1610–60; Corp. of London RO, City Repertories, 49, ff. 261–3; *Returns of Aliens*, pp. 168, 170, 171, 173.

[16] Bodleian Library, MS Wills Oxon. 85/5/39; 131/5/24; 32/1/16; 295/1/72; 51/2/9; MS Wills Peculiars 56/4/13; 48/1/20; Wadham Coll., Oxford, Muniments 78/1 & 2; Harvey, *op.*

especially noted for market gardening could indicate that there was a rural demand for vegetables, although these gardeners may have been in private employment at country houses. Pontefract and Worksop continued to be areas where liquorice was grown.[17]

Many towns were still not served by market gardeners in 1640. The period from then until the end of the century, however, saw a steady advance in all types of commercial horticulture. London in the second half of the seventeenth century continued to lead the country in the size and sophistication of its market gardening. The loss of garden ground in the suburbs as the city expanded was more than made up as commercial gardening spread into Middlesex, Surrey, Essex, and Kent, and as many gardeners increased the intensity of their production. In Surrey the common fields of Croydon were tilled and dug for vegetables by farmer-gardeners, and Godalming became well known for its liquorice and root crops. Market gardeners in southern Essex and along the north Kent coast began to cultivate land to supply London and local markets. Gardeners at Sandwich and Colchester let some of their vegetables stand for seed which was sent to London. Garden ground in the vicinity of London was estimated to have expanded from 10,000 acres in 1660 to 110,000 acres in 1721.[18]

Away from the influence of London, gardeners began to exploit the very favourable soils around Evesham in the second half of the seventeenth century, sending produce south to Bristol and north to the Midlands. In the Vale of Taunton Dean in Somerset gardeners grew carrots and other vegetables for consumption in Bristol. Further west, around Exeter, Plymouth, along the South Hams seaboard, and in south-east Devon, market gardening developed well before 1700. Gardeners sold their produce at Leeds in the 1690s, and in the same county liquorice growing overflowed from Pontefract to nearby Featherstone.[19]

cit., pp. 63–4; John H. Harvey, 'The Family of Telford, Nurserymen of York', Yorks. Arch. J., XIII, 167, 1969, pp. 352–7; Charles Deering, Nottinghamia Vetus et Nova, Nottingham, 1751, pp. 93, 97; Bristol RO, Invs. of Joanne Weston, 25 Mar. 1625; John Carpenter, 10 Oct. 1643; Norden, op. cit., p. 168; Beavington, 'Early Market Gardening in Bedfordshire', p. 93.

[17] Bodleian Library, MS Wills Oxon., 7/2/9; 76/1/10a; Norfolk RO, INV 49A/16; INV 30/57.

[18] Richard Bradley, A General Treatise of Husbandry and Gardening, II, London, 1726, p. 273; Greater London RO (M), AM/PI(1) 1682/35; E. C. Willatts, Middlesex and the London Region, ed. L. D. Stamp, LUS 79, London, 1937, pp. 284, 294; John Aubrey, The Natural History and Antiquities of Surrey, IV, London, 1718, p. 16; LPL, UH 96/1,062; PRO, E 134, 20 & 21 Chas II, Hil. 14.; E 134, 33 & 34 Chas II, Hil. 26; K. H. Burley, 'The Economic Development of Essex in the Later Seventeenth and Early Eighteenth Centuries', unpub. London Univ. Ph.D. thesis, 1957, pp. 57, 278; Kent AO, PRC 11/57/55; PRC 11/59/248; DRb/Pi 1/20; DRb/Pi 3/40; DRb/Pi 5/42; DRb/Pi 8/58; DRb/Pi 18/17; DRb/Pi 18/43; U269 E21.

[19] R. C. Gaut, A History of Worcestershire Agriculture, Worcester, 1939, p. 112; R. W. Sidwell, 'A Short History of Commercial Horticulture in the Vale of Evesham', Vale of Evesham Hist. Soc. Research Papers, II, 1969, pp. 43–51; PRO, E 190, 1,250/4; E 190, 1,251/15; E 190, 1,253/14; William Tindal, The History and Antiquities of the Abbey and Borough of Evesham, Evesham, 1794, p. 208; Leeds City Archives, TN/EA/13/49; Borthwick Inst., Tithes R VII H 4,529.

The spread of market gardening continued during the first half of the eighteenth century so that by 1750 most large towns in England and quite a few smaller centres of population were supplied with locally grown fresh vegetables. In the north of England gardening was expanding in Lancashire and Cheshire, supplying the growing northern towns. In Wales, Llandaff produced vegetables for Cardiff and sent garden produce across the Severn to Bristol. The fashionable resort of Abergavenny also had a market-gardening hinterland.[20]

The substantial increase in market gardening was largely due to the continuing demand from the poor for vegetables. Roots, beans, peas, cabbages, and other common garden produce poured into London markets. Tolls totalling £1,816 10s., levied at the rate of 2d. a horseload and between 3d. and 6d. a cartload per day were taken in 1696 on peas, beans, and roots brought into the Stocks, Newgate, and Leadenhall markets. Vegetables were consumed in London in such quantities that "in some seasons the gardens feed more people than the fields". In the second half of the seventeenth century it was claimed that garden produce was "meat, bread and drink in such years that corn hath been scarce".[21] It was even suggested in the 1670s that so much were the poor substituting vegetables for grain in their diet that it was a cause of "the deadness of the market for corn". This may have been so in London, but the advocacy by some writers on agricultural matters at this time of more market gardening to help feed the poor indicates that much of the population was still dependent on other foods. Even so, Gregory King estimated that English *per capita* consumption of vegetables and fruit in 1696 was higher than that of Holland, the home of European market gardening, and another writer thought that the English ate more vegetables than the French.[22]

Garden vegetables were more in evidence on the tables of the middle and upper classes than they had been before the Civil War as more of the rich copied the French in regarding vegetables as acceptable foods. At the end of the seventeenth century a 'respectable' household served boiled beef "besieged with five or six heaps of cabbage, carrots, turnips or some other herbs or roots". A foreign visitor to London in 1748 found that his hosts ate butcher's meat as the main ingredient of their dinners, accompanied by

[20] D. J. Davies, *Economic History of South Wales prior to 1800*, Cardiff, 1933, p. 110; Cheshire RO, DUA/5 Agden Tithes. See eighteenth-century plans of such towns as Birmingham (1731), Bristol (1743), York (1851), Salisbury (1751), Canterbury (1768).

[21] Figures calculated from P. V. McGrath, 'The Marketing of Food, Fodder, and Livestock in the London Area in the Seventeenth Century', unpub. London Univ. M.A. thesis, 1948, pp. 195–6; Fuller, *Worthies of England*, p. 543; John Worlidge, *Systema Horti-Culturae, or the Art of Gardening*, London, 1677, p. 173.

[22] Worlidge, *op. cit.*, pp. 173, 174; Gregory King, *Natural and Political Observations and Conclusions*, 1696, in *The Earliest Classics*, ed. Peter Laslett, Farnborough, 1973, p. 67; *M. Misson's Memoirs and Observations*, tr. Mr Ozell, London, 1719, pp. 125–6.

boiled roots or cucumbers, lettuce, salad, and spinach, and also served green beans and peas when they were in season.[23]

Although by the eighteenth century the rich would eat even common root vegetables, throughout the period they demanded exotic vegetables and vegetables grown out of season. The latter demand stimulated technical advances in commercial gardening by inducing kitchen gardeners to use glassware and artificial heat to extend their growing season. The demand for the exotic was often self-defeating: the taste for new vegetables which could be easily grown tended to move down the social scale – artichokes, once sold for "crownes apiece" were in 1629 "so common here with us at London, that even the most vulgar begin to despise them".[24]

The great increase in the size and number of private gardens from the sixteenth century encouraged the trades of nurseryman and seedsman. The monarchy and nobility set the fashion for such gardens, but they were emulated by those lower in the social scale so that during the seventeenth and early eighteenth centuries gentlemen of quite modest means created ornamental and kitchen gardens beside their houses. The large scale of new gardens laid out by the nobility, extensive remodelling of existing ones according to the dictates of fashion, the constant desire of all those with gardens for new plants, trees, shrubs, and flowers, and the inability of the poorest gentlemen to make any provision for their own plants and seeds all added to the trade of seedsman and nurseryman.[25]

Access to market was the most important consideration for a market gardener choosing the site of his garden. Most market gardens were in or near towns, being some distance from population centres only when such a location was particularly favourable to gardening. Good transport as well as proximity to the market influenced the siting of gardens. The importance of the Thames and the main roads from London to the north and west can be clearly seen in the location of market gardening in Middlesex by the 1750s. Kitchen gardeners near the Thames in St Martin-in-the-Fields owned their own boats, and fleets of gardeners' boats from some miles upstream were to be seen in the early morning sailing down the Thames to Queenhithe and Billingsgate markets. Coastal shipping allowed gardeners in Kent, Essex, Suffolk, and Norfolk to send produce to London, and river transport was important in opening up markets for gardeners at Evesham and

[23] M. Misson's Memoirs, p. 314; The Diary of Samuel Pepys, ed. Robert Latham and William Matthews, I, 1660, London, 1970, p. 269; Pehr Kalm, Kalm's Account of his Visit to England on his Way to America in 1748, ed. J. Lucas, London, 1892, p. 14.

[24] The Tatler, no. 148, 18–21 Mar. 1709; Thomas Muffet, Health's Improvement, London, 1655, pp. 215, 216; Parkinson, Paradisi in Sole, p. 518.

[25] Miles Hadfield, A History of British Gardening, London, 1969, pp. 40–179; Stephen Switzer, Ichnographia Rustica, London, 1718, pt I, pp. 1–97; Elstob, Garden Book of Sir Thomas Hanmer Bart., pp. xvii–xix; Worlidge, op. cit., 'Preface to the Reader'; David Green, Gardener to Queen Anne: Henry Wise and the Formal Garden, Oxford, 1956, pp. 107–11, 135–51.

Tewkesbury.[26] Nevertheless, market gardening also flourished in places like Sandwich and Colchester and in some land-locked areas of Middlesex and Surrey despite their distance from main markets.

Gardeners who had to transport produce overland used pack horses with panniers, or carts. Strings of pack horses left Evesham in the eighteenth century with garden produce bound for the Midland towns. The more robust vegetables – root crops, peas, and beans – could be piled into carts and taken several miles over difficult roads without undue damage. Carts laden with such vegetables caused serious congestion in London markets before the Great Fire, and in the eighteenth century cartloads of roots probably made the long journey from Sandy to London.[27] However they travelled, vegetables and fruit benefited from careful packing, and a variety of wickerwork containers were used for this purpose – baskets, flaskets, maunds, hampers, skips, barges, pots, combs, and sieves.

Intensive gardening requires large amounts of fertilizer, so the availability of manure influenced the location of gardening and also production methods. Those gardeners near towns received animal and human waste from stables, streets, and privies. Again, water transport was important, for, in the early seventeenth century, "The soyle of the stables of London, especially neere the Thames-side, is carried westward by water to Chelsey, Fulham, Battersey, and Putney and those parts for their sandie grounds". Throughout the period manure from London was delivered to farmers and gardeners by barge on the tidal part of the Thames at a fraction of the cost of overland transport. Londoners were glad to be rid of the manure, and the gardeners were quick to point out to the City the service they were doing in removing it.[28]

With the aid of manure and other fertilizers the London gardeners could almost manufacture their own soils; good gardening soils occurring naturally in other areas encouraged market gardening. At Sandwich the land was "light, sandy and fresh" and particularly suitable for seed growing. Sandy also had a light soil: a deep sand, yellowish brown in colour, composed of smaller grains than other sand in the area. The best gardening soils at Evesham were "naturally black, fertile and easily worked". Within the walls of

[26] Greater London RO (M), AM/PI(1) 1682/18; AM/PI(1) 1718/10; The Spectator, VI, 414, Wed. 25 June 1712; Willatts, Middlesex and the London Region, Fig. 74, p. 294; Burley, thesis, p. 278; Boys, Collections for an History of Sandwich, pp. 742–3; PRO, E 190, 594/9; E 190, 474/17; E 190, 480/5; E 190, 477/8; E 190, 481/11; E 190, 1,250/4; E 190, 1,253/14; E 190, 1,251/15; Norden, Surveyor's Dialogue, p. 168.

[27] W. Pitt, A General View of the Agriculture of the County of Worcester, London, 1810, p. 147; Corp. of London RO, City Repertories, 34, f. 38; Guildford MR, MSS, vv, f. 129; Beavington, 'Early Market Gardening in Bedfordshire', p. 98.

[28] Thomas Read, A New Description of Gloucestershire, Hampshire, the Isle of Wight, etc., London, 1749, p. 445; Norden, op. cit., p. 191; Kalm, Visit to England, pp. 143–4; Cal. S.P., Venetian, 1618, London, 1909, p. 318; John Middleton, General View of the Agriculture of Middlesex, London, 1798, p. 303; W. T. Crosweller, The Gardeners' Company: A Short Chronological History, 1605–1907, London, 1908, p. 11.

Colchester the soil was sandy, rich, and black – very suitable for gardening. Further north in Suffolk the hot sands near the coast were good for root crops. Godalming and Pontefract both had the deep sandy soils essential to successful liquorice growing.[29]

Market gardening was labour-intensive, so the availability of cheap labour or the need for extra income of those with smallholdings was a factor in the establishment of horticulture in some areas. Acquiescence on the part of landlords and others whose interests were affected by big changes in land use and methods of cultivation was a precondition for the successful establishment of horticulture, as was a willingness to experiment on the part of the cultivators of the land.

Labour, enterprise, and a lack of institutional or landlord constraints were frequently found together. In the vales of Evesham and Tewkesbury vigorous peasant communities, where manorial control was often lax and freeholders were numerous, adopted market gardening in the course of the seventeenth century, along with other forms of intensive agriculture and industrial by-employment. These developments utilized the surplus labour in the area which owed its existence to a social and institutional structure which over a long period of time encouraged population expansion.[30] At Sandy, where market gardening fitted comfortably into the open fields, there were a large number of small freeholders engaged in gardening. Neithrop, a suburban hamlet of Banbury, had market gardeners among its inhabitants from the early seventeenth century. Its common fields were, long before enclosure, largely cultivated by freeholders. Always the most populous hamlet of Banbury owing to immigration, Neithrop degenerated in the early nineteenth century into a crowded slum.[31] At Sandwich, Colchester, and Norwich, the arrival of Dutch and Flemish refugees gave an initial impetus to market gardening, and the settlement of these industrious people played no small part in determining the location of market gardening in the seventeenth century.

Once established, market gardening encouraged population growth; at Evesham, population increase between the third quarter of the seventeenth century and 1801 was many times the national average. In the early

---

[29] Read, op cit., p. 411; Thomas Batchelor, General View of the Agriculture of the County of Bedford, London, 1808, p. 456; Tindal, History of Evesham, p. 208; K. M. Buchanan, Worcestershire, LUS 68, London, 1944, p. 628–31; Morant, History of Colchester, p. 1; Holmes, History of Pontefract, I, p. 239; William Ellis, The Modern Husbandman...October, IV, Dublin, 1743, p. 172; Norden, op. cit., p. 168; L. D. Stamp, E. C. Willatts, and D. W. Shave, Surrey, LUS 81, London, 1941, p. 382.

[30] Joan Thirsk, 'New Crops and their Diffusion: Tobacco-Growing in Seventeenth Century England', in Rural Change and Urban Growth, 1500–1800, ed. C. W. Chalklin and M. A. Havinden, London, 1974, pp. 88–93.

[31] Arthur Young, ed., The Annals of Agriculture, 46 vols., London, 1784–1815, XLII, p. 28; VCH Oxon., X, pp. 27, 44, 54.

nineteenth century at Evesham it was claimed that the availability of jobs in the gardens encouraged early marriage or bastardy, and in 1906 in the vale it was "almost possible to pick out the market gardening area from the agricultural parishes by the increase or decrease in the population".[32]

Other factors of local significance influenced the location of individual gardens – the dissolution of religious houses in towns in the sixteenth century made monastery gardens near to markets available to kitchen gardeners. Tithes were burdensome, and at least one gardener at Colchester sought to avoid tithes by occupying land in the precincts of the defunct castle, claiming that the land was tithe-free because it was within the tithing area of the redundant castle chapel. Further research may bring to light similar instances of tithe avoidance.[33]

The high output associated with gardening was achieved by technical efficiency; this was especially true of kitchen gardening. Kitchen gardens were usually small in comparison with other arable holdings, generally under ten acres and often a good deal smaller. Ten acres was established as the maximum holding of members of the London Gardeners' Company in 1649: some members, however, evaded this regulation by working land outside the company's jurisdiction, more than six miles from the City.[34] In the 1630s, enclosed gardens at Fulham, producing bush fruit and flowers, were commonly under three acres in size, and in the 1660s Samuel Hartlib knew "divers, which by 2 or 3 acres of land maintain themselves and family, and imploy other [sic] about their ground". The optimum size for a kitchen garden was only a few acres, because rents were high, as were the costs per acre of labour and manure needed to maintain a large output of crops. Therefore, only the richest of gardeners could afford a large establishment. In some instances, kitchen gardeners rented several small patches of land near to towns rather than one large garden – an indication either of land shortage in surburban areas or that gardeners were willing to rent pieces of land with very productive soils despite the inconveniences of a scattered holding.[35]

Kitchen gardens were cultivated with hand tools. The soil was dug, stirred, pulverized, and cleansed with the spade, fork, hoe, rake, mattock, and stone

[32] Tindal, op. cit., pp. 213–14; L. A. Clarkson, The Pre-Industrial Economy in England, 1500–1750, London, 1971, p. 26; VCH Worcs., IV, p. 472; William Salt Library, Stafford, Salt MS/33, p. 135; B. R. Mitchell and P. Deane, Abstract of British Historical Statistics, Cambridge, 1962, p. 8; Evesham Public Library, An Account of Proceedings in the Parish of All Saints in the Borough of Evesham towards Obtaining an Act of Parliament...to Erect a House of Industry, 24 Oct. 1806.

[33] John Stow, A Survey of London, 1603, ed. C. L. Kingsford, I, Oxford, 1908, pp. 126, 131; Tindal, op. cit., p. 208; PRO, E 134, 3 Wm & Mary, Mich. 5, Essex.

[34] Crosweller, Gardeners' Company, pp. 15–16; Greater London RO (M), AM/PI(1) 1682/18; Guildford MR, MS 3,389/2, Abstracts of Wills in P.C.C. 1610–60.

[35] Corp. of London RO, City Repertories 49, ff. 261–3; Hartlib, His Legacie, 2nd edn, p. 8; Norfolk RO, Norwich Archdeaconry Invs., case 33 shelf F pcl 124 no. 54; case 33 shelf F pcl 12 no. 91; Notts. RO, PRNW Mary Parkinson, 12 July 1712; Kent AO, PRC 10/60 no. 111.

roller. Gardeners evolved variants of these tools for particular tasks – carrot and asparagus forks for lifting those vegetables from the soil, dung forks for manuring, and a variety of hoes for weeding. They used reels and lines and dibbers to set crops in rows. For irrigation, watering pots – earthenware vessels with narrow necks and broad bases pierced by small holes – were in general use early in the period, later being superseded by metal watering cans. For larger-scale watering, tubs mounted on barrows were employed. Dung barrows carried manure to various parts of the gardens and wheelbarrows were used for general carrying. To shelter growing crops London gardeners put up reed 'hedges' or hurdles and 'bass' mats made from woven reeds. All these tools and pieces of garden equipment were relatively inexpensive; most kitchen gardeners owned under £1 worth.[36]

One type of garden utensil was expensive, namely, glassware. The introduction of glass utensils was the most important technical innovation in market gardening in the seventeenth century. Glass covers gave plants protection from wind, precipitation, and the cold while allowing access to sunlight. With glass a gardener could force crops to grow faster and grow them out of season. Bell glasses were the most versatile pieces of garden glassware; these were bell-shaped covers, sometimes called 'hand-', 'mellon', or 'moving-glasses', which were placed over individual plants or groups of seedlings. Flat glass panes, known as 'lights', were set against each other tentwise to form cloches, and also fitted into frames which were put on top of boxes of boards to enclose completely small patches of garden while letting in the sunlight. Often, two sides of the boxes were tapered, so that the frames were angled toward the sun's rays.[37]

For most of the period bell glasses were valued at between 6d. and 9d. each. Towards the middle of the eighteenth century, however, 1s. 6d. each was the usual price. The price of lights and frames depended on size; those employed by London gardeners in the mid eighteenth century were worth between 4s. and 7s. each.[38]

Certainly London kitchen gardeners made the earliest and most extensive use of glassware, beginning to employ it in the third quarter of the seventeenth century. Previously its use had been confined to private gardens. By the eighteenth century some London kitchen gardeners had invested

---

[36] Stephen Blake, *The Compleat Gardener's Practice*, London, 1664, p. 140; Kent AO, PRC 27/33/2; Norfolk RO, INV/79 box 20/B no. 8; case 33 shelf E pcl 4 f. 148; Greater London RO (M), AM/PI(1) 1718/10; AM/PI(1) 1682/35; PRO, PROB 3 49/21. The average value of hand tools listed in 18 kitchen gardeners' inventories from between 1681 and 1747 was 15s. 7d.

[37] Kalm, *Visit to England*, p. 7.

[38] Norfolk RO, INV/78 box 200 A no. 41; INV/79 box 201 E no. 23; case 33 shelf F pcl 124 no. 54; PRO, PROB 3/26/198; Bodleian Library, MS Wills Peculiars 52/1/38; Greater London RO (M), AM/PI(1) 1681/11; Oxford City Library, Quarter Sess., 1706 Mich., 15; Surrey RO, Quarter Sess., 6/2/Midsummer 1750/62 to /105; Corp. of London RO, Orphans Invs. Box 12, Common Serjeant's Book II, f. 331.

considerable sums in glassware. At his death in 1718, a gardener of St Martin-in-the-Fields possessed 1,240 bell glasses and a number of lights, together worth between £30 and £40. Forty-three gardeners of Bermondsey, Southwark, Lambeth, Camberwell, and Walworth had their glassware extensively damaged by a hailstorm in the summer of 1750. Together their losses were reckoned at £2,537, eleven of them losing over £100 worth of glass each.[39] Outside the London area kitchen gardeners took to glassware more slowly and on a more modest scale. A Canterbury gardener died in 1718 owning £2 worth of glass; six Norfolk kitchen gardeners who died between 1719 and 1748 possessed glass worth on average 63s. each; a gardener of Banbury owned 3s. worth of bell glasses in 1712.[40]

Those gardeners incorporated in the London Gardeners' Company in 1649 claimed to employ among them 1,500 men, women, and children, and 400 apprenticies, an average of up to 6 labourers and 1 or 2 apprentices per gardener. In the 1770s, Hammersmith kitchen gardeners employed 8 men and 4 women per twenty acres the year round, and in addition hired 16 women per twenty acres during the summer. Just over twenty years later it was reported that London kitchen gardens gave work to an average of 10 persons per acre all year, and up to 25 more for the harvest. Many of the seasonal workers were women who had travelled to London from as far afield as Wales.[41]

Like their private counterparts, commercial kitchen gardens were carefully laid out. The cultivated area usually consisted of a number of rectangular pieces of ground, described variously as beds, patches, pieces, plots, plats, spots, and quarters. Some London gardeners constructed sloping beds angled towards the sun. Narrow paths separated the beds and gave access to each. All available space was pressed into cultivation; even borders under walls and between paths were planted with crops. Garden walls, useful as shelter and protection from thieves, often supported fruit frees which benefited from the warmth absorbed by the walls from the summer sun. Gardens without walls in London had reed fences, plank fences, or stout hedges around them.[42]

It was an advantage for kitchen gardeners to be near to fresh water for irrigation. Gardeners at the Neat Houses in Westminster constructed irrigation channels and 'dip holes' to bring Thames water into their gardens.

[39] Greater London RO (M), AM(PI(1) 1718/10; AM/PI(1) 1684/93; Surrey RO, Quarter Sess., 6/2/Midsummer 1750 /62 to /106.

[40] Bodleian Library, MS Wills Peculiars 52/1/38; Norfolk RO, Archdeaconry Invs. INV/78 box 200 A no. 4; INV/79 box 201 B no. 8; INV/79 box 201 E no. 23; case 33 shelf F pcl 22 no. 28; case 33 shelf F pcl 124 no. 54; Kent AO, PRC 11/74/31.

[41] Arthur Young, A Six Months Tour through the North of England, 4 vols., London, 1770, IV, pp. 24–5; Crosweller, op. cit., pp. 15–16; McGrath, thesis, p. 200; W. H. Pyne, The Costume of Great Britain, London, 1808, p. 17; Kalm, op. cit., p. 83; T. Baird, General View of the Agriculture of the County of Middlesex, London, 1793, p. 46.

[42] Greater London RO (M), AM/PI(1) 1718/10; Kalm, op. cit., pp. 7, 27–8, 32–4.

On the Surrey bank of the Thames opposite London, pumps raised water to the gardens.[43]

Much of the high output of kitchen gardeners was achieved by dint of careful soil preparation; frequent digging was the hallmark of kitchen gardening. The Dutch at Norwich were said to have done much digging in order to produce large quantities of roots, and the first Dutch gardeners to arrive in Surrey dug their land so regularly that they worried their landlords, who feared they would damage the soil. Seventeenth-century gardening books exhorted their readers to dig their ground like 'ordinary' or market gardeners.[44]

Thorough digging involved turning the soil to a depth of at least two spade blades, starting with a trench into which adjacent soil was turned, and so continuing across the garden, carefully extracting weeds as the digging progressed. Winter was the main digging season, with more done in the spring to remove weeds and reopen the soil to the air.[45] Dung and other additives such as sand, soot, ashes, and marls were often put into the soil when it was dug; London gardens were said to have been "in a manner made new and fresh once in two or three years, by dung and soil, and good trenching" so that the same crops could be continually grown on them without fear of rot or canker.[46] Manure was kept in carefully managed heaps, not being used to fertilize growing crops until it was quite rotted and odourless, for fear it would taint them. Gardeners also employed dung to heat soil and growing crops, forcing them to mature quickly or out of season. Kitchen gardeners formed hot dung, still decomposing, into long beds about three feet high and broad, on top of which a few inches of fine soil or mould were sprinkled. On these 'hot beds' were forced such crops as radishes, mushrooms, cucumber plants, asparagus, and seedlings, sometimes under glass. Alternatively, hot dung dug deep into the soil provided a more gentle heat.[47]

The most common kitchen-garden crops were edible roots – parsnips, carrots, and turnips; cabbages and coleworts; peas and beans; and salad stuffs such as cucumbers, radishes, and lettuces. Flowers and herbs were sometimes grown by kitchen gardeners, and some produced also bush fruits – gooseberries and currants – and tree fruit. Some kitchen gardeners in the early eighteenth century had begun to specialize in just a few food crops, vegetables such as asparagus, celery, or cucumbers, for which there was a consistent demand. Others used glassware and hot beds extensively to grow vegetables

[43] Greater London RO (M), AM/PI(1) 1718/10; Middleton, *General View of the Agriculture of Middlesex*, p. 261; PRO, PROB 3 49/21.

[44] *The Walloon Church of Norwich*, p. 262; Hartlib, *op. cit.*, p. 9.

[45] Leonard Meager, *The English Gardener*, London, 1670, pp. 164–5. [46] *Ibid.*, p. 165; Norden, *Surveyor's Dialogue*, p. 191.

[47] Middleton, *op. cit.*, pp. 259–61; Kalm, *op. cit.*, pp. 54–5; Meager, *op. cit.*, pp. 170–1; Blake, *op. cit.*, pp. 134, 136.

out of season and to grow less common crops such as melons and mushrooms to excite the palates of the rich.[48]

All kitchen gardeners sowed their crops and arranged their rotations to achieve a high output. Gardeners pioneered row cultivation; in the 1660s the London practice was to set carrots in rows and thin them to ten inches apart, and to set peas and beans with a reel and line. Frequent hoeing between the rows kept the crops clean. To achieve a succession of maturing crops from one piece of ground, vegetables maturing at different times were sown together, or seeds and seedlings were sown between other growing crops. In London in the mid seventeenth century radishes, lettuces, carrots, and parsnips were sown together; the two salad crops matured first, and next the carrots were harvested, leaving the parsnips to be taken up in the late autumn.[49]

The following is a one-year succession of crops on the same soil, typical of the intensively worked London kitchen gardens of the mid eighteenth century. Cauliflower seeds sown on hot beds in August were planted in November or October under bell glasses set four feet apart, with six plants to each glass. The ground between the glasses was sown with lettuces and spinach. In March, the cauliflowers were thinned to two per bell glass, the spinach and lettuces harvested, and cucumber plants raised on hot beds planted in place of the spinach. The glasses were transferred to the cucumbers. In July or August the cauliflowers were harvested and endive planted in their place. Soon afterwards the cucumber vines ceased to fruit, and were taken up and replaced by cauliflower plants under glass which would mature by Michaelmas.[50]

Thus were some London kitchen gardens fully under crops the year round. In the winter month of February 1718 Robert Gascoine's garden in St Martin-in-the-Fields contained a great many growing crops. Large numbers of cauliflower plants grew there, some already planted out under glass and interplanted with coleworts, cabbages, lettuces, and artichokes. Radish and carrot seed had been newly sown in one bed, and nearby stood a small patch of celery. Gascoine's asparagus was at various stages of maturity: young plants on hot beds, some planted out that year, and some mature 'cutting' asparagus ready for the market. One quarter of ground contained 45 rods of artichokes.[51]

Not all kitchen gardeners, however, worked their ground with such intensity. Many outside the London area grew little during the winter except

[48] Kalm, *op. cit.*, pp. 24–5; *The Spectator*, no. 454, Mon. 11 Aug. 1712; Surrey RO, Quarter Sess. 6/2/Midsummer 1750 /62 to /105.

[49] Blake, *op. cit.*, pp. 138–9, 140; Kalm, *op. cit.*, pp. 34–5; Robert Sharrock, *The History of the Propagation and Improvement of Vegetables*, Oxford, 1660, p. 15.

[50] Richard Weston, *Tracts on Practical Agriculture and Gardening*, London, 1773, pp. 53–60.

[51] Greater London RO (M), AM/PI(1) 1718/10.

roots and cabbages, having neither glass nor hot dung to raise tender crops in cold weather.[52]

Farm-gardens were arable farms on which both field and garden crops were grown, the garden crops being cultivated by methods similar to those used in kitchen gardens. In that a certain proportion of their land was under labour-intensive cultivation, farmer-gardeners differed little from other farmers who at this time incorporated such crops as madder, woad, saffron, flax, hemp, tobacco, and teasels in their husbandry. Some farmer-gardeners, indeed, grew these crops as well as garden vegetables. We will, however, confine our definition of farmer-gardeners to those who raised by garden methods crops widely grown also in kitchen gardens.[53]

Within this narrower definition wide variations in the size of holdings and the proportion of arable devoted in any one year to garden crops are found. A Surrey farmer-gardener in 1697 had only 4 acres of his 75 acres of arable under garden crops; another from the same county put $4\frac{1}{2}$ out of $56\frac{1}{2}$ acres under vegetables in 1673. A seventeenth-century Sandwich husbandman grew 5 acres of garden crops and 19 acres of field crops in one year, and a Fulham farmer-gardener cropped 25 acres of arable with 3 acres of wheat, 9 acres of peas, and 3 acres of carrots.[54]

Garden crops were grown in rotation with field crops by farmer-gardeners, but while no part of the farm was set aside to be continuously cropped with vegetables, often they were grown only on the most favourable soils or sheltered plots. The garden ground was usually spade-dug and cultivated with hand tools. Such careful digging and weeding not only facilitated the growing of garden vegetables, it also improved the quality and yield of subsequent field crops.[55] The garden vegetables were often grown in small patches, although bed cultivation was not used by farmer-gardeners. The sophisticated techniques used by kitchen gardeners to lengthen the growing season and hasten crop maturity were not seen on farm-gardens. As a result, farmer-gardeners used less labour per acre than kitchen gardeners.[56]

For a number of reasons farmer-gardeners were forced to limit the intensity of their gardening and to devote only part of their arable acreage

[52] Worcs. RO, Wills, Susannah Hughes, 19 Oct. 1742; Notts. RO, PRNW, Thomas Boulds, Radford, 19 May 1724; Mary Parkinson, 12 July 1712; Norfolk RO, Archdeaconry Invs., INV/67 box 190 no. 44; case 33 shelf F pcl 12 no. 91.

[53] Joan Thirsk, 'Seventeenth-Century Agriculture and Social Change', in Land, Church and People: Essays Presented to Professor H. P. R. Finberg, AHR, XVIII, 1970, supp., pp. 148–77; Thirsk, 'New Crops'; Kent AO, PRC 10/57/6; PRC 27/35/221; PRC 11/57/55; PRC 11/59/248; PRC 11/76/85; PRC 11/49/74; PRC 11/80/142.

[54] Kent AO, PRC 11/76/85; PRO, E 134, 2 & 3 Anne, Hil. 1; LPL, UH 96/414; UH 90/2,945.

[55] Corp. of London RO, City Repertories 49, ff. 261–3; PRO, E 134, 33 & 34 Chas II, Hil. 26; William Ellis, The Practical Farmer, or The Hertfordshire Husbandman, London, 1732, p. 20; F. Beavington, 'Market Gardening in Eastern and Central Bedfordshire', unpub. London Univ. Ph.D. thesis, 1961, pp. 19–20, 27.

[56] Kent AO, PRC 11/57/55; PRC 11/63/110; Young, Northern Tour, I, pp. 48–51.

to garden crops. Many farmer-gardeners were situated some distance from their most important markets, either beyond the kitchen gardeners on the outskirts of large towns or concentrated in areas where their combined output was larger than the local markets could absorb, so that produce had to be sent to towns some miles away. In these circumstances they either confined their gardening activities purely to producing for the local market or they surmounted the high transport costs involved in supplying the distant markets by using only the best of their gardening soil and keeping costs to a minimum.

Another limitation on their gardening activities was the availability of manure. Many farmer-gardeners were too far away from towns to obtain manure, and were restricted to that produced by their own livestock. At Sandy, the farmers depended upon extensive common grazing to maintain sufficient cattle to manure adequately both field and garden ground. Surplus and waste vegetables could augment the diet of farm animals, and it may well be that farmer-gardeners were the first to feed their animals with root crops and cabbages.[57]

The concentration of farmer-gardeners in areas some distance from their main markets occurred because these places were peculiarly favourable to gardening. Farmer-gardeners took advantage of such factors as very favourable soils and lack of tenurial restraints on innovation to raise large quantities of vegetables in such areas as Sandy and Sandwich.[58]

Being some miles from their markets, the garden produce grown by farmer-gardeners had to withstand transportation, so roots, beans, peas, onions, cabbages, pickling cucumbers, and, in the eighteenth century, potatoes were crops favoured by them. Those at Sandwich grew garden crops for seed, and others may well have done so at Colchester and Evesham. The Sandwich men also cultivated flax, teasels, and canary seed.[59]

Open fields do not appear to have been a barrier to farm-gardening; garden crops were cultivated in common fields in Middlesex, Surrey, Oxfordshire, Bedfordshire, and Somerset. In some places only a few enterprising farmers grew garden crops, but in others many of those holding land were farmer-gardeners. Gardening was an important part of the agriculture of Sandy by the mid eighteenth century, and the open-field husbandry there had been modified to accommodate it. At Fulham farm-gardening was well established in the common fields.[60]

---

[57] Young, *Annals of Agriculture*, XLII, p. 28; Adolphus Speed, *Adam Out of Eden*, London, 1659, pp. 20–1.

[58] Beavington, thesis, p. 27; Young, *Annals of Agriculture*, XLII, p. 28. Some examples of Sandwich farmer-gardeners' inventories are: Kent AO, PRC 10/57/25; PRC 11/79/74; PRC 11/59/248; PRC 11/76/85.

[59] Corp. of London RO, City Repertories 49, ff. 261–3; Norden, *op. cit.*, p. 168; Thomas Read, *New Description of Gloucestershire, etc.*, p. 411; Batchelor, *General View of the Agriculture of Bedford*, p. 457; Beavington, 'Early Market Gardening in Bedfordshire', pp. 97–8; Pitt, *General View of the Agriculture of Worcester*, p. 135.

[60] Corp. of London RO, City Repertories 49, ff. 261–3; Guildford MR, MS 3,389/2, unpaged,

The size of the businesses of kitchen gardeners and farmer-gardeners varied considerably, as did the costs and profits of individual gardeners. Nevertheless, it is possible to make some general remarks about the commercial activities of both types.

For all but the poorest kitchen gardeners, who hired little or no outside labour, wages were the largest item of costs. Journeyman gardeners' wage rates varied according to skill; the Middlesex justices recognized two grades of garden labourer in their 1666 wage assessment – 2s. 6d. per day without food and 1s. 6d. with food for the best labourers, and 2s. a day without food and 1s. a day with food for the second grade. At Twickenham in Middlesex, garden labourers were paid 1s. 6d. per day in 1730, and in 1747 journeyman gardeners in London received between 9s. and 15s. per week according to skill.[61] London garden labourers were paid at the same rate the year round, emphasizing that kitchen gardens were never fallow. More labour was, however, employed during summer than in the winter; many of the extra hands were women and children whose wages were much less than the men's. With over 100 hands employed on larger kitchen gardens in the summer, wage bills were very heavy.[62]

Kitchen-garden rents, especially around London, were high in comparison with those for arable lands in general and varied considerably according to the quality and location of the land. In the middle of the seventeenth century rents of £2 to £9 per acre were paid by London gardeners. In the 1770s London kitchen-garden ground let at anything from £1 to £6 per acre. Outside London, kitchen gardeners at Evesham paid up to £3 per acre at this time and at Sandy up to £5 per acre.[63]

Kitchen gardeners faced varying capital equipment costs according to the intensity of their production. Hand tools were relatively inexpensive, but the use of glass sharply increased costs, both in the initial purchase and in the replacement of breakages. The already laid-out gardens of former monasteries and town houses were readily rented by kitchen gardeners, thereby avoiding the initial costs of garden construction.[64]

Manure, both as a fertilizer and for hot beds, was bought in such quantities by some London kitchen gardeners that its cost per year could approach the

extracts from PCC Wills, 1610–60; PRO, E 134, 33 & 34 Chas II, Hil. 26; Bodleian Library, MS Wills Oxon. 121/5/22; 2/3/11; 32/1/16; Beavington, thesis, pp. 24–7. For Somerset, see pt I, ch. 11, p. 373.

[61] L. Martindale, 'Demography and Land Use in the Late Seventeenth and Eighteenth Centuries in Middlesex', unpub. London Univ. Ph.D. thesis, 1968, pp. 460–3; E. Ironside, *The History and Antiquities of Twickenham*, London, 1797, p. 152; R. Campbell, *The London Tradesman*, London, 1747, p. 274.

[62] Martindale, thesis, pp. 360, 462–3; Young, *Northern Tour*, IV, pp. 24–5.

[63] Young, *Northern Tour*, I, pp. 48–51; III, pp. 391–2; IV, pp. 24–5; Fuller, *Worthies of England*, p. 77; Hartlib, *His Legacie*, 2nd edn, p. 8; Weston, *op. cit.*, pp. 57, 62.

[64] Wadham Coll., Oxford, Muniments, 78/1 & 2; Tindal, *History of Evesham*, p. 208; Stow, *Survey of London*, I, p. 131.

figure for the annual rent of the garden, for many of them had no livestock to supplement their manure supplies. Away from London, most kitchen gardeners kept one or more horses for transport, and either one or two cows or a few pigs. Seeds and plants were relatively inexpensive, and in some cases could be provided from inside the garden.[65]

A detailed estimate of the costs of multiple cropping in a London kitchen garden was published in 1773. To raise two crops of cauliflowers under glass, interspersed with successive crops of spinach, lettuce, cucumber, and endive cost an estimated £30 per acre. This cost was broken down as follows: labour, £7 13s.; seeds and the labour of sowing and raising plants on hot beds, £7 4s.; dung and the repair and replacement of broken glasses, £10 3s.; rent, £5. In this example, the intensity of production was such that the rent, high as it was, was an insignificant item in the total cost.[66]

Production costs per acre of garden ground were lower for farmer-gardeners than for kitchen gardeners. Many of them paid rural rather than town wage rates, and they used more extensive techniques and so less labour per acre. As in most cases the ground employed by farmer-gardeners for gardening had only an agricultural alternative use, rents were lower than those of suburban kitchen gardens. Nevertheless, they were higher than most arable rents: at Sandy in the 1770s garden ground was let at between £2 and £5 per acre, and at Evesham at between £2 10s. and £3 per acre; in both cases the lower figure probably applied to farm-gardening ground. At Hammersmith in the late eighteenth century the going rate was £3 per acre.[67]

Farmer-gardeners used no glassware, and so their equipment costs were light; neither did they have the expense of laying out a garden, since their garden crops were grown in the fields. Manure was not a direct cost for those farmer-gardeners who used only that provided by their own livestock. For those who purchased manure off the farm, its cost depended very much on how far and by what means it had to be transported.[68]

Partially offsetting the generally lower costs enjoyed by farmer-gardeners were the higher charges they had to bear to transport their produce to distant markets. Those near Colchester, Sandwich, and elsewhere along the East Anglian and Kent coasts sent their produce to London by ship, some in the Vale of Evesham used pack horses to supply towns in the Midlands, and from Sandy garden produce was carted over fifty miles to London.[69]

[65] Martindale, thesis, pp. 362–3; Middleton, *General View of the Agriculture of Middlesex*, p. 262; PRO, PROB 3/26/198; Corp. of London RO, Orphans Invs. box 12, Common Serjeant's Book II, f. 331; Kent AO, DRb/Pi 8/52.

[66] Weston, *op. cit.*, pp. 53–60.

[67] Young, *Northern Tour*, I, pp. 48–51; III, pp. 391–2.

[68] Norden, *op. cit.*, p. 191; Young, *Annals of Agriculture*, XLII, p. 28; Middleton, *op. cit.*, p. 303.

[69] PRO, E 190, 536/7; E 190, 477/8; E 190, 491/4; E 190, 481/11; E 190, 479/16; E 190, 480/5;

Examples of the costs per acre for garden crops grown by farmer-gardeners at Sandy in the 1770s are: carrots, total cost £6 7s. 6d., of which rent was £3, labour £2 19s. 6d., and seed 8s.; onions, total cost £14 11s., of which rent was £3, labour £5 16s., manure £5, and seed 15s.; and potatoes, total cost £12 18s. 6d., of which rent was £3, labour £3 5s., manure £5, and seed £1 13s. 6d.[70]

The absence of business records of farmer- or kitchen gardeners precludes detailed discussion of the profits to be gained by gardening. However, many writers in the seventeenth and early eighteenth centuries had no doubts that gardening was a lucrative occupation, and some of them backed up their claims with numerical estimates of its profitability. Most of their examples were drawn from the London area, for here commercial gardening reached its peak and the most advanced techniques were used. The numerical estimates must, however, be treated with caution, for, in addition to demonstrating the common trait of exaggerating statistics to give weight to an argument, their examples were frequently of the maximum, not the average, profits which could be expected.

The earliest detailed estimate of the profitability of multiple cropping in kitchen gardens dates from the 1770s. A London gardener to the west of the City, growing early and late cauliflowers, spinach, lettuce, cucumbers, and endive in succession over a year, could expect a gross profit of £90 5s. per acre, reduced to about £70 when marketing costs had been deducted, this profit being on a total outlay of £30 per annum. Another calculation by the same author, based on one acre planted with young currant bushes and undersown in one year with spinach, potatoes, and two crops of coleworts, yielded a gross profit of £47 7s. on an initial outlay of £20.[71]

In 1659 the gross returns per acre for the following garden crops were said to be: teasels, £25; French beans, £20; asparagus, £20. Walter Blith, writing in the same decade, believed that turnips could yield a profit of £8, £10, or £12 per acre and that occasionally garden ground might yield £100 per acre. Richard Weston in 1773 put the gross profit from growing early turnips at £12 per acre, these roots occupying the ground for only three months in the spring. An acre of carrots grown at Sandy a few years earlier earned a profit of £13 12s. 6d. per acre, potatoes £7 17s. 6d. per acre, and onions £2 2s.[72]

Potentially high profits however, were matched by high risks. The weather was a constant hazard to all agriculture but especially to gardening.

E 190, 594/9; E 190, 628/6; E 190, 630/14; E 190, 713/19; E 190, 718/11; Boys, *History of Sandwich*, pp. 742, 743; Pitt, *General View of the Agriculture of Worcester*, p. 147; Beavington, 'Early Market Gardening in Bedfordshire', p. 98.   [70] Young, *Northern Tour*, I, pp. 48–51.

[71] Weston, *op. cit.*, pp. 53–60, 61–3.

[72] Speed, *Adam Out of Eden*, pp. 19, 51, 143, 144; Walter Blith, *The English Improver Improved*, 3rd edn, London, 1652, pp. 272–4; Weston, *op. cit.*, p. 68; Young, *Northern Tour*, I, pp. 54–5.

Unseasonal frosts could destroy plants; especially as kitchen gardeners often sowed and planted out early so as to enjoy high prices for early crops. Hot, dry summers destroyed salad vegetables inadequately irrigated. Although infrequent, summer hailstorms ruined crops and did such damage to glassware that gardeners could be reduced to penury by a heavy storm.[73] In an age without chemical pesticides, garden crops were prone to pests and diseases. Thieves posed a problem to gardeners in urban areas. Some sought protection in high walls topped with broken glass; others formed protection and prosecution societies.[74]

The state of the market had a bearing on gardeners' profits, especially those of kitchen gardeners, since prices fluctuated widely according to season. In the late summer, carrots, turnips, parsnips, beans, and peas, cabbages, and such-like vegetables came on the market in abundance and were cheap enough to be bought by the poor. These selfsame 'common' vegetables, when raised or stored and sold out of season, commanded high prices as delicacies for the tables of the rich. J. C. Loudon's table of Covent Garden prices published in 1822 showed an eighteenfold difference between the cheapest and dearest monthly average price for turnips, a sevenfold difference in the case of lettuce prices, sixfold for carrots, and twenty-one-fold for cucumbers. Vegetables such as asparagus, which demanded some skill to grow and took some time to mature, always commanded relatively high prices. The rich were prepared to pay for novelty; when new vegetables first made their appearance on the market they could be sold very dear.[75]

Some garden produce was sold at the garden gate, especially by kitchen gardeners working in the suburbs of large towns. Most garden wares, however, were taken to the open markets. Many London markets handled vegetables: Queenhithe and Billingsgate received much waterborne garden produce, and Cheapside had a thriving fruit and vegetable market before its removal to St Paul's in 1657. After the Fire, the New Leadenhall and New Stocks markets both contained purpose-built accommodation for fruit and vegetable selling. New markets which appeared in the growing London suburbs during the course of the seventeenth century were patronized by gardeners; one, Covent Garden, during the eighteenth century became the premier London fruit and vegetable market.[76]

[73] Weston, op. cit., p. 55; Sharrock, History of the Propagation and Improvement of Vegetables, p. 13; Surrey RO, Quarter Sess., 6/12/Midsummer 1750 /62 to /105.

[74] Bodleian Library, GA Oxon. 4° 835/1. Eileen Cavanagh Davies, "Chronological Synopsis and Index to Oxfordshire Items in Jackson's Oxford Journal, 1753–1780", vol. 1: issue no. 537, p. 2, Mon., 5 Sept. 1763; Kalm, Visit to England, pp. 29–30.

[75] Muffet, Health's Improvement, pp. 215, 216; Loudon, Encyclopaedia of Gardening, p. 1,223; J. E. Thorold Rogers, A History of Agriculture and Prices in England from 1259 to 1793, 7 vols., Oxford, 1866–1902, VI, pp. 230, 234.

[76] Kalm, op. cit., p. 34; McGrath, thesis, pp. 59, 204; John Strype, A Survey of London and Westminster, London, 1720, bk 2, pp. 89, 199; Ronald Webber, Covent Garden, Mud-Salad Market, London, 1969, p. 85.

Gardeners' stalls were a familiar sight in many market towns throughout the country. Although most gardeners appeared in the market at Billericay in Essex from May to September in the early eighteenth century, some attended throughout the year. At Nottingham, similarly, gardeners attended the market regularly throughout the year in the seventeenth and early eighteenth centuries.[77]

Most gardeners retailed their own wares or employed hawkers to sell in the streets and market-places. Specialist retailers, however, appeared in London in the second half of the eighteenth century who bought garden vegetables in the larger markets to retail elsewhere. By the early eighteenth century, regular stall holders at Covent Garden received produce for sale from market gardeners to the west of the city. Wholesaling also grew in importance; in the 1630s the London Company of Gardeners complained of forestallers who enhanced prices by buying whole crops still in the ground. Greengrocers' shops, however, were not known in the seventeenth century, and there were few in London before 1750.[78]

Liquorice was raised in England by methods akin to those used in kitchen gardens. Throughout the period the liquorice gardens at Pontefract, Godalming, and Worksop produced much of England's output, although no liquorice was grown at Worksop after the 1770s, and production there was probably in decline for some years before that. The profitability of liquorice encouraged gardeners outside these areas to take it up; by the middle of the eighteenth century it was being grown at Croydon and in Norfolk, and from the seventeenth century onwards kitchen and nursery gardeners around London grew it in favourable soils.[79] Its use was mainly medicinal. The juice of the root was administered to relieve infections of the lungs, throat, bladder, and kidneys. English liquorice was preferred to that imported from Spain because of its "farre more weake sweete taste".[80]

The unusual soil conditions needed to grow liquorice explain why it was raised in only a few places. The roots were the only useful part of the plant. To encourage a profusion of roots, liquorice had to be planted in a deep, easily worked soil, either naturally rich or capable of heavy dunging. Before planting, the ground was thoroughly dug to a depth of three and a half to four feet at Pontefract and two and a half feet at Croydon. During digging,

[77] Essex RO, D/DP M 992; Deering, Nottinghamia, pp. 71, 97–8.

[78] Kalm, op. cit., p. 34; Cogan, Haven of Health, p. 61; McGrath, thesis, pp. 52, 74; Richard Dering, Cries of London, ed. Denis Stevens, Penn. State Music Ser.,v, 1964, pp. 14, 15, 16, 17, 18, 21, 28; Guildford MR, MS 3,389/2.

[79] Parkinson, Paradisi in Sole, p. 533; Holmes, History of Pontefract, I, p. 240; Aubrey, Natural History and Antiquities of Surrey, IV, p. 16; Blith, op. cit., p. 251; J. Mortimer, The Whole Art of Husbandry, London, 1707, pp. 127–9; Museum Rusticum et Commerciale, I, London, 1764, pp. 252–8; Borthwick Inst., Tithes R vii H 4,529, 1696; Norfolk RO, How 220 (1750); Camden, Britannia, pp. 485, 715, 712; John H. Harvey, 'Leonard Gurle's Nurseries and Some Others', Garden Hist., III, 3, 1975, pp. 44, 45, 46; John Holland, History of Worksop, Worksop, 1826, p. 6; William Ellis, Modern Husbandman...October, IV, p. 172.   [80] Parkinson, op. cit., p. 533.

manure was added to the soil, comprising one spit's depth of rotten dung at Pontefract, and at Croydon a mixture of rotten dung, coal ashes, and lime. Above the manure the soil was raised in ridges three feet wide separated by narrow paths. Three rows of liquorice slips (small pieces of live root) were set three or four inches apart on each ridge. At Pontefract the gardeners sowed lettuces, onions, or spinach on the ridges in the first and sometimes the second year of liquorice growth. No subsidiary crops were grown in the third year, but the space between the liquorice plants was frequently hoed until the roots were taken up. To harvest liquorice, trenches up to three feet deep were dug beside each row, and the roots were carefully extracted from the soil by hand. The producers sold the roots to wholesalers who resold to apothecaries either the fresh or dried and powdered roots or a solidified juice extracted by boiling them.[81]

At Pontefract liquorice was grown in small gardens often only an acre or so in size; the total acreage of 50 to 100 acres of liquorice garths cultivated there in the second half of the eighteenth century was shared amongst a large number of growers.[82]

The small acreages of individual growers reflect the high costs and high profits per acre associated with this crop. The total cost of growing liquorice in London over three years in the mid seventeenth century was estimated at £23 per acre and in 1730 at £50 16s. per acre. Two-thirds of these costs were wages. Rents were high; at Pontefract they averaged £5 per acre and at Godalming £3 to £4 per acre at the end of the eighteenth century. Profits, without tithe payments, were put at £50 to £100 per acre in 1653, at around £40 per acre in 1730, and at £60 per acre for a good crop in 1763 – a high return even when the costs and the three years it took to grow the crop are taken into consideration.[83]

From about the middle of the seventeenth century some market gardeners established themselves as general nurserymen, making all or most of their living by raising for sale young trees, shrubs, flower roots, bulbs, and seeds. At least fifteen nurseries were in business in or near London between 1691 and 1700. One of these, Brompton Park in Kensington, was far bigger than the rest, and dominated the nursery trade until the second decade of the eighteenth century.[84]

It was not until the third decade of the eighteenth century that any number of nurseries existed outside London. Initially, only in the London area was there sufficient demand for nursery wares to support many full-time

[81] Holmes, op. cit., I, p. 239; Young, Northern Tour, I, pp. 382–7; Museum Rusticum, I, pp. 252–8; Ellis, op. cit., pp. 172–6.

[82] Young, Northern Tour, I, pp. 382–3; Celia Fiennes, The Journeys of Celia Fiennes, ed. C. Morris, London, 1947, pp. 94–5.

[83] Young, Northern Tour, I, pp. 345–7; Museum Rusticum, I, pp. 252–8; Thomas Hale, A Compleat Body of Husbandry, London, 1756, pp. 517–19; Ellis, op. cit., p. 175; Blith, op. cit., pp. 250–2.   [84] Harvey, Early Nurserymen, pp. 5–6, 55–6.

nurserymen. Once established, these London nurseries so dominated the trade that it was difficult for provincial nurseries to compete with them. The first provincial nurseries were in the west and north of the country, where distance sheltered them from the competition of the London firms. In 1730 about thirty nurseries existed in the provinces and roughly an equal number in London. By 1760 perhaps a hundred nurseries were in operation throughout the whole of England.

The rise of the general nurseryman after 1640 coincided with the decline of joint nursery and kitchen gardeners. Throughout the period, however, non-specialists sold small amounts of nursery wares to local customers.[85] Many of the early nurserymen were former gardeners in noble or gentle households, and such establishments continued to supply recruits to the trade who, having learnt their skills in private gardens, saw the commercial opportunities in setting up their own businesses. The leading London nurserymen were literate and educated men, not only versed in the practice of gardening, but also often skilled garden designers, botanists, and in some cases authors. Consequently, the nursery trade was the branch of market gardening with the most prestige. Nurserymen were, on average, richer than other market gardeners, and some regarded themselves, or were regarded by others, as gentlemen.[86]

Most nurseries were of similar size to kitchen gardens; Brompton Park was an exception. It may have been well over fifty acres in extent in the late seventeenth century. It was on a compact site, whereas some London nurserymen rented several small parcels of land, either because of suburban land shortage or because land of the right quality was important to nurserymen. By the eighteenth century nurserymen knew that poor soils made the best nursery grounds because plants raised in such soils throve when transplanted.[87]

Like kitchen gardens, nurseries were laid out in a number of plots and beds of varying sizes with narrow walks between. The separation of crops and easy access to them were particularly important to the nurseryman, because his plants were sold live and had to be taken from the soil for delivery to the customer without disturbing the other stock still growing there.[88] Nurserymen used the same hand tools as kitchen gardeners: London nurserymen also used substantial quantities of glassware, and some of their nurseries were equipped with greenhouses, allowing sizeable delicate plants to be stored during the winter. In the eighteenth century the taste among the nobility and gentry for exotic plants encouraged more nurserymen

[85] *Ibid.*, pp. 5–6, 36–7; Hartlib, *His Legacie*, 2nd edn, p. 10.

[86] Harvey, *Early Nurserymen*, pp. 9–13, 37, 45.

[87] *Ibid.*, pp. 5, 45, 55–6; John H. Harvey, 'The Nurseries on Milne's Land-Use Map', *London & Middx Arch. Soc.*, XXIV, 1973, pp. 177–98; PRO, PROB 3 20/88; PROB 3 33/73; PROB 3 48/2; E 134 16 Chas II, Easter 1; Kalm, *Visit to England*, p. 25.

[88] PRO, PROB 4 23/6; PROB 3 33/73; C 110 174.

to invest in greenhouses and to add stoves to them for artificial heating.[89]

The introduction of plants and trees from abroad, many of them from the Americas, widened the range of stock kept by general nurserymen, as can be seen from their ever lengthening trade catalogues.[90] If the number of plants is any guide to the size of nurseries, then London nurseries increased in size over the period. Robert Standard of St Giles Cripplegate had over 10,000 trees and tree stocks growing in his nursery in 1684; William Cox of Kew had a stock of 30,000 plants on his death in 1722; Peter Mason's nursery at Isleworth contained 115,000 plants in 1730. These nurseries were dwarfed by Brompton Park, where an estimated 10,000,000 plants grew for sale in 1705. Such numbers of plants were of considerable value; those at Brompton Park were estimated to be worth between £30,000 and £40,000, and other London nurseries had stocks of plants worth many hundreds of pounds. Nurseries were thus substantial businesses. In the 1740s between £500 and £1,000 was needed to set up a London nursery, and to finance, in addition to stocks of plants, such costly items as equipment, wages, and loans to customers in the form of unpaid bills.[91]

Not all of these large London nurserymen concerned themselves wholly with nursery gardening; some also produced fruit and vegetables and occasionally field crops for the market. Others worked as private gardeners for part of their time.[92] However, many nurserymen, although keeping a wide range of plants in stock, were specialists in certain types of plants. In 1691 Rickets of Hoxton kept a large selection of flowers, trees, and 'greens', but was a specialist in Assyrian thyme; Pearson's nursery nearby had a great choice of flowers, including the best anemones in London, while Darby of Hoxton was an expert in raising 'greens'. From the early seventeenth century gardeners at Isleworth and Twickenham specialized in growing young fruit trees for sale, and throughout the period there continued to be specialist tree nurserymen and florists. When larger formal gardens and landscaped parks became fashionable and the demand for 'forest trees' was thus increased, some nurserymen, like Thomas Raty of Cheshunt, raised nothing but many thousands of such trees.[93]

Nursery wares sold in the public markets were usually grown and sold by non-specialists. Nurserymen sold direct to customers at their nurseries,

[89] PRO, PROB 4 23/6; C 108 353; Harvey, 'Leonard Gurle's Nurseries', p. 176; *Archaeologia*, XII, 1796, pp. 189, 191, 192; Harvey, *Early Nurserymen*, p. 51.

[90] John H. Harvey, *Early Gardening Catalogues*, London, 1972.

[91] PRO, PROB 4 22/60; PROB 3 4/77; PROB 3 29/111; John H. Harvey, 'The Stocks Held by Early Nurseries', AHR, XXII, 1, 1974, pp. 18–35; Harvey, *Early Nurserymen*, p. 160; PRO, PROB 3 20/88; LPL, UH 96/271; Campbell, *London Tradesman*, p. 337.

[92] PRO, PROB 3 2/77; PROB 4 22/60; Harvey, 'Leonard Gurle's Nurseries', pp. 43–6.

[93] *Archaeologia*, XII, 1796, p. 181; (map) Glover, *Istelworth*; Harvey, *Early Nurserymen*, pp. 1, 41–2; PRO, PROB 3 20/88; E 126/199; E 134, 16 Chas II, Easter 1.

or despatched plants to the country in response to orders received by post. Plants were often sent considerable distances by carriers' waggon, coastal vessel, or hired cart, carefully wrapped in sacking and tied in bundles or placed in wicker baskets.[94] To attract custom, and also to facilitate business at a distance, first London and later provincial nurserymen published printed catalogues of their wares. The earliest of these were single broadside sheets, while later ones were in pamphlet form, sometimes illustrated.[95]

Some London nurserymen spent part of each year travelling the country visiting their customers, collecting orders, and giving advice on garden improvements. Many of those who travelled had reputations as garden designers, a profitable skill in that they would be likely to secure the contract for plants required to stock a new or extended garden.[96]

The seed and nursery trades were closely linked. Seedsmen bought trees and plants from nurserymen to sell in their shops, and they in turn supplied nurserymen with seeds for their customers. Some seed merchants loaned money to nurserymen, enabling them in turn to extend credit to their customers.[97] The wholesale and most of the retail trade in garden seeds, and much of that in agricultural seeds, was concentrated in London. This was a consequence of the heavy dependence on European seed imported through London in the sixteenth and seventeenth centuries, the continued import of considerable amounts of seed well into the eighteenth century, easy access to London from the main English seed-growing areas, and the large number of seedsmen's customers who lived in or visited London or could easily communicate with the capital by post or carrier.[98]

Throughout the period home production could not satisfy the whole of the demand for garden seeds. Nearly $2\frac{3}{4}$ tons of them were imported during a two-month period in 1682. A leading London seedsman in 1729 obtained garden seeds from Italy, Denmark, and France, and a writer in the 1770s echoed many before him in complaining that for want of home-produced seed we were forced to import much which was often of low quality.[99] Indigenous seed growing did, however, increase in the late seventeenth and eighteenth centuries. Small amounts of garden seeds were grown by London

[94] M. de la Quintinye, tr. G. London and H. Wise, *The Complete Gard'ner*, London, 1701, p. ii; Webber, *Covent Garden*, p. 86; HMC, *Egmont*, I, p. 531; PRO, SP 46/100 ff. 218, 219; Harvey, *Early Nurserymen*, pp. 171–85; Bodleian Library, 4 Rawlinson 323, MS letter from Philip Miller.

[95] Harvey, *Early Gardening Catalogues*, pp. 7–34 and illustrations between pp. 68 and 69; John H. Harvey, *Early Horticultural Catalogues: A Checklist*, Bath, 1973, pp. 1–23.

[96] Harvey, *Early Nurserymen*, pp. 53–5, 180.

[97] Corp. of London RO, Orphans Invs. box 11, Common Serjeant's Book II, f. 325b; La Quintinye, *op. cit.*, p. ii; Harvey, *Early Nurserymen*, pp. 4, 12–13.

[98] Harvey, *Early Nurserymen*, p. 31; Harrison, *Description of England*, p. 26; Dietz, *Port and Trade of Early Elizabethan London: Documents*, pp. 68, 78.

[99] John Houghton, *A Collection for Improvement of Husbandry and Trade*, ed. R. Bradley, 4 vols., London, 1727–8, IV, p. 169; Stephen Switzer, *A Compendious Method for the Raising of Italian Brocoli…* London, 1729, pp. 55, 56; Weston, *Tracts on Practical Agriculture and Gardening*, pp. 5–6.

nurserymen and seedsmen, some of whom perfected the seeds of new strains of garden plants. Farmers, market gardeners, and private gardeners within striking distance of London grew seeds for the London market. In many cases this seed too was of poor quality, obtained from vegetables or flowers too small or old for table use which were left to stand for seed. Some, however, was grown in a more systematic way. Selected seeds for sowing were sent to the grower, and the seedsman travelled from London to see the resulting crop and to buy the harvest of seeds. Some places were noted for particular types of seed – Barnes for peas, Battersea for cabbage, and Deptford for onion. Much home-produced seed, however, arrived in London from further afield.[100]

Three gardening areas in England raised large quantities of seed: the Vale of Evesham, Sandwich, and Colchester. Sandwich carrot, bean, pea, and radish seed was sold by London seedsmen in the seventeenth century. As well as vegetable and herb seeds, the area also grew flax and canary seed for sale to London wholesalers. This latter crop was grown exclusively in east Kent and was sold as food for caged birds. Conditions for raising seeds at Sandwich were good; "the ground being pretty low, the seeds do not often recieve a blight, as in many other places".[101]

At Colchester seed production was well established by the second half of the seventeenth century. In 1664 $49\frac{3}{4}$ cwt of seed left the port of Colchester for London, in 1676 $133\frac{1}{2}$ cwt was shipped, and 8 cwt in 1700. Considerable amounts of garden seed were taken down the Severn via the port of Gloucester towards the end of the seventeenth century, and it is most likely that they came from Evesham. Certainly by the end of the eighteenth century seed growing, especially onion seed, was well established in this region.[102]

Seed taken to London was either sold direct to seedsmen or exposed for sale at the wholesale seed market at Mark Lane. The number of firms in London concerned with seeds was small – three or four in the 1680s and perhaps a dozen by 1760. It is doubtful if there were any full-time London seed merchants much before the 1770s, and throughout the period no sharp distinction existed between wholesale and retail seedsmen. Seedsmen bought seeds wholesale from merchants who shipped them into London, or direct from the growers, retailed them to the public, and also acted as wholesalers

[100] Kalm, *Visit to England*, p. 25; Harvey, 'Stocks Held by Early Nurseries', p. 19; Sharrock, *History of the Propagation and Improvement of Vegetables*, p. 33; Loudon, *Encyclopaedia of Gardening*, p. 1,212; Weston, *op. cit.*, pp. 4–13; Kent AO, U 269 E 21; Daniel Lysons, *The Environs of London*, IV, London, 1796, p. 576.

[101] Kent AO, U 269 E 21; PRC 10/57/25; PRC 11/57/55; PRC 11/59/248; PRC 11/76/85; PRC 11/79/74; Read, *New Description of Gloucestershire, etc.*, p. 411; Boys, *History of Sandwich*, pp. 742–3; R. Avis, *The Canary*, London, 1886, p. 19; Corp. of London RO, Orphans Invs., box 11, Common Serjeant's Book II, f. 325b.

[102] Burley, thesis, Table xxxi, p. 278; PRO, E 190, 1,250/4; E 190, 1,253/14; E 190, 1,251/15; Pitt, *General View of the Agriculture of Worcester*, p. 135.

to nurserymen and those shopkeepers who sold seeds. Outside London, shopkeepers, innkeepers, and market gardeners retailed garden seeds purchased mainly from London wholesalers.[103]

The major seedsmen were of similar wealth and social status to nurserymen; their methods of trading were similar to those of nurserymen and they too derived their custom largely from the nobility and gentry. They frequently issued printed catalogues of their wares which confirm that they sold an extensive range of nursery goods and garden implements as well as garden and agricultural seeds.[104]

The latter were listed under the head "Seeds to improve land". In a catalogue from the 1680s the seeds of clover, trefoil, sainfoin, lucerne, ryegrass, French furze, and Riga or Danzig flax were advertised in this section. By the 1760s the improving farmer could also obtain the seeds of cow grass, buckwheat, spurrey, hemp, canary seed, rape, opium poppy, and lentils from a London seedsman.[105] In the mid seventeenth century much of this agricultural seed was imported from the Continent, chiefly from the Low Countries and France. Imported seed, however, was often costly; Dutch clover seed retailed at 2s. a pound in the 1650s and was frequently of low quality. The persistence of such enthusiasts as Andrew Yarranton in popularizing Dutch clover and in organizing its importation on a large scale brought down the price to 7d. a pound for good quality seed in the early 1660s, and it was under half that price in some years in the early eighteenth century.[106]

As more English and Welsh farmers deliberately sowed their land with the seeds of clover, trefoil, sainfoin, and such-like plants, there developed indigenous production of these seeds. Farmers, innkeepers, and provincial seedsmen were selling locally raised seed towards the end of the seventeenth century. A method of threshing trefoil to extract the seed, patented in 1673, brought its price down to 4d. a pound in London in 1678. However,

[103] Harvey, Early Nurserymen, pp. 3–4; Leeds City Archives, TN/EA/13/49; E. Melling, Kentish Sources, III, Maidstone, 1961, p. 40; T. Donnelly, 'Arthur Clephane, Edinburgh Merchant and Seedsman', AHR, XVIII, 2, 1970, 151–60; Corp. of London RO, Orphans Invs., box 11, Common Serjeant's Book II, f. 325b; Alan Everitt, 'The English Urban Inn, 1560–1760', in Perspectives in English Urban History, ed. id., London, 1973, p. 105.

[104] Harvey, Early Nurserymen, pp. 3, 47–8, 80; Corp. of London RO, Orphans Invs., box 11, Common Serjeant's Book II, f. 325b; Oxon. RO, DIL xxvi/4; Kent AO, U 269 E 21; Donnelly, op. cit., pp. 151–60; PRO, SP 46/100 ff. 218, 219, 242, 245.

[105] Oxon. RO, DIL xxvi/4; Kent AO, U 269 E 21.

[106] Sir Richard Weston, A Discours of Husbandrie Used in Brabant and Flanders, 2nd edn, London, 1652, endpiece; Walter Blith, The English Improver Improved, 4th edn, London, 1653, pp. 253, 261, 187; Andrew Yarranton, The Improvement Improved, by a Second Edition of the Great Improvement of Lands by Clover, London, 1663, pp. 4, 6–7, 44, 45; Andrew Yarranton, England's Improvement by Sea and Land, London, 1677, p. 194; Speed, Adam Out of Eden, pp. 33–7; Frank V. Emery, 'The Mechanics of Innovation: Clover Cultivation in Wales before 1750', J. Hist. Geog., II, 1, 1976, p. 41.

considerable quantities of clover seed were still being imported from Flanders in the 1720s and sold at competitive prices, the Flemish being able to thresh out twenty-five to thirty pecks of it per man per day with the aid of machines, whereas an English expert could hand-thresh only half a peck in the same time. Some other 'improved seeds', most notably flax, continued to be imported in quantity because the climate of the British Isles was not suitable for ripening the seed.[107]

London, and later provincial, seedsmen gave away printed instructions for sowing the seeds of the pasture plants they sold; leaflets varied from a single page of advice to a four-page pamphlet.[108]

C. CONCLUSION

The role of market gardening in helping to feed the population of England and Wales between 1640 and 1750 was substantial. Gregory King estimated the value of fruit and vegetables consumed in England in 1695 at £1.2 million, roughly $5\frac{1}{4}$ per cent of the value of all food and drink consumed in that year. It may well be, however, that the long-term contribution of market gardening to economic advance, through its influence on the rest of agriculture, was more important than its supplementation of the nation's diet.[109]

That "improved agriculture was in some sense the result of the application of garden methods to the arable" was recognized by the many writers of the period who made explicit or implicit references to gardening when describing agricultural innovations. John Laurence quoted Houghton as advising "country farmers, to send their sons they design to breed in their own way, to the husbandmen about London, that are partly gardeners and partly ploughmen, or at least take some servants that have been thus bred". How many took the advice of these authors is difficult to determine. The absence then or later of some of the innovations enthusiastically advocated for farms shows them to have been inapplicable, while the presence of others points to their success.[110]

[107] Everitt, op. cit., p. 105; Melling, op. cit., III, p. 39; Patent Office Library, no. 166, 3 Feb. 25 Chas II; London Gazette, Mon. 17 Feb. 1678; Richard Bradley, A General Treatise of Husbandry and Gardening, I, London, 1726, pp. 175–6, 177; Blith, op. cit., 3rd edn, pp. 253, 261; Houghton, Collection, ed. Bradley, II, pp. 332–3, 374, 378; IV, pp. 169, 194.

[108] Bodleian Library, JJ Hort. 1, A Catalogue of Several Sorts of Grass Seeds, sold by Nathaniel Powell, etc., n.d.; Cambridge, Botanical Garden, A Catalogue of Several Sorts of Grass Seeds, Sold by John Turner, etc., n.d.; Emery, op. cit., pp. 38, 39, 40.

[109] King, Natural and Political Observations, p. 67. See also below, ch. 19, pp. 581ff.

[110] G. E. Fussell, 'Low Countries' Influence on English Farming', EHR, LXXIV, 1959, p. 614; Blith, op. cit., 3rd edn, pp. 271–4; Sir Hugh Plat, The New and Admirable Arte of Setting of Corne, London, 1600, p. 1; John Worlidge, Systema Agriculturae, London, 1675, pp. 42, 49; Hartlib, His Legacie, 2nd edn, pp. 6–8; John Laurence, A New System of Agriculture, London, 1726, p. 90.

One such unsuccessful 'improvement' was digging. Initially looked upon with suspicion by some landlords, digging was soon recognized as beneficial to deep soils. Samuel Hartlib believed deep digging to be worth three ploughings as a preparation for corn, as it buried weeds and killed noxious grasses. Over seventy years later John Laurence was no less enthusiastic; where soil was at least twenty inches deep, trenching which went half as deep again as the plough was excellent husbandry, "throwing down that which is worn out to the bottom, and raising up a new and fresh soil, which may last four or five crops together, without any other advantage but continued stirring". He cautioned however, against digging a shallow soil, as being likely to bring up "a hungry soil worse than the surface".[111]

Hartlib claimed digging to be no more expensive than ploughing if the land was mellow, and Laurence quoted a cost of £1 6s. 8d. per acre for land previously in cultivation, a price amply repaid, he argued, by the benefits which accrued. There is little evidence, however, that this academic praise of digging induced the husbandman or yeoman to take it up.[112]

Setting seeds individually at measured distances in holes made by a dibber or some more complex instrument was another idea borrowed by some authors from the gardeners. It too was a costly and laborious process. While generally agreed to be economic in the case of field beans and some types of peas, most interest surrounded its use in growing grain, in particular wheat. Writers of agricultural books from Sir Hugh Plat at the very beginning of the seventeenth century onwards advocated setting corn; some advised the use of boards; and others, setting instruments of their own invention. Hartlib, however, regarded the practice as "an infinite trouble and charge", of no advantage unless done correctly, and liable to lead to a deficient crop if the seed was attacked by pests or disease.[113]

An alternative suggestion was that the seeds should be drilled in rows, dropping them in a furrow made by a hoe. Such 'hoeing in' saved seed, allowed the crop to be hoed in spring between the rows to control weeds, and at the same time raised mould about the roots. Nor, wrote Hartlib, were such operations costly; a gardener would hoe in an acre of wheat for 5s. per acre and remove weeds by a hoeing in spring at even less charge. In 1707 hoeing an acre of turnips to weed and space the crop cost between 4s. and 9s. per acre, while in 1726, 4s. would pay for hoeing an acre of turnips. It was not until the process had been successfully mechanized, however, that drilling and row cultivation became normal farming operations.[114]

[111] Hartlib, op. cit., pp. 6–9; Laurence, op. cit., pp. 90–1.
[112] Hartlib, op. cit., p. 6; Laurence, op. cit., p. 90.
[113] G. E. Fussell, The Farmer's Tools, 1500–1900, London, 1952, pp. 92–114; Hartlib, op. cit., pp 6–7.
[114] Hartlib, op. cit., p. 7; Mortimer, Whole Art of Husbandry, p. 123; Laurence, op. cit., p. 110; Fussell, Farmer's Tools, pp. 92–114.

Garden vegetables were urged on farmers as fodder crops and were adopted in the field. Carrots, parsnips, cabbages, and even pumpkins were recommended, but most interest surrounded the turnip. We can trace the acceptance of turnips as a field rather than garden crop through the phraseology of the husbandry books. Blith recommended farmers to sow turnips principally to supply the vegetable markets, although if the crop was good and prices low "then may they be disposed of to the feeding of sheep and cattel". Worlidge in 1675 wrote of turnips, "although this be a plant usually nourished in gardens, and properly a garden plant, yet it is to the very great advantage of the husbandman sown in his fields". Both Meager in 1697 and Mortimer in 1707 wrote that turnips were commonly grown for human consumption, but were also good for cattle and sheep. By the second quarter of the eighteenth century the emphasis had changed; according to Laurence in 1726, "The turnep hath been formerly to be a root only fit for the garden and kitchen use; but the industrious farmer finds it now to be one of his chief treasures". Ellis in 1747 claimed that "This root is become very much in use in divers countries in this kingdom, and become the food of beast and sheep etc."[115]

Market gardens were often the proving grounds for crops new to both field and garden, and the source of supply for farmers anxious to experiment with them. Madder roots could be purchased from London gardeners in the 1650s. In the late sixteenth century tobacco was grown in London gardens before it was taken up in the provinces for field cultivation. Liquorice was also grown by market gardeners around the capital. Sandwich farmer-gardeners pioneered the production of canary seed, as well as growing quantities of flax and teasels.[116] Yet another agency promoting the introduction of new field crops was the seed trade. Complementing the efforts of the agricultural writers (in whose books they were often advertised), seedsmen, through their catalogues and pamphlets and through personal contact with their customers or their agents, could offer gentlemen the seeds of new crops and advise on their cultivation.[117] In short, by demonstrating garden practices and crops which could also be grown in the field, commercial horticulture stimulated agricultural progress.

[115] Kerridge, Agricultural Revolution, pp. 268–78; Speed, Adam Out of Eden, pp. 18–29, 48–54; Blith, op. cit., 3rd edn, pp. 273–4; Worlidge, Systema Agriculturae, p. 42; Leonard Meager, The Mystery of Husbandry, London, 1697, p. 99; Mortimer, op. cit., p. 121; Laurence, op. cit., pp. 109–12; William Ellis and Samuel Trowell, The Farmer's Instructor, London, 1747, p. 63.

[116] Blith, op. cit., 3rd edn, p. 236; C. M. MacInnes, The Early English Tobacco Trade, London, 1926, p. 79; PRO, PROB 4 22/60; PROB 4 19/04; PROB 4 23/16.

[117] Corp. of London RO, Orphans Invs., box 11, Common Serjeant's Book, II, f. 325b; Donnelly, 'Arthur Clephane', pp. 151–160.

7

AGRICULTURAL INNOVATIONS AND
THEIR DIFFUSION, 1640–1750

A recurring theme in all the regional chapters of this volume is the gradual diffusion of agricultural innovations and improvements within regions and between one region and another. Many new crops and systems of cultivation had been introduced into England and Wales in the period 1500–1640 (see Volume IV), but their impact still remained in 1640 relatively limited and local. In the following century, between 1640 and 1750, they were much more widely and successfully advertised. And since this century laid the foundation of the next hundred years of "agricultural revolution", the spread of innovation in this period was plainly a motor carrying men forward into a new age. This chapter attempts to show more precisely *how* innovations were diffused. It does not aim to measure the pace of diffusion of every innovation, which is plainly an impossible task. It concentrates on examples that illustrate the process.

A. SETTING THE SCENE IN 1640

At first sight the spread of new crops or new systems of farming seems random and unpredictable. An innovation, adopted by one man in one village, might spread quickly in the same district; on the other hand, it could remain confined to one farm and then die out. Sometimes it leapt long distances, and established itself firmly in a seemingly unrelated area. To explain the phenomenon in all cases is impossible, but all need not be dismissed as irrational and inexplicable. Many diverse examples finally reveal the web of favourable circumstances needed to promote novelties. The first responsibility for innovation lay with single individuals, who were goaded by economic and/or intellectual interest, and had the determination and persistence, zest, energy, and money to experiment. Thereafter it was the social and agricultural requirements of the new crop or farming system which encouraged, or discouraged, its diffusion geographically and socially. Finally economic, political, and cultural factors again came into play, mingling with agricultural and social considerations, to prescribe for the innovation a long or short life. The failure of men to recognize their best interests has little place in the story.

The spread of agricultural improvements was an outstanding achievement of the period 1640–1750, but many fertile seeds were sown between 1500 and 1640, and it is necessary, therefore, to look back at the way in which the ground was being prepared before 1640. For the pioneers, the first enlightenment dawned in the sixteenth century with the publication of an entirely new class of books of husbandry. Later developments cannot be fully understood unless they are set against this bibliographical history. When the first works appeared, nothing of their kind had been written for some two hundred years. The new literature not only opened men's eyes to new possibilities; it offered them an account of the farming methods of the ancients, and also made them aware of the intellectual curiosity and varied practices of their contemporary countrymen on the continent of Europe. When once English authors started to copy this example, they in turn revealed to their readers the highly diverse farming procedures of fellow Englishmen living in other parts of the kingdom. Such books were intellectually exciting, and stimulated action. They appeared at a moment when English landlords and large farmers were perceiving in rising food prices a growing demand for food that brought benefits and problems: it increased *their* incomes, but it brought small advantage to poor subsistence farmers, and positive hardship to agricultural labourers who were their tenants or neighbours. For various different reasons reflective men were forced to look afresh at traditional farming systems.

English authors of agricultural textbooks in the sixteenth century all seem to have belonged to the same social class. They were gentry who wished to see their estates efficiently administered. To this end, they preached hard work and conscientious supervision by the master of his household and his fields. Some authors had influence in high places; others were often the younger sons of gentlemen, who moved in the same circle, but had to earn their living. They finished up as farmers, even driving the plough themselves, not simply watching their servants do so. Such was Thomas Tusser who farmed at Braham Hall in Suffolk, and wrote with knowledge of Suffolk and of Essex where he was born; such was Reynolde Scot, who wrote the first book on hop growing, was a younger son from Kent (a successful hop-growing county from the moment that hops were introduced into England), and whose work, in Fussell's words, was "the work of a practical man, written for practical men".[1]

Sixteenth-century books on husbandry deserve careful reading, for their authors were usually competent and in some cases exceptionally highly qualified in their subject. The tradition was preserved, and the standards even raised, by early-seventeenth-century writers. John Norden's *Surveyor's Dialogue* (1607), for example, reveals local knowledge of remarkable range and precision. Norden was a surveyor of crown forests and of the duchy of Cornwall estates, a mapmaker, and a topographer. He planned a series of county histories, of which those on Middlesex and Hertfordshire were

[1] G. E. Fussell, *The Old English Farming Books from Fitzherbert to Tull, 1523 to 1730*, London, 1947, pp. 9, 11–12.

published in 1593 and 1598. Work of this kind requires a keen, observant eye, a sensitive feeling for landscape and geological differences, and a shrewd, practical cast of mind. All these qualities are reflected in Norden's writing, with its exact references to districts and villages, types of soil, even including some bold generalizations on the kinds of people inhabiting them.[2]

The next generation of agricultural writers came into still closer contact with working farmers. The most popular of these was Gervase Markham, a poor younger son of a country gentleman, Robert Markham of Cotham in the Vale of Trent, Nottinghamshire. His father's association with eminent men like Sir Francis Walsingham and his own (probable) sojourn in the stables of the earl of Rutland at Belvoir Castle gave direction to his early years, but his living had to be earned by hard work, and he tried his hand at several different occupations. "Although a piece of my life was scholar, a piece soldier, and all horseman", he wrote, "yet did I for nine years apply myself to the plough." This experience imbued him with respect for the farming fraternity. "For divers years, wherein I lived most happily, I lived a husbandman, amongst husbandmen of most excellent knowledge", he wrote. Hence in his farming books he wrote for "honest, plain dealing English husbandmen", and was sufficiently successful in his purpose to recruit readers somewhat lower in the social scale than the sons of gentry. "Markham's books were so popular in his own day that they were almost literally read to pieces", writes F. N. L. Poynter, his bibliographer.[3]

Markham not only wrote of English farming, but also, like other authors, maintained wider interests in the European literature on husbandry. He supervised in 1616 a new edition of a famous French text: he amended Richard Surflet's English translation of the French work of Estienne and Liebault, entitled *Maison Rustique*. He similarly promoted a fresh edition of Barnaby Googe's much-read translation of the German work of Konrad Heresbach, first published in England in 1577. He was a bridge between the older generation of landowners, who kept up a lively interest in agricultural improvement at an exalted social level, and the new generation which wished to extend the influence of books lower down the social scale to yeomen and husbandmen. Markham wrote "carefully and clearly, and seemed always aware that the readers for whom he was writing were not accustomed to receiving instructions from books but by word of mouth".[4] By the time of his death in 1637 this viewpoint and missionary purpose had become commonplace among writers in all branches of agriculture.[5]

---

[2] *DNB, sub nomine*; for some extracts from Norden, see T & C, pp. 106–7, 109–15.

[3] F. N. L. Poynter, *A Bibliography of Gervase Markham, 1568?–1637*, Oxford, 1962, pp. 6–11, 18–19, 21–2.

[4] *Ibid.*, pp. 27, 29–30; see also below, pp. 272–3.

[5] See e.g. the tone of the dialogue in R. C., *An Old Thrift Newly Revived*, London, 1612, instructing practical woodwards on measuring timber. The author, Rocke Church, was James I's surveyor of royal forests – J. Thirsk, review of Blanche Henrey, *British Botanical and Horticultural Literature before 1800*, AHR, XXVI, 1, 1978, pp. 59–61.

A serviceable collection of agricultural textbooks was thus available to literate farmers by 1640. General works on husbandry stood alongside specialist treatises, such as those by Sir Hugh Plat (1600 and 1601) and Edward Maxey (1601) on setting corn in rows, by Thomas Hill (1579) and others on bee keeping, by Gervase Markham on wildfowling (1621), by Leonard Mascall on tree grafting (1572), by Reynolde Scot on hop gardens (1576), and by Rowland Vaughan on floating water meadows (1601). They were stimulating to the knowledgeable and essential to beginners. Gentleman readers copied useful tips into their commonplace books, underlined their own copies, wrote exclamations of approval or disapproval in the margins, corresponded with one another to exchange opinions about these books, and exchanged the books themselves, sometimes sending them on very long journeys across the Atlantic in their missionary quest. The good ship *Supply* taking victuals and equipment in September 1620 to furnish a new settlement in Virginia took Markham's works on "all kinds of English husbandry and huswifry", Barnaby Googe's translation of Heresbach, and two other treatises "for the ordering of silk and silkworms". Their recipient across the Atlantic was advised to guard the books under his own hands, "otherwise you will be defrauded of them".[6]

The contents of books, and what is known of their authors, make it clear that agricultural literature did not stand aloof from farming practice. "I did by proof find that action and discourse went even hand in hand together", wrote Gervase Markham,[7] and with these words he spoke for all the best authors. Their books described standard procedures in one locality for the benefit of farmers in others; they presented novel ideas, like setting corn in rows, that had not yet been perfected but deserved further experiment; and they gave information about new plants like tobacco, coleseed, and madder that were grown on the continent of Europe but were not yet seriously tried in England. Writers had no way of knowing which of the new plants would eventually succeed in the English climate and which would fail, and we should not judge them with hindsight. Rather they should be admired for keeping open minds on everything, and doing their best to match theory with practice.

English farming books by 1600, however, were only the visible tip of an iceberg. Another influential group of people consisted of gardeners, herbalists, and botanists who were continually on the lookout for better varieties of

[6] Susan M. Kingsbury, *Records of the Virginia Company of London, III* (1607–22), London, 1906, p. 400. For examples of memoranda books in which notes from agricultural authors are copied, see BL, Sloane MS 1,607, containing Markham's printed work *The Inrichment of the Weald of Kent*, London, 1625, together with other manuscript notes on the use of marl (c. 1642); BL, Sloane MS 3,095, a manuscript treatise on horses, including notes from Markham and Blundeville; and Norfolk Rural Life Museum, Gressenhall Dereham, NCM 547–971, which contains long notes from Jethro Tull and a reference to Blith. I am grateful to Miss Bridget Yates for making this last document known to me.   [7] Poynter, *op. cit.*, p. 12.

old and new plants, and exhorted all travellers in Europe, Asia, and America to bring them back fresh specimens from abroad. If a new plant promised well, then somewhere an interested gentleman or merchant was sure to give it a trial. Books thus give only a small idea, which must be magnified ten times, of the energy that was being devoted by gentleman farmers, gardeners, merchants, nurserymen, and herbalists to grow new crops and improve old ones.

Is it possible to penetrate more deeply the bookish surface, to gauge more exactly the inspiration that impelled innovators in agriculture? The pioneers were gentlemen with intellectual curiosity and above-average financial resources. If the explanations of Konrad Heresbach are a fair guide to the attitude of European humanists, many took delight in estate and farm management as a relaxation from other more taxing and disagreeable duties. Seeing the land produce bountifully, managing their households prudently, knowing that the foodstuffs on their table were of their own growing gave them deep satisfaction.[8] Moreover, their standard of living was rising. For these men, therefore, some of the most beguiling novelties in agriculture were luxuries, like vines and peach and mulberry trees. But the published descriptions of plants contained many more useful suggestions that also excited them as a challenge. And, on further reflection, many of the novelties took on other virtues. They promised to reduce imports, and so might aid the economy; they employed labour intensively, and so might give more work to the poor. Such motives, mingling with a fervent dedication to the ideas of the commonweal, encouraged experiments. By the second or third decade of the seventeenth century one could be sure that the appearance of a book about a new plant meant that practical experiments were already in train. Books were stimulating action, not initiating it.

Many practical experiments were put under way in the early seventeenth century by men who were deliberately secretive, guarding their knowledge in order to make the highest profit from a pioneering success. But if their first trials succeeded and more labouring people became involved in the work of cultivation, the crop was publicized whether the pioneers liked it or not. Books continued to explain procedures and reassured men that the innovation was a practical possibility, but men could now count on having seen the crop growing at home, and sometimes also abroad. It became a talking point among friends and neighbours, and no obstacles impeded the spread of news. Now it was wider economic, social, agricultural, and political considerations that governed the future of the innovation.

Much light is shed on these steps in the development of new crops by the history of woad, madder, mulberry trees, and tobacco. The right agricultural environment had to be found for these crops, their labour

[8] Konrad Heresbach, *Vier Bücher über Landwirtschaft, I, Vom Landbau*, ed. W. Abel, Meisenheim, 1970, preface and pp. 1a ff.

requirements had to accord with the social resources of the neighbourhood, and the financial rewards had to be sufficient to make the crop more profitable than other crops competing for the same land. Woad, for example, became a thoroughly successful first crop on old pasture land that was being broken up for several seasons of arable cultivation. It required an ample supply of casual labour throughout the summer, and it required large acreages in one district to justify the temporary erection of a woad mill. The milling and balling of the leaves required expert woad men; and so itinerant woad growers, leasing land for a year or two and then moving on, proved to be the answer. Where all these conditions were met, the crop became commonplace in the seventeenth-century landscape. Madder, in contrast, did not require so much hand labour, but did call for long-term planning and investment, for it had to be in the ground for three years before a crop was gathered. Whenever foreign (mostly Dutch) madder became too expensive – in the early 1620s, the 1660s, and again between about 1758 and 1775 – it enjoyed popularity, but it lost favour when foreign madder fell in price. Mulberry trees, which were needed to feed silkworms in order to nourish a domestic silk industry, were energetically publicized and taken up by gentlemen who had sufficient spare land to accommodate them. Some gentry in the 1650s had the satisfaction of wearing waistcoats woven from their own home-made silk. But in the end mulberry trees proved difficult to propagate, and trials were being made with the wrong variety. They failed to compete with fruit trees for the same ground. Tobacco quickly found a market among all classes in society, and, as it demanded much hard labour and little land, it proved successful wherever large numbers of smallholders existed alongside landless poor who lacked other work. In such places it persisted for decades – until about 1690 – despite the government's ban on tobacco growing in 1619 in order to favour the crop of the Virginia colony.[9]

The years between 1600 and 1640, then, were extremely fruitful for the introduction of new crops and other improvement schemes. Contacts between the nobility and gentry of England and the Continent, which had been greatly strengthened in the previous century, were maintained, and the flow of fresh ideas on economic projects of all kinds showed no signs of running dry. The system of patents and monopolies granted to individuals by the crown had encouraged innovators, especially merchants of gentry origin, in Elizabeth's reign, and the same system continued to exercise some influence despite mounting disenchantment among ordinary people.[10] That

[9] On woad, see Joan Thirsk, *Economic Policy and Projects: The Development of a Consumer Society in Early Modern England*, Oxford, 1978, pp. 28–30. On madder and mulberry trees I propose to write at greater length elsewhere. On tobacco, see Joan Thirsk, 'New Crops and their Diffusion: Tobacco-Growing in Seventeenth Century England', in C. W. Chalklin and M. A. Havinden, eds., *Rural Change and Urban Growth, 1500–1800*, London, 1974, pp. 76–103.

[10] Thirsk, *Economic Policy and Projects*, chs. II–IV.

patents were still an incentive to young adventurers in the early 1620s is shown by the pioneers of madder and tobacco.[11]

Nevertheless, most pioneers in agriculture broke free of the patent system; and this was just as well, for grain and wool were embarked on a long price decline which of itself gave sufficient stimulus to the search for new crops and livestock outside the traditional farming system. Freedom was necessary for these crops to be tried and tested. Until the 1650s the full significance of falling agricultural prices was not everywhere understood, but once conventional corn and livestock farmers found themselves after 1660 in increasingly straitened circumstances, the merits of innovations became more obvious. Their diffusion then became a faster and also a more refined process, both socially and geographically.

Looking back to the period before 1600, we should not underrate the role of policy makers in encouraging agricultural innovation. An idea put to ministers by a foreigner could result in important initiatives being taken by the government; and foreign inventors and innovators sent a steady stream of petitions and advice to Privy Councillors. If their advice was accepted, the government was ready to give much practical assistance, licensing foreigners to come to England, while officials employed or entertained them in their households, making land available for experimental plantations, and soliciting reports on progress. Simultaneous consultations with business men and landowners enlisted them on the side of the new project. Alternatively, merchants or gentry put their ideas to the government and sought favours, whether patents of monopoly or other protection from foreign competition. They might be disappointed of such favours, but their very canvassing gave the scheme publicity, and immediately stimulated competition under watchful government eyes. Negotiations for the madder patent illustrate one such competitive bid; the letters of George Bedford to his stepfather, when he was still a hopeful applicant for a patent that finally went to William Shipman, the king's gardener, reveal how much time and patience were needed, waiting endlessly in antechambers, before such favours were granted.[12]

Strong financial incentives urging men to take the risk of promoting novelties were compounded with other motives which should not be overlooked. A sense of obligation to one's fellow men to strengthen the economy, promote the commonweal, and provide work for the poor was part of an accepted philosophy, inspired by religious and political conviction. It was not idle talk. All labour-intensive crops, like woad, madder, and tobacco, were commended for their value in employing many poor, alongside the financial gain to individual planters. Public statements usually

[11] For madder, see above, p. 168. For tobacco, see Thirsk, 'New Crops and their Diffusion', pp. 79, 101 n. 45. See also PRO, SP 14/187/22A for a patent in 1613 for a liquor for steeping grain seed to discourage birds.   [12] Hants. RO, 44M69/XXXIII, nos. 29–37.

combined careful analyses of the profits such crops could yield in good years with equally precise accounts of their labour needs. Both sets of considerations weighed heavily with many Puritans and other public-spirited men. In short, new crops were canvassed as commendable examples of mutual aid and won support on both counts.[13]

Other measures for increasing profits from the land, which found favour with thoughtful men by the beginning of the seventeenth century, started from a different source. They concerned the improvement of run-down, long-neglected grassland, and took much inspiration from writers like John Norden who claimed that no land, however barren, was incapable of improvement. A "discreet and industrious husband" could always find means to enrich his soil, if he took pains. "There must be observation to mark how others thrive, inclination and imitation to do the like endeavour and charge. And if one experiment fail, try a second, a third, and many."[14] Gentlemen read these exhortations, and, knowing the efforts of their monarchs, Elizabeth, James, and Charles, at reclaiming newly silted marshland along the coast, draining the fens, and disafforesting the forests, they took them seriously. The original lessons seem to have been learned by English sovereigns from their peers in Europe. They in turn now taught the same lessons to the gentry, who noticed the increasingly positive, even aggressive, tone of the crown surveyors. When advising on the improvement of fens, forests, and chases, professional servants of the king advocated enclosure against all contrary arguments, whether coming from lawyers, agriculturalists, commoners, or taxpayers.[15] Private gentlemen took courage from this royal example. Thus John Smyth of Nibley, Gloucestershire, drew the attention of his son, who was a commissioner for the crown engaged in disafforesting the Forest of Dean in 1639, to observe the crown's policy in this regard. It accorded with his own prejudices, formed by his experience as landowner in the parish of Slimbridge: large commons and wastes burdened a village with beggarly cottages and idle people. They were better enclosed. The same consideration, he maintained, was "none of the least why King James and the king that now is have reduced into severalty, and into smaller parcels, let to private men's uses and farmers thereof, so many of their forests, chases, and wild and waste grounds...to the private benefit of themselves and the general good of the commonwealth, both in the breed of serviceable men and subjects, and of answerable estates and abilities". The improvement of

[13] J. Thirsk, 'Projects for Gentlemen, Jobs for the Poor: Mutual Aid in the Vale of Tewkesbury, 1600–1630', in *Essays in Bristol and Gloucestershire History*, ed. P. McGrath and John Cannon, Bristol, 1976, *passim*; *id.*, *Economic Policy and Projects*, pp. 18–22.

[14] T & C, pp. 111–12.

[15] See e.g. the report of the king's surveyor on the improvement of forests in 1612 – *ibid.*, pp. 116–20. For plans for royal forest improvements in James I's time, see BL, Cotton MS Titus B v, no. 138; no. 84 ff. 268ff; Add. MS 38,444.

fens, forests, and chases became the slogan of all dedicated seventeenth-century improvers.[16]

Beyond the large, well-defined areas of under-used, mostly common, land, the greatest scope for development lay in scattered pockets of old pasture and woodland, often on former monastic land that had been passing from hand to hand since the 1540s without being put to maximum use. Behind some of the brisk sales of former monastic and crown land in certain west Midland counties in James I's reign, for example, seem to lie lively plans and hopes for redevelopment. Shortly after their sale, some of these sites, often comprising run-down pasture, were chosen for experiments with new crops. They lay in places where no one objected; indeed, men positively welcomed their more productive use. At Winchcomb, in Gloucestershire, for example, old pasture had been let for £2 an acre, but under tobacco it earned a rent of £5–8. A site for woad growing in 1594 at Ashcombe in the parish of Berwick St John, Wiltshire, was in part a former rabbit warren. A site chosen in the 1590s for woad growing in Blagdon Park in Martin parish, next to Cranborne Chase, was formerly a royal park, disparked in 1570. Three sites for madder growing, Appledore on the edge of Romney Marsh, and Barn Elms and Deptford along Thames-side, were all low-lying, probably ill-drained lands, possibly semi-derelict.[17]

Finally, the means of passing information between agricultural improvers was growing more efficient as interested persons formed circles of like-minded friends, and kept up a flow of correspondence and discussion. They were often kinsmen, visiting each other's houses, or friends who met regularly at Quarter Sessions and Assizes. Rowland Vaughan's first experiments with the floating of water meadows in Herefordshire were next copied on the Wiltshire lands of the earl of Pembroke, to whom Vaughan dedicated his book on the subject, and then taken up in Surrey by Sir Richard Weston, who had links with Herefordshire, seemingly through his wife, and who also held land there; Weston may even have met Rowland Vaughan.[18] The tobacco-growing experiments in Gloucestershire in 1618–19 involved a closely knit group of gentlemen who were kinsmen, neighbours, and old school friends. Many of them were well educated and well travelled, had much time on their hands, and positively relished the challenge of a fresh interest. They read any books that came their way, and took seriously those on country subjects which exhorted them to respect the skills of the farmer, to appreciate their good

---

[16] T & C, pp. 122–3.

[17] Thirsk, 'New Crops', pp. 90, 85; J. Bettey, 'The Cultivation of Woad in the Salisbury Area during the Late Sixteenth and Early Seventeenth Centuries', *Textile Hist.*, IX, 1978, p. 113.

[18] *Rowland Vaughan, His Booke*, ed. E. B. Wood, London, 1897, pp. x–xi, 25. The connection with Herefordshire is suggested by the fact that Weston's wife was Grace Harper, daughter of John Harper. John Harper of Hereford gave evidence in a dispute involving Weston in 1631; but his exact relationship to Weston was not explained. I owe this information to Michael Nash, citing PRO, E 178/5,669.

fortune in escaping the harassment of city life, and positively to enjoy the contentment it brought. Such works fostered an intelligent and professional view of agriculture, and filled some readers, at least, with a self-conscious pride in their efforts to mend their land, and sustain their local community in productive work.

The wisdom learned from books shines through many of the doings and writings of gentlemen. John Smyth of Nibley, Gloucestershire, plainly shared John Norden's optimism about improving all soils, no matter how poor, for it underlies the argument of a manuscript in his hand that scarce any manor in England, however barren, lacked marl which would enrich the ground. Konrad Heresbach's praise of country life, newly rendered into English by Gervase Markham in 1634, is echoed in Smyth's description of husbandry as "the only vocation wherein innocency remaineth", in contrast with the life in cities and market towns where men "seek means and busy themselves how to deceive and beguile one another". In this passage also Smyth disclosed another source of his inspiration by commending to his readers "Mr. Markham's books of husbandry". He had plainly learned much from them himself.[19]

The emphasis that must be laid in the period before 1640 on gentlemen and merchants as innovators, to the exclusion of yeomen and husbandmen, explains itself when the financial risks of novelties are considered. Some grand schemes for woad, madder, and tobacco went awry, and their projectors lost substantial sums. Poorer men could not contemplate such hazardous ventures. Even to procure publicity for a novel idea required money, time, and patience which working men could not spare from the daily routine of getting a living. So while merchants and gentry were cheerful gamblers, though commonly setting up partnerships among themselves to spread their risks, workaday farmers waited and watched carefully. If a new crop worked well and suited their circumstances, they were quick to learn and imitate. London gardeners plainly did so: on their small plots of land they could mingle a new crop with a number of old and reliable ones, and not risk bankruptcy if it failed. Outside London the news of novelties waited upon merchants and gentlemen to blaze a trail. But a new crop could spread like wildfire among small peasants, if its social, economic, and agricultural requirements suited their circumstances. That is proven beyond all dispute by the history of tobacco growing.[20]

B. 1640–1660

Between 1640 and 1660 one of the chief lessons learned by attentive farmers was the scope for selling at the market a multitude of foodstuffs that had hitherto been relatively neglected as items of trade. The argument was clearly

[19] J. Smith, *Lives of the Berkeleys*, Gloucester, 1883, pp. 40–3; Heresbach, *op. cit.*, I, pp. 1a ff.
[20] Thirsk, 'New Crops', pp. 83–6.

set out in print in the highly popular French work *Maison Rustique*, by Estienne and Liebault, first made available to English readers in a translation by Richard Surflet in 1600, and reissued by Gervase Markham in 1616. Its lessons were then driven home by adversity. It underlined the financial rewards to be earned by those who attended to the refined tastes of the well-to-do in foodstuffs, and the cumulative profit to be had from exploiting many small and neglected natural assets. "We see it in common experience", it reminded its readers, "that such cooks as can contrive and make of some one stuff (and that in itself little regarded and less used), either by adding of some few things (and those not costly), or else by their labour or manner of preparing many both pleasant and wholesome dishes, are had in high account and estimation." The same attention to refined detail had brought large returns to the French in the sixteenth century in the production of manufactured consumer goods like fancy shoes and perfumed gloves. The same attention could be equally profitable to farmers and gardeners. The second lesson concerned the economical use of every available natural resource, however trifling. "When all is said a good farmer will make profit of everything, and there is not (as we say) so much as the garlic and onion which he will not raise gain of, by selling them at fairs most fitting for their time and season, and so help himself thereof and fill his purse with money."[21]

By 1660 countrymen were exploiting many more ways of getting a livelihood than in 1600. As Adam Speed made clear in his work *Adam Out of Eden* in 1659, the possibilities were endless, and men had no need to go to Jamaica in search of more land. On the most barren soils, rabbits were profitable, or French furze could be grown from seed, with spreading tops "far transcending our English furze", thereby providing a much superior fuel.[22] With fern and furze one could fuel a malthouse, and anyone could make a living buying barley and selling malt. Alternatively, swine, pigeons, geese, turkeys, ducks, and bees were all profitable. Buckwheat was worth a trial on heathy ground and would feed poultry to perfection. On richer soils, the prizes were even more alluring: liquorice might earn £200 an acre, saffron £40, mustard £30, teasels £30, osiers £20, and hops £40–£120. Carrots on sand made many small fortunes. In London gardeners prospered by growing clove gillyflowers and red roses. Moreover, some of these field and garden crops interlocked with animal husbandry to provide a double

[21] *Maison Rustique, or The Countrey Farme*...ed. Gervase Markham, London, 1616, f. A3, p. 311.

[22] A. Speed, *Adam Out of Eden*, London, 1659, pp. 2–10, 65, 'To the Reader'. For a Welshman's interest in French furze in 1685, see the letter of Owen Hughes, London, replying to an enquiry from John Owen of Penrhos concerning its cost and special virtues. "It is like our furze", he said, "but some say it grows thicker" – UCNWL, Penrhos Coll., v, 96. John Houghton also stressed the value of furze for fuel where wood was scarce, and the value of the tops for horse fodder – J. Houghton, *A Collection for Improvement of Husbandry and Trade*, 4 vols., ed. R. Bradley, London, 1727–8, *IV*, p. 29.

reward. Coleseed when crushed for oil left a residue for making rape cake to be fed to milking cows; furze gave cover to pheasants; waste vegetables from market gardens and green tops from the fields fed cows and swine.[23]

The many ideas here being offered to the thrifty and resourceful were taken up at all social levels. Among town dwellers, male and female, many who lacked other means bought barley and made malt. Of many towns between 1540 and 1640 it was said that their principal occupation was malting, so that in this case Adam Speed's advice plainly followed behind common knowledge. That rabbits attracted increasing interest from gentlemen at this time can be seen in Samuel Hartlib's letters in the 1650s. One of his correspondents found some *Directions for Keeping Tame Conies*, dating from fifty years earlier, among "Mr. Slegger's Writings". Though he did not realize it, these *Directions* were those published by Robert Payne, the woad grower, in 1589 in a little book designed to encourage settlement in Ireland. This rediscovery set its finder hunting through other literature for more advice on keeping conies. Gervase Markham had a few words on them; so did the French work *The Country Farm*; so did *Le Théâtre d'Agriculture*. A fresh discussion on rabbit keeping ensued, leading one writer to suggest that rabbits be stocked on slightly better land than sandy heaths, and at a higher density. It was reckoned possible to keep 200 couples, worth £20 per annum, at a cost of only £2. As this yield was higher than for any other livestock, it was bound to rouse someone somewhere to action.[24]

Thus the agricultural scene was enriched between 1640 and 1660, even though war and political uncertainty put an end to the most adventurous schemes of improvement in the 1640s, and the highest gambling fever died away. Expensive works like dykes for fen drainage were destroyed by angry peasants who had the chance to turn back the clock and recover their lost commons amid the devastation that accompanied civil strife. But the war also placed the need for agricultural improvement higher on the agenda than ever before, for it inflicted great financial losses on landowners of both parties, and those who had earlier shown an interest in land improvement naturally turned back to these possibilities in the quieter days of the 1650s. Two particular circumstances impelled them. A reduction in the official rate of interest in 1651 from 8 per cent to 6 per cent encouraged expenditure on improvements, while the bad harvest years of 1646–51, coupled with a trade depression, gave extra urgency to their schemes. More food had to be grown, and more work had to be found. By reclaiming neglected land, men argued

---

[23] Speed, *op. cit.*, 'To the Reader' and pp. 9, 37, 65, 114 *et passim*. Although not stated, these returns almost certainly represent gross values, and costs would be high.

[24] Sheffield Univ. Library, Hartlib MSS, 67/5/1–4; R. Payne, *A Briefe Description of Ireland*, London, 1589, pp. 15–16; Hartlib MSS, 62/32/1; J. Sheail, 'Rabbits and Agriculture in Post-Medieval England', *J. Hist. Geog.*, IV, 4, 1978, p. 347. For the active interest in rabbits of one landowner in 1655, leading him to plan the import of Dutch conies, see Northants. RO, Isham Correspondence, IC 537.

that more farms could be created which would produce more food and give peacetime employment to demobilized soldiers. The powerful slogan of the period 1600–40 exhorting men to improve fens, forests, and chases was reiterated, even while the content of those schemes was modified to show greater consideration for the rights of commoners.[25]

The career of a notable gentleman improver, Sir Richard Weston, which spanned the reigns of James I and Charles I and did not end until 1652, mirrors both the difficult economic circumstances of landowners between 1640 and 1660 and the opportunities of the age. For thirty years Weston conscientiously managed his estate at Sutton in west Surrey. But in his fifties, probably in 1643 or early in 1644, he made a journey to Brabant in Flanders, forced upon him by the sequestration of his estate. This opened his eyes to the potential for improvement of his land, greater than he had ever perceived at home.[26] In Holland, between Antwerp and Ghent, he saw sandy heathlands, similar to his own, in much more productive use. Moreover, they were deemed more profitable to their owners than rich wheat, barley, and peas lands, for they were worked on a rotation of flax, turnips, oats, and clover, each of which crops paid far better than wheat. The flax crop was worth four to five times more than corn; the turnips were also worth more than corn, *and* fed dairy cows to perfection; the clover crop lasted four or five years without further cultivation, and fed cattle and cows as well as the best natural meadows; alternatively, it was left for seed. Weston walked the fields in April when flax and clover were being sown, questioning farmers, purchasing a rod of grown flax to test its price in the market, as well as investigating other ways of improving heathland by planting orchards, timber trees, and hops. Weston uncovered in Holland a fact of life which was slowly learned in seventeenth-century England, namely, that specialized industrial crops like flax, or new fodder crops like turnips and clover, were financially more rewarding to many farmers than bread grains. In 1644 in Holland one acre of flax was said to be worth £40–50, one acre of turnips £8–10, and one acre of clover £10–12, whereas wheat was worth only £5–6 an acre, and best meadow grass £4–5 an acre. Faced with these economic realities, Holland had come to rely increasingly on Baltic grain for its bread, and was concentrating its efforts on the growing of other crops, some of which plainly preferred heathy, sandy soils, and flourished there better than on the deep loams of older cultivated corn country.[27]

Sir Richard Weston's observations in Flanders and Brabant gave him valuable ideas for improving heathlands at Sandie Chapel in Surrey, in

---

[25] See ch. 4 above, pp. 128 ff. Sir Josiah Child in *New Discourse of Trade*, 1694 (pp. 10, 48–9), thought that the reduction of interest in 1651 promoted draining, marling, and liming by landlords and tenants.   [26] *DNB, sub nomine.*

[27] *A Discours of Husbandrie Used in Brabant and Flanders*, 2nd edn, 1652, *passim*, but esp. pp. 7–15, 18, 24–5.

Windsor Forest, Berkshire, and in St Leonard's Forest, Sussex.[28] And although his treatise of advice was originally written only for his sons who would inherit his estate, it reached a much larger readership when it was published by Samuel Hartlib in 1650. Not only did it confirm the faith of others in the virtue and wisdom of agricultural improvement all over England, but its precise observations also taught them to study details rather than to sweep the landscape with a grand, but unseeing, eye. Writers like Gervase Markham had already written of the great variety of England's regions, its diverse soils, and diverse systems of cultivation and cropping.[29] The essential next step was to match soils to crops more carefully, using the right system of management in each case. Flax, turnips, and clover were already grown in numerous places in England, but, as Weston emphasized the system of management was as different from the Dutch system as a crop grown in a garden was different from one growing wild in the fields. New plants had to be fitted into new and satisfactory systems of cultivation, and one system was not necessarily right in all situations. Success in discovering the best system was the key to that crop's wider diffusion.

Agricultural improvement was becoming a task for those with an eye for detail, who did not expect everything to grow everywhere, but who selected as scientifically as they could between alternative uses for land, alternative crops, and alternative methods of cultivation, and examined costs and profits in a local context.[30] The foundation was being laid for the new kind of agricultural literature, which flourished increasingly after 1649, when parsons and landed gentry with enquiring minds gathered practical information and wrote it up faithfully and clearly. With the execution of Charles I, moreover, a Commonwealth was set up by men who saw a new age dawning. Parliamentarians saw new hopes and new opportunities as church lands, crown lands, and royalist lands were seized and sold, and first surveyors and then purchasers became acquainted with new tracts of country inviting improvement.

The career of Walter Blith exemplifies the professionalism of the next generation of agricultural writers, as well as showing their intimate contact with practising farmers. Walter Blith wrote much the best general work on agricultural improvement during the Interregnum, and owed his wide experience to the chances that war and its aftermath put in his path. His father was a yeoman grain and dairy farmer from the Forest of Arden, Warwickshire;

---

[28] See AHEW, vol. v, pt 1, ch. 9, p. 297.

[29] G. Markham, *Farewell to Husbandry*, London, 1625, pp. 150–1.

[30] Some idea of Weston's continuing experiments was later given by Adam Speed in *Adam Out of Eden*, pp. 34–6. He tested the productivity of different seeds by sowing 8 acres with Flemish clover seed and 8 acres with his own seed in order to compare results. He found Flemish seed yielded better if it was of good quality, but since so much was adulterated, he thought it better to rely on English seed. He also tested the right time to sow, whether clover throve best when undersown with barley or not, and how best to thresh seed.

he was a parliamentary captain, surveyor of crown lands in 1649–50, and a modest purchaser of such lands in Northamptonshire. In various ways he saw much Midland land, good, bad, and indifferent.[31]

Blith's first book on agricultural improvement in 1649 was a modest but creditable effort, in which he strove to write in countryman's language, using homespun terms in order to enlighten plain husbandmen. But between 1649 and 1652, when a new edition of his book appeared, Blith accumulated a lot of new experience. He then added six new measures of land improvement to the six that had appeared in the first edition, and incorporated many new or rewritten passages. His readers had plainly informed him of the virtues and profits to be had from new crops that were unknown to him in 1649 – clover; sainfoin and lucerne; weld, woad, and madder; hops, saffron, and liquorice; coleseed, hemp, and flax; orchard and garden fruits.[32]

It is also likely, judging from the differing content of the two books, that between 1650 and 1652 Blith saw drainage in the fens at close quarters; perhaps he even supervised some of the work. In short, Blith rewrote his first book of husbandry partly on the basis of new experience culled at first hand.[33]

Walter Blith was only one of a circle of authors writing in the 1650s on the basis of practical experience that was continually being enlarged. The fullest view of their activities is obtained from the correspondence and diary of Samuel Hartlib, who kept in touch with them all, prodded them into writing, and was always looking for more authors. At his house in London Hartlib sat as if at the centre of a spider's web, drawing all interested persons to him, to talk, argue, plan, and exchange books and ideas. His letters and diary explain the origins of several books of husbandry published in the 1650s, as well as describing many experiments and improvements by other men, who did not write books but who read the literature avidly and consulted all the experts by letter or in person. One of his authors was Cressy Dymock, of a Lincolnshire family, who visited him on 17 May 1648 and imparted "the design of his agriculture". Dymock had the chance of taking land at Wadsworth near Doncaster in Yorkshire, where access to markets was good, and the land was excellent. Thereafter Dymock was a regular visitor at Hartlib's house, brimming over with ideas and reporting his doings as he

[31] J. Thirsk, 'Plough and Pen: Agricultural Writers in the Seventeenth Century', in *Social Relations and Ideas*, ed. T. H. Aston *et al.*, Cambridge, 1983, pp. 306–13.

[32] W. Blith, *The English Improver*, London, 1649, p. 2; Joan Thirsk, 'Seventeenth-Century Agriculture and Social Change', in *Land, Church and People: Essays Presented to Professor H. P. R. Finberg*, ed. Joan Thirsk, AHR, XVIII, supp., 1970, p. 159.

[33] Thirsk, 'Plough and Pen'; W. Blith, *The English Improver Improved*, 4th edn, London, 1653, pp. 45–64. Dr Child, writing to Hartlib from Ireland in June 1652, expressed the hope that Blith would write more about draining, since the English were busy draining bogs in Ireland and needed all the information they could get. This may have been written after Blith's revised work had already appeared – Sheffield Univ. Library, Hartlib MS, 15/5/9.

tested them out. He was indefatigable with plans to use labour and seed more economically, and improve the efficiency of farm tools. Starting with an invention for winnowing corn cleaner than by any other method, he moved on to schemes for fattening hogs and geese, keeping rabbits, curing sheep rot, and growing teasels.[34] He planned a more rational layout of land by which fields radiated from the farm at the centre of a circle, and offered his proposal to the fen drainers as one that might immediately be implemented. They turned it down, but Hartlib published Dymock's scheme in 1653 for the benefit of other fen drainers, whether in England or Ireland.[35] It was one of many publications by Hartlib, instigated and assembled in a similar way.

Visitors to Hartlib's house and correspondents were all given the same sympathetic hearing, and their ideas and problems were freely discussed with the next visitor. In this circle of men the secretive spirit was fiercely denounced. Advances could be made only if men gave their knowledge freely. Hence they all exchanged books, invited each other to view their farms and fields, and explained their failures to one another as frankly as their successes. Colonel Blunt put himself outside this circle, for, although he was known to busy himself with all kinds of agricultural improvements on his estate near Blackheath, had invented several new kinds of ploughs, and prospered far above his neighbours, he was "all for himself and not the public".[36]

While acting as go-between for English improvers Hartlib also kept in touch with many foreign friends who sent him news or specimens. Unmussig (Johann Brun), the much-travelled Paracelsian physician, undertook to send from somewhere in Europe, via Cologne, a new sort of apple. A year later he was writing in recommendation of Borsdorf's apple, one of the best varieties in Germany, of which he promised to procure pips to send to England for planting. Francis Lodwick (Frederick Lodowick) commended, for drying purposes, the great black cherries of Flanders, which he undertook to send to Hartlib. Grundman wrote of the excellence of the Brunswick turnip in 1648, and suggested that they might be sent to England from Hamburg. From Hamburg also Mrs Dury sent Hartlib a new breed of hens in 1648, producing bigger chicks than ordinary.[37]

[34] Sheffield Univ. Library, Hartlib MSS, "Ephemerides", 1648, O–P1 to O–P7; 1649, C–D5, B–C7.

[35] S. Hartlib [C. Dymock], *A Discovery for Division or Setting Out of Land*, London, 1653, *passim*, but esp. Hartlib's 'Preface to the Reader'. Dymock's original scheme was put to Hartlib in a long and detailed letter (now Hartlib MS 62/29/1–2) from which the text of the printed treatise was edited. See R. Grove, 'Cressey Dymock and the Draining of the Fens: An Early Agricultural Model', *Geog. J.*, CXLVII, 1, 1981, pp. 27–37. [36] Hartlib, "Ephemerides", 1648, V–W6.

[37] C. Webster, *The Great Instauration*, London, 1975, pp. 78, 302; Hartlib, "Ephemerides", 1648, T–S1; 1649, H–J3; 1650, F–G2; 1648, S–T8, P–Q1. Hartlib can never have passed for an Englishman. He remained essentially a European: his diary was written up daily in a mixture of Latin, German, and English.

Through personal introductions and correspondence, often initiated by the reading of Hartlib's books, Hartlib started many friendships with people whom he subsequently persuaded to become authors. His first agricultural publication in 1650 had been Sir Richard Weston's *Discours of Husbandrie Used in Brabant and Flanders*, when he was ignorant of its authorship. The treatise had evidently passed in manuscript from hand to hand and the writer had been forgotten. The true author was acknowledged in the next edition in 1651, and when Sir Richard Weston proved to be "of a free and communicative disposition" he was drawn to the very edge of the Hartlib circle. Being a Papist, he could never enter into wholehearted membership, but men who discussed clover growing with Hartlib sometimes visited Weston in Surrey and were shown his pastures.[38] Of all Hartlib's books on agriculture, his printing of Weston's manuscript was the most influential.[39] Further editions were issued in 1652 and 1655, and through them many people were persuaded to try the Dutch rotations for themselves, and inform Hartlib of their progress. Hartlib's correspondence is liveliest on the subject of clover, as the account below will show.

Hartlib's methods of publication made authorship as easy as possible for his friends. He did not ask them to write long, comprehensive treatises. He merely solicited letters describing their doings or observations, which he then edited for publication. Dymock's plan for setting out land originated in this way, as a letter. Hartlib printed it as a book, filling up with short items from other correspondents. Gradually his books took on something of the appearance of journals, though they appeared irregularly, and each bore a different title, determined by the subject matter of the principal article. His publication in 1655, for example, was *The Reformed Commonwealth of Bees*, containing a miscellany of contributions on beekeeping and honey production, but concluding with a restatement of the success of Virginia mulberry trees in feeding silkworms. This last had been advertised by Hartlib in 1652, and had infused new life into James I's silkworm project. The introduction of Virginian mulberry trees seemed to offer hopes of better success in feeding silkworms, and so the project was given fresh publicity.

Another theme for a book which was urged on Hartlib by his acquaintances concerned orchard and timber trees. Interest grew noticeably from 1648 onwards as a rational response to the political and economic uncertainties of the time. As one writer put it, "in time of war this is one of the most honest and safe ways of hiding a man's spare moneys". In 1648 Hartlib heard of a Mr Dawson with ideas on tree planting and soft-fruit growing, and in 1651 Benjamin Worsley offered him a manuscript by the same Dawson for

[38] This modifies the verdict of A. R. Michell that Hartlib's circle was totally separated from Weston – 'Sir Richard Weston and the Spread of Clover Cultivation', AHR, XXII, 2, 1974, pp. 160–1.

[39] This was explicitly stated later in *Philos. Trans. Roy. Soc.*, x, 1675, p. 321.

publication. *A Designe for Plentie, by an Universall Planting of Fruit-Trees*, by an unknown author, which Hartlib published a year later, possibly owed something to Dawson, but it promised a larger work to follow.[40] This was supplied by Ralph Austen in his *Treatise of Fruit Trees, Showing the Manner of Grafting, Setting, Pruning and Ordering of them in All Respects*, published in 1653. Austen was both scholar and skilled gardener. Registrar to the University Visitors, he read up his subject in the Bodleian Library, and ran his own busy nurseries in south-west Oxford. He gave a more intelligible account than was previously available of such techniques as grafting and pruning, with the result that his book was reissued in 1657 and in 1665.[41]

In 1657 another enthusiast for orchards, parson John Beale, published *Herefordshire Orchards, a Pattern for All England*. His knowledge was based on firm practical experience in a celebrated fruit-growing county. Both his father and grandfather had been experts on orchards and cider. Then Hartlib put Beale and Austen in touch, to correspond and thrash out their differences of opinion on such matters as grafting methods and the best varieties of apples for cider making. His intention was to stimulate debate which would furnish material for another publication.[42]

Yet another theme for Hartlib's books in the later 1650s was vegetable cultivation, an occupation that was of equal interest to the gentry, wishing to see choice and exotic vegetables on the dinner table, and to the poor, needing a substitute or supplement for bread. Vegetables meant spade cultivation, which had a further interest; it was considered by some to be the key to increasing the productivity of land. "Let me but dig land", wrote Dr Child, "if it be not extremely barren, I'll wager to have the same increase [i.e. 100-fold] without all these slibber slops" (a deprecating reference to French friars, who steeped seed in nitre, and whose technique was publicized by Hartlib). Hartlib listened to gardeners with increasing attention and sought out suitable authors. John Thomas, a gardener of St Albans, had proposed to the Council of State ways of encouraging fruit, hemp, and flax growing and beekeeping. Hartlib hoped he would write a book, but the author who eventually answered the call was Robert Sharrock, parson and Baconian scientist, educated at Oxford, who published *The History of the Propagation*

---

[40] Webster, *op. cit.*, pp. 473, 477–9; Fussell, *op. cit.*, p. 48; R. Austen, *The Spiritual Use of an Orchard; or Garden of Fruit Trees*, Oxford, 1653, 'Preface to the Reader'. See Blanche Henrey, *British Botanical and Horticultural Literature before 1800*, 3 vols., Oxford, 1975, I, p. 169, for evidence that the author of *A Designe for Plentie* was a parson of Lothingland, near Lowestoft.

[41] Fussell, *op. cit.*, pp. 48–9; Webster, *op. cit.*, pp. 479–80; Henrey, *op. cit.*, I, pp. 171–2; J. Turner, 'Ralph Austen, an Oxford Horticulturist of the Seventeenth Century', *Garden Hist.*, VI, 2, 1978, pp. 39 45.

[42] T. Birch, *The History of the Royal Society of London*...4 vols., London, 1756–7, IV, p. 235. I wish to thank Mrs Mayling Stubbs for information on John Beale's parentage. For further details, see *id.*, 'John Beale, Philosophical Gardener of Herefordshire, Part I: Prelude to the Royal Society (1608–1663)', *Annals of Science*, XXXIX, 1982, pp. 463–89.

and Improvement of Vegetables... in 1660. This was a disappointing work, quoting other writers, but lacking the backbone of personal experience. It did not measure up to Hartlib's usual standards.[43]

Books faithfully mirror, but cannot measure, the full agricultural achievement of these two decades. This is conclusively shown in the correspondence passing among members of the Hartlib circle. Books inspired much practical work among the same class, but of this last only a very small part is documented. When a farm belonging to Sir Cheney Culpeper fell into his hands in 1645, he wrote to Hartlib saying he "would willingly make some advantage of that inconvenience by making several trials". He was particularly interested in laying a rich compost on corn, and asked for advice from "Mr. Plattes' books or elsewhere". In 1646 Culpeper asked for more information on a new plough, seed drill, and compost barrow invented by a Mr Shaw. If they worked, he intended to use them on his barley in the spring. He was still waiting in 1648 for Shaw's seed drill to use on his wheat. In 1647 he was willing to try breeding rabbits on a quarter of an acre of walled ground before turning them out into an open warren.[44] Dr Samuel Coxe, parson of Downton (Wilts.), wrote to Hartlib in August 1652 explaining that he had been for five months a husbandman. "I never was before", he confessed. He needed advice on the best time of year to buy clover seed cheap, and had written to Cressy Dymock for advice. He had also read Walter Blith, and was seeking information further afield on several different matters: he applied to a Sussex gentleman about fruit tree growing, and to a Devon gentleman on the uses of furze.[45] William Petty, who in 1658 had two pieces of land of fifty acres each in the fens, sown the previous year with coleseed, wrote to Dymock for advice on the best crops to grow there. He favoured turnips as the next crop; but would they succeed, he asked? If so, how should he use the turnips? Blith's book suggested boiling them for cattle feed; but would he not be better advised to use the turnip seed for oil, even though it would involve finding a mill to grind it? Perhaps he should buy pigs or calves on which to feed the turnips. Or perhaps carrots or Irish potatoes would be better? If Dymock recommended another crop of rapeseed, Petty asked him to buy the seed for him, but confessed himself ignorant about how often rapeseed should be grown on the same plot. He was plainly a solicitous landowner seeking knowledge. He was about to spend five or six weeks in the fens, consulting his tenants, deciding what to plant, and hoping to meet Dymock personally; as landlord, he evidently expected to influence the farming of his tenantry.[46] Petty was unique in his intimate friendship with

[43] S. Hartlib, *His Legacie, or An Enlargement of the Discours of Husbandrie Used in Brabant and Flanders*, 2nd edn, London, 1652, p. 8; Hartlib, [Dymock], *A Discovery for Division*, p. 15; "Ephemerides", 1653, EE–EE5; Hartlib MS 62/12/1–3; *CSPD*, 1659–60, p. 438; Webster, *op. cit.*, pp. 478–9.   [44] Hartlib MSS 13/66–7; 127–8; 233; 13/202–3.

[45] *Ibid.*, 26/35/1; 8/5/1.

[46] Hartlib MS 66/23/1. Cf. vol. II of the paperback series, pp. 361ff.

Hartlib and in his personal involvement in government schemes of land improvement in England and Ireland, but his blend of scientific and practical interests was far from unusual.

An impressive figure in the Hartlib circle was Peter Smith, who farmed "barren Dyffrin" in Wales in the 1650s. He read the *Discours of Husbandrie in Brabant and Flanders* as soon as it was published in 1650, and *c.* 1657 visited Holland to see things at first hand. His letters to his uncle, John Beale, illustrate how much careful art, study, and thought went into some gentlemen's farming. And reading his descriptions of Dutch methods makes one understand why so many improvers in England at this time were concentrating on perfecting "instruments" and "engines". Dutch experience showed what might be achieved. In Holland Smith never saw more than two horses drawing one plough, even on stiff land. Plough drivers were unnecessary, for the ploughman controlled the team by the use of reins and whip. He was convinced that half the labour and charge of ploughing and carting at home might be saved with the right tools and machines. His other letter to John Beale described improvements in Herefordshire, in Irchenfield (with lime), and in Bromyard (with paring and burning and hop growing). His own achievements in Dyffrin included using gardening techniques, growing fruit, watering the land, and planting coppices.[47]

From the writings of men in the Hartlib circle, we have a fairly full explanation of the failure of improvements to spread more rapidly. Chief among them was the fact that many men were content to make a living and sought no more. Husbandmen, after all, had a different view of life and its purpose from gentry. Thus wrote Cressy Dymock: "a great error in husbandmen why they grow not richer is because they are only content with so much as gives them a livelihood, whereas if they would manage more acres, they might come to great riches".[48] Moreover, as Dymock later learned by bitter experience, farmers who were eager to introduce new methods of farming had to persuade unwilling labourers, and this could tax the patience of the most dedicated agriculturalist. Mr Nichols talked to Hartlib of the same problems in terms that showed he had quite lost patience and hope. "The invincible impediment against husbandry" was the servants "who will never be faithful and diligent, etc." These same words were echoed by Jethro Tull in the 1720s, but in his case determination to get round this obstacle was sharpened, not dulled, by the truculence of his servants. Yet Tull paid a heavy price for that resolution, for his obsessive suspicion and hatred of servants bordered on paranoia.[49]

Finally, the financial risks of innovation were a deterrent. Sir Cheney Culpeper expressed them when he poured cold water on one of Cressy

[47] Hartlib MSS 62/23/4; 67/23/3, 4, 5, 8, 10.
[48] Hartlib, "Ephemerides", 1649, G–H3.
[49] *Ibid.*, 1652, CC–CC1. See also below, p. 315.

Dymock's grand schemes, which called for 160 acres of land. Who would venture so much, he asked, "for an uncertain gain and in a project where £30 must be laid out in instruments, besides the hazards of a new way, upon which nobody will be induced to hazard his whole year's crop, being the produce not only of his lands but also of his stock and pains?" And in this case the recompense did not even equal the cost of the instruments.[50] The financial risks of innovations, tussles with servants, the fear that improvements would mean higher rents, and placid contentment with an adequate living – all these considerations deterred many would-be improvers for thoroughly good reasons.

When books were read by gentlemen and parsons, then, only the first step had been taken towards transforming theory into practice. Continuing practice depended on gentlemen instructing, or bullying, their stewards and bailiffs, and – less often, no doubt – prevailing upon their tenants. The home farms of the gentry were the spearhead of agricultural improvement, and things could not have been otherwise. But the achievements of this spearhead are effectively demonstrated in the history of clover growing. The need for grassland improvement attracted urgent attention as a result of several years of bad weather from 1646 onwards. Hay rotted, fodder was short, and meat prices rose alarmingly. A pamphlet, thought to be by Hartlib, in 1652 described the "very great destruction of beans and peas these late years by worms and other creeping things, men being ignorant of any remedy therefore". It is not surprising that clover was a major talking point from 1649 onwards. That year Cressy Dymock promised to show Hartlib a useful work on clover by a French author, explaining how it fattened cattle and horses. Colonel Hutchinson was also reported to him as a great experimenter with clover.[51] Mr Boyle had earlier promised to send Culpeper a manuscript in his possession about sowing clover, and by return of post (July 1648) Culpeper had written asking to see it, returning it the following month.[52] Almost certainly this last manuscript was Sir Richard Weston's *Discours*, which Hartlib duly published a year later. Ringing in his ears as he prepared it for publication were the cogent words of Dr Child: "The right knowledge of all manner of grass is a principal foundation of good pasturage and that of husbandry." "Therefore it should be more studied than hitherto it hath been." Such study was helped by the publication of William Howes's *Phytologia* in 1650, listing the grasses and distinguishing each one botanically.[53] By 1652 Hartlib was writing to Dr Child in Ireland giving an optimistic account of the way clover growing was spreading in England,[54] and in 1653 Hartlib was being consulted and informed by all and sundry on clover: Mr

[50] Hartlib MS 13/239.
[51] [S. Hartlib], *Cornucopia*, 1652?, f. B; Hartlib, "Ephemerides", 1649, D–E5, F–G8.
[52] Hartlib MSS 13/227; 13/239.
[53] Hartlib, "Ephemerides", 1650, F–G4, F–G5.   [54] Hartlib MS 15/5/18–19.

Bedingfield brought experience from Norfolk; Mr Marmaduke James came personally for advice; Ralph Austen wrote for the names of seedsmen.[55]

Publicity for clover was now so considerable that the difficulties of getting enough clover seed loomed large. Dr Wilkins offered the name of a merchant who would get the right seed from overseas, and noted in passing how profitable it would be for anyone wishing to set up in business as a supplier. Clover cost 4d. a pound in the Low Countries and 1s. 6d. in England. He proposed that the next edition of Weston's book should state the name of a dealer who could supply the seed.[56]

Even a supply of seed from Holland, however, did not dispose of all the difficulties. The quality of Dutch seed was often poor, and people were urged to send a trusted servant to Holland to get it personally. Petty reported Sir Richard Weston's admission that he never managed to get true clover seed until he threshed his own. But threshing out the seed was not easy, and so Hartlib set himself to pick the brains of all he met on the best method. He was told in 1652 that it could be prised from the husk by a mill, and that Lady Ranelagh would give further information. Cressy Dymock favoured hand rubbing, which would give work to poor children. Sir Richard Weston advised letting it dry out for about nine months before threshing. When the problem was solved, the price of seed fell from 2s. a pound in 1650 to 7d. by 1662.[57]

Hartlib continued all through the 1650s, collecting first-hand accounts of different men's results with clover. He may even have sent out a questionnaire to Ireland requesting information, for Robert Wood sent Hartlib four foolscap pages from Dublin in 1656, answering those who maintained that clover left the land barren and unfit for any other crop. He had grown it himself, had undertaken a special enquiry on behalf of a Norfolk friend, and had personally inspected Sir Richard Weston's clover fields. Wood could only conclude that those who argued against clover were repeating gossip without verifying its truth. Perhaps, he added darkly, some feared that other kinds of grassland would lose value if clover gained too high a reputation. A campaign vilifying clover was becoming sufficiently strident to be taken seriously. Wood therefore suggested to Hartlib a publication that dealt with the prejudices, that stated plainly on what soils it would succeed and where it might fail, on what soils it lasted longest, how it could be managed (so many failures were due to faulty management at critical times – after

[55] Hartlib, "Ephemerides", 1653, EE–EE5, JJ–JJ4; Hartlib MS 41/1/66.

[56] Hartlib, "Ephemerides", 1651, A–B8.

[57] *Ibid.*, 1651, C–C3; 1652, BB–BB8; 1653, EE–EE8, FF–FF3. See also Michell, 'Sir Richard Weston', pp. 160–1; Thirsk, 'Seventeenth-Century Agriculture and Social Change', pp. 152–3. John Aubrey, writing some twenty years later, claimed that in Herefordshire they ground the clover seed in a cider mill, then threshed it four or five times over – Bodleian Library, Bodley MS Aubrey 2. For the final solution to the problem, see below, p. 299.

drought, in wet weather, or when the seed was ripening), and what crop should follow clover. Wood's final advice to prospective clover growers was to ascertain the "custom of Flanders" in order to avoid mistakes.[58]

Hartlib evidently invited Wood to write something for publication about clover, but Wood declined in á letter of November 1656, giving the most judicious and carefully considered reasons for his reluctance. "I cannot find those conjectures of mine, whereof I discoursed unto you at your house, to hold water in every particular, especially if the grass be constantly mowed and carried off the land. And therefore till I have further satisfied myself, I thought it better to leave men to their own experience, than to endeavour to persuade them unto that which might possibly mislead and betray them."[59] The exchange of experience continued, provoking forthright language from Moses Wall of Caversham, the purchaser of a forfeited royalist estate of Lord Craven, who thought clover an utter failure. He wrote at length in 1659 of his disastrous experiment with fourteen acres over a period of two years. The clover even ruined his barley crop in the third year, he claimed; at best his cows would only eat it for a month from May to June and then left it. He reckoned he lost £20 on his trials with clover, and was altogether disgruntled about the new grasses.[60] His neighbours, moreover, had been as unsuccessful as he, and one dubbed it "a great cheat to the nation". "Let us have no more discourse about it", Wall concluded.[61]

Other fodder crops besides clover, namely lucerne, sainfoin, and spurry, all became the subject of lively debate and publicity in the Hartlib circle in the 1650s in the effort to improve fodder supplies. Hartlib first heard of lucerne in 1650: the French had got seeds, as Hartlib thought, from Switzerland, though almost certainly they came from Italy. It was found to have a deep root, and was not liable to scorching like other grasses. Sainfoin was already better known. It had come to the attention of English gentlemen in Charles I's reign by means later described so circumstantially by Lord Halton that his must be credited as a true description of one, if not the only, channel by which sainfoin reached England. Horses sent by a French nobleman as a gift to Charles I were so fatigued by their journey through France that it seemed they would not survive the Channel crossing. They were taken in hand at a northern port by a Normandy farmer who grazed them on sainfoin, and they recovered. The marquis (later duke) of Newcastle, a horse fancier of the first rank, and Sir John Walters of Oxfordshire both showed lively interest when they heard this story, and immediately sent to France for seed. In 1636 Bulstrode Whitelocke's diary showed him trying

---

[58] Hartlib MS 26/67/1–2.   [59] *Ibid.*, 33/1/7.

[60] *Ibid.*, 34/4/21. Adam Speed in *Adam Out of Eden*, p. 41, seemed to be replying to some of Hartlib's correspondents, including Wall, when he wrote that clover grew little in the first summer but grew stronger in the next three years. Wall had put out his cattle to eat the clover in the first summer.   [61] Hartlib MS 34/4/25.

out sainfoin on his estate at Fawley, near Henley on Thames, and in the 1630s (or possibly the 1640s) the duke of Lennox imported sainfoin seed, and was said to have had success with it – again a credible story, since the family had strong French connections. The news of sainfoin circulated within a limited upper-class circle from the 1630s onwards. In the 1640s Sir Richard Weston mentioned it in his work and may have aroused Hartlib's interest. At all events, when Hartlib heard more of sainfoin from a correspondent, Normandy was still regarded as the fount of information on how to sow it, and its greatest value was deemed to be as horse feed.[62]

Sainfoin proved successful on the Wiltshire chalklands by 1651 when Pensa, the club at Oxford, undertook to describe the husbandry of sainfoin growing round Salisbury. The sainfoin here referred to may have been the same as "Tooker's grass", of which Dr Coxe of Downton (Wilts.) gave Hartlib news in the same year; this was a very productive grass cultivated by Mr Tooker of Maddington, on Salisbury Plain.[63] Sainfoin continued to make cautious headway. It was introduced to Barton Seagrave (Northants.) by Bishop Henchman, a native of that place, who was canon and precentor at Salisbury from 1660–3. It was growing on many light soils by the 1670s – on the North Downs in Kent, in the Cotswolds, on the Norfolk heaths, and even in some common fields, such as those of East Chadlington (Oxon.), by 1673. But it could never suit as many different situations as clover.[64] Similarly with spurry. Hartlib first heard of it in 1652 from John Pell, an academic friend of long standing. He called it "the new seed of Brabant". As soon as news of it arrived in England, Culpeper sowed 3 acres but got nothing from it; Mr Ford tried 3–4 acres and got 60 lb of spurry. Spurry continued on trial for a century or more.[65]

Among gentleman farmers with intellectual curiosity and a strong practical urge to improve agriculture, novel ideas were implemented with the minimum of delay. Converting the sceptical was an uphill task, to be undertaken with good humour and patience. Moses Wall belonged in the latter category. "You have been theorical [sic] and I have been practical", he wrote to Hartlib. "I have tried divers of your experiments about bees

[62] I wish to thank Professor Mauro Ambrosoli for information on the origins of lucerne. Hartlib, "Ephemerides", 1650, F–G4; C. Kirkham, *Two Letters to a Friend*, London, 1726, pp. 32–6. I wish to thank Mr Frank Emery for this reference; I owe the reference from Whitelocke's diary to Miss Ruth Spalding, who is at present editing it for publication. Hartlib, "Ephemerides", 1650, F–G4; Hartlib MS 52/153; "Ephemerides", 1651, A–B3, Z–ZZ.

[63] Hartlib, "Ephemerides", 1651, A–B3, Z–ZZ. On the Tookers of Maddington, a Puritan gentry family, see Rev. J. Offer and Sir R. C. Hoare, *The History of Modern Wiltshire: Hundred of Branch and Dole*, London, 1825, p. 37.

[64] E. Kerridge, *The Agricultural Revolution*, London, 1967, pp. 278–9, though the sequence in the geographical spread of sainfoin given by Kerridge is here revised; M. A. Havinden, 'Agricultural Progress in Open Field Oxfordshire', AHR, IX, 2, 1961, p. 76.

[65] Webster, *op. cit.*, pp. 37, 83–4; Hartlib, "Ephemerides", 1652, CC–CCI. Spurry was recommended by John Houghton in his *Collection*, ed. Bradley, II, pp. 373–4.

and they signify nothing." He preferred to stick to the countryman's rules and observations, "about which I find less trouble and more profit".[66] This was one point of view. Elsewhere, scattered over England, from Cheshire, Lancashire, and Yorkshire southward, enough gentlemen were thinking and acting differently to begin to dissolve these hard prejudices. And by 1658 one author addressed himself direct to the gentry and parsons of the four northern counties, hoping to extend to them knowledge through books that would lead to practical results.[67]

At all times Hartlib was alert to record in his papers any names mentioned in his hearing of men and women who wrote nothing and were not members of his immediate group of enthusiasts, but were practical improvers. One Buckner at Blackfriars was studying a hundred varieties of grass "upon which we tread so ignorantly", noting their differences. An Italian gentleman had brought wheat grains from Italy to Obadiah Walker of University College, Oxford, and Lady Hilliard had planted them at East Horsley in Surrey. The earl of Thanet was one of the country's great husbandmen, with excellent gardens. A Mr Middleton kept a quantity of mulberry trees and silkworms and made very good silk. Mr Cruckenden, now dead, had been a great husbandman in Kent, skilful in ordering vines. The earl of Southampton had had thousands of fruit trees planted in his hedges.[68] But even Hartlib did not hear of every enterprising farmer with a fund of practical experience. A farming book from an estate at Puttenham, Surrey, between 1653 and 1655 arouses the suspicion that some of Walter Blith's recommended rotations were being tried out here in a methodical way. Six acres, newly enclosed in 1653, were sown with barley in the first year and with oats and clover in the second, and then laid down to pasture in the third. Other plots were being put under different rotations: barley, then tares, then wheat was one. Some pieces were being limed, some were dunged, some were folded. Their owner was evidently trying many different recipes to see which worked best.[69]

In short, the bookish circle of improving farmers was only the smallest of innumerable concentric rings of lively, enthusiastic improvers with a zest for experiment and a profound belief in the future of agricultural improvement. "The genius of this age", wrote one contemporary, "is very much bent to advance husbandry." Government policy was spurring men on. Their scientific and philosophical creeds urged them in the same direction as their political aspirations. John Beale believed every improver he knew to be an "excellent republican". Many were, indeed, excellent republicans,

  66 Hartlib MS 34/4/25.
  67 W. London, *A Catalogue of the Most Vendible Books*, London, 1657, 'Epistle Dedicatory', p. A3.
  68 Hartlib, "Ephemerides", 1649, J–Z; Hartlib MS 62/50/13; "Ephemerides", 1650, F–G4; 1652, DD–DD2, DD–DD5.   69 GMR, 51/5/67.

old soldiers in fact, but not all: some like Sir Richard Weston and Sir William Dugdale were less than excellent but found in the 1650s a congenial atmosphere in which to collaborate with their former parliamentary opponents.[70]

To measure the sum of all these efforts in quantitative terms is plainly impossible, but enough documents survive to show how often systems of cultivation entered into the conversation of the gentry class, and drew ideas from yeomen and gardeners. All aspects of farming routine were somewhere being scrutinized afresh, and the successes were conspicuous in southern, eastern, and Midland England by the end of the 1650s. They are most readily identified in the spread of crops like clover, coleseed, woad, fruit, and vegetables, all of which were destined to become thoroughly commonplace in the later decades of the seventeenth century. Less well documented, but supporting these advances, was the greater use of fertilizers of all kinds.[71] To understand the major successes, moreover, we have to appreciate the multitude of trials and experiments that failed to make any lasting impact. Without the failures, there would have been no outstanding successes. Together they were the necessary foundation of everything, and the fact that they were so broadly distributed geographically was essential for success. Different soils produced different results. If enthusiasm had not been widely aroused, one or two trials, concentrated in the wrong place, could have spelt the end of a new crop.

Fortunately, the gentry were travellers, living in a small social world where they reckoned to know most of their peers. Among a total population of 5 million it was easy to make contact with others of a like mind – it is not so very difficult nowadays in a population of 55 million – and so a fraternity of farming improvers was built up, without any formal association or society, exchanging experience over long distances. Samuel Hartlib was effectively president, secretary, and sometimes even treasurer (he certainly financed Cressy Dymock when he was short of cash for his experiments).[72] The way was being prepared for the setting up of formal scientific and agricultural societies after 1660.

The achievements of gentleman farmers at one end of the social scale must be coupled with the efforts of smallholders, gardeners, and cottage labourers at the other end, who were, as always, canny enough to spot opportunities that came within the scope of their different resources. Gentlemen had land and cash but encountered serious problems in getting satisfactory hands to work. The poor lacked much land and cash but were not short of labour. Since Dutch agriculture was the principal model for English improvers in this period, and since much of its success derived from the labour-demanding

---

[70] Webster, op. cit., p. 474; J. Beale, Herefordshire Orchards, London, 1657, p. 39.

[71] For one example, see the depositions in a Chancery suit of 1657 showing that lime to dress land was an innovation at Witley and Thursley, Surrey, c. 1607, but had become general practice by 1650 – GMR, 70/38/4.   [72] Hartlib, "Ephemerides", 1649, A–B1.

cultivation of special crops, poor peasants could learn as many useful, though different, lessons from the foreigner as the gentry. Of course, they had to choose the right crop for the right place, but then so did the gentry. It was simply common sense, as Peter Smith, writing from the Welsh border, pointed out, that cherry trees were worth planting round London, because London palates valued "delicacies above necessaries". They were not a sensible choice on the Welsh border where men wanted bread and beef. John Beale, with the concerns of Herefordshire farmers in mind, wrote in the same vein to criticize Gabriel Plattes's ideas. His recommendation of spade cultivation was fitter for cottagers than for yeomen: "to bring the world from the plough to the spade is a vain attempt", he wrote.[73] True enough, seen from the viewpoint of the yeoman. But yeomen were not the only men needing to get more from the land to make a livelihood. Smallholders and cottagers were a far larger class, and the Dutch and Frenchmen's ways of growing vegetables, industrial crops, fruit, and hops were as instructive to them as was the method of growing clover to gentlemen and yeomen.

Not all novel, foreign ways could be imitated by every cottager in England, of course; choices had to be made in the light of the available markets. But vegetable growing round London was one story of remarkable success; tobacco in Gloucestershire was another, one which might have been still more successful had the government not opposed it so bitterly; hop gardens proliferated with astonishing speed in many localities, not only in Kent around Canterbury, but at Farnham in Surrey, and in scattered places in the south-west like Buckland Brewer, Devon, where there were said to be three times as many hop gardens in the parish in 1660 as in 1640. Saffron, liquorice, teasels, herbs, flax, and hemp all flourished in parts of the country far from London. In short, gardeners, cottagers, and smallholders were quite as successful in exploiting their chief asset — their labour — as were gentlemen in exploiting theirs.[74]

The most cautious people, resisting innovation until absolutely convinced of its utility, were the intermediate classes of yeomen and husbandmen who had most to lose in risky enterprise. Their existing way of life gave them self-sufficiency and often more; some yeomen enjoyed considerable comforts, but they wisely deemed them precarious. Agricultural improvements demanded of such men too high a price, asking that they put self-sufficiency and a relatively secure livelihood at risk. This was not the case with gentlemen whose living was not endangered by a farming experiment; nor was it the case with smallholders and labourers who never knew security and always lived from hand to mouth. Yeomen and husbandmen who had achieved a successfully balanced farming system that assured them a living had a precious asset not to be surrendered lightly. Theirs were the best of reasons for pursuing the familiar ways.

[73] Hartlib MSS 67/23/3; 62/23/4.   [74] See AHEW, vol. v, pt 1, ch. 11, p. 385.

C. 1660–1700

The restoration of Charles II in 1660 created different and, in some respects, somewhat less favourable circumstances for improving agriculture. The momentum generated by the Hartlib circle in bringing gentry and working farmers together to debate agriculture improvements was slowly dissipated by unfavourable economic conditions and the subtly altered climate of social intercourse. But in practice by 1660 virtually all the agricultural improvements of this century were known in general terms, though possible refinements of detail were endless, and since they were being implemented somewhere, no social barriers could bar their spread by demonstration and example.

Some of the similarities and the differences between the political climate of the 1650s and that of the 1660s are mirrored in two different editions of Ralph Austen's *Treatise of Fruit Trees*. The 'Dedicatory Epistle' of his work in 1653 was written with one ear alert to the parliamentary discussions of policy that were designed to promote economic development including enclosure and the improvement of wastelands and commons. The urgent need to employ the poor was a major justification throughout the book, whereas the financial profit to the grower was a secondary consideration, and only third came the need to supply cider in quantity in order to save malt and the fuel for malting, and so save barley and the land it occupied. The new edition of Austen's book in 1665 was substantially the same work, but its newly written prefaces shifted the emphasis of its justifying argument. The new dedication was to Robert Boyle, and Austen hoped the book would promote the endeavours of the Royal Society. The chief case for fruit trees was now to provide cider. To ensure success, legislation was necessary, plus administrative officers to enforce it. At much greater length than in 1653 Austen underlined the need for books on fruit trees that were small in bulk and price, and written in plain language for husbandmen to buy and read. The benefits to the poor were put very briefly. Authors and landowners were already viewing husbandmen at a greater distance. They were less immediately involved in their poverty and the need to alleviate it, though they still strove to reach them through books and through faceless statutes and administrative officials. Already it was becoming clear that the Royal Society was not dedicated in quite the same way to ideas of the commonweal as were Hartlib and his circle. Adopting a paternal role, its members stood aloof; they ordained, and through the medium of officialdom hoped to be obeyed. They did not encourage husbandmen to knock at their doors for instruction and advice.

In this different atmosphere, Walter Blith's book of husbandry was cold-shouldered. He had been in close sympathy with parliamentary policy makers, and had deliberately written in simple language for plain husbandmen. Occasionally after 1660 men referred to Captain Blith, but his book hardly ever appeared in gentlemen's libraries. While other authors had their works of the 1650s reprinted, and men wrote eloquently of the value of Gervase Markham's books, "of noble Heresbachius" and Barnaby Googe, men said little of Blith.[75] And when John Worlidge published his *Systema Agriculturae* in 1669, he incorporated so much from Blith that Blith's book was entirely superseded.

Less favourable circumstances for improvement were the result of falling rents and falling prices. Yet they undoubtedly galvanized some into more energetic activity and expenditure than ever before. Many royalists returned to their estates with a new determination to maximize the income from their land. For some, of course, it was a compelling necessity. The much-quoted remark of John Houghton about royalist energies being poured into estate improvement at this time rings true. Referring to extravagant young men who wasted their estates and then had to learn to manage them more efficiently in order to pay off their debts, Houghton wrote: "witness, the great improvement made of lands since our inhuman civil wars, when our gentry, who before hardly knew what it was to think, then fell to such an industry, and caused such an improvement as England never knew before".[76] The chances of spreading innovations geographically were thereby much increased.

Longer distances were traversed and bolder ventures instigated for yet another reason. Some royalists during the Interregnum had gone overseas, and during their involuntary exile they had observed many different systems of farm management that they thought worth trying in England. When they returned, these activities helped to fill their days with interest – a plain necessity after the stimulation of overseas travel. Estate improvement, therefore, became one of their hobbies; and while it led some into exotic frivolities, like devising intricate water fountains, others concentrated on their gardens and orchards, woodlands, deer parks, and fish ponds.[77] The principal interest of William Cavendish, duke of Newcastle, for example, was his horse stud. He had set up a stable in Antwerp in the 1650s, and had spent his days meeting and vying with European horse fanciers of all nations. He had learned much about different breeds of horses and different regimes of feeding and housing, as well as training horses. He returned to England with an attitude of contempt for what the parliamentarians had done for English horse breeding, and determination to raise the standard. Gentry like the Verneys of Claydon in Buckinghamshire concerned themselves with more fundamental farming matters like enclosures, land tenancies, and fertilizers. Lime, salt, and coal ash were applied and compared, and new grasses tested (sainfoin

---

[75] *Philos. Trans. Roy. Soc.*, x, 1675, p. 320.

[76] Houghton, *Collection*, ed. Bradley, *IV*, p. 56.

[77] Some of these conceits are described in R. Plot, *The Natural History of Oxfordshire*, 2nd edn, Oxford, 1705. See, for example, "waterworks of pleasure", pp. 240–1.

was sown at Claydon in 1689). They too gave careful attention to their vegetable garden, fruit orchard, and woodlands.[78]

Other gentry who looked upon the restoration of the king more sourly retreated from politics into a quiet country life, and also devoted their energies to improving their estates. Lord Lisle, for example, retired to his house at Sheen, and, from the correspondence he had with Sir William Temple when the latter was minister in Holland, we may guess at the way his energies were employed. Their letters discussed their books and their gardens.[79]

Gentlemanly interest in improved agriculture was channelled formally after 1660 through the Royal Society. Founded in 1662, it was not the direct descendant of the Hartlib circle, but rather of a group of scholars, tired of the fierce religious and political controversies of the 1640s, who had started to meet in London, and then in Oxford c. 1645–59, in order to debate dispassionately with one another the safer subject of natural philosophy. The first members in Oxford did not overlap with the Hartlib circle, nor did they do so when they moved their meetings back to London in 1659.[80] But after the Royal Society was founded men like Ralph Austen and John Beale, old correspondents of Hartlib, became members, while other friends of Hartlib who did not belong to the Royal Society were in indirect contact. Cressy Dymock did not appear as a member, but when Lord Brereton, who subsequently became a member of the Royal Society's Georgical Committee, went to Cheshire in 1661 to survey and sell family land to pay his father's debts, Cressy Dymock accompanied him.[81]

The first sign of the Royal Society's interest in promoting food production came in response to a letter from John Beale on 21 December 1662 proposing that the society promote the growing all over England of cider fruit. A committee was appointed, which was plainly the forerunner of the Georgical Committee, for it met in the same place – at Arundel House in Charles Howard's lodgings – and included members of the later Georgical Committee. John Evelyn was asked to read over the papers on cider fruit sent to the society by John Beale with a view to publication, and Viscount Scudamore and his father, celebrated growers of fruit trees, were asked to take an interest. On 20 March 1663 Mr Buckland, a Somerset gentleman, proposed that potatoes

[78] J. Thirsk, *Horses in Early Modern England: For Service, for Pleasure, for Power*, Stenton Lecture, 1977, Reading, 1978, pp. 26–7; J. Broad, 'Sir Ralph Verney and his Estates, 1630–96', Oxford Univ. D.Phil. thesis, 1973, esp. pp. 226, 240, 242, 225. I wish to thank Dr Broad for permission to quote from his unpublished thesis.

[79] Julia Cartwright, *Sacharissa: Some Account of Dorothy Sidney, Countess of Sutherland...1617–84*, London, 1893, pp. 128–9.

[80] T. Sprat, *The History of the Royal Society of London...* London, 1667, pp. 53–8; Birch, *History of the Royal Society*, I, pp. 2–3. See also Webster, *The Great Instauration*, esp. pp. 154–6.

[81] *Correspondence of Hartlib, Haak, Oldenburg and Others...with Governor Winthrop...1661–72*, ed. R. C. Winthrop, Boston, Mass., 1878, pp. 12–13.

be planted throughout England, and his plan was put to the same committee. Mr Buckland explained the usefulness of potatoes when other food was scarce, and Mr Boyle described how potatoes had saved thousands of poor from starving in Ireland. Potatoes were not as yet regarded exclusively as a vegetable, but were being recommended as a flour for bread when mixed with wheat, for pastry making, for cakes, for drink, and as a feed for poultry and other livestock. The committee agreed to urge all members of the society having land to begin planting potatoes and persuade their friends to do the same. Mr Buckland, Mr Howard, and Mr Boyle promised to supply seed potatoes, and John Evelyn agreed to insert some instructions on growing them in the treatise he was in process of publishing "by order of the Society" on trees. The committee went on to discuss Dr Wilkins's way of setting corn, and asked him to demonstrate it. Many useful tasks to be undertaken by an agricultural committee were being formulated.[82]

The decision to set up a Georgical Committee of thirty-two members was taken in March 1664, and Mr Charles Howard was appointed chairman. Members at an early meeting in June 1664 included Dr Merret from Winchcomb in Gloucestershire, who was doubtless familiar with tobacco growing there, John Evelyn, the expert on trees, Ralph Austen, the expert on fruit trees, and Edward Waterhouse, who was familiar with rapeseed growing in Essex and promised a history of rape oil crushing.[83]

As fresh topics came up for discussion by Charles Howard's committee, John Evelyn's book was made the receptacle for additional information, until it threatened to become, like one of Hartlib's publications, a miscellany.[84] But the kernel of the book remained its discussion of timber and fruit trees, and, when published, it had immeasurable influence. Evelyn's *Sylva* passed through many editions and was an almost indispensable text in gentlemen's libraries.[85] It was published at the right psychological moment when landowners could not fail to see the damage done by earlier neglect, and nurserymen were setting up businesses on a scale that enabled them to supply the gentry with young trees in abundance. Jonathan Rogers, an attorney of Chippenham, who raised banks to plant ash trees "after Mr. John Evelyn's ways" was only one of hundreds of gentlemen moved to action by this seminal book.[86]

[82] Birch, *op. cit.*, I, pp. 172, 179, 207, 213, 219; Royal Soc., Domestic MSS. v, no. 60. The best-known early publication advocating potatoes is J. Forster, *England's Happiness Increased*, London, 1664. Forster wrote from Hanslope, Bucks., but his knowledge of potato growing came from Ireland, though he was aware that they were already prospering in Wales and northern England (p. 3). He mentioned 1661 as a year of high grain prices in England when potatoes would have benefited the poor.   [83] Royal Soc., Domestic MSS, v, no. 65.

[84] Birch, *op. cit.*, I, pp. 212–13, 215, 347; John Evelyn, *Sylva...to which is annexed Pomona*, London, 1664, *Sylva, passim*.   [85] Henrey, *British Botanical Literature*, I, pp. 103ff.

[86] John H. Harvey, *Early Gardening Catalogues*, London, 1972, pp. 25–6; Bodleian Library, Bodley MS Aubrey, 2.

Another purpose of the Georgical Committee was to compose "a good history of agriculture and gardening in order to improve the practice thereof". Its members were steeped in the Baconian tradition that theory and practice should go hand in hand, so that, despite the academic atmosphere in which it conducted its proceedings, its ultimate objective was to encourage experiments that would improve the general standard of farming. It proposed to send to acquaintances in England, Scotland, and Ireland a questionnaire to discover "what is practised already, and [how] every place be enriched with the aids that are found in any place". At first the committee seemed to be pursuing a narrow path of interest: its enquiry proposed questions only on the management of arable and meadows. But Dr Merret, with a temperament that leaned towards the compiling of catalogues (he became the first librarian of the Royal College of Physicians), drew up a list of cultivated crops in England, and persuaded the committee to broaden its enquiry to consider the cultivation of the many new crops now in vogue, woad, hops, flax, hemp, madder, buckwheat, liquorice, and rapeseed. Charles Howard added to this list "materials for kitchen garden and...winter greens", in other words, herbs, vegetables, and fruit; and Dr Wilkins, Mr Henshaw, and Dr Holder undertook to question skilful gardeners of their acquaintance and report their answers.[87] Gardeners had high social status at this time, and talked as equals with gentlemen, so this did not involve any descent into the market-place.[88] One of the products of this interest was the work of John Evelyn on vegetables, *Acetaria: A Discourse of Sallets*, which drew on information given by Charles II's principal gardener, Mr London, and revealed what advances had been made since 1600 in multiplying the varieties and improving the quality of greenstuff. Radishes, for example, raised on a monthly hot bed, were now available almost the whole year round.[89]

Finally, Charles Howard asked the committee to consider how wastes, heaths, and bogs might be improved, and undertook to assemble his own knowledge and get advice from others. Although the committee had not started with the same broad programme that had been taken for granted by the republicans of the 1650s, it quickly came round to it. But just as the literature of the 1650s had never fundamentally reassessed livestock breeding – it was considered only in so far as it might benefit from better hay and fodder crops – so the new literature continued to exclude this topic. Contemporary notions of what was possible set certain bounds to the

[87] Royal Soc., Domestic MSS, v, no. 65.

[88] For an example of a gardener who plainly considered himself his master's equal, see the letter of the Rev. I. Lawrence to Sir Justinian Isham, 1714 – Northants. RO, IC 2,802. S. Switzer thought gardeners should be as knowledgeable as stewards – *Ichnographia Rustica*, London, 1718, pt I, pp. xxix–xxxi.

[89] John Evelyn, *Acetaria: A Discourse of Sallets*, London, 1699, pp. 56–7 et passim.

programme of agricultural improvement, and experiments in livestock breeding lay beyond the mental horizon of this age. Men relied instead on making their choices between existing breeds of livestock. Here lay a mental barrier which men did not surmount until the eighteenth century.[90]

The questionnaire that was circulated by the Georgical Committee to gentlemen, and especially to parsons, all over England remained confined to the subject of arable and meadows. The questions ranged over soils and their appropriate manures, systems of cultivation and fallowing, ploughs used, methods to improve heathland, how to find marl in the subsoil and how to use it, what varieties were favoured of grains and legumes, hemp, flax, and rape. Correspondents were asked which plants flourished best in different soils, what steeps for seeds were used, what quantities sown and with what implements, what were the yields and the pests, and what were the methods of harvesting, threshing, and storing crops. Questions on meadows concerned management, measures to reduce mosses, bracken, and brambles, ways of draining wet land, varieties of grass, haymaking procedures, and what grasses made the best hay and suited different livestock best.[91]

Eleven replies survive in the Royal Society's archives, covering only a small part of England, but as late as February 1668 one report on Devon and Cornwall was received from Samuel Colepresse, later vicar of Plympton St Mary, which gave members the occasion to prod their fellows to collect reports as they had earlier promised. All reports summarized a larger body of information collected by letter or in conversation from friends. Thus they dealt not with unusual systems of agriculture, but with those which gentlemen and parsons considered standard in their neighbourhood, i.e. those followed by themselves and by yeomen and husbandmen among their tenants with whom they had regular contact. Such informants inevitably excluded people living in districts that were not generally frequented by gentlemen. Thus poor peasant areas beyond the influence of the gentry went unremarked. Nevertheless, the reports justified the original enquiry by showing something of the variety of local farming systems: ploughs differed, as did the size and composition of the plough team and the number and method of ploughings for different crops; manures were similarly varied in composition; and, along with bushels and acres that were far from uniform, sowing rates seem to have been substantially different.[92]

[90] See also AHEW, vol. v, pt 1, p. xxix, and ch. 2, p. 54. The only glimmering of concern for selective animal breeding so far found appears in a letter from Oldenburg to John Winthrop in America. He plied Winthrop with questions about the plants of New England, and the animals. He was considering the cross-breeding of dogs with a good scent which might locate mines. He had read of Irish wolfdogs. "What crossbreeds can be encouraged?" he asked – Correspondence of Hartlib, p. 38.

[91] R. V. Lennard, 'English Agriculture under Charles II: The Evidence of the Royal Society's "Enquiries"', EcHR, iv, 1932, pp. 23–45 passim.

[92] Ibid.; R. G. F. Stanes, ed., 'A Georgicall Account of Devonshire and Cornwalle in Answer

The Royal Society's activities were in one sense extremely limited in their impact. In the 1660s and 70s it had only about 200 members, and attendance at anniversary meetings was usually 50 to 60; at ordinary meetings, 20. The majority of members lived in London; only 10 per cent in 1673 lived outside. Aristocrats and courtiers, gentlemen, doctors, scholars, and clerics were the backbone of the society, and when lectures on agricultural topics were delivered the immediate audience was tiny.[93] Yet to contemporaries it went almost without saying that influence *must* spread out from London because only there could groups of interested people from different counties meet to talk, exchange experience, and advance their practice. In the view of one writer in 1675, London must take responsibility for the progress of horticulture throughout England. "The adventures of all the expert gardeners" could only be communicated in London, "where there are clubs of expert gardeners, apt to assay novelties and rarities; and where they may have the fullest intelligence from other parts and can most effectually disperse all over England what is most for common good." The clubs were probably informal, but very efficient in the small world of seventeenth-century England. They had their counterpart at a lower social level in the coffee houses where all classes met. John Houghton, writing in 1700, was convinced of the value of the latter in bringing learned and unlearned together to spread knowledge further. An inquisitive man, he believed, could learn more in an evening in the coffee house than he could learn from books in a month.[94]

The records of the Georgical Committee are too fragmentary to document its later activities adequately. It may have lapsed into inactivity after 1668, but the gentry who read the *Philosophical Transactions*, published by the society, continued to receive a miscellany of agricultural news and views, interspersed with many other matters. They learned where to get garden seeds, how to dehusk clover seed, where to inspect the latest cider engine, and how to plant saffron. They could also read reviews of all the new books of husbandry.[95]

In 1681 John Houghton wrote of the society's Committee for Agriculture having been revived. He was probably referring to the fresh stimulus offered

to Some Queries concerning Agriculture', *Devonshire Assoc.*, XCVI, 1964, pp. 269–302. Colepresse was vicar at Plympton from 1669 onwards, after he had submitted his report to the Georgical Committee. In Feb. 1667 he wrote to say he had distributed several copies of the Royal Society's questionnaire to other parts of Devon, from which he awaited replies. See also A. R. Hall and M. B. Hall, eds., *The Correspondence of Henry Oldenburg, III, 1666–67*, Madison and Milwaukee, 1966, pp. 90, 311n, 333, 395, 545.

[93] M. Hunter, 'The Social Basis and Changing Fortunes of an Early Scientific Institution: An Analysis of the Membership of the Royal Society, 1660–1685', *Notes & Rec. of the Roy. Soc.*, XXXI, 1976, pp. 9–114.

[94] *Phil. Trans. Roy. Soc.*, X, 1675, p. 303; Houghton, *Collection*, ed. Bradley, III, p. 132.

[95] *Philos. Trans. Roy. Soc.*, X–XII, 1675–7, pp. 820–46; J. Lowthorp, ed., *The Philosophical Transactions and Collections to the End of the Year 1700 Abridg'd...II*, London, 1705, pp. 635–8.

by the appointment of Christopher Wren as president of the society in 1681–2. In a New Year's speech in the 1660s Wren had revealed his interests in this direction by laying much emphasis on the study of agriculture. But his concern now was not with assessing the value of new crops or manures in different situations – the preoccupation of the Georgical Committee's earlier questionnaire – but with the study of weather in relation to the various operations of land cultivation and the occurrence of plant diseases.[96] Wren's programme should correct any impression that the Royal Society's members had become more interested in scientific theories than in practical problems. At a stage in the seventeenth century when almost no new plants were waiting to be introduced into England, agriculturalists had to concentrate on making the best of those means of improvement already known to them, understanding the effect of weather on crops, reducing disease, exploiting all the known fertilizers to improve poor quality land, and selecting the crops most appropriate to particular soils.[97] This last aspiration convinced Dr Martin Lister of the need for a soil and mineral map, and inspired the continuing exhortations to persist with vines, mulberry trees, chestnuts, walnuts, figs, and almonds, as well as sainfoin and garden vegetables. Somewhere or other they would prove appropriate and profitable.[98] Underlying this propaganda lay the fundamental seventeenth-century assumption that diversity in agricultural production was advantageous. Experience had taught that it was more beneficial to diversify production than to rationalize and limit the range of agricultural products. To be sure of a market, producers had to supply a wide range of produce and a wide range of qualities, not undifferentiated quantity. And if they did this, consumers were ready to take all their output.[99]

Thus when Joseph Blagrave published his derivative work *The Epitome of the Whole Art of Husbandry* in 1669 (other editions followed in 1670, 1675, and 1685) he received a more kindly review in the *Philosophical Transactions* than he has received from modern commentators. He was not criticized by contemporaries for his plagiarism, but praised for his innovations, of which the most notable was the advice on breeding and teaching singing birds for cages, aviaries, parks, or chamber windows.[100] As a source of income this might not seem of interest to many farmers, but it was just one more suggestion for diversifying production in the countryside. Canary grass was already a lucrative crop in east Kent, including Thanet – John Evelyn saw

[96] Sir Henry Lyons, *The Royal Society, 1660–1940*, Cambridge, 1944, pp. 91–3; Stephen Wren, ed., *Parentalia; or Memoirs of the Family of the Wrens*, London, 1750, p. 221.

[97] This problem was carefully explored by Robert Mellish in his "Discourse concerning the Best Way of England's Improvement", in Royal Soc., Classified Papers, x, iii.

[98] Lowthorp, *op. cit.*, II, pp. 450–1, 749–50.

[99] This argument is pursued in Joan Thirsk, *Economic Policy and Projects*, pp. 106ff.

[100] Fussell, *Old English Farming Books*, pp. 76–7. The review of Blagrave was of the 1675 edition – *Philos. Trans. Roy. Soc.*, x, 1675, pp. 323–4.

"whole fields of canary seed" near Sandwich and Deal in the 1660s – and it continued to be a profitable crop in this quarter of Kent until at least the mid nineteenth century. The breeding of birds also offered a source of extra cash to resourceful smallholders. And the ingenuity and success of these many jacks-of-all-trades were recognized when John Houghton in 1694 urged country farmers to send their sons to learn from farmer-gardeners round London.[101]

In the advice offered to more conventional farmers greater precision in writers' instructions on agricultural improvement emerges clearly in the work of Andrew Yarranton, urging the growing of clover in the 1660s. He did not attempt to advocate the growing of clover all over the kingdom, but sought rather to remedy the weakness of the ryelands in the west Midlands, especially in Worcestershire, Gloucestershire, Herefordshire, Shropshire, and Staffordshire, which had suffered from long years of tillage and liming. A serviceable variety of grass was needed that would thrive on sandy, gravelly land where the light soil conditions and over-ready drainage caused conventional grasses to burn up in a hot summer. The answer lay with clover, which would not only remedy the shortage of pasture in common-field townships, but would reduce labour costs. In place of grass or hay people at present had to grow peas and beans, which were expensive in labour, because they were set by hand and had to be weeded. Robert Plot's description of the care given to improving the Staffordshire ryelands matches Yarranton's work in demonstrating how books both reported on and argued for more scientific trials.[102]

Writers of articles in the *Philosophical Transactions* believed that their articles wrought many agricultural improvements all over England. They did so by feeding readers with a steady stream of information, fresh ideas, and new topics for discussion. This could have been the source for the note by Samuel Bagshawe of Ford Hall, Yorkshire, in his memorandum book for 1687–8, reminding himself where he could buy a book of directions, as well as seeds, flowers, plants and trees for land improvement, flax seed, and all artificial grasses.[103] The special role of London as a centre for information is illustrated in a modest letter from John Witter to his parents in Cheshire in April 1669, sending four pecks of sainfoin, bought from a London

---

[101] Canary seed, like all other special crops, varied greatly in price according to quality and market conditions. According to one writer, it varied from 30s. to £10 a quarter. I owe this information to Dr D. A. Baker's Kent Univ. Ph.D. thesis, 1976, entitled 'Agricultural Prices, Production and Marketing, with Special Reference to the Hop Industry: North-East Kent, 1680–1760', I, pp. 238–42. Houghton, *Collection*, ed. Bradley, *I*, p. 234.

[102] Andrew Yarranton, *The Improvement Improved, by a Second Edition of the Great Improvement of Lands by Clover*, London, 1663, pp. 32, 39. Yarranton listed in his book suppliers of clover seed in the west Midlands. He had been a soldier in the parliamentary army and a purchaser of crown land. I owe this information to Dr Ian Gentles. R. Plot, *The Natural History of Staffordshire*, Oxford, 1686, pp. 341–3. See also AHEW, vol. v, pt 1, ch. 6, p. 174.

[103] Sheffield City Library, OD 1,416.

salesman, with full instructions how to sow and graze it. He recommended it for a barren piece of their estate, Windmill Hill Ground, where, if the sainfoin succeeded, he promised more nourishment to their horses and cattle in four weeks than any afforded by their natural grass in seven.[104] Outside London, the Botanical Gardens at Oxford, the gardens of famous men like the earl of Pembroke at Wilton, and other nurseries around Salisbury were recognized for their contribution to agricultural advance in selling plants.[105] From 1681 onwards John Houghton, in his weekly journal entitled *A Collection for Improvement of Husbandry and Trade*, issued in a cheap format bookish and practical wisdom on all varieties of crops, whether usual or unusual, and the latest information on cultivation methods and current prices. He also gave more prominence than earlier writers to systems of livestock production and dairying and the feeding of veal, as well as the cures found effective for outbreaks of cattle disease and sheep rot in the 1690s. Regional isolation seemed to be an obstacle to progress, and more than one writer had commented on county boundaries as barriers inhibiting the spread of knowledge. Houghton's publication attempted to break these down.[106]

Books became more scrupulous and reasonable in their judgments. The best examples of influential general handbooks are John Worlidge's *Systema Agriculturae* published in 1669, and *Systema Horti-Culturae* (1677), both of which proved extremely popular and found a place in many gentlemen's libraries; five editions of the agricultural textbook and three of the horticultural appeared in the lifetime of their author, a country gentleman, living at Petersfield in Hampshire, who was also said to have been at one time woodward to the earl of Pembroke. The work on agriculture was a well-considered, compendious survey of arable and livestock husbandry, repeating the factual information in Blith's and Hartlib's books and adding more. The section on clover, for example, was sober, realistic, and yet encouraging to the farmer who wished to grow it. It cited the best results, but fostered no illusions about the results to be expected from poor land. Poor land must first be improved by denshiring, liming, marling, or other kinds of manuring. Its careful instructions made it clear that the perfect dehusking of clover seed was no longer thought necessary. Clover had to be well dried (until March) before threshing, but men were finding they got a better, thicker growth without dehusking.

Writing on horticulture, Worlidge dealt first with pleasure gardens, then with vegetables and fruits for food, underlining the interests of husbandmen as well as gentry in this latter subject for thoroughly practical reasons. Fruit and vegetables created much work and used less land for much greater profit. Turnips, carrots, and onions produced four to five times the profit per acre

[104] Cheshire RO, DAR A/30/1.

[105] John Beale and A. Lawrence, *Nurseries, Orchards*…London, 1677, p. 2.

[106] Houghton, *Collection*, ed. Bradley, *IV*, pp. 33–5, 56; *II*, p. 461.

of wheat and barley. Not only did fruit and vegetables find a good market among those with "curious palates", they afforded food for husbandmen's families, which diversified diet in normal years and served as a substitute for meat, bread, and drink in scarce years. Vegetables, moreover, reduced the need for drink, so that vegetarian diets were less charge and trouble than flesh, bread, and cheese. The scale of gardening activity in the kingdom was now such that it even seemed to Worlidge to be one principal cause for the deadness of the market for corn.[107]

The range of topics covered in new books showed how much interest was now concentrated on special activities — fruit trees, timber trees, vineyards, kitchen gardens, deer parks, and fish ponds — rather than on the production of basic grains and livestock. The literature reflected not merely gentlemen's eagerness to beautify their mansions and gardens and diversify their diet; it reflected also the greater financial profit to be had from such activities as compared with routine farming systems. And in this connection Stephen Switzer, the noted gardener and adviser to wealthy lords and gentry, voiced the opinion in 1718 that gentlemen benefited so much from the profits of gardening that for some these were its main justification.[108]

The declining prices of grain, wool, and even some meat continued remorselessly. These had to be endured. The government's bounties, malt drawbacks, and statutes to encourage exports helped some farmers, but did nothing positively to reverse the price trend. Farmers of all classes gradually groped their way to salvation by adding special crops or livestock to their existing routines, or, less often, by specializing in them alone. Thus the survival of the agricultural community in the period 1660–1750 depended partly on improved yields from conventional farming — in this activity the supremely efficient corn–wool areas like the Wiltshire downlands made a brave showing — and partly on the adoption of new sidelines or specialities. To pass over special crops and luxury fish, fowl, and other flesh as the trivialities of this age is to pass over activities that were veritable lifesavers. Among the special crops, the animals, and the fish keeping there was something to suit every class of farmer. And in the period 1660–1750 the selection of preferences was increasingly rationalized. Gentlemen favoured orchards, vineyards, vegetable gardens, woodland plantations, deer parks, fish ponds, rabbit warrens and dovecotes, and duck decoys; it was unfortunate that some of these ventures were greedy in appropriating derelict land that had formerly been shared with others, and so were responsible for creating social tensions over hunting rights that had long lain dormant in rural areas.

[107] J. Worlidge, *Systema Agriculturae*, London, 1669, *passim*; *id.*, *Systema Horti-Culturae, or The Art of Gardening*, London, 1677, pp. 173–7; Fussell, *op. cit.*, p. 68; J. H. Thomas, *Petersfield under the Later Stuarts: An Economic and Social Study*, Petersfield Papers, no. 6. Petersfield Area Hist. Soc., 1980, pp. 39–40; Thirsk, 'Plough and Pen'. See also ch. 6 above, pp. 238–9.

[108] Switzer, *Ichnographia Rustica*, pt I, pp. viii, xxvii.

The middle ranks of yeomen and husbandmen favoured orchards and hops, coleseed and dye crops, which could be inserted into existing rotations. Smallholders turned to vegetable gardening for reasons which John Houghton explained crisply in 1677: "A great deal (of enclosed) land will be turned into orchards and gardens, four or five acres of which sometimes maintains a family better and employs more labourers than fifty acres of other shall do. Hops, saffron, liquorice, onions, potatoes, madder, artichokes, aniseed and coleseeds...I suppose none will deny an acre of these to yield more money than so much wheat." The result was Gregory King's calculations at the end of the seventeenth century which valued new industrial crops, fruit, and vegetables at £2,200,000 per annum, which represented 9 per cent of total agricultural production. Very little of this was being produced, let alone marketed, in 1540.[109]

D. 1700–1750

In the half-century 1700–50 a certain broadening of interest in new ways of agricultural improvement can be discerned, clearing paths that eventually developed into important highroads to the agricultural revolution. But all agricultural development was slow, and we should not expect it to have been otherwise; the seeds of development in the future took a long time to germinate. Meanwhile special crops and special activities continued to arouse most interest. Low prices for conventional farm produce persisted, and, in consequence, improvements that assisted mainstream farming remained tentative. Enclosure had to await the emergence of a more favourable economic climate for corn production before large capital outlay could be contemplated. Fortunately, many special crops needed little land, and could usually find a place in ground that was already enclosed. What is noticeable in this period is the way the merits of each crop were gradually made clearer, thereby enabling the different classes in rural society to select them with more discrimination.

Among the literate classes books were now treated as basic reference works, to be consulted as a routine alongside other forms of advice. This is illustrated in the accounts of Sir Edward Filmer of Kent dating from the later 1730s. His seedsmen sent him four varieties of peas with advice on each. He checked this against information in Ellis's book *Chiltern and Vale Farming* and duly recorded both sets of directions in his account book. Stephen Switzer, as author, had a thoroughly practical end in view when he wrote his work on gardening and farming. He aimed at a work "in handy parts", to serve as "complete pocket companions in the field, easily pulled out and read on any occasion".[110]

[109] J. Houghton, *England's Great Happiness*...London, 1677, p. 12; Thirsk, *Economic Policy and Projects*, p. 177. See also ch. 6 above, p. 238.
[110] Kent AO, U120 A19; Switzer, *op. cit.*, pt 1, p. vi.

A basic set of reliable textbooks found its place on the library shelves of the gentry as a matter of course. William Brockman of Beachborough, east Kent, had a library in 1742 plainly pointing to agriculture as one of several different interests. He read Richard Baxter on non-conformity, Francis Bacon's *The Advancement of Learning*, Burton's *Melancholy*, and Dr Barebones's *Trade*. On agrarian matters he had Evelyn's *Sylva*, Gervase Markham's works, Leonard Meager's *English Gardener* (1670), and John Worlidge's *Systema Agriculturae* (first edition, 1669).[111] This might be deemed a very basic library of the period. A better selection was in the possession of Sir Wyndham Knatchbull at Hatch in Kent in 1731. Markham's *Country Farm* was the oldest work on his shelves, standing alongside the up-to-date writing of Richard Bradley, the most prolific author of the period 1700–30, John Mortimer's *Art of Husbandry* (1707), William Gibson's *The Farrier's New Guide* (1720), Quintiny's *Compleat Gard'ner* in translation from the French, and the *Husbandman's Instructor* by A. S. Gent (1697).[112] Authors like Worlidge, Mortimer, Meager, and Bradley were found in so many gentlemen's libraries, and their works passed through so many editions, that their popularity as reading matter can hardly be gainsaid. As for their practical influence, it can sometimes be perceived in estate accounts that produce carbon copies of bookish precepts. An estate account of 1718, for example, shows hedges at Chippenham in Cambridgeshire planted with quicksets, interspersed with crab apple trees and elms, exactly following the procedures recommended by John Mortimer in *The Whole Art of Husbandry* (1707).[113].

Thus through the efforts of country gentlemen, first and foremost, initiatives were taken to spread innovations to the ends of the realm, bringing the use of clover and sainfoin to Wales, of marl to Roxburghshire and Berwickshire in Scotland, and fine vegetables to the neighbourhood of Edinburgh. Thomas Pitt, owner of an estate in east Cornwall, even wrote off to Bordeaux in 1722 for lucerne, having heard that France was the source of this grass that afforded four or five crops a year. A willingness to entertain the idea of changes was now more widespread, and prejudices were being prized from their anchorage in the rock of routine farming. In the Lincolnshire fens, a region which could not nurse too many conservative notions – it had seen too much rapid change in the course of the previous hundred years – we see a relatively young prejudice against potatoes in process of being worn down in Wildmore Fen in 1758 in a landlord's admission that the potato crop was indeed of great value to the poor and of benefit in breaking up ground.[114]

---

[111] BL, Add. MS 42,614.

[112] Kent AO, U951 E14A. For an even larger selection in Mr Talbot's library in Glamorgan, c. 1750, see Glamorgan RO, D/DP885. See also AHEW, vol. v, pt 1, ch. 8, p. 263, and ch. 9, p. 297.

[113] J. H. Harvey, 'Hedges and Local History', *Local Historian*, XII, 2, 1976, p. 84.

[114] See AHEW, vol. V, pt i, ch. 12. For an example of a gentleman growing sainfoin from 1668 onwards

The wider influence of the printed word can best be understood by considering the content of agricultural literature in the early eighteenth century, and its form. Authors made considerable efforts to give their readers the best help possible. Writers themselves read all the available literature, investigated the practice of the most diligent husbandmen, and added their own experience. Books became more encyclopaedic in the sense that they were more comprehensive and descended into greater detail. Their writers set themselves ever higher standards in their endeavour to help the practical farmer, offering more and more illustrations as well as an exact, descriptive text. Some works showed a laudable open-mindedness in their advocacy of different methods; they did not advance their own arguments by first quarrelling with other writers, as had been common in the sixteenth century. Any and every agricultural operation could be performed in several different ways, and one method was not necessarily the only one to fit all circumstances. Edward Lisle's book, *Observations in Husbandry*, illustrates the painstaking gathering of experience from a multitude of sources. The author was a country gentleman who in the words of his son "determined to make the study of agriculture one of the chief amusements of his life". Country gentlemen were still leaders in enquiry and curiosity. They had much time on their hands, but the "amusement" they sought should not be misunderstood. Work and leisure were not separate segments of life. The study of agriculture was satisfying because it was, at one and the same time, useful in improving the efficiency of a man's estate and farm, educational in introducing him to books, and interesting in sharpening his observation as he travelled. Lisle settled at Crux Easton, Hampshire, in 1693–4, and thereafter sought out reputable farmers in the immediate neighbourhood, and on all his journeys, whether to see his father-in-law, Sir Ambrose Phillips, at Garendon, Leicestershire, to see his estates in Wiltshire or the Isle of Wight, or to see his friends. He did not intend publication at first: his notebooks were for his own use. It was not until about 1713 that he thought they might be useful to a wider public and began an index. He died in 1722 and his son published the work in 1757, at a time when it seemed to him that "every day produces new inventions and improvements in agriculture".[115]

Lisle's notes reveal how he read, travelled, and questioned indefatigably. He talked to Mr Bobart at the Botanical Gardens in Oxford in 1708, and taxed innumerable farmers and labourers in Wiltshire, Hampshire, and

in north Wales who made personal visits to view other farmers' sainfoin between Uxbridge and Aylesbury, in Surrey and Oxfordshire, and then used a pamphlet of advice and instruction to persuade his agent, see Frank V. Emery, 'The Mechanics of Innovation: Clover Cultivation in Wales before 1750', *J. Hist. Geog.*, II, 1, 1976, pp. 38–9. For marl in Scotland, see Robert A. Dodgshon, 'Land Improvement in Scottish Farming: Marl and Lime in Roxburghshire and Berwickshire in the Eighteenth Century', AHR, XXVI, 1, 1978, pp. 1–2; for lucerne, see AHEW, vol. V, pt 1, ch. 11, p. 366; for potatoes, LAO, Ancaster Coll., 3 Anc. 7/3/12.

[115] Edward Lisle, *Observations in Husbandry*, London, 1757, *passim*.

Leicestershire with questions on every subject under the sun: how to burn lime, how to improve meadows, what plough was best. He stopped farmers at work in the fields and asked them why they did certain things; he experimented at home with the early sprouting of different varieties of oats, barley, etc.; he critically examined the barley on sale at Banbury market as he passed through, argued with his threshers about the small quantities they threshed per day, finally explaining the differences in their performance by the quality of the crops from cold hill lands compared with warm vale soils.

Lisle's contacts suggest that certain parishes scattered round the counties had a reputation for improved farming which drew visitors to them and further enhanced their reputation. Mr Clerk at Ditchley, Leicestershire, was often consulted, and it may be no accident that Ditchley was where Robert Bakewell was to farm later. Garendon and Gracedieu, places that have a high reputation in the history of the later agricultural revolution, are also mentioned. The rathe-ripe barley of Patney in Wiltshire had been advertised by Robert Plot when writing his *Natural History of Oxfordshire*; the same barley and the same place are mentioned by Lisle also. The recurrence of these same names of places and people in progressive farming circles underlined the continuing influence of books throughout the period. Just as Sir Richard Weston's work and Samuel Hartlib's publications had brought to both men a stream of visitors, so now bookish references brought visitors to Ditchley, Garendon, Gracedieu, and Patney. In exactly the same way after 1760 the books of Arthur Young induced German and Russian farmers from well-to-do families to make their round of visits to the English improvers named in his works. Improved farms might be islands in a sea of commonplace husbandry, but their fame spread abroad and attracted visitors directly to them.

While gentleman farmers opened their minds to new ideas, inspected the practice of "the most diligent husbandmen" (Mortimer's phrase), read the literature, married theory with practice in the Baconian manner, husbandmen began to be catered for by pamphlets of up to four pages which were cheap to produce and made no great demands on the reader. Recommending clover or other grasses, such pamphlets might be found on sale in the same shops that sold seeds.[116] Later on, generally after 1770, farmers became sufficiently interested in new ideas to launch farmers' clubs. The first in England, namely the Faversham Farmers Club, belongs to this period, however, having been set up in 1727. But it seems to have started as a club of farmers, both yeomen and gentlemen, meeting to eat, drink, and play cards rather than to promote good farming. The next, with a more serious improving purpose, was the Bath Society, not founded until 1777.[117]

[116] I owe this information to Mr Malcolm Thick. See ch. 6 above, p. 260 and n. 108.

[117] P. G. Selby, *The Faversham Farmers' Club and its Members*, Canterbury, 1927, pp. 6–10. For later clubs and societies, see K. Hudson, *Patriotism with Profit: British Agricultural Societies in the Eighteenth and Nineteenth Centuries*, London, 1972.

Among the novel influences of the period 1700–50, and one that would almost certainly repay more investigation, was the interest of the Hanoverian kings and their court circle in extending, intensifying, and perhaps making fashionable a lively interest in improved farming. George III was known as Farmer George, but George I also seems to have shown a desire to keep abreast of new ideas on land cultivation and management. At the king's *levée* in London in August 1726, he questioned Lord Cathcart about his new woodland plantations.[118] Two years earlier, in 1724, a letter from A. Stanyan to his brother in Turkey had informed the latter of George I's desire to acquire the seeds of foreign plants for the improvement of kitchen gardening in England.[119] These fragmentary glimpses of royal interest in agricultural pursuits, both grand and modest, prompt the question whether English landowners who moved in court circles benefited in any way from a closer acquaintance with landowners in Hanover. We have already suggested that royal policy towards the English forests after 1700 may have been influenced by German examples. Did English statesmen pick up other ideas on their visits to Hanover in the company of their monarch? One small clue suggests that these contacts may not have been unfruitful. When Earl Cathcart wrote an article in 1891 on Jethro Tull, drawing on information in the diary of his ancestor, the eighth baron, between 1725 and 1731, he stated categorically that Lord Townshend studied turnip husbandry while attending his master, George I, on his visits to Hanover, and subsequently introduced that system into his own county of Norfolk. Earl Cathcart did not add supporting evidence to this statement, but it is possible that the fact of the matter was an oral tradition in the family. The surviving records of the Townshend estate at Rainham are too meagre to offer more than very slight supporting clues. A group of eighteen letters dating from 1706 reveals some discussion between Townshend and his steward concerning crop sequences, which implies some experimentation and uncertainty about the best rotation involving oats or barley, clover, and turnips. Since Thomas Pope wrote of Lord Townshend that his favourite subject of conversation was "that kind of rural improvement which arises from turnips", it is not impossible that, in his meetings with landowners in Hanover, Townshend discussed rotations incorporating turnips with lively, practical interest.[120]

Among nobility and gentry several specialized activities made noticeable headway in this half-century, representing an effective alternative, or supplement, to traditional agriculture. One was the keeping of pigeons, which aroused fresh interest after 1660, and resulted in the rebuilding, or new

[118] Earl Cathcart, 'Jethro Tull, his Life, Times and Teaching', *J. RASE*, 3rd ser., II, 1, 1891, p. 24.

[119] PRO, SP 35/54, f. 7. I am much indebted to Mr Jeremy Black for this reference.

[120] Cathcart, *op. cit.*, p. 24 (the original diary, consulted by courtesy of the present Lord Cathcart, does not give any clues on the matter); H. W. Saunders, 'Estate Management at Rainham, 1661–86 and 1706', *Norfolk Arch.*, XIX, 1917, pp. 63–6; *DNB*, *sub nomine*.

building, of some dovecotes (though gentlemen did not manage to preserve their former monopoly rights over this activity). The pigeons adorned the dinner table, while the dung was highly prized for bringing on special crops, like the Portugal onions which John Cockburn urged his gardener to grow in Scotland in 1735. Another enterprise was the keeping of fish ponds. Examples from eastern Europe of fish ponds of carp and pike had been made known to the English gentry in the later sixteenth century, and in one English translation of a foreign work in 1599 the high financial return had been underlined. The price of fish excelled other produce, it was said, and yet the labour needs were low. John Norden in the first decade of the seventeenth century had recommended fish ponds, and marvelled at their increase in Sussex and Surrey; when John Aubrey copied out the same words into his notebook eighty years later, it is likely that interest was reviving. Certainly other scattered evidence, like that in 1677 showing Edward James, a grazier of Kinvaston, Staffordshire, tending carp in his ponds called The Pits (old marlpits, perhaps?) suggests it. By the early eighteenth century the literature and the practice left no doubt about the enthusiasm for fish farming. A general textbook on agricultural pursuits by Sir Jonas Moore in 1703, addressed to gentlemen and farmers, made attractive claims for the financial profit from carp breeding in fish ponds, though the essential condition, as he wisely pointed out, was a market locally where nobility and gentry resided. (Doubtless this was why the counties of Surrey and Sussex had pioneered fish ponds in an earlier age.) In 1713 Roger North published *A Discourse of Fish* to help those wanting to breed carp in clay country where fresh springs or rivers were lacking. His ponds were intended to be ornamental, but again their principal recommendation was their profitable use of a gentleman's landed resources. Assuming that four acres of water bred about 1,000 carp, with some pike, perch, and tench in addition, the author expected an income of £25 a year. This represented a gain of £6 5s. per acre, compared with £2 from meadow. North's book of advice was highly practical, and was intended to encourage others with experience of fish keeping in other soil regions to offer their knowledge. Roger North believed there was as much variety in fish and fish keeping as in cattle.[121]

As a source of protein, adding further variety to the foods at the dining table, the same could be said of wildfowl. The many ponds constructed by gentlemen with islands in the middle seem to have been designed with the

[121] James Colville, ed., *Letters of John Cockburn of Ormistoun to his Gardener, 1727–44*, Scottish Hist. Soc., XLV, 1904. See also AHEW, vol. v, pt 1, ch. 6, p. 191, and vol. 5 of the paperback series, pp. 168, 355; George Churchey, *A New Book of Good Husbandry...*London, 1599, p. 3; J. Norden, *The Surveyor's Dialogue*, London, 1607, pp. 218–20; Bodleian Library, Aubrey MS 2, f. 94; Staffs. RO, Account Book, 237/27; Sir J. Moore, *England's Interest, or the Gentleman and Farmer's Friend*, London, 1703, pp. 161–5; [R. North], *A Discourse of Fish and Fish-Ponds...*London, 1713, 'Introduction' and pp. 71–3. Dudley North in his *Observations and Advices Oeconomical* in 1669 had recommended fish ponds as a gentleman's help towards housekeeping.

preservation of waterfowl in mind. Certainly wildfowl decoys attracted more and more gentlemanly interest at this period. They had first been introduced into Norfolk in the early seventeenth century, almost certainly with Dutch expertise. The word 'decoy' derives from a Dutch word *Eendekooy*, meaning 'a duck cage or trap'. They multiplied most in eastern England when the drainage of the fens circumscribed the breeding areas, and so made it desirable to conserve more systematically those watery habitats that remained. But they appeared elsewhere also; Defoe in the 1720s described two in Dorset, of which one had been newly laid out "at great expense". Large expenditure presupposed a certain level of market demand, which Defoe confirmed in his description of "an infinite number of wildfowl such as duck and mallard, teal and widgeon, brand geese, wild geese, etc." which "are sent up to London; the quantity indeed is incredible". Richard Blome's *Gentlemen's Recreation* was thought to give the best advice on the construction of a decoy, and the extent of gentlemanly interest is further reflected in the legislation of 1711 to protect this asset.[122]

Wildfowl decoys exemplify a costly recreational pursuit of the gentry which then turned into a profitable business enterprise. Deer parks seem to have followed the same course. Improvement of wasteland and forest left less land for wild deer, and obliged the gentry to preserve them more carefully in parks. Deer in parks guaranteed a larger supply of venison, and a market developed as the taste for this meat began to be cultivated among classes below the gentry. Venison as a foodstuff was produced, and may also have been traded, by the gentry. It was certainly traded by poachers. In other words, it deserves the same attention as the market for rabbit meat. This last plainly encouraged the more careful tending of warrens and the gentry's increasing expenditure on them.[123]

Another capital-intensive pursuit much favoured by gentlemen was horse breeding. Early interest stemmed from government policy in the reigns of Henry VIII and Elizabeth to improve the strength, quality, and training of English horses, so inferior did they seem to other breeds like the Flemish, Italian, Spanish, and Arabian. As a gentlemen's recreation the pleasures of horse racing were added to those of hunting in the late sixteenth century, and much experience of cross-breeding resulted from the desire to breed the fastest race horses. By the mid seventeenth century English horses were

[122] See RCHM, *Northants.*, II, p. lix, for islands in ponds; J. Wentworth Day, *History of the Fens*, Wakefield, 1970, pp. 116–17; D. Defoe, *A Tour through England and Wales*, 2 vols., Everyman edn, I, pp. 209, 214; II, pp. 97–100; Houghton, *Collection for Improvement of Husbandry and Trade*, 10 Sept. 1702 (vol. XIX, no. 581). See also Gervase Markham, *Hunger's Prevention, or the Whole Art of Fowling by Water and Land*, 1621 and 1665. For a legal dispute concerning damage to a decoy in 1712 in Borough Fen, Northants, see *House of Lords Papers, NS, IX*, 1710–12, p. 728. On the legislation, see ch. 4 above, pp. 193ff.

[123] See ch. 4 above, pp. 193ff; on rabbit warrens, see above, p. 274 and Sheail, 'Rabbits and Agriculture', pp. 343–55.

evidently much improved, for a high European reputation stimulated export demand, which persisted in the eighteenth century. Thus the breeding of horses both for the coach and for recreation made good business for gentlemen, as Sir Jonas Moore stressed in 1703. Since the peace treaty with France, he claimed, English farmers had been offered by Frenchmen three times the accustomed price for their horses, and, following the present war, they could expect still higher returns. In this case, quality had been improved not only by cross-breeding, but also by careful attention to feeding on the new grasses.[124]

For want of proof, one can only hazard guesses when exactly the lessons learned from horse breeding influenced breeders of other livestock. The ample choice among many different breeds of cattle, sheep, and pigs satisfied for a long time; farmers plainly exploited the many alternatives available to them. But the possibilities of cross-breeding were well known, and experience with in-breeding was acquired willy-nilly on open commons where all men's livestock grazed together. But when Robert Bakewell, a gentleman farmer of Dishley, Leicestershire, established by the 1770s his reputation as the best-known expert on the selective breeding of cattle and sheep, it may be no accident that he farmed in good hunting country, which was recognized as having "for many years abounded with intelligent and spirited breeders". Hugo Meynell, the first Master of the Quorn Hunt, was breeding foxhounds in the 1760s on the same principles as Bakewell, and Quorn Hall lies only six miles from Dishley Grange. As in so many other instances where progress was a long-drawn-out affair, over-much credit was given to the foremost publicist. Other substantial contributors did not seek the limelight, but seem to have been at work for many decades before.[125]

Economic self-interest and social convenience obliged different farming classes to choose different agricultural options, and yeomen and husbandmen could hardly compete with the gentry's fish ponds, deer parks, wildfowl decoys, or horse studs. They preferred enterprises requiring medium quantities of capital, modest amounts of land, and moderate labour. Another decisive factor in their selection was the way the labour requirements of the new crops fitted into slack periods in the existing pattern of work. Dye crops and hops were eminently satisfactory in this respect. In north-east Kent, for example, when madder flourished, it was not only because the price was right, but because it was harvested after hop picking came to an end. Canary grass dovetailed well on farms where bread grains were a major crop: canary seed

---

[124] The evidence for this argument is set out in Thirsk, *Horses in Early Modern England, passim*. See also Moore, *op cit.*, p. 94. On the organization of the horse fairs, see vol. 4 of the paperback series, pp. 187–8, and P. R. Edwards, 'The Horse Trade of the Midlands in the Seventeenth Century', AHR, XXVII, 2, 1979, pp. 90–100.

[125] Joan Thirsk, 'Agrarian History, 1540–1950', in *VCH Leics.*, II, pp. 221–2; G. E. Mingay, *The Agricultural Revolution: Changes in Agriculture, 1650–1880*, London, 1977, pp. 28–30, 143–58.

was harvested after the corn. Nevertheless, from time to time the labour shortages in this area so close to London pressed hard, especially in wartime when many Kentish men were attracted by higher pay into the navy. No wonder that north-east Kent was more advanced than many other regions in the use of seed drills for economizing on labour.[126]

Turnips fitted comfortably into existing arable rotations in many parts of the country, without calling for special enclosures. Their increasing popularity is recorded in Norfolk and Suffolk where farmers fed more livestock than in the seventeenth century in order to offset the low prices of grain. Whereas only 10 per cent of probate inventories surviving for the period 1585 to 1680 mentioned turnips, between 1680 and 1710 50 per cent of inventories recorded them.[127] In a contrasting county of the west Midlands, in the vicinity of the Clee Hills in Shropshire, middling farmers were plainly trying a wider variety of alternatives. More careful attention was being paid to improving the quality of grassland by liming. But at the same time, hop gardens, fruit orchards, and hemp and flax growing, as well as horse breeding and dairying, were all gaining ground at the expense of mainstream arable crops and livestock. The vicar of Cleobury Mortimer, to take but one example, first grew hops in 1658 and first received tithe hops in 1662. In this region, hops did not prove as successful a crop as fruit, but the fact that the experiment occurred is significant; if they had fitted the circumstances better, they would have spread at this auspicious time.[128]

Finally among the small and very small landholders, market gardening was more widely publicized for its advantages in requiring next to no capital but employing family labour. Sandwich in Kent had been a pioneer in late-sixteenth-century England. In 1749 a writer caught sight of a similar, yet recent, development in the same county, near Gravesend: land was being turned over to kitchen gardens using town dung to enrich the soil, with the result that Gravesend asparagus now bore a better price than any other, even that of Battersea. This was evidently a new success story of southern England. In the west Midlands, in the inventory (1742) of the goods of Susannah Hughes of Evesham, Worcestershire, we perceive another specialized gardening area that was now being developed, according a living to very modest cultivators. Susannah's assets included a little bag of turnip seed (2s.), a little lettuce seed, a little cabbage seed (1s.), a little cucumber seed, onion seed (10s.),

[126] Letter from Dr Dennis Baker to the author; John Lyons, *A Description of the Isle of Thanet*...Margate, 1763, p. 8. I owe this reference to Dr Baker also.

[127] Mark Overton, 'Computer Analysis of an Inconsistent Data Source: The Case of Probate Inventories', *J. Hist. Geog.*, III, 4, 1977, pp. 325–6.

[128] Kenneth W. G. Goodman, 'Hammerman's Hill: The Land, People, and Industry of the Titterstone Clee Hill Area of Shropshire, from the 16th to the 18th Centuries', unpub. Keele Univ. Ph.D. thesis, 1978, pp. 79, 170, 175, 190. Cf. the case of a Hampshire farmer in 1745 in financial straits who considered planting 100 acres with hops – E. L. Jones, 'Eighteenth-Century Changes in Hampshire Chalkland Farming', *AHR*, VIII, 1, 1960, p. 9.

a strike of beans, a few kidney beans (1s.), odd seed in little bags (1s.), and hops growing on their poles.[129]

For an Evesham gardener, the main market for vegetables probably lay in Birmingham, though it was not yet as voracious a consumer as London. Intelligent observers saw great opportunities in the vicinity of most towns. But they were most perceptively and eloquently described by John Cockburn, a Scottish landowner living in London, who wrote private letters to his gardener at home urging him to grow more of his fruit and vegetables commercially, and set the same movement under way around Edinburgh. If only his gardener would offer his wares to appreciative gentry roundabout, he was sure he would gradually coax into existence more sophisticated and refined tastes, and a large market would gradually emerge. A letter in June 1735 firmly set out the main objective, based on Cockburn's observations in London: it involved "drawing in the people to a better taste towards garden stuff", thus putting an end to the dull conviction that "an apple is only an apple, and people don't distinguish". "If you produce good kinds such as Nonpareil's Russedines and the like, and put them into the hands of a few at Edinburgh who know the difference, you'll soon find a demand for all you can have, and by having such, you will even get customers for other things. Depend upon it there are people in Edinburgh who have taste, and if you can once get into the custom of some who have it, [it] will put others upon enquiring where they had good things, and this will hold in your herbs, etc., as well as in your fruit." No more eloquent argument in favour of specialized horticulture – in this case for a highly finicky upper-class market – could be found than in these letters. The writer advocated the growing of mulberries, quinces (more profitable than pears or apples), "better kinds of pears and apples [which] yield more than the common kinds", peas and beans that could be got ready in July and August rather than later, raspberries for raspberry brandy or for the apothecaries, and gooseberries for sauces and fruit. The model throughout was the London market gardeners, who carried their wares carefully packed in baskets, on horse-drawn carts, so that they were not "wet, bruised or broiled in the sun, the cart being covered"; they "took care to have something for the market every day the year round"; and every day such men were knocking at Cockburn's door offering beans, peas, cauliflowers, and cabbages for sale. Why did Edinburgh's upper and middle classes not offer the same opportunities? Cockburn had the answer. "All the people of Scotland are not so void of taste or their other senses as you incline to think them. It is the not being able to get good things which makes people not have them"; if they were once introduced to customers, they would soon

[129] Thos. Read, *A New Description of Gloucestershire, Hampshire...and the County of Kent*, London, 1749, p. 445; R. W. Sidwell, 'A Short History of Commercial Horticulture in the Vale of Evesham', *Vale of Evesham Hist. Soc. Research Papers*, II, 1969, p. 45. See also AHEW, vol. v, pt I, ch. 6, pp. 167ff.

catch on. "People would presently come to distinguish", just as they came in to buy when garden stuff was first introduced. "Besides having uncommon things brings customers to take of the common."[130]

In these exhortations intended to extend the horticultural business into lowland Scotland, we have a clear analysis of the way market demand had been built up around London, and how it was taking shape in other large towns. We also see how much skill and careful attention to detail were demanded not only in marketing the produce but in cultivation as well. The ground had to be carefully dug and redug to eliminate weeds, the weeding hoe had to be in constant use, all seed and new plants were chosen with discrimination, and top dressings were especially selected for each plant. Cockburn promised his gardener some new Portugal onion seed, and recommended that a bed be prepared with a top dressing of pigeon dung mixed with ashes. For watering the plants, soft water was better than hard. London gardeners evidently took "pains even to soften their water, which generally is softer than ours", he wrote. And to meet such standards, labourers had to work meticulously: "don't get triflers, and keep the men to work", he advised.[131]

E. THE INTERACTION OF HORTICULTURE AND AGRICULTURE

For many decades – almost a century, in fact – the success of horticulture proffered lessons to agriculture, and they did not pass unheeded. Many writers commented on the high productivity of land that was dug with the spade, and the fears of some gentry that soils would be spoiled by so much digging were gradually dissipated.[132] Then in the early eighteenth century, men who positively hankered for the more meticulous cultivation of arable land by methods akin to those of the gardeners added a further consideration to their reflections, namely, the rising cost of labour. In this conjuncture of circumstances there developed a more positive interest in using wheeled implements in the fields for drilling and hoeing. In the more encouraging circumstances after 1750 this was to usher in a revolution in techniques of cultivation.

Jethro Tull's innovations with horse-drawn cultivators in the 1720s cannot be seen in correct perspective without noticing the long period of preparation beforehand. As early as 1600–1 two authors, Sir Hugh Plat and Edward Maxey, had both publicized in books the idea of setting corn seed so that it was regularly spaced in, and between, rows. Maxey's device, illustrated on the title page of his book, was a wooden setting board with holes through

---

[130] Colville, *op. cit.*, pp. 22–8.

[131] *Ibid.*, pp. 30, 32–3, 51, 48.

[132] See e.g. John Beale in *Philos. Trans. Roy. Soc.*, x–xii, 116, 1675, p. 363. On damage by digging, see Hartlib, *His Legacie*, 1651, pp. 11–12; see also ch. 6 above, p. 245.

which the corn was dropped.[133] Interest in such matters at this time may be explained by the severe grain shortages of the 1590s. Setting corn promised economies that were urgent in years of dearth. And when once the idea was mooted in print, it circulated publicly and continuously, being revived whenever circumstances gave fresh practical urgency to economies in seed. For this reason corn setting again attracted interest in the midst of grievous harvest failures between 1646 and 1651. In 1648 Samuel Hartlib recorded in his diary a querulous remark by Sir William Petty, wanting to know why men should trouble their brains about the setting of corn when all it would do would be to save seed. But the same diarist's notice in September 1649 suggests that Petty had by then seen the sense of it all; he himself had an engine that seemed successful in practice. At the same time a Shropshire gentleman, Peter Cole, had devised another implement for the same purpose; so had a Mr Steward of Hampshire in 1653 (evidently Nicholas Steward of Hartley near Odiham).[134]

Hartlib's diary set out the theoretical and practical problems as contemporaries saw them in the 1650s. Practical observation showed how much seed was normally lost when sown by hand; much of it fell into the furrows instead of on the ridges. On newly broken ground, this meant that much seed was hardly covered because the earth was not deep enough in the furrows. For this reason, oats were often sown rather than wheat as a first crop. Yet this had its disadvantages, for the oat seed then lingered in the ground for years after. If seed were set, it could be placed on the ridges, and, because of the greater certainty of germination in a deeper soil, wheat could be grown rather than oats, and less land would need to be planted. The costs of tillage would be somewhat greater than under the old hand-sowing methods – 10s. as opposed to 6s. an acre – but only one-third the amount of seed would be used, and less land would require less manure to keep it in heart.[135]

Practical experiments with the setting of grain were carried out by Cressy Dymock at Wadsworth, near Doncaster, in 1653. His worst trials and tribulations were in dealing with truculent labourers, which he graphically described in his letters to Hartlib. The exact form of his implement was kept a secret, but Dymock described it as an "engine that serves for a plough", and he called the method of setting "blowing". The plough evidently opened the land, let in the seed at whatever depth and distance was required, and closed it again. In one of his notes, Hartlib claimed that it would plough,

[133] Fussell, *Old English Farming Books*, p. 15. See also ch. 6 above, p. 261.

[134] Hartlib, "Ephemerides", 1648, S–T3; 1649, E–F8, F–G8; 1649, H–J6; 1653, JJ–JJ1; 1655, 25–257. Yet another modest inventor was mentioned by Sir Cheney Culpeper in 1655 – a plain Kentish countryman, using a plain wooden instrument of his own devising to set corn – *ibid.*, 1655, 30–307.

[135] *Ibid.*, 1655, 30–307. It should be emphasized that these were tillage, not merely sowing, costs.

sow or set corn, harrow, and dung in one operation. When oxen, which were slower than horses, drew the engine, Dymock found it possible to set sixteen acres with barley in ten days, a task which formerly would have taken sixteen days. Since labour in fenland areas was unusually expensive (the new system of farming after drainage had called for far more labour than the old pastoral system), this was an encouraging start. Moreover, Dymock used ten to twelve bushels of seed instead of the usual forty bushels. He went ahead and set beans by the same method.[136]

Dymock's servants who started by being obstructive were won over. Their "secret slanders" turned to "open commendation". And in April 1653, when the seed germinated, everyone watched carefully to learn more lessons about the correct density of seed. Dymock was satisfied with the performance of his drill plough, and was anxious to demonstrate it nearer London, possibly at Deptford.[137]

How many other experiments with seed drilling were carried out in the years up to 1700 it is impossible to say, but it is reasonable to guess that inventive farmers in different places kept the idea and the experiments alive. In 1657 a plough for setting corn was said to have been devised at Oxford, though it did not work well on stony ground. In the same year Mr Steward in Hampshire was still improving his drill plough. Cressy Dymock resorted to print in 1668 with a flysheet called *The New and Better Art of Agriculture*, in which he calculated how much grain would be saved over the whole kingdom by setting seed in his way – enough to feed one million people with bread and drink. And in 1697 a "drill plough", mentioned in a probate inventory of Samuel Hayworth of Richmond, Surrey, shows that the theories were still matched by practical experiments.[138] This was not surprising, for, as we have seen, gardeners demonstrated the merits of hand setting seed every day of the week.

Nevertheless, the practical drawbacks of copying gardening procedures in the fields can readily be imagined. The Reverend John Beale, an intelligent and thoughtful agricultural improver with experience in Herefordshire and Somerset, summed them up in 1657. "Sowing engines", he wrote, "are fitter for cottagers and for the shift of one year upon barren ground than for a yeoman that must till much and hold on his course." Yet he recognized their potential. "The helps of the plough and other carriages do properly belong to human art, and undoubtedly ease the charge of the family, free [them] from cumbersome servants and double the value of arable land."[139] Some years later when Andrew Yarranton was publicizing clover growing and experimenting with various different ways of handling the crop, he thought

---

[136] Hartlib MS 55/2/2–6; "Ephemerides", 1652, CC–CC5; 1655, 30–307.

[137] Hartlib MSS 55/2/4; 55/2/5; 67/7/1.

[138] Hartlib, "Ephemerides", 1657, 51–51–3, 53–53–8; PRO, SP 29/251, no. 182. See AHEW, vol. v, pt 1, ch. 9, p. 306.   [139] Hartlib MS 62/23/2.

it might even be possible to sow clover in rows, so that it could be hoed once or twice in the summer. But he too recognized the impracticality of such a suggestion to a husbandman "till some more expeditious instrument than the common hoe is found out". Even so, he believed that to an ingenious man such an invention should be a work of "no great difficulty".[140]

Reflections of this kind were evidently widespread by the early eighteenth century, with the result that in north-east Kent, where farming most resembled garden cultivation, the impractical was actually practised. Garden beans and even canary seed were dibbled or drilled and hoed in rows. John Lewis described two different procedures in his account of Thanet farming in 1723. Most laborious was the planting of canary seed, which was drilled into specially made furrows by passing it "through the spout of a teapot or some such thing". Others who thought this method tedious sowed the seed by hand, but built up ridges as sharp as they could so that seed would fall more surely into the furrows. Either way farmers reaped the advantages of row cultivation in easier weeding and a heavier crop — $1\frac{1}{2}$ sems per acre heavier than by conventional methods.[141]

The author of this account remarked on the tedium of such procedures but not on their high cost. This was hardly surprising: family farmers predominated on Thanet, and cultivators specialized in crops of high value grown on small acreages. Thus most attention was focused on high yields rather than on any notional calculation of the labour cost of family members. But the cost of labour and its scarcity were a recurring theme in other men's writings. Roger North had fulminated because "both year and day men's wages are risen almost as much as the profits on land have fallen; and chiefly in the tillage countries". Low food prices made matters worse, for they allowed the poor to subsist too easily in semi-idleness. Beggar's status "hath a sort of freedom as well as luxury, if there be any truth in common fame, in it", he moaned. Thus when more conventional farmers attempted to exploit the benefits of row cultivation on large units of land, they had to reckon with high costs and the sullen resistance of their labourers to tedious work. Even so, the advantages were compelling in the seed saved, the weeding made easy, and the much heavier yields. One writer even suggested "candying" the seed (coating it to the size of a small bean) so that the seed could be more easily and regularly spaced, and birds and worms deterred. Men were further spurred on by the observation that plants grew quicker and larger when better spaced out. Again the lesson was learned from the

---

[140] Yarranton, *The Improvement Improved*, pp. 37–8.

[141] John Lewis, *The History and Antiquities...of the Isle of Tenet, in Kent*, 2nd edn, London, 1736 (1st edn 1723), pp. 19–21. I owe this reference to Dr Dennis Baker; J. Mortimer in *The Whole Art of Husbandry*, London, 1707, p. 131, referred to safflower, growing in Oxfordshire, which "they plant in rows about a foot distant for the convenience of hoeing it". This also signifies field cultivation in rows.

gardeners: it was a contemporary cliché to say that gardeners produced ten times more food than farmers from the same ground.[142]

Against the background of this writing Jethro Tull's concerns with wheeled implements for drilling and hoeing do not appear as the singular interests of a unique individual. He was only singular in the vexation, verging on neurosis, that he felt towards his expensive and unreliable labourers, and towards new labour and wage regulations and judgments by county magistrates which, to his mind, favoured labourers against their masters. But his innovations resulted not from this circumstance alone so much as from a conjuncture. He had a farm in hand that he could not manage to let. To escape the thrall of servants, he resolved to plant the whole farm with sainfoin, since sainfoin yielded a higher return than grain. But sainfoin seed was scarce and dear, and, knowing that much seed was wasted by being buried too deep, Tull pondered ways of using less. At harvest time he noticed that the crop was heaviest when one plant occupied one square foot of land. Yet at Tull's usual rate of sowing (7 bushels per acre), 140 seeds were scattered over a square foot. So he determined the best depth of sowing, and employed people on a ten-acre plot to make channels, set the seed, and cover it to the correct depth. In this experiment Tull was following the same procedures as those used in Thanet. But family farmers in Thanet worked for themselves and were prepared to suffer such tedious labour; Tull's labourers were not so amenable. Well pleased with the harvest from his experimental plot, Tull planned the next year to plant more, but "his labourers conspired to thwart him", and he had to abandon his scheme. He turned to the idea of an engine to drill sainfoin, and then to drill grain. Drilling facilitated hand hoeing, which turned his mind to the possibilities of horse hoeing.[143]

By the 1730s, then, detailed procedures for drilling and hoeing had become a matter for highly varied experiments and argument among a wide circle. To those who were already hand sowing turnips under barley (thereby growing stunted turnips that were useful only as a green crop) Tull recommended drilling turnips in rows after the barley was off the land, or, alternatively, as he had tried himself, drilling turnips between rows of barley,

---

[142] Lewis, op. cit., pp. 13, 14, 17, 24; R. North, Discourse of the Poor, 1753 edn, pp. 58, 15; [L. Braddon], To Pay Old Debts without New Taxes by Charitably Relieving, Politically Reforming, and Judiciously Employing the Poor, London, 1723, pp. xiv–xv, xvii–xviii, xx, 36–7. A similar verdict on high productivity is given by A. Klima, writing on agrarian development in Bohemia. Czech historians are convinced, he says, that yields on peasants' smallholdings were higher in the seventeenth and eighteenth centuries than on demesnes, because smallholders practised more labour-intensive farming – PP, no. 85, 1979, p. 59.

[143] J. Tull, A Supplement to the Essay on Horse-Hoing Husbandry...London, 1736, pp. 225–6, 234, 250. Tull's references to labour regulations are somewhat enigmatic: he refers to statutes "which are new laws" and to "judgements thereupon", especially "the famous judgement given by some country magistrates, four of them in particular" – id., The New Horse-Houghing Husbandry...Dublin, 1731, pp. vii–ix.

oats, or wheat. For this last method, however, Tull was still uncertain what distances between rows served best. In short, men now generally recognized many alternative possibilities when exploiting the basic idea of row cultivation; the best method was not yet a settled matter, and innumerable experiments were afoot. Tull gained most publicity because he wrote the first book, but he moved in a circle of well-to-do agriculturalists, all of whom were experimenting with the same zest.[144]

The experiments of others are made clear in the diary of one of Tull's enthusiastic supporters, Lord Cathcart. He mentioned Lord Ducie (who died in 1735), who had drilled hundreds, even thousands, of acres, starting almost as early as Tull himself. He also named Lord Halifax (George Montague, who died in 1739), who had made many trials with drilling, had entertained Cathcart at Bushey, Hertfordshire, and at Abbs Court, near Walton on Thames, and had taken him to visit Tull. In 1731 Cathcart watched sainfoin and barley being drilled together on Lord Halifax's estate, in the very same year in which Tull published his first work on horse-hoeing husbandry. In short, an active concern for labour-saving methods in arable farming was being shared by a number of influential nobility and gentry who were in regular contact with Tull. Cathcart's diary, moreover, referred to a wider circle of friends who were interested improvers – Lord Townshend; Robert Walpole; Lords Bathurst, Litchfield, and Stair; Mr Thomas Hope of Rankielor, president of the Scotch Society of Improvers; and Mr Hall, a papist attorney near Hungerford.[145]

This account of innovations in farming has dwelt on the process of diffusing novelties rather than on the publicity given to adjustments and transformations within the structure of traditional farming. But it is important not to forget the more familiar alternatives. An important one for the conventional farmer was the conversion of arable or convertible land (cultivated under a ley farming system) to permanent pasture. This was a cost-cutting measure to counter the effects of low grain prices, which did not encounter the prejudices against new-fangled ways. Its scale is difficult to measure, but it has been judged by John Broad a substantial transformation in the south and east Midlands after 1650. Even in East Anglia such a trend, however weak, may possibly be inferred from the rising total valuation of fodder crops and the declining valuation of grain crops between 1660 and 1750. Permanent grassland, however, did not always prove a satisfactory solution, since the demand for deep stock-feeding pastures slackened when farmers produced

[144] Tull, *Supplement*, pp. 259–69. Subsequently, under the inspiration of Tull's work, Frenchmen, especially du Hamel and Chateauvieux, carried out trials with row cultivation in France. By 1809–12 when Albrecht Daniel Thaer published his *Principles of Agriculture* (English tr., London, 1844, *II*, p. 444) he deemed Tull's methods nearly out of date, but only because the rows were now cultivated much closer together.

[145] Cathcart, 'Jethro Tull', pp. 14–17, 20–30.

more of their own fodder crops, by growing clover, sainfoin, lucerne, and turnips. Occasionally, of course, an eccentric notion could save the situation, as when Grahame of Levens urged Lord Weymouth in 1698 to use Scotch cattle to feed on his coarse grass at Drayton (Northants.). Weymouth was at first sceptical, but later was so satisfied with the results that he ordered more Scotch beasts to be sent to his main estate at Longleat in Wiltshire.[146] In many regions of England, however, the problems of finding a satisfactory farming scheme within the traditional framework were insoluble, and this seems to explain why the enclosure movement tended to lose some of its momentum. In north-west Northamptonshire, for example, interest weakened noticeably between 1670 and 1740, even though this was an area where conversion to pasture might have seemed a wise recourse.[147] Only in regions that were dedicated to corn like the Wiltshire–Hampshire chalklands, high farming systems, which avoided major transformations, managed to counter the depressing effects of low grain prices. The spread of water meadows, for example, greatly enlarged the capacity of these farms to keep livestock, which in turn promoted the productivity of their corn lands. This kind of adaptation, of course, also enhanced the role of livestock, instead of giving it the distinctly subsidiary place which it had formerly occupied on the best-quality corn lands.

F. CONCLUSION

This survey of innovations underlines their hazards and uncertainties, which should not be brushed aside by after-knowledge. The risks of experiments were daunting to the great majority of farmers, who could not afford to gamble and lose. And as regional farming systems became more inter-dependent, interpolated novelties created many practical problems which the outsider cannot always readily perceive. Even when an interest in innovation was settled in principle, it raised innumerable questions on procedure in detail. Tull's writing sheds light on the debate about which crops to drill and at what distances. Interested gentry embarked on a long-drawn-out process of trial and error. Is it any wonder that other farmers were content to stand back and let the dust settle before they were convinced?

Nevertheless, the intricate dovetailing of farming systems gave scope to many ingenious farmers and gardeners to devise new combinations that made a livelihood. Variety, diversity, and unique specialization – these were characteristics of the age, and in every decade more distinctive regions came into existence as a result. Markets by the first half of the eighteenth century

[146] John Broad, 'Alternate Husbandry and Permanent Pasture in the Midlands, 1650–1800', AHR, xxviii, 2, pp. 77–89. On East Anglia, see the computer map of crops, based on inventories of Dr Mark Overton. On cattle in Northamptonshire, see J. V. Beckett, 'Landownership in Cumbria, c. 1680 – c. 1750', unpub. Lancaster Univ. D.Phil. thesis, 1975, p. 305.

[147] RCHM, *Northants.*, III, 1981, p. lii.

had developed a prodigious appetite for agricultural produce that was highly varied in quality and price. It was to move in the century after 1750 towards satisfying demand of another kind, for quantity and uniformity. The impressive list of local varieties of grain, compiled by Robert Plot in the later seventeenth century, was to be whittled away by standardization in the nineteenth century.[148] But until 1750 innovation multiplied individuality, and the pace of this process was probably as rapid in the years 1640 to 1750 as at any time before or since.

Nevertheless, in a period of increasing *laissez-faire*, when individuality flourished, many people still clung to conservative ways. While alternative agricultural systems were taking root in all corners of the kingdom, a multitude of farmers adhered to the ways of their forefathers. Arthur Young was not the fairest critic of small farmers, but we may judge him fair in placing his best hopes of advance on the gentlemen. "I would not ... be understood to expect too much from the common farmers reading this or indeed any book; I am sensible that not one farmer in five thousand reads at all. But the country abounds in gentlemen farmers whose ideas are more enlarged and whose practice is founded less on prejudice."[149] Even so, with a longer perspective on agricultural development, Young might have given more credit to the small farmer for shrewd intelligence. He was not slow to espouse new crops and ways when they plainly served his interests.

Alternative agriculture enjoyed a flourishing life so long as traditional agriculture was depressed. After 1750 it receded as mainstream products resumed their importance. We lack a general survey of the published literature on farming which could demonstrate this shift of interest. But it is helpful to notice that similar evidence has been assembled by a French historian, examining libraries in the Lyonnais between 1730 and 1770. Given the fact that the major interests of book collectors were history and literature and not the arts and sciences, the average proportion of books on these last subjects amounted to only 18 per cent. But within this small class of works, 40 per cent were agricultural textbooks, of which much the largest number (25 per cent) were concerned with horticulture and tree growing, 6 per cent with vines, and only 9 per cent with traditional corn–grass farming. Publication dates showed, furthermore, when interest in special crops waxed and when it waned. Between 1646 and 1720, over half of all extant books published were horticultural, and between 1720 and 1743 almost two-thirds.

[148] Baker, thesis, pp. 198–9, citing Kent Field Club, III, 4, 1971, pp. 215–16. Cf. J. Banister, *A Synopsis of Husbandry*, London, 1799, pp. 56–7: "Scarcely a market town but has a favourite species, which, having been successfully cultivated by some farmer in the neighbourhood, is by him dignified with a pompous title, and becomes the fashionable grain."

[149] A. Young, *A Six Weeks' Tour through the Southern Counties*, London, 3rd edn, 1772, p. viii. I wish to thank Dr Roger Richardson for this reference.

But between 1743 and 1765 conventional corn–grass farming came into its own again, and three-quarters of the textbooks were devoted to these matters. It is likely that a thorough survey of English libraries would reveal subject matter distributed on a similar pattern.[150]

[150] Georges Durand, *Vin, Vigne, et Vignerons en Lyonnais et Beaujolais (XVIe — XVIIIe siècles)*, Paris, 1979, pp. 184–91.

8

SELECT BIBLIOGRAPHY, 1640–1750

Addison, W. *English Fairs and Markets*. London, 1953.

Airs, M. *The Making of the English Country House, 1500–1640*. London, 1975.

Albert, W. A. *The Turnpike Road System in England and Wales, 1663–1840*. Cambridge, 1972.

Alcock, N. W. *Stoneleigh Houses*. Birmingham, 1973.

Allison, K. J. *The East Riding of Yorkshire Landscape*. London, 1976.

'Flock Management in the Sixteenth and Seventeenth Centuries', EcHR, 2nd ser., XI, 1958.

'The Norfolk Worsted Industry in the Sixteenth and Seventeenth Centuries', *Yorks. Bull. Ec. & Soc. Research*, XII–XIII, 1960–1.

'The Sheep–Corn Husbandry of Norfolk in the Sixteenth and Seventeenth Centuries', AHR, V, 1, 1957.

Ambler, L. *Old Halls and Manor Houses of Yorkshire*. London, 1913.

Amery, C. *Period Houses and their Details*. London, 1974.

Andrews, J. H. 'The Port of Chichester and the Grain Trade, 1650–1750', *Sussex Arch. Coll.*, XCII, 1954.

Andrews, L. S. 'Vaynor Lands during the Eighteenth Century', *Mont. Coll.*, XLVI, 1940.

Appleby, A. B. 'Disease or Famine? Mortality in Cumberland and Westmorland, 1580–1640', EcHR, 2nd ser., XXVI, 1973.

Ashton, T. S. *Economic Fluctuations in England, 1700–1800*. Oxford, 1959.

An Economic History of England: The Eighteenth Century. London, 1955.

Ashworth, G. J. 'A Note on the Decline of the Wealden Iron Industry', *Surrey Arch. Coll.*, LXVII, 1970.

Astbury, A. K. *The Black Fens*. Cambridge, 1957.

Atwell, G. *The Faithfull Surveyor*. Cambridge, 1662.

Aubrey, J. *The Natural History of Wiltshire*, ed. J. Britton. London, 1847.

Austen, R. *The Spiritual Use of an Orchard; or Garden of Fruit Trees*. Oxford, 1653.

Bailey, J. *A General View of the Agriculture of Durham*. London, 1810.

Bailey, J. and Culley, G. *General View of the Agriculture of Cumberland*. London, 1794.

General View of the Agriculture of the County of Northumberland. 3rd edn. London, 1805.

Baker, A. H. R. and Butlin, R. A. (eds.). *Studies of Field Systems in the British Isles*. Cambridge, 1973.

Banister, J. *A Synopsis of Husbandry*. London, 1799.

Bankes, J. and Kerridge, E. *The Early Records of the Bankes Family at Winstanley*. Manchester, 1973.

Barley, M. W. 'The Double-Pile House', *Arch. J.*, CXXXVI, 1979.

The English Farmhouse and Cottage. London, 1961.

'A Glossary of Names for Rooms in Houses of the Sixteenth and Seventeenth Centuries', in *Culture and Environment*, ed. I. Ll. Foster and L. Alcock. London, 1963.

The House and Home. London, 1963.

Barley, M. W. and Summers, N. 'Averham Park Lodge and its Paintings', *Thoroton Soc.*, LXV, 1961.

Barnes, D. G. *A History of the English Corn Laws from 1660–1846*. London, 1930. Repr. New York, 1965.

Barratt, D. M. (ed.). *Ecclesiastical Terriers of Warwickshire Parishes, II*. Dugdale Soc., 1971.

Batchelor, T. *General View of the Agriculture of the County of Bedford*. London, 1808.

Batey, Mavis. 'Oliver Goldsmith: An Indictment of Landscape Gardening', in P. Willis (ed.), *Furor Hortensis*. Edinburgh, 1974.

Baxter, R. *The Reverend Richard Baxter's Last Treatise*, ed. F. J. Powicke. Manchester, 1926.

Beale, J. *Herefordshire Orchards*. London, 1657.

Beale, J. and Lawrence, A. *Nurseries, Orchards, Profitable Gardens and Vineyards Encouraged...* London, 1677.

Beastall, T. W. *A North Country Estate*. London and Chichester, 1975.

Beavington, F. 'Early Market Gardening in Bedfordshire', *Inst. Brit. Geographers*, XXXVII, 1965.

Beckett, J. V. *Coal and Tobacco: The Lowthers and the Economic Development of West Cumberland, 1660–1760*. Cambridge, 1981.

'English Landownership in the Later Seventeenth and Eighteenth Centuries: The Debate and the Problems', EcHR, 2nd ser., XXX, 4, 1977.

'Regional Variation and the Agricultural Depression, 1730–50', EcHR, 2nd ser., XXXV, 1982.

Bell, V. *To Meet Mr. Ellis: Little Gaddesden in the Eighteenth Century*. London, 1956.

Bennett, M. K. 'British Wheat Yield per Acre for Seven Centuries', *Ec. Hist.*, III, 1935.

Beresford, M. W. 'The Common Informer, the Penal Statutes, and Economic Regulation', EcHR, 2nd ser., X, 1957.

'Glebe Terriers and Open Field Leicestershire', in *Studies in Leicestershire Agrarian History*, ed. W. G. Hoskins. Leicester, 1949.

'Glebe Terriers and Open-Field Yorkshire', *Yorks. Arch. J.*, XXXVII, 1951.

'Habitation versus Improvement', in *Essays in the Economic and Social History of Tudor and Stuart England*, ed. F. J. Fisher. Cambridge, 1961.

Best, Henry. *Rural Economy in Yorkshire in 1641, being the Farming and Account Books of Henry Best of Elmswell, East Riding of Yorkshire*. Surtees Soc., XXXIII. 1851.

Bettey, J. 'The Cultivation of Woad in the Salisbury Area during the Late Sixteenth and Early Seventeenth Centuries', *Textile Hist.*, IX, 1978.

Bigmore, P. *The Bedfordshire and Huntingdonshire Landscape*. London, 1979.

Billing, R. *An Account of the Culture of Carrots*. London, 1765.

Blake, S. *The Compleat Gardener's Practice*. London, 1664.

Blith, W. *The English Improver*. London, 1649. 2nd edn. 1649.

The English Improver Improved. 3rd edn. London, 1652. 4th edn. 1653.

Blome, R. *Britannia*. London, 1673.

Blomefield, F. *An Essay towards a Topographical History of Norfolk*. 5 vols. Norwich and King's Lynn, 1739–75. 2nd edn. 11 vols. 1805–20.

Blundell, N. *The Great Diurnall of Nicholas Blundell of Little Crosby*, ed. J. S. Bagley. 3 vols. Lancs. & Cheshire Rec. Soc. Manchester, 1968–72.

Bonfield, L. 'Marriage Settlements and the "Rise of Great Estates": The Demographic Aspect', EcHR, 2nd ser., XXXII, 1979.

Bonser, K. J. *The Drovers*. London, 1970.

Bouch, C. M. L. and Jones, G. P. *The Lake Counties, 1500–1830*. Manchester, 1961.

Bowden, P. J. *The Wool Trade in Tudor and Stuart England*. London, 1962.

Boys, J. *General View of the Agriculture of the County of Kent*. London, 1813.

Brace, H. W. *A History of Seed Crushing in Great Britain*. London, 1960.

[Braddon, L.]. *To Pay Old Debts without New Taxes by Charitably Relieving, Politically Reforming, and Judiciously Employing the Poor*. London, 1723.

Bradley, R. *A General Treatise of Husbandry and Gardening, II*. London, 1726.

Brigg, M. 'The Forest of Pendle in the Seventeenth Century', *Hist. Soc. Lancs. & Cheshire*, CXIII, 1961.

Broad, J. 'Alternative Husbandry and Permanent Pasture in the Midlands, 1650–1800', AHR, XXVIII, 2, 1980.

Brodrick, G. C. *English Land and English Landlords*. London, 1881.

Brooks, C. E. P. *Climate through the Ages*. 2nd edn. London, 1949.

Brown, E. H. Phelps and Hopkins, S. V. 'Builders' Wage-Rates, Prices and Population: Some Further Evidence', *Economica*, NS, XXVI, 1959.

'Seven Centuries of the Prices of Consumables, compared with Builders' Wage-Rates', *Economica*, NS, XXIII, 1956.

Brown, J. *General View of the Agriculture of the County of Derby*. London, 1794.

Brunskill, R. W. *Illustrated Handbook of Vernacular Architecture*. London, 1970.

Buchanan, K. M. 'Studies in the Localisation of Seventeenth-Century Worcestershire Industries, 1600–1650', *Worcs. Arch. Soc.*, XVII, 1940; XIX, 1943.

Bulkeley, W. 'The Diary of William Bulkeley of Brynddu, Anglesey', ed. H. Owen, *Anglesey Antiq. Soc.*, 1931.

Campbell, Colin. *Vitruvius Britannicus, or the British Architect*. 3 vols. London, 1715–25.

Campbell, M. *The English Yeoman*. New Haven, 1942.

Carter, E. *A History of Cambridgeshire*. London, 1819.

Carter, W. *The Proverb Crossed*. London, 1677.

Cartwright, J. J. (ed.). *The Travels through England of Dr. Richard Pococke*. 2 vols. Camden Soc., NS, XLII, XLIV, 1888–9.

Cathcart, Earl. 'Jethro Tull, his Life, Times and Teaching', *J. RASE*, 3rd ser., II, I, 1891.

Chalklin, C. W. 'The Rural Economy of a Kentish Wealden Parish, 1650–1750', AHR, X, 1962.

Seventeenth Century Kent: A Social and Economic History. London, 1965.

Chalklin, C. W. and Havinden, M. A. (eds.). *Rural Change and Urban Growth, 1500–1800: Essays in English Regional History in Honour of W. G. Hoskins*. London, 1974.

Chambers, J. D. *Nottinghamshire in the Eighteenth Century*. London, 1932.

Chambers, J. D. and Mingay, G. E. *The Agricultural Revolution, 1750–1880*. London, 1966.

Chapman, S. D. 'The Genesis of the British Hosiery Industry, 1600–1750', *Textile Hist.*, III, 1972.

Chartres, J. A. *Internal Trade in England, 1500–1700*. London, 1977.
  'Road Carrying in England in the Seventeenth Century: Myths and Reality',
    EcHR, 2nd ser., XXX, 1977.
Chauncy, H. *Historical Antiquities of Hertfordshire* (1700). Bishop's Stortford, 1826.
Chesney, H. E. 'The Transference of Lands in England, 1640–60', *Trans. RHS*, 4th
    ser., XV, 1932.
Chibnall, A. C. *Sherington: The Fiefs and Fields of a Buckinghamshire Village*.
    Cambridge, 1965.
Child, Sir J. *Discourse about Trade*. London, 1690.
  New Discourse of Trade. London, 1694.
Clapham, Sir John. *A Concise Economic History of Britain from the Earliest Times to
    1750*. Cambridge, 1949.
Clarke, P. and Slack, P. (eds.). *Crisis and Order in English Towns, 1500–1700*. London,
    1972.
Clarkson, L. A. 'The Leather Crafts in Tudor and Stuart England', AHR, XIV, 1,
    1966.
  The Pre-Industrial Economy in England, 1500–1750. London, 1971.
Clay, C. '"The Greed of Whig Bishops"? Church Landlords and their Lessees,
    1660–1760', *PP*, no. 87. 1980.
  'Marriage, Inheritance, and the Rise of Large Estates in England, 1660–1815',
    EcHR, 2nd ser., XXI, 3, 1968.
  'The Misfortunes of William, Fourth Lord Petre', *Recusant Hist.*, XI, 2, 1971.
  'The Price of Freehold Land in the Later Seventeenth and Eighteenth Centuries',
    EcHR, 2nd ser., XXVII, 2, 1974.
  Public Finance and Private Wealth. Oxford, 1978.
Cliffe, J. T. *The Yorkshire Gentry from the Reformation to the Civil War*. London,
    1969.
Clifton-Taylor, A. *The Pattern of English Building*. London, 1972.
Coate, M. *Cornwall in the Great Civil War and Interregnum*. 2nd edn. Truro, 1963.
Coleman, D. C. *The Economy of England, 1450–1750*. Oxford, 1977.
  'Growth and Decay during the Industrial Revolution: The Case of East Anglia',
    Scand. Ec. Hist. Rev., X, 1962.
  'An Innovation and its Diffusion: The "New Draperies"', EcHR, 2nd ser., XXII,
    1969.
  'Labour in the English Economy of the Seventeenth Century', EcHR, 2nd ser.,
    VIII, 1956.
  'Naval Dockyards under the Later Stuarts', EcHR, 2nd ser., VI, 1953.
  Sir John Banks – Baronet and Businessman. Oxford, 1963.
Coleman, D. C. and John, A. H. (eds.). *Trade, Government and Economy in Pre-Industrial
    England*. London, 1976.
Colville, James (ed.). *Letters of John Cockburn of Ormistoun to his Gardener, 1727–1744*.
    Scottish Hist. Soc., XLV. 1904.
Colvin, H. M. *Biographical Dictionary of British Architects*. London, 1978.
  History of the King's Works, V. London, 1976.
Colvin, H. M. and Harris, J. (eds.). *The Country Seat*. London, 1970.
Colvin, H. M. and Newman, J. (eds.). *Of Building – Roger North's Writings on
    Architecture*. Oxford, 1981.

Colyer, R. J. 'Cattle Drovers in the Nineteenth Century', *Nat. Lib. Wales J.*, XVIII, 1973–4.
　The Welsh Cattle Drovers. Cardiff, 1976.
Cooper, J. P. 'Patterns of Inheritance and Settlement by Great Landowners', in J. Goody *et al.* (eds.), *Family and Inheritance*. Cambridge, 1976.
　'The Social Distribution of Land and Men in England, 1436–1700', EcHR, 2nd ser., XX, 1967.
Cordingley, R. A. 'British Historical Roof-Types and their Members', *Ancient Monuments Soc.*, NS, IX, 1961.
Cornwall, J. C. K. 'Agricultural Improvement, 1560–1640', *Sussex Arch. Coll.*, XCVIII, 1960.
Court, W. H. B. *The Rise of the Midland Industries, 1600–1838*. Rev. edn. Oxford, 1953.
Cox, T. *Magna Britannia*. London, 1720.
Cracknell, B. E. *Canvey Island*. Leicester, 1959.
Cranfield, G. A. *The Development of the Provincial Newspaper, 1700–1760*. Oxford, 1962.
Crosweller, W. T. *The Gardeners' Company: A Short Chronological History, 1605–1907*. London, 1908.
Darby, H. C. *The Draining of the Fens*. Cambridge, 1940. 2nd edn. 1956.
Davies, Margaret G. 'Country Gentry and Falling Rents in the 1660s and 1670s', *Midland Hist.*, IV, 2, 1977.
Davies, Walter. *A General View of the Agriculture and Domestic Economy of South Wales*. 2 vols. London, 1815.
Davis, O. R. F. 'The Wealth and Influence of John Holles, Duke of Newcastle, 1694–1711', *Renaissance & Mod. Stud.*, IX, 1965.
Davis, R. *General View of the Agriculture of the County of Oxford*. London, 1794.
Davis, T. *General View of the Agriculture of the County of Wiltshire*. London, 1794.
Deane, P. and Cole, W. A. *British Economic Growth, 1688–1959*. Cambridge, 1962. 2nd edn. 1969.
Defoe, Daniel. *The Complete English Tradesman*. 2 vols. London, 1745.
　A Tour through the Whole Island of Great Britain, ed. G. D. H. Cole and D. C. Browning. 2 vols. London, 1962.
Dell, R. F. 'The Decline of the Clothing Industry in Berkshire', *Newbury & Dist. Field Club*, X, 1954.
Dexter, K. and Barber, D. *Farming for Profits*. London, 1961.
Dodd, A. H. 'Caernarvonshire in the Civil War', *Caerns. Hist. Soc.*, XIV, 1953.
　'The Civil War in East Denbighshire', *Denbs. Hist. Soc.*, III, 1954.
　'Flintshire Politics in the Seventeenth Century', *Flints. Hist. Soc.*, 1953–4.
　The Industrial Revolution in North Wales. Cardiff, 1933.
　Life in Wales. London, 1972.
　'The North Wales Coal Industry during the Industrial Revolution', *Arch. Cambrensis*, LXXXIV, 1929.
　'The Pattern of Politics in Stuart Wales', *Hon. Soc. Cymmrodorion*, 1948.
　Studies in Stuart Wales. 2nd edn. Cardiff, 1971.
Doddington, George Bubb. *The Political Journal of George Bubb Doddington*, ed. J. Carswell and L. A. Dralle. London, 1965.

Donnelly, T. 'Arthur Clephane, Edinburgh Merchant and Seedsman', AHR, xviii, 2, 1970.

Dony, J. G. *A History of the Straw Hat Industry*. Luton, 1942.

Doughty, H. M. *Chronicles of Theberton*. London, 1910.

Douglas, J. 'The Culture of Saffron', *Philos. Trans. Roy. Soc.*, xxxv, 1728.

Downes, K. *English Baroque Architecture*. London, 1966.

Driver, A. and Driver, W. *General View of the Agriculture of the County of Hampshire*. London, 1794.

Drummond, J. C. and Wilbraham, A. *The Englishman's Food*, rev. D. Hollingsworth. London, 1957.

Dugdale, W. *The History of Imbanking and Drayning*. London, 1662.

Dyer, Alan. 'Growth and Decay in English Towns, 1500–1700', *Urban Hist. Yearbook*, 1979.

Eaton, Daniel. *The Letters of Daniel Eaton to the Third Earl of Cardigan, 1725–32*, ed. Joan Wake and Deborah Champion Webster. Northants. Rec. Soc., xxiv. 1971.

Edie, C. A. *The Irish Cattle Bills: A Study in Restoration Politics*. Amer. Philos. Soc., NS LX. 1970.

Edmunds, Henry. 'History of the Brecknockshire Agricultural Society, 1755–1955', *Brycheiniog*, iii, 1957.

Edwards, J. K. 'The Gurneys and the Norwich Clothing Trade in the Eighteenth Century', *JFHS*, L, 1962–4.

Edwards, P. R. 'The Cattle Trade of Shropshire in the Late Sixteenth and Seventeenth Centuries', *Midland Hist.*, vi, 1981.
 'The Development of Dairy Farming on the North Shropshire Plain in the Seventeenth Century', *Midland Hist.*, iv, 3–4, 1978.
 'The Horse Trade of the Midlands in the Seventeenth Century', AHR, xxvii, 2, 1979.

Ellis, W. *Chiltern and Vale Farming Explained*. London, 1733.
 A Compleat System of Experienced Improvements. London, 1749.
 The Compleat Planter and Cyderist. London, 1756.
 The Practical Farmer, or The Hertfordshire Husbandman. London, 1732. 2nd edn., 2 pts. 1732.
 The Modern Husbandman. 8 vols. London, 1750.

Emery, Frank V. 'Early Cultivation of Clover in Gower', *J. Gower Soc.*, xxvi, 1975.
 'The Mechanics of Innovation: Clover Cultivation in Wales before 1750', *J. Hist. Geog.*, ii, 1, 1976.
 'A New Account of Snowdonia, 1693, Written for Edward Lhuyd', *Nat. Lib. Wales J.*, xviii, 1974.

Emery, Frank V. and Smith, C. G. 'A Weather Record from Snowdonia, 1697–98', *Weather*, xxxi, 1976.

Evans, E. J. *The Contentious Tithe*. London, 1976.
 'Tithing Customs and Disputes: The Evidence of Glebe Terriers, 1698–1850', AHR, xviii, 1, 1970.

Evans, G. N. 'The Artisan and Small Farmer in Mid-Eighteenth Century Anglesey', *Anglesey Antiq. Soc.*, 1933.

Evelyn, John. *Acetaria: A Discourse of Sallets*. London, 1699.
 Diary, ed. E. S. de Beer. 6 vols. Oxford, 1955.
 Sylva...to which is annexed Pomona. London, 1664.

Everitt, Alan M. 'The English Urban Inn, 1560–1760', in *Perspectives in English Urban History*, ed. Alan Everitt. London, 1973.
'Social Mobility in Early Modern England', *PP*, no. 33, 1966.
Eversley, D. E. C. 'A Survey of Population in an Area of Worcestershire from 1660 to 1850 on the Basis of Parish Registers', in *Population in History*, ed. D. V. Glass and D. E. C. Eversley. London, 1965.
Ferris, J. P. and Oliver, R. C. B. 'An Agricultural Improvement of 1674 at Trewern, Llanfihangel-Nant-Melan', *Radnors. Soc.*, XLII, 1972.
Fieldhouse, R. T. 'Agriculture in Wensleydale from 1600 to the Present Day', *Northern Hist.*, XVI, 1980.
Fieldhouse, R. T. and Jennings, B. *A History of Richmond and Swaledale*. Chichester, 1978.
Fiennes, Celia. *The Journeys of Celia Fiennes*, ed. C. Morris. London, 1947.
Firth, C. H. and Rait, R. S. (eds.). *Acts and Ordinances of the Interregnum, 1642–60*. 3 vols. London, 1911.
Fisher, F. J. 'The Development of London as a Centre of Conspicuous Consumption in the Sixteenth and Seventeenth Centuries', in *Essays in Economic History, II*, ed. E. M.Carus-Wilson. London, 1962. (Repr. from RHS, 4th ser., xxx, 1948.)
'The Development of the London Food Market, 1540–1640', in *Essays in Economic History, I*, ed. E. M. Carus-Wilson. London, 1954. (Repr. from EcHR, v, 1935.)
Fisher, F. J. (ed.). *Essays in the Economic and Social History of Tudor and Stuart England*. Cambridge, 1961.
Fisher, H. E. S. 'Anglo-Portuguese Trade, 1700–1770', EcHR, 2nd ser., XVI, 1963.
Fletcher, A. J. *A County Community in Peace and War: Sussex, 1600–1660*. London, 1975.
Flinn, M. W. 'The Growth of the English Iron Industry, 1660–1760', EcHR, 2nd ser., XI, 1958.
Fowler, J. and Cornforth, J. *English Decoration in the Eighteenth Century*. London, 1974.
Fox, Sir Cyril and Raglan, Lord. *Monmouthshire Houses*. 3 vols. Nat. Museum of Wales, 1953–4.
Fox, H. S. A. and Butlin, R. A. (eds.). *Change in the Countryside: Essays on Rural England, 1500–1900*. Inst. Brit. Geographers, Special Publ., no. 10. London, 1979.
Freeman, C. *Pillow Lace in the East Midlands*. Luton, 1958.
Fuller, T. *The Worthies of England*, ed. J. Freeman. London, 1952.
Fussell, G. E. *The English Dairy Farmer, 1500–1900*. London, 1966.
'Four Centuries of Farming Systems in Hampshire, 1500–1900', *Hants. Field Club & Arch. Soc.*, XVII, 3, 1949.
'Four Centuries of Leicestershire Farming', in *Studies in Leicestershire Agrarian History*, ed. W. G. Hoskins. Leicester, 1949.
'History of Cole (*Brassica* sp.)', *Nature, London*, 9 July 1955.
The Old English Farming Books from Fitzherbert to Tull, 1523 to 1730. London, 1947.
Fussell, G. E. and Goodman, Constance. 'Eighteenth-Century Traffic in Livestock', *Ec. Hist.*, III, 1936.
Garret[t], Daniel. *Designs and Estimates for Farm Houses...* 3rd edn. London, 1772.
Gazley, J. G. *The Life of Arthur Young, 1741–1820*. Philadelphia, 1973.

Gentles, I. 'The Sales of Bishops' Lands in the English Revolution, 1646–1660', EHR, XCV, 1980.

'The Sales of Crown Lands during the English Revolution', EcHR, 2nd ser., XXVI, 4, 1973.

Gerarde, John. *The Herbal, or General Historie of Plantes.* London, 1636.

Gill, H. and Guilford, E. L. (eds.). *The Rector's Book of Clayworth, Notts.* Nottingham, 1910.

Girouard, M. *Robert Smythson.* London, 1966.

Girouard, Mark. *Life in the English Country House: A Social and Architectural History.* New Haven and London, 1978.

Godber, Joyce. *History of Bedfordshire, 1066–1888.* Bedford, 1969.

Godfrey, W. H. *The English Almshouse.* London, 1955.

Gooder, A. *Plague and Enclosure: A Warwickshire Village in the Seventeenth Century.* Coventry & N. War., Hist. Pamphlets, no. 2. 1965.

'The Population Crisis of 1727–30 in Warwickshire', *Midland Hist.*, I, 4, 1972.

Gough, R. *Antiquityes and Memoyres of the Parish of Myddle.* London, 1875.

Grainger, J. *General View of the Agriculture of Co. Durham.* London, 1794.

Granger, C. W. J. and Elliott, C. M. 'A Fresh Look at Wheat Prices and Markets in the Eighteenth Century', EcHR, 2nd ser., XX, 1967.

Gras, N. S. B. *The Evolution of the English Corn Market from the Twelfth to the Eighteenth Century.* Harvard Ec. Stud., XIII. Cambridge, Mass., 1915.

Gray, H. L. *English Field Systems.* Cambridge, Mass., 1915.

'Yeoman Farming in Oxfordshire from the Sixteenth Century to the Nineteenth Century', *Qtly J. Ec.*, XXIV, 1910.

Green, D. *Gardener to Queen Anne: Henry Wise and the Formal Garden.* Oxford, 1956.

Green, F. 'The Stepneys of Prendergast', *W. Wales Hist. Rec.*, VII, 1917–18.

Green, I. M. 'The Persecution of Parish Clergy during the English Civil War', EHR, XCIV, 1979.

Gunther, R. T. *The Architecture of Sir Roger Pratt.* Oxford, 1928.

Habakkuk, H. J. 'Daniel Finch, 2nd Earl of Nottingham: His House and Estate', in *Studies in Social History*, ed. J. H. Plumb. London, 1955.

'The English Land Market in the Eighteenth Century', in *Britain and the Netherlands*, ed. J. S. Bromley and E. H. Kossmann. London, 1960.

'English Landownership, 1680–1740', EcHR, X, 1940.

'The Land Settlement and the Restoration of Charles II', RHS, 5th ser., XXVIII, 1978.

'Landowners and the Civil War', EcHR, 2nd ser., XVIII, 1965.

'Marriage Settlements in the Eighteenth Century', RHS, 4th ser., XXXII, 1950.

'Public Finance and the Sale of Confiscated Property during the Interregnum', EcHR, 2nd ser., XV, 1962–3.

'The Rise and Fall of English Landed Families, 1600–1800', RHS, 5th ser., XXIX–XXX, 1979–80.

Hadfield, Miles. *A History of British Gardening.* London, 1969.

Halfpenny, William. *Twelve Beautiful Designs for Farmhouses.* London, 1750.

Hammersley, G. 'The Charcoal Iron Industry and its Fuel, 1540–1750', EcHR, 2nd ser., XXVI, 1973.

'The Crown Woods and their Exploitation in the Sixteenth and Seventeenth Centuries', *Bull. IHR*, XXX, 1957.

Harris, A. 'The Agriculture of the East Riding before the Parliamentary Enclosures', *Yorks. Arch. J.*, XL, 1962.

The Open Fields of East Yorkshire. York, 1959.

Hartley, M. and Ingilby, J. *The Old Hand-Knitters of the Dales*. Clapham, 1951.

Hartlib, S. *His Legacie, or An Enlargement of the Discours of Husbandrie Used in Brabant and Flanders*. London, 1651. 2nd edn. 1652.

[C. Dymock]. *A Discovery for Division or Setting Out of Land*. London, 1653.

Harvey, John H. *Early Gardening Catalogues*. London, 1972.

Early Nurserymen. London, 1974.

'The Family of Telford, Nurserymen of York', *Yorks. Arch. J.*, XLII, 167, 1969.

'Leonard Gurle's Nurseries and Some Others', *Garden Hist.*, III, 3, 1975.

'The Nurseries on Milne's Land-Use Map', *London & Middx Arch. Soc.*, XXIV, 1973.

'The Stocks Held by Early Nurseries', AHR, XXII, 1, 1974.

Havinden, M. A. 'Agricultural Progress in Open Field Oxfordshire', AHR, IX, 2, 1961.

Henrey, Blanche. *British Botanical and Horticultural Literature before 1800*. 3 vols. Oxford, 1975.

Henstock, A. 'Cheese Manufacture and Marketing in Derbyshire and North Staffordshire, 1670–1870', *Derbs. Arch. J.*, LXXXIX, 1969.

Hervey, Lord Francis (ed.). *Suffolk in the Seventeenth Century: A Breviary of Suffolk by Robert Reyce, 1618*. London, 1902.

Hey, D. *An English Rural Community: Myddle under the Tudors and Stuarts*. Leicester, 1974.

Packmen, Carriers and Packhorse Roads. Leicester, 1980.

The Rural Metalworkers of the Sheffield Region. Leicester, 1972.

Hill, M. C. 'The Wealdmoors, 1560–1660', *Shrops. Arch. J.*, LIV, 1951–3.

Hill, O. and Cornforth, J. *English Country Houses: Caroline*. London, 1966.

Holderness, B. A. 'The Agricultural Activities of the Massingberds of South Ormsby, Lincolnshire, 1638 – c. 1750', *Midland Hist.*, I, 3, 1972.

'Capital Formation in Agriculture', in *Aspects of Capital Investment in Great Britain, 1750–1850*, ed. J. P. P. Higgins and S. Pollard. London, 1971.

'Credit in English Rural Society before the Nineteenth Century', AHR, XXIV, 1976.

'The English Land Market in the Eighteenth Century: The Case of Lincolnshire', EcHR, 2nd ser., XXVII, 4, 1974.

Holiday, P. G. 'Land Sales and Repurchases in Yorkshire after the Civil Wars, 1650–1670', *Northern Hist.*, V, 1970.

Holland, H. *General View of the Agriculture of Cheshire*. London, 1808.

Hollingsworth, T. H. 'The Demography of the British Peerage', suppl. to *Pop. Stud.*, XVIII, 1964.

Holmes, G. S. 'Gregory King and the Social Structure of Pre-Industrial England', RHS, 5th ser., XXVII, 1977.

Holt, J. *General View of the Agriculture of the County of Lancaster*. London, 1795.

Hopkins, E. 'The Bridgewater Estates in North Shropshire during the Civil War', *Shrops. Arch. Soc.*, LVI, 2, 1960.

'The Re-Leasing of the Ellesmere Estates, 1637–42', AHR, X, 1, 1962.

Hoskins, W. G. 'Harvest Fluctuations and English Economic History, 1620–1759', AHR, XVI, 1, 1968.

Houghton, John. *A Collection for Improvement of Husbandry and Trade.* 9 vols. London, 1692–1703. Ed. R. Bradley. 4 vols. London, 1727–8.

A Collection of Letters for the Improvement of Husbandry and Trade. 2 vols. London, 1681–3.

Howard, C. 'The Culture of Saffron', *Philos. Trans. Roy. Soc.*, XII, 1678.

Howells, B. E. (ed.). *A Calendar of Letters relating to North Wales.* Cardiff, 1967.

Hughes, E. *North Country Life in the Eighteenth Century: The North-East, 1700–1750.* Oxford, 1952.

North Country Life in the Eighteenth Century, II, Cumberland & Westmorland, 1700–1830. Oxford, 1965.

Hull, F. 'The Tufton Sequestration Papers', *Kent Rec.*, XVII, 1960.

Hussey, C. *English Country Houses: Early Georgian.* London, 1965.

Innocent, C. F. *The Development of English Building Construction.* Cambridge, 1916. Newton Abbot, 1971.

Jacob, G. *The Country Gentleman's Vade Mecum.* London, 1717.

James, M. 'The Political Importance of the Tithes Controversy in the English Revolution, 1640–60', *Hist.*, XXVI, 1941.

James, W. and Malcolm, J. *General View of the Agriculture of the County of Buckingham.* London, 1794.

General View of the Agriculture of the County of Surrey. London, 1793.

Jancey, E. M. 'An Eighteenth-Century Steward and his Work', *Shrops. Arch. Soc.*, LVI, 1, 1957–8.

'The Hon. and Rev. Richard Hill of Hawkstone, 1655–1727', *ibid.*, LV, 1954–6.

Jenkins, J. G. *The Welsh Woollen Industry.* Cardiff, 1969.

The English Farm Waggon: Origins and Structure. Newton Abbot, 1972.

Jenkins, R. 'Suffolk Industries: An Historical Survey', *Newcomen Soc.*, XIX, 1940.

Jennings, B. (ed.). *A History of Harrogate and Knaresborough.* Huddersfield, 1970.

A History of Nidderdale. Huddersfield, 1976.

John, A. H. 'Agricultural Productivity and Economic Growth in England, 1700–1760', *J. Ec. Hist.*, XXV, 1965.

'The Course of Agricultural Change, 1660–1760', in *Studies in the Industrial Revolution*, ed. L. S. Pressnell. London, 1960. Repr. in W. E. Minchinton (ed.), *Essays in Agrarian History*, I. Newton Abbot, 1968.

'English Agricultural Improvement and Grain Exports, 1660–1765', in D. C. Coleman and A. H. John (eds.), *Trade, Government and Economy in Pre-Industrial England.* London, 1976.

The Industrial Development of South Wales, 1750–1850. Cardiff, 1950.

'Iron and Coal on a Glamorgan Estate, 1700–40', EcHR, XIII, 1943.

Johnson, George W. *A History of English Gardening.* London, 1829.

Jones, E. L. 'Agricultural Conditions and Changes in Herefordshire, 1600–1815', *Woolhope Naturalists' Field Club*, XXXVII, 1962.

'Agricultural Origins of Industry', *PP*, no. 40, 1968.

'Agricultural Productivity and Economic Growth, 1700–1760', in E. L. Jones (ed.), *Agriculture and Economic Growth in England, 1650–1815.* London, 1967.

'Agriculture and Economic Growth in England, 1660–1750: Agricultural Change', *J. Ec. Hist.*, XXV, 1965.

'Eighteenth-Century Changes in Hampshire Chalkland Farming', AHR, VIII, 1, 1960.

Seasons and Prices: The Role of Weather in English Agricultural History. London, 1964.

Jones, F. 'The Old Families of Wales', in *Wales in the Eighteenth Century*, ed. D. Moore. Swansea, 1976.

'A Squire of Anglesey', *Anglesey Antiq. Soc.*, 1940.

'The Vaughans of Golden Grove. I, The Earls of Carbery', *Hon. Soc. Cymmrodorion*, 1963, pt 1.

'The Vaughans of Golden Grove. II, Anne, Duchess of Bolton, 1690–1715', *ibid.*, 1963, pt 2.

'The Vaughans of Golden Grove. III, Torycoed, Shenfield, Golden Grove', *ibid.*, 1964, pt 2.

Jones, G. P. 'Sources of Loans and Credits in Cumbria before the Rise of Banks', *CW2*, LXXV, 1975.

Jones, Stanley and Smith, J. T. 'Breconshire Houses', *Brycheiniog*, IX, 1963.

Kalm, Pehr. *Kalm's Account of his Visit to England on his Way to America in 1748*, ed. J. Lucas. London, 1892.

Kelch, R. A. *Newcastle: A Duke without Money: Thomas Pelham-Holles 1693–1768*. London, 1974.

Kent, N. *General View of the Agriculture of Norfolk*. London, 1796.

Hints to Gentlemen of Landed Property. London, 1775.

Kenyon, G. H. 'Kirdford Inventories, 1611 to 1776, with Particular Reference to the Weald Clay Farming', *Sussex Arch. Coll.*, XCIII, 1955.

'Petworth Town and Trades, 1610–1760', *ibid.*, XCVI, 1958.

Kerridge, E. *The Agricultural Revolution*. London, 1967.

Agrarian Problems in the Sixteenth Century and After. London, 1969.

'The Sheepfold in Wiltshire and the Floating of the Water Meadows', EcHR, 2nd ser., VI, 1954.

'Turnip Husbandry in High Suffolk', EcHR, 2nd ser., VII, 1956.

Lambton, L. *Temples of Convenience*. London, 1978.

Lane, Carolina. 'The Development of Pastures and Meadows during the Sixteenth and Seventeenth Centuries', AHR, XXVIII, 1980.

Langley, Batty. *The City and Country Builder's and Workman's Treasury of Designs*. London, 1745. Repr. 1969.

La Quintinye, M. de. *The Complete Gard'ner*, tr. G. London and H. Wise. London, 1701.

Laurence, Edward. *The Duty of a Steward to his Lord*. London, 1727.

Laurence, John. *A New System of Agriculture*. London, 1726.

Law, C. M. and Hooson, D. J. M. 'The Straw Plait and Straw Hat Industries of the South Midlands', *E. Midlands Geographer*, IV, 6, 1968.

[Lee, J.]. *Considerations concerning Common Fields*. London, 1654.

Lees–Milne, J. *English Country Houses: Baroque, 1685–1715*. London, 1970.

Leigh, C. *The Natural History of Lancashire, Cheshire and the Peak of Derbyshire*. Oxford, 1700.

Lennard, R. V. 'English Agriculture under Charles II: The Evidence of the Royal Society's "Enquiries"', EcHR, IV, 1932.

L'Estrange, R. *A Treatise of Wool and Cattel*. London, 1677.

Lewis, W. J. 'The Cwmsymlog Lead Mine', *Ceredigion*, II, 1, 1952.

Lightoler, Thomas. *Gentleman and Farmer's Architect*. London, 1762.

Linnard, W. 'A Glimpse of Gwydyr Forest and the Timber Trade in North Wales in the Late 17th Century', *Nat. Lib. Wales J.*, XVIII, 1974.

Linnell, C. D. 'The Matmakers of Pavenham', *Beds. Mag.*, 1, 1947.

Lisle, Edward. *Observations in Husbandry*. London, 1757. 2nd edn. 2 vols. London, 1757.

Lloyd, T. H. *The Movement of Wool Prices in Medieval England*. EcHR suppl., no. 6. Cambridge, 1973.

Lodge, E. C. (ed.). *The Account Book of a Kentish Estate, 1616–1704*. Oxford, 1927.

Long, W. H. 'Regional Farming in Seventeenth-Century Yorkshire', *AHR*, VIII, 2, 1960.

Loudon, J. C. *An Encyclopaedia of Gardening*. London, 1822.

Lowe, N. *The Lancashire Textile Industry in the Sixteenth Century*. Manchester, 1972.

Lowe, R. *General View of the Agriculture of Nottinghamshire*. London, 1798.

McCutcheon, K. L. *Yorkshire Fairs and Markets*, Thoresby Soc., XXXIX. 1940.

Machin, R. 'The Great Rebuilding: A Reassessment', *PP*, no. 77, 1977.

Machin, R. (ed.). *Probate Inventories and Memorial Excepts of Chetnole, Leigh and Yetminster*. Bristol, 1976.

Madge, S. J. *The Domesday of Crown Lands*. London, 1938.

Manley, G. *Climate and the British Scene*. London, 1952.

Manning, B. *The English People and the English Revolution*. London, 1976.

Markham, G. *The Inrichment of the Weald of Kent*. London, 1625.

Marshall, G. 'The "Rotherham" Plough', *Tools & Tillage*, III, 3, 1978.

Marshall, J. D. *Furness and the Industrial Revolution*. Barrow in Furness, 1958.
    Kendal, 1661–1801: The Growth of a Modern Town. Kendal, 1975.
    Old Lakeland. Newton Abbot, 1971.

Marshall, W. *Review and Abstract of the County Reports to the Board of Agriculture*. 5 vols. London and York, 1808–17. 5 vols. in 1. 1818.
    The Rural Economy of Gloucestershire. 2 vols. Gloucester, 1789.
    The Rural Economy of the Midland Counties. 2 vols. London, 1790. 2nd edn. 1796.
    The Rural Economy of Norfolk. 2 vols. London, 1787.
    Rural Economy of the Southern Counties. 2 vols. London, 1798.
    The Rural Economy of Yorkshire. 2 vols. London, 1788.

Mathias, P. *The Brewing Industry in England, 1700–1830*. Cambridge, 1959.

Mavor, W. *General View of the Agriculture of Berkshire*. London, 1809.

Meager, Leonard. *The English Gardener*. London, 1670.

Meek, M. 'Hempen Cloth Industry in Suffolk', *Suffolk Rev.*, II, 1961.

Mercer, Eric. *English Vernacular Houses: A Study of Traditional Farmhouses and Cottages*. RCHM (England). London, 1975.

Meredith, R. 'A Derbyshire Family in the Seventeenth Century: The Eyres of Hassop and their Forfeited Estates', *Recusant Hist.*, VIII, 1965.

Michell, A. R. 'Sir Richard Weston and the Spread of Clover Cultivation', *AHR*, XXII, 2, 1974.

Middleton, J. *General View of the Agriculture of Middlesex*. 2nd edn. London, 1807.

Millward, R. 'The Cumbrian Town between 1600 and 1800', in *Rural Change and Urban Growth, 1500–1800*, ed. C. W. Chalklin and M. A. Havinden. London, 1974.

Mingay, G. E. 'The Agricultural Depression, 1730–1750', EcHR, 2nd ser., VIII, 1956.
  'The Eighteenth Century Land Steward', in *Land, Labour and Population in the Industrial Revolution*, ed. E. L. Jones and G. E. Mingay. London, 1967.
  English Landed Society in the Eighteenth Century. London, 1963.
  'Estate Management in Eighteenth-Century Kent', AHR, IV, 1, 1956.
  'The Size of Farms in the Eighteenth Century', EcHR, 2nd ser., XIV, 3, 1962.
Mitchell, B. R. with Deane, P. *Abstract of British Historical Statistics.* Cambridge, 1962.
Moore, B. J. S. *Goods and Chattels of our Forefathers: Frampton Cotterell and District Probate Inventories, 1539–1790.* Chichester, 1976.
Morant, P. *A History of Essex.* London, 1768.
Mordant, J. *The Complete Steward.* 2 vols. London, 1761.
Mortimer, J. *The Whole Art of Husbandry.* London, 1707.
Mullett, C. F. 'The Cattle Distemper in Mid-Eighteenth Century England', *Agric. Hist.*, XX, 3, 1946.
Munby, L. N. (ed.). *East Anglian Studies.* Cambridge, 1968.
Myddelton, W. M. (ed.). *Chirk Castle Accounts, 1666–1753.* Manchester, 1931.
Neve, Richard. *City and Country Purchaser and Builder's Dictionary.* 3rd edn. London, 1736. Repr. Newton Abbot, 1969.
Nichols, J. *The History and Antiquities of the County of Leicester…* 4 vols. London, 1795–1811.
Norden, J. *The Surveyor's Dialogue.* London, 1607.
North, Roger. *The Lives of the Norths*, ed. A. Jessopp. 3 vols. London, 1890.
Oliver, J. 'The Weather and Farming in the Mid-Eighteenth Century in Anglesey', *Nat. Lib. Wales J.*, X, 1958.
Ormrod, D. J. 'Dutch Commercial and Industrial Decline and British Growth in the Late Seventeenth and Early Eighteenth Centuries', in *Failed Transitions to Modern Industrial Society: Renaissance Italy and Seventeenth-Century Holland*, ed. F. Krantz and P. M. Hohenberg. Montreal, 1975.
Osborne, B. S. 'Glamorgan Agriculture in the Seventeenth and Eighteenth Centuries', *Nat. Lib. Wales J.*, XX, 1979.
Outhwaite, R. B. 'Dearth and Government Intervention in English Grain Markets, 1590–1700', EcHR, 2nd ser., XXXIII, 3, 1981.
Overton, M. 'Computer Analysis of an Inconsistent Data Source: The Case of Probate Inventories', *J. Hist. Geog.*, III, 4, 1977.
Owen, L. 'Letters of an Anglesey Parson', *Hon. Soc. Cymmrodorion*, 1961, pt 1.
Owen, W. *Owen's Book of Fairs.* London, 1756.
Parker, R. A. C. *Coke of Norfolk: A Financial and Agricultural Study 1707–1842.* Oxford, 1975.
Parkinson, John. *Paradisi in Sole.* London, 1629.
Parkinson, R. *General View of the Agriculture of Huntingdonshire.* London, 1813.
Patten, J. 'Patterns of Migration and Movement of Labour to Three Pre-Industrial East Anglian Towns', *J. Hist. Geog.*, II, 1976.
  'Population Distribution in Norfolk and Suffolk during the Sixteenth and Seventeenth Centuries', *Inst. Brit. Geographers*, LXV, 1975.
  'Village and Town: An Occupational Study', AHR, XX, 1972.
Peate, I. C. 'A Flintshire Barn at St. Fagan's', *Country Life*, July–Dec. 1952.
  The Welsh House. Liverpool, 1944.

Pelham, R. A. 'The Agricultural Revolution in Hampshire, with Special Reference to the Acreage Returns of 1801', *Hants. Field Club & Arch. Soc.*, XVIII, 1953.

Penney, N. (ed.). *The Household Account Book of Sarah Fell*. Cambridge, 1920.

Perkins, J. A. *Sheep Farming in Eighteenth- and Nineteenth-Century Lincolnshire*. Occ. Papers in Lincs. Hist. & Arch., no. 4, Soc. Lincs. Hist. & Arch. Sleaford, 1977.

Peters, J. E. C. *The Development of Farm Buildings in... Staffordshire*. Manchester, 1969.

Pettit, P. A. J. *The Royal Forests of Northamptonshire: A Study in their Economy, 1558–1714*. Northants. Rec. Soc., XXIII. 1968.

Petty, W. *Economic Writings*...ed. C. H. Hull, Vol. I. Cambridge, 1899.

Pilkington, J. *A View of the Present State of Derbyshire*. Derby, 1789.

Plot, Robert. *The Natural History of Oxfordshire*. Oxford, 1676/7. 2nd edn. 1705.
The Natural History of Staffordshire. Oxford, 1686.

Plumb, J. H. *Sir Robert Walpole*. 3 vols. London, 1956.
'Sir Robert Walpole and Norfolk Husbandry', EcHR, 2nd ser., V, 1952.

Plumb, J. H. (ed.). *Studies in Social History*. London, 1955.

Plymley, J. *General View of the Agriculture of Shropshire*. London, 1803.

Postgate, M. R. 'The Field Systems of Breckland', AHR, X, 1961.

Postlethwayt, Malachy. *Britain's Commercial Interest Explained and Improved...I*. London, 1757.

Poynter, F. N. L. *A Bibliography of Gervase Markham, 1568?–1637*. Oxford, 1962.

Prichard, M. F. Lloyd. 'The Decline of Norwich', EcHR, 2nd ser., III, 1951.

Priest, St John. *General View of the Agriculture of Buckinghamshire*. London, 1813.

Prince, H. *Parks in England*. Shalfleet Manor, I.O.W. 1967.

Pringle, A. *General View of the Agriculture of Westmorland*. Edinburgh, 1794.

Radley, J. 'Holly as a Winter Feed', AHR, IX, 2, 1961.

Raistrick, A. and Jennings, B. *A History of Lead Mining in the Pennines*. London, 1965.

Ramsay, G. D. *The Wiltshire Woollen Industry in the Sixteenth and Seventeenth Centuries*. Oxford, 1943.

Ravensdale, J. R. *Liable to Floods*. Cambridge, 1974.

Rawson, H. Rees. 'The Coal Mining Industry of the Hawarden District on the Eve of the Industrial Revolution', *Arch. Cambrensis*, XCVI, 1941.

Rees, Alwyn. *Life in a Welsh Countryside*. Cardiff, 1950.

Rennie, G. B., Brown, R., and Shirreff, S. *General View of the Agriculture of the West Riding*. London, 1794.

Reyce, R. *See* Hervey (ed.).

Riches, N. *The Agricultural Revolution in Norfolk*. Chapel Hill, 1937.

Roberts, P. 'The Decline of the Welsh Squires in the Eighteenth Century', *Nat. Lib. Wales J.*, XIII, 1963–4.

Roebuck, P. 'Absentee Landownership in the Late Seventeenth and Early Eighteenth Centuries: A Neglected Factor in English Agrarian History', AHR, XXI, 1, 1973.
'The Constables of Everingham: The Fortunes of a Catholic Royalist Family during the Civil War and Interregnum', *Recusant Hist.*, IX, 1967.

Roebuck, P. (ed.). *Constables of Everingham Estate Correspondence, 1726–43*. Yorks. Arch. Soc. Rec. Ser., CXXXVI. 1974.

Rogers, Benjamin. *The Diary of Benjamin Rogers, Rector of Carlton*, ed. C. D. Linnell. Beds. Rec. Soc., XXX. 1950.

Rogers, J. E. T. *A History of Agriculture and Prices in England from 1259 to 1793*. 7 vols. Oxford, 1866–1902.

Rogers, Nathan. *Memoirs of Monmouthshire*. London, 1708.

Rowlands, Henry. *Idea Agriculturae*. Dublin, 1764.

Rowlands, M. B. *Masters and Men in the West Midland Metalware Trades before the Industrial Revolution*. Manchester, 1975.

Salaman, R. N. *The History and Social Influence of the Potato*. Cambridge, 1949.

Salmon, N. *The History of Hertfordshire*. London, 1728.

Scarfe, N. *The Suffolk Landscape*. London, 1972.

Schumpeter, E. B. *English Overseas Trade Statistics, 1697–1808*. Oxford, 1960.

Seaborne, M. *The English School*. London, 1971.

Sharp, Lindsay. 'Timber, Science and Economic Reform in the Seventeenth Century', *Forestry*, XLVIII, 1, 1975.

Sharrock, Robert. *The History of the Propagation and Improvement of Vegetables*. Oxford, 1660.

An Improvement to the Art of Gardening. London, 1694.

Sheail, J. 'Rabbits and Agriculture in Post-Medieval England', *J. Hist. Geog.*, IV, 4, 1978.

Sheppard, J. A. *The Draining of the Hull Valley*. York, 1958.

Sidwell, R. W. 'A Short History of Commercial Horticulture in the Vale of Evesham', *Vale of Evesham Hist. Soc., Research Papers*, II, 1969.

Simpson, A. 'The East Anglian Fold-Course: Some Queries', AHR, VI, 1958.

Skipp, V. *Crisis and Development: An Ecological Case Study of the Forest of Arden, 1570–1674*. Cambridge, 1978.

'Economic and Social Change in the Forest of Arden, 1530–1649', in *Land, Church and People: Essays Presented to Professor H. P. R. Finberg*, ed. Joan Thirsk. Suppl. to AHR, XVIII, 1970.

Slicher van Bath, B. H. 'Yield Ratios, 810–1820', *A.A.G. Bijdragen*, X, 1963.

Smith, J. T. 'The Evolution of the English Peasant House in the Late Seventeenth Century: The Evidence of Buildings', *J. Brit. Arch. Assoc.*, XXXIII, 1970.

'The Long-House in Monmouthshire, a Reappraisal', in *Culture and Environment*, ed. I. Ll. Foster and L. Alcock. London, 1963.

'Medieval Roofs: A Classification', *Arch. J.*, CXII, 1958.

Smith, Peter. *Houses of the Welsh Countryside*. London, 1975.

Smith, W. J. (ed.). *Calendar of Salusbury Correspondence*. Cardiff, 1954.

Herbert Correspondence. Cardiff, 1963.

Smout, T. C. *Scottish Trade on the Eve of Union, 1660–1707*. Edinburgh, 1963.

Speed, Adolphus [Adam]. *Adam Out of Eden*. London, 1659.

Spenceley, G. F. R. 'The Origins of the English Pillow Lace Industry', AHR, XXI, 1973.

Spufford, Margaret. *A Cambridgeshire Community: Chippenham*. Leicester, 1965.

Contrasting Communities: English Villagers in the Sixteenth and Seventeenth Centuries. Cambridge, 1974.

Stanes, R. G. F. (ed.). 'A Georgicall Account of Devonshire and Cornwalle in Answer to Some Queries concerning Agriculture, by Samuel Colepresse, 1667', *Devonshire Assoc.*, XCVI, 1964.

Steer, F. W. (ed.). *Farm and Cottage Inventories of Mid-Essex, 1635–1749*. Chelmsford, 1950.

Steers, J. A. *The Coastline of England and Wales.* Cambridge, 1946.

Steers, J. A. (ed.). *Cambridge and its Region.* Cambridge, 1965.

Stern, W. M. 'Cheese Shipped Coastwise to London towards the Middle of the Eighteenth Century', *Guildhall Misc.*, IV, 1973.

Stone, L. *Crisis of the Aristocracy, 1538–1641.* Oxford, 1965.

  Family and Fortune: Studies in Aristocratic Finance in the Sixteenth and Seventeenth Centuries. Oxford, 1973.

  The Family, Sex and Marriage in England, 1500–1800. London, 1977.

Stone, Lawrence and Stone, Jeanne C. F. 'Country Houses and their Owners in Hertfordshire, 1540–1879', in *The Dimensions of Quantitative Research in History*, ed. W. O. Aydelotte *et al.* Princeton and Oxford, 1972.

Stout, William. *The Autobiography of William Stout of Lancaster, 1665–1752*, ed. J. D. Marshall. Manchester, 1967.

Straker, E. *Wealden Iron.* London, 1931.

Strickland, H. E. *General View of the Agriculture of the East Riding of Yorkshire.* London, 1812.

Summerson, J. *Architecture in Britain 1530 to 1830.* London, 1953.

  'The Classical Country House in 18th-Century England', *J. Roy. Soc. Arts*, CVII, 1959.

Switzer, Stephen. *A Compendious Method for the Raising of Italian Brocoli.* London, 1729.

Tate, W. E. 'Cambridgeshire Field Systems', *Proc. Cambridge Arch. Soc.*, XL, 1939–42.

  A Domesday of English Enclosure Acts and Awards, ed. M. Turner. Reading, 1978.

  'Inclosure Movements in Northamptonshire', *Northants. Past & Present*, I, 2, 1949.

Taylor, C. C. *The Cambridgeshire Landscape.* London, 1973.

Thirsk, Joan, 'Agrarian History, 1540–1950', in *VCH Leics.*, II. London, 1954.

  Economic Policy and Projects: The Development of a Consumer Society in Early Modern England. Oxford, 1978.

  English Peasant Farming: The Agrarian History of Lincolnshire from Tudor to Recent Times. London, 1957. Repr. London, 1981.

  'The Fantastical Folly of Fashion: The English Stocking Knitting Industry, 1500–1700', in *Textile History and Economic History*, ed. N. B. Harte and K. G. Ponting. Manchester, 1973.

  'Horn and Thorn in Staffordshire: The Economy of a Pastoral County', *N. Staffs. J. Field Stud.*, IX, 1969.

  Horses in Early Modern England: For Service, for Pleasure, for Power. Stenton Lecture, 1977. Reading, 1978.

  'Industries in the Countryside', in *Essays in the Economic and Social History of Tudor and Stuart England*, ed. F. J. Fisher. Cambridge, 1961.

  'New Crops and their Diffusion: Tobacco-Growing in Seventeenth Century England', in *Rural Change and Urban Growth, 1500–1800*, ed. C. W. Chalklin and M. A. Havinden. London, 1974.

  'Plough and Pen: Agricultural Writers in the Seventeenth Century', in T. H. Aston *et al.*, *Social Relations and Ideas.* Cambridge, 1983.

  'Projects for Gentlemen, Jobs for the Poor: Mutual Aid in the Vale of Tewkesbury, 1600–1630', in *Essays in Bristol and Gloucestershire History*, ed. P. McGrath and J. Cannon. Bristol. 1976.

'The Restoration Land Settlement', *JMH*, XXVI, 4, 1954.

'The Sales of Royalist Land during the Interregnum', EcHR, 2nd ser., V, 1952–3.

'Seventeenth-Century Agriculture and Social Change', in *Land, Church and People: Essays Presented to Professor H. P. R. Finberg*, ed. Joan Thirsk. Suppl. to AHR, XVIII, 1970.

Thirsk, Joan (ed.). *The Agrarian History of England and Wales, IV, 1500–1640*. Cambridge, 1967.

Thirsk, Joan and Cooper, J. P. (eds.). *Seventeenth-Century Economic Documents*. Oxford, 1972.

Thomas, D. 'The Social Origins of the Marriage Partners of the British Peerage', *Pop. Stud.*, XXVI, 1972.

Thomas, H. *A History of Wales, 1485–1660*. Cardiff, 1972.

Thomas, K. R. 'The Enclosure of Open Fields and Commons in Staffordshire', *Staffs. Hist. Coll.*, 1931.

Thompson, E. P. 'The Moral Economy of the English Crowd in the Eighteenth Century', *PP*, no. 50, 1971.

Whigs and Hunters: The Origins of the Black Act. London, 1975.

Thompson, F. M. L. 'The Social Distribution of Landed Property in England since the Sixteenth Century', EcHR, 2nd ser., XIX, 1966.

'Landownership and Economic Growth in England in the Eighteenth Century', in *Agrarian Change and Economic Development*, ed. E. L. Jones and S. J. Woolf. London, 1969.

Thomson, G. Scott. *Family Background*. London, 1949.

Life in a Noble Household, 1641–1700. London, 1937.

Tibbutt, H. G. *Bedfordshire and the First Civil War*. 2nd edn. Elstow, 1973.

Torrington Diaries, ed. C. Brayn Andrews. London, 1954.

Trinder, B. S. *The Industrial Revolution in Shropshire*. Chichester, 1973.

Trinder, B. S. and Cox, J. *Yeomen and Colliers in Telford*. Chichester, 1980.

Trow-Smith, R. *A History of British Livestock Husbandry to 1700*. London, 1957.

A History of British Livestock Husbandry, 1700–1900. London, 1959.

Tubbs, C. R. 'The Development of the Smallholding and Cottage Stock-Keeping Economy of the New Forest', AHR, XIII, 1965.

Tucker, G. S. L. 'Population in History', EcHR, 2nd ser., XX, 1967.

Tuke, J. *General View of the Agriculture of the North Riding of Yorkshire*. London, 1800.

Tull, J. *A Supplement to the Essay on Horse-hoing Husbandry...* London, 1736.

Tupling, G. H. 'The Early Metal Trades and the Beginnings of Engineering in Lancashire', *Lancs. & Cheshire Arch. Soc.*, LXI, 1951.

Turner, J. 'Ralph Austen, an Oxford Horticulturist of the Seventeenth Century', *Garden Hist.*, VI, 2, 1978.

Turner, M. *English Parliamentary Enclosure: Its Historical Geography and Economic History*. Folkestone, 1980.

Underdown, D. 'A Case concerning Bishops' Lands', EHR, LXXVIII, 1963.

Unwin, R. W. 'The Aire and Calder Navigation, Part II: The Navigation in the Pre-Canal Age', *Bradford Antiq.*, NS XLIII, 1967.

Utterström, G. 'Climatic Fluctuations and Population Problems in Early Modern History', *Scand. Ec. Hist. Rev.*, III, 1955.

Vanbrugh, Sir John. *The Complete Works, IV, Letters*. London, 1928.

Vancouver, C. *General View of the Agriculture in the County of Cambridge*. London, 1794.

General View of the Agriculture of Essex. London, 1795.

General View of the Agriculture of Hampshire. London, 1813.

Verney, F. P. *Memoirs of the Verney Family during the Civil War*. 2 vols. London, 1892.

Verney, F. P. and Verney, M. M. *Memoirs of the Verney Family during the Seventeenth Century*. 2nd edn. 2 vols. London, 1904.

Veysey, A. G. 'Col. Philip Jones, 1618–74', *Hon. Soc. Cymmrodorion*. 1966, pt 2.

Warner, J. 'General View of the Agriculture of the Isle of Wight', in A. and W. Driver, *General View of the Agriculture of the County of Hampshire*. London, 1794.

Watts, S. J. 'Tenant-Right in Early Seventeenth-Century Northumberland', *Northern Hist.*, VI, 1971.

Weatherill, L. *The Pottery Trade and North Staffordshire, 1660–1760*. Manchester, 1971.

Webber, Ronald. *Covent Garden, Mud-Salad Market*. London, 1969.

Market Gardening. Newton Abbot, 1972.

Webster, C. *The Great Instauration*. London, 1975.

Westerfield, R. B. *Middlemen in English Business, Particularly between 1660 and 1760*. Conn. Acad. Arts & Sci., XIX. New Haven, 1915. Repr. Newton Abbot, 1968.

Weston, R. *A Discours of Husbandrie Used in Brabant and Flanders*. London, 1605 [*recte* 1650].

Weston, Richard. *Tracts on Practical Agriculture and Gardening*. London, 1773.

Whetter, J. *Cornwall in the Seventeenth Century: An Economic Survey of Kernow*. Padstow, 1974.

Whistler, L. *The Imagination of Vanbrugh*. London, 1954.

White, Gilbert. *The Natural History of Selborne*, ed. G. Allen, London, 1908.

Wiliam, Eurwyn. 'Adeiladau Fferm Traddodiadol yng Nghymru' (with English summary), *Amgueddfa*, XV, 1973.

Willan, T. S. *The English Coasting Trade 1600–1750*. Manchester, 1938.

The Inland Trade. Manchester, 1976.

'The River Navigation and Trade of the Severn Valley, 1600–1750', *EcHR*, VIII, 1937–8.

River Navigation in England, 1600–1760. Oxford, 1936. New impr. London, 1964.

[William, Richard]. *Wallography, or the Britton Described*. London, 1673.

Williams, Glanmor (ed.). *The Glamorgan County History, IV*. Cardiff, 1976.

Williams, J. E. 'Whitehaven in the Eighteenth Century', *EcHR*, 2nd ser., VIII, 1956.

Williams, L. A. *Road Transport in Cumbria in the Nineteenth Century*. London, 1975.

Williams, Michael. *The Draining of the Somerset Levels*. Cambridge, 1970.

Wilson, C. H. *England's Apprenticeship, 1603–1763*. London, 1965.

Wood-Jones, R. B. *Traditional Domestic Architecture of the Banbury Region*. Manchester, 1963.

Woodward, D. M. 'The Anglo-Irish Livestock Trade in the Seventeenth Century', *Irish Hist. Stud.*, XVIII, 72, 1973.

'Cattle Droving in the Seventeenth Century: A Yorkshire Example', in *Trade and Transport: Essays in Economic History in Honour of T. S. Willan*, ed. W. H. Chaloner and B. M. Ratcliffe. Manchester, 1977.

'A Comparative Study of the Irish and Scottish Livestock Trades in the Seventeenth Century', in *Comparative Aspects of Scottish and Irish Economic and Social History, 1600–1900*, ed. L. M. Cullen and T. C. Smout. Edinburgh, 1977.

Wordie, J. R. 'Social Change on the Leveson-Gower Estates, 1714–1832', EcHR, 2nd ser., XXVII, 4, 1974.

Worlidge, J. *Systema Agriculturae*. London, 1669.

Systema Horti-Culturae, or the Art of Gardening. London, 1677.

Wrigley, E. A. 'A Simple Model of London's Importance in Changing English Society and Economy, 1650–1750', PP, no. 37, 1967.

Yarranton, Andrew. *England's Improvement by Sea and Land*. London, 1677.

The Improvement Improved, by a Second Edition of the Great Improvement of Lands by Clover. London, 1663.

Yates, E. M. 'Aspects of Staffordshire Farming in the Seventeenth and Eighteenth Centuries', *N. Staffs. J. Field Stud.*, xv, 1975.

'Enclosure and the Rise of Grassland Farming in Staffordshire', *ibid.*, XIV, 1974.

Yelling, J. A. 'Changes in Crop Production in East Worcestershire, 1540–1867', AHR, XXI, 1, 1973.

'The Combination and Rotation of Crops in East Worcestershire, 1540–1660', AHR, XVII, 1, 1969.

Common Field and Enclosure in England, 1450–1850. London, 1977.

Youd, G. 'The Common Fields of Lancashire', *Hist. Soc. Lancs. & Cheshire*, CXIII, 1961.

Young, A. *The Farmer's Tour in the East of England*. 4 vols. London, 1771.

General View of the Agriculture of Hertfordshire. London, 1804.

General View of the Agriculture of the County of Lincoln. London, 1799.

General View of the Agriculture of the County of Norfolk. London, 1804.

General View of the Agriculture of Oxfordshire. London, 1809.

A Six Months Tour through the North of England. 4 vols. London, 1770.

A Six Weeks' Tour through the Southern Counties. 3rd edn. London, 1772.

Tours in England and Wales (Selected from 'The Annals of Agriculture'). London, 1932.

Young, A. (ed.). *The Annals of Agriculture*. 46 vols. London, 1784–1815.

Young, the Rev. A. *General View of the Agriculture of the County of Sussex*. London, 1813.

INDEX

Abergavenny (Mon.), 238
Agarsely Park (Staffs.), 217
Agistment, 37
Agreements of the People, 220
agricultural change: financial involvement,
    269–70, 282–3, 291; growth patterns, 131,
    274; role of improvers, 270–2, 273ff.,
    286ff., 290ff.; innovatory, 263ff., 282–3,
    290ff., 305ff., 311ff.; policies for, 125ff.,
    131ff., 151ff., 198–9, 213–15; regional
    comparisons, 175, 177–8, 180, 182, 196–7,
    288; resistance to, 263, 317; see also Estate
    management; Market gardening; Royal
    agricultural unrest, 140, 150 Society
Aire, river, 187
Aisby (Lincs.), 107
alcohol consumption, 164; see also
    drunkenness
ale, exports, 161, 172; substitutes for, 15; see
    also beer; brewing
Allen, William, 160
Alphamstone (Essex), 29
Alsace: safflower, 168
Althorp, 104
America: commodity trade, 134, 190, 256;
    grain trade, 160
Anabaptists, 222
Ancholme Level, 200
Anglesey, earl of, 177, 179
Anglesey, livestock, 40
Antwerp, 291
apothecaries, 204
Appledore (Kent), 271
apples, 50
apricots, 50
arable land, conversion to pasture, 2, 61, 68f.,
    79, 81; ploughing, sowing, and manuring,
    20–2
Archenfield (Herefords.), 23
Arden, 65
Argyll estates, 204
Armstrong, Clement, 94
army, victualling, 129–30, 137
Ashcombe (Wilts.), 271
Ashdown Forest, 144, 202
ashes, as fertilizer, 34
Ashley, Lord, 179

Aubrey, John, 306
Austen, Ralph, 137, 139, 148, 280, 284, 290,
    292, 293
Axholme, Isle of (Lincs.); hemp industry, 31;
    population growth, 58

bacon, 47
Bacon, Francis, 302
Bagshawe, Samuel, 298
Bagshot (Surrey), 26
Bakewell, Robert, 302, 308
Baltic trade, 160, 162, 275
Banbury (Oxon.), 236, 244
Bankes, James, 17, 51
Barebones, Dr, 302
Barebones Parliament, 8
barges, 240
barley, as breadcorn, 23; exports, 159, 163;
    uses of, 24; varieties, 24; see also malt and
    malting
Barn Elms (Thames-side), 271
Barnes, D.G., 157
Barnes (Middx), 29, 258
Barrow on Soar (Leics.), 230
Bartholmley (Cheshire), 226
Barton Seagrave (Northants.), 286
Baswick (Staffs.), 231
Bates, Thomas, 184–6
Bath Society, 304
Bathurst, Earl, 316
Battesea, 51, 258, 309
Bawdsey (Suffolk), 38
Baxter, Richard, 302
Beachborough (Kent), 302
Beale, John, 30, 172, 280, 282, 287, 289, 292,
    313
beans, as fodder, 26; varieties, 26
Bedford, earl of: estates, 187, 204; drainage,
    199, 228
Bedford, George, 269
Bedford Level, 150, 201; see also Great Level
Bedfordshire, enclosure in, 89; market
    gardening, 233, 248; patterns of tenure,
    219; pigeons, 22; woad, 29
Bedingfield, Mr, 284
bee-keeping, 48
beef production, 129

339